Fundamentals of
ORGANIZATIONAL BEHAVIOR

Fundamentals of
ORGANIZATIONAL BEHAVIOR

4e

Andrew J. DuBrin
Professor of Management
College of Business
Rochester Institute of Technology

THOMSON
™
SOUTH-WESTERN

Australia · Brazil · Canada · Mexico · Singapore · Spain · United Kingdom · United States

THOMSON
™
SOUTH-WESTERN

Fundamentals of Organizational Behavior, Fourth Edition
Andrew J. DuBrin

VP/Editorial Director:
Jack W. Calhoun

Editor-in-Chief:
Melissa S. Acuña

Senior Acquisitions Editor:
Joe Sabatino

Developmental Editor:
Mike Guendelsberger

Senior Marketing Manager:
Kimberly Kanakes

Content Project Manager:
Margaret M. Bril

Editorial Assistant:
Ruth Belanger

Manager of Technology, Editorial:
Vicky True

Technology Project Manager:
Kristen Meere

Senior Manufacturing Coordinator:
Doug Wilke

Production House:
Interactive Composition Corporation

Printer:
Transcontinental
Louiseville, QC

Art Director:
Tippy McIntosh

Internal Designer:
Stratton Design, Michael Stratton

Cover Designer:
Stratton Design, Michael Stratton

Cover Images:
© Brian Jensen, images.com

Library of Congress Control
Number:
2006927121

For more information about our
products, contact us at:

Thomson Learning Academic
Resource Center

1-800-423-0563

Thomson Higher Education
5191 Natorp Boulevard
Mason, OH 45040
USA

Brief Contents

Contents

Contents

Preface

Welcome to the fourth and slightly expanded edition of *Fundamentals of Organizational Behavior*. This book is designed for courses in organizational behavior and management that focus on the application of organizational behavior knowledge to achieve enhanced productivity and satisfaction in the workplace.

Organizational behavior is about human behavior on the job. Knowledge of organizational behavior is, therefore, an important source of knowledge from which any manager may draw. The same information that can drive a manager to excel can also assist individual organizational contributors in becoming more adaptive and effective. Nonmanagerial professionals, technology workers, sales representatives, and service providers benefit from the insight and analysis that organizational behavior provides, just as do managers and prospective managers. All are welcome under the umbrella of organizational behavior.

Organizational behavior, because of its key contributions in driving workforce productivity, is a standard part of the curriculum in schools and colleges of business, management, and public administration. As a result, research and writing about the field proliferates. To provide just an overview of this vast amount of information, many introductory textbooks are quite lengthy, easily filling 800 pages or more. To soften the impact of such encyclopedic approaches to the study of organizational behavior, many of these books also lavishly layer figures and photographs onto their extended narratives. Many of the new, briefer textbooks are simply condensed versions of the longer books.

Fundamentals of Organizational Behavior takes a briefer, more focused, and more applied approach to learning about the field. Instead of trying to dazzle with a baffling array of concepts, research findings, theories, and news clippings, this book concentrates on only the most useful ideas. It blends clear and thoughtful exposition of traditional topics, such as motivation, with topics of more recent origin, such as creativity, virtual teams, knowledge management, diversity, and cultural intellgence.

And although each chapter packs a lot of information, chapters consistently emphasize the essential and the practical. A major strategy was to de-emphasize elaborate theories and findings that are no longer the subject of active research, practice, or training programs. However, we did not permit a concern for brevity to strip the text down to a sterile outline devoid of human interest, examples, and useful applications. Most of the brief textbooks in organizational behavior sacrifice cases, self-quizzes, discussion questions, and in-action inserts. *Fundamentals of Organizational Behavior*, however, injects all of these elements into its pages and still stays concise.

The size and scope of this book are well suited to college courses that supplement a core textbook with journal articles, major projects, specialty textbooks, or other instructional media. In addition, the comprehensiveness of *Fundamentals of Organizational Behavior*, combined with its brevity, makes it suitable for workplace organizational training programs about human behavior. The student who masters this textbook will not only acquire an overview of and appreciation for organizational behavior research, literature, theory, and opinion but will also develop a feel for managing and influencing others through the application of systematic knowledge about human behavior.

THE FEATURES

In addition to summarizing and synthesizing relevant information about essential organizational behavior topics and providing concrete examples of theories in action, *Fundamentals of Organizational Behavior* incorporates many useful features to make the material more accessible, collaborative, and incisive. It also works hard to be technologically relevant, such as by describing how information technology is used to enhance group decision making.

New videos, available for viewing online at **www.thomsonedu.com/ management/dubrin,** demonstrate the usefulness of organizational behavior knowledge at a diverse range of organizations. And the InfoTrac® integration feature—in every chapter—identifies passages in the text for which related information on a specific topic is available online using the Gale Group's InfoTrac extensive database.

- *Learning Objectives* introduce the major themes of each chapter and provide a framework for study.
- *Definitions* of boldfaced key terms are highlighted in the text and are reinforced at the end of each chapter and in an end-of-book glossary.
- *Opening vignettes* explore real organizational issues, highlighting the stake all types of organizations have in using human capital well.
- *Organizational Behavior in Action* boxes describe the actions of managers and professionals in dealing effectively with the human aspects of management, making visible the connection between theory and practice.
- *Self-Assessments and Skill-Development Exercises* support self-directed learning while driving the connections among research, theory, and practice down to the personal level. They not only provide a point of departure for students in understanding and valuing their own individual attitudes and behaviors but they also serve to create an ongoing dialogue, as each assessment and exercise can be returned to many times over the course of a semester.
- *InfoTrac Examples* appear in the margin alongside text passages where additional, contrasting, or current news stories can be searched for and read online from a database of over 5000 journals.
- *Video* selections are cued to places in the text where they have particular applicability.
- *Implications for Managerial Practice* boxes, located near the end of each chapter, set off several smart suggestions for applying organizational behavior information in a managerial context.
- *Summaries of Key Points,* located at the end of each chapter, integrate all key topics and concepts into several cogent paragraphs and link them with the chapter's stated learning objectives.
- *Key Terms and Phrases* provide a useful review of each chapter's terminology.
- *Discussion Questions and Activities,* located at the end of each chapter, are suitable for individual or group analysis. Included are Collaboration Questions aimed at fostering group activity.
- *Organizational Behavior Online* combines "To Do" exercises and "To Bookmark" resources.

Collaboration

- *Case Problems,* located at the end of each chapter, illustrate major themes of the chapter and are suitable for individual or group analysis. Case Problems are uniquely designed to complement this textbook, and include relevant follow-up discussion questions and links to related websites when appropriate.

THE FRAMEWORK

Fundamentals of Organizational Behavior is a blend of description, skill development, insight, and prescription. Divided into four parts, it moves from the micro to the macro, beginning with a brief introduction to the discipline. It then progresses to an exploration of the individual, to a discussion of groups and intergroup dynamics, and to an examination of organizational systems.

As just noted, Part 1 provides an introduction to organizational behavior. Chapter 1 focuses on the nature and scope of organizational behavior and provides the foundation for what is to come.

Part 2 includes seven chapters that deal with the individual in the organization. Chapter 2 describes fundamental aspects of understanding individuals in terms of individual differences, diversity, mental ability, and personality. Chapter 3 describes individuals from the standpoint of learning, perception, and attributions. Chapter 4 describes attitudes, values, and ethics as they relate to behavior in organizations. Chapter 5 is about individual decision making and creativity. Chapter 6 presents basic concepts of motivation, and Chapter 7 discusses techniques for enhancing motivation.

Part 3, about groups and intergroup relations, contains six chapters. Chapter 8 is about interpersonal communication, and Chapter 9 covers group dynamics, including the characteristics of an effective work group. Chapter 10 is devoted to teams and teamwork. Chapter 11 deals with leadership, a cornerstone topic in organizational behavior and management. Chapter 12 extends the study of leadership by describing power, politics, and influence. Chapter 13 describes the nature and management of conflict and stress. (This chapter deals in part with interpersonal phenomena and in part with individual phenomena.)

Part 4, about the organizational system and the global environment, contains four chapters covering macro issues in organizational behavior. Chapter 14 deals with organization structure and design. Chapter 15 is about organizational culture and knowledge management. Chapter 16 is about organizational change, but it also deals with the individual profiting from change. Chapter 17 covers cultural diversity and cross-cultural organizational behavior.

THE FACTS—THE FOURTH EDITION, NEW AND EXPANDED

The fourth edition expands and thoroughly updates the second edition. Sixteen of the seventeen chapter-opening vignettes are new, and all Organizational Behavior in Action boxes are new. Sixteen of the seventeen case problems are new, and new research findings can be found in every chapter. Major additions and new or enhanced topical coverage are listed here, chapter by chapter:

Chapter 1:   The Nature and Scope of Organizational Behavior
Explicit emphasis is placed on the positive organizational behavior movement, or what is right with people in organizations, rather than focusing on problems.

Chapter 2:   Individual Differences, Mental Ability, and Personality
Presented are a new section on generation stereotypes influencing work behavior, a new quiz, the conscientiousness scale, and the NEO Personality Inventory, which measures the Five Factor Model of personality, including the subfactors of the Five Factor Model of personality.

Chapter 3:   Learning, Perception, and Attribution
Exhibit 3-1 describes sources of learning on the job. The chapter includes more about e-learning and about visual, auditory, and kinesthetic learning styles. We cover self-assessment of VAK learning styles, and discuss blame as part of attribution theory.

Chapter 4:   Attitudes, Values, and Ethics
Exhibit 4-1, The 2004 *Job Satisfaction Survey,* suggests what job factors are important to workers. Exhibit 4-3 shows responses to ethical questions given by visitors to *Fast Company's* website.

Chapter 5:   Individual Decision Making and Creativity
Exhibit 5-3 is a list of the world's top 20 innovative companies, and includes a few words of explanation for the ranking. The chapter also explains the "Seven Whys" tool, used for finding the root cause of a problem.

Chapter 6:   Foundation Concepts of Motivation
This chapter discusses the influence of culture on motivation.

Chapter 7:   Motivational Methods and Programs
In this chapter, potentially effective rewards based on employee perception of job satisfaction and retention factors are displayed in Exhibit 7-5, and we discuss pride as a motivator.

Chapter 8:   Interpersonal Communication (Chapter 9 in previous edition)
We cover company blogs as a communication vehicle, and present more information about the distributed workforce.

Chapter 9:   Group Dynamics (part of Chapter 10 in previous edition)
This chapter introduces a new type of group, crews.

Chapter 10: Teams and Teamwork (new chapter, stems from team section of Chapter 10 in previous edition)
The chapter covers key mechanisms for continuous learning by teams, including team learning orientation, unusual problems and crises, collective problem solving, and team coaching, in addition to managing on-site and virtual teams.

Chapter 11: Leadership in Organizations
This chapter offers new research on consideration and initiating structure that supports classical findings. Servant leadership is presented as a leadership behavior and attitude, Situational Leadership II replaces the older situational leadership model, and a new exercise, "My Leadership Journal," aids your development as a leader.

Chapter 12: Power, Politics, and Influence
We show how implicit leadership theory relates to influence, and present two new negative political tactics to watch out for: good mouthing an incompetent to make him or her transferable, and placing a weak manager under you to help secure your position.

Chapter 13: Conflict and Stress (Chapter 7 in previous edition)
Factional groups (subgroups) are a source of conflict. Task versus relationship conflict replaces C-type conflict versus A-type conflict. We discuss negotiating and bargaining as a method of conflict resolution.

The Yerkes–Dodson law shows the impact of strain on a complex task. And we explain the freeze-frame technique for managing stress.

Chapter 14: Organization Structure and Design (Chapter 13 in previous edition)
I simplified this chapter by reducing the number of alternative organization structures. "Two in a box" is a form of power sharing. We discuss the product and service organization structure at Microsoft, take account of extended coverage of outsourcing and offshoring and their link to organization structure, and cover more focused criteria for an effective organization design.

Chapter 15: Organization Culture and Knowledge Management (consolidation of portion of old Chapters 14 and 15 in previous edition)
Belief in a higher purpose as a dimension of culture replaces organizational spirituality. We discuss organizational types or personalities. The role of transformational and transactional leadership in institutionalizing knowledge is presented. The subjects of knowledge management and the learning organization are now reduced to about one-third of the chapter.

Chapter 16: Organizational Change (was the larger part of Chapter 14 in previous edition)
Changing the values of an organization can be used as a change method. Linkage analysis can be a tool to spread the positive effects of organization development. And the chapter deals with the changes created by the "flat world," or globalization and computerization of the economy in many countries.

Chapter 17: Cultural Diversity and Cross-Cultural Organizational Behavior
Potential problems with cultural diversity are included, along with its advantages. Performance orientation is added to dimensions of cultural values. GLOBE findings show how culture can influence the acceptability of the participative leadership style. We discuss cultural assumptions as a barrier to effective cross-cultural relations and talk about cultural intelligence training.

THE RESOURCES

Fundamentals of Organizational Behavior is supported by comprehensive instructional and learning support materials:

InfoTrac® College Edition: Packaged free with every new copy of *Fundamentals of Organizational Behavior* is a 4-month subscription to InfoTrac College Edition, an online research database that amasses over 5 million full-text articles from nearly 5000 scholarly and popular periodicals. With InfoTrac, your students have anytime, anywhere access to *Business Week, Fast Company, Fortune, Harvard Business Review,* and *Newsweek,* to name a few. Routinely incorporating extra readings or research assignments into your course outline and directing your students to log on to InfoTrac to access particular articles or to conduct their own searches provides them with a quick and convenient way to gain a comprehensive view of the business environment from the most influential journals from around the world. For more information on InfoTrac, visit www.thomsonedu.com/infotrac.

Interactive Self-Assessments (ISBN 0-324-35499-1): If your course includes a self-assessment component designed to start your students thinking about the skills they have acquired to date or to evaluate their strengths and developmental needs, a series of online self-assessments is available for free use in conjunction with *Fundamentals*. During a quick visit to **http://selfassessments.swlearning.com,** instructors may register and tour the site. Place your order using the designated ISBN, and *Fundamentals of Organizational Behavior* will ship to your bookstore with preassigned passcodes for entering the site. For additional details contact your South-Western/Thomson sales representative (800-423-0563).

Instructor's Manual with Test Bank (ISBN 0-324-53646-1): Available in print or for download at **www.thomsonedu.com/management/dubrin,** this author-generated manual includes a comprehensive array of instructional resources, all geared to offering instructors insights into how course content might be taught. Each chapter includes an outline, along with key lecture notes; answers to end-of-chapter discussion questions and activities, usually in the form of a comment rather than an absolute answer; and notes about the self-assessments and skill-development exercises. An examination for each chapter is also included, with 25 multiple-choice questions, 25 true/false questions, and three or four essay questions.

PowerPoint™ Slides (ISBN 0-324-53644-5): An entirely new set of over 125 slides to supplement course content is available for download at **www.thomsonedu. com/management/dubrin.** A duplicate set can also be found on the Instructor's Resource CD-ROM. For use by students as note-taking guides and by instructors to enhance lectures, these full-color images were designed to help you get the most out of your experience with *Fundamentals of Organizational Behavior.* Taken together, many students have found these slides to be an effective study guide. However, the slides are not designed to replace studying the text.

ExamView Testing Software: ExamView, South-Western's computerized testing program, contains all the questions in the printed Test Bank and is available on the Instructor's Resource CD-ROM (ISBN 0-324-53648-8) to instructors who adopt *Fundamentals of Organizational Behavior.* This easy-to-use test-creation program is compatible with both Microsoft® Windows and Macintosh systems and enables instructors to create printed tests, Internet tests, and LAN-based tests quickly. Blackboard- and WebCT-ready versions of *Fundamentals'* Test Bank are also available to qualified instructors. Contact your South-Western/Thomson sales representative for more information.

Video: Videos featuring a diverse group of businesses are available for viewing at **www.thomsonedu.com/management/dubrin** via streaming media. These high-interest video assets provide an inside look at how companies address organizational behavior issues every day, showing managers—at all levels of an organization—in action. All videos are also available to instructors on DVD (ISBN 0-324-53775-1) or VHS cassette (ISBN 0-324-53772-7).

Product Support Site: The dedicated *Fundamentals of Organizational Behavior* site provides broad online support. Visit **www.thomsonedu.com/management/ dubrin** to view available video, download supplements, take a quiz, and find links to and repositories of related resources.

Instructor's Resource CD-ROM (ISBN 0-324-53648-8): This CD-ROM contains the Microsoft Office application files of various teaching resources (the Instructor's Manual with Test Bank and the PowerPoint slides), along with our ExamView testing program and test files.

ALSO AVAILABLE FROM THE PUBLISHER

eCoursepacks: Create a tailor-fitted, easy-to-use online companion for your organizational behavior course with eCoursepacks, from Thomson Business, South-Western, and Gale. eCoursepacks give educators access to current content from thousands of popular, professional, and academic periodicals, from North American Case Research Association (NACRA) and Darden cases, and from the Gale Group's business and industry data. eCoursepacks also give you the ability to easily add your own material—even collecting a royalty if you choose. Permission to reprint all eCoursepack content has already been secured, saving you time and worry in securing rights.

Online publishing tools from eCourspacks allow you to search our content databases and make selections quickly, to organize your selections, and to publish a final online product in a clear, uniform, and full-color format. To learn more visit **http://ecoursepacks.swlearning.com** or contact your South-Western/Thomson sales representative (800-423-0563).

ACKNOWLEDGMENTS

The final topical content and organization of this text were heavily influenced by the results of a survey of professors who expressed interest in using a shorter, more concise textbook. Instructors from 60 colleges provided their opinions on what subjects form the foundation of their courses. They also provided feedback on the types of pedagogical activities and features that provide real value to the introductory organizational behavior course. My writing also benefited from the suggestions of numerous reviewers, some of whom, for reasons of confidentiality, must remain anonymous. Grateful acknowledgment is made to

Lori Abrams
University of Minnesota

David C. Baldridge
Oregon State University

Talya N. Bauer
Portland State University

Dr. Dorothy Brandt
Brazosport College

Neil S. Bucklew
West Virginia University

Glenna Dod
Wesleyan College

Debi Griggs
Bellevue Community College

Mary Humphrys
University of Toledo

Avis L. Johnson
University of Akron

Marianne W. Lewis
University of Cincinnati

Jalane M. Meloun
Kent State University

Linda Morable, Ph.D.
Richland College

Claire Marie Nolin, Ph.D.
Eastern Connecticut State University

Regina M. O'Neill
Suffolk University

Douglas Palmer
Trinity College

Sarah Robinson, M.S.
IUPUI

John W. Rogers
American International College

James Smas
Kent State University

Darrin Sorrells, Ph.D.
Oakland City University

Mary Anne Watson
University of Tampa

Dr. Bonnie Tiell
Tiffin University

Thanks also to the staff at Thomson South-Western who worked with me to publish this new edition of *Fundamentals of Organizational Behavior*: Acquisitions Editor Joe Sabatino, Developmental Editor Mike Guendelsberger, Marketing Manager Kimberly Kanakes, Content Project Manager Marge Bril, Editorial Assistant Ruth Belanger, and Art Director Tippy McIntosh. My special thanks also go to Professors Douglas Benton of Colorado State University, Terri Scandura of the University of Miami, and Ann Welsh of the University of Cincinnati, who read the entire first-edition manuscript and made many valuable suggestions that continue to inform my work.

Finally, writing without loved ones would be a lonely task. My thanks therefore go to my family: Drew, Douglas, Gizella, Melanie, Will, Rosie, Clare, Camila, and Sofia. I thank also Tammy, the woman in my life, for her encouragement.

Andrew J. DuBrin

ABOUT THE AUTHOR

Andrew J. DuBrin is professor emeritus of management in the College of Business at the Rochester Institute of Technology, where he has taught courses and conducts research in management, organizational behavior, leadership, and career management. He has served the college as chairman of the management department and as team leader. He received his Ph.D. in industrial psychology from Michigan State University. His business experience is in human resource management, and he consults with organizations and with individuals. His specialties include leadership and career management.

Professor DuBrin is an established author of both textbooks and trade titles. He also writes for professional journals, magazines, and newspapers. He has written textbooks on the principles of management (including *Essentials of Management,* now in its seventh edition for Thomson South-Western), leadership, organizational behavior, industrial psychology, and human relations. His trade titles cover many current issues, including coaching and mentoring, team play, office politics, coping with adversity, and overcoming career self-sabotage.

The Nature and Scope of Organizational Behavior

The Healthy Workplace Awards recognize organizations for their commitment to programs and policies that enhance employee health and well-being. Evaluators consider companies for the state-level awards across five areas: employee involvement, work–life balance, employee growth and development, health and safety, and employee recognition. The top 10 companies are selected from a pool of more than 180 previous state-level winners.

"It is important to highlight those companies' efforts in this era of business challenges and workplace pressures," says Russ Newman, the executive director for professional practice at the American Psychological Association. "Many organizations are struggling to stem the forces that are whittling away at their employees' morale, productivity, and health," says Newman. "These Best practices honorees are setting an example by creating strong, vibrant organizational cultures that contribute to both employee health and well-being and the company's bottom line."

Three of the winners are:

Liberty Precision Industries. Based in New York, this machine-building company helps its employees develop new, versatile job skills. Liberty employees work with a consulting psychologist to identify specific areas in which they can improve job performance.

South Carolina Bank and Trust. The company's employee expectation survey has cut turnover rates in half by allowing employees to

Source: Adapted from Mark Greer, "A Happier, Healthier Workplace," *Monitor on Psychology*, December 2004, pp. 28–29.

OBJECTIVES

After reading and studying this chapter and doing the exercises, you should be able to:

(1) Explain what organizational behavior means.

(2) Summarize the research methods of organizational behavior.

(3) Identify the potential advantages of organizational behavior knowledge.

(4) Explain key events in the history of organizational behavior.

(5) Understand how a person develops organizational behavior skills.

anonymously voice concerns about the workplace. Management listens: It has added employee recognition programs and new stock purchase options.

Sysco Food Services of New Mexico. The company partnered with the University, of New Mexico to develop a coaching skills class that taught all executives, managers, and supervisors skills such as collaborative decision-making, employee development, and team-building. Employees report less stress and increased job satisfaction.

Now Ask Yourself: **In what way does the information just presented illustrate that paying careful attention to human behavior in the workplace is an important part of an organization's being successful?** The purpose of this book is to present systematic knowledge about people and organizations that can be used to enhance individual and organizational effectiveness. Managers and potential managers are the most likely to apply this information. Yet the same information is important for other workers, including professionals, sales representatives, customer service specialists, and technical specialists.

In the modern organization, workers at every level do some of the work that was formerly the sole domain of managers. Team members, for example, are often expected to motivate and train each other. One reason organizations get by with fewer managers than previously is that workers themselves are now expected to manage themselves to some extent. Self-management of this type includes the team scheduling its own work and making recommendations for quality improvement.

In this chapter, we introduce organizational behavior from several perspectives. We will explain the meaning of the term, see why organizational behavior is useful, and take a brief glance at its history. After describing how to develop skills in organizational behavior, we present a framework for understanding the field. An important goal in studying organizational behavior is to be able to make sense of any organization in which you are placed. For example, you might be able to answer the question, "What is going on here from a human standpoint?"

THE MEANING AND RESEARCH METHODS OF ORGANIZATIONAL BEHAVIOR

Explain what organizational behavior means.

A starting point in understanding the potential contribution of organizational behavior is to know the meaning of the term. It is also important to be familiar with how information about organizational behavior is acquired.

The Meaning of Organizational Behavior

Organizational behavior (OB) is the study of human behavior in the workplace, of the interaction between people and the organization, and of the organization itself.[1] The major goals of organizational behavior are to explain, predict, and control behavior.

Explanation refers to describing the underlying reasons or process by which phenomena occur. For example, an understanding of leadership theory would explain why one person is a more effective leader than another. The same theory would help predict which people (such as those having charismatic qualities) are likely to be effective as leaders. Leadership theory could also be useful in controlling (or influencing) people. One leadership theory, for example, contends that group members are more likely to be satisfied and productive when the leader establishes good relationships with them.

Data Collection and Research Methods in Organizational Behavior

To explain, predict, and control behavior, organizational behavior specialists must collect information systematically and conduct research. The purpose of collecting data is to conduct research.

Summarize the research methods of organizational behavior.

Methods of Data Collection

Three frequently used methods of collecting data in organizational behavior are surveys, interviews, and direct observation of behavior. The *survey questionnaire* used by a specialist in organizational behavior is prepared rigorously. Before preparing a final questionnaire, a scientist collects relevant facts and generates hypotheses (educated guesses) about important issues to explore. The questionnaire is carefully designed to measure relevant issues about the topic being surveyed. Among the surveys included in this textbook is the Creative Personality Test in Chapter 5.

Research about human behavior in the workplace relies heavily on the *interview* as a method of data collection. Even when a questionnaire is the primary method of data collection, interviews are usually used to obtain ideas for survey questions. Interviews are also helpful in uncovering explanations about phenomena and furnishing leads for further inquiry. Another advantage of interviews is that a skilled interviewer can probe for additional information. One disadvantage of the interview method is that skilled interviewers are required.

Observers placing themselves in the work environment collect much information about organizational behavior. *Systematic observations* are then made about the phenomena under study. One concern about this method is that the people under observation may perform atypically when they know they are being observed. A variation of systematic observation is *participant observation*. The observer becomes a member of the group about which he or she collects information. For example, to study stress experienced by customer service representatives, a researcher might work temporarily in a customer service center.

Research Methods

Four widely used research methods of organizational behavior are case studies, laboratory experiments, field experiments (or studies), and meta-analyses. Although *cases* are a popular teaching method, they are often looked on negatively as a method of conducting research. Case information is usually collected by an observer recording impressions in his or her mind or on a notepad. People have a tendency to attend to information specifically related to their own interests or needs. Despite this subjective element in the case method, cases provide a wealth of information that can be used to explain what is happening in a given situation.

An *experiment* is the most rigorous research method. The essence of conducting an experiment is making sure that the variable being modified (the independent variable) influences the results. The independent variable (such as a motivational technique) is thought to influence the dependent variable (such as productivity). The dependent variable is also known as the *criterion* (or measure).

4

A major characteristic of the *laboratory experiment* is that the conditions are supposedly under the experimenter's control. A group of people might be brought into a room to study the effects of stress on problem-solving ability. The stressor the experiment introduces is an electronic beeping noise. In a field setting, assuming the experiment was permitted, the experimenter might be unaware of what other stressors the subjects faced at that time. A key concern about laboratory experiments, however, is that their results might not apply to the outside world.

Field experiments (or studies) attempt to apply the experimental method to real-life situations. Variables can be controlled more readily in the laboratory than in the field, but information obtained in the field is often more relevant. An example of a field experiment would be investigating whether giving employees more power would have an effect on their motivation to produce a high quantity of work. The independent variable would be empowerment, while the dependent variable would be quantity of work.

A widely used approach to reaching conclusions about behavior is to combine the results of a large number of studies. A **meta-analysis** is a quantitative or statistical review of the literature on a particular subject, and is also an examination of a range of studies for the purpose of reaching a combined result or best estimate. A meta-analysis is therefore a review of studies, combining their quantitative information. You can also view meta-analysis as a quantitative review of the literature on a particular subject. For example, a researcher might want to combine the results of 100 different studies about the job performance consequences of group decision making before reaching a conclusion. Many of the research findings presented throughout this book are based on meta-analysis rather than on the results of a single study.

An important use of meta-analysis in organizational behavior is to understand how certain factors, referred to as *moderator variables,* influence the results of studies.[2] For example, in the experiment mentioned previously about stress and problem-solving ability, a moderator variable might be the amount of stress a study participant faces in personal life. Individuals who enter the experiment already stressed might be influenced more negatively by the electronic beeping noise.

Meta-analysis gives the impression of being scientific and reliable because so much information is assimilated, using sophisticated statistical tools. One might argue, however, that it is better to perform one rigorous study than to analyze many poorly conducted studies.

HOW YOU CAN BENEFIT FROM STUDYING ORGANIZATIONAL BEHAVIOR

③

Identify the potential advantages of organizational behavior knowledge.

Studying organizational behavior can enhance your effectiveness as a manager or professional. Yet the benefits from studying organizational behavior are not as immediately apparent as those derived from the study of functional fields such as accounting, marketing, purchasing, and information systems. Such fields constitute the *content* of managerial and professional work. Organizational behavior, in contrast, relates to the *process* of conducting such work. An exception may be seen with organizational behavior specialists whose content, or functional knowledge, deals with organizational behavior concepts and methods.

Visualize an information systems specialist who has extremely limited interpersonal skills in communicating, motivating, and resolving conflict. She will have a difficult time applying her technical expertise to organizational problems. She will therefore fail in serving her clients because she lacks the ability to use effective interpersonal processes. In contrast, if the same information systems specialist had solid interpersonal skills, she could do a better job of serving her clients. (She would probably also hold onto her job longer.)

Studying and learning about organizational behavior offers four key advantages: (1) skill development, (2) personal growth, (3) enhancement of organizational and individual effectiveness, and (4) sharpening and refinement of common sense.

Skill Development

An essential requirement for entering into, surviving, and succeeding in the modern workplace is to have the appropriate skills. A person needs both skills related to his or her discipline and generic skills such as problem solving and dealing with people. The study of organizational behavior contributes directly to these generic skills. Later in this chapter, we provide details about how one develops skills related to organizational behavior.

Organizational behavior skills have gained in importance in the modern workplace. A relevant example is that many CIOs (chief information officers) now need information technology professionals to get more involved in business concerns, to interact with other departments, and to communicate more effectively with colleagues. Soft skills such as business acumen, communication, leadership, and project management become more important as specialists such as information technology professionals get more involved in the overall business. A survey of 1420 CIOs found that 53 percent of these managers offered information technology employees training in areas outside of technology.[3]

The distinction between *soft* skills and *hard* skills is relevant for understanding the importance of skill development in organizational behavior. Soft skills are generally interpersonal skills such as motivating others, communicating, and adapting to people of different cultures. Hard skills are generally technical skills, such as information technology and job design. Some skills, such as those involved with decision making, have a mixture of soft and hard components. To make good decisions you have to be creative and imaginative (perhaps a soft skill), yet you also have to weigh evidence carefully (most likely a hard skill). The aforementioned survey classified *business acumen* as a soft skill, yet some business strategy specialists would classify such knowledge as a hard skill.

Personal Growth through Insight into Human Behavior

As explained by Robert P. Vecchio, an important reason for studying organizational behavior is the personal fulfillment gained from understanding others.[4] Understanding fellow human beings can also lead to enhanced self-knowledge and self-insight. For example, while studying what motivates others, you may gain an understanding of what motivates you. Participating in the experiential exercises and self-assessments included in this textbook provides another vehicle for personal growth. A case in point is the study of leadership in Chapter 11. You will be invited to take a self-quiz about readiness to assume a leadership role. Taking the test and reviewing the results will give you insight into the types of attitudes and behaviors you need to function as a leader.

Personal growth, through understanding others and self-insight, is meritorious in and of itself, and it also has practical applications. Managerial and professional

Log on to **www.thomsonedu.com/infotrac**. Perform a search on "soft skills" and find out what specific skills employers look for in "well-rounded" job applicants.

positions require sharp insights into the minds of others for tasks such as selecting people for jobs and assignments, communicating, and motivating. Sales representatives who can size up the needs of prospects and customers have a competitive advantage. Another value of understanding others and self-insight is that they contribute to continuous learning because the needs of others change over time, and so might your needs. For example, people are more strongly motivated by the prospects of job security today than they might have been in years past. Continuous downsizings and outsourcing have enhanced the value of job security.

Enhancement of Organizational and Individual Effectiveness

A major benefit from studying organizational behavior is that it provides information that can be applied to organizational problems. An important goal of organizational behavior is to improve **organizational effectiveness**—the extent to which an organization is productive and satisfies the demands of its interested parties. Each chapter of this book contains information that is applied directly or indirectly by many organizations. One visible example is the widespread use of teams in the workplace. Certainly, organizational behavior specialists did not invent teams. We suspect even prehistoric people organized some of their hunting forays by teams. Nevertheless, the conclusions of organizational behavior researchers facilitated the shift to teams in organizations.

The accompanying box presents fresh evidence about the link between treating employees well and a firm's financial performance. The argument is particularly interesting because it is presented by a financial analyst.

Why does paying more attention to the human element improve business performance? One explanation Jeffrey Pfeffer offers is that people work harder when they have greater control over their work environment and when they are encouraged by peer pressure from teammates. Even more advantage comes from people working smarter. People-oriented management practices enable workers to use their wisdom and to receive appropriate training. Another contribution to improved performance stems from eliminating positions that focus primarily on watching and controlling workers.[5] Much of organizational behavior deals with people-oriented management practices. Many of these practices will be described in later chapters.

Understanding organizational behavior also improves organizational effectiveness because it uncovers factors that contribute to or hinder effective performance. Among these many factors are employee motivation, personality factors, and communication barriers. Furthermore, an advanced understanding of people is a major contributor to managerial success. This is especially true because so much of a manager's job involves accomplishing tasks through people.

Organizational behavior also contributes insights and skills that can enhance individual effectiveness. If a person develops knowledge about subjects such as improved interpersonal communication, conflict resolution, and teamwork, he or she will become more effective. A specific example is that knowledge about organizational behavior can contribute to high performance. Executive coach Lisa Parker observes that managers sometimes neglect to give encouragement and recognition to good performers because these workers are already performing well. Yet if these same solid performers were given more encouragement, coaching in the form of advice, and recognition, they will often develop into superstars (high performers).[6]

ORGANIZATIONAL BEHAVIOR *In Action*

Equity Analyst Evaluates the Importance of Treating Employees Well

I have been an equity research analyst for more than 15 years, the past 10 devoted to analyzing consumer service stocks, including restaurants, hotels, casinos, and cruise companies. These are labor-intensive sectors. As part of my analyses, I have quizzed senior management on the steps they take to manage labor costs. It has been conventional wisdom that reducing wages and benefits improves profit margins, earnings, and even stock price because, generally, investors reward companies that cut these expenses. In reality, it's not that simple.

I don't think enough investors have asked the more important question: Can companies be even more successful by focusing on optimizing each employee's contribution, rather than simply looking for ways to reduce the cost of employing them? Perhaps, we as investors, need to be more conscious of how these people who clean our hotel rooms, cook our meals, and deal our cards are treated and paid, rather than simply looking to see whether the expense can be cut further. Staff motivation, although difficult to quantify, should be part of the investment analysis.

At the risk of stating the obvious, it is apparent that treating employees with respect and paying them fairly goes a long way to establishing an efficient and creative organization. Most corporate executives say that they do this and that they don't put shareholder interests ahead of their workers. But, a significant number of companies who say they subscribe to this philosophy don't live up to it.

This is surprising because the service companies that go that extra mile often derive tangible benefit from adopting these practices.

They produce a higher quality of customer service, which becomes a competitive advantage for the company.

Working in a busy coffee bar can be a tough job, but Starbucks Corporation is at the forefront of trying to treat its workers with respect. Howard Schultz, who has led Starbucks through more than 18 years of growth, has set the tone from the top and made it clear that his company is not going to leave its people behind. For instance, employees who complete a minimum of 20 hours of work or more a week could become eligible for health benefits and may receive a stock option grant. There is a financial benefit: Starbucks' employee turnover is toward the bottom of the industry range and its service levels are high. And since the IPO [initial public offering] in June 1992, the shares of Starbucks have risen an eye-popping 3500%.

Treating employees well is certainly not the only reason that the companies alluded to here have outperformed. The strength of their products, the skills of management, and market conditions have also had a significant impact. I believe that investors should look beyond cost-cutting initiatives and ask whether the company is getting the very best out of its people. In other words, is it well managed?

Questions

1. What in your mind constitutes being treated well by an employer?
2. What is the tie-in between this opinion piece and organizational behavior?

Source: Steven Kent, "Happy Workers Are the Best Workers," *The Wall Street Journal*, September 6, 2005, p. A20.

Sharpening and Refining of Common Sense

A manager commented after reading through several chapters of an organizational behavior textbook, "Why should I study this field? It's just common sense. My job involves dealing with people, and you can't learn that through a book." Many other students of organizational behavior share the sentiments expressed by this manager.

However logical such an opinion might sound, common sense is not an adequate substitute for knowledge about organizational behavior. This knowledge sharpens and enlarges the domain for common sense. It markedly reduces the amount of time necessary to learn important behavior knowledge and skills, much as law school reduces the amount of time that a person in a previous era would have had to spend as a law apprentice.

You may know through common sense that giving recognition to people is generally an effective method of motivating them toward higher performance. By studying organizational behavior, however, you might learn that recognition should be given frequently but not every time somebody attains high performance. (You specifically learn about intermittent rewards in your study of motivation.) You might also learn that the type of recognition you give should be tailored to the individual's personality and preferences. For example, some people like flamboyant praise, while others prefer praise focused tightly on the merits of their work. Formal knowledge thus enhances your effectiveness.

Organizational behavior knowledge also refines common sense by challenging you to reexamine generally accepted ideas that may be only partially true. One such idea is that inactivity is an effective way to reduce stress from a hectic schedule. In reality, some hard-driving people find inactivity more stressful than activity. For them, lying on a beach for a week might trigger intense chest pains. For these people, diversionary activity—such as doing yard work—is more relaxing than inactivity.

(4) A BRIEF HISTORY OF ORGANIZATIONAL BEHAVIOR

Explain key events in the history of organizational behavior.

The history of organizational behavior is rooted in the **behavioral approach to management,** or the belief that specific attention to workers' needs creates greater satisfaction and productivity. In contrast to the largely technical emphasis of scientific management, a common theme of the behavioral approach is the need to focus on people. Scientific management did not ignore people altogether, and in some ways it contributed to organizational behavior. For example, scientific management heavily emphasized financial incentives to increase productivity. Yet the general thrust centered on performing work in a highly efficient manner.

Organizational behavior is also heavily influenced by sociology in its study of group behavior, organization structure, diversity, and culture. In addition, the insights of cultural anthropologists contribute to an understanding of organizational culture (the values and customs of a firm). In recent years, several companies have hired anthropologists to help them cultivate the right organizational culture. Organizational behavior also gains insights from political science toward understanding the distribution of power in organizations.

Five key developments in the history of organizational behavior are the classical approach to management, the Hawthorne studies, the human relations movement, the contingency approach to management and leadership, and positive organizational behavior.

The Classical Approach to Management

The study of management became more systematized and formalized as a by-product of the Industrial Revolution that took place from the 1700s through the 1900s. Managing these factories created the need for systems that could deal with large numbers of people performing repetitive work. The classical approach to management encompassed scientific management and administrative management, and contributed some insights into understanding workplace behavior.

The focus of **scientific management** was the application of scientific methods to increase an individual worker's productivity. An example would be assembling a lawn mower with the least number of wasted motions and steps. Frederick W. Taylor, considered the father of scientific management, was an engineer by background. He used scientific analysis and experiments to increase worker output. A key part of his system was to convert individuals into the equivalent of machines parts by assigning them specific, repetitive tasks. Other key contributors to scientific management were Henry Gantt and Frank and Lillian Gilbreth. (Gantt charts for scheduling activities are still used today.)

Taylor tackled the dilemma of management wanting to maximize profits, and workers wanting to maximize possible wages. Disputes between management and labor centered on what each side saw as incompatible goals. Taylor believed that his system of scientific management could help both sides attain their goals, providing each would undergo a "mental revolution." Each side had to conquer its antagonistic view of the other. Taylor believed that management and labor should regard profit as the result of cooperation between the two parties. Management and labor each needed the other to attain their goals.[7]

Scientific management is based on four principles, all of which direct behavior in the workplace:[8]

- Careful study of the jobs to develop standard work practices, with standardization of the tools workers use in their jobs
- Selection of each worker using scientific principles of personnel selection
- Obtainment of cooperation between management and workers to ensure that work is accomplished according to standard procedures
- Plans and task assignments developed by managers, which workers should carry out

According to these principles of scientific management, there is a division of work between managers and workers. Managers plan and design work, assign tasks, set performance goals, and make time schedules. Managers also select and train workers to do the tasks according to standard procedures, and give the workers feedback about their performance. Workers are rewarded with financial incentives when they increase their productivity.[9]

Administrative management was concerned primarily with the management and structure of organizations. The French businessman Henri Fayol and the German scholar Max Weber were the main contributors to administrative management. Based on his practical experience, Fayol developed 14 management principles through which management engaged in planning, organizing, commanding, coordinating, and controlling. Weber suggested that bureaucracy is the best form of organization because it makes highly efficient management practices possible.

The core of management knowledge lies within the classical school. Its key contributions come from studying management from the framework of planning, organizing, leading, and controlling. The major strength of the classical school was providing a systematic way of measuring people and work that still exists in some form today. For example, United Parcel Service (UPS) carefully measures the output and work approaches of the delivery workers. The major limitation of the classical school is that it sometimes ignores differences among people and situations. In addition, some of the classical principles for developing an organization are not well suited to fast-changing situations.

The Hawthorne Studies

Many scholars pinpoint the Hawthorne studies (1923–1933) as the true beginning of the behavioral approach to management.[10] Without the insights gleaned from these studies, organizational behavior might not have emerged as a discipline. The purpose of the first study conducted at the Hawthorne plant of Western Electric (an AT&T subsidiary) was to determine the effect of changes in lighting on productivity. In this study, workers were divided into an experimental group and a control group. Lighting conditions for the experimental group varied in intensity from 24 to 46 to 70 foot-candles. The lighting for the control group remained constant.

As expected, the experimental group's output increased with each increase in light intensity. But unexpectedly, the performance of the control group also changed. The production of the control group increased at about the same rate as that of the experimental group. Later, the lighting in the experimental group's work area was reduced. This group's output continued to increase, as did that of the control group. A decline in the productivity of the control group finally did occur, but only when the intensity of the light was roughly the same as moonlight. Clearly, the researchers reasoned, something other than illumination caused the changes in productivity.

The relay assembly test room produced similar results over a 6-year period. In this case, relationships among rest, fatigue, and productivity were examined. First, normal productivity was established with no formal rest periods and a 48-hour week. Rest periods of varying length and frequency were then introduced. Productivity increased as the frequency and length of rest periods increased. Finally, the original conditions were reinstated. The return to the original conditions, however, did not result in the expected productivity drop. Instead, productivity remained at its usual high level.

One interpretation of these results was that the workers involved in the experiment enjoyed being the center of attention. Workers reacted positively because management cared about them. The phenomenon is referred to as the **Hawthorne effect.** It is the tendency of people to behave differently when they receive attention because they respond to the demands of the situation. In a research setting, this could mean that the people in an experimental group perform better simply because they are participating in an experiment. In a work setting, this could mean that employees perform better when they are part of any program—whether or not that program is valuable.

The Hawthorne studies also produced other findings that served as the foundation for the human relations movement. Although many of these findings may seem obvious today, documenting them reinforced what many managers believed to be true. Key findings included the following:

1. Economic incentives are less potent than generally believed in influencing workers to achieve high levels of output.
2. Dealing with human problems is complicated and challenging.
3. Leadership practices and work-group pressures profoundly influence employee satisfaction and performance.
4. Personal problems can strongly influence worker productivity.
5. Effective communication with workers is critical to managerial success.
6. Any factor influencing employee behavior is embedded in a social system. For instance, to understand the impact of pay on performance, you have to understand the climate in the work group and the leadership style of the manager. Furthermore, work groups provide mutual support and may resist management schemes to increase output.

Despite the contributions of the Hawthorne studies, they have been criticized as lacking scientific rigor. The most interesting criticism contends that the workers in the control group were receiving feedback on their performance. Simultaneously, they were being paid more as they produced more. The dual impact of feedback and differential rewards produced the surprising results—not the Hawthorne effect.[11]

The Human Relations Movement

The **human relations movement** is based on the belief that there is an important link among managerial practices, morale, and productivity. Workers bring various social needs to the job. In performing their jobs, workers typically become members of several work groups. Often these groups provide satisfaction of some of the workers' needs. Satisfied workers, it was argued, would be more productive workers. The challenge for managers was to recognize workers' needs and the powerful influence that work groups can have on individual and organizational productivity.

A second major theme of the human relations movement is a strong belief in workers' capabilities. Given the proper working environment, virtually all workers would be highly productive. Significant amounts of cooperation between workers and managers prove critical to achieving high levels of productivity. A cornerstone of the human relations movement is Douglas McGregor's analysis of the assumptions managers make about human nature, delineated in two theories.[12] Theory X is a set of traditional assumptions about people. Managers who hold these assumptions are pessimistic about workers' capabilities. They believe that people dislike work, seek to avoid responsibility, are not ambitious, and must be supervised closely. McGregor urged managers to challenge these assumptions about human nature because they may be untrue in most circumstances.

Theory Y is an alternative, and optimistic, set of assumptions. These assumptions include the ideas that people do accept responsibility, can exercise self-control, have the capacity to innovate, and consider work to be as natural as rest or play. McGregor argued that these assumptions accurately describe human nature in far more situations than most managers believe. He therefore proposed that these assumptions should guide managerial practice.

The Contingency Approach

Beginning in the early 1960s, organizational behavior specialists emphasized the difficulties in finding universal principles of managing people that can be applied in all situations. To make effective use of knowledge about human behavior, one must understand which factors in a particular situation are most influential.

The **contingency approach to management** emphasizes that there is no one best way to manage people or work. A method that leads to high productivity or morale in one situation may not achieve the same results in another. The contingency approach is derived from the study of leadership styles. Experienced managers and leaders know that not all workers respond in the exact same way to identical leadership initiatives. A recurring example is that well-motivated, competent team members require less supervision than those who are poorly motivated and less competent. In Chapter 11, we present more information about the contingency approach to leadership.

The strength of the contingency approach is that it encourages managers and professionals to examine individual and situational differences before deciding on a course of action. Its major problem is that it is often used as an excuse for not acquiring formal knowledge about organizational behavior and management. If management depends on the situation, why study organizational behavior or management? The answer, of course, is that a formal study of management helps a manager decide which factors are relevant in particular situations. In the leadership example just cited, the relevant factors are the skills and motivation of the group members.

Positive Organizational Behavior

An emerging movement in organization behavior is a focus on what is right with people. The human relations movement was a start in this direction. However, the movement toward focusing on strengths rather than weaknesses stems directly from *positive psychology,* with its emphasis on what is right with people, such as love, work, and play. Fred Luthans defines **positive organizational behavior** as the study and application of human resource strengths and psychological capacities that can be measured, developed, and managed for performance improvement.[13]

The criteria of being measurable and developmental are significant because they separate positive organizational behavior from simply giving pep talks and inspirational speeches to employees. An example would be the concept of *self-efficacy,* or having confidence in performing a specific task. A worker might be asked how confident he or she is to perform a difficult task, such as evaluating the risk of a particular investment. If his or her self-efficacy is not strong enough, additional experience and training might enhance the person's self-efficacy.

An everyday application of positive organizational behavior would be for a manager to focus on employee strengths rather than weaknesses. It is well accepted that encouraging a worker to emphasize strengths will lead to much more performance improvement than attempting to patch weaknesses. Assume that a person is talented in interpersonal relationships but weak in quantitative analysis. This person is likely to be more productive by further developing strengths in a position calling for relationship building. The less productive approach would be overcoming the weakness in quantitative analysis and attempting to become a financial specialist. (The point here is not that working on weakness is fruitless, but that capitalizing on strengths has a bigger potential payoff.)

In general, positive organizational behavior focuses on developing human strengths, making people more resilient, and cultivating extraordinary individuals, work units, and organizations.[14] All of this is accomplished by careful attention to well-developed principles and research, rather than simply cheering people on.

SKILL DEVELOPMENT IN ORGANIZATIONAL BEHAVIOR

Understand how a person develops organizational behavior skills.

Developing skill in organizational behavior means learning to work effectively with individuals, groups, and organizational forces. The greater one's responsibility, the more one is expected to work well at these three levels.

The distinction between hard skills and soft skills mentioned previously is not necessarily the distinction between difficult and easy. Hard skills are not better than soft skills, and vice versa. A chief executive officer (CEO) may have a difficult job, yet she uses mostly *soft* skills such as leading others and bringing about organizational change. In contrast, an entry-level financial analyst might use *hard* skills in preparing an analysis. His job, however, might be considered easier than the CEO's. Notice also that possessing soft skills often helps a person earn hard money.

Developing most organizational behavior skills is more complex than developing a structured skill such as conducting a physical inventory or arranging an e-mail address book. Nevertheless, you can develop organizational behavior skills by reading this textbook and doing the exercises. The book follows a general learning model:

1. *Conceptual knowledge and behavioral guidelines.* Each chapter in this book presents research-based information about organizational behavior, including a section titled "Implications for Managerial Practice."

Exhibit **1-1**   13

A Model for Developing Organizational Behavior Skills

Organizational behavior skills can be developed by using a systematic approach.

2. *Conceptual information and examples.* These include brief descriptions of organizational behavior in action, generally featuring managers and leaders.

3. *Experiential exercises.* The book provides an opportunity for practice and personalization through cases and self-assessment exercises. Self-quizzes are included because they are an effective method of helping you personalize the information, assisting you in linking conceptual information to your own situation. For example, you will read about creative problem solving and also complete a quiz about creativity.

4. *Feedback on skill utilization, or performance, from others.* Feedback exercises appear at several places in the book. Implementing organizational behavior skills outside the classroom will provide additional opportunities for feedback.

5. *Frequent practice.* Readers who look for opportunities to practice organizational behavior skills outside the classroom will acquire skills more quickly. An important example is the development of creative thinking skills. The person who looks for imaginative solutions to problems regularly is much more likely to become a more creative thinker, and be ready to think creatively at a given moment. Contrast this with the individual who participates in a creative-thinking exercise once, and then attempts the skill a year later when the need is urgent. As in any field, frequently practicing a skill the right way leads to skill improvement.

As you work through the book, keep the five-part learning model in mind. To help visualize this basic learning model, refer to Exhibit 1-1.

Developing organizational behavior skills is also important because it contributes to your lifelong learning. A major theme of the modern organization is that to stay competitive, a worker has to keep learning and developing. A relevant example is that as work organizations have become more culturally diverse, it is important to keep developing one's skills in working effectively with people from different cultures.

A FRAMEWORK FOR STUDYING ORGANIZATIONAL BEHAVIOR

A challenge in studying organizational behavior is that it lacks the clear-cut boundaries of subjects such as cell biology or French. Some writers in the field consider organizational behavior to be the entire practice of management. Others focus organizational behavior much more on the human element and its interplay with the total organization. Such is the orientation of this textbook. Exhibit 1-2 presents a basic framework for studying organizational behavior. The framework is simultaneously a listing of the contents of Chapters 2 through 17.

Proceeding from left to right, the foundation of organizational behavior is the study of individual behavior, presented in Chapters 2 though 7. No group or organization is so powerful that the qualities of individual members do not count.

14

Exhibit **1-2**

A Framework of Studying Organizational Behavior

To better understand organizational behavior, recognize that behavior at the individual, group, and organizational system and global environment levels is linked.

Visualize a famous athletic team with a winning history. Many fans contend that the spirit and tradition of the team, rather than individual capabilities, carry it through to victories against tough opponents. Yet if the team has a couple of poor recruiting years or loses a key coach, it may lose more frequently.

Key factors in understanding how individuals function include individual differences, mental ability and personality, learning, perception, attitudes, values, attribution, and ethics. It is also important to understand individual decision making, creativity, foundation concepts of motivation, and motivational programs.

As suggested by the arrows in Exhibit 1-2, the various levels of study are interconnected. Understanding how individuals behave contributes to an understanding of groups and interpersonal relations, the second level of the framework. This will be studied in Chapters 8 through 13. The topics include communication, group dynamics (how groups operate), teams and teamwork, and leadership. Although leadership relates directly to interpersonal relationships, top-level leaders are also concerned with influencing the entire organization. The study of power, politics, and influence is closely related to leadership. Conflict, stress, and well-being might be classified at the individual level, yet these processes are heavily dependent on interaction with others.

Finally, the third level of analysis in the study of organizational behavior is the organizational system and the global environment, as presented in Chapters 14 through 17. Components of the organizational and environmental level studied here include organizational structure and design, organizational culture, organizational change and knowledge management, cultural diversity, and international (or cross-cultural) organizational behavior. International organizational behavior could just as well have been studied before the other topics. Our position, however, is that everything else a person learns about organizational behavior contributes to an understanding of cross-cultural relations in organizations.

The connecting arrows in Exhibit 1-2 emphasize the interrelatedness of processes and topics at the three levels. Motivation provides a clear example. A person's motivational level is dependent on his or her individual makeup as well as work-group influences and the organizational culture. Some work groups and organizational cultures energize new members because of their highly charged atmospheres. The arrows also run in the other direction. Highly motivated workers, for example, improve work-group performance, contribute to effective interpersonal relationships, and enhance the organizational culture.

IMPLICATIONS FOR MANAGERIAL PRACTICE

Each of the following chapters includes a brief section explaining how managers and professionals can use selected information to enhance managerial practice. Our first lesson is the most comprehensive and perhaps the most important: Managers should raise their level of awareness about the availability of organizational behavior information. Before making decisions in dealing with people in a given situation, pause to search for systematic information about people and organizations. For example, if you need to resolve conflict, first review information about conflict resolution, such as that presented in Chapter 13. The payoff could be improved management of conflict.

Another key implication from this chapter is to search for strengths and talents in others and yourself, and then capitalize on these strengths as a way of improving organizational and individual effectiveness. Weaknesses should not be ignored, but capitalizing on strengths has a bigger potential payoff.

CVS Stands for Consumer Value Store

Visit **www.thomsonedu. com/management/dubrin** and watch the video for this chapter. In what ways do you think the Emerging Leaders Program helps achieve good person–job fit at CVS?

SUMMARY OF KEY POINTS

 Explain what organizational behavior means.
Organizational behavior is the study of human behavior in the workplace, the interaction between people and the organization, and the organization itself. Organizational behavior relates to the process, rather than the content, of managerial work.

 Summarize the research methods of organizational behavior.
Three frequently used methods of collecting data on organizational behavior are surveys (typically questionnaires), interviews, and direct observation of behavior. Four widely used research methods are case studies, laboratory experiments, field experiments, and meta-analysis. The essence of conducting an experiment is to make sure that the independent variable influences the results.

 Identify the potential advantages of organizational behavior knowledge.
Knowledge about organizational behavior offers four key advantages: skill development, personal growth, the enhancement of organizational and personal effectiveness, and sharpening and refinement of

common sense. Substantial evidence has accumulated that substantiates that emphasizing the human factor increases productivity and gives a firm a competitive advantage. Organizational behavior skills have increased in importance in the modern workplace, partly because of the prevalence of diverse teams.

 Explain key events in the history of organizational behavior.
The history of organizational behavior parallels the behavioral approach to management, including contributions from classical management. The classical approach to management encompasses both scientific and administrative management, and contributes some insights into understanding workplace behavior. The behavioral approach formally began with the Hawthorne studies. Among the major implications of these studies were that leadership practices and work-group pressures profoundly influence employee satisfaction and performance. The human relations movement and the contingency approach to management are also key developments in the history of organizational behavior. The human

relations movement was based on the belief that there is an important link among managerial practices, morale, and productivity. Analysis of Theory X versus Theory Y (pessimistic versus optimistic assumptions about people) is a key aspect of the movement. The contingency approach emphasizes taking into account individual and situational differences in managing people. An emerging movement in the field is positive organizational behavior, which focuses on measurable human resource strengths and capacities.

 Understand how a person develops organizational behavior skills.

Organizational behavior skills can be developed by following a general learning model that includes the use of conceptual knowledge and behavioral guidelines, experiential exercises, feedback on skill utilization, and frequent practice. The framework for studying organizational behavior in this textbook emphasizes the interconnectedness of three levels of information: individuals, groups and interpersonal relations, and the organizational system and the global environment.

KEY TERMS AND PHRASES

Organizational Behavior, 2
The study of human behavior in the workplace, the interaction between people and the organization, and the organization itself.

Meta-Analysis, 4
A quantitative or statistical review of the literature on a particular subject; an examination of a range of studies for the purpose of reaching a combined result or best estimate.

Organizational Effectiveness, 6
The extent to which an organization is productive and satisfies the demands of its interested parties.

Behavioral Approach to Management, 8
The belief that specific attention to the workers' needs creates greater satisfaction and productivity.

Scientific Management, 9
The application of scientific methods to increase workers' productivity.

Administrative Management, 9
A school of management thought concerned primarily with how organizations should be structured and managed.

Hawthorne Effect, 10
The tendency of people to behave differently when they receive attention because they respond to the demands of the situation.

Human Relations Movement, 11
An approach to dealing with workers based on the belief that there is an important link among managerial practices, morale, and productivity.

Contingency Approach to Management, 11
The viewpoint that there is no one best way to manage people or work but that the best way depends on certain situational factors.

Positive Organizational Behavior, 12
The study and application of human resource strengths and psychological capacities that can be measured, developed, and managed for performance improvement.

DISCUSSION QUESTIONS AND ACTIVITIES

1. Find somebody in your network who works for, or has worked for, Starbucks (including you) to comment on employee treatment by management.
2. What contributions might organizational behavior knowledge make in the Internet age?
3. What does it mean to say that organizational behavior relates to the *process*—as opposed to the *content*—of a manager's job?
4. Give a possible explanation why meta-analysis is considered so important in evaluating the effectiveness of prescription drugs.

5. Work by yourself, or form a small brainstorming group, to furnish an example from physical science in which common sense proves to be untrue.
6. Have you ever worked for a manager who held Theory X assumptions about people? What was the impact of his or her assumptions on your motivation and satisfaction?
7. Get together with a few classmates. Develop a list of strengths of group members that you think if further developed would be career assets, and explain why these strengths might be assets.

CASE PROBLEM: The Hands-On CEO of JetBlue

The first thing you notice when getting on board is the new-car smell. "No wonder," says the flight attendant, hearing your remark. She points to a metal plaque on the doorway rim that says the Airbus A320 was delivered 1 month ago. Other notable features are the free cable on your personal video screen and the leather seats. Flight attendants are trained on how to give service with a retro flair. All attendants have to learn how to strut proudly, as if there were an imaginary string between their chin and belly button.

JetBlue attendants have a sense of fun about their jobs, and the can-do pilot informs over the public address system that yes, there's a major storm coming into the New York City area but that we'll get there on time anyway. And the plane and passengers do. So the traveler wonders. Is this for real? Or maybe the right question is, "How long can they keep up this nonsense?" JetBlue was rated highest in customer satisfaction of all U.S. airlines in *Condé Nast Traveler* magazine's 2005 Business Travel Awards—the fourth time in 6 years.

Just as discontent with airlines was mounting in 2000, JetBlue Airlines came into being with a new attitude, new planes, and a new concept of service. What perfect takeoff timing for a carrier that is trying to bring pleasure and even style back to flying. JetBlue is low-price and all-coach, like Southwest Airlines, yet hip and sassy, like Virgin Atlantic. In the air, JetBlue offers the plush seats and satellite TV; on the ground it offers a high level of efficiency.

JetBlue has achieved an impressive profit picture. Of the hundreds of start-ups since the industry was deregulated in 1978, only Southwest Airlines and JetBlue have sustained their success. For 2005, JetBlue had a net income of approximately $60 million for $1.3 billion in revenue, with over 80 percent of seats being filled.

Credit CEO David Neeleman, who founded the firm at age 41, for piloting JetBlue past the early disasters that typically befall fledgling carriers. For starters, Neeleman raised $160 million from investors—almost triple what other new airline entrants have managed to obtain. The hefty sum is insurance against any unforeseen cash crunch.

Consumers are usually concerned about the safety issue with "new" airlines that fly 25-year-old planes. JetBlue flies only factory-fresh, state-of-the-art A320s. Neeleman has fitted each with 162 seats—versus the

A320's 180-seat maximum. Flyers are ecstatic about the JetBlue experience. It begins with pricing, which is competitive and doesn't torture consumers with requirements like Saturday-night stays. JetBlue is attracting business travelers, the industry's most valuable passengers and the source of up to 50 percent of its profits.

A JetBlue spokesperson said, "We see our customers as the same ones who can afford more but shop at Target because their stuff is hip but inexpensive." That kind of thinking drove decisions like JetBlue's choice of leather seats instead of less expensive cloth. "It's a nicer look, a better feel," says Neeleman, in full salesman mode. Nevertheless, as JetBlue became several years old, their sections of airline terminals, such as JFK (serving New York City), had the same worn-down look with cracked leather seats as other airlines.

Neeleman obsesses over keeping employees happy, and with good reason. Airline watchers say JetBlue's ability to stay union-free is critical to its survival as a low-cost carrier. The industry's labor-relations record is weak. "But if there is anyone who realizes the importance of treating their employees right, it's the management team at JetBlue," says airline analyst Holly Hegeman.

JetBlue employees get profit-sharing checks, amounting to 17 percent of their salary in recent years. Also, 84 percent of JetBlue employees participate in a company stock purchase program, in which they can buy stock at a 15 percent discount.

On September 21, 2005, JetBlue Flight 292 in Los Angeles narrowly escaped a crash when its front landing gear stuck sideways, so the plane had to land while metal scraped the runway instead of the wheels rolling in their intended manner. The day after the mishap Neeleman released a statement acknowledging the problem, and thanking everyone concerned for their assistance and emotional support. Neeleman's public statement included these words:

> The crew of Flight 292 has asked us to communicate their appreciation to the 140 customers on board for their cooperation, and they are also grateful for the messages of support sent to JetBlue by thousands of people. The crew looks forward to returning to their families and loved ones, and to their normal lives as quickly as possible.

Neeleman is one of seven siblings, and has nine children of his own. He has been dreaming about

(continued)

18

CASE PROBLEM (Continued)

airplanes since he saw a red one on his second birthday cake. A serial travel entrepreneur, he has launched four airlines, including Morris Air and Canada's WestJet Airlines, with each one being more successful than the last. Neeleman, with a strong interest in information technology, developed the computer system that became the basis for e-ticketing.

Neeleman notes that despite heavy competition, JetBlue's profit margins are the highest in the industry. He attributes part of the company's success to selecting the right people, which is especially important because an airline is a people business. "We have a saying at Jet-Blue that you're either serving a customer or serving someone who is serving a customer."

An example of the selection process at JetBlue was an applicant pilot who was furious about being rejected. The pilot telephoned Neeleman and explained that he had 15,000 hours of flying experience. Neeleman then spoke to the interviewer, who said that she asked the pilot, "You've flown for 15,000 hours, tell us one thing that you've done besides just sitting there and flying the airplane." He couldn't come up with a single example. He retorted, "What do you mean by that? I'm a pilot, and that's what I do." The interviewer explained that the pilot was not somebody JetBlue wants in the company.

To manage the company, Neeleman emphasizes the quality of supervisors. The company has one supervisor for every 80 employees. Neeleman tells the supervisors, "You can know 80 people. You can know who they're married to, you can know who their kids are, and what their challenges are." In this way JetBlue employees know there is a personal touch to the company.

Case Questions

1. In what way does Neeleman demonstrate an understanding of organizational behavior?

2. So what's wrong with a pilot staying in the cockpit in terms of being a contributor to a people-oriented business?

3. How else might Neeleman make use of organizational behavior knowledge to improve the chances of JetBlue Airlines staying successful?

Sources: Sally B. Donnelly, "Blue Skies: Is Jet Blue the Next Great Airline— Or Just a Little Too Good to Be True?," July 30, 2001 *Time*, pp. 24–27; Eric Gillin, "JetBlue Soars Past Profit Targets," *TheStreet.com*, July 25, 2002; (http://www.thestreet.com/pf/tech/earnings/10034305.html); "On the Record: David Neeleman, JetBlue Airways, http://www.sfgate.com, September 12, 2004; JetBlue Airways Voted Best in Class and Best Value for Cost . . . Again," www.primezone.com, September 29, 2005; "Statement by JetBlue CEO David Neeleman Regarding Flight 292, http://www.primezone.com, September 22, 2005.

ENDNOTES

1. Gregory Morehead and Ricky W. Griffin, *Organizational Behavior: Managing People and Organizations,* 4th ed. (Boston: Houghton Mifflin, 1995), p. 3.
2. Piers D. Steel and John D. Kammeyer-Mueller, "Comparing Meta-Analytic Techniques under Realistic Conditions," *Journal of Applied Psychology,* February 2002, p. 107.
3. Jon Surmacz, "The Hard Truth: Soft Skills Matter," *CIO Magazine*, January 15, 2005, p. 1.
4. Robert P. Vecchio, *Organizational Behavior: Core Concepts, 6th ed.* (Mason, OH: South-Western/Thomson Learning, 2003), pp. 5–6.
5. Jeffrey Pfeffer, *The Human Equation* (Boston: Harvard Business School Press, 1998), p. 59.
6. Cited in Anne Fisher, "Turn Star Employees into Superstars," *Fortune*, December 13, 2004, p. 70.
7. Joseph E. Champoux, *Organizational Behavior: Essential Tenets* (Mason, OH: South-Western/Thomson Learning, 2003), pp. 11–12; Edward G. Wertheim, "Historical Background of Organizational Behavior," http://web.cba.neu.edu/~ewertheim/introd/history.htm, accessed March 16, 2006.
8. Frederick W. Taylor, *Principles of Scientific Management* (New York: W. W. Norton, 1911), p. 9.
9. Champoux, *Organizational Behavior,* p. 12.
10. E. J. Roethlisberger and W. J. Dickson, *Management and the Worker* (Cambridge, MA: Harvard University Press, 1939); Wertheim, pp. 2–3.
11. H. McIlvaine Parsons, "What Caused the Hawthorne Effect? A Scientific Detective Story," *Administration & Society,* November 1978, pp. 259–283.
12. Douglas McGregor, *The Human Side of Enterprise* (New York: McGraw-Hill, 1960), pp. 33–57.
13. Fred Luthans, "Positive Organizational Behavior: Developing and Managing Psychological Strengths," *Academy of Management Executive*, February 2002, p. 59.
14. Kim Cameron, Jane Dutton, Rover Quinn, and Gretchen Spreitzer, "What Is Positive Organizational Scholarship?" http://www.bus.umich.edu/Positive/WhatisPOS/, accessed September 29, 2005.

Individual Differences, Mental Ability, and Personality

Google Inc. executives say they can't expand as rapidly as they would like to because they can't find enough qualified employees or deploy new computers fast enough. At the company's first analyst meeting since its August initial public offering, the executives said they are aggressively adding products and staff, but are limited by their own recruitment standards and ability to expand Google's technical infrastructure. The web-search company is known for a rigorous hiring process, which can include tests of the candidate and more than a half-dozen interviews.

"Can we hire the quality and quantity of people we want to? No," said cofounder Sergey Brin, speaking before several hundred analysts at Google's Mountain View, California, headquarters. "We're underinvesting in our business because of the limitations on hiring." Google said it has more than 3000 employees, up from 2292, seven months ago.

Now Ask Yourself: **What does this anecdote from Google tell you about the importance of understanding individual differences and human capability when managing a very successful enterprise?** The purpose of this chapter is to explain how individual differences affect performance. In addition, we describe key sources of individual differences: demographic diversity, mental ability,

Source: Kevin J. Delaney, "Google Expansion is Being Held Back by Hiring Process," *The Wall Street Journal,* February 10, 2005, p. B5.

OBJECTIVES

After reading and studying this chapter and doing the exercises, you should be able to:

1. Explain how individual differences influence the behavior of people in organizations.

2. Describe key factors contributing to demographic diversity.

3. Explain how mental ability relates to job performance.

4. Identify major personality variables that influence job performance.

5. Explain how emotional intelligence is an important part of organizational behavior.

and personality. In Chapters 3 and 4 we will consider other sources of individual differences that influence behavior in organizations: learning, perception, attributions, attitudes, values, and ethics. Although our focus in this chapter is on individual differences, we also describe principles of human behavior that apply to everyone. For example, everyone has different components to his or her intelligence. We all have some capacity to deal with numbers, words, and abstract reasoning.

INDIVIDUAL DIFFERENCES

Explain how individual differences influence the behavior of people in organizations.

People show substantial **individual differences,** or variations in how they respond to the same situation based on personal characteristics. An extraverted production planner might attempt to influence a plant superintendent by taking him to lunch and making an oral presentation of her ideas. In the same situation, an introverted planner might attempt to influence the superintendent by sending him an elaborate report. Understanding individual differences helps to explain human behavior, but environmental influences are also important.

The importance of understanding individual differences for managing people is highlighted by the research of Marcus Buckingham, who studied over 80,000 managers, using both survey questionnaires and interviews. He concluded that exceptional managers come to value the particular quirks and abilities of their employees. Exceptional managers analyze how to capitalize on the strengths of workers and tweak the environment to adapt to employee strengths. For example, the manager might modify a job description so the worker can do more work that fits his or her talents, such as giving a very bright employee more opportunity to troubleshoot.[1]

A basic proposition of psychology states that behavior is a function of a person interacting with his or her environment.[2] The equation reads $B = f(P \times E)$, where B stands for behavior, P for the person, and E the environment. A key implication of this equation is that the effects of the individual and the environment on each other determine a person's behavior. For example, working for a firm that requires many levels of approval for a decision might trigger a person's tendencies toward impatience. The same person working in a flatter organization (one that requires fewer layers of approval) might be more patient. Have you ever noticed that some environments, and some people, bring out your best traits? Or your worst traits?

Another way of understanding the impact of individual differences in the workplace is to say that these differences *moderate* how people respond to situations. Assume that a new organization structure results in most professional-level workers having two bosses. (Each worker has a manager in his or her own discipline, plus a project leader.) Workers who have a difficult time tolerating ambiguity (a personality trait) will find the new structure to be frustrating. In contrast, workers who tolerate ambiguity well will enjoy the challenge and excitement of having two bosses.

Here we identify seven consequences of individual differences that have a major impact on managing people.

1. *People differ in productivity.* A comprehensive analysis of individual differences illustrates the magnitude of human variation in job performance.[3] Researchers synthesized studies involving over 10,000 workers. They found that as jobs become more complex, individual differences have a bigger impact on work output. An outstanding industrial sales representative might produce 100 times as much sales revenue as a mediocre one. In contrast, an outstanding production specialist might produce only twice as much as a mediocre one. (An industrial sales position is more complex than the job of production specialist. Industrial

selling involves a variety of activities, including persuading others, analyzing problems, and mining data via a computer.)

2. *Quality of work varies because people vary in their propensity for achieving high-quality results.* Some people take naturally to striving for high quality because they are conscientious, have a good capacity for precision, and take pride in their work. Workers who are less conscientious, less precise, and have little pride will have more difficulty achieving quality targets.

3. *Empowerment is effective with some workers, but not with all.* People differ in how much they want to be empowered and involved. A major thrust of the modern workplace is to grant workers more authority to make decisions by themselves and to involve them in suggesting improvements. Many workers welcome such empowerment and enrichment because they seek self-fulfillment on the job. However, many other workers are not looking for more responsibility and job involvement. They prefer jobs that require a minimum of mental involvement and responsibility.

4. *A given leadership style does not work with all people.* People differ in the style of leadership they prefer and need. Many individuals prefer as much freedom as possible on the job and can function well under such leadership. Other individuals want to be supervised closely by their manager. People also vary with respect to the amount of supervision they require. In general, less competent, less motivated, and less experienced workers need more supervision. One of the biggest headaches facing a manager is to supervise people who need close supervision yet resent it when it is administered.

5. *People differ in their need for contact with other people.* As a by-product of their personality traits and occupational interests, people vary widely in how much human contact they need to keep them satisfied. Some people can work alone all day and remain highly productive. Others become restless unless they are engaged in business or social conversation with another employee. Some workers will often drop by the work area of other workers just to chat. Sometimes a business luncheon is scheduled more out of a manager's need for social contact than a need for discussing job problems.

6. *Company management will find that commitment to the firm varies considerably.* The reason is that people differ in their commitment and loyalty to the firm. Some employees are so committed to their employers that they act as if they are part-owners of the firm. As a consequence, committed and loyal employees are highly concerned about producing high-quality goods and services. They also maintain excellent records of attendance and punctuality, which helps reduce the cost of doing business. At the other extreme, some employees feel little commitment or loyalty toward their employer. They feel no pangs of guilt when they produce scrap or when they miss work for trivial reasons.

7. *Workers vary in their level of self-esteem, which, in turn, influences their productivity and capacity to take on additional responsibilities.* People with high self-esteem believe that they can cope with the basic challenges of life (self-efficacy) and also that they are worthy of happiness (self-respect). A group of economists found that self-esteem, as measured by a personality test, had a big impact on the wages of young workers. The researchers found that human capital—schooling, basic skills, and work experience—predictably had a significant impact on wages. Yet 10 percent of this effect was really attributable to self-esteem, which highly correlated with human capital. It was also found that differences in productivity, as measured by comparative wages, related more to differences in self-esteem than to differences in human capital.[4]

22

The sampling of individual differences creating the consequences cited is usually attributed to a combination of genetic makeup and environmental influences. Some workers are more productive because they have inherited better problem-solving abilities and have lived since childhood in environments that encourage the acquisition of knowledge and skills. Many other personality traits, such as introversion, also are partially inherited.

Despite the importance of heredity, a person's environment—including the workplace—still plays a significant role in influencing job behavior. The manager must therefore strive to create a positive environment in which workers are able to perform at their best.

DEMOGRAPHIC DIVERSITY

Describe key factors contributing to demographic diversity.

Workers vary widely with respect to background, or demographic characteristics, and these differences sometimes affect job performance and behavior. **Demographic diversity** refers to the differences in background factors relating to the workforce that help shape workers' attitudes and behavior. Key sources of demographic diversity include gender, generational differences and age, and ethnicity. As is well known, the U.S. workforce is becoming increasingly diverse. Understanding demographic differences among workers can help the manager both capitalize on diversity and avoid negative stereotyping. For example, some managers still hold the stereotype that single people are less conscientious than married people.

Sex and Gender Differences

A topic of intense debate and continuing interest is whether men and women differ in aspects of behavior related to job performance. (*Sex differences* refer to actual biological differences, such as the average height of men versus that of women. *Gender differences* refer to differences in the perception of male and female roles.) A series of studies suggest that gender differences in personality exist. These findings include the following:

- Women are better able to understand nonverbal communication.
- Women are more expressive of emotion.
- The average woman is more trusting and more nurturing than the average man.[5]

More closely related to job behavior, much has been written about the different styles and communication patterns of men and women. Chapter 8 presents more details about male–female differences in communication patterns. A major finding is that men more typically communicate to convey information or establish status. Men also tend to emphasize immediate goals and communicate to exchange facts and ideas. Women are more likely to communicate to establish rapport and solve problems.

Men are generally more aggressive than women and therefore less sensitive to the feelings of others. Women, according to this generalization, tend to be more courteous and polite. Another gender difference, according to James Q. Wilson, is that men are more likely to value equity, whereas women value equality. *Equity* refers to people being treated fairly, such as people in a department getting the salary increases they deserve. *Equality* refers to people sharing equally, such as all people in a department receiving an identical salary increase.[6]

Despite the existence of these gender differences, the overall evidence suggests that there are few differences between men and women in factors such as ability and motivation that will affect job performance. A meta-analysis of the evidence about gender differences suggests that the similarities between men and women far outweigh the differences. According to the gender-similarities hypothesis, as advanced by Janet Shibley Hyde, males and females are alike on most, but not all, behavioral variables. An example of a slight difference is that males tend to be slightly more aggressive than females. Hyde observes that overinflated claims of gender differences can do harm in the workplace.[7] Two examples would be denying a woman a job as a bill collector because women are thought to be less aggressive than men, or denying a man a job as a home health care aid because men are thought to be less nurturing than women.

Generational and Age-Based Differences

The generation to which a person belongs may have a strong influence on his or work behavior and attitudes, as outlined in Exhibit 2-1. Greg Hammill observes that this is the first time in American history that we have had *four* different generations interacting in the workplace.[8] In Chapter 4, we will explore these generational differences more specifically from the standpoint of values. The general point is that people may behave differently on the job based somewhat on the behaviors and attitudes typical of many members of their generation. We emphasize that we are dealing in stereotypes that represent tendencies of the typical worker in a generational category. An extreme negative stereotype is that younger workers are lazy and older workers are workaholics. In reality, some younger workers are workaholics and some older workers are lazy.

According to Constance Patterson, every generation is influenced by the major economic, political, and social events of its era, such as the Great Depression, the women's movement, and advances in information technology.[9] Emerging standards of etiquette also influence work-related behavior. A middle-aged recruiter was aghast when a young job candidate put her on hold twice to respond to call waiting during a telephone job interview. The candidate, in turn, thought it was natural to interrupt one person to accept a telephone call from another. As this example illustrates, generational differences can lead to communication problems.

Generational differences can sometimes cause clashes, especially among members of the same work group. For example, baby boomers may believe that generation Xers are too impatient and willing to reject reliable work procedures. In contrast, generation Xers may perceive baby boomers as always trying to please people in

Traditionalists (Veterans) (1925 to 1945)	Baby Boomers (1946 to 1960)	Generation X (1961 to 1980)	Generation Y (Millennials) (1981 to present)
Practical	Optimistic	Skeptical	Hopeful
Patient, loyal, and hardworking	Teamwork and cooperation	Self-reliant	Meaningful work
Respectful of authority	Ambitious	Risk-taking	Value diversity and change
Rule followers	Workaholics	Balance work and personal life	Technology savvy

Exhibit **2-1**

Generation Stereotypes Influencing Work Behavior

Source: Adapted from Constance Patterson, "Generational Diversity: Implications for Consultation and Teamwork." Paper presented at the meeting of the Council of Directors of School Psychology Program on Generational Differences, Deerfield Beach, Florida, January 2005.

power and being inflexible to change. Traditionalists may view baby boomers as being self-absorbed and too quick to share information. Baby boomers may perceive traditionalists as being dictatorial and rigid. Furthermore, members of generation X may perceive members of generation Y as too spoiled and self-absorbed, while members of generation Y may perceive members of generation X as being too cynical and negative. Patterson encourages members of mixed-generation groups to seek a balance between building on traditional procedures and supporting flexibility and imaginative thinking to effectively blend the work ethics of the several generations.[10]

Age is related to generational differences with a subtle difference—age differences include a focus on mental and physical capabilities. Potential differences in productivity and job behavior based on age are topical. According to demographic trends, many baby boomers will retire around 2010. Because the next generation is smaller than its predecessor, workers with the skills and experience needed to fill positions left open by retiring boomers may be in short supply. A potential solution would be to encourage many people to keep working longer and to employ a larger number of older people in general. In its emphasis on hiring older workers, Home Depot now offers "snowbird specials"—fall, winter, and spring work in Florida, and summers in Maine. Another factor keeping more seniors in the workforce was the downturn in the stock market at the turn of the century and its aftermath. With retirement funds having shrunk in value, many seniors elected to postpone retirement until their funds appreciated substantially.

Age and experience are not synonymous. For example, a person age 35 might have 14 years' experience as a restaurant manager, whereas a person age 65 might have 5 years' experience in such a position. Nevertheless, age and experience are usually related.

The research evidence about job-related consequences of age is mixed. One study of 24,000 federal workers found that age was barely related to performance. Not surprisingly, both age and experience predicted performance better for high-complexity jobs than for other, less complicated jobs.[11] A review of articles spanning 22 years studying the relationship between age and performance (involving almost 40,000 workers) found that age and job performance were generally unrelated. However, among workers in the 17- to 21-year-old category, the 21-year-olds tended to be more productive than the 17-year-olds.[12] Advances in technology are now helping workers compensate for mental losses, such as less acute memory, associated with age. Two examples are memory-enhancing drugs and the use of Internet search engines to quickly retrieve information that the worker may have forgotten.[13]

Even if being older and more experienced does not always contribute to job performance, older workers do have notable attributes. In contrast to younger workers, they have lower absenteeism, illness, and accident rates; higher job satisfaction; and more positive work values.[14] For top-level executive positions, age is often valued because the older executive may have more wisdom based on experience. An example is that in 2004, struggling Delta Airlines Inc. picked outside board member Gerald Grinstein, 71, to replace the existing CEO.[15] The discussion of practical intelligence later in this chapter reintroduces the topic of wisdom based on experience.

Ethnic, Racial, and Cultural Differences

Differences in job performance and behavior are sometimes attributed to ethnic group and racial differences. However, these differences are usually more attributable to culture than to ethnicity itself. For example, it is part of the culture of European countries to take long lunch breaks. An Italian manager working in an Italian subsidiary might take a 2-hour lunch break, while her American counterpart might take a 45-minute break. The Italian manager's behavior reflects cultural values rather than the fact of being Italian. Also, the cultural group with which people affiliate, such as middle class versus lower class, influences their behavior much more than does their race.[16]

Chapter 16 presents more details about cross-cultural differences in job behavior. As will be described there, demographic diversity will often give an organization a competitive advantage. Diversity also affects employee behavior and attitudes. A study of almost 1600 insurance company employees found that an individual's demographic similarity to his or her work group positively influenced the individual's perception of group productivity and commitment to the work group. (The demographic characteristics studied were race and ethnicity.) Another key finding was that the greater the similarity between an individual's demographic characteristics and others in the work group, the more positive the individual's perceptions of advancement opportunities would be.[17] In short, job satisfaction tends to be higher for employees when others of similar demographic characteristics are present in the workplace.

MENTAL ABILITY (COGNITIVE INTELLIGENCE)

Mental ability, or **intelligence** (the capacity to acquire and apply knowledge, including solving problems), is a major source of individual differences that affect job performance and behavior. Intelligent workers can best solve abstract problems. More than 100 years of research findings consistently indicate that intelligence, as measured by mental ability tests, is positively related to job performance.[18] General mental ability is also a good predictor of job performance and success in training for a wide variety of occupations in the European Community.[19] An example of the widespread use of mental ability tests to predict job performance is that most NFL (National Football League) teams use the Wonderlic Personnel Test, a standardized measure of cognitive ability, as part of the selection process. An informal study indicated that the four franchises with the highest average Wonderlic score achieved by the players each played in the Super Bowl (the championship game) during a span of five seasons. In general, quarterbacks—the position calling for the most analytical skills—tend to have the highest mental ability test scores.[20]

Few people seriously doubt that mental ability is related to job performance. Controversy does abound, however, about two aspects of intelligence. One is how accurately and fairly intelligence can be measured. It is argued, for example, that intelligence tests discriminate against environmentally disadvantaged people. The second controversial aspect is the relative influence of heredity and environment on intelligence. Some people believe that intelligence is mostly the product of genes, while others believe that upbringing is the key factor.

The late Hans J. Eysenck, a leading authority in the field of intelligence and personality, concluded that a large component of mental ability is inheritable. Evidence for the genetic contributor to scores in intelligence tests has been reinforced by twin and adoption studies demonstrating that monozygotic (identical) twins, whether reared apart or together, exhibit relatively high correlations in intelligence. In contrast, dizygotic (fraternal) twins, whether reared apart or together, have correlations that are substantially lower.[21]

The argument that environment is the major contributor to intelligence centers on evidence that many people, if placed in an enriched environment, are able to elevate their intelligence test scores. People with genes favoring high intelligence will gravitate toward mentally enriching experiences, thereby relying on the environment

Explain how mental ability relates to job performance.

Log on to **www.thomsonedu.com/infotrac**. Perform a keyword search on 'Kinko's' and founder Paul Orfalea.' How did he use street smarts and more conventional notions of intelligence?

to boost their natural cognitive advantage.[22] Related to this argument is the fact that IQs have been steadily rising worldwide, with the average IQ of each successive generation higher than that of the previous generation. Possible explanations for gains in mental ability (as measured by IQ tests) include better nutrition, more training in mental tasks, and more sophistication in taking tests. All of these reasons indicate that environment heavily influences intelligence.[23] (If it is true that mental ability can be improved by a stimulating environment, giving employees ample opportunity to stretch themselves mentally will help them improve their intellectual skills.)

Based on hundreds of studies, it appears that heredity and environment contribute about equally to intelligence.[24] This finding does not mean that a person with extremely limited mental capacity can be made superintelligent through specialized training. Nor does it mean that a naturally brilliant person does not need a mentally stimulating environment.

Here we describe several aspects of mental ability that have implications for organizational behavior: the components of intelligence, the triarchic theory of intelligence that features practical intelligence, and multiple intelligences. Emotional intelligence is described under the category of personality.

Components of Intelligence

Intelligence consists of multiple components. A component of intelligence is much like a separate mental aptitude. A standard theory of intelligence explains that intelligence consists of a **g (general) factor** along with **s (special) factors** that contribute to problem-solving ability. Another way of describing g is that it represents a general cognitive factor that pervades almost all kinds of mental ability. Scores on tests of almost any type (such as math or creative ability) are influenced by g. High scores on g are associated with good scholastic performance. In the workplace, g is the best predictor of success in job training, job performance, occupational prestige, and accomplishment within occupations. Also, g is related to many social outcomes, including early death due to vehicular accidents.[25] The g factor helps explain why some people perform so well in many different mental tasks—they have the *right stuff*.

Various researchers have identified different s factors contributing to overall mental aptitude. Exhibit 2-2 lists and defines seven factors that have been consistently

Exhibit 2-2

Special Factors Contributing to Overall Mental Aptitude

- **Verbal comprehension:** The ability to understand the meanings of words and their relationship to one another, and to comprehend written and spoken information.
- **Word fluency:** The ability to use words quickly and easily, without an emphasis on verbal comprehension.
- **Numerical:** The ability to handle numbers, engage in mathematical analysis, and do arithmetic calculations.
- **Spatial:** The ability to visualize forms in space and manipulate objects mentally, particularly in three dimensions.
- **Memory:** Having a good rote recall for symbols, words, and lists of numbers, along with other associations.
- **Perceptual speed:** The ability to perceive visual details, to pick out similarities and differences, and to perform tasks requiring visual perception.
- **Inductive reasoning:** The ability to discover a rule or principle and apply it in solving a problem, and to make judgments and decisions that are logically sound.

Source: These seven factors stem from the pioneering work of L. L. Thurstone, "Primary Mental Abilities," *Psychometric Monographs, 1* (1938).

noted. Being strong in any mental aptitude often leads to enjoyment of work associated with that aptitude. Conversely, enjoyment of an activity might lead to the development of an aptitude for that activity.

The Triarchic Theory of Intelligence (Emphasis on Practical Intelligence)

Many people, including specialists in organizational behavior, are concerned that the traditional way of understanding intelligence inadequately describes mental ability. An unfortunate implication of intelligence testing is that intelligence as traditionally calculated consists largely of the ability to perform tasks related to scholastic work. Thus, a person who scored high on an intelligence test could follow a complicated instruction manual but not have street smarts; which would, for example, be needed to operate a successful small business.

To overcome the limited idea that intelligence mostly involves the ability to solve abstract problems, the **triarchic theory of intelligence** has been proposed, as presented in Exhibit 2-3. This theory holds that intelligence is composed of three different subtypes: analytical, creative, and practical. The *analytical* subtype is the traditional type of intelligence needed for solving difficult problems with abstract reasoning. Analytical intelligence is required to perform well in most school subjects. The *creative* subtype is the type of intelligence required for imagination and combining things in novel ways. The *practical* subtype is the type of intelligence required for adapting to an environment to suit an individual's needs. Practical intelligence is a major contributor to being street smart.[26]

The idea of practical intelligence helps explain why a person who has a difficult time getting through school can still be a successful businessperson, politician, or

(handwritten margin note: 3 different subtypes - analytical - creative - practical)

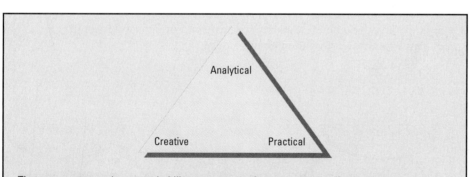

Exhibit 2-3

The Triarchic Theory of Intelligence

Three managers took a mental ability test as part of a career counseling program.

Analytical. Manager A scored well on mental ability tests and was good at both test taking and analytical thinking. He exemplifies the analytical aspect of intelligence and has excellent skills in budgeting.

Creative. Manager B had mediocre test scores, but she was a creative thinker and insightful in sizing up people and business situations. She exemplifies the creative aspect of intelligence and has achieved good success as a branch manager.

Practical. Manager C also had mediocre test scores, but he had street smarts and understood how to manipulate his environment in a variety of contexts. Before becoming a manager, he was an excellent sales representative.

Source: Based on information in Robert J. Trotter, "Three Heads Are Better than One," *Psychology Today*, August 1986, pp. 56–62; modified and updated with information from Robert J. Sternberg, book review in *Personnel Psychology*, Summer 1999, pp. 471–476.

visual artist. Practical intelligence incorporates the ideas of common sense, wisdom, and street smarts. One reservation about practical intelligence is the implication that people who are highly intelligent in the analytical sense are not practical thinkers. In truth, most executives and other high-level workers score quite well on tests of mental ability. Also, leaders at many levels in business who receive higher performance evaluations and actual productivity tend to score slightly higher on mental ability tests. These tests usually measure analytical intelligence.[27]

For organizations, an important implication about practical intelligence centers on problem-solving ability and age. Analytical intelligence may decline from early to late adulthood. Ability of this type is referred to as *fluid intelligence,* and is needed for on–the-spot reasoning, abstraction, and problem solving. However, the ability to solve problems of a practical nature is maintained or increased through late adulthood. Such ability is referred to as *crystallized* intelligence, and centers around accumulated knowledge such as vocabulary, arithmetic, and general information.[28] As people become older, they compensate well for declining raw mental energy by focusing on things they do well. In job situations calling for wisdom, such as resolving conflicts, age and experience may be an advantage.

Multiple Intelligences

Another approach to understanding the diverse nature of mental ability is the theory of **multiple intelligences,** developed by Howard Gardner. According to Gardner's theory, people know and understand the world in distinctly different ways, or look at it through different lenses. Individuals possess the eight intelligences (or faculties), in varying degrees, as listed here and depicted in Exhibit 2–4.

1. *Linguistic:* Enables people to communicate through language, including reading, writing, and speaking
2. *Logical–Mathematical:* Enables individuals to see relationships between objects and solve problems, such as in calculus and statistics
3. *Musical:* Gives people the capacity to create and understand meanings made out of sounds and to enjoy different types of music

Exhibit **2-4**

The Theory of Multiple Intelligences

Individuals possess eight different types of intelligence in varying degrees.

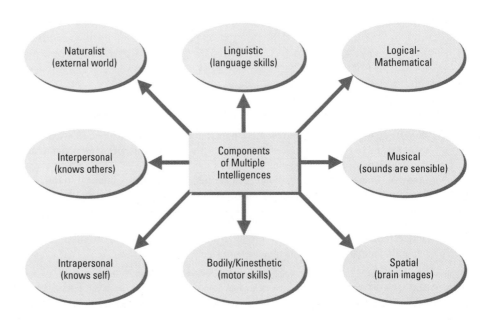

4. *Spatial:* Enables people to perceive and manipulate images in their brain and to re-create them from memory, such as in making graphic designs

5. *Bodily–kinesthetic:* Enables people to use their body and perceptual and motor systems in skilled ways, such as dancing, playing sports, and expressing emotion through facial expressions

6. *Intrapersonal:* Enables people to distinguish among their own feelings and acquire accurate self-knowledge

7. *Interpersonal:* Makes it possible for individuals to recognize and make distinctions among the feelings, motives, and intentions of others, as in managing and parenting

8. *Naturalist:* Enables individuals to differentiate among, classify, and use various features of the physical external environment

Your profile of intelligences influences how you will best learn, and for which types of jobs you are best suited. Gardner believes that it is possible to develop these separate intelligences through concentrated effort. Another consideration is that any of these intelligences will fade if not used.[29] These separate types of intelligences might also be perceived as different talents or abilities. Having high general problem-solving ability would therefore contribute to high standing on each one of the eight intelligences.

A concern about the theory of multiple intelligences is that it is not as well documented as theories of intelligence that emphasize general cognitive ability. Should evidence be collected to support the existence of multiple intelligences, the theory could be applied to improve productivity. Workers could be assigned positions that best fit their profile of intelligences. A person who was not strong in linguistic intelligence or logical–mathematical intelligence might have high enough interpersonal intelligence to be effective as a customer service representative.

PERSONALITY DIFFERENCES

Identify major personality variables that influence job performance.

Personality characteristics such as conscientiousness and extraversion contribute to success in many jobs. Most job failures are not attributed to a person's intelligence or technical competence but to personality characteristics. The subject of personality is therefore important in organizational behavior. However, some controversy still centers on the concept of personality, despite hundreds of studies linking personality to job performance (several are referred to later). There is disagreement as to whether personality can be accurately measured and whether it is influenced more by heredity or environment.

Personality refers to the persistent and enduring behavior patterns of an individual that are expressed in a wide variety of situations. Your personality is the combination of attributes, traits, and characteristics that makes you unique. Your walk, talk, appearance, speech, and creativity all contribute to your personality. Personality can therefore be regarded as the core of who you are.[30]

We approach the topic of personality by first describing eight key personality traits related to job performance and behavior, including a sampling of relevant research. Two experiential activities related to personality will also be presented.

Eight Major Personality Factors and Traits

According to the Five Factor Model (also known as the Big Five) of personality, the basic structure of human personality is represented by five broad factors: neuroticism, extraversion, openness to experience, agreeableness, and conscientiousness. Although the Five Factor Model of personality is well documented, other aspects of personality still have merit. We therefore also present three other factors of particular significance to job behavior: self-monitoring, risk taking and thrill seeking, and optimism versus pessimism. People develop all eight factors to different degrees, partially from growing up in a particular environment. For example, a person might have a natural tendency to be agreeable. An environment in which agreeableness was encouraged would help him or her become even more agreeable.

All eight factors have a substantial impact on job behavior and performance. The interpretation and meaning of these factors provide useful information because they help you to pinpoint areas for personal development. Although these factors are partially inherited, most people can improve their development in them.

1. *Neuroticism.* This trait reflects neuroticism versus emotional stability. People with high neuroticism are prone to psychological distress and coping with problems in unproductive ways. Traits associated with this personality factor include being anxious, insecure, angry, embarrassed, and worried. A person of low neuroticism—or high emotional stability—is calm and confident and usually in control.

2. *Extraversion.* Traits associated with extraversion include being social, gregarious, assertive, talkative, and active. An outgoing person is often described as extraverted, whereas a shy person is described as introverted. Many successful leaders are extraverted, yet some effective leaders are introverted because they rely on other factors such as giving feedback and encouraging others. (Note that *extraversion* in everyday language is spelled *extroversion*.)

3. *Openness to experience.* People who score high with openness have well-developed intellects. Traits associated with this factor include being imaginative, cultured, curious, original, broad-minded, intelligent, and artistically sensitive. Many successful managers and professionals search printed information and the Internet for useful ideas. Also, many top-level executives support the arts.

4. *Agreeableness.* This factor reflects the quality of a person's interpersonal orientation. An agreeable person is friendly and cooperative. Traits associated with the agreeableness factor include being courteous, flexible, trusting, good natured, cooperative, forgiving, softhearted, and tolerant. Agreeableness is a plus for customer service positions, such as the greeters at Wal-Mart.

5. *Conscientiousness.* A variety of meanings have been attached to the conscientious factor, but it generally implies dependability. Recent studies of conscientiousness suggest it consists of six subfactors: industriousness, order, self-control, responsibility, traditionalism, and virtue.[31] Other related traits include being hardworking, achievement oriented, and persevering. Being conscientious to the extreme, however, can lead to workaholism and perfectionism. Take the accompanying (self-assessment 2-1) quiz to think about your tendencies toward being conscientious.

6. *Self-monitoring behavior.* The self-monitoring trait refers to the process of observing and controlling how we appear to others. High self-monitors are pragmatic and are even chameleon-like actors in social groups. They often say what others want to hear. Low self-monitors avoid situations that require them to adopt different outer images. In this way, their outer behavior adheres to their inner values. Low self-monitoring can often lead to inflexibility. People who are skilled at office politics usually score high on the self-monitoring factor.

7. *Risk taking and thrill seeking.* Some people crave constant excitement on the job and are willing to risk their lives to achieve thrills. The willingness to take risks and pursue thrills is a personality trait that has grown in importance in the

SELF-ASSESSMENT 2-1

The Conscientiousness Scale

Responding to the following statements will help you think through your standing on the personality dimension of conscientiousness, including its various facets. Answer mostly true or mostly false, even when the correct answer might be "completely true" or "completely false."

	Mostly True	Mostly False
1. I have a reputation for "getting it done."	X	
2. I procrastinate too much.	X	
3. I am strong willed.	X	
4. My attendance record at school has been excellent.		X
5. My attendance record at work has been excellent.		X
6. I have been frequently late for class.		X
7. I have been frequently late for work.		X
8. I am great with details.	X	
9. I have been complimented about being dependable.		X
10. My self-discipline could use a lot of improvement.	X	
11. My desk is a mess.		X
12. The documents on my hard drive are neatly organized into easily identifiable folders.	X	
13. I carefully follow rules on the job and in school.		X
14. I will read the user manual before jumping in to use a new electronic device, such as a cell phone.		X
15. I seem to try harder than most people to accomplish whatever goal I am pursuing.	X	
16. My checkbook rarely balances accurately.		X
17. I am easily distracted when I attempt to complete a task.		X
18. I quite often exceed the speed limit when driving a vehicle.	X	
19. I am quite prompt in paying my bills.	X	
20. I am very conscientious.	X	

Give yourself 1 point each time you answer agrees with the key. If you scored 16–20, you are probably a highly conscientious person, and this trait will be an asset to your career. 9–15: you are moderately conscientious. 0–8: you will need to become more conscientious and dependable to be successful at work.

1. MT	6. MF	11. MF	16. MF
2. MF	7. MF	12. MT	17. MF
3. MT	8. MT	13. MT	18. MF
4. MT	9. MT	14. MT	19. MT
5. MT	10. MF	15. MT	20. MT

high-technology era. Many people work for employers, start businesses, and purchase stocks with uncertain futures. The search for giant payoffs and daily thrills motivates these individuals. A strong craving for thrills may have some positive consequences for the organization, including the willingness to perform dangerous feats such as setting explosives, capping an oil well, controlling a radiation leak, and introducing a product in a highly competitive environment. However, extreme risk takers and thrill seekers can create problems such as involvement in a disproportionate number of vehicular accidents and

SELF-ASSESSMENT 2-2

The Risk-Taking Scale

Answer true or false to the following questions to obtain an approximate idea of your tendency to take risks, or your desire to do so:

	True	False
1. I eat sushi or other raw fish.	☐	☐
2. I think that amusement park roller coasters should be abolished.	☐	☐
3. I don't like trying foods from other cultures.	☐	☐
4. I would choose bonds over growth stocks.	☐	☐
5. I like to challenge people in positions of power.	☐	☐
6. I don't always wear seat belts while driving.	☐	☐
7. I sometimes talk on my cell phone while driving at highway speeds.	☐	☐
8. I would love to be an entrepreneur (or I love being one).	☐	☐
9. I would like helping out in a crisis such as a product recall.	☐	☐
10. I would like to go cave exploring (or already have done so).	☐	☐
11. I would be willing to have at least 1/3 of my compensation based on a bonus for good performance.	☐	☐
12. I would be willing to visit a maximum security prison on a job assignment.	☐	☐

Give yourself one point each time your answer agrees with the key. If you score 10–12, you are probably a high risk taker. 6–9: You are a moderate risk taker. 3–5: You are cautious. 0–2: You are a very low risk taker.

1. T	5. T	9. T
2. F	6. T	10. T
3. F	7. T	11. T
4. F	8. T	12. T

Source: The idea of a test about risk-taking comfort as well as several of the statements on the quiz come from psychologist Frank Farley.

imprudent investments. Take the accompanying (self-assessment 2-2) quiz to measure your tendency toward risk taking.

8. *Optimism* refers to a tendency to experience positive emotional states and to typically believe that positive outcomes will be forthcoming from most activities. The other end of the scale is *pessimism*—a tendency to experience negative emotional states and to typically believe that negative outcomes will be forthcoming from most activities. Optimism versus pessimism is also referred to in more technical terms as positive affectivity versus negative affectivity and is considered a major personality trait. A person's tendency toward having positive affectivity (optimism) versus negative affectivity (pessimism) also influences job satisfaction. Being optimistic, as you would suspect, tends to enhance job satisfaction.[32]

Although personality is relatively stable, new research suggests that as measured by the Five Factor Model, some aspects of personality improved with age. Based on a sample of 132,000 subjects who took the personality tests on the Internet, it appears that people generally become more responsible, organized, and focused with age. The study examined traits over time. Conscientiousness tended to increase in adulthood, particularly in a person's 20s. Both men and women scored higher on agreeableness and openness as they reached age 30.[33] Readers interested in testing themselves can visit http://www.outofservice.com.

Research Evidence about Personality and Job Behavior

Evidence for the relevance of the Five Factor Model of personality in understanding human behavior comes from a cross-cultural study involving 7134 individuals. The five-factor structure of the American personality was also found to hold true for German, Portuguese, Hebrew, Chinese, Korean, and Japanese samples when the personality test questions were translated into each of these languages. Based on this extensive study, it was concluded that personality structure is universal, much like the structure of the brain or the body. [34]

Depending on the job, any one of the eight personality factors mentioned previously can be important for good job performance. The most consistent finding is that conscientiousness is positively related to job performance for a variety of occupations. Furthermore, the combination of intelligence ("can do") with conscientiousness ("will do") is especially important for job performance. In a study of 91 sales representatives for an appliance manufacturer, the combination of intelligence and conscientiousness made accurate predictions of job success. Representatives who scored high on intelligence and conscientiousness tended to sell more appliances and receive better performance ratings from their supervisors. In a related study with the same sales representatives, extraversion was a good predictor of job performance.[35]

You may recall that moderator variables are important in understanding many aspects of organizational behavior, and this proves to be true with conscientiousness. A series of four studies with several different occupations found that workers needed good social skills for conscientiousness to be related to aspects of job performance related to interpersonal effectiveness.[36] For example, a conscientious sales rep still needs good social skill to close deals.

A meta-analysis of 73 studies demonstrated a relationship between the Five Factor Model and the two criteria of leadership effectiveness, and stepping forth as a leader. Extraversion was the factor most frequently associated with the two leadership criteria.[37]

Self-monitoring is another personality factor whose relationship to job behavior has been supported by extensive research. Meta-analyses were conducted for 136 samples and over 23,000 employees to understand the relationship between work-related behaviors and self-monitoring. It was found that high self-monitors tend to receive better performance ratings and more promotions than low self-monitors. High self-monitors were also more likely to emerge as leaders.[38] In short, it pays to tell people what they want to hear if you want to succeed in business.

The accompanying box insert illustrates how some companies rely on personality measures for key work assignments.

In general, favorable results when using personality measures to predict job performance are more likely to occur when the job requirements are carefully analyzed. For example, agreeableness is more important for an airline reservations assistant than a Web designer. Another essential requirement for the use of personality testing for job selection and employee development is that the test be scientifically constructed by experts in human behavior. Robert Hogan, a leader in the field of

ORGANIZATIONAL BEHAVIOR *In Action*

Franchisers Seek Franchisees with the Right Personality Traits

Robert Bingham was interviewing a prospective franchisee when he realized something was wrong. The woman had "sounded outgoing and warm on the phone," says Bingham, chief executive of Little Gym International Inc., a 170-unit chain based in Scottsdale, Ariz. "But when she got here, she seemed very reserved."

That could spell trouble, since Little Gym owners spend their days leading children through gymnastics, dance and exercise classes. "We need operators who are comfortable interacting with kids and their parents," Bingham says.

In tricky cases like this, Bingham used to rely on his intuition. But about a year ago, his company discovered a safeguard to back up its hunches: a personality test. The exam asks applicants to rank how well a series of words describes them. The results are then compared with the profile of a successful franchisee to see how they match up. "This woman's personality profile showed us she'd rather be in the back office crunching numbers," Bingham says. "We suggested she find another business."

For companies that are sniffing out potential franchisees, a clean financial history isn't enough anymore. A growing number of franchisers are turning to personality tests to see whether potential franchisees will be a good fit with the company's vision—and generate big royalty revenue.

Scott Lehr, vice president of development and marketing for the International Franchise Association (IFA) in Washington, estimates that 30 to 40% of the group's 1000 franchise members use some type of personality profile to award franchises, "and the number is growing.

Franchisers have discovered that they can't spend a couple of hours, or even a few days, with someone, and know if that person will fit into their system."

Personality-assessment tests are common in other parts of the business world, but they have only begun to catch on among franchisers—a reflection of how much the industry has matured in recent years. "Franchisers are much more sophisticated today than they were a generation ago, and are more ready to embrace analytical tools, including personality evaluations," says Matt Shay, president of the IFA.

Changing demographics are also helping to drive the popularity of these tests. Today's prospective franchisees tend to be midlevel or senior corporate managers with lots of experience and definite ideas about how to run a business, says Shay. Franchisers need to know whether a candidate "who interviews well really has the mind-set to exchange some of his or her independence and autonomy for a recognized brand and business plan."

Questions

1. Are franchisers placing too much faith in personality testing?
2. What do you speculate would be the right personality profile for the operator of a Little Gym International Franchise? Use some of the personality traits described in this chapter to help you develop your answer.

Source: Excerpted from Julie Bennett, "Do You Have What it Takes? Companies Are Using Personality Tests to Find Franchisees with the Right Stuff," *The Wall Street Journal,* September 19, 2005, p. R11.

personality assessment in industry, contends that only a handful of personality tests are legitimate in terms of being substantiated by research.[39]

The role plays in the accompanying skill-development exercise give you an opportunity to practice managing for individual differences in personality. Remember that a role player is an extemporaneous actor. Put yourself in the shoes of the character you play and visualize how he or she would act. Because you are given only the general idea of a script, use your imagination to fill in the details.

SKILL-DEVELOPMENT EXERCISE

Personality Role Plays

Run each role play for about 7 minutes. The people not involved in the role play will observe and then provide feedback when the role play is completed.

1. *The Extravert.* One student assumes the role of a successful outside sales representative who has just signed a $3 million order for the company. The elated sales rep returns to the office. Another student assumes the role of the sales manager. He or she decides that this is a splendid opportunity to build a good relationship with the triumphant sales rep.

2. *Openness.* One student plays the role of an experienced worker in the department who is told to spend some time showing around a new co-op student. It appears that this worker is open to experience. Another student plays the role of the co-op student, who is also open to experience and eager to be successful in this new position.

3. *Conscientiousness.* One student plays the role of a team member who is dependent on another team member for his or her contribution to a team project for which the entire team will receive the same grade. The second student was to have collected extensive data about how energy companies establish wholesale and retain prices for gasoline, but is not ready with the input. The first team member has observed from the start of the group project that the second team member is the opposite of a conscientious person. The report is due in 5 days, and the professor is known for not accepting excuses for late papers.

Collaboration

The NEO Personality Inventory for Measuring the Big Five Factors

As you would suspect from the positive research results described previously, the Five Factor Model is widely used by organizations to measure personality and help make selection decisions about job candidates. The NEO Personality Inventory (another name for *test* or *instrument*) measures the five factors, and six more specific traits or facets within each domain. All factors and facets have been scientifically developed. As implied by the description of the Big Five Factors, each factor consists of several facets of behavior, such as self-discipline being part of conscientiousness.

Exhibit 2–5 lists the factors and associated facets of the NEO Personality Inventory. You can use this exhibit for self-reflection, by thinking through your standing

Exhibit 2-5

The Five Factors and Associated Facets Measured by the NEO Personality Inventory

Neuroticism	Extraversion	Openness	Agreeableness	Conscientiousness
(N1) Anxiety	(E1) Warmth	(O1) Fantasy	(A1) Trust	(C1) Competence
(N2) Angry hostility	(E2) Gregariousness	(O2) Aesthetics	(A2) Straight-forwardness	(C2) Order
(N3) Depression	(E3) Assertiveness	(O3) Feelings	(A3) Altruism	(C3) Dutifulness
(N4) Self-consciousness	(E4) Activity	(O4) Actions	(A4) Compliance	(C4) Achievement striving
(N5) Impulsiveness	(E5) Excitement-seeking	(O5) Ideas	(A5) Modesty	(C5) Self-discipline
(N6) Vulnerability	(E6) Positive emotions	(O6) Values	(A6) Tender-mindedness	(C6) Deliberation

Source: Table assembled from information in Paul T. Costa and Robert R. McCrae, "Your NEO PI-R™ Summary," PAR Psychological Assessment Resources, Inc. Copyright © 1985, 1988, 1992, 1994, 2000.

36

on each factor and its associated facets. For example, a truly agreeable person would trust others, be straightforward, be altruistic, comply with others, and be modest. Fortunately, all the technical definitions of the facets are quite close in meaning to the general use of the terms.

A key difference exists between a personality inventory like the NEO and the many self-assessment quizzes presented throughout this text. A standardized personality inventory is scientifically developed and restricted in use to specialists in the field. The self-quizzes presented in this text are designed for self-reflection and self-development, and are not designed to be used for employee selection or professional diagnosis of personality traits.

EMOTIONAL INTELLIGENCE

Explain how emotional intelligence is an important part of organizational behavior.

Research into the functioning of the human brain has combined personality factors with practical intelligence, indicating that how effectively people use their emotions has a major impact on their success. The topmost layers of the brain govern componential intelligence functions, such as analytical problem solving. The innermost areas of the brain govern emotional functions, such as dealing with anger when being criticized by a customer.

Emotional intelligence refers to qualities such as understanding one's own feelings, empathy for others, and the regulation of emotion to enhance living. As the concept of emotional intelligence has gained in popularity, many definitions have been proposed and more and more behavior has been incorporated into emotional intelligence.

Emotional intelligence has to do with the ability to connect with people and understand their emotions. A worker with high emotional intelligence can engage in behaviors such as sizing up, pleasing, and influencing people. Based on research in dozens of companies, Daniel Goleman discovered that the most effective leaders are alike in one essential way: They all have a high degree of emotional intelligence. Without a high degree of emotional intelligence, a person can have excellent training, superior analytical skills, and many innovative suggestions. However, he or she will still not make a great leader. According to a recent conceptualization by Goleman and his associates, the four key factors included in emotional intelligence are as follows:[40]

1. *Self-awareness.* The ability to understand one's own emotions is the most essential of the four emotional intelligence competencies. Having high self-awareness allows people to know their strengths and limitations and have high self-esteem. Effective leaders use self-awareness to accurately measure their own moods, and to intuitively understand how their moods affect others. Effective managers seek feedback to see how well their actions are received by others. A manager with good self-awareness would recognize factors such as whether he or she was liked, or was exerting the right amount of pressure on people.

2. *Self-management.* The ability to control one's emotions and act with honesty and integrity in a consistent and adaptable manner. The right degree of self-management helps prevent a person from throwing temper tantrums when activities do not go as planned. Effective workers do not let their occasional bad moods ruin their day. If they cannot overcome the bad mood, they let work associates know of the problem and how long it might last. A manager with high

self-management would not suddenly decide to fire a group member because of one difference of opinion.

3. *Social awareness.* Having empathy for others and having intuition about organizational problems are key aspects of this dimension of emotional intelligence. Socially aware leaders go beyond sensing the emotions of others by showing that they care. In addition, they accurately size up political forces in the office. A team leader with social awareness, or empathy, would be able to assess whether a team member has enough enthusiasm for a project to assign him to that project. A CEO who has empathy for a labor union's demands might be able to negotiate successfully with the head of the labor union to avoid a costly strike.

4. *Relationship management.* Includes the interpersonal skills of being able to communicate clearly and convincingly, disarm conflicts, and build strong personal bonds. Effective leaders use relationship management skills to spread their enthusiasm and solve disagreements, often with kindness and humor. A leader with good relationship-management skills would not burn bridges and would continue to enlarge his or her network of people to win support when support is needed.[41] Many training programs are designed to improve emotional intelligence, but the earlier that people develop skills in handling emotional reactions the better. This is because the key to emotional intelligence lies in the way the brain is programmed in childhood. People learn most of their emotional habits when they are young, but can still learn to improve inappropriate responses later in life.

Among the many practical outcomes of having high emotional intelligence is the ability to cope better with setbacks. A review of many studies concluded that low emotional intelligence employees are more likely than their high emotional intelligence counterparts to experience negative emotional reactions to job insecurity, such as high tension. Furthermore, workers with low emotional intelligence are more likely to engage in negative coping behaviors, such as expressing anger and verbally abusing a immediate supervisor for the organization failing to provide job security.[42]

A concern about the concept of emotional intelligence is that a person with good cognitive intelligence would also engage in many of the behaviors of an emotionally intelligent person. Another concern is that the popularized concept of emotional intelligence has become so broad it encompasses almost the entire study of personality. Some approaches to presenting emotional intelligence appear to present a long list of desirable qualities, such as resiliency and vision.[43]

Tests of emotional intelligence typically ask you to respond to questions on a 1-to-5 scale (never, rarely, sometimes, often, consistently). For example, indicate how frequently you demonstrate the following behaviors:

I can laugh at myself.	1	2	3	4	5
I help others grow and develop.	1	2	3	4	5
I watch carefully the nonverbal communication of others.	1	2	3	4	5

Emotional intelligence underscores the importance of being practical-minded and having effective interpersonal skills to succeed in organizational life. Many topics included in the study of organizational behavior, such as communication, conflict resolution, and power and politics, are components of emotional intelligence.

The message is an old one: Both cognitive and noncognitive skills are required for success!

IMPLICATIONS FOR MANAGERIAL PRACTICE

A major implication of individual differences in personality and abilities is that these factors have a major impact on the selection, placement, job assignment, training, and development of employees. When faced with such decisions, the manager should seek answers to questions such as:

- Is this employee intelligent enough to handle the job and deal with out-of-the-ordinary problems?
- Is this employee too intelligent for the assignment? Will he or she become bored quickly?
- Is this employee's personality suited to the assignment? For instance, is the employee conscientious enough? Is the employee open to new learning?

Many employees perform below standard not because they are not motivated but because their abilities and personality traits are not suited to the job. For instance, an employee who writes garbled update reports may be doing so because of below-average verbal comprehension, not low motivation. Training programs and coaching can be useful in making up for deficits that appear on the surface to be motivational problems.

SUMMARY OF KEY POINTS

 Explain how individual differences influence the behavior of people in organizations.

Understanding individual differences helps to explain human behavior. Nevertheless, behavior is a function of the person interacting with the environment, as expressed by the equation $B = f(P \times E)$. Seven consequences of individual differences that have an impact on managing people are (1) productivity, (2) quality of work, (3) effectiveness of empowerment, (4) which leadership style is effective will vary, (5) people differ in their need for social contact, (6) commitment and loyalty to the firm will vary, and (7) self-esteem differences will influence productivity.

 Describe key factors contributing to demographic diversity.

Understanding demographic differences among workers can help the manager capitalize on diversity and avoid negative stereotyping. Key sources of demographic diversity include sex and gender, generational and age-based differences, ethnicity, race, and culture.

 Explain how mental ability relates to job performance.

Mental ability, or intelligence, is one of the major sources of individual differences that affect job performance and behavior. Intelligence consists of many components. One perspective is that intelligence includes a general factor (g) along with special factors (s) that contribute to problem-solving ability. A related perspective is that intelligence consists of seven components, including verbal and numerical comprehension. To overcome the limited idea that intelligence involves mostly the ability to solve abstract problems, the triarchic theory of intelligence has been proposed. Its three component types of intelligence are analytical, creative, and practical (adapting to your environment to suit your needs). The theory of multiple intelligences proposes eight types of intelligence: linguistic, logical–mathematical, musical, spatial, bodily–kinesthetic, intrapersonal, interpersonal, and naturalist.

Identify major personality variables that influence job performance.

Personality is one of the major sources of individual differences. Eight major personality factors are neuroticism, extraversion, openness to experience, agreeableness, conscientiousness, self-monitoring, risk taking and thrill seeking, and optimism. Depending on the job, any one of these personality factors can be important for success.

The NEO Personality Inventory measures a person's standing on the Five Factor Model, including the factors and associated facets.

 Explain how emotional intelligence is an important part of organizational behavior.

The concept of emotional intelligence helps explain how emotions and personality factors contribute to success. A worker with high emotional intelligence would be able to engage in such behaviors as sizing up, pleasing, and influencing people. The components of emotional intelligence are self-awareness, self-management, social awareness, and relationship management.

KEY TERMS AND PHRASES

Individual Differences, 20
Variations in how people respond to the same situation based on personal characteristics.

Demographic Diversity, 22
Differences in background factors about the workforce that help shape workers' attitudes and behavior.

Intelligence, 25
The capacity to acquire and apply knowledge, including solving problems.

***g* (General) Factor, 26**
A major component of intelligence that contributes to problem-solving ability.

***s* (Special) Factors, 26**
Components of intelligence that contribute to problem-solving ability.

Triarchic Theory of Intelligence, 27
The theory that intelligence is composed of three different types of intelligence: analytical, creative, and practical.

Multiple Intelligences, 28
The theory that people know and understand the world in distinctly different ways, or look at it through different lenses.

Personality, 29
The persistent and enduring behavior patterns of an individual that are expressed in a wide variety of situations.

Emotional Intelligence, 36
Qualities such as understanding one's own feelings, empathy for others, and the regulation of emotion to enhance living.

DISCUSSION QUESTIONS AND ACTIVITIES

1. Give an example from your own life of how $B = f(P \times E)$.

2. Ten years into the future, your classmates will show wide variations in terms of their career achievements. How might individual differences explain some of these differences in accomplishment?

3. Work together in a small discussion group to uncover several positive demographic stereotypes about workers. Give examples of how these stereotypes might be used in selecting new hires or in making work assignments for present employees.

4. Suppose you or a family member were taking a transcontinental flight. Would you want the pilot for your ship captain a pilot who claims he has good practical intelligence, even though he has below-average analytical intelligence? Explain your reasoning.

5. What is your opinion of the usefulness of using a standardized mental ability test to help screen college football plays for a position in the NFL?

6. Which of the personality traits described in this chapter do you think are particularly important for managers who would conduct their work in a highly ethical manner? Explain.

7. Why does having high self-esteem contribute to being more productive and earning a higher income?

CASE PROBLEM: The Sought-After Military Vets

Mark Mandel is the sales manager for Precision Machines, a company that customizes machines bought from other companies for use by its customers. The original manufacturer of the machine is often not interested in reconfiguring its machines for an unusual application. Precision Machines works closely with its customers to understand their unique manufacturing needs. As American companies strive to become competitive with companies from other countries, the need for machine efficiency has increased. As a consequence, Precision Machines has experienced a steady increase in sales. A deterrent to the growth of the company, however, has been a shortage of highly capable sales representatives. In addition to having sales skills, the representatives must have an in-depth understanding of machines and information technology.

Mandel has given considerable thought to innovative recruiting methods for finding the type of sales reps that could help the company. While reading the business section of the local newspaper one Sunday morning, Mandel came upon a report that presented some promising ideas for finding sales reps. He called the company owner, Liz Barton, that evening to schedule a Monday morning meeting to discuss his ideas.

"Let's get right to the heart of the matter," said Mandel at the meeting. "I've made a copy of the report for you, and I've also prepared a few PowerPoint slides with bulleted points. The study assumes that a company is looking for sales reps who handle rejection well, plow ahead in a difficult environment, and stay focused on the mission at hand. That is certainly the type of rep we need at Precision."

Mandel and Bartow then start reviewing the report together, including an occasional glance at the PowerPoint slides. Details of the report follow:

A study from Wright State University, sponsored in part by Recruiting Military LLC, concluded that those with military training may be a good choice for an account executive slot. Drew Myers, president of RecruitMilitary, wasn't surprised by the findings. "Military personnel are keenly focused on issues, able to define obstacles, and then efficiently remove them," he said. "These are terrific attributes."

Many of the tens of thousands of Americans serving in the military around the world will be looking for jobs when they return home, and the report says traits of most military veterans tend to make them suitable for sales positions or strategic development roles with customers.

The report from RecruitMilitary and the HR Chally Group evolved from the results of assessment tests given in 2004 to 250 veterans seeking sales positions. Those names were drawn from the 74,000-name database of RecruitMilitary, which were then compared with civilian test-takers in the 150,000-person database managed by the Chally Group.

Differences were profiled and ranked in the report by Corey E. Miller, assistant professor of psychology, along with two doctoral students, at Wright State University in Dayton.

While critics of military training maintain that the military structure tends to drain initiative and entrepreneurial drive and create organizational followers, Miller insisted that the opposite was true. "When I started off, that was my perspective," Miller said. "We found that veterans are comfortable weighing risks and rewards, and when it makes sense to take the risk, they do."

Generally, veterans in sales jobs are more likely to:

- Focus on customer problems. "In Iraq and Afghanistan, small-unit leaders had to solve problems as mundane as traffic issues and as complicated as tribal disputes," said Meyers. "Few rules, few operating procedures, and here's a guy [or gal] who's 24. He or she is a first lieutenant and already he or she has had to solve a lot of problems."
- Treat customers with courtesy. "When they ask a question (to close a deal), they are able to do it without being abrupt or aggressive," Myers said.
- Welcome accountability for core business results. "The discipline necessary to succeed in any of the services carries over very well into sales," said Howard Stevens, chief executive of HR Chally.

CASE PROBLEM (Continued)

"My thoughts right now, Liz," said Mandel "are to start recruiting military veterans for our sales positions. We will work with employment agencies to find vets, we will post our openings on job boards, and indicate a preference for vets. The careers section of our company Web site will also indicate a preference for vets."

"Hold on Mark," replied Bartow. "The study did not conclude that every military veteran had such sterling qualities. I've met some ex-soldiers who are unsuited for sales in terms of their people skills and their mental ability. Also, do we really want to publicly discriminate against candidates who are not military veterans? Wouldn't significant experience in the Boy Scouts or Girl Scouts also prepare a person for technical sales? What about experience on a highly disciplined sports team. Wouldn't that help prepare a person for industrial selling?"

"It looks like I have to give my recruiting plans a little more thought," concluded Mandel. "Let's meet again in a few days."

Case Questions

1. What is your evaluation of the accuracy of the study conclusions that military veterans are well suited for sales?
2. If Precision Machines does look to hire military veterans for sales positions, how can the company avoid charges of discriminating against nonveterans?
3. What advice can you offer management at Precision to make good use of the study results to help with the recruitment of sales representatives?

Source: The facts in this case are based on John Eckberg, "Need a Good Salesman? Hire a Vet: New Report Finds Military Training, Experience Make Worthy Prospects," Gannett News Service, April 1, 2005.

ENDNOTES

1. Marcus Buckingham, "What Great Managers Do," *Harvard Business Review*, March 2005, pp. 70–79.
2. Kurt Lewin, *A Dynamic Theory of Personality* (New York: McGraw-Hill, 1935).
3. John E. Hunter, Frank L. Schmidt, and Michael E. Judiesch, "Individual Differences in Output Variability as a Function of Job Complexity," *Journal of Applied Psychology,* February 1990, pp. 28–42.
4. "The Vital Role of Self-Esteem: It Boosts Productivity and Earnings," *Business Week,* February 2, 1998, p. 26.
5. A brief review of the literature is presented in Leonard Sax, "Maybe Men and Women are Different," *American Psychologist,* June/July 2002, p. 444.
6. James Q. Wilson, *The Moral Sense* (New York: The Free Press, 1993).
7. Janet Shibley Hyde, "The Gender Similarities Hypothesis," *American Psychologist*, September 2005, pp. 581–592.
8. Greg Hammill, "Mixing and Managing Four Generations of Employees," *FDUMagazine Online,* Winter/Spring 2005 (http://www.fdu.edu/newspubs/magazine/05ws/generations.htm).
9. Cited in Melissa Dittman, "Generational Differences at Work," *Monitor on Psychology*, June 2005, pp. 54–55.
10. Dittman, "Generational Differences at Work," p. 55.
11. Bruce J. Avolio, David A. Waldman, and Michael A. McDaniel, "Age and Work Performance in Nonmanagerial Jobs: The Effects of Experience and Occupational Type," *Academy of Management Journal,* June 1990, pp. 407–422.
12. Glen M. McEvoy and Wayne F. Cascio, "Cumulative Evidence of the Relationship between Employee Age and Job Performance," *Journal of Applied Psychology,* February 1989, pp. 11–17.
13. Scott Goldsmith with Diane Brady, "Old, Smart, Productive," *Business Week,* June 27, 2005, p. 80.

14. Susan R. Rhodes, "Age-Related Differences in Work Attitudes and Behavior: A Review and Conceptual Analysis," *Psychological Bulletin,* March 1983, pp. 328–367; Milt Freudenheim, "More Help Wanted: Older Workers Please Apply," *nytimes.com,* March 23, 2005, p. 1.
15. Joann S. Lublin, "Aged to Perfection? More Companies Seek Older Leaders," *The Wall Street Journal*, December 2, 2003, p. B1.
16. Janet E. Helms, Maryam Jernigan, and Jackquelyn Mascher, "The Meaning of Race in Psychology and How to Change It," *American Psychologist*, January 2005, p. 35.
17. Christine M. Riordan and Lynn McFarlane Shore, "Demographic Diversity and Employee Attitudes: An Empirical Examination of Relational Demography within Work Units," *Journal of Applied Psychology,* June 1997, pp. 342–358.
18. Orlando Behling, "Employee Selection: Will Intelligence and Conscientiousness Do the Job?" *Academy of Management Executive,* February 1998, p. 78.
19. Jesús F. Salgado, et al., "A Meta-Analytic Study of General Mental Ability Validity for Different Occupations in the European Community," *Journal of Applied Psychology*, December 2003, pp. 1068–1081.
20. Sam Walker, "The NFL's Smartest Team," *The Wall Street Journal*, September 30, 2005, pp. W1, W10.
21. Hans J. Eysenck, *Intelligence: A New Look* (New Brunswick, NJ: Transaction, 1998).
22. Research cited in Sharon Begley, "Good Genes Count, But Many Factors Make Up a High IQ," *The Wall Street Journal*, June 20, 2003, p. B1.
23. James R. Flynn, "The Discovery of IQ Gains Over Time," *American Psychologist,* January 1999, pp. 5–20; Tomoe Kanaya, Matthew H. Scullin, and Stephen J. Ceci, "The Flynn Effect and U.S. Policies," *American Psychologist*, October 2003, p. 779.

42

24. Saul Kassin, *Psychology,* 3rd ed. (Upper Saddle River, NJ: Prentice Hall, 2001), p. 467; Eysenck, *Intelligence: A New Look.*

25. Arthur R. Jensen, *The g Factor: The Science of Mental Ability* (Westport, CT: Praeger, 1998).

26. Robert J. Sternberg, *Beyond IQ: A Triarchic Theory of Human Intelligence* (New York: Cambridge University Press, 1995).

27. Timothy A. Judge, Amy E. Colbert, and Remus Ilies, "Intelligence and Leadership: A Quantitative Review and Test of Theoretical Propositions," *Journal of Applied Psychology*, June 2004, pp. 542–552.

28. Kanaya, Scullin, and Ceci, "The Flynn Effect and U.S. Policies," p. 779.

29. Howard Gardner, *Leading Minds: An Anatomy of Leadership* (New York: Basic Books, 1996).

30. "From 'Character' to 'Personality,'" *APA Monitor,* December 1999, p. 22.

31. Brent W. Roberts, Oleksandr S. Chernyshenko, Stephen Stark, and Lewis R. Goldberg, "The Structure of Conscientiousness: An Empirical Investigation Based on Seven Major Personality Questionnaires," *Personnel Psychology*, Spring 2005, pp. 103–139.

32. Remus Ilies and Timothy A. Judge, "On the Heritability of Job Satisfaction: The Mediating Role of Personality," *Journal of Applied Psychology*, August 2003, pp. 750–759.

33. Research reported in Rosemarie Ward, "Ripening with Age: Key Traits Seem to Improve as We Grow Older," *Psychology Today*, July/August 2003, p. 12.

34. Robert R. McCrae and Paul T. Costa, Jr. "Personality Trait Structure as a Human Universal," *American Psychologist,* May 1997, pp. 509–516.

35. These studies and similar ones are reviewed in Leonard D. Goodstein and Richard I. Lanyon, "Applications of Personality Assessment to the Workplace: A Review," *Journal of Business and Psychology,* Spring 1999, pp. 293–298.

36. L. A. Witt and Gerald R. Ferris, "Social Skill as Moderator of the Conscientiousness-Performance Relationship: Convergent Results Across Four Studies," *Journal of Applied Psychology*, October 2003, pp. 809–820.

37. Timothy A. Judge, Joyce E. Bono, Remus Ilies, and Megan W. Gerhardt, "Personality and Leadership: A Quantitative and Qualitative Review," *Journal of Applied Psychology,* August 2002, pp. 765–780.

38. David B. Day, Deidra J. Schleicher, Amy L. Unckless, and Nathan J. Hiller, "Self-Monitoring Personality at Work: A Meta-Analytic Investigation of Construct Validity," *Journal of Applied Psychology,* April 2002, pp. 390–401.

39. Cited in Arielle Emmett, "Snake Oil or Science? That's the Raging Debate on Personality Testing," *Workforce Management,* October 2004, p. 90.

40. Daniel Goleman, Richard Boyatzis, and Annie McKee, "Primal Leadership: The Hidden Driver of Great Performance," *Harvard Business Review,* December 2001, pp. 42–51.

41. Peter J. Jordan, Neal M. Ashkanasy, and Charmine E. J. Hartel, "Emotional Intelligence as a Moderator of Emotional and Behavioral Reactions to Job Insecurity," *Academy of Management Review,* July 2002, pp. 361–372.

42. Patrick A. McGuire, "Teach Your Children Well—and Early, Goleman Says," *APA Monitor,* October 1998, p. 15.

43. Gerald Matthews, Moshe Zeidner, and Richard Roberts, *Emotional Intelligence: Science and Myth* (Cambridge, MA: MIT Press, 2003), p. 531.

Learning, Perception, and Attribution

Randy MacDonald, Senior Vice President of Human Resources at IBM Corp., wrote a letter to the editor of *The Wall Street Journal* explaining some of the company's initiatives to help its workforce retrain for the future. He wrote, "That's the price of entry for leadership in a world where expertise and the quality of your work force are the most important points of competitive differentiation.

"The Chief Executive Officer of IBM will commit $25 million in seed money for this project to help our people develop and refresh their skills and find work with our 90,000 business partners world-wide. In the technology universe, none of our competitors have done anything like this to help their work force—and to help their partners add critical skills that are hard to find and develop.

"IBM currently invests more than $750 million annually to develop the knowledge and expertise of its work force. Employees spend an estimated 17 million hours each year (about 55 hours per employee) in formal training—either through online learning activities or in a traditional classroom. And as part of our training emphasis, we've earmarked $200 million specifically to emerging 'hot' skill areas such as high-value services, the skills to do executive business integration, open standards and pervasive/wireless technologies.

"We are determined to give IBM employees every opportunity to be retrained in skills that will be valuable inside and outside IBM. It's inefficient

Source: Randy MacDonald, "IBM Retrains Employees to Find Work World-Wide," Letters to the Editor, *The Wall Street Journal*, March 15, 2004, p. A17.

OBJECTIVES

After reading and studying this chapter and doing the exercises, you should be able to:

1. Explain the basics of modeling and shaping, cognitive learning, and e-learning.

2. Describe how learning styles influence workplace learning.

3. Describe key aspects of the perceptual process, along with common perceptual problems.

4. Describe how attribution theory and blaming others contribute to an understanding of human behavior in the workplace.

and undesirable to part with members of the IBM community when we can train them, in many cases for new jobs of the future. It is consistent with the company's values, and it's an important part of our desire to constantly improve our value to our clients.

IBM is hiring world-wide and in the U.S.—and unlike many other companies, we're working hard to retrain existing workers and keep them in this industry, even while we hire for the emerging jobs of the new century."

Now Ask Yourself: **What is the relevance of employee learning to the welfare of a firm?** For one, the fact that IBM invests so much time in employee training and learning suggests that on-the-job training affects a firm's financial position and competitive advantage. In this chapter, we describe three aspects of individual functioning: learning, perception, and attributions. Understanding these aspects of behavior helps managers deal more effectively with people. Understanding these aspects of behavior should also make job seekers realize that technical skill alone is not enough to survive in today's information-age economy.

TWO KEY LEARNING PROCESSES AND E-LEARNING

Explain the basics of modeling and shaping, cognitive learning, and e-learning.

Given that most organizations emphasize continuous learning, it is useful to understand how people learn. Workers at all levels are expected to acquire both new hard skills and soft skills throughout their career. For example, a worker might have to learn the new technology to work at a call center and also develop an ability to understand the accents of people from different cultures, which is necessary to deal with call-center customers. **Learning** is a relatively permanent change in behavior based on practice or experience. A curiosity about learning is that it is possible to learn something and store it in your mind without changing your behavior.[1] For example, you might read that if you press "F12" in Windows you open the "Save As" function. You keep it in mind but do not use the command yet. The new knowledge is stored in your upper brain but is not yet put into action.

A person does not learn how to grow physically, digest food, hear sounds, or see light. These are innate, inborn patterns of behavior. But a person does learn how to conduct a performance evaluation, use an Internet search engine to access information, or prepare a report. Unless learning takes place, few employees would be able to perform their jobs satisfactorily.

Our concern here is with two methods of learning complex material: (1) modeling and shaping, and (2) cognitive learning, including informal learning. We also describe a popular method of delivering material for learning, e-learning. In recognition of the fact that people learn in different ways, we will also discuss learning styles.

Modeling and Shaping

When you acquire a complicated skill such as coaching a team member, you experience much more than the acquisition of a few habits. You learn a large number of habits, and you learn how to put them together in a cohesive, smoothly flowing pattern. Two important processes that help in learning complicated skills are modeling and shaping.

Modeling (or imitation) occurs when you learn a skill by observing another person perform that skill. Many sales representatives acquire sales skills by observing a competent sales representative in action. DVDs are widely used to facilitate modeling of skills such as interviewing, resolving conflict, and conducting a meeting. Modeling often brings forth behaviors that people did not previously seem to have in their repertoire. To model effectively, one must carefully observe the demonstration and then attempt the new skill shortly thereafter. Although modeling is an effective learning method, the learner must have the proper capabilities and motivation.

Shaping occurs when a person learns through the reinforcement or rewarding of small steps that build up to the final or desired behavior. It is another way in which complicated skills are learned. At each successful step of the way, the learner receives positive reinforcement. As the learner improves his or her ability to perform the task, more skill is required to receive the reward.

A clerical worker might be shaped into an inside sales representative (taking telephone and computer orders). He acquires a series of small skills, beginning with learning the computerized inventory system. He receives a series of rewards as he moves along the path from a support specialist to an inside sales representative who can understand and satisfy customer requirements. Among the forms of positive reinforcement he receives are approval for his new skills, incremental pay increases, and the feeling of pride as new small skills are learned. Among the punishments he receives to assist learning are negative statements from customers when he fills an order incorrectly.

Cognitive Learning

Cognitive learning theory emphasizes that learning takes place in a complicated manner involving much more than acquiring habits and small skills. Learners also strive to learn, develop hunches, and have flashes of insight. Furthermore, they use many aspects of their personality (such as openness to experience) in acquiring knowledge. Suppose that a safety and health specialist discovers the cause underlying a mysterious rash on the skin of many employees. Cognitive learning theory would emphasize that the specialist may have reached the conclusion by acquiring bits of information that formed a cohesive pattern. The theory would also emphasize the goal orientation of the safety and health specialist, along with the person's reasoning and analytical skills. Dedication to the cause and problem-solving ability would also contribute to the learning.

Another type of learning in organizations that fits a cognitive theory explanation is **informal learning.** This is defined as any learning that occurs in which the organization does not determine or design the learning process. You might learn by observing others, asking tech support a question, or working with knowledgeable people.[2] The central premise of such learning is that employees acquire some important information outside of a formal learning situation. The employees capitalize on a learning situation outside of a formal structure, in which the rewards stemming from the learning situation are not explicit.

Informal learning can be spontaneous—such as receiving a suggestion on how to calculate the value of an American dollar in terms of a euro, and vice versa, while having lunch in a company cafeteria. Or the company might organize the work to encourage such informal learning. The company might provide common areas such as an atrium or food and beverage lounges that encourage employee interaction. Sometimes these common work areas are furnished with white boards and markers to facilitate exchanging ideas.

Exhibit **3-1**

Sources of Learning on the Job

Capital Works reported that we learned through the following means.

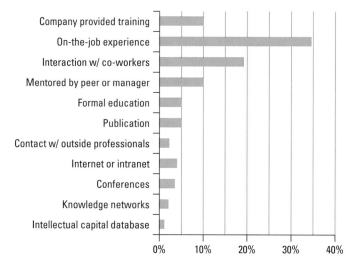

Source: Capital Works, LLC as reprinted in Marcia L. Conner, "Informal Learning," *Ageless Learner*, 1997–2005. http://agelesslearner.com/intros/informal.html, p. 2.

Research conducted by the Center for Workforce Development indicated that up to 70% of learning takes place informally.[3] Exhibit 3-1 presents a similar picture, with approximately 65% of learning stemming from on-the-job experience, interaction with coworkers, mentoring, and contact with outside professionals. Informal learning frequently does not have an expressed goal. You might be chatting in an atrium with a coworker and learn something valuable even though you had not established a learning goal for the conversation. According to the study in question, informal learning can be divided into four types:

- *Practical skills:* Examples include job-specific skills and knowledge, and technical competence.
- *Intrapersonal skills:* Examples include problem solving, critical thinking, exploring boundaries for risk taking, and stress management.
- *Interpersonal skills:* Examples include peer-to-peer communications, presentation skills, and conflict resolution.
- *Cultural awareness:* Examples include professional awareness, professional advancement, social norms, understanding company goals, quality standards, and company expectations and priorities.

An important implication of informal learning for managers is that knowledgeable and well-motivated employees can help one another with learning. However, the manager must still be on guard against misinformed and poorly motivated employees who would create negative learning. Classroom training is helpful in increasing the chances that the right type of learning takes place.

A factor influencing how much cognitive learning takes place is the orientation of the learner. A *mastery orientation* relates to a dedication to increasing one's competence with a task. These learners are eager to improve their ability with tasks. For example, a person might want to learn how to make more effective oral presentations so he or she could better enjoy presenting at meetings. With a *performance orientation,* learners focus on how well they perform a task and make comparisons with others.

Learners with a performance orientation are keenly interested in displaying their ability to (or performing for) others. Evidence has been collected from college students that a mastery orientation is associated with greater effort and more complex learning strategies. (An example of a complex learning strategy would be paraphrasing and generating questions with answers.) In contrast, performance orientation is associated with less effort devoted to the task and less frequent use of complex learning strategies.[4]

E-learning

Important innovations in learning have taken place in both schools and industry through the use of distance learning, technology-based learning, and e-learning. Here, the learner studies independently outside of a classroom setting and interacts with a computer in addition to studying course material. **E-learning** is a Web-based form of computer-based training. Many learning programs are computer based without being delivered over the Internet. For example, the tutorials included in many software packages are a form of computer-based training. An e-learning course usually is carefully structured, with specific lessons plans for the student. E-learning is more of a method of delivering content than a method of learning, yet the process helps us understand more about learning.

A major impetus behind e-learning is that many employees are geographically dispersed, making it difficult to gather them in one place for learning. A germane example is the marketing communications firm, Fleishman-Hillard with 2000 employees spread across 80 locations in 22 countries. The company uses web-based technology to make information sharing more accessible and interactive.[5]

Although e-learning is technologically different from more traditional forms of learning, it still is based on basic methods of learning. For example, the learner will often need reinforcement to keep going. Trainers at GE Capital found that when managers gave reinforcement to employees about attendance, made them feel important, and tracked their progress, employees were more likely to complete the course.[6]

Another relevant aspect of e-learning here is that its success depends on cognitive processes of the learner, particularly self-motivation and self-discipline. Self-motivation is important because an assignment to take an e-learning course by the company is often not enough to motivate a person to work independently. Self-discipline is necessary to create a regular time for performing class work and to prevent distractions by work or home activities. In educational settings, successful distance learning also requires high motivation. Some students may not take e-learning seriously. Corporate e-learning programs have a high dropout rate; most students need the structure of a face-to-face instructor, a classroom, and other students to keep them focused on the course.[7]

E-learning has gained momentum, yet most companies prefer to use blended learning (Web and classroom) because it combines the personal nature of classroom training with the cost efficiencies of learning via the Internet. The cost efficiencies include decreases in travel and lodging costs and payments to classroom instructors.[8] However, classroom training provides the difficult-to-measure benefit of employees spontaneously exchanging ideas that could lead to a creativity breakthrough. In general, e-learning is most effective in delivering conceptual subject matter, such as product information, whereas classroom training is more effective for learning interpersonal skills.[9]

The accompanying Organizational Behavior in Action describes an extensive application of e-learning by a company that owns one of America's best-known brands.

ORGANIZATIONAL BEHAVIOR *In Action*

Nike Teaches Sports Knowledge Underground through e-Learning

Mike Donahue, who is in charge of e-learning at Nike, was asked to design an online training program that the company could offer to employees in its stores as well as at other stores that sell its products. He knew that he and his team would have to design a program that would convey a lot of information quickly, but also would be easy to digest.

"We knew that we did a great job of advertising and that we could drive people into the stores, but ultimately the person that is talking to the customer is a 16- to 22-year old," he says. "We wanted them to have a better dialogue with the consumer."

Nike faced a challenge that a number of retailers today are confronting as they adopt e-learning: Many of these companies face more than 100% turnover in their stores, and to train their staffs in a classroom setting is just not cost-effective or even possible for retailers that have stores scattered throughout the country, according to Claire Shooley, senior industry analyst at Forrester Research.

Donahue and his team knew they wanted their program to deliver information in short increments to make it easy for associates to take in—and keep them out on the floor.

"We were throwing out ideas, and someone suggested that we need to come up with something edgy, something underground," Donahue says. That's when the idea for the Sports Knowledge Underground was born. It was by pure coincidence that the acronym for the new program, SKU, also stands for the retail stocking term "stock keeping unit," Donahue says.

The layout for the Sports Knowledge Underground resembles a subway map, with different stations representing different training themes. For example, Apparel Union Station branches off into the apparel technologies line, the training products line, and the Nike Pro products line. The Cleated Footwear Station offers paths to football, whereas the Central Station offers such broad lines as customer skills.

Each segment is 3 to 7 minutes long and gives the associate the basic knowledge he or she needs about basic products. As new products are introduced each season, the training is updated and Nike customizes the program for each retailer if requested. Associates are quizzed at the end of the training, and asked for feedback, which gets routed back to Donahue and his team. "If we get feedback that something is confusing, we can go back and change it immediately," Donahue says.

Nike ran a pilot program in its own stores but now has Sports Knowledge Underground running at external retailers too, reaching about 20,000 associates. Donahue expects that number to quadruple in the next few months as the company continues to place the program in more stores.

Already Nike has seen results. Stores that have implemented Sports Knowledge Underground have seen a 4 to 6% increase in sales. "The bottom line is if you can move the necessary handle on the sales floor, it's worth it," Donahue says.

For Nike, one of the most appealing aspects of introducing e-learning is that it sets a standard of learning for diverse workforces. The culture of one store may be vastly different from the next. "One of the problems that a lot of organizations face is that training is not usually a centralized activity," says Peter McStravick, senior research analyst in learning services at IDC.

Questions

1. Why is e-learning supposedly of particular value in a company with high employee turnover?
2. How effective do you think Sports Knowledge Underground would be at teaching customer service skills?

Source: Jessica Marquez, "Faced with High Turnover, Retailers Boot Up e-Learning Programs for Quick Training," *Workforce Management,* August 2005, pp. 74–75.

LEARNING STYLES

Another important concept in understanding learning is **learning style,** the fact that people learn best in different ways. For example, some people acquire new material best through passive learning. Such people quickly acquire information through studying textbooks, manuals, and magazine articles. They can juggle images in their mind as they read about abstract concepts such as supply and demand, cultural diversity, and customer service. Others learn best by doing rather than by studying—for example, learning hands-on about customer service by dealing with customers in many situations.

Another key dimension of learning styles is whether a person learns best by working alone or cooperatively, such as in a study group. Learning by oneself allows for more intense concentration, and one can proceed at one's own pace. Learning in groups and through classroom discussion allows people to exchange viewpoints and perspectives. Considerable evidence has been accumulated that peer tutoring and cooperative learning are effective for acquiring knowledge.[10] Another advantage of cooperative learning is that it is more likely to lead to changes in behavior. Assume that a manager holds group discussions about the importance of achieving high customer satisfaction. Employees participating in these group discussions are more likely to assertively pursue high customer satisfaction on the job than those who only read about the topic.

Learning styles have also been studied more scientifically, and two approaches are described in the following sections.

Visual, Auditory, and Kinesthetic Learning Styles

According to the visual, auditory, and kinesthetic (VAK) learning style categorization, people learn best using one of three main sensory receivers.[11] *Visual learners* learn best by seeing, and they have two subchannels, linguistic and spatial. Learners who are *visual–linguistic* prefer to learn through written language, such as reading and writing assignments. This type of learner would carefully pore over an instruction manual before using a new electronic device. Learners who are *visual–spatial* prefer graphics, demonstrations, and videos or DVDs over written information.

Auditory learners prefer to learn by hearing, and they tend to move their lips and read out loud. An auditory learner would much prefer a spoken explanation of how to do something, such as using a new electronic device, than reading a manual. The same learners would prefer the interaction of a classroom over e-learning. *Kinesthetic learners* learn best while touching and moving and rely on two subchannels, kinesthetic (movement) and tactile (touch). These learners like to take notes while listening to lectures, tend to use highlighters, and frequently doodle while listening. When reading, the kinesthetic learner prefers to take an overview of the material first, to obtain the big picture, and focuses on details later.

Most learners combine all three styles to some degree, even if they are dominant in one. For example, the visual learner might want to read the manual first to learn how to use a new electronic device. Yet the same learner might welcome a discussion about using the device and would also like to handle the device while reading the manual.

The accompanying self-assessment quiz gives you an opportunity to measure your standing on the VAK dimensions.

Describe how learning styles influence workplace learning.

Log on to **www.thomsonedu.com/infotrac.** Search for articles concerning workplace learning and the four styles of learning.

49

SELF-ASSESSMENT

Visual, Auditory, and Kinesthetic Survey

Read each statement carefully. To the left of each statement, write the number that best describes how each statement applies to you by using the following guide:

1	2	3	4	5
Almost never applies	Applies once in a while	Sometimes applies	Often applies	Almost always applies

Answer honestly, as there are no correct or incorrect answers. It is best if you do not think about each question too long, as this could lead you to the wrong conclusion. Once you have completed all 36 statements (12 statements in three sections), total your score in the spaces provided.

Section One—Visual

_____ 1. I take a lot of notes and I like to doodle.

_____ 2. When talking to someone else I have the hardest time handling those who do not maintain good eye contact with me.

_____ 3. I make lists and notes because I remember things better if I write them down.

_____ 4. When reading a novel I pay a lot of attention to passages picturing the clothing, description, scenery, setting, etc.

_____ 5. I need to write down directions so I remember them.

_____ 6. I need to see the person I am talking to in order to keep my attention focused on the subject.

_____ 7. When meeting a person for the first time I notice the style of dress, visual characteristics, and neatness first.

_____ 8. When I am at a party, one of the things I love to do is stand back and "people-watch."

_____ 9. When recalling information, I can see it in my mind and remember what I saw.

_____ 10. If I had to explain a new procedure or technique, I would prefer to write it out.

_____ 11. During my free time I am most likely to watch television or read.

_____ 12. If my boss has a message for me, I am most comfortable when he or she sends an e-mail or hard-copy memo.

Total for Visual _____ (The minimum score is 12 and maximum 60.)

Section Two—Auditory

_____ 1. When I read, I read out loud or move my lips to hear the words in my head.

_____ 2. When talking to someone else I have the hardest time handling those who do not talk back with me.

_____ 3. I do not take a lot of notes but I still remember what was said. Taking notes distracts me from the speaker.

_____ 4. When reading a novel I pay a lot of attention to passages involving conversations, talking, speaking, dialogues, etc.

_____ 5. I like to talk to myself when solving a problem or writing.

_____ 6. I can understand what a speaker says, even when I am not focused on the speaker.

_____ 7. I remember things more easily by repeating them again and again.

_____ 8. When I am at a party, one of the things I love to do is talk in-depth about a subject that is important to me with a good conversationalist.

_____ 9. I would rather receive information from the radio than from a newspaper (or online newspaper).

SELF-ASSESSMENT

(continued)

_____ 10. If I had to explain a new procedure or technique, I would prefer telling about it.
_____ 11. During my free time I am most likely to listen to music.
_____ 12. If my boss has a message for me, I am most comfortable when he or she calls on the phone.

Total for Auditory _____ (The minimum score is 12 and maximum score 60.)

Section Three—Kinesthetic

_____ 1. I am not good at reading or listening to directions. I would rather just start working on the task or project at hand.
_____ 2. When talking to someone else, I have the hardest time handling those who do not show any kind of emotional support.
_____ 3. I take notes and doodle but I rarely go back and look at them.
_____ 4. When reading a novel, I pay a lot of attention to passages revealing feelings, moods, action, drama, etc.
_____ 5. When I am reading, I move my lips.
_____ 6. I will exchange words and place and use my hands a lot when I can't remember the right things to say.
_____ 7. My desk appears disorganized.
_____ 8. When I am at a party, one of the things I love to do is enjoy the activities such as dancing, games, and totally losing myself in the action.
_____ 9. I like to move around. I feel trapped when seated at a meeting or a desk.
_____ 10. If I had to explain a new procedure or technique, I would prefer actually demonstrating it.
_____ 11. During my free time I am most likely to exercise.
_____ 12. If my boss has a message for me, I am most comfortable when he or she talks to me in person.

Total for Kinesthetic _____ (The minimum is 12, and the maximum 60.)
Total each section: Visual _____; Auditory_____; Kinesthetic_____.

The area in which you have the highest score represents your best learning style. Note that you learn in all *three* styles, but you typically learned best using one of the three styles.

Source: "Learning Styles," http://www.nwlink.com/~donclark/hrd/vak.html. (Updated October 24, 2000.)

Learning Styles Based on Four Learning Stages

Learning styles have also been studied more scientifically. Some researchers have divided learning styles into four orientations, based on four stages of the learning process.[12] As shown in Exhibit 3-2, learning can be regarded as a four-stage cycle: (1) Concrete experience is followed by (2) observation and reflections, which lead to (3) the formation of abstractions and generalizations, followed by (4) hypotheses to be tested in future actions, which in turn lead to new experiences. People may not be aware that these four stages are taking place as they acquire new information. Three points about this model are especially important.

First, according to this model of the learning process, the learning cycle operates continuously. People continue to test their concepts through experience and modify

Exhibit **3-2**

The Learning Process

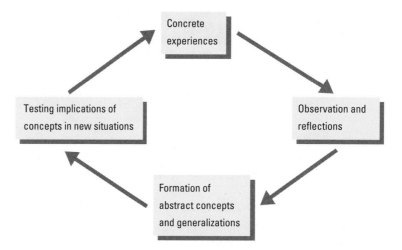

Source: Joyce S. Osland, David A. Kolb, and Irwin M. Rubin, *Organizational Behavior: An Experiential Approach,* 7th ed. (Upper Saddle River, NJ: Prentice Hall, 2001), p. 43. Reprinted by permission of Pearson Education, Inc. Upper Saddle River, NJ.

them as a result of their observations of the experience. For example, a person might learn that the euro is worth less than the U.S. dollar (which may be true during a given time period). However, as the person reads the business pages regularly, he or she learns that the euro is often worth more than the American dollar. So the person modifies his or her original knowledge, recognizing that currency values fluctuate.

Second, a person's internal needs and goals control the direction that learning takes. People seek experiences that are related to their goals, and interpret these experiences in light of their goals. Simultaneously, the person would test implications of the concept that are relevant to these needs and goals. Returning to the example at hand, the person seeking to learn more about the American dollar versus the euro would search for information on this topic. Here, the person might test the implication that the values of currencies change too rapidly to make definitive statements about their relative value.

Third, because the learning process is directed by a person's needs and goals, learning style is individualistic in both direction and process. A production manager might favor concrete experience, whereas a research and development scientist might favor abstract conceptualization.

The four learning orientations (or styles) stemming from this information are as follows:

1. An *orientation toward concrete experiences* emphasizes involvement in experiences and dealing with human interactions in a personal way. The person with this orientation is more intuitive and artistic than systematic and scientific.
2. An *orientation toward observation and reflections* emphasizes understanding the meanings of ideas, situations, and things and describing them in an unbiased way. The person with this orientation is predisposed to reflection rather than action and looking at situations from different perspectives and appreciating different points of view.
3. An *orientation toward formation of abstract concepts and generalizations* emphasizes applying logic, ideas, and concepts. This person prefers thinking as opposed to feeling and has a scientific rather than an artistic approach to problems.
4. An *orientation toward testing implications of concepts in new situations* emphasizes actively influencing people and changing situations. The person with this orientation prefers practical applications as opposed to reflective understanding, with an emphasis on doing rather than observing.

Considerable practice would be required to develop such a four-barreled approach to learning. Yet the payoff would be substantial in terms of learning complex activities such as motivating people and developing business strategy. A person with an attention-deficit disorder would usually prefer the orientation toward concrete experiences because he or she lacks the patience required for the other three orientations.

People tend to develop a learning style that has both strong points and weak points instead of making good use of the four stages of learning. A person might benefit from concrete experiences (stage 1) yet not profit fully from reflecting on the lessons to be learned from these experiences (stage 2).

A manager can apply the concept of learning styles by asking group members to reflect on how they learn best. When new work-related material has to be learned, group members can select the learning method that is most effective for them. Some group members might study manuals, while others might find work in study groups valuable. A more cautious approach to capitalizing on learning styles is to encourage learners to use more than one mode of learning. They should invest some time in individual study and also interact with others to enhance learning.

Individual Differences Related to Skill Acquisition

The various approaches to learning, including learning styles, help us understand how people learn. How *much* people learn is another important consideration in understanding learning in the workplace. In general, people with higher mental ability and personality traits that allow them to concentrate better (such as emotional stability and conscientiousness) acquire knowledge and skills more readily.

A large-scale research study supports the idea that cognitive skills and personality traits contribute to a person profiting from training, and then using the acquired information to enhance job performance. The sample consisted of 9793 trainees accepted into the FAA (Federal Aviation Administration) training program for air-traffic controllers. The average age of the trainee was 26 years; 84% were male, and 16% were female. Trainees took a cognitive skill test when applying for the program, whereas the personality test was administered as part of the medical examination of the air-traffic-control selection process.

The study found that air-traffic controllers who rate high on general cognitive ability demonstrated greater skills acquisition than controllers who rate lower on general cognitive ability. A combination of personality traits, known as *Factor A (warmth),* proved useful in predicting skill acquisition. High Factor A people are warm, outgoing, attentive to others, cooperative, generous, and trusting. *Warmth* predicted skill acquisition, particularly when training was based on group work. The study also demonstrated that trainees who performed well in the training program were more likely to achieve full performance status when employed as an air-traffic controller.[13]

PERCEPTION

Most of us interpret what is going on in the world around us as we perceive it—not as it really is. This tendency is much more pronounced when interpreting meanings rather than tangible physical phenomena. Five members of a team might give varying interpretations to receiving a 4% salary increase for the upcoming year. Yet the same five people would share the same accurate perception that an office tower is under construction across the street. **Perception** deals with the various ways in

Describe key aspects of the perceptual process, along with common perceptual problems.

which people interpret things in the outside world and how they act on the basis of these perceptions.

Perceptions on the job are important. Many studies, for example, have investigated the consequence of employees' job perceptions. The results show that employees who perceive their job to be challenging and interesting have high job satisfaction and motivation. In addition, these favorable perceptions lead to better job performance.[14] Our concern here is with two aspects of perception of most concern to managerial workers: (1) perceptual distortions and problems, and (2) how people attribute causes to events.

Perceptual Distortions and Problems

Under ideal circumstances, people perceive information as it is intended to be communicated or as it exists in reality. For example, it is hoped that an executive from the home office who is assigned to a task force at a company division will perceive the assignment as a compliment. Yet the executive given such an assignment may perceive it as a way of being eased out the door. As shown in Exhibit 3-3, both characteristics of the stimulus and people's perceptual processes can lead to perceptual distortions. Chris Argyris has observed that people are unaware of how they form perceptions; moreover, they are unaware that they are unaware.[15] So studying perception may help reduce some of the mystery.

Characteristics of the Stimulus

Perceptual problems are most likely encountered when a stimulus or cue affects the emotional status of the perceiver. If you have strong attitudes about the issue at stake, you are most likely to misperceive the event. The perception of a stimulus or an

Exhibit 3-3

Contributors to Perceptual Distortions

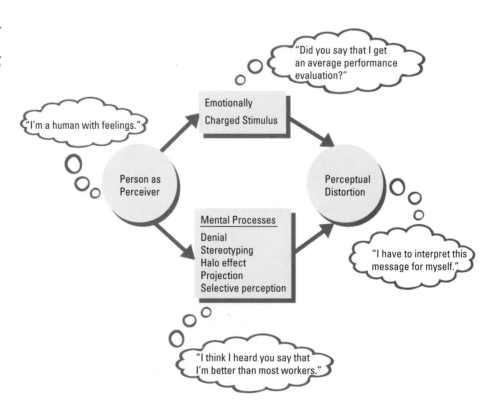

event depends on the emotions, needs, attitudes, and motives of a person. Imagine that an irate customer writes a letter to a CEO complaining about shabby service received when asking for a refund on a defective product. The CEO widely distributes this letter by e-mail. Among the possible perceptions of this event are the following:

> *Interpretation by customer service manager:* "*I'm really in trouble now.* It's my job to ensure top-quality service throughout the organization. The CEO thinks I've messed up big time."
> *Interpretation by customer service specialist immediately involved with the case:* "It's nice to have a laugh once in a while. One customer out of 2000 I've dealt with in the past year is upset. The other 99.9 percent have no gripe, so why worry?"
> *Interpretation by merchandising manager:* "It's obvious the big boss is upset with the customer service group. I don't blame him. We get no complaints about the quality of merchandise. I hope those customer service reps can get their act together."

Mental Processes of People

The devices people use to deal with sensory information play a major role in creating perceptual problems. The general purpose of these perceptual shortcuts is usually to make the reality of a situation less painful or disturbing. As such, these mental processes are types of defensive behavior.

Denial   If the sensory information at hand is particularly painful to us, we often deny to ourselves and others that the information even exists. A purchasing agent was confronted by her manager with the accusation that a supplier entertained her so lavishly that it was tantamount to a kickback. The purchasing agent replied that she thought the company was only concerned about sales incentives involving tangible goods or money. Yet the agent had been on a committee 6 months previously that formulated the new regulations on kickbacks.

Another frequently seen example of denial in organizations is when a manager ignores hints that he is falling out of favor and thus may soon lose his job. He then loses any advantage by not conducting a job search until he has been terminated.

The implication for the managerial worker is to stand ready for a message to be distorted by the receiver if the issue is emotional. Be prepared to clarify and repeat messages and to solicit feedback to ensure that the message was received as intended. Chapter 8 deals at length with the topic of overcoming communication barriers.

Stereotyping   A common shortcut to the perceptual process is to evaluate an individual based on the group or class to which he or she belongs. Stereotypes reduce tension in an unusual way. Encountering a person who does not fit our stereotype of that person's group can be painful to our ego. We lessen the discomfort by looking for behavior that conforms to the stereotype. Assume that you believe that Asian workers are meticulous. When you meet an Asian on the job, you might have a tendency to search for evidence of meticulousness.

An important workplace consequence of stereotypes is that they typically lead to performance standards or expectations based on an individual's group membership. Based on her own research and that of colleagues, Monica Biernat concluded that if one holds the stereotype that men are better leaders than women, he or she is likely to judge the leadership ability of a specific woman relative to lower standards *for women*. In contrast, the leadership ability of a specific man is judged relative to higher standards of competence *for men*. As a consequence of the stereotype about leadership, "good" for a woman does not mean the same thing as "good" for a man.[16] The fact that stereotypes influence standards is not always harmful. When you say "My 6-year old nephew is great at math," you are using a different standard than when you say, "My statistics professor is great at math."

Halo Effect   A tendency exists to color everything that we know about a person because of one recognizable favorable or unfavorable trait. When a company does not insist on the use of objective measures of performance, it is not uncommon for a supervisor to give favorable performance ratings to persons who dress well or smile frequently. The fine appearance or warm smile of these people has created a halo around them. Group members often create a positive halo about one member who is articulate and witty. In reality, the person's professional competence may be average.

Projection   Another shortcut in the perceptual process is to project our own faults onto others instead of making an objective appraisal of the situation. A manager might be asked to recommend a group member for a difficult troubleshooting assignment out of town. The manager might hesitate, saying, "Most of the people in my group do not handle pressure well." In reality, handling pressure poorly is the manager's key weakness.

Selective Perception   People use this mechanism when they draw an unjustified conclusion from an unclear situation. A feedback letter from the manager might be interpreted as a letter of documentation to help the company build a case for firing the individual. Selective perception can have negative consequences when it leads to self-deception about potentially bad news. A worker planning for retirement, for example, might not pay attention to the trend toward companies doing away with traditional pensions. She observes only the encouraging news that many companies still do have traditional pensions. As a result, the worker may not embark on a serious investment program for retirement.

What can managerial workers do with knowledge about perceptual distortions? If it appears that a work associate is making obvious use of a perceptual distortion, one should gently confront the person about the discrepancy in his or her thinking. In the pension example, a coworker might have said, "Look, I claim no great foresight about our company pension plan, but our company could eliminate pensions anytime—particularly if we are bought out. If you want to fulfill your retirement dreams, you'd better start investing now."

 ATTRIBUTION THEORY AND BLAME

Describe how attribution theory and blaming others contribute to an understanding of human behavior in the workplace.

Another important aspect of perception is how people perceive the causes of behavior in themselves and others. **Attribution theory** is the process by which people ascribe causes to the behavior they perceive. Two attribution errors are quite common. The **fundamental attribution error** is the tendency to attribute behavior to internal causes when focusing on someone else's behavior. We might therefore think that a vice president achieved that position because of his or her ambition and talent. The other error, **self-serving bias,** takes place when focusing on one's own behavior. People tend to attribute their achievements to good inner qualities, whereas they attribute failure to adverse factors within the environment. A manager thus would attribute increased productivity to his or her superior leadership skills but blame low productivity on poor support from the organization. (The self-serving bias takes place more frequently than the fundamental attribution error.)

According to attribution theory as developed by Harold H. Kelley, people attribute causes after gathering information about three dimensions of behavior: consensus, consistency, and distinctiveness.[17]

- *Consensus* relates to comparing a person's behavior with that of peers. High consensus exists when a person acts similarly to others in the group, and low consensus exists when the person acts differently. If others cannot perform the same feat you can, your feat will be attributed to your internal qualities.
- *Consistency* is determined by assessing whether a person's performance on a given task is consistent over time. If you are consistent over time, people will attribute your accomplishment to your internal qualities.
- *Distinctiveness* is a function of comparing a person's behavior on one task with that person's behavior on other tasks. High distinctiveness means that the person has performed the task in question quite differently from his or her performance on other tasks. Low distinctiveness refers to stable performance or quality from one task to another. If you turn in high-quality performance on many tasks, your internal characteristics will receive credit.

Observe that consensus relates to other people, consistency involves time, and distinctiveness relates to other tasks. The combination of these factors leads to attribution of causes. People attribute behavior to external (or environmental) causes when they perceive high consensus, low consistency, and high distinctiveness. People attribute behavior to internal (or personal) factors when they perceive low consensus, high consistency, and low distinctiveness.

What might this approach to attribution theory mean in practice? A manager would attribute poor-quality work to external factors, such as poor equipment and resources, under these conditions: All workers are producing low-quality work (high consensus), the low quality occurs only one or two times (low consistency), and the low quality occurs on only one of several tasks (high distinctiveness). In contrast, the manager will attribute low quality to personal characteristics of the workers under these conditions: Only one person is performing poorly (low consensus), the low-quality work has persisted over time (high consistency), and the low-quality work occurs for several tasks (low distinctiveness). Exhibit 3-4 presents another example of this complicated attribution process.

Locus of Control

A logical extension of attribution theory is the concept of **locus of control**—the way in which people look at causation in their lives. Some people have an internal locus of control because they perceive their outcomes as being controlled internally. As a result, they generally feel in control of their lives. Some people have an external locus of control because they perceive much of what happens to them as being controlled by circumstances.[18] People with an internal locus of control feel that they create their own opportunities in life, while those with an external locus attribute much of their success and failure to luck. Workers with an internal locus of control are generally more mature, self-reliant, and responsible.

Attribution theory, including the locus of control theory, has another important implication for organizational behavior aside from those already mentioned. People search for causes of events and alter their behavior because of these perceptions. Managers should therefore invest time in explaining the causes of events to workers, to avoid misperceptions and counterproductive behavior.

Exhibit **3-4**

Kelley's Theory of Attributing Causes—An Example

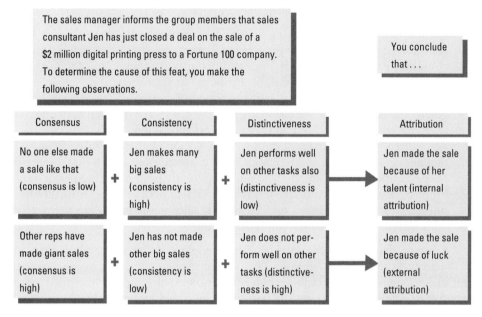

To determine whether another person's behavior stems mainly from internal or external causes, we focus on three types of information: consensus, consistency, and distinctiveness.

The sales manager informs the group members that sales consultant Jen has just closed a deal on the sale of a $2 million digital printing press to a Fortune 100 company. To determine the cause of this feat, you make the following observations.

You conclude that . . .

Consensus	Consistency	Distinctiveness	Attribution
No one else made a sale like that (consensus is low) +	Jen makes many big sales (consistency is high) +	Jen performs well on other tasks also (distinctiveness is low) →	Jen made the sale because of her talent (internal attribution)
Other reps have made giant sales (consensus is high) +	Jen has not made other big sales (consistency is low) +	Jen does not perform well on other tasks (distinctiveness is high) →	Jen made the sale because of luck (external attribution)

Blame as an Attribution

Another aspect of attribution that merits highlighting is **blame,** the tendency to place the responsibility for a negative outcome on a person, a thing, or the environment. Thus, the workers may blame the CEO for sending work overseas, and the CEO blames the workers' high wages and benefits for making outsourcing essential. Blame is an innate tendency at least a million years old. Blame researcher Mark Alicke concludes that "the human impulse to blame grew out of the evolutionary need to avert harm."[19] Frequently, blame takes the form of blame shifting, as we attribute a negative outcome to someone other than ourselves.

Blame is most likely to take place when harmful events take place, from minor transgressions to international disasters. Blaming and punishing harmdoers will sometimes discourage people who imperil the physical and psychological well-being of others, such as blaming a bus driver for an accident that took place during an ice storm.[20]

A negative consequence of blame is that it can block problem solving. As the adage says, "Instead of fixing the problem, we fix the blame." Blame focuses on the past, whereas problem solving focuses on what needs to be done so the problem will not recur. A positive consequence of blame is that it can lead to change for the good. An airline company might blame high fuel costs for recent financial losses. As a result, the airline managers figure out a way to have passengers pay for more of the fuel costs, find a way to economize on fuel, or both.

IMPLICATIONS FOR MANAGERIAL PRACTICE

In addition to the suggestions made for applying information throughout this chapter (as is done in all chapters of this book), here we make a few additional practical suggestions. The first two suggestions are from Kenneth Neal, e-learning solutions practice leader with KPGM Consulting in New York.[21]

1. With e-training, the structure should be in three steps: Show me, let me practice, and watch me do it. A good course has quizzes throughout. You also need cases and business simulations in which participants get a chance to practice what they have learned. Exams are also needed to provide feedback and enhance learner motivation.

2. Not all subject matter and skills are suitable for e-learning. For example, if employees are taught teamwork skills or how to make presentations, underlying concepts can be taught online. However, the trainees also need instructor-led classes in which employees actually give presentations.

3. Be aware of the pervasive effect of selective perception in organizational behavior. Many of the perceptions that people have, for example, are based on their needs at the time. A manager who has to fill a position by a tight deadline may judge the qualifications of applicants too positively. The judgment of a second party, who is not facing the same need, can be helpful in arriving at an objective judgment.

4. Employees who are talented in one aspect of work might become stereotyped as being capable of and interested in only that type of work. An example would be thinking that a competent financial analyst wants to remain in the finance department and would have no interest in serving on a product development team. Managers who form rigid opinions about what workers can and cannot do might waste the talents of these employees and deny them the broad experience they need to advance.[22]

SUMMARY OF KEY POINTS

 Explain the basics of modeling and shaping, cognitive learning, and e-learning.

Modeling and shaping, and cognitive learning are two ways of learning complex material. Modeling involves imitating another person performing the task correctly, then repeating the task. Shaping occurs when a person learns through the reinforcement of small steps that build up to the final or desired behavior.

In cognitive learning, learners strive to learn, develop hunches, have flashes of insight, and use many aspects of personality. Cognitive learning includes informal learning, which occurs outside a formal learning situation.

An important innovation in learning is e-learning, whereby the learner studies independently outside a classroom setting and interacts with a computer in addition to studying course material. E-learning is a Web-based form of computer-based training. Although e-learning is different from traditional forms of learning, it still is based on basic methods of learning. Self-motivation and self-discipline are required for successful e-learning. The most successful e-learning experiences combine features of technology-based learning with the emotional support and interaction possible in the classroom.

 Describe how learning styles influence workplace learning.

People learn best in different ways; for example, some people acquire information best through passive learning. A preference for working alone versus cooperatively is another difference in learning style. A useful classification of learning styles is the preference of visual, auditory, or kinesthetic learning. Most learners use a combination of the three styles. Learning styles have also been classified based on the four stages in the learning process. The styles are orientations toward (a) concrete experiences, (b) reflective observation, (c) abstract conceptualization, and (d) active experimentation.

 Describe key aspects of the perceptual process, along with common perceptual problems.

Perception deals with the various ways in which people interpret things in the outside world and how they act on the basis of these perceptions. Perceptual problems are most likely encountered when the stimulus or cue to be perceived affects the emotional status of the perceiver. The devices people use to deal with sensory information play a major role in creating perceptual problems. Among these devices are denial, stereotyping, the halo effect, projection, and selective perception.

Describe how attribution theory and blaming others contribute to an understanding of human behavior in the workplace.

Attribution theory is the process by which people ascribe causes to the behavior they perceive. The fundamental attribution error is to attribute behavior to internal causes when focusing on the behavior of others. The self-serving bias leads us to attribute good results to ourselves and poor results to the environment.

People attribute causes after gathering information about consensus (comparison among people), distinctiveness (comparison across tasks), and consistency (task stability over time). Blame is an important part of attribution that sometimes blocks problem solving yet at other times leads to positive change.

KEY TERMS AND PHRASES

Learning, 44

A relatively permanent change in behavior based on practice or experience.

Modeling, 45

Imitation; learning a skill by observing another person performing that skill.

Shaping, 45

Learning through the reinforcement or rewarding of small steps to build to the final or desired behavior.

Cognitive Learning Theory, 45

A theory emphasizing that learning takes place in a complicated manner involving much more than acquiring habits and small skills.

Informal Learning, 45

A planned learning that occurs in a setting without a formal classroom, lesson plan, instructor, or examination.

E-Learning, 47

A Web-based form of computer-based training.

Learning Style, 49

A person's particular way of learning, reflecting the fact that people learn best in different ways.

Perception, 53

The various ways in which people interpret things in the outside world and how they act on the basis of these interpretations.

Attribution Theory, 56

The process by which people ascribe causes to the behavior they perceive.

Fundamental Attribution Error, 56

The tendency to attribute behavior to internal causes when focusing on someone else's behavior.

Self-Serving Bias, 56

An attribution error whereby people tend to attribute their achievements to good inner qualities, whereas they attribute their failure to adverse factors within the environment.

Locus of Control, 57

The way in which people look at causation in their lives.

Blame, 58

The tendency to place the responsibility for a negative outcome on a person, a thing, or the environment.

DISCUSSION QUESTIONS AND ACTIVITIES

1. Give an example from your own life in which you have learned through modeling.
2. What relatively inexpensive steps might a company take to promote informal learning among employees?
3. If e-learning is so effective, why haven't most colleges and universities shifted almost entirely to distance learning?
4. What implications might e-learning have for assisting customers with problems involving information technology–based products, including business hardware, software, and consumer electronics?
5. How can a person capitalize on the halo effect in managing his or her career?
6. Work together in a group to supply several examples of how you might have different performance standards for people from different demographic groups.
7. Create a scenario in which, according to attribution theory, most people would agree that the success of a person who picked a winning stock was caused by his or her inner qualities.

CASE PROBLEM: Trying to Get Out of the Pigeonhole

Jenny Lo majored in management information systems at a college of business. Her expectation was that her technical skills along with her people skills would set her on a path to exciting and high-paying work. To Lo's delight, her job search was quick, easy, and successful. She landed a position as an information systems specialist in the cereal division at a major food manufacturer.

Lo's first assignment was serving on a team whose mission was to implement customer relationship manager (CRM) software. Several of her team members had about 5 years of experience at implementing large software systems, and similar to Lo, another team member was just getting started in his professional career.

Lo enjoyed the work, and received an outstanding performance evaluation after her first 6 months on the job. Pete Talbot, her team leader, said that she was learning the system rapidly and was quite helpful to users in answering implementation questions. Lo was encouraged by the positive feedback, and tried even harder in the upcoming months. Soon one of the more technically oriented members of the team left for a promotion within the company. Talbot asked Lo to replace the departing team member.

Lo remarked, "Pete, I'm really not so deep technically. Maybe I'm not the best person for this assignment." Talbot, however, insisted that Lo could do the job after some careful studying of the more technical features of the system.

Lo thought to herself that she was being dragged into a more technical direction than she wanted, yet being a good team player was the best way to build her reputation in the company. After a year in the new team role, Lo received another outstanding performance evaluation, signed by both Talbot and his manager, Kate Clancy. Talbot said to Lo, "Kate and I both agree that you are a gem. You are making a stronger technical contribution, yet you are not losing your human touch with the users."

Lo was happy with her progress at the company, yet she was concerned about her career path. She began to envy people in the marketing side of cereals, and thought it would be great to become a brand manager and eventually become a marketing executive. Lo felt that her information technology background had helped sharpen her analytical skills and that such capability would give her an edge in marketing.

She also believed that her knowledge of information technology would help her in any future marketing position. She thought, for example, that her knowledge of information systems would help her understand distribution systems for cereals or any other product.

Three months later, Lo mustered up the courage to speak to Talbot about a transfer into a marketing position within the cereal division. Talbot replied, "Are you kidding, Jenny? Do you think I would voluntarily give up one of my best technical people so she could help sell corn flakes? Besides, you have established a great niche for yourself in the company."

Lo brought up the topic again in a few months, and received a similar response from Talbot. She then asked if she could at least talk to a marketing manager about the possibilities of someday entering the brand-manager track. Talbot replied that it was a free company, and that she therefore had the right to interview anywhere. He also said, "You are a key player for both our team and the company as a whole."

Lo then arranged an exploratory interview with Michelle Vara, the director of brand management. Lo went into detail about her aspirations for working in brand management, and that she wanted to engage in work that relied more heavily on soft skills than hard skills. Toward the end of the interview Vara said to Lo, "I can see that you would have some potential in brand management. But you are so good technically that your best contribution to the company would be in staying where you are for now. Besides, your salary is already a little too high for an entry-level position in the marketing group. Maybe we can talk again in the future."

Lo left the interview encouraged that the company saw her as a strong contributor, yet discouraged that it would be exceedingly difficult to move into brand management. She thought to herself, "How do I get out of this pigeonhole?"

Case Questions

1. In what way does this case relate to stereotyping?
2. What advice can you give Jenny Lo to get out of her pigeonhole?
3. What advice can you give the company for dealing with Jenny Lo's request?

ENDNOTES

1. John W. Donahoe and David C. Palmer, *Learning and Complex Behavior* (Boston: Allyn & Bacon, 1994), p. 2.
2. Nancy Day, "Informal Learning Gets Results," *Workforce,* June 1998, p. 31; Jay Cross, *Internet Time Group,* http://internettime.com, May 8, 2003, p. 2.
3. Day, "Informal Learning," pp. 31–32.
4. Sandra L. Fisher and J. Kevin Ford, "Differential Effects of Learner Effort and Goal Orientation on Two Learning Outcomes," *Personnel Psychology,* Summer 1998, pp. 397–420.
5. Michael A. Tucker, "E-Learning Evolves," *HR Magazine,* October 2005, p. 75.
6. Karen Frankola, "Why Online Learners Drop Out," *Workforce,* October 2001, p. 54.
7. "Assessing Online Learning: Defining the Efficacy of Online Learning," *Keying In,* March 2001, p. 3.
8. Tucker, "E-Learning Evolves," p. 78.
9. Joe Mullich, "A Second Act for E-Learning," *Workforce Management,* February 2004, p. 52.
10. Wanda L. Stitt-Gohdes, "Teaching and Learning Styles: Implications for Business Teacher Education," in *The 21st Century: Meeting the Challenges to Business Education* (Reston, VA: National Business Education Association, 1999), p. 10.
11. "Learning Styles," http://www.nwlink.com/~donclark/hrd/styles.html, pp. 4–6.
12. Joyce S. Osland, David A. Kolb, and Irwin M. Rubin, *Organizational Behavior: An Experiential Approach,* 7th ed. (Upper Saddle River, NJ: Prentice Hall, 2001), pp. 43–44.
13. David W. Oakes, et al., "Cognitive Ability and Personality Predictors of Training Program Skill Acquisition and Job Performance," *Journal of Business and Psychology,* Summer 2001, pp. 523–548.
14. Ricky W. Griffin, "Effects of Work Redesign on Employee Perceptions, Attitudes, and Behaviors: A Long-Term Investigation," *Academy of Management Journal,* June 1991, p. 426.
15. Chris Argyris, *On Organizational Learning* (Oxford, England: Blackwell, 1994), p. 7.
16. Monica Biernat, "Toward a Broader View of Social Stereotyping," *American Psychologist,* December 2003, pp. 1019–1027.
17. Harold H. Kelley, "The Process of Causal Attribution," *American Psychologist,* February 1973, pp. 107–128.
18. Julian P. Rotter, "Generalized Expectancies for Internal vs. External Control of Reinforcement," *Psychological Monographs, 80* (1966), pp. 1–28.
19. Cited in Jeffrey Zaslow, "'It's All Your Fault': Why Americans Can't Stop Playing the Blame Game," *The Wall Street Journal,* September 15, 2005, p. D1.
20. Mark D. Alicke, "Culpable Control and the Psychology of Blame," *Psychological Bulletin, 4,* July 2000, pp. 1–30.
21. Cited in Eilene Zimmerman, "Better Training Is Just a Click Away," *Workforce,* January 2001, p. 38.
22. Carol Hymowitz, "Bosses Who Pigeonhole Workers Waste Talent, Contribute to Turnover," *The Wall Street Journal,* May 24, 2005, p. B1.

Attitudes, Values, and Ethics

For years, Jefferies Group Inc. coveted more brokerage business with Fidelity Investments, the mutual-fund giant. So in 2002, the midsize securities firm hired Kevin Quinn, an experienced trader with contacts at Fidelity. To reel in new business, Quinn said he would need a lot of bait, and that is what Jeffries game him, in the form of a huge $1.5 million annual expense account.

Quinn, who worked in Boston, where Fidelity is based, promptly put his entertainment budget to work. At his expense, Fidelity employees enjoyed expensive dinners, private air travel, ritzy golf outings, and tickets to premier sports events like the Wimbledon tennis championships. Sure enough, Jeffries won more assignments to buy and sell stocks for Fidelity mutual funds.

In early 2002, Jeffries ranked roughly 50th among securities firms in terms of brokerage commissions received from Fidelity. By early 2005, Jeffries had surged to 15th. Fidelity attributed the jump to a significant improvement in Jeffries' trading operations and services. But Jeffries and Fidelity now agree that the entertaining got out of hand. Quinn, who is 39 years old, was fired in October 2004 for allegedly abusing his expense account, according to regulatory records. He did not hit his limit, but from 2002 through 2004, he spent more than $1 million on entertainment and an additional $600,000 on gifts. Fidelity traders enjoyed junkets to resorts such as Bellagio in Las Vegas and the Breakers in Palm Beach, Fla. They received wine worth thousands of dollars and even free golf clubs. Jeffries has also accused Quinn of falsifying expense paperwork and improperly treating friends and family to free air travel.

Source: Reprinted with permission from Susanne Craig and John Hechinger, "Entertaining Excess: Fishing for Fidelity Business, One Firm Employed Lavish Bait," *The Wall Street Journal,* August 11, 2005, pp. A1, A7.

4

OBJECTIVES

After reading and studying this chapter and doing the exercises, you should be able to:

1. Describe the importance of attitudes and emotions to behavior in organizations.

2. Describe how organizational citizenship behavior contributes to individual and organizational effectiveness.

3. Summarize why values are an important part of organizational behavior.

4. Describe three ethical decision-making criteria, along with several explanations for the existence of ethical problems.

5. Describe the eight-step guide to ethical decision making.

6. Describe what organizations can do to enhance ethical and socially responsible behavior.

Now Ask Yourself: **How high (or low) does a corporate professional go to influence another company to purchase services from his or her firm? Who gets hurt when a brokerage firm spends $1.6 million in several years to entertain a customer?** Ethical business conduct is one topic presented in this chapter about attitudes and emotions, values, and ethics. Understanding these aspects of behavior helps managers to deal more effectively with people and guide their own behavior toward high performance.

ATTITUDES AND EMOTIONS

Describe the importance of attitudes and emotions to behavior in organizations.

"You've got an attitude," said the supervisor to the store associate, thus emphasizing the importance of attitude to job performance. For mysterious reasons, the term *attitude* in colloquial language often connotes a *negative* attitude. More accurately, an **attitude** is a predisposition to respond that exerts an influence on a person's response to a person, a thing, an idea, or a situation. Attitudes are an important part of organizational behavior, because they are linked with perception, learning, emotions, and motivation. For example, your attitude toward a coworker influences your perception of how favorably you evaluate his or her work. Also, emotions such as joy and anger contribute to attitude formation. First, we examine the components of attitudes and their relationship to organizational behavior, and then we explain how emotions influence behavior in the workplace.

Components of Attitudes

Attitudes are complex and have three components. The *cognitive* component refers to the knowledge or intellectual beliefs an individual might have about an object (an idea, a person, a thing, or a situation). A market researcher might have accumulated considerable factual information about statistics (such as sampling procedures) and software for running data. The researcher might therefore have a positive attitude toward statistics.

The feeling, or *affective* component, refers to the emotion connected with an object or a task. The market researcher mentioned might basically like statistical analysis because of some pleasant experiences in college associated with statistics.

The *behavioral* component refers to how a person acts. The market researcher might make positive statements about statistical methods or emphasize them in his or her reports.

The cognitive, affective, and behavioral aspects of attitudes are interrelated. A change in one of the components will set in motion a change in one or more of the others. If you have more facts about an object or process (cognitive), you form the basis for a more positive emotional response to the object (affective). In turn, your behavior toward that object would probably become more favorable. For example, if you have considerable information about the contribution of feedback to personal development, you might have a positive feeling toward feedback. When receiving feedback, therefore, you would act favorably.

At times, people do not experience the type of consistency just described, and they feel compelled to search for consistency. **Cognitive dissonance** is the situation in which the pieces of knowledge, information, attitudes, and beliefs held by an individual are contradictory. When a person experiences cognitive dissonance, the relationship between attitudes and behaviors is altered. People search for ways to reduce internal conflicts when they experience a clash between the information they receive and their actions or attitudes. The same process is used when a person has to resolve two inconsistent sets of information.

A typical example of cognitive dissonance on the job might occur when a worker believes that the report she submits to team members is of high quality; her teammates, however, tell her the report is flawed and requires substantial revisions. To reduce the dissonance, the worker might conveniently ignore the criticism. Or the worker might reason that she is the resident expert on the topic of the report, and her teammates are therefore not qualified to judge the merits of her report.

Emotions in the Workplace

A traditional viewpoint contends that emotions in the workplace should be minimized, and decisions should be based on rational analysis. Nevertheless, the importance of emotion in influencing job behavior has long been recognized. For example, customer-contact workers need training to deal with angry customers; and supervisors have been trained how to give emotional support to a distressed group member. Current interest in workplace emotion has surged, as evidenced by the growth of research and writing in this area.[1]

In Chapter 2, we described the importance now attached to having emotional intelligence. An **emotion** is a feeling—such as anger, fear, joy, or surprise—that underlies behavior. Emotions might lead an employee who has just solved a difficult problem to shout "Yes!" and punch his or her fist into the air. Unfortunately, intense negative emotion might trigger an employee to stab another employee with a knife. A study commissioned by the Department of Homeland Security found that corporate insiders who attack computer systems are typically angry over disciplinary actions, missed promotions, or layoffs.[2]

Similar to an attitude, an emotion consists of three interacting components: (1) internal physiological arousal, (2) expressive behavior in the face or body, and (3) a cognitive appraisal.[3] Imagine that a production worker has just been informed that he has won a $50,000 award for a suggestion that will save the company millions of dollars. The worker will experience a surge of physiological arousal, such as an accelerated pulse or an elevated breathing rate. His facial expressions will most likely communicate joy and surprise. The cognitive appraisal deals with quick thoughts, such as saying to himself, "Now, I will get the respect I deserve," and "Here's my chance to buy something great for my family and invest a little money also."

Managing Emotion

Neal M. Ashkanasy and Catherine S. Daus regard emotion in the workplace as the new challenge facing managers.[4] Given that every worker, top executives included, is an organism governed partly by emotion, constructive use should be made of emotion. Two suggestions by Ashkanasy and Daus provide practical starting points in managing emotions well. First, the manager should create a friendly emotional climate by setting a positive example. Managers might serve as a model of healthy emotional expression that includes being emotionally perceptive. ("Kelly, I notice that you are quite anxious about the credit-card processing unit possibly being outsourced. How can I help you with your concerns?") Warm and sincere expression of positive emotion is usually effective, as is appropriate expression of negative emotion. The leader might indicate, for example, that he or she is also worried about a downturn in sales that could lead to cutbacks.

Another recommendation is to include a positive attitude as one factor in selecting individuals and teams. A candidate might be evaluated in part based on his or her emotional skills demonstrated during a job interview and by checking his or her references. Within the organization, teams might be selected for key assignments in part based on their cheerful outlook. Positive attitudes contribute to organizational health, whereas consistently negative attitudes create an unfavorable work climate.

A caution to workers about emotional regulation is that anger derived from one set of interactions might be displaced toward others, with the result being poor coworker relationships.[5] For example, a call-center technician angry with customers or the boss might take out this anger on other call-center technicians.

Emotional Labor and Dissonance

Another aspect of emotional behavior in the workplace receiving recent attention is the problem of faking emotions. Alicia Grandey defines **emotional labor** as the process of regulating both feelings and expressions to meet organizational goals. Emotional labor involves both surface acting and deep acting. *Surface acting* means faking expressions, such as smiling, whereas *deep acting* involves controlling feelings, such as suppressing anger toward a customer whom you perceive to be uncivil. Sales workers and customer service representatives carry the biggest emotional labor among all workers because so often they have to take on facial expressions and feelings to please customers.[6]

Emotional dissonance is a key aspect of emotional labor and refers to the mismatch between felt and expressed emotions. The greater the gap between actual and expressed feelings, the more frequently workers report feeling emotional exhaustion, dissatisfaction with their jobs, and cynicism toward customers.[7] Imagine making a PowerPoint presentation to top management, and being interrupted with what you perceive to be foolish questions and ridicule. You want to retaliate, but instead keep smiling and making comments such as "good question."

A variation of emotional labor can occur when workers create a façade in relation to conforming to corporate values. Façade creation might include conforming to the dress code despite disliking such attire, expressing agreement with one's manager although one thinks the manager is wrong, and going along with a group decision that one thinks is ridiculous. Maintaining a façade for a long time can lead to emotional distress.[8]

An analysis of hundreds of jobs revealed that workers who experience the most emotional labor do not uniformly receive higher financial compensation. One finding was that occupations with high cognitive demands (such as a psychiatrist) tend to receive higher wages when emotional labor demands are high. Another finding was that occupations low in cognitive demands (such as a supermarket cashier) tend to receive low wages when emotional labor demands are high.[9]

One implication of emotional labor is that managers need to take into account job characteristics in creating rules for displays of emotion. Rules that conflict with job characteristics may trigger unhealthy levels of tension. For instance, asking cashiers to be overly polite to customers may conflict with a fast work pace. Cashiers facing a long line of impatient customers may need to decrease displays of courtesy to avoid having customers wait even longer. (It takes more time to be polite and conversational.)[10]

Attitudes and Job Satisfaction

Another reason attitudes are important in the study of organizational behavior is that they form the basis for how satisfied people are with their jobs. **Job satisfaction** is the amount of pleasure or contentment associated with a job. Workers will have high job satisfaction when they have positive attitudes toward job factors such as the work itself, recognition, and opportunity for advancement. According to a 2005 Conference Board survey of 5000 households, about half of U.S. workers are satisfied with their jobs, down from nearly 60% a decade earlier. About 14% of the workers sampled said they were very satisfied, down from 18% in 1995. The biggest decline in contentment with the job was among workers earning $25,000 to $35,000 and among workers between the ages of 35 and 44. The most satisfied workers were those earning $50,000 or more, and those at least 65 years old. Rapid technological changes, increasing productivity demands, and changing employee expectations all contributed to the decline in satisfaction, according to the report.[11]

Exhibit 4-1 provides a sampling of issues that influence employee satisfaction.

A practical view of job satisfaction is that it centers on employees having fun on the job. *Fun* can be anything from doing exciting work to engaging in sports during the lunch break. Companies today are likely to provide a working environment that provides key satisfying elements such as casual dress, flexible working hours, and telecommuting. Managers are concerned about maintaining high levels of job

Exhibit 4-1

Rank According to Employees	Rank According to You
1. Benefits	
2. Compensation/pay	
3. Feeling safe in the work environment	
4. Job security	
5. Flexibility to balance work–life issues	
6. Communication between employees and senior management.	
7. Relationship with immediate supervisor	
8. Management recognition of employee job performance	
9. Opportunities to use skills/abilities	
10. The work itself	
11. Overall corporate culture	
12. Autonomy and independence	
13. Career development opportunities	
14. Meaningfulness of the job	
15. Variety of work	
16. Career advancement opportunities	
17. Contribution of work to organization's business goals	
18. Organization's commitment to professional development	
19. Job-specific training	
20. Relationship with coworkers	
21. Networking	

Question: Why do you think modern employees rank benefits (e.g., medical insurance and life insurance) among the most important job-satisfaction factors?

Suggestion: Make your own ranking of the 21 factors. What big differences do you see between your ranking and the national ranking at the left?

The 2004 Job Satisfaction Survey Conducted by the Society for Human Resource Management and CNN Found the Factors Listed in this Exhibit Listed as "Very Important" by 600 Employees at a Variety of Companies. The List Shows the Order of Importance of Job-Satisfaction Factors Among Employees as a Group.

Source: Adapted from Pamela Babcock, "Find What Workers Want," *HR Magazine,* April 2005, p. 53.

satisfaction, including enthusiasm, because of its consequences, which include the following:

- High productivity when the work involves contact with people
- A stronger tendency to achieve customer loyalty
- Loyalty to the company
- Low absenteeism and turnover
- Less job stress and burnout
- Better safety performance
- Better life satisfaction, including a better mood at home[12]

The job satisfaction consequence of loyalty is especially important because it enhances employee retention (keeping valuable employees). Employee turnover is particularly expensive and involves costs such as recruitment, selection, training, and lost productivity while the replacement is trained. Management consultant Diane Arthur observes that if employees feel loyal to a company, they are likely to be more productive and make an extra effort for the employer. They are also likely to stay with the company, keeping the firm stable and allowing management to concentrate on sales, operations, and earnings, not on hiring replacement workers.[13]

High job satisfaction is correlated with high organizational performance. However, an analysis of 35 companies over 8 years suggests that high organizational performance leads to satisfaction rather than vice versa. According to this reasoning, when a firm excels it makes employees happy. The study in question found that measures of company financial performance were more accurate predictors of employee satisfaction than the reverse. Nevertheless, the study concluded that managers should not neglect attempting to satisfy employees and instead just concentrate on organizational performance. For example, a prosperous firm that did not offer good rewards to employees might find that job satisfaction would decrease.[14]

Many of the methods and techniques described in this book, such as empowerment and modified work schedules, are aimed at sustaining job satisfaction. Almost any positive management practice, however, might be linked to improving job satisfaction.

ORGANIZATIONAL CITIZENSHIP BEHAVIOR

Describe how organizational citizenship behavior contributes to individual and organizational effectiveness.

A broader consequence of job satisfaction is that it contributes to **organizational citizenship behavior** (OCB), or the willingness to work for the good of the organization even without the promise of a specific reward. Five important components of organizational citizenship behavior are conscientiousness, altruism, civic virtue, courtesy, and sportsmanship. A good organizational citizen would engage in behaviors such as assisting a person with a computer problem outside his or her team or department, or picking up a broken bottle on the company lawn. People who are good organizational citizens are likely to achieve some of the consequences of job satisfaction, including higher customer loyalty, higher productivity, and better safety performance.

According to George A. Neuman and Jill R. Kickul, organizational citizenship behavior has received increased theoretical attention as organizations face the challenge of global competition and the need for continuous innovation. The good organizational citizen goes "above and beyond the call of duty," or engages in *extrarole* behavior.[15]

Although OCB is often a consequence of job satisfaction, personality factors are sometimes linked to OCB. Workers may be predisposed to being good, or poor, organizational citizens. A study with customer-contact workers supports the personality–OCB link. The employee-disposition (or personality) factors of service orientation and empathy were found to be related to engaging in good citizenship behavior in relation to customers. Four examples of service-oriented OCBs are when a person does the following:

- Encourages friends and family to use firm's products and services
- Follows up in a timely manner to customer requests and problems
- Contributes many ideas for customer promotions and communication
- Frequently presents creative solutions to customer problems[16]

Similar to job satisfaction, OCB has been linked to voluntary turnover. A study conducted in 11 companies in China found that employees rated low in OCB by their supervisors were more likely to quit than those who were rated as exhibiting high levels of such behavior.[17]

A concern about the construct (similar to a concept) of organizational citizenship behavior is that some employees may perceive going beyond their job description as part of their job. An employee might think, for example, "I'm paid a good salary to do whatever it takes to make my company successful, whether or not it is strictly my job." In a study of master of business administration students and their supervisors, four OCB behaviors were generally perceived to be *in role* (part of the job) if workers felt they were working for a just and fair organization. The four specific behaviors are as follows:

- Interpersonal helping (helping coworkers on their job when needed)
- Individual initiative (communications designed to improve individual and group performance)
- Personal industry (performing tasks in a way that goes above and beyond the call of duty)
- Loyalty boosterism (promoting the organization to outsiders)[18]

One implication of this study is that when workers perceive their organization to be fair and just, they are more likely to believe that OCB is part of their job. So the organization can facilitate good citizenship behavior by being fair and just.

Although OCB benefits the organization and will often facilitate career growth, being an exceptional organizational citizen may have negative consequences for the individual. A study with 98 couples investigated the impact of one type of organizational citizenship behavior—individual initiative—on adverse personal consequences. Examples of individual initiative include working on weekends, taking work home, and working longer than most others. These types of initiative were rated by spouses or significant others. The results indicated that greater initiative was positively associated with feelings of being overworked, job stress, and conflict between work and family.[19] An implication of this study is that managers should discourage good organizational citizens from going overboard.

VALUES

Another key factor influencing behavior in organizations is the values and beliefs of people. A **value** refers to the importance a person attaches to something that serves as a guide to action. Values are also tied in with enduring beliefs that one's mode of conduct is better than the opposite mode of conduct. One person may highly value quantitative analysis and will look down on people who present a position without

Summarize why values are an important part of organizational behavior.

	Baby Boomers (1946–1964)	Generation X (1961–1980)	Generation Y (1981–2000)
Exhibit 4-2 *Value Stereotypes for Several Generations of Workers*	Uses technology as necessary tool	Techno-savvy	Techno-savvy
	Appreciates hierarchy	Teamwork very important	Teamwork very important
	Tolerates teams but values independent work	Dislikes hierarchy	Dislikes hierarchy; prefers participation
	Strong career orientation	Strives for work–life balance but will work long hours for now	Strives for work–life balance but will work long hours for now
	More loyalty to organization	Loyalty to own career and profession	Believes in informality; wants to strike it rich quickly
	Favors diplomacy	Candid in conversation	Ultracandid in conversation
	Favors old economy	Appreciates old and new economy	Prefers the new economy
	Expects a bonus based on performance	Would appreciate a signing bonus	Expected a signing bonus before the dot-com crash
	Believes that issues should be discussed formally	Believes that feedback can be administered informally	Believes that feedback can be given informally, even on the fly

Sources: Several of the ideas in this table are from Robert McGarvey, "The Coming of Gen X Bosses," *Entrepreneur*, November 1999, pp. 60–64; Joanne M. Glenn, "Teaching the Net Generation," *Business Education Forum*, February 2000, pp. 6–14; Anita Bruzzese, "There Needn't Be a Generation Gap," Gannett News Service, April 22, 2002; Gregg Hammill, "Mixing and Managing Four Generations of Employees," *FDUMagazine Online*, Winter/Spring 2005, p. 5.

Note: Disagreement exists about which age bracket fit baby boomers, Generation X, and Generation Y, with both professional publications and dictionaries showing slight differences.

providing quantitative evidence. As described in Chapter 2, values are a major factor creating generational differences among employees.

The topic of values is a perennial favorite, as baby boomers are compared with younger people in Generations X and Y. With baby boomers being more conservative and respectful of authority and hierarchy, the differences in values between the generations can cause job conflict. As with other group stereotypes, generation differences are often exaggerated. Exhibit 4-2 outlines several generational differences in values and shows both new information and some overlap with Exhibit 2-1. Understanding generational differences is critical to managing people effectively.[20] For example, the oldest employees in an organization may prefer adhering closely to policies and procedures, whereas the youngest employees might prefer to improvise when faced with a problem. The manager may have to intervene to resolve these differences.

We discuss values from three standpoints: how they are learned, how they are clarified, and the mesh between individual and organizational values. Values will be mentioned again in the discussion of ethics because values are the foundation of ethics.

How Values Are Learned

People are not born with a particular set of values. Rather, values are learned in the process of growing up; many values are learned by age 4. One important way we acquire values is through modeling. Often a person who takes considerable pride in work was reared around people who had a strong work ethic. Models can be parents, teachers, friends, siblings, and even public figures. If we identify with a particular person, the probability is high that we will develop some of his or her major values.

Communication of attitudes is another major way in which values are learned. The attitudes we hear expressed directly or indirectly help shape our values. If using credit to purchase goods and services was talked about as an undesirable practice among your family and friends, you might hold negative values about installment purchases.

Unstated but implied attitudes may also shape values. If key people in your life showed no enthusiasm when you talked about work accomplishment, you might not place a high value on achieving outstanding results. In contrast, if your family and friends centered their lives on their careers, you might develop similar values. (Or you might rebel against such a value because it interfered with a more relaxed lifestyle.)

Many key values are also learned through religion and thus become the basis for society's morals. A basic example is that all religions emphasize treating other people fairly and kindly. Members of the clergy teach many ethics courses and seminars because it is often assumed that a religious person has special expertise with constructive values.

Clarifying Values

The values you develop early in life are directly related to the kind of person you are now and will be, and the quality of relationships that you form.[21] Recognizing this fact has led to exercises designed to help people clarify and understand some of their own values. Value-clarification exercises ask you to compare the relative importance you attach to different objects and activities. The accompanying self-assessment exercise gives you an opportunity to clarify your values.

The Mesh between Individual and Organizational Values

Under the best of circumstances, the values of employees mesh with those required of the job and organization. When this state of congruence exists, job performance is likely to be higher. For example, a person who values workplace democracy is likely to perform better in a firm that gives workers more say in decision making than if he or she worked in one that was more authoritarian.

The "Founding Values" of Enterprise Rent-A-Car contain elements found in the value statements of many consumer companies:

- Our brand is the most valuable thing we own.
- Personal honesty and integrity are the foundations of our success.
- Customer service is our way of life.
- Enterprise is a fund and friendly place, where teamwork rules.
- We work hard . . . and reward hard work.
- Great things happen when we listen . . . to our customers and to each other.
- We strengthen our communities, one neighborhood at a time.
- Our doors are open.

Enterprise management communicates these values to every employee and job applicant. Management reinforces the message that there is no room at Enterprise for anything less than full adoption of all company values.[22]

Not every business firm claiming to have such values carries them out in practice. As a result, problems are created for some employees. When the demands made by the organization or a manager clash with the basic values of the individual, that person suffers from **person–role conflict.** The employee wants to obey

SELF-ASSESSMENT

Clarifying Your Values

Directions: Rank from 1 to 21 the importance of the following values to you. The most important value on the list receives a rank of 1, the least important a rank of 21. Use the space next to the two "Other" blanks to include important values of yours not on the list.

_____ Having my own place to live	_____ Helping people less fortunate than myself
_____ Performing high-quality work	_____ Loving and being loved by another person
_____ Having one or more children	_____ Having physical intimacy with another person
_____ Having an interesting job and career	
_____ Owning a detached house, a condominium, or an apartment	_____ Earning an above-average income
	_____ Being in good physical condition
_____ Having good relationships with coworkers	_____ Being a knowledgeable, informed person
_____ Having good health	_____ Leading an information technology lifestyle, including having up-to-date high-technology devices to be in touch frequently with work associates, friends, and family
_____ Watching my favorite television shows	
_____ Participating in sports or other pastimes	
_____ Being neat, clean, and orderly	
_____ Being active in a professional society in my field	
	_____ Other
_____ Being a religious person	_____ Other

1. Discuss and compare your ranking of these values with the person next to you.
2. Perhaps your class, assisted by your instructor, can arrive at a class average on each of these values. How does your ranking compare to the class ranking? What evidence will you need before you conclude that a given rank is representative of the class?
3. Are there any surprises in the class ranking? Which values did you think would be the highest and lowest?
4. How do you think average ranks for these values would be influenced by a person's culture?

Collaboration

orders but does not want to perform an act that seems inconsistent with his or her values. A situation of this type might occur when an employee is asked to help produce a product or service that he or she feels is unsafe or of no value to society. Unfortunately, both safety and value to society are not easy to specify objectively. Assume that a person is a supervisor in the pet insurance department of an insurance company. She might suffer from role conflict because she believes that pet insurance policies are a waste of resources. Yet many human resource professionals believe that pet insurance is an employee benefit that builds company loyalty, reduces worries for pet caretakers, and helps animals. One could argue that any product or service is of value to society because it creates employment for somebody.

What constitutes a good fit between personal values and organizational values may change at different stages of a person's career because of a change in values. At one point in a person's career, he or she may think that founding a business is important because the new firm might create employment. At another stage of the same person's career, he or she might believe that working for the nonprofit sector is more meritorious.

A starting point in finding a good fit between individual and organizational values is to identify what type of work would be the most meaningful. Po Bronson writes that people "thrive by focusing on the question of who they really are—and connecting to work that they truly love (and, in so doing, unleashing a productive and creative power that they never imagined)."[23] After identifying your passion in terms of work, you would then seek an employment opportunity that provides such work. For example, a manager might discover that helping young people learn useful job skills brings her the most professional excitement. She might then seek an opportunity to manage a manufacturing apprenticeship program in her company.

ETHICS

Describe three ethical decision-making criteria, along with several explanations for the existence of ethical problems.

Our last key factor for understanding individuals in organizations is **ethics,** which is the set of the moral choices a person makes based on what he or she ought to do. Ethics is based on an individual's beliefs about what is right and wrong or good and bad. Ethics can also be regarded as the vehicle that converts values into action. You might value a clean environment; the corresponding ethical behavior is not to place a television set or computer in a landfill. Ethics is a major consideration in studying the actions of managerial workers and the functioning of organizations. The prominent financial scandals in business during the first several years of the new century have intensified recognition of the importance of ethics. We will therefore refer to ethics at various places in this book.

The ethical behavior of organizational members, whether individual contributors (nonmanagers) or managers, exerts a major force on how outsiders and insiders will perceive the firm. If the behavior of one or more organizational members is outrageously unethical, it may violate the law, thus leading to outside intervention. Furthermore, if top-level management in the company is unethical, the result can be an erosion of employee trust and organizational loyalty.[24]

Here we approach ethics as it relates to individuals from four perspectives. First we look at three somewhat philosophical criteria for making ethical decisions. Second, we describe major causes of ethical problems. Third, we present an eight-part guide to ethical decision making. Fourth, we describe the role of organizations in promoting ethical and socially responsible behavior.

Ethical Decision-Making Criteria

A standard way of understanding ethical decision making is to understand the philosophical basis for making these decisions. When attempting to decide what is right and wrong, people can focus on (1) consequences; (2) duties, obligations, and principles; or (3) integrity.[25]

Focus on Consequences

When attempting to decide what is right and wrong, people sometimes focus on the consequences of their decision or action. According to this criterion, if nobody gets hurt, the decision is ethical. Focusing on consequences is often referred to as *utilitarianism*. The decision maker is concerned with the utility of the decision. What really counts is the net balance of good consequences over bad.

To focus on consequences, the decision maker would have to be aware of all the good and bad consequences of a given decision. A financial vice president might decide that if all travel-expense reimbursements were delayed by 10 days, the company could earn $1 million per year nationwide. The earnings would stem from holding on to money longer, thus collecting interest. How would this vice president know how many family arguments and how much job stress would be created by these delayed reimbursements? How many good performers would quit in disgust?

Focus on the Rights of Individuals

Another approach to making an ethical decision is to examine one's duties in making the decision. The theories underlying this approach are referred to as *deontological,* from the Greek word *deon* (or duty). Deontology also refers to moral philosophies that center on the rights of individuals and the intentions associated with a particular behavior. A fundamental idea of deontology is that equal respect must be given to all persons. The deontological approach is based on universal principles such as honesty, fairness, justice, and respect for persons and property. Rights, such as the right to privacy and safety, are the key aspects of deontology. From a deontological perspective, the principles are more important than the consequences. If a given decision violates one of these universal principles, it is automatically unethical, even if nobody gets hurt.

The financial vice president pondering whether to defer payments on travel expenses would not have to spend much time with deontology. She would say to herself, "Delaying these payments may earn the company another $1 million per year, but it is not honest, fair, or just. Furthermore, employees have a right to prompt payment."

Focus on Integrity (Virtue Ethics)

The third criterion for determining the ethics of behavior focuses on the character of the person involved in the decision or action. If the person in question has good character and genuine motivation and intentions, he or she will be judged to have behaved ethically. The criteria for good character will often include the two other ethical criteria. For example, one might judge a person to have good character if he or she follows the right principles and respects the rights of others.

Trustworthiness has emerged in recent years as a virtue of major importance for managers and professionals, in part because of many well-publicized incidents of executives being untrustworthy. The name Enron has become almost synonymous with untrustworthy behavior. Research suggests that trust makes a major contribution to organizational effectiveness. Two major contributors to trust are consistent behavior and clear communication. Any act of bad management is likely to engender distrust. At the top of the list are inconsistent messages from top management and inconsistent standards.[26]

The decision maker's environment, or community, helps define what integrity means. You might have more lenient ethical standards for a person selling you investment derivatives (high-risk investments used to hedge other investments, with their value derived from the existence of other securities) than you would for a bank vice president who accepted your cash deposit.

The virtue ethics of managers and professionals who belong to professional societies may be readily inferred. Business-related professions having codes of ethics include accountants, purchasing managers, and certified financial planners. To the extent that the person abides by the tenets of the code, he or she behaves ethically. An example of such a tenet would be for a financial planner to be explicit about any commissions he or she stands to gain from a client accepting the advice.

Ethical Question	% Yes	% No
Have you inflated numbers in a forecast?	12	88
Have you taken office supplies home?	69	31
Have you ever inflated your company's sales to win a client?	19	81
Have you ever put a personal cost on your expense report or company credit card?	19	81
Have you booked an order that wasn't yet contracted?	6	94

Exhibit 4-3

Responses to Ethical Questions by 374 Visitors to Fast Company's *Web Site*

Source: Jennifer Alsever, "The Ethics Monitor," *Fast Company*, August 2005, p. 27.

Major Causes of Ethical Problems

Individuals, organizations, and society must share some of the blame for the prevalence of unethical behavior in the workplace. Exhibit 4–3 presents a sampling of unethical behavior in business. Major contributors to unethical behavior are an *individual's greed and gluttony,* or the desire to maximize self-gain at the expense of others. Former Federal Reserve Chairman Alan Greenspan said that "an infectious greed" had contaminated the business community in the late 1990s, as one executive after another manipulated earnings or resorted to fraudulent accounting to capitalize on soaring stock prices.[27] The decision makers at Fidelity (in the chapter opener) who accepted lavish gifts from a brokerage house might have been experiencing greed and gluttony.

Another key contributor to a person's ethics and morality is his or her *level of moral development.*[28] Some workers are morally advanced, while others are morally challenged—a condition that often develops early in life. People progress through three developmental levels in their moral reasoning. At the *preconventional level,* a person is concerned primarily with receiving external rewards and avoiding punishments. A manager at this level of development might falsify earnings statements for the primary purpose of gaining a large bonus.

At the *conventional level,* people learn to conform to the expectations of good behavior as defined by key people in their environment, as well as societal norms. A manager at this level might be just moral enough to look good, such as being fair with salary increases and encouraging contributions to the United Way campaign. At the *postconventional level,* people are guided by an internalized set of principles based on universal, abstract principles that may even transcend the laws of a particular society. A manager at the postconventional level of moral behavior would be concerned with doing the most good for the most people, whether or not such behavior brought him or her recognition and fortune. If the manager just described wanted to direct an apprenticeship program, he or she might also be at the postconventional level of moral behavior.

Another major contributor to unethical behavior is an *organizational atmosphere that condones such behavior.* If leaders at the top of the organization take imprudent, quasilegal risks, other leaders throughout the firm might be prompted to behave similarly. The ethical violations of the financial services giant, Citi, were attributed to an aggressive culture that encouraged daring risks. For example, Japanese regulators accused Citi of numerous instances of unfair transactions in which excessive profits were obtained through unsound means. The megabank admitted to failing to comply with regulatory requirements.[29]

Unethical behavior is often triggered by *pressure from higher management to achieve goals.* One study found that 56% of all workers feel some pressure to act unethically or illegally.[30] Another cause of unethical behavior emphasizes the *strength of relationships among people* as a major factor.[31] Assume that two people have close ties to each other, such as having worked together for a long time or knowing each other both on and off the job. As a consequence, they are likely to behave ethically toward each other on the job. In contrast, if a weak relationship exists between the two people, either party is more likely to engage in an unethical relationship. Executives who do not feel that they have a personal relationship with employees well below them in the hierarchy are more likely to behave unethically toward them than if a bond had been formed.

A final cause of unethical behavior to be mentioned here are *unconscious biases* that lead us to make unfair judgments and lead us toward discriminatory practices. Suppose a real-estate manager believes that women are much better at selling homes than men are, and the manager is not aware of his bias. His unconscious belief may lead him to hire a woman rather than a man when the two have comparable qualifications. It is difficult to overcome an unconscious bias, yet progress can be made by remembering to broaden one's options when making a workplace decision.[32]

AN EIGHT-STEP GUIDE TO ETHICAL DECISION MAKING

Describe the eight-step guide to ethical decision making.

Linda K. Treviño and Katherine A. Nelson have developed a guide to ethical decision making that incorporates the basic ideas found in other ethical tests.[33] After studying this guide, you will be asked to ethically screen a decision. The eight steps to sound ethical decision making are described here.

1. *Gather the facts.* When making an important business decision, it is necessary to gather relevant facts. Ask yourself such questions as, "Are there any legal issues involved here?" "Is there a precedent in our firm with respect to this type of decision?" "Do I have the authority to make this decision?" "Are there company rules and regulations governing such a decision?"

2. *Define the ethical issues.* The ethical issues in a given decision are often more complicated than suggested at first glance. When faced with a complex decision, it may be helpful to talk over the ethical issues with another person. The ethical issues might involve common ethical problems such as:

   - Lying to customers
   - Job discrimination
   - Sexual harassment
   - Offering or accepting bribes or kickbacks
   - Overstatement of the capability of a product or service
   - Use of corporate resources for personal gain

3. *Identify the affected parties.* When faced with a complex ethical decision, it is important to identify those who will feel the impact of the decision. Brainstorming may be helpful to identify all the parties affected by a given decision. Major corporate decisions can affect thousands of people. If a company decides to shut down a plant and outsource manufacturing to a low-wage country, thousands of individuals and many different parties are affected. Workers lose their jobs, suppliers lose their customers, the local government loses out on tax revenues, and local merchants lose many of their customers.

   The people affected by the decision to delay expense-account reimbursements include the workers owed the money and their families. In some instances, the creditors of the workers owed money may also receive late payments.

4. *Identify the consequences.* After you have identified the parties affected by the decision, the next step is to predict the consequences for each party. It may not be necessary to identify every consequence. Yet it is important to identify the

consequences with the highest probability of occurring and those with the most negative outcomes.

Both short-term and long-term consequences should be specified. The company closing a plant might create considerable short-term turmoil but might be healthier in the long term. A healthy company would then be able to provide for more workers. The short-term consequences of delaying expense reimbursements might be a few grumbles; ill will probably will be created for the long term.

The symbolic consequences of an action are important. Every action and decision sends a message (the message is a symbol of something). If a company moves manufacturing out of a community to save on labor costs, it means that the short-term welfare of domestic employees is less important than the welfare of shareholders. Delaying expense-account reimbursements symbolizes more concern about optimizing cash flow than treating employees fairly.

5. *Identify the obligations.* When making a complex decision, identify the obligations and the reason for each one. A manufacturer of automotive brakes has an obligation to produce and sell only brakes that meet high safety standards. The obligation is to the auto manufacturer who purchases the brakes, and more importantly to the ultimate consumer, whose safety depends on effective brakes. The ultimate reason for the obligation to make safe brakes is that lives are at stake.

6. *Consider your character and integrity.* A core consideration when faced with an ethical dilemma is to consider how relevant people would judge your character and integrity. What would your family, friends, significant others, teachers, and coworkers think of your actions? How would you feel if your actions were publicly disclosed in the local newspaper or through e-mail? If you would be proud for others to know what decision you made when you faced an ethical dilemma, you are probably making the right decision.

7. *Think creatively about potential actions.* When faced with an ethical dilemma, put yourself in a creative-thinking mode. Stretch your imagination to invent several options rather than thinking you have only two choices—to do or not to do something. Creative thinking may point toward a third choice, or even more alternatives. Visualize the ethical dilemma of a purchasing agent who is told by a sales rep that he will receive a Blackberry as a token of appreciation if his company signs a contract. The agent says to himself, "I think we should award the contract to the firm, but I cannot accept the gift. Yet if I turn down the gift, I will be forfeiting a valuable possession that the company simply regards as a cost of doing business."

By thinking creatively, the agent finds another alternative. He tells the sales rep, "We will grant the contract to your firm because your product fits our requirements. I thank you for the offer of the Blackberry but instead please give it to the Southside Young Entrepreneur's Club in my name."

8. *Check your intuition.* So far we have emphasized the rational side of ethical decision making. Another effective way of conducting an ethics screen is to rely on intuition. How does the contemplated decision feel, taste, and smell? Would you be proud of yourself or would you be disgusted with yourself if you made the decision? Of course, if a person lacks a conscience, checking intuition is not effective.

Another type of decision that often requires an ethical test is choosing between two rights (rather than right versus wrong). Joseph L. Badaracco, Jr., refers to these situations as *defining moments,* because such decisions over time form the basis of a person's character. The defining moment challenges a person by asking him or her to choose between two ideals in which he or she deeply believes.[34] Suppose a blind worker in the group has personal problems so great that her job performance suffers. She is offered counseling but does not follow through seriously. Other members of

SKILL-DEVELOPMENT EXERCISE

Ethical Decision Making

Working in small groups, take one or both of the ethical dilemmas presented in this exercise through the eight steps for an ethical screening of contemplated decisions. Compare your answers for the various steps with other groups in the class.

Scenario 1: The Enormous Omelet Sandwich by Burger King. You and three other students are placed on an ethics task force at Burger King being asked to investigate the ethics of selling the Enormous Omelet Sandwich. The sandwich is composed of one sausage patty, two eggs, two American cheese slices, and three strips of bacon on a bun, and contains 730 calories and 47 grams of fat. The Enormous Omelet sells particularly well with males between 18 and 35. "Food police" outside the company claim that the Enormous Omelet is so loaded with fat and bad cholesterol that it could lead to heart disease. Yet the position of company management is that there are plenty of options on the Burger King menu for customers who want to make healthy choices. The Enormous Omelet Sandwich has been a major financial

success for the restaurant chain. You and your teammates are asked to present top management with an evaluation of the ethics of continuing to sell the Enormous Omelet Sandwich.

Scenario 2: The High-Profit Toys. You are a toy company executive starting to plan your holiday-season line. You anticipate that the season's hottest item will be RoboWoman, a battery-operated crime fighter and superheroine. RoboWoman should have a wholesale price of $20.50 and a retail price of $40.00. Your company anticipates a gross profit of $12 per unit. You receive a sales call from a manufacturing broker who says he can produce any toy you want for one-third of your present manufacturing cost. He admits that the manufacturer he represents uses prison labor in China but that his business arrangement violates no law. You estimate that your firm can earn a gross profit of $16 per unit if you do business with the manufacturing broker. The decision you face is whether to do business with him.

Collaboration

the team complain about the blind worker's performance because it interferes with the group achieving its goals. If the blind worker is dismissed, she may suffer severe financial consequences. (She is the only wage earner in the family.) However, if she is retained, the group will suffer consequences of its own. The manager must now choose between two rights, or the lesser of two evils.

The accompanying skill-development exercise gives you an opportunity to practice the eight-part guide to ethical decision making.

ORGANIZATIONAL APPROACHES TO ENHANCING ETHICAL AND SOCIALLY RESPONSIBLE BEHAVIOR

(6)

Describe what organizations can do to enhance ethical and socially responsible behavior.

Establishing an ethical and socially responsible workplace is not simply a matter of luck and common sense. Top-level managers, assisted by other managers and professionals, can develop strategies and programs to enhance ethical and socially responsible attitudes and behavior. **Social responsibility** is the idea that firms have obligations to society beyond their economic obligations to owners or stockholders, and beyond those prescribed by law or contract. Both ethics and social responsibility relate to the goodness or morality of a firm. However, social responsibility is broader than ethics because it relates to an organization's impact on society beyond doing what is ethical. The accompanying Organizational Behavior in Action box presents a large-scale example of social responsibility. We turn now to initiatives executive leadership can take to help create an ethical and socially responsible culture.

ORGANIZATIONAL BEHAVIOR *In Action*

Wal-Mart Reaches Out to Hurricane Disaster Victims

At 8 A.M. on Wednesday August 31, as New Orleans filled with water, Wal-Mart chief executive H. Lee Scott, Jr., called an emergency meeting of his top lieutenants and warned them he did not want a "measured response" to the hurricane. "I want us to respond in a way appropriate to our size and the impact we can have," he said, according to an executive who attended the meeting. Over the next few days, Wal-Mart's response to Katrina—an unrivaled $20 million in cash donations, 1500 truckloads of free merchandise, food for 100,000 meals, and the promise of a job for every one of its displaced workers—has turned the chain into an unexpected lifeline for much of the Southeast and earned it near-universal praise at a time when the company is struggling to burnish its image.

While state and federal officials have come under harsh criticism for their handling of the storm's aftermath, Wal-Mart is being held up as a model for logistical efficiency and nimble disaster planning, which have allowed it to quickly deliver staples such as water, fuel, and bathroom tissue to thousands of evacuees. At the Brookhaven, Miss., distribution center, for example, the company had 45 trucks full of goods loaded and ready for delivery before Katrina made landfall. To keep operating near capacity, Wal-Mart secured a special line at a nearby gas station to ensure that its employees could make it to work.

Wal-Mart had much to gain through its conspicuous largesse—it has hundreds of stores in Gulf Coast states and an image problem across the country—but even those who have criticized the company in the past are impressed. "Wal-Mart has raised the ante for every company in the country," said Adam Hanft, chief executive of a branding and marketing firm. "This is going to change the face of corporate giving."

Scott, Wal-Mart's folksy chief executive and its chief defender against a chorus of critics, was singled out by former presidents George H. W. Bush and Bill Clinton during a joint news conference. The praise comes at a time when the chain faces a series of lawsuits over allegations of wage-an-hour-law violations and gender discrimination.

But the chain's huge scale is suddenly an advantage in providing disaster relief. The same sophisticated supply chain that has turned the company into a widely feared competitor is now viewed as exactly what the waterlogged Gulf Coast needs. The Bentonville, Ark., company rushed to set up mini-Wal-Marts in storm-ravaged areas, handing out clothing, diapers, baby wipes, toothbrushes, and food. With police escorts, it delivered two truckloads of ice and water into New Orleans. It shipped 150 Internet-ready computers to shelters caring for evacuees.

During a tearful interview on "Meet the Press," Aaron F. Broussard, president of a parish in suburban New Orleans, said that if "the American government would have responded like Wal-Mart has responded, we wouldn't be in this crisis."

Asked what motivated the chain's relief efforts and how he thought critics would respond, Scott said: "We have never claimed to be flawless. But on the other hand, we have always demanded that we as a company do care. If anything, this week has shown we do care. We can't do more than our own part. We are not the federal government. There is a portion we can do, and we can do it darn well."

Questions

1. In what way was Wal-Mart being ethical and socially responsible in the story presented?
2. To what extent do you believe that top-level management at Wal-Mart capitalized on hurricane Katrina to build its image?
3. What impact, if any, has this story about Wal-Mart had on your willingness to shop at Wal-Mart?

Source: Excerpted from Michael Barbaro and Justin Gillis, "Wal-Mart at Forefront of Hurricane Relief," *washingtonpost.com*, September 6, 2005.

Log on to **www
.thomsonedu.com/
infotrac.** Search for
articles on the now-
disgraced executives
of the business world,
such as Kenneth Lay
and Jeffrey Skilling of
Enron, or L. Dennis
Kozlowski of Tyco.

Leadership by Example and Establishing an Ethical Culture

A high-powered approach to enhancing ethics and social responsibility is for corporate leaders to behave in such a manner themselves. If people throughout the firm
believe that behaving ethically is "in" and behaving unethically is "out," ethical
behavior will prevail. Marc Benniof, founder of Salesforce.com, urges other corporations to adopt his philanthropy model of donating 1% of the company's time,
equity, and profits to assist the people and communities the business serves. Top management at Salfesforce.com grants employees 6 days a year of paid time to do
volunteer work. The company has also used company profits to offer nonprofit
organizations its customer relationship management software without charge.[35]

Leading by example contributes to establishing a culture in which ethical behavior is expected, and unethical behavior is not tolerated. The Vanguard Group, one
of the largest mutual fund companies, represents a good example. Known for its
low-cost funds, the company was not involved in the mutual fund scandals involving late trading and market timing. To help establish an ethical culture, company
leaders talk about commitment to client service—and they establish tight controls,
including audits.[36]

Written Codes of Ethical Conduct

Many organizations use written codes of conduct as guidelines for ethical and socially responsible behavior. Such guidelines continue to grow in importance because
workers in self-managing teams have less leadership than previously. An ethical code
is sometimes established to help a company repair a tarnished reputation. Several
years ago two key executives at Tyco International were convicted of, and sent to
prison for, stealing $600 million in company funds. While the executives were still
being tried, the new CEO hired an ethics officer who developed an ethical code for
the company soon after her arrival.[37] Some general aspects of ethical codes require
people to conduct themselves with integrity and candor. Here is a statement of this
type from the Johnson & Johnson (medical and health supplies) code of ethics:

> We believe our first responsibility is to the doctors, nurses, and patients, to
> mothers and fathers and all others who use our products and services. In
> meeting their needs everything we do must be of high quality.[38]

Formal Mechanisms for Dealing with Ethical Problems

Large organizations frequently establish ethics committees to help ensure ethical and
socially responsible behavior. Committee members generally include a top management representative plus other managers throughout the organization. An ethics and
social responsibility specialist from the human resources department might also join
the group. The committee establishes policies about ethics and social responsibility,
and may conduct an ethical audit of the firm's activities. In addition, committee
members might review complaints about ethical problems.

Accepting Whistle-Blowers

A **whistle-blower** is an employee who discloses organizational wrongdoing to parties who can take action. Whistle-blowers will sometimes report wrongdoing to a
company insider such as a vice president, or blow the whistle externally, such as to a

government agency. Emotion is a mediating factor in whistle-blowing. A team of re-searchers concluded that to the extent potential whistle-blowers experience anger and resentment toward the perceived wrongdoers, they will decide to blow the whistle.[39] For example, a manager angry about top management using the corporate jet for personal travel might report top management's misdeeds to the board.

It was a whistle-blower who began the process of exposing the scandalous financial practices at Enron, such as hiding losses. Enron vice president Sherron Watkins wrote a one-page anonymous letter exposing unsound, if not dishonest, financial reporting. Enron had booked profits for two entities that had no assets. She dropped the letter off at company headquarters the next day.

The Sarbanes–Oxley Act is supposed to prevent retaliation against whistle-blowers by top management. Despite the Act, whistle-blowers are often ostracized and humiliated by the companies they hope to improve, by means such as halting promotions or giving poor performance evaluations. Of the hundreds of people who lost jobs during the first 3 years of the Act, only two were back at their jobs. Others were still waiting or settled out of court.[40]

More than half the time, the pleas of whistle-blowers are ignored. It is impor-tant for leaders at all levels to create a comfortable climate for legitimate whistle-blowing. The manager needs the insight to sort out the difference between a trou-blemaker and a true whistle-blower. Careful investigation is required, because only 15% of Sarbanes–Oxley complaints are found to have merit, according to the U.S. Department of Labor.

Training in Ethics and Social Responsibility

Many companies train managerial workers about ethics. Forms of training include messages about ethics and social responsibility from company leadership, classes on ethics at colleges, and exercises in ethics. These training programs reinforce the idea that ethically and socially responsible behavior is both morally right and good for business. Ethics training received a boost in 2004 in response to an amendment to the Federal Sentencing Guidelines for Organizations (FSGO) of 1991. The amend-ment calls for much stricter training requirements and emphasizes establishing a legal and ethical company culture.[41] Much of the content of this chapter reflects the type of information communicated in such programs.

Awareness of Cross-Cultural Influences on Ethics

A key part of encouraging ethical behavior is to know what constitutes good ethics. The answer is not so easy to ascertain in dealing with companies from other coun-tries, which vary in what they consider to be ethical and socially responsible behav-ior. For example, both the United States and China make extensive use of prison labor—an activity some countries would consider highly unethical. Bribes to foreign officials to conduct business within their country are usually considered unethical and illegal. Yet these bribes, reclassified as *offsets,* are widespread in the armaments industry. An offset is presenting a lavish package to a foreign government for the right to do business in that country. Offsets can be any form of financial or nonfinancial aids such as direct investments, agreements to help countries export their goods, agreements to use more foreign components in the weapons sold, and even outsourcing production jobs overseas.

An experiment was conducted to examine if the national location in which people work influences their attitudes and intended behavior toward ethical scenarios provided by the experimenters. The sample consisted of Americans working in Russia and the United States. Location did make a difference in ethical attitudes and intended behavior; however, the type of ethical scenario also exerted an influence. When the two groups of workers responded to scenarios about universal norms reflecting basic human rights, they did not differ in their responses. A specific universal norm would be upholding employees' rights to physical security. When local norms were involved, such as those relating to bribery or being late with employee pay, differences were found. Americans in Russia differed from Americans in the United States with respect to their attitudes and intended behaviors. An inference to be drawn from this study is that cultural attitudes can influence a worker's perception of what type of behavior is ethical.[42]

Financial Consequences of Being Ethical and Socially Responsible

The initiatives for ethics and social responsibility just described can benefit the organization. Research evidence suggests that high ethics and social responsibility are related to good financial performance. According to the International Business Ethics Institute, socially responsible behavior does enhance profits. One study found that the overall financial performance of a list of the 100 Best Firms was significantly better than the remaining companies in the S&P 500. The study took into account measures of responsibility, reflecting quality service to seven stakeholder entities: the community, minorities, women, employees, the environment, foreign stakeholders, and customers.[43]

The relationship between social responsibility and profits can also work in two directions. More profitable firms can better afford to invest in social responsibility initiatives, and these initiatives can in turn lead to more profits. Sandra A. Waddock and Samuel B. Graves analyzed the relationship between corporate social performance and corporate financial performance for 469 firms, spanning 13 industries, for a 2-year period. Many different measures of social and financial performance were used. An example of social performance would be helping to redevelop a poor community.

Levels of corporate social performance were influenced by prior financial success. The results suggest that financial success creates enough money left over to invest in corporate social performance. The study also found that good corporate social performance contributes to improved financial performance as measured by a company's return on assets and return on sales. Waddock and Graves concluded that the relationship between social and financial performance may be a **virtuous circle,** meaning that corporate social performance and corporate financial performance feed and reinforce each other.[44]

Being ethical also helps avoid the costs of paying huge fines for being unethical, including charges of discrimination and class action lawsuits because of improper financial reporting. Charges of age discrimination and sex discrimination are the two leading sources of lawsuits against companies.

IMPLICATIONS FOR MANAGERIAL PRACTICE

In addition to the suggestions made for applying information throughout this chapter (as is done in all chapters of this book), here we make a few additional practical suggestions:

1. Recognize emotion in the workplace as a potentially constructive force rather than a human condition to be ignored or suppressed. For example, enthusiasm

and joy should be encouraged because they are symptoms of feelings of accomplishment and high job satisfaction. Also, anger can be a constructive force if directed toward overcoming problems.

2. An important interpersonal skill in the workplace is to recognize both generational and individual values, and then make some concession to satisfying the reasonable job demands stemming from these values. For example, to appeal to the value system of the stereotypical member of Generation Y, you would grant that person flexibility in choosing methods of work and working hours, frequent feedback, and meaningful projects. Also, if you were working with a member of the veteran generation (born between 1922 and 1943), you would make concessions to his or her interest in abiding by rules and regulations.

3. When facing a major decision, you will want to use many of the guidelines for problem solving and decision making presented in the next chapter. In addition, major decisions should be subject to the eight-step guide for ethical decision making presented here. For a quick check on the ethical soundness of your decisions, use steps 6 (consider your character and integrity) and 8 (check your intuition).

Timberland: Ethics and Social Responsibility "Visit **www. thomsonedu.com/ management/dubrin** and watch the video for this chapter. What organizational forces exist at Timberland to support ethical and socially responsible behavior?"

83

SUMMARY OF KEY POINTS

 Describe the importance of attitudes and emotions to behavior in organizations.

Attitudes influence organizational behavior in many ways. The three components of attitudes are cognitive, affective, and behavioral. A state of cognitive dissonance leads people to reduce their internal conflict when they experience a clash between the information they receive and their actions or attitudes. Attitudes are especially important because they are the basis for job satisfaction, which is linked to important consequences such as absenteeism and turnover and job stress. Job satisfaction contributes to organizational performance, and being part of a high-performing organization might elevate job satisfaction.

An emotion consists of three interacting components: internal physiological arousal, expressive behavior, and a cognitive appraisal. Emotional labor takes place when workers adjust their feelings and expressions to meet organizational goals, such as pleasing customers. Managers should make good use of emotions. Two key steps are to establish a friendly emotional climate, and to include a positive attitude as one factor in selecting individuals and teams.

 Describe how organizational citizenship behavior contributes to individual and organizational effectiveness.

Job satisfaction also contributes to organizational citizenship behavior. The good organizational citizen goes above and beyond the call of duty, or engages in extrarole behavior. Personality factors, such as service orientation and empathy, contribute to organizational citizenship behavior. Low organizational citizenship behavior has been linked to turnover. When workers perceive their organization to be fair and just, they are more likely to believe that OCB is part of their job. Being too strong an organizational citizen by taking on extra work can lead to conflict in personal life.

 Summarize why values are an important part of organizational behavior.

A *value* refers to the importance a person attaches to something that serves as a guide to action. Many values are acquired early in life, often through modeling. The values a person develops early in life are directly related to the kind of person he or she is now and will be, as well as the quality of his or her personal relationships. Job performance tends to be higher when there is congruence between individual and organizational values. A person suffers from person–role conflict when the demands made by the organization or a manager clash with the basic values of the individual.

 Describe three ethical decision-making criteria, along with several explanations for the existence of ethical problems.

A philosophical approach to understanding ethics gives three possible focuses: on consequences; on duties, obligations, and principles; or on integrity.

When focusing on consequences, the decision maker is concerned with the utility, or net balance of good and bad consequences, of a decision. The deontological approach focuses on the rights of individuals, and is based on universal principles such as honesty, fairness, justice, and respect for persons and property. The integrity, or virtue, criterion focuses on the character of the ethical action.

Major causes of ethical problems include an individual's greed and gluttony, an individual's level of moral development; a culture that condones unethical behavior; pressure from higher management; weak relationships between people; and unconscious biases.

 Describe the eight-step guide to ethical decision making.

An eight-step guide to ethical decision making follows these steps: (1) Gather the facts, (2) define the ethical issues, (3) identify the affected parties, (4) identify the consequences, (5) identify the obligations, (6) consider your character and integrity, (7) think creatively about potential actions, and (8) check your intuition. Choosing between two rights, or defining moments, may require an ethical test.

 Describe what organizations can do to enhance ethical and socially responsible behavior.

Managers can develop strategies and programs to enhance ethical and socially responsible attitudes and behaviors. Among these approaches are: leading by example and establishing an ethical culture, establishing written codes of ethical conduct, and formal mechanisms for dealing with ethical problems, accepting whistle-blowers, giving training in ethics and social responsibility, and gaining awareness of cross-cultural influences on ethics.

KEY TERMS AND PHRASES

Attitude, 64
A predisposition to respond that exerts an influence on a person's response to a person, a thing, an idea, or a situation.

Cognitive Dissonance, 64
The situation in which the pieces of knowledge, information, attitudes, and beliefs held by an individual are contradictory.

Emotion, 65
A feeling, such as anger, fear, joy, or surprise, that underlies behavior.

Emotional Labor, 66
The process of regulating both feelings and expressions to meet organizational goals.

Job Satisfaction, 67
The amount of pleasure or contentment associated with a job.

Organizational Citizenship Behavior, 68
Behaviors that express a willingness to work for the good of an organization even without the promise of a specific reward.

Value, 69
The importance a person attaches to something that serves as a guide to action.

Person–Role Conflict, 71
A condition that occurs when the demands made by the organization or a manager clash with the basic values of the individual.

Ethics, 73
An individual's moral beliefs about what is right and wrong or good and bad.

Social Responsibility, 78
The idea that firms have an obligation to society beyond their economic obligations to owners or stockholders and beyond those prescribed by law or contract.

Whistle-Blower, 80
An employee who discloses organizational wrongdoing to parties who can take action.

Virtuous Circle, 82
The idea that corporate social performance and corporate financial performance feed and reinforce each other.

DISCUSSION QUESTIONS AND ACTIVITIES

1. One study showed that more intelligent workers are more likely to experience job satisfaction. How might you explain this relationship between intelligence and job satisfaction?

2. In what way can being a very strong organizational citizen potentially lead to a worker becoming stressed out?

3. For what reasons do you think most workers are reluctant to cry in front of other workers when something goes wrong such as receiving a poor performance review or losing data on their computer? How does your answer fit with the idea that emotional expression is supposed to be welcome on the job?

4. Give an example of a situation in which you would most likely experience person–role conflict within an organization.

5. What can a manager do to teach the right values to employees?

6. What can business schools do to increase the probability that business graduates will behave ethically on the job?

7. The Vice Fund (**http://www.vicefund.com**) bills itself as a "socially irresponsible fund" because it puts investor's assets into four industry sectors: tobacco, gambling, liquor, and defense. What is your opinion of: (a) the ethics of the founders of the fund, and (b) the advisability of investing money in such a fund?

CASE PROBLEM: The Not-So-Harmless Cage Divers

Every morning, tourist boats leave the southern Cape coast for a patch of sea called Shark Alley. Off a rocky outcrop populated by seals and washed by crashing waves, the boat crews throw mesh bags of ground-up fish into the water. Great White sharks soon pick up the scent of blood and start circling. Occasionally shrieking with fear, paying customers climb into a steel cage, about 8 feet by 4 feet, four people at a time. They are then lowered into the frigid ocean. Baited by the crew, 10-foot long sharks arrive, snapping their jaws at the cage railing and raising gnashing teeth above the water. Most of the customers have other thrills on Cape vacations: bungee jumping, sky diving, and jungle safaris.

This shark-diving industry, established in the late 1990s, has become big business on the Cape coast of South Africa. Drawing in some 35,000 mostly American and European adrenaline junkies a year, shark divers pay some $6.3 million in fees to 12 licensed operators, or as much as $200 a dive, and more for hotel, food, and airfare.

But there isn't just fish blood in the water. As the cage-diving industry flourishes, Cape Town beaches—a Mecca for surfers—have been hit by a spate of gruesome shark attacks on people. Critics blame the deaths on shark-diving practices such as baiting and chumming (the throwing of ground fish into the ocean). Cage-diver operators, these critics say, may have taught sharks to associate humans with food, turning the ocean's apex predators into man-eaters.

Amid the outcry, a shark-diving boat was burned here last year, though the motivation for the incident remains unclear. In June, after a lethal shark attack, a coalition of surfers, fishermen, ecologists, and sailors demanded that the South African government ban chumming and baiting by shark-diving boats. "These people are attracting the sharks to right where we swim," says the group's leader, Craig Bovim. "The reality is that the sharks are rewarded constantly, and so the chances of something going wrong are considerably high."

Bovin, a 38-year-old owner of an engineering company, knows this firsthand. On Christmas Eve 2002, he was snorkeling off the Cape peninsula, hoping to catch lobsters for dinner. A 5-yard-long Great White shark swam up alongside. As Bovim blew the air out of his snorkel, producing a sound like a seal's, the shark opened its jaws and lunged for his hands. The shark took a generous bite out of both, leaving Bovin's right hand snapped in two and flapping back.

Bovin somehow managed to undo his weight belt and swim to shore, some 50 yards away. After much surgery, he is still in only partial command of his hands. In 2003, a Great White killed a 19-year-old surfer. A year later, an abalone poacher was bitten to death near Shark Alley, and 77-year-old Tyna Webb was torn apart by a shark in full view of sunbathers at a popular Cape Town beach. In June 2005, medical student Henri Murray was killed by a shark while spear-fishing in nearby waters. Great Whites usually don't like human flesh. But Webb and Murray appeared to have been swallowed and digested, with little apart from blood, a red bathing cap and a tattered wetsuit left behind. "Emotionally, it's a lot harder when people get consumed," says Gregg Oelofse, the Cape Town city government's environmental policy coordinator. "It changes perceptions."

An avid surfer, Oelofse is part of a working group of officials and academics set up last year to evaluate the effects of cage-diving on shark behavior. Scientists consider sharks to be smart and fast learners. As summer approached in the southern hemisphere, researchers began deploying electronic monitors and human shark-spotters to track shark movements around Cape Town to see if these predators are moving closer to the shore and showing an increased interest in bathers. A report

(continued)

CASE PROBLEM (Continued)

that may lead to new regulations was anticipated in 2006. So far, Oelofse says he sees no link between recent shark attacks and practices such as chumming.

In the United States, both Florida and California have banned commercial chumming. This means South Africa is the only place where encounters with Great Whites can be virtually guaranteed on a day trip from a major city. South African businesses are eager to preserve this gold-mine, painting the controversy as uninformed paranoia. "Every time they try to bite the cage, they taste metal," says Craig Ferreira, owner of White Sharks Projects, one of the 12 South-African operators. "If you were conditioning the shark to anything, it's that humans taste like metal."

South Africa recently banned the common practice of using fresh bait such as tuna heads, seeking to discourage aggressive shark behavior. Operators are also forbidden from actually feeding the sharks, though they can tease them by dangling chum in front of them.

Regardless of whether chumming changes shark behavior, such close encounters with humans will have consequences, environmentalists and officials warn. "You cannot interact with nature without affecting nature," says Oelofse. "We are affecting things—we just don't know how."

Case Questions

1. What ethical issues appear to be involved with the Cape Town cage-diving operators and their customers?

2. What social responsibility issues are present in the above story?

3. What rights (if any) do Great White sharks have that should be taken into account in making decisions about cage-diving?

4. What would you guess would be the most likely demographic groups to which the cage-diving customers belong? Explain your reasoning.

Source: Yaroslav Trofimov, "Angry Surfers Say Cage-Diving Changes Great White's Way," *The Wall Street Journal*, September 24–25, 2005, pp. A1, A6.

ENDNOTES

1. Stephen Fineman, *Understanding Emotion at Work* (Thousand Oaks, CA: Sage, 2003).
2. Department of Homeland Security study cited in "U.S. Studies Root of Sabotage," Associated Press, May 17, 2005.
3. Saul Kassin, *Psychology*, 3rd ed. (Upper Saddle River, NJ: Prentice Hall, 2001), p. 330.
4. Neal M. Ashkanasy and Catherine S. Daus, "Emotion in the Workplace: The New Challenge for Managers," *The Academy of Management Executive*, February 2002, pp. 82–83.
5. Stéphane Côté, "A Social Interaction Model of the Effects of Emotion Regulation on Work Strain," *Academy of Management Review*, July 2005, p. 525.
6. Alicia A. Grandey, "Emotion Regulation in the Workplace: A New Way to Conceptualize Emotional Labor," *Journal of Occupational Health Psychology, 5*(1), 2000, pp. 95–110; Alicia A. Grandey, "When the 'Show Must Go On': Surface Acting and Deep Acting as Determinants of Emotional Exhaustion and Peer-Related Service Delivery," *Academy of Management Journal*, February 2003, pp. 86–96.
7. Reported in book review of Neal M. Ashkanasy, Charmine E. J. Härtel, and Wilfred J. Zerbe (eds.), *Emotions in the Workplace: Research, Theory, and Practice* (Westport, CT: Quorum Books/Greenwood, 2000) in *Contemporary Psychology*, April 2002, p. 165.
8. Patricia Faison Hewlin, "And the Award for Best Actor Goes to. . . : Facades of Conformity in Organizational Settings," *Academy of Management Review*, October 2003, pp. 633–642.
9. Theresa M. Glomb, John D. Kammeyer-Mueller, and Maria Rotundo, "Emotional Labor Demands and Compensating Wage Differentials," *Journal of Applied Psychology*, August 2004, pp. 700–714.
10. Review of Ashkanasy, Härtel, and Zerbe, *Emotions in the Workplace*, p. 165.
11. "U.S. Job Satisfaction Keeps Falling, the Conference Board Reports Today," http://www.conference-board.org/utilities/press, February 28, 2005.
12. Arthur P. Brief, *Attitudes in and Around Organizations* (Thousand Oaks, CA: Sage, 1998), Chapter 2; David Sirota, *The Enthusiastic Employee: How Companies Profit by Giving Workers What They Want* (Upper Saddle River, NJ: Wharton School Publishing/Pearson, 2005); "Employee Retention . . . Attitudes to Make Them Stay," *Managers Edge,* November 1999, p. 8; Timothy A. Judge and Remus Ilies, "Affect and Job Satisfaction: A Study of Their Relationship at Work and at Home," *Journal of Applied Psychology*, August 2004, pp. 661–673.
13. "Success Linked to Worker Loyalty," Associated Press, May 13, 2002.
14. Benjamin. Schneider, Paul J. Hanges, D. Brent Smith, and Amy Nicole Salvaggio, "Which Comes First: Employee Attitudes or Organizational Financial and Market Performance?" *Journal of Applied Psychology,* October 2003, pp. 836–851; Christian Kiewitz, "Happy Employees and Firm Performance: Have We Put the Cart before the Horse?" *Academy of Management Executive,* February 2004, pp. 127–128.
15. George A. Neuman and Jill R. Kickul, "Organizational Citizenship Behaviors: Achievement Orientation and Personality," *Journal of Business and Psychology,* Winter 1998, pp. 263–264.
16. Lance A. Bettencourt, Kevin P. Gwinner, and Matthew L. Meuter, "A Comparison of Attitude, Personality, and Knowledge Predictors of Service-Oriented Organizational Citizenship Behaviors," *Journal of Applied Psychology,* February 2001, pp. 29–41.

86

17. Xiao-Ping Chen, Chun Hui, and Douglas J. Sego, "The Role of Organizational Citizenship Behavior in Turnover: Conceptualization and Preliminary Tests of Key Hypotheses," *Journal of Applied Psychology,* December 1998, pp. 922–931.

18. Bennett J. Tepper, Daniel Lockhart, and Jenny Hoobler, "Justice, Citizenship, and Role Definition Effects," *Journal of Applied Psychology,* August 2001, pp. 789–796.

19. Mark C. Bolino and William H. Turnley, "The Personal Costs of Citizenship Behavior: The Relationship between Individual Initiative and Role Overload, Job Stress, and Work-Family Conflict," *Journal of Applied Psychology*, July 2005, pp. 740–748.

20. Ron Zemke, "Generation Veneration," in *Business: The Ultimate Resource*™ (Cambridge, MA: Perseus Books, 2002), pp. 39–40.

21. David C. McClelland, "How Motives, Skills, and Values Determine What People Do," *American Psychologist,* July 1985, p. 815.

22. "Putting People First," *BizEd*, July/August 2003, p. 19.

23. Po Bronson, "What Should I Do With My Life?" *Fast Company,* January 2003, p. 72.

24. Jennifer Schramm, "Perceptions on Ethics," *HR Magazine*, November 2004, p. 176.

25. Linda K. Treviño and Katherine A. Nelson, *Managing Business Ethics: Straight Talk about How to Do It Right* (New York: Wiley, 1995), pp. 66–70; O. C. Ferrell, John Fraedrich, and Linda Ferrell, *Business Ethics: Ethical Decision Making and Cases*, 4th ed. (Boston: Houghton Mifflin, 2000), pp. 52–61.

26. Robert Galford and Anne Seibold, "The Enemies of Trust," *Harvard Business Review,* February 2003, pp. 88–95.

27. "Fed Chief Points to Cautious Recovery," *Gannett News Service,* July 17, 2002.

28. Research synthesized in Richard L. Daft, *Leadership: Theory and Practice* (Mason, OH: Thomson South-Western, 2003), pp. 369–370.

29. Mara Der, "Can Chuck Prince Clean Up Citi?" *Business Week*, October 4, 2004, pp. 32–35.

30. Samuel Greengard, "50% of Your Employees Are Lying, Cheating, and Stealing," *Workforce,* October 1997, p. 46.

31. Daniel J. Brass, Kenneth D. Butterfield, and Bruce C. Skaggs, "Relationships and Unethical Behavior: A Social Network Perspective," *The Academy of Management Review,* January 1998, pp. 14–31.

32. Mahzarin R. Banaji, Maz H. Bazerman, and Dolly Chugh, "How (Un)ethical Are You?" December 2003, pp. 56–64.

33. Treviño and Nelson, *Managing Business Ethics,* pp. 71–75.

34. Joseph L. Badaracco, Jr., "The Discipline of Building Character," *Harvard Business Review,* March–April 1998, pp. 114–124.

35. April Y. Pennington, "A World of Difference," *Entrepreneur*, October 2004, p. 82.

36. Jonathan Pont, "Doing the Right Thing to Instill Business Ethics," *Workforce Management,* April 2005, p. 27.

37. Andy Meisler, "Clean Slate," *Workforce Management*, March 2004, p. 30.

38. Excerpted from http://www.jnj.com/our_company/our_credo/index.htm.

39. Michael J. Gundlach, Scott C. Douglas, and Mark J. Martinko, "The Decision to Blow the Whistle: A Social Information Processing Model," *Academy of Management Review*, January 2003, p. 112.

40. Jayne O'Donnell, "Blowing Whistle Hasn't Lost Its Risks," *USA Today*, August 7, 2005.

41. Kathryn Tyler, "Do the Right Thing: Ethics Training Programs Help Employees Deal with Ethical Dilemmas," *HR Magazine*, February 2005, pp. 99–102.

42. Andrew Spicer, Thomas W. Dunfee, and Wendy J. Bailey, "Does National Context Matter in Ethical Decision Making? An Empirical Test of Integrative Social Contracts Theory," *Academy of Management Journal*, August 2004, pp. 610–620.

43. Study reported in http://www.business-ethics.org.

44. Sandra A. Waddock and Samuel B. Graves, "The Corporate Social Performance-Financial Performance Link," *Strategic Management Journal,* Spring 1997, pp. 303–319.

5

OBJECTIVES

After reading and studying this chapter and doing the exercises, you should be able to:

1 Work through the classical/behavioral decision-making model when faced with a major decision.

2 Identify and describe factors that influence the effectiveness of decision making.

3 Understand the nature of creative decision making in organizations.

4 Enhance your creative problem-solving ability.

Individual Decision Making and Creativity

Most people might think of Starbucks as a fancy coffee joint. Not Chairman Howard D. Schultz. He sees the 8000-store chain as a "third place" for people to hang out besides home and work. That's why a seemingly unrelated service—offering wireless Net access in its stores starting in 2002—turned out to be a winner. Although Starbucks Corp. won't quantify the revenue impact, people using the service stay nine times longer than the usual 5 minutes, almost certainly buying more lattés. And 90% of its customers who log on are doing so after peak morning hours, filling stores during previously light periods, says Anne Saunders, Starbucks' senior vice-president of marketing: "If we'd only thought of ourselves as a coffee company, we wouldn't have done this."

The wireless network also inspired a new initiative that could remake the Seattle-based company. Its new Hear Music Coffeehouses were rolled into existing stores in Seattle at first, and then expanded to about 1000 sites in 2005. The stores feature dozens of listening stations from which people can make custom CDs (legally), at about a buck a tune, from hundreds of thousands of songs. In addition to offering a new service to 30 million weekly customers, Shultz has said he thinks Starbucks could transform the music business. At the least, he's transforming Starbucks once again.

Source: Robert D. Hof, "Building An Idea Factory," *Business Week*, October 11, 2004, p. 200.

Now Ask Yourself: **Why should this story about Starbucks expanding into technology services interest students of organizational behavior?** The key idea is that companies have to go beyond traditional thinking in order to prosper. (Starbucks did not invent the Internet café, but its foray into music was more original.) Going beyond traditional thinking sometimes leads to breakthrough ideas. The traditional thinking here is that a café focuses on serving coffee and closely related products such as pastries and bagels.

To be an effective decision maker, a person must think creatively. In this chapter, we study creativity in the context of individual decision making in organizations. First, we describe a model of the decision-making process; then we examine key influences on decision making, followed by a careful look at the nature and development of creativity. We return to the study of decision making in Chapter 9 with a description of group decision making. The steps in ethical decision making have already been described in Chapter 4.

The creative aspects of decision making are emphasized in this chapter because employee creativity contributes enormously to organizational success. An analysis of high-performing organizations observed that a company's most important asset is *creative capital*, defined as an arsenal of creative thinkers whose ideas can be converted into valuable products and services.[1]

TYPES OF DECISIONS

A **decision** takes place when a person chooses among two or more alternatives in order to solve a problem. People attempt to solve problems because a **problem** is a discrepancy between the ideal and the real. The ability to make good decisions is enormously valuable for a person's career and job performance. Choosing the right career will most likely mean more job satisfaction, less stress, and a longer life. (Stress-related disorders often shorten life.) Making good business decisions is more complex and difficult than most people recognize. The research of Paul C. Nutt suggests that half the decisions made in organizations fail—meaning that the decisions were not fully used after 2 years. His conclusions stem from a database of more than 400 decisions made by top-level managers in a variety of firms in the United States, Canada, and Europe. The typical reason for failure is that managers use poor decision-making tactics, such as taking shortcuts when faced with time pressures. Managers will often grab the first possible solution without analyzing the possible causes of problems and their remedies.[2]

Programmed versus Nonprogrammed Decisions

Managerial workers sometimes face routine, uncomplicated problems involving alternatives that are specified in advance. The standard responses to these uncomplicated problems are called **programmed** (or **routine**) decisions. Procedures already exist for how to appropriately handle the problem. Examples of programmed decisions include the procedures for accepting a check or whether to grant an employee a day of personal leave.

Managerial workers frequently face complex, nonrecurring problems for which the alternatives are not specified in advance. The unique responses to these complex problems are called **nonprogrammed** (or **nonroutine**) decisions. Making a nonprogrammed decision requires imaginative or creative thinking. An important characteristic of a complex problem requiring a decision is that more than one solution is possible, such as how to reduce costs in operating a store. Higher-level managers spend more of their time making nonprogrammed decisions, while lower-level managers face a higher proportion of programmed decisions. An example of a nonprogrammed decision would be whether or not to outsource the company call center.

Degree of Risk and Uncertainty Associated with Decisions

Another useful way of classifying decisions is by dividing the degree of risk and uncertainty associated with them into three categories: certainty, risk, and uncertainty. A condition of *certainty* exists when the facts are well known and the outcome can be predicted accurately. A retail store manager might predict with certainty that more hours of operation will lead to more sales. (It might be uncertain, however, whether the increased sales would cover the increased expenses.) Problem solving and decision making are easiest under conditions of certainty, but few major decisions are easy to make. In other words, few business decisions are truly "no-brainers."

A condition of *risk* involves incomplete certainty regarding the outcomes of various alternative courses of action. Nevertheless, there is some awareness of the probability associated with the alternatives. Based on past experience, predictions can be made about the various outcomes. An executive might be able to estimate how employees will react to an early retirement program based on previous company experience.

A condition of *uncertainty* exists when a decision must be based on limited or no factual information. In this type of decision environment, the decision maker is unable to assign probabilities to the problem-solving alternatives. When faced with a condition of uncertainty, managers rely on intuition. Michael Dell, the founder of Dell, Inc., founded his company in an uncertain business environment. He predicted intuitively that enough demand existed for purchasing personal computers by telephone. His intuition proved to be eminently correct.

A CLASSICAL/BEHAVIORAL DECISION-MAKING MODEL

Work through the classical/behavioral decision-making model when faced with a major decision.

Two different versions of how managerial workers make decisions are widely studied. The **classical decision model** views the manager's environment as certain and stable and the manager as rational. Many economists view decision making in this manner. The **behavioral decision model,** in contrast, points out that decision makers have cognitive limitations and act only in terms of what they perceive in a given situation.[3] Furthermore, decision making is influenced by many emotional and personal factors. According to the behavioral model, decision making has a messy side. For example, job performance alone may not decide who obtains big promotions in a family-controlled business.

The decision-making model described here blends the classical and behavioral decision models. Managers may make decisions in a generally rational framework. Nevertheless, at various points in the model (such as choosing creative alternatives), intuition and judgment come into play. Furthermore, the discussion in the following section about influences on decision making is based heavily on the behavioral decision model.

The seven steps in the decision-making process, reflecting both the classical and behavioral models, are outlined in Exhibit 5-1 and described in the following paragraphs. The model is useful for making nonprogrammed decisions of both a personal and an organizational nature. You might therefore want to use the model in purchasing a car, choosing a career, or deciding whether to drop a product line.

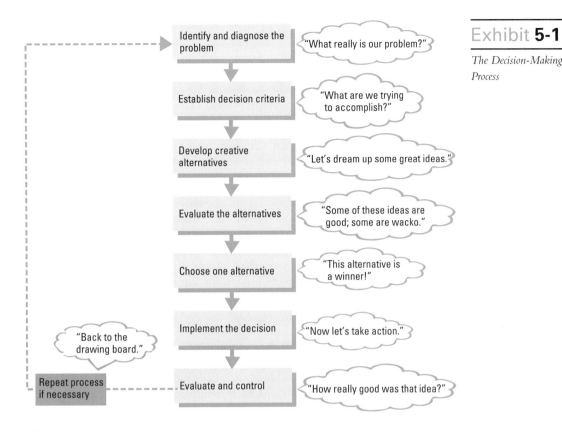

Exhibit **5-1**

*The Decision-Making
Process*

Identify and Diagnose the Problem

Problem solving and decision making begins with the awareness that a problem exists. In other words, the first step in problem solving and decision making is identifying a gap between desired and actual conditions. A problem occurs when something has gone wrong or has deviated from the norm. At times, a problem is imposed on a manager, such as a demand from upper management to increase e-tailing sales by 20%. At other times, the manager has to search actively for a worthwhile problem or opportunity. For example, a human resources manager sought a way for her firm to celebrate cultural diversity.

Finding a problem lies at the heart of being a successful entrepreneur. A classic example is why Howard Schultz expanded Starbucks into a chain of cafés in the United States. (Starbucks already existed as a seller of coffee beans to stores.) According to legend, Schultz was traveling in Italy when he noticed that Italians were passionate about strong coffee and their local cafés. The insight hit him that "If it works in Italy, why not at home too?" He would offer Americans something they were not used to, thereby creating a new market.[4]

A thorough diagnosis of the problem is important because the real problem may be different from the one suggested at first look. To diagnose a problem properly, you must clarify its true nature. For example, what might at first glance seem like a problem of quality is really one of consumer misuse of the product. To resolve the problem, one would need to better inform the consumer, not modify the product. An extreme example is that of an owner of a new digital camera complaining that the camera shot only partial images, with a horizontal dark spot across the pictures, when the true problem was that the camera user held his index finger across the lens while shooting photos.

Establish Decision Criteria

When solving a problem, it pays to know what constitutes a good decision. **Decision criteria** are the standards of judgment used to evaluate alternatives. The more explicit the criteria, the better the decision will be. In seeking to reduce costs, several of the decision criteria might include the following:

1. Product (or service) quality should not suffer as a result of the cost cutting.
2. Profits should increase as a result of the cost cutting.
3. Employee turnover should not increase because of the cost cutting.
4. Employee morale should not decrease as a result of the cost cutting.

A good starting point in establishing decision criteria, according to the late management guru Peter Drucker, is to ask, "What needs to be done?" rather than "What do I want to do?"[5] In the present example, the manager would ponder whether cost cutting is even worthwhile. Perhaps increasing spending would lead to improvements that would more than pay for themselves, such as hiring a highly talented worker who would make money for the company.

Develop Creative Alternatives

The third step in decision making is to generate alternative creative solutions. All kinds of possibilities are explored in this step even if they seem unrealistic. Often the difference between effective and mediocre decision makers is that the former do not accept the first alternative they think of. Instead, they keep digging until they find the best solution. The research of Nutt with executives found that failed decisions often result from a limited search for alternatives.[6] For example, a corporate executive who was downsized out of a job wanted to purchase a business to operate. Impatient to renew his career, he purchased a well-known—but poorly performing—franchise. Trying to make the franchise operation profitable drained the rest of his cash reserve and he sold back the franchise at a big loss. Had he researched better alternatives, he might have succeeded. Creativity is such a key part of decision making that it receives separate treatment later in this chapter.

Evaluate the Alternatives

The next step involves comparing the relative value of the alternatives. The problem solver examines the pros and cons of each alternative and considers its feasibility. Part of evaluating the pros and cons of alternative solutions is to compare each against the decision criteria established in the second step. Some alternatives would appear attractive, but implementing them would be impossible or counterproductive. For example, one alternative solution a couple chose for increasing their income was to open an entirely new restaurant and bar in a mall. When they discovered that the start-up costs would be approximately $600,000, they decided that the alternative was impossible for the time being.

Choose One Alternative

After investing a reasonable amount of time in evaluating the alternative solutions, it is time to choose one of them—to actually make a decision. An important factor influencing this process is the degree of uncertainty associated with it. People who prefer not to take risks choose alternatives that have the most certain outcomes. In contrast, risk takers are willing to choose alternatives with uncertain outcomes if the potential gains appear to be substantial. Despite a careful evaluation of the alternatives, in most decisions ambiguity remains. The decisions faced by managers are often complex, and the factors involved in them are often unclear.

Implement the Decision

Converting the decision into action is the next major step. Until a decision is implemented, it is not really a decision. Many decisions represent wasted effort because nobody is held responsible for implementing them. Much of a manager's job involves helping group members implement decisions. A fruitful way of evaluating a decision is to observe its implementation. A decision is seldom a good one if workers resist its implementation or if it is too cumbersome to implement.

Evaluate and Control

The final step in the decision-making framework is to evaluate how effectively the chosen alternative solved the problem and met the decision criteria. The results of the decision obtained are controlled when they are the ones set forth during the problem-identification stage. Getting back to the example in the section "Establish Decision Criteria," the decision to cut costs would be considered good if service did not suffer, profits were higher, turnover did not increase, and morale did not decrease.

BOUNDED RATIONALITY AND INFLUENCES ON DECISION MAKING

Decision making is usually not entirely rational, because so many factors influence the decision maker. Awareness of this fact stems from the research of psychologist and economist Herbert A. Simon. He proposed that bounds (or limits) to rationality are present in decision making. These bounds are the limitations of the human organism, particularly related to the processing and recall of information.[7] **Bounded rationality** means that people's finite (somewhat limited) mental abilities, combined with external influences over which they have little or no control, prevent them from making entirely rational decisions. Updated research and opinion on bounded rationality emphasizes that humans use problem-solving strategies that are reasonably rapid, reasonably accurate, and that fit the quantity and type of information available.[8] In short, people do the best with what they have while making decisions.

Identify and describe factors that influence the effectiveness of decision making.

As a result of bounded rationality, most decision makers do not have the time or resources to wait for the best possible solution. Instead, they search for **satisficing** decisions, or those that suffice in providing a minimum standard of satisfaction. Such decisions are adequate, acceptable, or passable. Many decision makers stop their search for alternatives when they find a satisficing one.

Accepting the first reasonable alternative may only postpone the need to implement a decision that truly solves the problem and meets the decision criteria. For example, slashing the price of a pickup truck to match the competition's price can be regarded as the result of a satisficing decision. A superior decision might call for the firm to demonstrate to end users that the difference in quality is worth the higher price, which in the long term will increase sales.

Partly because of bounded rationality, decision makers often use simplified strategies, also known as **heuristics.** A heuristic becomes a rule of thumb in decision making, such as the policy to reject a job applicant who does not smile during the first 3 minutes of a job interview. A widely used investing heuristic is as follows: The percent of equity in your portfolio should equal 100 minus your age, with the remainder being invested in fixed-income investments including cash. A 25-year-old would therefore have a portfolio consisting of 25% interest-bearing securities such as bonds and 75% in stocks. Heuristics help the decision maker cope with masses of information, but their oversimplification can lead to inaccurate or irrational decision making.

A host of influences on the decision-making process contribute to bounded rationality. We describe eight such influences, as outlined in Exhibit 5-2.

Intuition

Intuition is a key personal characteristic that influences decision making. Effective decision makers do not rely on analytical and methodological techniques alone. Instead, they also use hunches and intuition. **Intuition** is an experience-based way of knowing or reasoning in which weighing and balancing evidence are done automatically. Intuition can be based mostly on experience, or mostly on feeling.[9] A loan officer may have evaluated the risks of hundreds of business owners and received feedback about their payment records. So she makes good decisions about making loans to business owners based on her experience. A new loan officer in the same bank may not have much experience but "he knows a good or bad risk when he sees it." His feelings about who is a good risk and who is a poor risk help him lend money to good risks.

When relying on intuition, the decision maker arrives at a conclusion without using a step-by-step logical process. The fact that experience contributes to intuition

Exhibit **5-2**

Influences on Decision Making Contributing to Bounded Rationality

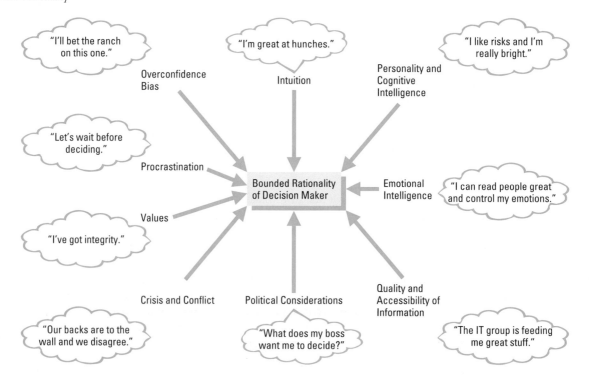

means that decision makers can become more intuitive by solving many difficult problems. A historically important example follows:

> Ray Kroc has been described as a legend of intuition on the basis of how he started the McDonald's chain. A milkshake-mixer salesman at the time, he came to deliver eight machines to the McDonald brothers' restaurant in 1952. Kroc had a flash that fast-food hamburgers would dominate in the future. So, he made the McDonalds a buyout offer, based on what he later termed his "funny-bone instinct."[10]

Although the use of intuition in organizational decision making is now widely recognized, researchers have also found limitations to intuition. When the stakes are high, such as a CEO contemplating acquiring a company in a different field, rational analysis is recommended. The analysis might include receiving input from many people and asking knowledgeable people loads of questions.[11] At the same time, however, intuition could help point the executive in the right direction, such as sizing up the overall merits of the company to be acquired. In short, you need to use your intuition to decide when intuition or extensive rational analysis is best!

Personality and Cognitive Intelligence

The personality and cognitive intelligence of the decision maker influence his or her ability to find effective solutions. One relevant personality dimension is cautiousness and conservatism. A cautious, conservative person typically opts for a low-risk solution. If a person is extremely cautious, he or she may avoid making major decisions for fear of being wrong. Cautiousness and conservatism can be in opposition to self-confidence. Confident people are willing to take reasonable risks because they have faith in the quality of their decisions.

Cautiousness and conservatism can lead to indecisiveness, in which the decision maker has a tendency to avoid or delay making a decision. Because a key part of a manager's role is to make decisions, indecisiveness can be a major flaw, and highly frustrating to subordinates who await a decision from the manager.[12] At the other extreme from indecisiveness is impulsiveness, in which the decision maker jumps quickly to a decision without much analysis.

Perfectionism is another personality factor that has a notable impact on decision making. People who seek the perfect solution to a problem are usually indecisive because they are hesitant to accept the fact that a particular alternative is good enough. **Self-efficacy,** the feeling of being an effective and competent person with respect to a task, also has an influence. Researchers note, for example, that having the right amount of "gall" contributes to innovative thinking.[13]

Rigid people have difficulty identifying problems and gathering alternative solutions. People who are mentally flexible perform well in these areas. Optimism versus pessimism is another relevant personality dimension. Optimists are more likely to find solutions than pessimists are. Pessimists are also likely to give up searching because they perceive situations as being hopeless.

Cognitive intelligence has a profound influence on the effectiveness of decision making. In general, intelligent and well-educated people are more likely to identify and diagnose problems and make sound decisions than are those who have less intelligence and education. A notable exception applies, however: Some intelligent, well-educated people have such a fondness for collecting facts and analyzing them that they suffer from analysis paralysis.

Emotional Intelligence

Emotional intelligence is important for decision making because how effectively you manage your feelings and read other people affects the quality of your decisions. For example, if you cannot control your anger, you are likely to make decisions that are motivated by retaliation, hostility, and revenge. You might shout and swear at your team leader because of a work assignment you received.

Your emotional intelligence could also influence career decision making. If you understand your own feelings, you are more likely to enter an occupation or accept a position that matches your true attitudes. A common problem is that many people pursue *hot* and/or well-paying fields even when they are not passionate about the field. As a result they are likely to become discouraged and leave the field—even as early as switching majors. Admitting this lack of passion to oneself might have prevented misdirected time and effort.

Quality and Accessibility of Information

Reaching an effective decision usually requires high-quality, valid information. One of the most important purposes of management information systems is to supply managers and professionals with high-quality information. A vice president of manufacturing might contemplate the establishment of a manufacturing plant in a distant city. She would more likely make an effective decision if the information systems group had accurate information about factors such as the quality of the workforce and environmental regulations.

Accessibility of information may be even more important than quality in determining whether or not information is used. Sometimes it takes so much time and effort to search for quality information that the manager relies on lower-quality information that is close at hand. Think of the decision-making process involved in purchasing a new automobile. Many people are more likely to rely on the opinion of friends than to search through reference sources for more systematic information.

Even when high-quality, accessible information is available, it will not lead to better decision making if the decision maker denies its importance. Sixteen months prior to the explosion of the space shuttle *Columbia* in 2003, the General Accounting Office concluded that the downsizing of NASA's workforce had left it ill equipped to manage its safety upgrade program for the shuttle. Furthermore, a Rand report released in late 2002 said that "Decaying infrastructure and shuttle component obsolescence are significant contributions to a future declining safety posture." Equally significant, NASA later released a batch of e-mails revealing that dozens of NASA workers at the Johnson Space Center were aware that engineers were concerned about a potentially catastrophic reentry for Columbia. A NASA official later said it would have been impossible for him to be aware of all the conversations among NASA's 18,000 employees.[14]

Political Considerations

Under ideal circumstances, organizational decisions are made on the basis of the objective merits of competing alternatives. In reality, many decisions are based on political considerations, such as favoritism, alliances, or the desire of the decision maker to stay in favor with people who wield power. Political factors sometimes influence which data are given serious consideration in evaluating alternatives. The decision maker may select data that support the position of an influential person whom he or she is trying to please. For instance, a financial analyst was asked to investigate the cost-effectiveness of outsourcing the payroll department, so he gave considerable weight to the "facts" supplied by a provider of payroll services. This allowed him to justify having an outside firm assume responsibility for the payroll function. Political factors in decision making, therefore, present an ethical challenge to the decision maker.

Pressure from top management has been cited as a political force that leads managers to make overly optimistic forecasts in analyzing proposals for substantial investments. By means of inflating the probable benefits of a project and minimizing the downside, these managers lead the organization into initiatives that are likely to fall short of expectations.[15] An example would be top management placing heavy pressure on an automotive marketing executive to come up with a dramatic new model that will enhance the company's prestige and profits. Facing this pressure, the marketing executive makes an optimistic proposal for a new vehicle that will compete against the Rolls Royce. The company proceeds to build a $375,000 luxury sedan that becomes a complete flop, partially because the automobile company is perceived by the public as a producer of ordinary—not prestigious—vehicles.

Crisis and Conflict

In a crisis, many decision makers panic. They become less rational and more emotional than they would be in a calm environment. Decision makers who are adversely affected by crisis perceive it to be a stressful event. As a consequence, they concentrate poorly, use poor judgment, and think impulsively. Under crisis, some managers do not bother dealing with differences of opinion because they are under so much pressure. A smaller number of managers perceive a crisis as an exciting challenge that energizes them toward their best level of problem solving and decision making.

Conflict is related to crisis because both can be an emotional experience. One study analyzed strategic decision making by top management teams in both the food-processing and furniture-making industries. The researchers found that the quality of a decision appears to improve with the introduction of conflict. However, the conflict often had the negative side effect of creating antagonistic relationships among some members of the top management team.[16] (More will be said about the positive and negative aspects of conflict in Chapter 13.)

Values of the Decision Maker

Values influence decision making at every step. Ultimately, all decisions are based on values. A manager who places a high value on the personal welfare of employees tries to avoid alternatives that create hardship for workers, and therefore implements decisions in ways that lessen turmoil. Another value that significantly influences decision making is the pursuit of excellence. A manager or professional who embraces the pursuit of excellence (and is therefore conscientious) will search for the high-quality alternative solution.

Attempting to preserve the status quo is a value held by many managers, as well as others. Clinging to the status quo is perceived as a hidden trap in decision making that can prevent people from making optimal decisions. People tend to cling to the status quo because they think they can prevent making a bad decision simply by not taking action at all.[17] If you value the status quo too highly, you may fail to make a decision that could bring about major improvements. At one company, the vice president of human resources received numerous inquiries about when the firm would begin offering benefits for domestic partners (of either the opposite or the same sex). The vice president reasoned that since the vast majority of employees rated the benefit package highly, a change was not needed. A few employees took

Log on to **www.thomsonedu.com/infotrac**. Search for articles pertaining to companies responding to stress and crisis. Firestone had a massive tire recall in 2000; popular fast food chain Wendy's was in the public eye a few years back after a falsified extortion scheme.

their complaints about "biased benefits" to the CEO. The chief executive then chastised the vice president of human resources for not suggesting an initiative that would keep the company in the forefront of human resources management.

Procrastination

Many people are poor decision makers because they **procrastinate,** or delay taking action without a valid reason. Procrastination results in indecisiveness and inaction and is a major cause of self-defeating behavior. People can overcome procrastination by learning how to become more self-disciplined. Part of the process involves setting goals for overcoming procrastination and conquering the problem in small steps. For example, a person might first practice making a deadline for a decision for a minor activity, such as responding to a group of e-mail inquiries.

Overconfidence Bias

The description of personality traits, values, and political factors as influences on decision making hints at the problem of biases when making decisions. These biases lead to predictable mistakes because the decision maker repeats the same error systematically. Among the many such biases investigated by decision theorists is overconfidence.[18] According to this bias, most of us are overconfident in our ability to estimate and we therefore do not acknowledge the true uncertainty. Overconfidence in our decisions can lead to ignoring some of the potential negatives in the situation. A person might take the position as a regional manager of a debt-collection business, knowing that he or she has profit-and-loss responsibility. The manager reasons, "Debt collection is a growth field with so many people getting in over their heads in debt. I can see a lot of profits." The manager neglects the reality that the turnover rate for debt collectors is about 85% per year, a factor that drains profits.

One of the managerial problems associated with overconfidence is that the person is likely to overlook the importance of contingency plans. For example, the executive cited previously in relation to political pressures did not develop a plan to exit the superluxury sedan business.

THE NATURE OF CREATIVITY

Understand the nature of creative decision making in organizations.

Creativity in organizations has surged in importance in recent years for several reasons. First, the high-velocity economy requires that business firms come up with new ideas frequently. Second, a creative business culture attracts, retains, and often motivates knowledge workers. Third, using creative techniques helps generate ideas that the normal mode of brain functioning might miss.[19] **Creativity** can be defined simply as the process of developing good ideas that can be put into action. The term *innovation* emphasizes the commercialization part of creativity, such as developing an innovative product. Until an invention or new idea for a product or service is placed on the market, it is not an innovation. The Crest Spinbrush™, a $6 retail battery-powered toothbrush that helped turn Crest into a billion-dollar brand, is considered to be an innovative product. Innovation also takes place with business models, such as eBay delivering goods and services by relying on Internet users to buy and sell to each other on a massive scale.

We approach the nature of creativity from three perspectives: steps in the creative process, characteristics of creative people, and conditions necessary for creativity. A good starting point in studying creativity is to take a creativity test, as presented in the accompanying self-assessment exercise.

SELF-ASSESSMENT

Rhyme and Reason

A noted creativity expert says that exercises in rhyming release creative energy; they stir imagination into action. While doing the following exercises, remember that rhyme is frequently a matter of sound and does not have to involve similar or identical spelling. This exercise deals with light and frivolous emotions. After each "definition," write two rhyming words to which it refers.

Examples:

1. Obese feline — Fat cat
2. Television — Boob tube
3. A computer command tool for the home — House mouse

Now try these:

1. Vehicle damage
2. Domestic insect
3. Software on CD about gambling
4. Impolite young lady
5. Profit from sale of airplane
6. Beautiful pig
7. Garment for a simian
8. Wooden Australian man
9. Slumber at a discount motel
10. Inventory of time pieces
11. Cutting instrument for a bride
12. Jump by an awful person
13. Extensive experience
14. Criticism lacking in effectiveness
15. Last-place team
16. Coloring for desert
17. Courageous person who is owned as property by another
18. Jumping off a building
19. Strange hair growing on the lower part of a man's face
20. Supporter of a computer criminal
21. A computer whiz with a ridiculous sense of humor
22. You make one up now for the most important question of all.

Answers and Interpretation: The more of these rhymes you were able to come up with, the higher your creative potential. You would also need an advanced vocabulary to score very high. Ten or more correct rhymes would tend to show outstanding creative potential, at least in the verbal area. Here are the answers:

1. Fender bender
2. House louse
3. Risk disk
4. Crass lass
5. Jet net
6. Fine swine
7. Ape cape
8. Oak bloke
9. Cheap sleep
10. Clock stock
11. Wife knife
12. Creep leap
13. Vast past
14. Weak critique
15. Cellar dweller
16. Pie dye
17. Brave slave
18. Tall fall
19. Weird beard
20. Hacker backer
21. Absurd nerd
22. Two bonus points

If you can think of a sensible substitute for any of these answers, give yourself a bonus point. For example, for number 21, how about a freak geek?

Source: The concept of the test traces back to Eugene Raudsepp with George P. Hough, Jr., *Creative Growth Games* (New York: Penguin, 1977). The current test contains just two of the original items.

Steps in the Creative Process

Understanding the steps involved in creativity helps a person become more creative and better manage creativity among others. An old but well-accepted model of creativity can be applied to organizations. The model divides creative thinking into five steps, as shown in Exhibit 5-3. Not all creative thinking follows these steps exactly, but the model works much of the time.

Step 1 is *opportunity or problem recognition:* A person discovers that a new opportunity exists or a problem needs resolution. Step 2 is *immersion:* The individual concentrates on the problem and becomes immersed in it. He or she will recall and collect information that seems relevant, dreaming up alternatives without refining or evaluating them. Step 3 is *incubation:* The person keeps the assembled information in mind for a while. He or she does not appear to be working on the problem actively, yet the subconscious mind takes over. While the information simmers, it is arranged into meaningful patterns. One way to capitalize on the incubation phase of creativity is to deliberately take a break from creative thinking. Instead, engage in a routine activity such as updating your electronic address book or sorting through mail. By immersing yourself in an entirely different and less taxing mental activity, a solution to the creative problem may emerge. Step 4 is *insight:* The problem-conquering solution flashes into the person's mind at an unexpected time, such as on the verge of sleep, during a shower, or while running. Insight is also called the "aha!" experience; all of a sudden, something clicks. Step 5 is *verification and application:* The individual sets out to prove that the creative solution has merit. Verification procedures include gathering supporting evidence, using logical persuasion, and experimenting with new ideas. Application requires tenacity because most novel ideas are at first rejected as being impractical.

Characteristics of Creative People

Creative workers are different in many ways from their less creative counterparts. The characteristics of creative people, including creative leaders, can be grouped into three key areas: knowledge, intellectual abilities, and personality. Yet, as explained by Robert J. Sternberg, so many things are true about some creative people, but there are exceptions. For example, most creative people are high in self-esteem,

Exhibit **5-3**

Steps in the Creative Process

but not all. Yet one consistent attribute of creative people stands out—the decision to be creative. Creative people decide that they will forge their own path and follow it, for better or worse.[20]

Knowledge

Creative problem solving requires a broad background of information, including facts and observations. This is particularly true because creativity often takes the form of combining two or more existing things in a new and different way. Internet search engines become more profitable by combining the exquisite technology of the search engines with the concept behind the Yellow Pages. For example, if you search for a singer, you will receive pop-up ads selling his or her music.

Intellectual Abilities

Creative problem solvers tend to be bright rather than brilliant. Intelligence and creativity tend to be moderately correlated up until an IQ of about 120 (the superior range of intelligence). Beyond that point, the relationship between intelligence and creativity becomes smaller.[21] Applying the triarchic theory of intelligence, the creative type of intelligence would obviously be important for creative problem solving. A good sense of humor and intellectual playfulness are outstanding characteristics of a creative problem solver. Humor helps release creativity, and some creativity is required to be funny.

Creative people maintain a youthful curiosity throughout their lives. The curiosity is not centered just on their field of expertise; they are enthusiastic about solving puzzling problems. Creative people score high on the dimension of Openness. Creativity consultant Juanita Weaver notes that when viewing the world with open and curious eyes, anything can trigger a new idea.[22] A person might be playing with a cat and observe how the cat's claws extend and contract based on the needs of the moment. Voila! The cat-watcher thinks of a new concept for a studded snow tire.

Creative people think divergently. They can expand the number of alternatives to a problem, thus moving away from a single solution. Yet the creative thinker also knows when it is time to think convergently, narrowing the number of useful solutions so innovation can occur.

Creativity can stem from both *fluid intelligence* and *crystallized intelligence*. As described in Chapter 2, fluid intelligence depends on raw processing ability, or how quickly and accurately you learn information and solve problems. Like raw athletic ability, fluid intelligence begins to decline by age 30, partly because our nerve conduction slows. Crystallized intelligence is accumulated knowledge that increases with age and experience. The implication for a manager who wants to assemble a creative group is to staff it with workers of varying ages. Generation X members of the group might have the wildest, most unique ideas. However, the baby boomers might have better intuition as to what will work.

Personality

Creative people tend to have a special type of self-confidence labeled **creative self-efficacy,** the belief that one can be creative in a work role. The major contributors to creative self-efficacy are self-efficacy about the job in general, experience

SKILL-DEVELOPMENT EXERCISE

The Forced Association Technique

The task is for individuals or groups to solve a problem by making associations between the properties of two objects. Working alone or within a group, select a word at random from a textbook or dictionary. If you choose a preposition or adverb instead of a noun, verb, or adjective, try again. Next, list properties and attributes of this word.

Assume that your problem is to improve the job satisfaction of employees. Assume also that the word you chose at random was *jaguar*. Its attributes might include "fast moving," "energetic," "intense," "self-sufficient," and "freedom loving." The forced association is supposed to help solve the problem. Look for a link between the properties of the jaguar and the problem object. To increase job satisfaction, you might give employees more autonomy (freedom loving) and offer them opportunities for job rotation (fast moving).

Collaboration

on the job, and a supervisor who serves as a good model and persuades the worker that he or she is capable of finding imaginative solutions.[23]

Creative people can tolerate the isolation necessary for developing ideas. Talking to others is a good source of ideas, yet at some point the creative problem solver has to work alone and concentrate. Creative people are frequently nonconformists and do not need strong approval from a group. Many creative problem solvers are thrill seekers who find developing imaginative solutions to problems to be a source of excitement. Creative people are also persistent, which is especially important because so many alternatives might have to be explored before finding a workable solution. For example, designers at Motorola Corp. explored dozens of possibilities for a fashionable new cell phone before they conceived of the Razr™ which became a runaway hit. Creative people enjoy dealing with ambiguity and chaos. Less creative people become quickly frustrated when task descriptions are unclear and disorder exists.

The accompanying skill-development exercise gives you a chance to apply your creative personal characteristics to a challenging problem.

Conditions Necessary for Creativity

Certain individual and organizational conditions are necessary for, or at least enhance, the production of creative ideas. The most consistent of these conditions are described here.

Expertise, Creative-Thinking Skills, and Internal Motivation

Teresa M. Amabile has summarized 22 years of research about the conditions necessary for creativity in organizations, and other observers have reported similar findings. Creativity takes place when three components join together: expertise, creative-thinking skills, and the right type of motivation.[24]

Expertise refers to the necessary knowledge to put facts together. The more facts floating around in your head, the more likely you are to combine them in some useful way. *Creative thinking* refers to how flexibly and imaginatively individuals approach problems. If you know how to keep digging for alternatives and avoid getting stuck in the status quo, your chances of being creative multiply. Persevering, or sticking with a problem to a conclusion, is essential for finding creative solutions. A few rest breaks to gain a fresh perspective may be helpful, but the creative person keeps coming back until a solution emerges. Quite often an executive will keep sketching different organization charts on paper or with a graphics program before the one that will help the firm run smoothly surfaces.

The right type of motivation is the third essential ingredient for creative thought. A fascination with or passion for a task is more important than searching for external rewards. People will be the most creative when they are motivated primarily by the satisfaction and challenge of the work itself. Although Jeff Bezos ultimately became wealthy from building Amazon.com, he was primarily motivated by the challenge of finding a way to capitalize on the potential of the Internet as a marketing vehicle.

Passion for the task and high intrinsic motivation contribute to a total absorption in the work and intense concentration, which is known as the **experience of flow.** When an experience is engrossing and enjoyable, the task becomes worth doing for its own sake regardless of the external consequences.[25] Perhaps you have had this experience when completely absorbed in a hobby or being at your best in a sport or dance. (*Flow* also means being "in the zone.") A highly creative businessperson, such as an entrepreneur developing a plan for worldwide distribution of a product, will often achieve the experience of flow.

Environmental Needs

Three factors outside the person play a key role in fostering creativity. An environmental need must stimulate the setting of a goal. This is another way of saying, "Necessity is the mother of invention." So often the light bulb is mentioned as an example of creativity, and there is a modern version to this tale. Light bulb manufacturers have observed that many aging people want to appear younger. In response to this need, the manufacturers have introduced dozens of new bulbs including a flattering array of fluorescent, halogen, and new incandescent bulbs that are an improvement over soft light. These "natural light" bulbs make wrinkles and blemishes appear less evident. By responding to this new environmental need, light bulb sales have increased about 6%.[26]

Conflict and Tension

Another condition that fosters creativity is the right amount of conflict and tension to put people on edge. Jerry Hirschberg, founder and president of Nissan Design International, says that people should be asked to hold what appears to be conflicting ideas in the mind simultaneously while encouraging their opposition to do the same. Understanding opposing ideas helps you gain a new perspective. An example Hirschberg offers is that Nissan asked his design team to produce a "world" car. Many staff members were threatened by the idea of a world car because it implied an ordinary vehicle of mass taste. A brave design manager, however, introduced a conflicting opinion. He said, "Whether we like it or not, there are some very successful world cars out there."

After someone in the group said that producing such a car would not mean designing one to appease some low common denominator, the group no longer felt threatened. The group became eager to accept the assignment. By moving past its fears, the group conquered those fears and "embraced the dragon."[27]

Encouragement from Others and Having Creative Coworkers

Another external factor in creativity is encouragement, including a permissive atmosphere that welcomes new ideas. A manager who encourages imaginative and original thinking, and does not punish people for making honest mistakes, is likely to receive creative ideas from employees. A study suggests that encouragement from family and friends, as well as from a supervisor, enhances creative thinking on the job. The participants in the study were both administrative and production employees in the Bulgarian knitwear industry. Support for creativity was measured by statements such as, "My family and friends outside this organization give me useful feedback about my ideas concerning the workplace." Supervisors rated employee creativity. The researchers concluded that: (a) supervisors and coworkers, and (b) family and friends each made their own contribution to worker creativity.[28]

The combination of receiving encouragement in the form of developmental feedback, along with the presence of creative coworkers, is another set of conditions that enhances creativity. (Developmental feedback focuses on giving constructive advice for personal improvement.) Jing Zhou conducted two studies with professional units within a university. Supervisory ratings of employee creativity were obtained, along with measures of how closely the employees believed they were monitored and their perception of coworkers' creative behavior. Key findings of the study were that the more creative coworkers were present, and the less supervisors engaged in close monitoring, the more creativity the workers exhibited. It was also found that workers without strong creative personalities were more likely to exhibit creativity when they perceived their coworkers to be creative and the supervisors provided developmental feedback. An important implication of the study is that the combination of creative coworkers and developmental feedback enhances creative output.[29]

Mood

You may have noticed that you think more creatively when you are in a good mood. A positive mood apparently also contributes to creative job performance, even if mood might not be truly classified as a condition necessary for creativity. A study of 222 employees in seven companies in three high-tech industries indicated that a positive mood made a positive, significant contribution to creativity. However, only weak evidence was found that producing a creative idea enhanced one's mood. Measurements of creativity were taken through both self-ratings and coworker ratings.[30]

Moderate Time Pressures

Some people are at their creative best when facing heavy time pressures. Several studies, however, suggest that feeling crunched leads to a creativity drop for most people. The greater the time pressure, the less likely workers are to solve a tricky problem, envision a new product, or have the type of "aha!" experiences that lead to innovation. Time pressure is a creativity dampener because it limits people's freedom to reflect on different options and directions. When workers believe they are faced with an urgent mission, the negative effects of time pressures are reduced.[31]

The accompanying Organizational Behavior in Action box illustrates several points about the creative person and the conditions necessary for creativity.

ORGANIZATIONAL BEHAVIOR *In Action*

King Gillette Decides to Throw Away the Blades

When a former bottle-cap salesman from Boston named King Camp Gillette started selling safety razors with disposable blades in 1903, people were not disposed to throw things away. The very idea of discarding something without reusing or repairing it ran counter to American notions of thrift. But Gillette, a part-time inventor whose earlier patents included an improved beer tap, had taken the advice of his boss at Crown, Cork & Seal, William Painter, inventor of the bottle cap. "Think of something which, once used, is thrown away," Painter told him, "and the customer keeps coming back for more."

Gillette was staring at his dull razor one morning when that thing came to him. Like other razors of the day, his blade required time-consuming "stropping" and professional resharpening to remain useful. Gillette spent the next 8 years figuring out how to cast a blade thin enough—and therefore cheap enough—to throw away when it got dull. In 1901, he patented the first razor with a disposable blade. Persuading men to buy it was easier than convincing them to dispose of it. Some barbers offered illicit resharpening services.

Contrary to myth, Gillette never did "give away the razor and sell the blade." The kit cost a hefty $5. But the U.S. Army gave 3.5 million Gillette razors and 32 million blades to soldiers during World War I, hooking a generation—and planting the beginnings of the throwaway culture.

Questions

1. Which characteristics of a creative person did Gillette display?
2. In what way is this story about decision making?
3. Over one hundred years later, how is Gillette's invention doing?

Source: Excerpted from "20 That Made History," *Fortune*, June 27, 2005, pp. 60–61. © 2005 Time Inc. All rights reserved.

ENHANCING AND IMPROVING CREATIVITY

Enhance your creative problem-solving ability.

A unifying theme runs through all forms of creativity training and suggestions for creativity improvement: Creative problem solving requires an ability to overcome traditional thinking. The concept of traditional thinking is relative and hard to pin down, but generally refers to a standard and frequent way of finding a solution to a problem. A traditional solution to a problem is thus a modal or recurring solution. For example, traditional thinking suggests that to increase revenue, a retail store should conduct a sale. Creative thinking would point toward other solutions, such as Starbucks' approach to increasing revenues described in the chapter opener.

The central task in becoming creative is to break down rigid thinking that blocks new ideas. A conventional-thinking manager might accept the long-standing policy that spending more than $5000 requires three levels of approval. A creative leader might ask, "Why do we need three levels of approval for spending $5000? If we trust people enough to make them managers, why can't they have budget authorization to spend up to $10,000?"

Overcoming traditional thinking is often characterized as *thinking outside the box*. A "box" in this sense is a category that confines and restricts thinking. During the aftermath of Hurricane Katrina that hit the Gulf Coast in 2005, rescue specialists thought outside the box of where to lodge rescue workers and construction workers. Cruise ships were hired, giving the workers temporary living quarters offshore. Here we describe several illustrative approaches and techniques for enhancing employee creativity. Recognize also that the conditions for creativity just described can be converted into techniques for creativity enhancement. For example, a manager might be able to enhance creativity by encouraging imaginative thinking. Exhibit 5-3 presents specific examples of what some of the most innovative companies in the world do to produce creativity and innovation.

1. *Brainstorming.* Brainstorming, which most of you have already done, is the best-known technique for developing mental flexibility. As a refresher, do the accompanying skill-development exercise (see page 108), which presents rules and guidelines for brainstorming and gives a challenging Internet business development task. Brainstorming is also accomplished online—participants from different locations enter their suggestions into a computer. Each participant's input appears simultaneously on the screen of the other participants. In this way, nobody feels intimidated by a dominant member, and participants think more independently. The forced-association technique presented in the skill-development exercise is a variant of brainstorming. To increase the efficiency of brainstorming, participants are sometimes told in advance of the problem or problems to be solved. Prethinking can result in some more refined ideas being brought to the brainstorming session.

2. *Idea quotas.* A straightforward and effective technique for enhancing worker creativity is to simply demand that workers come up with good ideas. Being creative therefore becomes a concrete work goal. Thomas Edison used idea quotas, with his personal quota being one minor invention every 10 days and a major invention every 6 months. Google company policy is that company engineers devote a quarter of their time to thinking up great new ideas, even with an uncertain financial payoff. Note that this Google policy refers to a *time* quota for ideas, yet the time allotted to ideas is likely to result in generating ideas. Another aspect of forcing the generation of ideas at Google is an intranet (internal website) that regularly collects fresh ideas from employees, even those without Internet savvy. Every employee spends a fraction of the workday on research and development. One of the tangible outcomes of the intranet technique is a news-search feature.[32]

3. *Heterogeneous groups.* Forming heterogeneous groups can enhance creativity because a diverse group brings various viewpoints to the problem at hand. Key diversity factors include professional discipline, job experiences, and a variety of demographic factors. Diverse groups encourage diverse thinking, which is the essence of creativity.[33] A culturally diverse group can be effective at developing creative marketing ideas to appeal to a particular cultural group. Levi-Strauss has on occasion included an adolescent in a problem-solving group to help understand what type of jeans appeal to members of that age group.

4. *Financial incentives.* A variety of laboratory studies have concluded that working for external rewards, particularly financial rewards, dampens creativity.[34] If you focus on the reward, you may lose out on the joy (internal rewards) of being creative. In work settings, however, financial incentives are likely to spur imaginative thinking. Such incentives might include paying employees for useful suggestions and paying scientists royalties for patents that become commercially useful. For example, IBM is consistently one of the leading companies with respect to being awarded patents. IBM employees who are awarded patents are paid cash bonuses.

5. *Architecture and physical layout.* Many companies restructure space to fire up creativity, harness energy, and enhance the flow of knowledge and ideas. Any

Exhibit **5-3**

Top 20 Innovative Companies in the World

The results of a poll of 940 senior executives in 68 countries by Boston Consulting Group, shown below, are particularly useful because they include an explanation of *why* the companies selected are perceived to be innovative.

Company	Responses (Percent of 940)	Why
Apple	24.84	Delivers **great consumer experiences with outstanding design;** steady flow of new ideas that redefine old categories, such as music players; continual evolution of business model and brand.
3M	11.77	Strong **internal culture of creativity with formal incentives** to innovate. Results in a high success rate in turning idea in health care, industrial components, and other areas into profitable products.
Microsoft	8.53	Strong **management pushes continuous improvement of products,** expansion into new markets and rapid strategy changes when necessary.
GE	8.53	Management **practices that are ahead of competition,** along with strong training, are allowing CEO to reinvent GE's business model and culture to promote innovation.
Sony	5.94	Understands **the importance of media convergence;** creates user-friendly electronic products with great design.
Dell	5.62	Superior business-process model **built on ruthless cost-cutting and innovations** in supply-chain management.
IBM	5.29	Wants to **use its powerful IT base to solve customers' problems** and even run their businesses.
Google	5.18	Steady stream of **new tools and services provide simple solutions** to complex problems. Dominates online search market and is growing fast in advertising; strong connection with customers.
P&G	4.21	Continuous **product innovation based on understanding of changing consumer lifestyles.** In a switch, now seeks outside partners for new expertise, ideas, and even products.
Nokia	4.21	Sharp **design, changes models rapidly and features** effortlessly, based on a close reading of customer desires in the emerging mobile lifestyle.
Virgin	4.00	Reframed **air travel as a lifestyle brand** and extended the brand into retail stores, cell-phone service, and other products; takes risks; attacks weak spots of traditional service providers.
Samsung	3.89	Catches **the pulse of the consumer;** good design; understands emotion; moved from commodity producer to brand leader; generates a flow of new products from cell phones to stunning flat-screen TVs.
Wal-Mart	3.24	Uses **supply-chain and logistics superiority** to move into new markets and product areas. Data mining tracks customer preferences on a daily basis, contributing to fast growth despite its size.
Toyota	3.02	Quality and manufacturing efficiency are constantly upgraded. Strategic use of **advanced technology yields big market advantages** in areas such as hybrid cars.
eBay	2.92	Forged a new retain business model based on **customer power, cheap prices, and community.**
Intel	2.70	Dynamic business model with the **ability to disrupt itself** to meet competition in areas such as wireless computing.
Amazon	2.70	Overturned retail distribution with **Internet technology and a focus on the consumer experience.**
Ideo	2.16	Top **consultant on the process of innovation;** uses design principles to guide companies through strategy changes that focus on consumer experience.
Starbucks	2.05	Reframed the **coffee business as a lifestyle brand** by watching customers; created a strong consumer affinity to the brand and uses that affinity to sell new products such as music.
BMW	1.73	Combines **sleek design, advanced technology, and Web-based marketing** to increase brand leadership and move into extensions, such as the revived MINI Cooper.

Questions
1. Is there any company not on this list that you would have voted to be included?
2. Is there any company on this list that you would not have voted to be included?

Source: Boston Consulting Group as presented in Bruce Nussbaum, "How to Build Innovative Companies," *Business Week*, August 1, 2005, p. 64.

SKILL-DEVELOPMENT EXERCISE

Brainstorming

Group Activity: Your group assumes the role of a team of GM workers who are told to formulate some sensible suggestions for cutting costs in the divisions of the company that produce vehicles. Top management informs you that it costs GM about $2000 more to produce a vehicle than it does its Asian competitors. You are also told, "Use your creative thinking to the best of your abilities. The survival of GM as a vehicle producer is at stake." Present your findings in a bulleted list to the rest of the class.

1. Use groups of five to seven people.
2. Encourage the spontaneous expression of ideas. All suggestions are welcome, even if they seem outlandish or outrageous at first glance. Avoid evaluating suggestions at this point, particularly with respect to making negative statements about suggestions.
3. Quantity and variety are important. The greater the number of ideas, the greater is the likelihood of a breakthrough idea.
4. Encourage combination and improvement of ideas. This process is referred to as "piggybacking" or "hitchhiking."
5. Use a room with natural light if possible. Sunlight, and the cheerfulness of a real window, facilitates creativity for many people.
6. One person serves as the secretary and records ideas, writing them on a sheet of paper, white board, chalkboard, flip chart, or computer.
7. Do not overstructure the session by following any of the rules too rigidly. Brainstorming is a spontaneous process.

Collaboration

configuration of the physical environment that decreases barriers to divergence, incubation, and convergence is likely to stimulate the flow of creative thinking.[35] The reasoning is that creative thinking is more likely to be enhanced by cubicles rather than corner offices, by elevators rather than escalators, and by atriums rather than hallways. In short, creating the opportunity for physical interaction facilitates the flow of ideas, which in turn facilitates creative thinking.

The establishment of *innovation laboratories* is another approach to making use of physical layout to enhance creativity. Members of the innovation team work in a remote location, such as a converted barn or a loft, rather than solely on traditional company premises. Innovation labs make use of structures that encourage open communication and teamwork, along with home-style furnishings such as comfortable couches and adjustable lighting. The concept is an old one that has come into renewed interest. For example, much of the critical work on the Razr cell phone was done at a downtown Chicago lab called Moto City, rather than at the Motorola's regular research and development facility. Decorated in trendy orange and gray, Moto City occupies the 26th floor of a high-rise once occupied by a dot-com.[36]

6. *Inspiration.* A leadership strategy for enhancing creativity and innovation is to inspire workers to think creatively. Inspiring creativity encompasses a wide range of behaviors, including establishing a permissive atmosphere. David Vasella, the chairman and CEO of a pharmaceutical company, offers an illustrative approach to inspiring innovation in product development and operations. Leadership at the company attempts to align business objectives with the company's ideals. Vasella says that people "do a better job when they believe in what they do and in how the company behaves, when they see that their work does more than enrich shareholders."[37] Similarly, when workers believe they are working for a cause, such as helping people plan their financial futures, or curing a disease, they are more likely to be creative.

7. *Creativity training.* A standard approach to enhancing individual and organizational creativity is to offer creativity training to many workers throughout the organization. About 30% of medium-size and large firms provide some sort of creativity training. Much of creativity training encompasses the ideas already covered in this chapter, such as learning to overcome traditional thinking and engaging in some type of brainstorming. Various techniques are used to encourage more flexible thinking, such as engaging in child's play, squirting each other with water guns, and having scavenger hunts. An extreme technique is to deprive participants of food and rest for 24 hours so their defenses are weakened, and they are then mentally equipped to "think differently." Other creativity training techniques are more cerebral, such as having participants solve puzzles and ask "what if" questions.

IMPLICATIONS FOR MANAGERIAL PRACTICE

1. A widely recommended decision tool for finding the root cause of a problem is to ask a series of questions, called the "Seven Whys" (or sometimes "Five Whys"). By asking "why?" seven times, you are likely to get to the core issue of a problem. As a CEO you observe that turnover is way above average in one division. The questioning might proceed in this manner:

   Question 1: "Why is turnover high?"
   Answer 1: "Because we have loads of people who decide to leave the firm."

   Question 2: "Why are they leaving?"
   Answer 2: "I guess they are not too happy."

   Question 3: "Why aren't they happy?"
   Answer 3: "They may not like the working conditions here too much."

   Question 4: "Why don't they like the working conditions?"
   Answer 4: "It's kind of a high-pressure atmosphere."

   Question 5: "Why is it a high-pressure atmosphere?"
   Answer 5: "The supervisors stay on people's backs."

   Question 6: "Why do the supervisors stay on people's backs?"
   Answer 6: "Most of them think that the best way to get results is to keep the pressure on employees."

   Question 7: "Why don't supervisors know more about supervising workers?"
   Answer 7: "A lot of them need more training in managing people, or they shouldn't have been chosen for supervisory positions in the first place."

2. Learning to be more creative is like learning other skills: Patience and time are required. As a manager, by practicing techniques and attitudes, you will gain the confidence and skill to build a group (or company) where creative thinking is widespread. A desirable goal is to find a way to tap the creativity of everyone for whom you are responsible.[38]

SUMMARY OF KEY POINTS

 Work through the classical/behavioral decision-making model when faced with a major decision. A decision takes place when a person chooses from among two or more alternatives in order to solve a problem. Programmed decisions are made in response to uncomplicated problems, while nonpro-grammed decisions are unique responses to complex problems. The degree of risk associated with a decision can be classified into three categories: certainty, risk, and uncertainty.

A classical/behavioral decision-making model in-corporates the ideas that managers make decisions in a generally rational framework, yet Intuition and judgment also enter the model. The seven steps in the model are as follows: (1) identify and diagnose the problem, (2) establish decision criteria, (3) develop creative alternatives, (4) evaluate the alternatives, (5) choose one alternative, (6) implement the decision, and (7) evaluate and control.

 Identify and describe factors that influence the effectiveness of decision making.

Bounded rationality means that people's limited mental abilities, combined with external influences over which they have little or no control, prevent them from making entirely rational decisions. Satisficing decisions result from bounded rationality. A host of influences contribute to bounded rationality, including intuition, personality and cognitive intelligence, emotional intelligence, quality and accessibility of information, political considerations, crisis and conflict, the values of the decision maker, procrastination, and the overconfidence bias.

 Understand the nature of creative decision making in organizations.

Understanding the steps involved in creativity can help a person become more creative and better manage creativity among others. The steps are as follows: (1) opportunity or problem recognition, (2) immersion, (3) incubation, (4) insight, and (5) verification and application.

Creative workers are different from others in several key areas. They typically have a broad background of knowledge, tend to be bright rather than brilliant, have a youthful curiosity, and think divergently. Both fluid intelligence and crystallized intelligence contribute to creativity. Creative workers tend to have a positive self-image, including creative self-efficacy, and are often nonconformists who enjoy intellectual thrills, along with ambiguity and chaos.

For creativity to occur, three components must join together: expertise, creative-thinking skills, and internal motivation characterized by a passion for the task. Total absorption in the work, also known as the experience of flow, is also important. An environmental need should be present, along with some conflict and tension, and encouragement from others and the presence of creative coworkers. A positive mood also contributes to creativity, as do moderate time pressures.

 Enhance your creative problem-solving ability.

A unifying theme runs through all forms of creativity training and suggestions for creativity improvement: Creative problem solving requires an ability to overcome traditional thinking. Techniques for enhancing creativity include brainstorming, imposing idea quotas, forming heterogeneous groups, offering financial incentives for creative problem solving in work settings, using a physical layout conducive to creative thinking, inspiring creative thinking, and creativity training.

KEY TERMS AND PHRASES

Decision, 89

The act of choosing among two or more alternatives in order to solve a problem.

Problem, 89

A discrepancy between the ideal and the real.

Programmed (or Routine) Decision, 89

A standard response to an uncomplicated problem.

Nonprogrammed (or Nonroutine) Decision, 89

A unique response to a complex problem.

Classical Decision Model, 90

An approach to decision making that views the manager's environment as certain and stable and the manager as rational.

Behavioral Decision Model, 90

An approach to decision making that views managers as having cognitive limitations and acting only in terms of what they perceive in a given situation.

Decision Criteria, 92

The standards of judgment used to evaluate alternatives.

Bounded Rationality, 93

The idea that people's limited mental abilities, combined with external influences over which they have little or no control, prevent them from making entirely rational decisions.

Satisficing Decision, 93

A decision that provides a minimum standard of satisfaction.

Heuristics, 94

Simplified strategies that become rules of thumb in decision making.

Intuition, 94

An experience-based way of knowing or reasoning in which weighing and balancing evidence are done automatically.

Self-Efficacy, 95

The feeling of being an effective and competent person with respect to a task.

Procrastinate, 98

To delay taking action, without a valid reason.

Creativity, 98
The process of developing good ideas that can be put into action.

Creative Self-Efficacy, 101
The belief that one can be creative in a work role.

Experience of Flow, 103
Being "in the zone"; total absorption in one's work.

DISCUSSION QUESTIONS AND ACTIVITIES

1. What was the problem that introducing wireless Internet and CD burning into Starbucks was intended to solve?
2. Can you give an example of a failed decision in business? Explain why you consider the decision to be a failure?
3. Which decision criteria are relevant for you in choosing a career?
4. How would the concept of bounded rationality apply to making decisions about financial investments?
5. A technique for creative problem solving is to remind oneself of a problem just before going to sleep. Upon waking up, a good solution often presents itself. How does this technique relate to the stages of creative thought?
6. Work together in a small group to reach a conclusion about several new products or services the world really needs. Explain why you need creative thinking to answer this.
7. Ask an experienced worker what he or she believes is the most important action a manager can take to enhance creative thinking among group members. Compare the response you get with the information in this chapter.

CASE PROBLEM: Staples' Annual Creativity Contest

Henry Ford. Thomas Alva Edison. Adrian Chernoff? Maybe Chernoff isn't a household name like the first two inventors, but the 33-year-old Royal Oak, Michigan, man certainly shows potential. Chernoff's claim to fame—a handy little office product called Rubber Bandits—started gracing the shelves of every Staples store in North America a few years ago. The labeling bands, which retail at $2.99, are also available online.

The General Motors Corp. employee was one of last year's finalists in Staples' Invention Quest. Now in its second year, the content is aimed at budding inventors looking to create the next Post-It note or better. About 10,000 entries were received in 2005. Besides giving inventors the gratification of seeing their ideas hit the shelves in 1600 office superstores, Staples promises to share the profits.

The contest has a grand prize of $25,000. Last year's winner was a California man who created WordLock, a combination lock that allows users to select their combinations using letters rather than the traditional set of numbers. Staples created the contest to develop private-label products that can compete against national brands or give Staples something unique.

Chernoff walked away with $5000, a licensing agreement with the office supply store, and the official title of

inventor. "The best part for me right now is seeing it actually make its way in the marketplace," Chernoff said. "The product is going into practice in the real world."

Maybe an extra-large rubber band with a wear- and tear-resistant label won't solve the world's problems. But Rubber Bandits do make it easier to bundle and label piles of paperwork. And they definitely make a nice workplace projectile, although Chernoff says that was not their original purpose.

Chernoff centered his career on creativity. Besides having a bachelor's degree and two master's degrees from the University of New Mexico in business and engineering, his résumé includes jobs working on robots for the National Aeronautics and Space Administration and designing new rides for The Walt Disney Co.

Rubber Bandits popped into his mind on a shuttle bus ride between Denver and Boulder, Colorado, where he was visiting a brother. He started pondering office efficiency and the problems people have of losing things in the shuffle.

Case Questions

1. Why should Rubber Bandits be classified as a creative idea?

(continued)

CASE PROBLEM (Continued)

2. What does this story illustrate about the stages of creative thought?

3. In what way might having studied both business and engineering helped Adrian Chernoff become an inventor?

4. Advise Staples' executives whether or not you think the Annual Creativity Contest is a good investment of time and money for the company.

Source: Karen Dyris, "Staples Hunting for Next Wave of Ideas, Inventors," Detroit News, May 10, 2005.

ENDNOTES

1. Richard Florida and Jim Goodnight, "Managing for Creativity," *Harvard Business Review*, July–August 2005, p. 125.
2. Paul C. Nutt, *Why Decisions Fail* (San Francisco: Berrett-Koehler, 2002).
3. James L. Bowditch and Anthony F. Buono, *A Primer on Organizational Behavior,* 5th ed. (New York: Wiley, 2001), p. 50.
4. "Starbucks' Schultz Played a Hunch," *Executive Leadership*, July 2004, p. 8.
5. Quoted in "How to Succeed in 2005," *Business 2.0*, December 2004, p. 118.
6. Paul C. Nutt, "Expanding the Search for Alternatives During Strategic Decision-Making," *Academy of Management Executive*, November 2004, p. 15.
7. Herbert A. Simon, "Rational Choice and the Structure of the Environment," *Psychological Review* 63, 1956, pp. 129–138.
8. Gerd Gigerenzer and Reinhard Selten (eds.), *Bounded Rationality: The Adaptive Toolbox* (Cambridge, MA: MIT Press, 2001).
9. Eugene Sadler-Smith and Erella Shefy, "The Intuitive Executive: Understanding and Applying 'Gut Feel' in Decision-Making," *The Academy of Management Executive*, November 2004, pp. 76–91.
10. Russell Wild, "Naked Hunch," *Success,* June 1998, p. 55.
11. C. Chet Miller and R. Duane Ireland, "Intuition in Strategic Decision Making: Friend or Foe in the Fast-Paced 21st Century?" *The Academy of Management Executive*, February 2005, pp. 19–30.
12. Jared Sandberg, "Deciders Suffer Alone; Nondeciders Make Everyone Else Suffer," *The Wall Street Journal*, November 8, 2005, p. B1.
13. Michael A. West and James L. Farr (eds.), *Innovation and Creativity at Work: Psychological and Organizational Strategies* (New York: Wiley, 1990).
14. The quote is from "Inquiry Puts Early Focus on Heat Tiles," *New York Times,* February 2, 2003; Larry Wheeler, "NASA Chief Calls on Columbia," *The New York Times,* February 28, 2003.
15. Dan Lovallo and Daniel Kahneman, "Delusions of Success: How Optimism Undermines Executives' Decisions," *Harvard Business Review*, July 2003, p. 56.
16. Allen C. Amason, "Distinguishing the Effects of Functional and Dysfunctional Conflict on Strategic Decision-Making Effectiveness," *Academy of Management Journal*, February 1996, pp. 123–148.
17. John S. Hammond, Ralph L. Keeney, and Howard Rafia, "The Hidden Traps in Decision Making," *Harvard Business Review,* September–October 1998, p. 50.
18. Max H. Bazerman, *Judgment in Managerial Decision Making,* 5th ed. (New York: Wiley, 2002), pp. 31–33.
19. Juanita Weaver, "The Missing Think," *Entrepreneur,* January 2003, p. 68.
20. Robert J. Sternberg, "Creativity as a Decision," *American Psychologist,* May 2002, p. 376.
21. Dorothy Leonard and Walter Swap, *When Sparks Fly: Igniting Creativity in Small Groups* (Boston: Harvard Business School Press, 1999).
22. Juanita Weaver, "The Mental Picture: Bringing Your Definition of Creativity Into Focus," *Entrepreneur*, February 2003, p. 69.
23. Pamela Tierney and Steven M. Farmer, "Creative Self-Efficacy: Its Potential Antecedents and Relationship to Creative Performance," *Academy of Management Journal,* December 2002, pp. 1137–1148.
24. Teresa M. Amabile, "How to Kill Creativity," *Harvard Business Review,* September–October 1998, pp. 78–79.
25. Mihaly Csikzentmihalyi, "If We Are So Rich, Why Aren't We Happy?" *American Psychologist,* October 1999, p. 824.
26. Sally Beatty, "The 2,500 Watt Makeover," *The Wall Street Journal,* August 5, 2005, p. W1.
27. "Creativity First," *Leadership* (American Management Association International), May 1998, pp. 5–6.
28. Nora Madjar, Greg R. Oldham, and Michael G. Pratt, "There's No Place Like Home? The Contributions of Work and Nonwork to Creativity Support to Employee's Creative Performance," *Academy of Management Journal,* August 2002, pp. 757–767.
29. Jing Zhou, "When the Presence of Creative Coworkers Is Related to Creativity: The Role of Supervisor Close Monitoring, Developmental Feedback, and Creative Personality," *Journal of Applied Psychology*, June 2003, pp. 413–422.
30. Teresa M. Amabile, Sigal G. Barsade, Jennifer S. Mueller, and Barry M. Staw, "Affect and Creativity at Work: A Daily Longitudinal Test," *Harvard Business School Working Papers*, 2002–2003.
31. Research cited in Bridget Murray, "A Ticking Clock Means a Creativity Drop," *Monitor on Psychology,* November 2002, p. 24; Teresa M. Amabile, Constance N. Hadley, and Steven J. Kramer, "Creativity Under the Gun," *Harvard Business Review*, August 2002, pp. 52–61.
32. "Google Aims for Perfection Before IPO," Knight Ridder syndicated story, May 27, 2003.
33. Leigh Thompson, "Improving the Creativity of Organizational Work Groups," *Academy of Management Executive*, February 2003, p. 102; G. Pascal Zachary, "Mighty Is the Mongrel," *Fast Company,* July 2000, p. 272.
34. Beth A. Hennessey and Teresa M. Amabile, "Reward, Intrinsic Motivation, and Creativity," *American Psychologist,* June 1998, pp. 674–675.
35. Dorothy Leonard and Walter Swap, "Igniting Creativity," *Workforce,* October 1999, pp. 87–89.
36. Joseph Weber, "'Mosh Pits' of Creativity: Innovation labs are Sparking Teamwork—and Breakthrough Products." *Business Week,* November 7, 2005, pp. 98–100.
37. Quoted in "Inspiring Innovation," *Harvard Business Review,* August 2002, p. 48.
38. Juanita Weaver, "Food for Thought," *Entrepreneur,* March 2003, pp. 62, 63.

Foundation Concepts of Motivation

Jessica Varga received no year-end bonus check one year. Not a share of stock or even a gift check from her employer, DVC Worldwide, a marketing firm in Morristown, New Jersey. Yet Varga, an assistant account executive who has never received a bonus, does not seem to mind: she was given her very first office—in fact, a coveted corner one.

She won the use of an office for one year as a prize at DVC's year-end party, held at a hotel in nearby Madison. Varga, 23, participated in a drawing to reward the company's less senior staff. Each employee received 10 raffle tickets to place in various boxes for prizes like dinner certificates, a dedicated spot in the front row of the company's parking lot, and the corner office.

Varga put all her tickets in the "corner office" box, and after her name was pulled out as the winner, the crowd cheered loudly. "I figured it would take me 10 years to get an office," said Varga, who has been with DVC for only 18 months. "It was the last thing I expected to be rewarded with."

Source: Melinda Ligos, "Those Year-End Bonuses Aren't Always Green," *The New York Times*, December 28, 2003.

6

Now Ask Yourself: **What does this woman's excitement about winning the opportunity to occupy a corner office for a year tell us about motivation?** Her excitement illustrates that people are motivated and satisfied by a variety of needs, including status. Money is not the only motivator. Need satisfaction in the workplace is one of the foundation explanations of motivation presented in this chapter. In the following chapter, we describe managerial techniques designed to enhance motivation, all based on motivation theory. This chapter also touches on practical approaches to motivation, but it starts with the basics of motivation. Knowledge and skill in motivating people is a topic of perennial interest to managers and professionals and is an important contributor to their eventual success.

Motivation (in a work setting) is the process by which behavior is mobilized and sustained in the interest of achieving organizational goals. We know a person is motivated when he or she actually expends effort toward goal attainment. Motivation is complex and encompasses a broad range of behaviors, many of which are described in this and the following chapter. To assess the effectiveness of your present knowledge of motivating others, take the accompanying self-assessment quiz.

NEED THEORIES OF MOTIVATION

Describe several need theories of motivation, including the needs hierarchy, the two-factor theory, and the achievement–power–affiliation triad.

The simplest explanation of motivation is one of the most powerful: People are willing to expend effort toward achieving a goal because it satisfies one of their important needs. Self-interest is thus a driving force. This principle is referred to as "What's in it for me?" or WIIFM (pronounced "wiff'em"). Reflect on your own experience. Before working hard to accomplish a task, you probably want to know how you will benefit. If your manager asks you to work extra hours to take care of an emergency, you will most likely oblige. Yet underneath you might be thinking, "If I work these extra hours, my boss will think highly of me. As a result, I will probably receive a good performance evaluation and maybe a better-than-average salary increase."

To apply the WIIFM principle you need to analyze the situation from the other person's point of view. A store manager might think that employees should be willing to restock merchandise after hours without compensation because they should be grateful to have a job. Yet from the employees' standpoint, they do not perceive that much is in it for them. From their point of view the desire to be paid for overtime is stronger than the feeling of gratitude for having a job. (Paying for overtime is a legal requirement that is widely ignored.)

Here we describe three classic need theories of motivation: the need hierarchy, the two-factor theory, and the achievement–power–affiliation triad.

Maslow's Hierarchy of Needs

Based on his work as a clinical psychologist, Abraham M. Maslow developed a comprehensive view of individual motivation.[1] **Maslow's hierarchy of needs** arranges human needs into a pyramid-shaped model with basic physiological needs at the bottom and self-actualization needs at the top (see Exhibit 6-1). Lower-order needs must be satisfied to ensure a person's existence, security, and requirements for human contact. Higher-order needs are concerned with personal development and reaching one's potential. Before higher-level needs are activated, the lower-order needs must be satisfied. The five levels of needs are described next.

SELF-ASSESSMENT

Motivating Others

Describe how often you act or think in the way indicated by the statements below when you are attempting to motivate another person. Use the following scale: very infrequently (VI); infrequently (I); sometimes (S); frequently (F); very frequently (VF).

	VI	I	S	F	VF
1. I ask the other person what he or she is hoping to achieve in the situation.	1	2	3	4	5
2. I attempt to figure out if the person has the ability to do what I need done.	1	2	3	4	5
3. When another person is heel-dragging, it usually means he or she is lazy.	5	4	3	2	1
4. I tell the person I'm trying to motivate exactly what I want.	1	2	3	4	5
5. I like to give the other person a reward up front so he or she will be motivated.	5	4	3	2	1
6. I give lots of feedback when another person is performing a task for me.	1	2	3	4	5
7. I like to belittle the person enough so that he or she will be intimidated into doing what I need done.	5	4	3	2	1
8. I make sure that the other person feels that he or she is being treated fairly.	1	2	3	4	5
9. I figure that if I smile nicely enough I can get the other person to work as hard as I need.	5	4	3	2	1
10. I attempt to get done what I need by instilling fear in the other person.	5	4	3	2	1
11. I specify exactly what needs to be accomplished.	1	2	3	4	5
12. I generously praise people who help me get my work accomplished.	1	2	3	4	5
13. A job well done is its own reward. I therefore keep praise to a minimum.	5	4	3	2	1
14. I make sure to let people know how well they have done in meeting my expectations on a task.	1	2	3	4	5
15. To be fair, I attempt to reward people about the same no matter how well they have performed.	5	4	3	2	1
16. When somebody doing work for me performs well, I recognize his or her accomplishments promptly.	1	2	3	4	5
17. Before giving somebody a reward, I attempt to find out what would appeal to that person.	1	2	3	4	5
18. I make it a policy not to thank somebody for doing a job he or she is paid to do.	5	4	3	2	1
19. If people do not know how to perform a task, their motivation will suffer.	1	2	3	4	5
20. If properly designed, many jobs can be self-rewarding.	1	2	3	4	5

Total Score _____

Scoring and interpretation: Add the numbers circled to obtain your total score.

90–100 You have advanced knowledge and skill with respect to motivating others in a work environment. Continue to build on the solid base you have established.

50–89   You have average knowledge and skill with respect to motivating others. With additional study and experience, you will probably develop advanced motivational skills.

20–49   To effectively motivate others in a work environment, you will need to greatly expand your knowledge of motivation theory and techniques.

Source: The idea for this quiz, and a few of the items, are from David A. Whetton and Kim S. Cameron, *Developing Management Skills*, 5th ed. (New York: HarperCollins, 2002), pp. 302–303.

Exhibit **6-1**

Maslow's Hierarchy of Needs

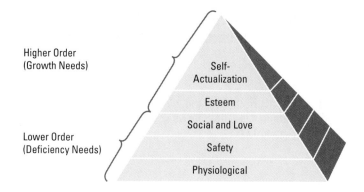

Higher Order
(Growth Needs)

Lower Order
(Deficiency Needs)

Self-Actualization

Esteem

Social and Love

Safety

Physiological

1. *Physiological needs.* At the first level are basic bodily needs such as the need for water, air, food, rest, and sleep. Should these needs be unfulfilled, the individual will be preoccupied with satisfying them. Once met, the second level of needs emerges.

2. *Safety needs.* At the second level are needs relating to obtaining a secure environment without threats to well-being. These include needs for security and freedom from environmental threat. Many employees who work at dangerous jobs, such as loggers and miners, would be motivated by the chance to have safer working conditions. Sexual harassment is an example of the safety need for security becoming frustrated, because the harassed person is subjected to an environmental threat. After a person feels safe and secure, a third level of needs emerges.

3. *Social and love needs.* Needs at this level include belonging to a group, affiliating with people, giving and receiving love, and engaging in sexual activity. Frustration of needs at this level can lead to serious personal problems. Managers can contribute to the satisfaction of social needs by promoting teamwork and encouraging social interaction in matters concerning work problems. When social and love needs are reasonably met, the person seeks to satisfy esteem needs.

4. *Esteem needs.* Needs at this level include self-respect based on genuine achievement, respect from others, prestige, recognition, and appreciation. Occupations with high status satisfy esteem needs. Managers can satisfy the esteem needs of employees by praising their work and giving them the opportunity for recognition. After reasonable satisfaction of esteem needs, most people will strive to achieve more of their potential through self-actualization.

5. *Self-actualization needs.* At the top of the hierarchy are needs for self-fulfillment and personal development and the need to grow to one's fullest potential. Self-actualized people are those who have become what they are capable of becoming. Managers can help employees move toward self-actualization by giving them challenging assignments, including the chance to do creative work. The U.S. Army ad campaign slogan "Be all that you can be" was pitched at self-actualization needs.

A key principle of the needs hierarchy is that, as needs at a given level are gratified, they lose their potency (strength). The next level of need is then activated. A satisfied need ceases to be a motivator. For instance, once employees can pay for the necessities of life, they ordinarily seek opportunities for satisfying social relationships.

Many people think that, for the vast majority of workers, the only sensible way to motivate them is to satisfy higher-level needs. Many exceptions still exist.

A program of providing backup child care helps workers deal with social and love needs. Another consideration is that, even during prosperous times, there are many corporate downsizings that pose a threat to satisfying basic needs, such as security. The many sweatshops still operating in the garment-manufacturing business pay workers wages that make paying for food and rent a major struggle. Also imagine the need frustration of construction workers doing basic work in the aftermath of Hurricane Katrina. In addition to the necessity of wearing face masks, many of the workers stayed at night in crowded tents. The practical implication here is that many workers today can be motivated by offering them an opportunity to satisfy basic needs through such means as job security and a living wage.

Herzberg's Two-Factor Theory

The study of the needs hierarchy led to the **two-factor theory of work motivation.** According to the research of Frederick Herzberg, there are two different sets of job factors.[2] One set, the motivators or satisfiers, can motivate and satisfy workers. The other set, dissatisfiers, or hygiene factors, can only prevent dissatisfaction. Motivators relate to higher-order needs, while hygiene factors relate to lower-order needs.

Key Points in the Theory

The two-factor theory explains how to design jobs to make them motivational. The motivational elements are the intrinsic, or job content, factors that make a job exciting. Motivator factors include achievement, recognition, advancement, responsibility, the work itself, and personal growth possibilities. The extrinsic, or job context, factors are hygienic. Although they are health maintaining and desirable, they are not motivational. Examples of hygiene factors are pay, status, job security, working conditions, and quality of leadership. Herzberg believed that motivation increases when one combines pay with a motivator such as challenging work. (Money is so widely used to enhance motivation that the topic will be treated separately in Chapter 7.)

According to the two-factor theory, only the presence of motivator factors leads to more positive energized behavior. For example, challenging work will motivate many people to exert increased effort. If intrinsic factors such as challenging work are not present, the result is neutral rather than negative, and the worker will feel bland rather than angry or unhappy. Although the presence of hygiene (or extrinsic) factors is not motivational, their absence can cause dissatisfaction, as in the following illustration. A police captain reported that when officers were assigned old patrol cars, they complained frequently. However, when assigned brand new patrol cars, they did not express much appreciation. Nor did they increase their productivity, as measured by the number of citations issued.

Evaluation

The two-factor theory has made two lasting contributions to work motivation. First, it has helped managers realize that money is not always the primary motivator. Second, it has spurred much of the interest in designing jobs to make them more intrinsically satisfying. The enrichment of individual jobs led to the enrichment of work-group activities, which in turn spurred the development of self-managing work teams. All these topics are discussed in subsequent chapters.

A major problem with the two-factor theory is that it de-emphasizes individual differences and glosses over the importance of hygiene factors in attracting and retaining workers. Hygiene factors such as good benefits and company management satisfy and motivate many people. Many working parents will work extra hard to keep their jobs at a company that offers on-site child care or flexible working hours. Furthermore, benefits such as company-subsidized health insurance and dental insurance and a retirement pension would motivate many workers today to work hard and stay with a firm. The reason is that many private and public employers have drastically reduced benefits in recent years.

Another problem with the two-factor theory is that some workers show no particular interest in motivators such as opportunities for growth and advancement. They work primarily so they can pay their bills and enjoy their time with family and friends.

McClelland's Achievement–Power–Affiliation Triad

Many other needs influence job behavior in addition to those mentioned specifically in the need hierarchy. (One example is the need for thrill seeking, as implied from the discussion of the trait for risk taking and thrill seeking described in Chapter 2.) David C. McClelland and his associates have provided a useful explanation of several of these needs.[3] They have proposed a theory of motivation based on the premise that people acquire or learn certain needs from their culture. Among the cultural influences are family, peer groups, television shows, and websites. When a need is strong enough, it prompts a person to engage in work activities to satisfy it. Three key acquired needs or motives driving workers are achievement, power, and affiliation.

The Need for Achievement

The **need for achievement** is the desire to accomplish something difficult for its own sake. People with a strong need for achievement frequently think of how to do a job better. Responsibility seeking is another characteristic of people with a high need for achievement. They are also concerned with how to progress in their careers. Workers with a high need for achievement are interested in monetary rewards primarily as feedback about how well they are achieving. They also set realistic yet moderately difficult goals, take calculated risks, and desire feedback on performance. (A moderately difficult goal challenges a person but is not so difficult as to most likely lead to failure and frustration.) In general, those who enjoy building business, activities, and programs from scratch have a strong need for achievement. Exhibit 6-2 outlines the preferences of workers with a strong achievement need.

The Need for Power

The **need for power** is the desire to control other people, to influence their behavior, and to be responsible for them. Managers with a high need for power wish to control resources (such as money and real estate) in addition to people. A person with a strong need for power spends time thinking about influencing and controlling others and about gaining a position of authority and status. Wanting to make a positive impact is also part of the power motive. Executives who have buildings named after themselves or buy professional athletic teams have strong power needs.

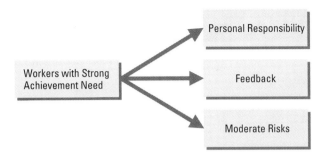

Exhibit **6-2**

*Preferences of Workers
with a Strong
Achievement Need*

For managing big companies, a manager's desire to have an impact and be strong and influential is more important than the need to get things done or the desire to be liked. One problem with someone with a strong achievement drive in a large company is that the manager will attempt to accomplish too much personally rather than spread the task among many workers.[4]

The Need for Affiliation

The **need for affiliation** is the desire to establish and maintain friendly and warm relationships with others. People motivated this way care about restoring disrupted relationships and soothing hurt feelings. They want to engage in work that permits close companionship. Successful managers have low affiliation needs, but managers with an extremely low need for affiliation may not show adequate concern for the needs of others.

The acquired needs theory has made an important contribution in identifying needs related to managerial performance. For example, many studies have shown that successful executives have a strong need for power. Another consistent finding is that entrepreneurs have a strong need for achievement. However, the achievement–power–affiliation triad is not a complete explanation of work motivation, because it focuses on just several key needs. Similarly, needs theories in general explain only part of motivation. The remaining sections of this chapter describe other approaches to understanding work motivation.

The direct implication of needs theories for managing and leading people is that to get the most from workers' talents, it is necessary to "push their hot buttons." Two examples are as follows:

- Employees with strong security needs are likely to seek assurance, be cautious, and carefully stay within their job description. The manager might encourage risk taking from these workers by telling them about other employees who have tried something new and been successful. It is best to avoid surprises about change and to offer frequent feedback.
- Employees with strong achievement needs are likely to display initiative and set personal goals, work well independently, take pride in work well done, and seek recognition for their good work. The manager might include them in the process of establishing work goals, give them ample resources, give them feedback on their work outcomes, and encourage professional growth opportunities.[5]

The accompanying skill-development exercise will help you focus on the importance of identifying psychological needs when attempting to motivate others—and perhaps yourself as well.

SKILL-DEVELOPMENT EXERCISE

Need Identification among Members of Generations X and Y

Following is a list of work preferences characteristic among members of Generations X and Y. Identify what psychological need or needs might be reflected in each work preference. Jot down the needs right after the work preference on the line indicated. In addition to the information presented in this chapter, the section about personality presented in Chapter 2 will give you some concepts for analysis.

- They like variety, not doing the same thing every workday. _____

- Part of their career goals is to face new challenges and opportunities. It is not all based on money, but on growth and learning. _____

- They want jobs that are cool, fun, and fulfilling. _____

- They believe that if they keep growing and learning, that is all the security they need. Advancing their skill set and continuous learning is their top priority. _____

- They have a tremendous thirst for knowledge. _____

- Unlike many baby boomers, who tend to work independently, members of Generations X and Y like to work in a team environment. _____

- They prefer learning by doing and making mistakes as they go along. _____

- They are apt to challenge established ways of doing things, reasoning that there is always a better way. _____

- They want regular, frequent feedback on job performance. _____

- Career improvement is a blend of life and job balance. _____

Source: Reprinted with permission from the TemPositions Group of Companies, 420 Lexington Ave., Suite 2100, New York, NY, 10170-0002.

GOAL THEORY

Summarize the key propositions of goal theory and reinforcement theory.

Log on to **www.thomsonedu.com/infotrac**. Search for articles regarding the CEOs of major companies (Steve Jobs, Bill Gates). How do these leaders motivate their workers? Does personality play a significant part?

Goal setting is a basic process that is directly or indirectly part of all major theories of work motivation. Managers widely accept goal setting as a means to improve and sustain performance. Based on several hundred studies, the core finding of goal-setting theory is as follows: Individuals who are provided with specific hard goals perform better than those given easy, nonspecific, or "do your best" goals—or no goals at all. At the same time, however, the individuals must have sufficient ability, accept the goals, and receive feedback related to the task.[6] Our overview of goal-setting theory elaborates on this basic finding.

The premise underlying goal-setting theory is that behavior is regulated by values and goals. A **goal** is what a person is trying to accomplish. Our values create within us a desire to behave consistently with them. For example, if an executive values honesty, she will establish a goal of trying to hire only honest employees. The executive would therefore make extensive use of reference checks and honesty testing. Edwin A. Locke and Gary P. Latham have incorporated hundreds of studies about goals into a theory of goal setting and task performance.[7] Exhibit 6-3 summarizes some of the more consistent findings, along with more recent developments. The list that follows describes these findings.

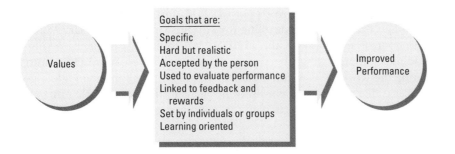

Exhibit **6-3**

Goal-Setting Theory

1. *Specific goals lead to higher performance than do generalized goals.* Telling someone to "do your best" is a generalized goal. A specific goal would be, "Decrease the cycle time on customer inquiries via the company website to an average of 3 hours." (Here is an example in which common sense can be wrong. Many people believe that telling others to "do your best" is an excellent motivator.)

2. *Performance generally increases in direct proportion to goal difficulty.* The more difficult one's goal, the more one accomplishes. An important exception is that when goals are too difficult, they may lower performance. Difficulty in reaching the goal leads to frustration, which in turn leads to lowered performance. At times when a major goal seems overwhelming, establishing smaller, interim goals is more motivational.

Goal theory now recognizes the importance of **superordinate goals,** overarching goals that capture the imagination of people.[8] The superordinate goal is similar to a vision because it relates to an ideal, and is often inspirational. The construction manager of a sewer-pipe company might explain to all workers that "We are working together to improve sanitation and help rid the world of deadly diseases stemming from poor sewage systems." Smaller goals then support the superordinate goals, such as installing a new sewer pipe under a given street within 10 days.

3. *For goals to improve performance, the worker must accept them.* If one rejects a goal, one will not incorporate it into planning. This is why it is often helpful to discuss goals with employees, rather than imposing goals on them. Updated research, however, suggests that the importance of goal commitment may be overrated. Two meta-analyses of studies conducted in laboratories about the effect of goal commitment on performance concluded that commitment has a small impact on performance. Goals appeared to improve performance whether or not people participating in the studies felt committed to their goal.[9] Despite these recent findings, many managers think employee commitment to goals is important. Participating in setting goals has no major effect on the level of job performance except when it improves goal acceptance. Yet participation is valuable because it can lead to higher satisfaction with the goal-setting process.

4. *Goals are more effective when they are used to evaluate performance.* When workers know that their performance will be evaluated in terms of how well they attained their goals, the impact of goals increases.

5. *Goals should be linked to feedback and rewards.* Workers should receive feedback on their progress toward goals and be rewarded for reaching them. **Feedback** is information about how well someone is doing in achieving goals. Rewarding people for reaching goals as a motivational technique is perhaps the most widely accepted principle of management.

6. *Deadlines improve the effectiveness of goals.* For most people, goals are more effective when they include a deadline for completion. Deadlines serve as a tool of time control and increase the motivational impact of goals. Knowing that a deadline is approaching, the typical worker will invest more effort into completing the work. In contrast, if plenty of time remains for attaining the goal, the worker is likely to slow down his or her pace to fill the available time. Yet when deadlines are too tight, particularly in complex jobs, work quality may suffer.[10]

7. *A learning goal orientation improves performance more than a performance goal orientation.* A person with a learning goal orientation wants to develop competence by acquiring new skills and mastering new situations. In contrast, the person with a performance goal orientation wants to demonstrate and validate his or her competence by seeking favorable judgments and avoiding negative judgments. A study with medical supply sales representatives found that a learning goal orientation had a positive relationship with sales performance. In contrast, a performance goal orientation was unrelated to sales performance.[11] An experiment conducted with business-school students found that a learning goal orientation was more strongly related to good performance on the Cellular Industry Business Game than was a performing goal orientation.[12]

8. *Group goal setting is as important as individual goal setting.* Having employees work as teams with a specific team goal, rather than as individuals with only individual goals, increases productivity. Furthermore, the combination of compatible group and individual goals is more effective than either individual or group goals alone. A related consideration is that when a team member perceives that other team members share his or her personal goals, the individual will be more satisfied and productive. A study of 324 members of 64 short-term project teams found that a perceived fit between individual and group performance goals brought about greater individual satisfaction and contribution to the team. Congruence had less of an impact on mastery goals.[13]

Despite the contribution of goals to performance, technically speaking, they are not motivational by themselves. Rather, the discrepancies created by what individuals do and what they aspire to do creates self-dissatisfaction. The dissatisfaction in turn creates a desire to reduce the discrepancy between the real and the ideal.[14] When a person desires to attain something, that person is in a state of arousal. The tension created by not having already achieved a goal spurs the person to reach the goal. If your goal is to update your company website in 10 days, your dissatisfaction with not having started would propel you into action.

An effective way to apply goal theory is for the manager to set short-term goals or to encourage others to do the same. The short-term goals should support the organization's long-term goals, but are established in "bites" that are more readily achievable. Assume, for example, that a manufacturing site wants to reduce absenteeism from 20 to 5% to remain competitive. Going from 20 to 5% in 3 months might not be achievable. However, moving down 2% per month would be feasible. As each 2% reduction in absenteeism is achieved, employees are fed back the results. The feedback serves as a reward for further progress.

Despite the many advantages of goal setting, goals can have negative consequences. A major concern is that some workers may behave unethically in the pursuit of goals, such as manipulating figures to attain a financial goal. Or a CEO might weaken an organization through cost cutting in order to reach a profit or stock price goal. Workers in the pursuit of individual goals may become so preoccupied with their own goals that they are reluctant to help others.[15] Also, the continual pursuit of goals that stretch your capability can be stressful, as workers keep extending their work week to "make their numbers."

The accompanying Organizational Behavior in Action box illustrates how challenging and complex goals in business can lead to better-than-anticipated performance.

ORGANIZATIONAL BEHAVIOR *In Action*

Liz Etling Points TransPerfect in the Right Direction with Goals

Liz Etling is the president and CEO of TransPerfect Translations Inc. in New York City, a company that provides translation, interpreting, typesetting, and multicultural marketing to companies worldwide. She was selected by *Entrepreneur* magazine as the woman entrepreneur who best exemplifies competitiveness, compassion, and clarity of vision. Etling does not measure success in sales alone. For her, success is wrapped up in the goals she meets for her business as well as the company culture she offers her more than 160 employees. "We are very entrepreneurial, very much a group of people building a company together," says Etling. "They're part of a professional organization with goals and a vision. It's a great place for overachievers."

People who want to control their own destinies flourish in the meritocracy that Etling has created. She prides herself on offering not only raises and opportunities for advancement (typically faster than other companies), but also benefit programs that include comprehensive medical coverage, a Caribbean vacation incentive, and company-wide celebrations that include networking and training exercises twice a year. Employees can even get their birthdays off. Though they work hard, long hours are not as painful with the free dinners and car service that anyone from vice presidents to interns can use when working late nights.

Starting in 1992 out of her dorm room at New York University (NYU) with $5,000 in start-up funding from credit cards, Etling set a goal. In 6 months, the company would move into office space. It did. She continues to set specific goals with her team each year, detailing the cities they want to expand into, the sales they want to reach, and the milestones needed to get there. "It's good to have a business plan," she says, "but you need annual goals."

This focus on goal setting and an employee-friendly culture have helped Etling achieve her competitive advantage. To gain the customer service edge, she says, she and her employees listen and go above and beyond their clients' needs: "You don't need a novel idea—you just need to do it better."

Etling rounds out her business/life strategy with charity and community service—from involvement at NYU, where she speaks to student groups and does seminars to encourage the next generation of business leaders, to her company's contributions to charities that help children, support cancer research, fight for human rights, and more. This entrepreneur, philanthropist, and mother says, "I haven't found that running a business is more difficult being a woman. It's more about what you do than whether you're a woman or a man."

Questions

1. In what way do Etling's goals fit in with goal theory?
2. What in addition to goal setting does Etling use to motivate her employees?

Source: Nichole L. Torres, "Winner's Circle: Meet the Winner of Our Woman of the Year Contest, and Learn What Sets Her Apart from the Competition," *Entrepreneur*, June 2004, pp. 38, 40. Reprinted with permission from Entrepreneur Magazine, June 2004. www.entrepreneur.com.

REINFORCEMENT THEORY

A well-established explanation of motivation is **reinforcement theory,** the contention that behavior is determined by its consequences. The consequences are the rewards and punishments people receive for behaving in particular ways. In Chapter 7 we describe behavior-modification programs that apply reinforcement theory to enhance motivation. Reinforcement theory, unlike needs-based theories of motivation, de-emphasizes understanding the needs a person attempts to satisfy. Instead, the manager looks for rewards that will encourage certain behaviors, and punishments that discourage other behaviors.

At the foundation of reinforcement theory is **operant conditioning,** or learning that takes place as a consequence of behavior. More specifically, people learn to repeat behaviors that bring them pleasurable outcomes and to avoid behaviors that lead to uncomfortable outcomes. After people learn a behavior through operant conditioning, they must be motivated by rewards to repeat that behavior.

According to the famous experimental psychologist B. F. Skinner, to train or condition people, and then later motivate them, the manager does not have to study the inner workings of the mind. Instead, the manager should understand the relationships between behaviors and their consequences. After these relationships are understood, the manager arranges contingencies to reward desirable behaviors and discourage undesirable behaviors.[16] Four basic strategies exist for arranging contingencies, which can modify individual (or group) behavior: positive reinforcement, avoidance motivation, extinction, and punishment.

Positive reinforcement is the application of a pleasurable or valued consequence when a person exhibits the desired response. After positive reinforcement, the probability increases that the behavior will be repeated. The term *reinforcement* means that the behavior (or response) is strengthened or entrenched. A manager who expresses appreciation when a team member works late strengthens the worker's propensity to work late.

Avoidance motivation is rewarding people by taking away an uncomfortable consequence. The process is also referred to as *negative reinforcement* because a negative situation is removed. Negative reinforcement is thus a reward, not a punishment, as commonly thought. Avoidance motivation is a way of strengthening a desired response by making the removal contingent on the right response. Assume that an employee is placed on probation because of poor attendance. After 30 consecutive days of coming to work, the employer rewards the employee by removing the probation.

Extinction is weakening or decreasing the frequency of undesirable behavior by removing the reward for such behavior. It is the absence of reinforcement. Suppose an employee engages in undesirable behavior such as creating a disturbance just to get a reaction from coworkers. If the teammates ignore the disturbance, the perpetrator no longer receives the reward of getting attention and therefore stops the disturbing behavior. The behavior is said to be extinguished.

Punishment is the presentation of an undesirable consequence for a specific behavior. An indirect form of punishment is to take away a privilege, such as working on an interesting project, because of some undesirable behavior.

The most direct managerial application of reinforcement theory is to reward the behaviors that support the goals of the organization. Punishment is widely used to maintain discipline within the organization. Avoidance motivation has less application than positive reinforcement and punishment, and extinction is mostly used to decrease disruptive or gross behaviors that are not rule violations.

The application of reinforcement theory is more obvious for basic jobs such as data entry or order shipment, yet positive reinforcement can also be applied to sustain the motivation of managers and professionals, as illustrated by the following anecdote[17]:

> A promotable, talented Director of Operations had just attended her company's annual leadership meeting and was presented with an award for improving the effectiveness of knowledge sharing across the organization. A few days later she returned to her desk to find her report analyzing a capital investment emblazoned with the comment "Nice job! Your ideas should help reduce our expenses on this project by 20%" written across the cover page by her boss. One month later, she received an invitation to join a special task force reporting directly to the CEO focused on detailing the operations portion of the 3-year strategic plan. Her desire and determination to contribute to the success of the management team continued to grow.
>
> Certainly she is talented, but in addition, various forms of reinforcement have kept her motivated and engaged.

EXPECTANCY THEORY OF MOTIVATION

According to **expectancy theory,** motivation results from deliberate choices to engage in activities in order to achieve worthwhile outcomes. People will be well motivated if they believe that a strong effort will lead to good performance and good performance will lead to preferred outcomes. The basic version of expectancy theory shown in Exhibit 6-4 is useful to managers and professionals. Components of the model, including an update about the effects of emotion, are described next, followed by the guidelines for motivation stemming from expectancy theory.[18]

Explain the expectancy theory of motivation.

Expectancy, Instrumentality, and Valence

The key components of expectancy theory are expectancy, instrumentality, and valence. Each of these components exists in each situation involving motivation. An **expectancy** is a person's subjective estimate of the probability that a given level of performance will occur. The effort-to-performance $(E \rightarrow P)$ expectancy refers to the individual's subjective hunch about the chances that increased effort will lead to the desired performance. If a person does not believe that he or she has the skill to accomplish a task, that person might not even try to perform it.

The importance of having high expectancies for motivation meshes well with a conception of work motivation that emphasizes the contribution of self-efficacy. If you have high self-efficacy about the task, your motivation will be high. Low self-efficacy leads to low motivation. Some people are poorly motivated to skydive because they doubt they will be able to pull the ripcord while free-falling at

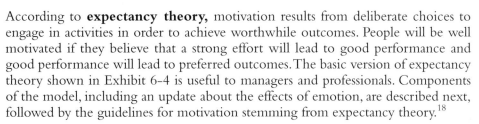

Exhibit **6-4**

A Basic Version of Expectancy Theory

120 mph. The following definition, which is more complete than the one presented in Chapter 5, will help you appreciate the contribution of self-efficacy to motivation:

> Self-efficacy refers to an individual's convictions (or confidence) about his or her abilities to mobilize the motivation, cognitive resources, and course of action needed to successfully execute a specific task within a given context.[19]

An **instrumentality** is the individual's estimate of the probability that performance will lead to certain outcomes. The $P \rightarrow O$ instrumentality refers to the person's subjective evaluation of the chances that good performance will lead to certain outcomes. Among the outcomes might be an increase in status and salary, a promotion, more job security, and appreciation from management. Performance almost always leads to multiple outcomes. In formulating the instrumentality, the employee seeks a subjective answer to the question: "If I do perform well, will the organization really make good on promises to me?" Expectancies and instrumentalities range from 0.00 to 1.00 because both are probabilities.

Valence refers to the value a person places on a particular outcome. People attach positive valences to rewards and negative valences to punishments. An advertising copywriter might place a high positive valence on making a presentation to a client and assign a high negative valence to having his work insulted by the manager or client. The maximum value of a positive valence is +100, while the maximum value of a negative valence is −100. Neutral outcomes (indifference) carry a valence of 0. (Most versions of expectancy theory limit the range of valences from −1.00 to +1.00. However, such a limited range fails to capture the intensity of highly preferred or feared outcomes.) The numerical values of valences are unknown in most situations, yet it is reasonable to assume that people attach values of "good," "bad," and "neutral" to potential outcomes derived from their efforts.

The Calculation of Motivation

In expectancy theory, motivation force $M = (E \rightarrow P) \times (P \rightarrow O) \times V$. The potential of an expected outcome increasing motivation can be high only if the expectancies, instrumentalities, and valences are high. Because anything multiplied by zero is zero, a zero value for $(E \rightarrow P)$, $(P \rightarrow O)$, or V will reduce motivation to zero. Suppose an employee places a maximum value on receiving a raise ($V = 100$). The employee is confident that she can perform the task required ($E \rightarrow P = 0.85$). And the employee is even more confident that the firm will come through with the raise if she performs well ($P \rightarrow O = 0.90$). Note that the values of 0.85 and 0.90 are subjective estimates, not true calculations. The employee's motivation is consequently $(100) \times (0.85) \times (0.90) = 76.5$ (above average, on a scale of −100 to +100).

A note of caution: The simple formula just presented does not tell the entire story because each task involves multiple expectancies, instrumentalities, and valences. Desirable and undesirable outcomes may cancel one another out, resulting in zero valence and therefore producing zero motivational force. For example, a person might not strive for a promotion because its positive valences (such as more money and status) are neutralized by its negative valences (such as having to relocate and leave friends behind). To create a situation of high motivation, the manager should take steps to elevate expectancies, instrumentalities, and valences. One approach would be for the manager to make sure the worker has the right training and to boost the worker's self-confidence—thus elevating expectancies. Assuring the worker that good performance would lead to a reward could boost instrumentalities. Choosing meaningful rewards would elevate the valences.

The Influence of Affect on Expectancy Theory

We have already mentioned the influence of affect on attitudes and creativity (Chapters 4 and 5). Positive affect may also exert influence on the components of expectancy theory, as suggested by two laboratory studies with 97 college students. The task was solving anagrams (rearranging letters to make new words such as *item* from *mite*). Affect, or mood, was manipulated by giving students in the experimental group a bag of candy. A key finding was that when the link between performance and outcomes was specified, being in the positive-affect group increased expectancies, instrumentalities, and valences.[20]

The implication is that managers might be able to increase the effectiveness of expectancy theory by finding ways to elevate the mood of group members. Dispensing bags of candy would be a short-term expedient, because as Chapter 7 will describe, the same reward repeated too often can become stale. Creating a positive work climate would probably be more effective for sustaining positive affect.

127

EQUITY THEORY AND SOCIAL COMPARISON

Explain how equity and social comparison contribute to motivation.

Expectancy theory emphasizes the rational and thinking side of people. Similarly, another theory focuses on how fairly people think they are being treated in comparison to certain reference groups. According to **equity theory,** employee satisfaction and motivation depend on how fairly the employees believe they are treated in comparison to peers. The theory contends that employees hold certain beliefs about the outcomes they receive from their jobs, as well as the inputs they invest to obtain these outcomes.

The outcomes of employment include pay, benefits, status, recognition, intrinsic job factors, and anything else stemming from the job that workers perceive as useful. The inputs include all the factors that employees perceive as being their investment in the job or anything of value that they bring to the job. These inputs include job qualifications, skills, education level, effort, trust in the company, support of coworkers, and cooperative behavior.

The core of equity theory is that employees compare their inputs and outcomes (making social comparisons) with others in the workplace.[21] When employees believe that they receive equitable outcomes in relation to their inputs, they are generally satisfied and motivated. When workers believe that they are being treated equitably, they are more willing to work hard. Conversely, when employees believe that they give too much as compared with what they receive from the organization, a state of tension, dissatisfaction, and demotivation ensues. The people used for reference are those whom the employee perceives as relevant for comparison. For example, an industrial sales representative would make comparisons with other industrial sales reps in the same industry about whom he has information.

There are two kinds of comparisons. People consider their own inputs in relation to outcomes received, and they also evaluate what others receive for the same inputs. Equity is said to exist when an individual concludes that his or her own outcome/input ratio is equal to that of other people. Inequity exists if the person's ratio is not the same as that of other people. All these comparisons are similar to those judgments made by people according to expectancy theory—they are subjective hunches that may or may not be valid. Inequity can be in either direction and of varying magnitude. The equity ratio is often expressed as follows:

$$\frac{\text{Outcomes of Individual}}{\text{Inputs of Individual}} \quad \text{compared to} \quad \frac{\text{Outcomes of Others}}{\text{Inputs of Others}}$$

According to equity theory, the highest level of motivation occurs when a person has ratios equal to those of the comparison person. When people perceive an inequity, they are likely to engage in one of the following actions:

1. *Alter the outcome.* The person who feels mistreated might ask for more salary or a bonus, promotional opportunities, or more vacation time. Some people might even steal from the company to obtain the money they feel they deserve. Others might attempt to convince management to give less to others. A few years back a sociology professor donated $2000 of his $60,000 annual salary to a custodial worker at his university. The professor's intent was to help create equity in the university pay system.

2. *Alter the input.* A person who feels treated inequitably might decrease effort or time devoted to work. The person who feels underpaid might engage in such self-defeating behavior by faking sick days to take care of personal business. Another extreme would be to encourage others to decrease their inputs so they will earn less money.

3. *Distort the perception.* To combat feelings of inequity, people can distort their perceptions of their own (or others') inputs or outcomes. Recognizing that she is overpaid in comparison to coworkers, a financial analyst might say, "Of course, I attended a much tougher program at college, so I deserve more money." Another distortion would be to look for evidence that coworkers are contributing less effort.

4. *Change the reference source.* A convenient way of restoring equity is to change to another reference source whose outcome/input ratio is similar to one's own. A recently graduated MBA accepted a job offer for $20,000 less per year than average compared with other graduates of her program. At first she grumbled about being underpaid but then reanalyzed the situation. Her conclusion was, "The MBAs I was comparing myself with took jobs in New York City or Boston, where the cost of living is much higher. If I compare myself to MBAs being hired outside of New York or Boston, I'm being paid well."

5. *Leave the situation.* As an extreme move, the person who feels treated inequitably might quit a job. He or she would then be free to pursue greater equity in another position.

Equity theory has much face validity and has direct relevance for pay systems. No matter how well designed a program of productivity or cost cutting might be, it must still provide equitable pay. Otherwise, the negative perceptions of workers might lead to less effort to accomplish the goals of management.

SOCIAL LEARNING THEORY

Use social learning theory to motivate yourself.

As described in Chapter 3, people learn various behaviors by observing and imitating others. At a later point, they are motivated to repeat the learned behaviors. **Social learning** is the process of observing the behavior of others, recognizing its consequences, and altering behavior as a result. According to social learning theory, individual behavior is influenced by a combination of a person's cognitions and social environment. A person has to make some interpretations of the efficacy and suitability of the behavior being observed; otherwise the model will not be imitated.

Social learning does not take place automatically just because environmental models are available. If social learning were that easy, almost every employee would be a model worker. Effective social learning, and therefore motivated behavior, is most likely to take place when several of the following conditions are met:[22]

1. The person should have high expectancies that he or she can learn the observed behavior, and high instrumentalities that the learned behavior will result in valued rewards. The high expectancies center on the person having high self-efficacy. Social learning will be facilitated when the person is confident of performing well in the modeled task.

2. Self-administration of rewards should take place. The person doing the modeling should find the behavior intrinsically satisfying and not have to rely exclusively on extrinsic rewards such as increased compensation and recognition. Modeling the new behavior should result in personal satisfaction and an enhanced self-image. Assume that you learned how to negotiate effectively by observing a mentor negotiate a deal. You would most likely experience increased personal satisfaction from having acquired a valuable new business skill. At a later point, external rewards would be forthcoming if your new skill led to a higher performance evaluation or saving money when purchasing a home.

3. The behavior to be learned should involve mostly tangible mechanical and verbal activities such as physical and interpersonal tasks. It is thus easier to be motivated by watching another person negotiate than to engage in strategic planning. We cannot readily imitate the cognitive processes of another person.

4. Social learning can only take place when we possess the physical and mental ability needed to imitate the behavior. A frail person cannot learn to move furniture by simply watching others do it correctly. Also, you cannot imitate effective negotiating practices if you are not intelligent enough to figure out what the other side really wants.

Social learning may appear to be more about learning than motivation, but the motivational aspects are still important. Workers typically model the behavior of people from whom they seek approval, such as superiors and high-performing teammates. Part of the motivation for learning and repeating the target behavior is to receive approval from significant people in the work environment. Have you ever noticed how people from the same organization often talk alike?

INTRINSIC VERSUS EXTRINSIC MOTIVATION

Recognize the importance of both intrinsic and extrinsic motivators.

Many management experts contend that if you make jobs more interesting, there may be less need for motivating people with external rewards. The two-factor theory of motivation is based on this idea. Also, attempting to motivate people by extrinsic rewards may not be sufficient. Motivating people through interesting work is based on the principle of **intrinsic motivation,** which refers to a person's beliefs about the extent to which an activity can satisfy his or her needs for competence and self-determination. The intrinsically motivated person has energy and passion for the task,[23] as implied in the discussion in Chapter 5 about the experience of flow. Values contribute to intrinsic motivation. People who highly value work tend to be intrinsically motivated, while people who place a low value on work have low intrinsic motivation. The contribution of intrinsic motivation to creativity was discussed in Chapter 5.

The Rationale behind Intrinsic Motivation Theory

Intrinsic motivation and self-determination theory are closely related. According to **self-determination theory,** workers are active agents of, rather than passive reactors to, environmental forces. Two factors influence the perception of intrinsic motivation. Certain characteristics of a task, such as challenge and autonomy, promote intrinsic motivation because they allow a person to satisfy the needs for competence and self-determination. Workers' perceptions of why they perform a task can also affect intrinsic motivation. Such motivation is likely to increase when people perceive that they perform tasks for themselves rather than for an external reward. To understand intrinsic motivation, visualize a computer programmer joyously working until midnight to write software that will give her company a competitive edge in satisfying customers. She is so wrapped up in her work that she is unaware of the time. Furthermore, she gives no particular thought to whether she will receive a bonus for her outstanding work.

When an individual performs a task to achieve an external reward such as money or recognition, a shift occurs. The individual believes that the external reward caused the behavior, and money or recognition now controls his or her actions. The worker no longer perceives that he or she is self-determining. As a result, intrinsic motivation may decrease.[24]

Kenneth W. Thomas presents a view, shared by many others, of the importance of intrinsic motivation in today's workplace. He reasons that the world of work has evolved from the command-and-control era to one in which encouraging workers to manage themselves plays a major role in leading workers. Intrinsic motivation is necessary for self-management because self-management implies that you find your work rewarding in itself.[25]

Problems Associated with Extrinsic Rewards

Intrinsic motivation theory is based on the fact that external rewards have disadvantages. Extrinsic rewards can sometimes lower a person's job performance and be demotivating, particularly when a creative task is involved. The appeal of extrinsic rewards can also cause people to:

- Focus narrowly on a task.
- Rush through a job to get a reward.
- Regard the task as a drudgery that must be suffered to receive a reward.
- See themselves as less free and less self-determining.[26]

Despite these problems, a firm should not abandon financial bonuses and other forms of extrinsic motivation. Even the people who enjoy work intensely still expect to be paid well and crave recognition from management. Also, people who love their work, such as top executives, successful novelists, entertainers, and athletes, demand huge fees. The sensible solution is for managers to balance intrinsic and extrinsic rewards. For example, a purchasing agent who saved the company $300,000 by finding a low-price alternative for a component might be rewarded with the opportunity to work on a cross-functional team. He might also be given a hefty year-end bonus.

A useful perspective on intrinsic versus extrinsic rewards is that the two can be combined into the same employee incentive program. (An incentive program uses extrinsic motivators.) Motivation consultant Bob Nelson offers managers guidelines on how to build intrinsic motivation into an incentive program. First, *set goals that have mutual benefits,* such as the employee learning new skills while pursuing a pro-ductivity goal. For example, an engineer might learn more about aerodynamics while helping design cars that sell better. Second, *form a partnership in the achievement of goals.* Offer the worker assistance in reaching the goal mandated by the incentive program so he or she can develop new skills. Third, *allow for individual choice in rewards.* When employees choose from a group of rewards in the incentive program, they are more likely to have a sense of self-determination. For example, a given employee might opt for tickets to a play instead of a gift certificate to a store he or she did not care for.[27]

THE INFLUENCE OF PERSONALITY
AND CULTURE ON MOTIVATION

Explain how personality and cultural factors are related to motivation.

131

Personality and culture can both influence a person's level of drive and the rewards he or she thinks are relevant. For many people, being well motivated comes easily because they have personality traits that predispose them to this. Two key examples are *conscientiousness* and the *achievement need.* (A need usually functions like a personality trait.) The conscientious person will strive to get the job done, and the achievement-driven person welcomes accomplishing tasks. Conversely, it will be more difficult for the manager to motivate people who score low on conscientiousness and have a weak achievement need.

A study involving 164 telemarketing sales representatives at a large financial services firm provides empirical evidence for the link between personality factors and motivation. As most readers would suspect, high motivation is crucial to perform well as a telemarketer—particularly in light of all the rejection a telemarketer encounters. Motivation was measured in relation to three factors. *Communion striving* represents actions directed toward being accepted in personal relationships and getting along with coworkers. *Status striving* refers to actions directed toward obtaining power and dominance within a status hierarchy, such as a business firm. *Accomplishment striving* reflects an individual's intention to accomplish tasks, as included in most definitions of work motivation. The Five Factor Model was used to study personality.

The strongest correlations found in the aspect of the study dealing with the personality–motivation relationship are listed here. We also include findings about job performance because motivation is assumed to be a major contributor to job performance:

- Extraversion was correlated with communion striving and status striving.
- Conscientiousness was correlated with accomplishment striving and status striving.
- Extraversion and conscientiousness were correlated with sales performance.
- Status striving and accomplishment striving were correlated with sales performance.[28]

The study therefore demonstrated that personality factors are correlated with motivation, and that both personality factors and motivation are related to job performance. The researchers thus provided one more brick in the wall of evidence that personality and motivation make a difference in job performance.

Cross-cultural factors typically influence which rewards or outcomes are likely to have the highest valence for a particular group. Hispanic people, for example, generally favor outcomes that enable them to maintain cordial relations with other members of the work group. Also, Asians would ordinarily prefer not to receive rewards that single them out for attention.

American managers are urged to be careful in assuming that rewards that are effective in their culture necessarily work well in other cultures. For example, increasing the salaries of one group of Mexican workers motivated them to worker fewer, not more, hours. As the Mexicans explained their behavior, "We can now make enough money to live and enjoy life in less time than previously. Now, we do not have to work so many hours." (The Mexicans placed a high valence on spending more time with family and friends.)

In another example of how culture influences the effectiveness of a reward, an expatriate manager in Japan rewarded a Japanese sales representative by promoting him to a management position (a status reward). However, the new manager experienced a decline in effort and performance. The promotion, an individualistic reward, separated the new manager from his colleagues and embarrassed him. As a result, he invested less effort in work.[29]

An extreme cross-cultural difference is that the promise of steady work and a regular wage is not a strong motivator in a select few cultures. To illustrate, several Canadian firms began mining for precious metals in Nunavut, Canada, several years ago. Many of the miners are recruited from the native Inuit population. On sunny days many of the workers chose to seal hunt or fish (a strong cultural tradition) instead of reporting to work even if it meant losing wages at the mine. Because some of the seal hunting and fishing generates revenue, we cannot assume that the Inuit are not motivated by money.

Expectancy theory is another illustration of how cultural factors influence motivation. As analyzed by Nancy J. Adler, expectancy theory depends on the extent to which workers believe they have control over the outcome of their efforts and how much faith they have in leaders to deliver rewards.[30] The assumption that workers believe they have control over their fate may be culturally dependent. In countries where individualism is strong, such as the United States, employees may believe more strongly that they can influence performance and outcomes. In collectivist societies, such as Taiwan, an individual may feel that group effort has a stronger influence on performance and outcomes. Taiwanese are also more likely to believe that the company has a moral obligation to deliver on outcomes.

IMPLICATIONS FOR MANAGERIAL PRACTICE

The explanations of motivation presented in this chapter all have implications for managerial practice. Nevertheless, we emphasize suggestions derived from expectancy theory because its components include ideas from other theories, and we also mention how procrastination influences goal attainment:

1. *Determine what levels and kinds of performance are needed to achieve organizational goals.* Motivating others proceeds best when workers have a clear understanding of what needs to be accomplished. At the same time, the manager should make sure that the desired levels of performance are possible.

2. *Train and encourage people.* Managers should give group members the necessary training and encouragement to be confident that they can perform the required task. Some group members who appear to be poorly motivated simply lack the right skills and self-confidence.

3. *Understand individual differences in valences.* To motivate workers effectively, managers must recognize individual differences in preferences for rewards. An attempt should be made to offer workers rewards to which they attach a high valence. Cross-cultural differences in valences may also occur.

132

4. *Use positive reinforcement more than punishment.* At times, punishment is necessary. Yet it can produce negative side effects such as anxiety and retaliation against the firm, including employees making costly mistakes intentionally.

5. *Be aware that procrastination can block goal attainment.* Now matter how carefully goals are established in accordance with goal theory, an employee who procrastinates will not achieve a given goal on time. A worker who appears to be procrastinating will need to be confronted about the problem and encouraged to get moving to attain the goal. To help the worker overcome the procrastination, emphasize attaining the easiest goal among the many goals involved in the task, such as establishing a computer file for the task.

SUMMARY OF KEY POINTS

 Describe several need theories of motivation, including the needs hierarchy, the two-factor theory, and the achievement–power–affiliation triad.

Motivation is the process by which behavior is mobilized and sustained in the interest of achieving organizational goals. As reflected in need theories of motivation, self-interest is a driving force. According to Maslow's needs hierarchy, human needs fall into five groups: physiological, safety, social and love, esteem, and self-actualization. As needs at one level are satisfied, they lose their strength and the next level of needs is activated.

Herzberg's two-factor theory of work motivation divides job factors into motivators and satisfiers versus maintenance factors or dissatisfiers. Motivational factors are the intrinsic or job content factors (such as achievement and recognition) that make a job rewarding. Maintenance factors are the extrinsic aspects of the job (such as working conditions and benefits). Dissatisfaction stems from substandard extrinsic factors.

McClelland's acquired needs theory explains that certain needs people strive to satisfy are acquired or learned from the culture. His research centers on three needs of particular significance in understanding entrepreneurs and managers: achievement, power, and affiliation. The need for power is the primary motivator of successful managers.

 Summarize the key propositions of goal theory and reinforcement theory.

Goal setting is an important part of all major theories of motivation. Specific and difficult goals result in higher performance than generalized goals. Goals must be accepted by workers, and goals are more effective when they are used to evaluate performance and linked to feedback and rewards. Deadlines improve the effectiveness of goals. A learning goal orientation is more effective than a performance goal orientation and group goal setting is as important as individual goal setting.

According to reinforcement theory, behavior is determined by its consequences, or rewards and punishments for behaving in particular ways. At the foundation of reinforcement theory is operant conditioning, or learning that takes place as a consequence of behavior. People learn to repeat behaviors that bring them pleasurable outcomes and to avoid behaviors that lead to uncomfortable outcomes. The four basic strategies for arranging contingencies to modify behavior are positive reinforcement, avoidance motivation, extinction, and punishment.

 Explain the expectancy theory of motivation.

Expectancy theory is based on the idea that work motivation results from deliberate choices to engage in certain activities in order to achieve worthwhile outcomes. The three components of expectancy theory are effort-to-performance expectancies, instrumentalities, and valence. Individual differences and cultural factors influence valence. Most situations have multiple outcomes and valences. Motivational force is the result of the multiplication of expectancies, instrumentalities, and valence. Positive affect may enhance any of these factors.

 Explain how equity and social comparison contribute to motivation.

Equity theory explains that workers compare their inputs and outcomes with relevant people in the workplace. When employees believe that they are receiving equitable outputs in relation to their inputs, they are generally satisfied and motivated. When workers believe they are giving too much in relation

133

to what they are receiving from the organization, dissatisfaction ensues. People will usually take action to bring their equity ratio into balance. Two such actions would be seeking greater outputs or decreasing input.

 Use social learning theory to motivate yourself.
According to social learning theory, individual behavior is influenced by a combination of a person's cognitions and social environment. People learn by imitating a model and becoming motivated to repeat the behavior. Conditions favoring social learning include high expectations, self-administration of rewards, observation of tangible behavior to imitate, and the necessary physical and mental ability.

 Recognize the importance of both intrinsic and extrinsic motivators.
The theory of intrinsic motivation, or self-determination, emphasizes that people are active agents rather than recipients of environmental forces. Passion and energy are part of being intrinsically motivated. Intrinsic motivation is tied in with needs for competence and self-determination. Extrinsic rewards can sometimes lower a person's job performance and be demotivating, particularly when a creative task is involved. A combination of intrinsic and extrinsic rewards is best for motivation, although intrinsic motivation is essential for self-management. Intrinsic motivators can sometimes be built into incentive programs.

 Explain how personality and cultural factors are related to motivation.
Certain personality traits can predispose a person to being well motivated. A study demonstrated various links between the Five Factor Model of personality and motivation, such as a correlation between extraversion and communion striving and status striving, and a correlation between conscientiousness and accomplishment and status striving. Motivation was also shown to be correlated with sales performance.

Cross-cultural factors typically influence which rewards or outcomes are likely to have the highest valence for a particular cultural group. A cross-cultural consideration in expectancy theory is that it depends on the extent to which workers believe they have control over the outcome of their efforts and how much faith they have in leaders to deliver rewards.

KEY TERMS AND PHRASES

Motivation, 114
In a work setting, the process by which behavior is mobilized and sustained in the interest of achieving organizational goals.

Maslow's Hierarchy of Needs, 114
A classical theory of motivation that arranges human needs into a pyramid-shaped model, with basic physiological needs at the bottom and self-actualization needs at the top.

Two-Factor Theory of Work Motivation, 117
Herzberg's theory contending that there are two different sets of job factors. One set can satisfy and motivate people (motivators or satisfiers); the other set can only prevent dissatisfaction (dissatisfiers or hygiene factors).

Need for Achievement, 118
The desire to accomplish something difficult for its own sake.

Need for Power, 118
The desire to control other people, to influence their behavior, and to be responsible for them.

Need for Affiliation, 119
The desire to establish and maintain friendly and warm relationships with others.

Goal, 120
What a person is trying to accomplish.

Superordinate Goals, 121
Overarching goals that capture the imagination of people.

Feedback, 121
Information about how well someone is doing in achieving goals. Also, messages sent back from the receiver to the sender of information.

Reinforcement Theory, 124
The contention that behavior is determined by its consequences.

Operant Conditioning, 124
Learning that takes place as a consequence of behavior.

Positive Reinforcement, 124
The application of a pleasurable or valued consequence when a person exhibits the desired response.

Avoidance Motivation, 124
Rewarding by taking away an uncomfortable consequence.

Extinction, 124
Weakening or decreasing the frequency of undesirable behavior by removing the reward for such behavior.

Punishment, 124
The presentation of an undesirable consequence for a specific behavior.

Expectancy Theory, 125
The theory that motivation results from deliberate choices to engage in activities in order to achieve worthwhile outcomes.

Expectancy, 125
A person's subjective estimate of the probability that a given level of performance will occur.

Instrumentality, 126
The individual's subjective estimate of the probability that performance will lead to certain outcomes.

Valence, 126
The value a person places on a particular outcome.

Equity Theory, 127
The theory that employee satisfaction and motivation depend on how fairly the employees believe that they are treated in comparison to peers.

Social Learning, 128
The process of observing the behavior of others, recognizing its consequences, and altering behavior as a result.

Intrinsic Motivation, 129
A person's beliefs about the extent to which an activity can satisfy his or her needs for competence and self-determination.

Self-Determination Theory, 130
The idea that workers are active agents of, rather than passive reactors to, environmental forces.

135

DISCUSSION QUESTIONS AND ACTIVITIES

1. How does WIIFM explain the fact that many busy managers and professionals devote considerable amounts of their time to community activities and charities?
2. How would you know if a particular person had a strong need for power? For achievement? For affiliation?
3. Get together in a group, and have each member give an example of how establishing a goal has been motivational for him or her.
4. How can a manager strengthen the expectancies of group members?
5. How does a person formulate an instrumentality for estimating the extent to which hard work will lead to a promotion?
6. Identify an outcome for which you have a strong negative valence. What type of motivated behavior would you engage in to avoid that outcome?
7. Which of your personality traits are likely to enhance your motivation to perform well on the job and at school? What evidence do you have for the strength of these traits?

CASE PROBLEM: Motivating the Staff at HROutsource

Kelly Winters is a program manager at HROutsource, a company that supplies human resource services to small and medium-size organizations, including businesses, hospitals, and a variety of nonprofit firms. The human resources services include administering payroll and employee benefits, bonus plans, and training. Winters is the program manager for training services, a small but growing part of client work for HROutsource.

The three members of Winters's staff are Christina Conway, Peter Wang, and Maria Sanchez, all of whom hold the job title of human resources consultant. All three

consultants are performing adequately, yet Winters has been thinking lately about enhancing their performance. Winters's immediate manager, the vice president of client programs, agrees that her staff has room for improvement in terms of effort and commitment. Winters's preliminary action plan for enhancing the motivation of her staff is to interview them to search for specific motivators.

In Winters's words, "As an HR professional, I'm not naïve enough to think that a one-size-fits-all approach to motivation is going to work. I'm going to offer each member of my team a gift certificate to their favorite

CASE PROBLEM (Continued)

online shopping service as a reward for outstanding performance. Gifts are nice, but I want to try something a little more sophisticated."

Excerpts from the interviews are as follows:

WINTERS: "Chris, what do you really want from working at HROutsource? What would it take to get you to the next level of effort?"

CONWAY: "Thanks for asking me, Kelly. I haven't given the issue much thought yet. But off the top of my head, I would say I want your job, and then keep moving. I see a great future in human resource programs being outsourced, and I want to be part of that future. I'm 26 right now, and I can see myself as a CEO of a human resources outsourcing firm by the time I hit 35. So if I could see some clear signs of career advancement, I would put a little more pressure on the accelerator."

WINTERS: "Peter, what do you want to get out of working for HROutsource? How could we get you to be even more strongly motivated?"

WANG: "I like what I see at the company, yet I'm falling into a little bit of a routine. I keep doing safety training and diversity training for clients. It's getting a little repetitious. I have to appear excited and enthused even if I've given the identical training program seven times in 1 month. I want to branch out, and maybe help install a bonus system for a client or two. I want to get into other aspects of HR.

"I don't want to feel like I'm finished growing as an HR professional. I'm only 31."

WINTERS: "Good morning, Maria. How are you doing today? I wanted to learn a little bit more about what makes you happy and motivated. What do you hope to get out of working for HROutsource? What type of work would get you even more fired up?"

SANCHEZ: "I thought I was pretty fired up. I think I could be more committed to the company if the company was more committed to me. I feel I am only as good as my last client assignment. Suppose the company runs out of client assignments for me. Does that mean I'm out the door?

"Stable employment is pretty important for me. I have a child, and my husband is a full-time student in a field with little prospect for high-paying work. I would like to wake up every morning and feel that my job at HROutsource will be there."

Case Questions

1. What needs are Conway, Wang, and Sanchez attempting to satisfy?
2. Make a suggestion to Winters and her manager for motivating Conway, Wang, and Sanchez.
3. Should Winters have asked each staff member exactly the same question in order to understand more clearly their potential motivators?

ENDNOTES

1. Abraham H. Maslow, "A Theory of Human Motivation," *Psychological Review,* July 1943, pp. 370–396; *Motivation and Personality* (New York: Harper & Row, 1954), Chapter 5.
2. Frederick Herzberg, Bernard Mausner, and Barbara Snyderman, *The Motivation to Work,* 2nd ed. (New York: Wiley, 1959); Herzberg, *Work and the Nature of Man* (Cleveland: World Publishing, 1966).
3. David C. McClelland, "Business Drive and National Achievement," *Harvard Business Review* July–August 1962, pp. 99–112; McClelland, *The Achieving Society* (New York: Van Nostrand, 1961).
4. David C. McClelland and David H. Burnam, "Power Is the Great Motivator," *Harvard Business Review,* January 2003, pp. 117–126, 142 (reprint of 1976 article plus *HBR* editor update).
5. Jane Churchouse and Chris Churchouse, *Managing People* (Hampshire, England: Gower, 1998); "Recognizing Workers' Needs," *Manager's Edge,* March 1999, p. 1.
6. Gary P. Latham, "Goal Setting: A Five-Step Approach to Behavior Change," *Organizational Dynamics,* Number 3, 2003, p. 311.
7. Edwin A. Locke and Gary P. Latham, *A Theory of Goal Setting and Task Performance* (Upper Saddle River, NJ: Prentice Hall, 1990).
8. Latham, "Goal Setting: A Five-Step Approach to Behavior Change," p. 309.
9. John J. Donavan and David J. Radosevich, "The Moderating Role of Goal Commitment on the Goal Difficulty-Performance Relationship: A Meta-Analytic Review and Critical Reanalysis," *Journal of Applied Psychology,* April 1998, pp. 308–315; Howard J. Klein, Michael J. Wesson, John R. Hollenbeck, and Bradley J. Alge, "Goal Commitment and the Goal-Setting Process: Conceptual Clarification and Empirical Synthesis," *Journal of Applied Psychology,* December 1999, pp. 885–896.
10. Yitzhak Fried and Linda Haynes Slowik, "Enriching Goal-Setting Theory with Time: An Integrated Approach," *Academy of Management Review,* July 2004, p. 407.
11. Don VandeWalle, Steven P. Brown, William L. Cron, and John W. Slocum, Jr., "The Influence of Goal Orientation and Self-Regulation Tactics on Sales Performance: A Longitudinal Field Test," *Journal of Applied Psychology,* April 1999, pp. 249–259.
12. Gerard H. Seijts, Gary P. Latham, Kevin Tasa, and Brandon W. Latham, "Goal Setting and Goal Orientation: An Integration of Two Different Yet Related Literatures," *Academy of Management Journal,* April 2004, pp. 227–239.

13. Amy L. Kristof-Brown and Cynthia Kay Stevens, "Goal Congruence in Project Teams: Does the Fit Between Members' Personal Mastery and Performance Goals Matter?" *Journal of Applied Psychology,* December 2001, pp. 1083–1095.

14. P. Christopher Earley and Terri R. Lituchy, "Delineating Goal and Efficacy Effects: A Test of Three Models," *Journal of Applied Psychology,* February 1991, p. 872.

15. Gary P. Latham, "The Motivational Benefits of Goal-Setting," *Academy of Management Executive,* November 2004, p. 129.

16. B. F. Skinner, *Science and Human Behavior* (New York: Macmillan, 1953).

17. *RHR International Executive Insights, 20*(3), 2004, p. 1.

18. Victor H. Vroom, *Work and Motivation* (New York: Wiley, 1964); Lynn E. Miller and Joseph E. Grush, "Improving Predictions in Expectancy Theory Research: Effects of Personality, Expectancies, and Norms," *Academy of Management Journal,* March 1988, pp. 107–122.

19. Alexander D. Stajkovic and Fred Luthans, "Social Cognitive Theory and Self-Efficacy: Going Beyond Traditional Motivational and Behavioral Approaches," *Organizational Dynamics,* Spring 1998, p. 66.

20. Amir Erez and Alice M. Isen, "The Influence of Positive Affect on the Components of Expectancy Motivation," *Journal of Applied Psychology,* December 2002, pp. 1055–1067.

21. J. Stacy Adams, "Toward an Understanding of Inequality," *Journal of Abnormal and Social Psychology, 67* (1963), pp. 422–436; M. R. Carrell and J. E. Dettrich, "Equity Theory: The Recent Literature, Methodological Considerations, and New Directions," *Academy of Management Review,* April 1978, pp. 202–210.

22. Robert Wood and Albert Bandura, "Social Cognitive Theory of Organizational Management," *Academy of Management Review,* July 1989, pp. 361–384.

23. Kenneth W. Thomas, *Intrinsic Motivation at Work: Building Energy and Commitment* (San Francisco: Berrett-Koehler Publishers, 2000).

24. Gregory Moorehead and Ricky W. Griffin, *Organizational Behavior: Managing People and Organizations,* 4th ed. (Boston: Houghton Mifflin, 1995), pp. 147–148; Robert P. Vecchio, *Organizational Behavior,* 2nd ed. (Mason, OH: South-Western/Thomson, 1991), p. 193.

25. Thomas, *Intrinsic Motivation at Work.*

26. Richard M. Ryan and Edward L. Deci, "Self-Determination Theory and the Facilitation of Intrinsic Motivation, Social Development, and Well-Being," *American Psychologist,* January 2000, pp. 68–78; Jeffrey Pfeffer, *Human Equation: Building Profits by Putting People First* (Boston: Harvard Business School Press, 1998), pp. 213–217.

27. Bob Nelson, "Build Intrinsic Motivation Into Your Incentive Programs." http://www.fed.org.

28. Murray R. Barrick, Greg L. Stewart, and Mike Piotrowski, "Personality and Job Performance: Test of Mediating Effects of Motivation among Sales Representatives," *Journal of Applied Psychology,* February 2002, pp. 43–51.

29. These studies and observations are reported in "Managing the Cross-Cultural Workforce," http://home.skif.net/%7Etodorov/036.htm.

30. Nancy J. Adler, *International Dimensions of Organizational Behavior,* 2nd ed. (Boston: PWS-Kent, 1991), pp. 157–160.

7

Motivational Methods and Programs

OBJECTIVES

After reading and studying this chapter and doing the exercises, you should be able to:

1. Explain how to enhance motivation through job enrichment, the job characteristics model, and job crafting.

2. Summarize the basics of a behavior-modification program in the workplace.

3. Identify rules and suggestions for motivating group members through behavior modification.

4. Explain why recognition and pride are good motivators, and discuss the nature of reward and recognition programs in the workplace.

5. Describe how to use financial incentives effectively to motivate others, including the use of employee stock ownership plans, stock options, and gainsharing.

6. Choose an appropriate motivational model for a given situation.

The insurance giant Allstate Corp. launched a pay-for-performance salary structure on January 1, 2005. Under the system, Allstate increased its compensation budget 3.8% for the year, but who gets how much of that cash depends on performance rankings. Supervisors rank the employees, and the rankings are reviewed and discussed with the supervisor's manager. This means one worker might receive, say a 5.5% increase, while a coworker in the next cubicle doing the exact same job—though less efficiently or productively—could receive only 2%.

"This allows us to attract better performers and keep the good talent we have," says Steve Scholl, Allstate's assistant vice president of human resources. To determine incentive pay, employees' individual performance is graded into one of five categories from below standard to outstanding.

Source: Adapted from Jeff D. Opdyke, "Getting a Bonus Instead of a Raise," *The Wall Street Journal*, December 29, 2004, pp. D1, D2.

Now Ask Yourself: **What does the incentive system at Allstate tell us about how companies use financial incentives systematically to motivate workers?** A standard practice for increasing employee productivity is to offer them more money for good performance, and less money for poor performance. Sometimes pay-for-performance achieves its intended results, and sometimes not, as described later.

Motivational programs continue in importance because many employees do not feel strongly motivated to help accomplish company goals. Several studies have found that most American workers are not fully engaged in their work. They do what is expected of them but do not contribute the extra mental and physical effort to be outstanding. Many of these workers want to be good organizational citizens, yet many of them feel they have a poor relationship with the supervisor or believe that the organization does not care about them. "We're running an economy at about 30 percent efficiency because so many employees are not investing their best effort on the job," says Curt Coffman of the Gallup Organization. According to a Gallup study, about 70% of employees are "disengaged," meaning that they are no longer committed to the company. Furthermore, the longer employees stay, the more disengaged they become.[1]

In this chapter, we describe motivational programs based on financial incentives, but we also examine motivation through job design, behavior modification, and reward and recognition programs. We also describe choosing an appropriate motivational model, a topic that relates to both the present and the previous chapter.

MOTIVATION THROUGH JOB DESIGN

A major strategy for enhancing motivation is to make the job so challenging and the worker so responsible that he or she is motivated just by performing the job. We will approach motivation through job design by explaining job enrichment, the job characteristics model, and job crafting. The self-managed work teams to be described in Chapter 10 are also a method of motivation through job design. Research and practice with motivation through job design has its roots in the two-factor theory described in Chapter 6.

Explain how to enhance motivation through job enrichment, the job characteristics model, and job crafting.

Job Enrichment

Job enrichment refers to making a job more motivational and satisfying by adding variety, responsibility, and managerial decision making. At its best, job enrichment gives workers a sense of ownership, responsibility, and accountability for their work. Because job enrichment leads to a more exciting job, it often increases employee job satisfaction and motivation. People are usually willing to work harder at tasks they find enjoyable and rewarding, just as they will put effort into a favorite hobby. Managers and professionals in organizations typically have enriched jobs. Professional-level workers at the beginning of their career are particularly eager for job enrichment because they see it as a vehicle to professional growth.

Characteristics of an Enriched Job

According to Frederick Herzberg, the way to design an enriched job is to include as many as possible of the characteristics described next.[2] Exhibit 7-1 summarizes an updated version of the characteristics and consequences of enriched jobs.

139

Exhibit **7-1**

Characteristics and Consequences of an Enriched Job

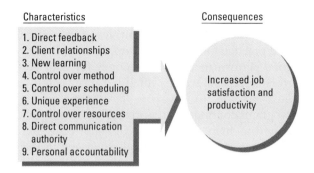

Characteristics

1. Direct feedback
2. Client relationships
3. New learning
4. Control over method
5. Control over scheduling
6. Unique experience
7. Control over resources
8. Direct communication authority
9. Personal accountability

Consequences

Increased job satisfaction and productivity

140

1. *Direct feedback.* Employees should receive immediate evaluation of their work. Feedback can be built into the job (such as the feedback that closing a sale gives a sales representative) or provided by the manager.

2. *Client relationships.* A job is automatically enriched when a worker has a client or customer to serve, whether that client is internal or external. Serving a client is more satisfying to most people than performing work solely for a manager. An information systems specialist at a bank who interacts with loan officers is said to have a client relationship. However, interacting with hostile and verbally abusive customers is demotivational and stressful rather than enriching.

3. *New learning.* An enriched job allows its holder to acquire new knowledge. The learning can stem from job experiences themselves or from training programs associated with the job.

4. *Control over method.* When a worker has some control over which method to choose to accomplish a task, his or her task motivation generally increases. An office manager, for example, might be told to decrease energy costs in the building by 10%. She would have control over the method if empowered to decide *how* to decrease costs, such as adjusting the thermostat or finding a lower-cost energy supplier.

5. *Control over scheduling.* The ability to schedule one's work contributes to job enrichment. Scheduling includes the authority to decide when to tackle which assignments and having some say in setting working hours, such as flexible working hours.

6. *Unique experience.* An enriched job has unique qualities or features. A public relations assistant, for example, has the opportunity to interact with visiting celebrities.

7. *Control over resources.* Another contributor to enrichment is the ability to have some control over resources, such as money, material, or people.

8. *Direct communication authority.* An enriched job provides workers the opportunity to communicate directly with other people who use their output. A software engineer with an enriched job, for example, handles complaints about the software she developed. The advantages of this dimension of an enriched job are similar to those derived from maintaining client relationships.

9. *Personal accountability.* In an enriched job, workers are responsible for their results. They accept credit for a job well done and blame for a job done poorly.

A highly enriched job has all nine of the preceding characteristics and gives the job holder an opportunity to satisfy growth needs such as self-fulfillment. A job with some of these characteristics would be moderately enriched. An impoverished job has none.

Empowerment and Involvement as a Type of Job Enrichment

A managerial practice that leads to job enrichment is to empower employees, as implied in characteristics 4, 5, and 7. **Empowerment** is the process of sharing power with group members, thereby enhancing their feelings of self-efficacy. Empowering workers usually enhances their motivation because having more power is intrinsically motivating. Involving employees in decisions that affect them is a form of empowerment and is also motivational. Involvement leads to greater commitment, and therefore facilitates making possible a change such as a new work method.[3] An example of empowerment and involvement follows:

> A construction company received a huge contract to rebuild a hotel in downtown New Orleans, 1 month after Hurricane Katrina struck. The project manager assigned the task said that it would be almost impossible to get the project completed on time because of the shortage of laborers and skilled workers in the Gulf Coast area. The project manager was then told by a company executive, "This job is your baby. If it were easy to accomplish, we would not have given you the assignment. Do whatever it takes to find the people you need to put the hotel back in shape. Spend all the money you want so long as we make a profit."
>
> The project manager wound up renting a fleet of recreational vehicles that served as temporary housing for the project. Workers were recruited from as far north as Wisconsin and Vermont, in addition to whatever workers were available locally. The hotel opened on time for a key convention.

Before implementing a program of job enrichment, a manager must ask if the workers need or want more responsibility, variety, and growth in the first place. Some employees' jobs are already enriched enough. Other employees do not want an enriched job because they prefer to avoid the challenge and stress of responsibility. A study conducted in a government service organization indicated that employees with a strong need for growth were more likely to respond to an opportunity for performing enriched work. The independent variable studied was the manager offering a case-processing specialist the opportunity to collaborate with him or her on a case.[4]

The Job Characteristics Model

The concept of job enrichment has been expanded to the **job characteristics model,** a method of job design that focuses on the task and interpersonal demands of a job.[5] The model is based on both needs theory and expectancy theory, with its emphasis on workers looking to satisfy needs through the job. To illustrate, a basic proposition of the model is that workers value outcomes to the extent that the outcomes can help satisfy their deficiency and growth needs. As Exhibit 7-2 shows, five measurable characteristics of a job can improve employee motivation, satisfaction, and performance. These characteristics are:

1. *Skill variety,* the degree to which there are many skills to perform
2. *Task identity,* the degree to which one worker is able to do a complete job, from beginning to end, with a tangible and possible outcome
3. *Task significance,* the degree to which work has a heavy impact on others in the immediate organization or the external environment
4. *Autonomy,* the degree to which a job offers freedom, independence, and discretion in scheduling and in determining procedures involved in its implementation
5. *Feedback,* the degree to which a job provides direct information about performance

As indicated in Exhibit 7-2, these core job characteristics relate to critical psychological states or key mental attitudes. Skill variety, task identity, and task significance

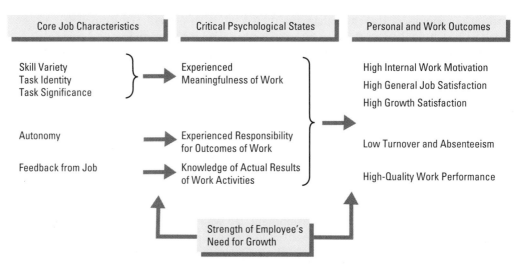

Source: J. R. Hackman and G. R. Oldham, *Work Redesign* (Reading, MA: Addison-Wesley, 1980), p. 77.

142

Exhibit 7-2

*The Job Characteristics
Model of Job Enrichment*

lead to a feeling that the work is meaningful. The task dimension of autonomy leads logically to a feeling that one is responsible for work outcomes. The feedback dimension leads to knowledge of results. According to the model, a redesigned job must lead to these three psychological states for workers to achieve the outcomes of internal motivation, job satisfaction, growth satisfaction, low turnover and absenteeism, and high-quality performance.

The task significance characteristic can be a potent motivator at all job levels. Donald Schneider, the owner and president of a major trucking firm, motivates truckers in this way: "I help them see that everything they do in their jobs contributes to America's economy. I'm always telling them that every idea or action they take to lower our logistics costs lowers the price of products we deliver."[6]

The job characteristics model combines the five characteristics into a single index that reflects the overall potential of a job to trigger high internal work motivation. Called the Motivating Potential Score (MPS), the index is computed as follows:

$$\text{MPS} = \frac{\overset{\text{Skill}}{\text{Variety}} + \overset{\text{Task}}{\text{Identity}} + \overset{\text{Task}}{\text{Significance}}}{3} \times \text{Autonomy} \times \text{Feedback}$$

Numeric values for each of the five job characteristics are obtained by tabulating the job holder's answers to the Job Diagnostic Survey, a written questionnaire. After computing the MPS, a researcher can evaluate whether redesigning a job actually changed employees' perceptions of its motivational value.

A potential problem in implementing the job characteristics model, as well as job enrichment in general, is that supervisors and group members may not agree on what constitutes an enriched job. A study conducted in a university office setting with a variety of jobs found that supervisors and subordinates perceived their job characteristics differently. (The dimensions studied were the same as those contained in the job characteristics model.)

The most notable difference was found for task significance, with the supervisors rating this dimension higher than group members did. A possible interpretation was that the supervisors had a clearer view of the "big picture," and thereby had a better understanding of the potential impact of a task. Another finding was that the group members perceived the enriched quality to have a bigger impact on job outcomes than did the supervisor's level. Your perception of task significance has a bigger impact on your satisfaction and motivation than your supervisor's perception of the same factor. An implication of these findings is that employees should play a major role in job redesign, since their perceptions of enrichment differ from their supervisors' perceptions.[7]

Job Crafting

The traditional view of a job is that a competent worker carefully follows a job description, and good performance means that the person accomplishes what is specified in the job description. A contemporary view is that a job description is only a guideline: The competent worker is not confined by the constraints of a job description. He or she takes on many constructive activities not mentioned in the job description.

One way workers frequently deviate from their job descriptions is to modify their job to fit their personal preferences and capabilities. According to the research of Amy Wrzesniewski and Jane E. Dutton, employees craft their jobs by changing the tasks they perform, and their contacts with others, to make their jobs more meaningful.[8] To add variety to his job, for example, a team leader might make nutritional recommendations to team members. The team leader has altered his task of coaching about strictly work-related issues to also coaching about personal health. He has also broadened his role in terms of his impact on the lives of work associates.

Job crafting refers to the physical and mental changes workers make in the task or relationship aspects of their job. Three common types of job crafting involve changing (1) the number and type of job tasks, (2) the interaction with others on the job, and (3) one's view of the job. The most frequent purpose of crafting is to make the job more meaningful or enriched. A cook, for example, might add a touch of decorative food to a meal just to inject a little personal creativity. Exhibit 7–3 illustrates these three forms of job crafting, including how crafting affects the meaning of work. After studying the exhibit, think through whether you have ever engaged in job crafting.

143

Exhibit 7-3

Forms of Job Crafting

Form	Example	Effect on Meaning of Work
Changing number, scope, and type of job tasks	Design engineers engage in changing the quality or amount of interactions with people, thereby moving a project to completion	Work is completed in a more timely fashion; engineers change the meaning of their jobs to be guardians or movers of projects
Changing quality and/or amount of interaction with others encountered in the job	Hospital cleaners actively caring for patients and families, integrating themselves into the workflow of their floor units	Cleaners change the meaning of their jobs to be helpers of the sick; see the work of the floor unit as an integrated whole of which they are a vital part
Changing the view of the job	Nurses taking responsibility for all information and "insignificant" tasks that may help them to care more appropriately for a patient	Nurses change the way they see the work to be more about patient advocacy, as well as high-quality technical care

Source: Adapted with permission from the Academy of Management Review from Amy Wrzesniewski and Jane E. Dutton, "Crafting a Job: Revisioning Employees as Active Crafters of Their Work," *Academy of Management Review*, April 2001, p. 185. Permission conveyed through the Copyright Clearance Center, Inc.

ORGANIZATIONAL BEHAVIOR MODIFICATION

Summarize the basics of a behavior-modification program in the workplace.

One of the more elaborate systems for motivating employees is based on reinforcement theory. **Organizational behavior modification (OB Mod)** is the application of reinforcement theory for motivating people in work settings. OB Mod programs typically use positive reinforcement rather than punishment to modify behavior. Linking behavior with positive consequences is more effective than using negative motivators, and positive consequences arouse less controversy. Tom Osbourne (R-Nebr.), former national championship–winning football coach at the University of Nebraska—and also an educational psychologist—says that rewards shape behavior better than punishment. He believes that his emphasis on positive motivators contributed to his winning attitude and dedication.[9] Here we present a framework for a formal OB Mod program, followed by suggestions for everyday managerial application of behavior modification.

Steps in a Formal OB Mod Program

As outlined in Exhibit 7-4, the OB Mod program begins with identifying behaviors that require change.[10] For example, the regional manager of a chain of convenience stores might believe strongly that cashiers should always ask "What else can I get for you?" before a customer pays. Market research has shown that this statement enhances sales. The behavior that needs to change is that the cashiers are not asking this question frequently enough.

The second step is for the manager to measure baseline performance; for example, how frequently cashiers ask the sales–inducing question. The behavior is stated in terms of a percentage frequency for various intervals. Store observers assigned by the regional manager might find, for example, that cashiers ask "What else can I get you?" only about 20% of the time.

Step 3 is to analyze the behavioral antecedents and contingent consequences in the performance-related context (analyzing the functional consequences). This analysis attempts to answer two questions: (1) What are the antecedents of the performance-related behavior measured in the first two steps?, and (2) What are the contingent consequences when workers make the desired response? Antecedents can include many factors, such as equipment, technological processes, job design, and/or performance training. However, here we are concerned with antecedents that set the occasion for the behavior to occur—a customer bringing goods to the counter.

The contingent consequences are the outcomes that stem from the behavior. The behavior is what the cashier does (asking the question). Consequences are the outcomes that stem from the behavior, such as the customer saying, "Yes, please get me six Beef Jerkies." A more general consequence would be that sales increase an average of $4.00 per customer when the cashier asks, "What else can I get for you?"

Next, the manager decides on an intervention strategy appropriate to the situation. Environmental variables affecting the linkage between reward and behavior include the nature of the industry, structure, size, processes, and technology. For example, the information technology built into the cash registers will influence how easy it is to record sales above baseline. The manager is now ready to apply an appropriate contingency strategy.

Positive reinforcement is applied to increase functional behaviors and decrease dysfunctional behaviors. Punishment of dysfunctional behaviors might also be used

Log on to **www.thomsonedu.com/infotrac**. Search for articles on online retailers (such as Amazon.com, Overstock.com, Bluefly.com, etc.) and compare them to shopping in a standard brick and mortar store. What do you like about the online experience? Dislike? Are online retailers adequately equipped to listen to their customer needs and feedback?

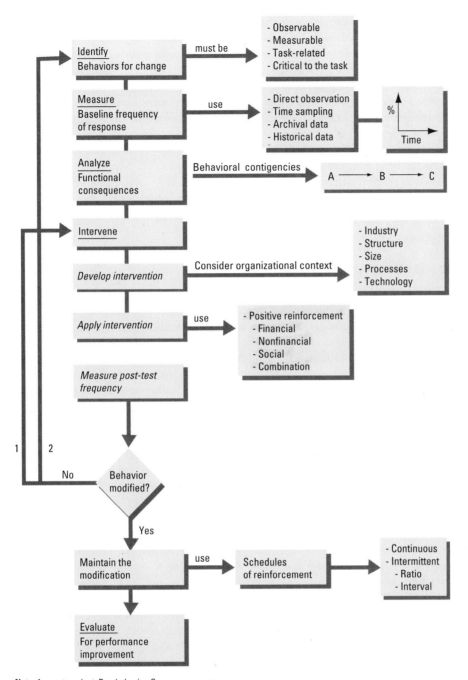

Exhibit **7-4**

OB Mod Application Model

145

Note: A = antecedent, B = behavior, C = consequences

Source: Reprinted with permission of the Academy of Management Review from Fred Luthans and Alexander D. Stajkovic, "Reinforce for Performance: The Need to Go Beyond Pay and Even Rewards," *Academy of Management Executive*, May 1999, p. 53.

as a last resort. Punishment, however, is followed by positive reinforcement as the worker improves.

After intervening, the manager measures performance again to assess whether the desired effect—asking the sales-inducing question frequently—has been achieved. If the appropriate behavior does not occur frequently, the manager must choose a new intervention strategy or repeat the entire process.

If performance increases as planned, the manager must maintain the desirable behavior through a schedule of reinforcement. Under a continuous schedule, the cashier receives a reward each time a customer responds positively to the question. An intermittent schedule offers rewards from time to time. (A ratio schedule gives the reward on a ratio, such as one reward per six right responses; an interval schedule gives the reward based on the amount of time between the right responses.) The cashier might receive continuous reinforcement in terms of earning a small commission on every sale. The fact that customers will not always respond "Yes" to the key question creates an intermittent schedule.

The last step answers the question of whether the OB Mod program leads to performance improvement in observable and measurable terms. The manager looks for improvements in the employee's behavior. A store observer might monitor how often the key question is asked; receipts might provide an index of change in sales volume.

Identify rules and suggestions for motivating group members through behavior modification.

146

Rules for the Application of OB Mod

Principles of behavior modification can also be applied outside a structured company program. Our focus here is on managers' day-to-day application of OB Mod, with an emphasis on positive reinforcement. An individual contributor attempting to motivate somebody else can also apply these rules. Following these eight rules increases the probability that an OB Mod program will achieve its intended result of increasing the motivation and productivity of individuals and groups. Although the rules have generally been developed with individuals, they also apply to rewarding group performance.

Rule 1: Choose an appropriate reward or punishment. An appropriate reward or punishment is effective in motivating a worker or group and is feasible from the company standpoint. Rewards should have a high positive attraction and punishments a negative one. (Attraction is the same idea as valence.) If one reward does not work, another should be tried. Some rewards are ineffective because the worker does not want the reward, such as giving tickets to a football game to a worker who dislikes football. Feasible rewards include money, company stock, recognition, challenging new assignments, and status symbols such as a private work area. Several years ago, top management at Procter & Gamble rewarded employees with two extra days of vacation, or two days' pay, because the company stock rose for four consecutive years. The attempt here was to recognize the contribution of all 98,000 employees at once.[11]

Often the most basic type of reward, such as an expression of appreciation, has the strongest effect in achieving higher productivity and employee retention.[12] It is generally best to use the mildest form of punishment that will motivate the person, such as verbally expressing disappointment. Although widely used, fear is a generally ineffective form of punishment because it may cause resentment, revenge, and a degree of immobilization.

Exhibit 7-5 presents some rewards of high valence as inferred from job satisfaction and retention factors preferred by employees. The inference is that if a given job factor (such as good compensation) will both satisfy an employee and encourage him or her to stay with the firm, that same factor will prompt the employee to work harder. In some instances this is not true, such as a given worker wanting high pay for little effort.

Rule 2: Reinforce the behaviors you really want to encourage. An axiom of behavior modification is that you get what you reinforce. If you give rewards to customer service representatives based on the number of requests for help they process, you will

2004 Job Satisfaction Survey (Top 10 of 21 Factors)	2005 Spherion Survey of Retention Factors (All Eight Factors Listed)	Exhibit **7-5**

2004 Job Satisfaction Survey
(Top 10 of 21 Factors)

1. Benefits
2. Compensation/pay
3. Feeling safe in work environment
4. Job security
5. Flexibility to balance work–life issues
6. Communication between employees and senior management
7. Relationship with immediate supervisor
8. Management recognition of employee performance
9. Opportunities to use skills/abilities
10. The work itself

2005 Spherion Survey
of Retention Factors
(All Eight Factors Listed)

1. Financial compensation
2. Benefits
3. Growth and earning potential
4. Time and flexibility
5. Management climate
6. Supervisor relationship
7. Culture and work environment
8. Training and development

Exhibit **7-5**

Potentially Effective Rewards Based on Employee Perception of Job Satisfaction and Retention Factors

Note: Observe that the 10 factors from the *2004 Job Satisfaction Survey* were also presented in the study of employee attitudes in Chapter 4.

Source: Synthesis of data from *2004 Job Satisfaction Survey* reported in "Views from Both Sides," *HR Magazine*, April 2005, p. 53; *Spherion Emerging Workforce Study*, http://www.spherion.com/press/releases/2005/Emerging_Workforce.jsp.

147

increase the number of calls. Customer service may not improve, however, because the representatives will feel compelled to process the calls for help quickly. Rewards for resolving customer problems have a greater probability of enhancing customer service. (It takes time and patience to resolve some problems received at a call center.)

Rule 3: Supply ample feedback. OB Mod tactics cannot work without frequent feedback to individuals. Feedback can take the form of simply telling people they have done something right or wrong. Brief e-mail messages or handwritten notes are another common form of feedback. Be aware, however, that many employees resent seeing a message with negative feedback on their computer monitor.

Rule 4: Rewards should be commensurate with the good deed. Average performance is encouraged when all forms of accomplishment receive the same reward. Suppose one employee made substantial progress in reducing customer complaints. She should receive more recognition (or a more valuable reward) than a group member who makes only a minor contribution to solving the problem.

Rule 5: Schedule rewards intermittently. Intermittent rewards sustain desired behavior longer and slow the process of desired behavior fading away when it is not rewarded. A reward that is given continuously may lose its impact. A practical value of intermittent reinforcement is that it saves time. Few managers have enough time to administer rewards for every appropriate response forthcoming from group members.

Rule 6: Rewards and punishments should follow the observed behavior closely in time. For maximum effectiveness, workers should be rewarded shortly after doing something right and punished shortly after doing something wrong. A built-in feedback system, such as software working or not working, capitalizes on this principle. If you administer rewards and punishments, strive to administer them the same day they are earned.

Rule 7: Make rewards visible to the recipient and to others. The person who receives the reward should be aware that it has been received. A person might receive a small bonus for good performance with the payment being virtually hidden in the paycheck. Because the reward is not noticed, it has a negligible impact on behavior.[13] Ideally, rewards should also be made visible to employees other than the recipient.

Rewards that are made public increase the status of the recipient and let other employees know what kinds of behavior get rewarded.

Rule 8: Change the reward periodically. Rewards do not retain their effectiveness indefinitely. A major criticism of positive reinforcement as a motivational technique is that rewards go stale. Employees and customers lose interest in striving for a reward they have received many times previously. This is particularly true with a repetitive statement such as "Nice job" or "Fantastic." It is helpful for the manager to formulate a list of feasible rewards and try different ones from time to time.

Now do the accompanying skill-development exercise to practice several of these rules for using behavior modification.

Behavior modification has a long history of improving productivity on the job. Fred Luthans and Alexander D. Stajkovic performed a meta-analysis of all the empirical findings of research conducted with the OB Mod method over a 20-year period. The study indicated a substantial 17% average improvement in performance. The overall improvement in manufacturing settings was 33%, and was 13% in service settings. Another notable finding was that social reinforcers such as recognition and positive feedback were as effective as monetary rewards.[14]

The same researchers conducted an experiment in the operations division of a company that processes and mails credit card bills for several hundred financial institutions, e-commerce customers included. The four reward groups in the study were (1) routine pay for performance; (2) monetary incentives based on behavior mod; (3) social recognition, such as public compliments; and (4) performance feedback. Monetary rewards based on the principles of behavior modification outperformed routine pay for performance, with a performance increase of 37% versus 11%. Behavior mod also had stronger effects on performance than social recognition and performance feedback.[15] Evidence like this is reassuring to the leader/manager who intends to apply behavior modification in the workplace.

SKILL-DEVELOPMENT EXERCISE

Organizational Behavior Modification

In both of the following scenarios, one student plays the role of the manager attempting to modify the behavior of, or motivate, the other individual. Another student plays the role of the recipient of these attempts at motivation.

Scenario 1: Rewarding a Debt-Collection Representative. The consumer debt manager reviews debt-collection reports and discovers that one debt-collection representative has collected the most money on overdue accounts for four consecutive weeks. Since this debt-collection representative has only been on the job for 6 months, the manager wants to ensure that the rep feels amply rewarded and appreciated. The manager also wants to sustain this high level of performance. The manager calls the debt-collection rep into the office to discuss this outstanding performance and administer an appropriate reward.

Scenario 2: Punishing a Debt-Collection Representative. The consumer debt manager reviews debt-collection reports and discovers that one debt-collection rep has resolved the fewest accounts for four consecutive weeks. Furthermore, three debtors have written the company complaining of rude treatment by this representative. Since this rep has only been on the job 6 months, the manager wants to make sure that the rep makes substantial improvements. The manager calls the rep into the office to discuss this poor performance and administer an appropriate punishment.

Others in the class should observe the two scenarios so they can provide feedback on how well OB Mod principles were applied.

Collaboration

MOTIVATION THROUGH RECOGNITION AND PRIDE

Motivating workers by giving them praise and recognition can be considered a direct application of positive reinforcement. Nevertheless, recognition is such a potentially powerful motivator that it merits separate attention. Also, reward and recognition programs are a standard practice in business and nonprofit firms. An example would be rewarding high-performing employees with electronic gift cards or designating them "employees of the month." A reward and recognition program essentially focuses on rewards as a form of recognition. The gift card just mentioned might have a commercial value of $100, but its main value is to recognize a job well done. Pride is a motive that makes recognition an effective motivator.

Explain why recognition and pride are good motivators, and discuss the nature of reward and recognition programs in the workplace.

Recognition as a Motivator

Recognition is a strong motivator because it is a normal human need to crave recognition. At the same time, recognition is effective because most workers feel they do not receive enough recognition. Several studies conducted over a 60-year time span indicate that employees welcome praise for a job well done as much as a regular paycheck. This finding should not be interpreted to mean that praise is an adequate substitute for compensation. Employees tend to regard compensation as an entitlement, whereas recognition is perceived as a gift.[16] Workers, including your coworkers, want to know that their output is useful to somebody.

To appeal to the recognition need of others, identify a meritorious behavior and then recognize that behavior with an oral, written, or material reward. The rules for the use of behavior modification are directly applicable. An example of employee recognition is as follows. As the team leader of a production unit, you observe that Janice, one of the manufacturing technicians, has the best safety record in the plant—zero accidents in 5 years. You send an e-mail message notifying every company employee of Janice's accomplishment.

An outstanding advantage of using recognition, including praise, as a motivator is that a person can give it with little or no cost, yet it can still be powerful. Recognition thus has an enormous return on investment in comparison to a cash bonus. The following are several more points to consider to better understand and implement reward and recognition programs:

1. *Feedback is an essential part of recognition.* Specific feedback about what the worker did right makes recognition more meaningful. For example, "The clever cartoon you inserted on our website increased sales by 22% for replacement keyboards."
2. *Praise is one of the most powerful forms of recognition.* Praise works well because it enhances self-esteem if the praise is genuine. As indicated previously, praise is a supplement to other rewards, such as compensation. A challenge in using praise as a form of recognition is that not everybody responds well to the same form of praise. A germane example is that highly technical people tend not to like general praise like "Great job." Instead, they prefer a laid-back yet factual statement about how their output made a contribution.[17]
3. *Reward and recognition programs should be linked to organizational goals.* Many organizations understand that the biggest return on reward and recognition programs takes place when the rewards and recognition are linked to a business strategy.[18] For example, if the company strategy is to develop a more culturally diverse workforce at all levels, an employee should be recognized for recruiting a Latino computer scientist.

4. *Employee input into what type of rewards and recognition are valued is useful.* A company might spend a lot of money giving away grandfather clocks to employees, only to find that they would prefer gift certificates to movies as a form of reward and recognition. Many employees enjoy having a meal with coworkers to celebrate accomplishments while at the same time building team spirit.[19] Yet here also individual differences are important. Some workers do not want to take time away from family responsibilities or social activities to participate in an after-hours meal. Cross-cultural factors can have a strong impact on what form of reward or recognition is motivational. In China, for example, a clock can backfire as a recognition symbol because the word for clock can suggest funeral or death. Instead of being a symbol of appreciation for good service, the clock's message could be interpreted as "Drop dead."[20]

5. *It is important to evaluate the effectiveness of the reward and recognition program.* As with all organizational behavior and human resources interventions, it is useful to assess how well the reward and recognition program is working. For example, the company could establish baseline measures of performance, administer the reward and recognition program, and then measure performance again. (Review the section about research methods on page 3 of Chapter 1.)

The accompanying Organizational Behavior in Action box illustrates one of the most basic forms of recognition a manager might use.

ORGANIZATIONAL BEHAVIOR *In Action*

Bank Vice President Recognizes Employees on the Cheap

Stephanie Wheeler, senior vice president of Sovereign Bank, used to run the Philadelphia-based bank's 175-employee call center. A reporter for an executive newsletter asked Wheeler, "When have you spent your own money to motivate your employees, and did it pay off?" Wheeler replied:

"One of the best investments I ever made in that job was spending $5 on a book of motivational stickers at Wal-Mart. The book came with 1252 bright, colorful stickers with messages like 'Dynamite!' 'Going Above and Beyond' and 'Great Work!'

"I'd put a sticker on a slip of paper and write a short note alongside it that praised the employee for a specific job well done. At the end of the day after everyone left, I'd place these notes on employees' desks. The next morning, they'd find this handwritten message

from me with this eye-catching sticker, and it would make their day. Later, I'd see my notes pinned up on their wall or taped to the side of their PC. It showed me they were proud to receive them."

Questions

1. What evidence does Wheeler present that her notes and motivational stickers resulted in stronger worker motivation?
2. How effective do you think these notes and motivational stickers would be with professional-level corporate employees?
3. Is it possible that the notes accompanying the stickers that had a bigger impact on pride than the stickers themselves?

Source: "Never Underestimate Cheap Motivation Tricks," *Executive Leadership,* September 2003, p. 4.

Pride as a Motivator

Wanting to feel proud motivates many workers even if *pride* is not exactly a psychological need. Workers who are proud of their accomplishments are eager to receive recognition for what they have achieved. Striving to experience the emotion of pride most likely stems from the desire to satisfy the needs for self-esteem and self-fulfillment. Being proud of what you accomplish is more of an intrinsic motivator than an extrinsic motivator such as receiving a gift. Giving workers an opportunity to experience pride can therefore be a strong internal motivator.

> Imagine that you are the assistant service manager at a company that customizes corporate jets to meet the requirements of individual clients. Your manager asks you to prepare a PowerPoint presentation of trends in equipment problems. You make your presentation to top management, the group applauds, executives shake your hand, and later you receive several congratulatory e-mail messages. One of the many emotions you experience is likely to be pride in having performed well. You are motivated to keep up the good work.

Workers can also experience pride in relation to recognition awards. For example, a worker might receive a crystal vase for having saved the company thousands of dollars in shipping costs. The vase might be more valuable to the worker as recognition for accomplishment than as a household decoration. The feeling of pride stems from having accomplished a worthwhile activity (saving the company money) rather than from being awarded a vase.

According to consultant Jon R. Katzenbach, managers can take steps to motivate through pride. A key tactic is for the manager to set his or her compass on pride, not money. It is more important for workers to be proud of what they are doing day by day than for them to be proud of reaching a major goal. The manager should celebrate "steps" (or attaining small goals) as much as the "landings" (the major goal). The most effective pride builders are masters at identifying and recognizing the small achievements that will instill pride in their people.[21]

MOTIVATION THROUGH FINANCIAL INCENTIVES

A natural reinforcer for workers at any level is to offer them financial incentives for good performance. As was shown in Exhibit 7-4, compensation is a major issue for modern workers. Using financial incentives as a motivator is another application of behavior modification. Financial incentives, however, predate behavior modification in the workplace and are an application of common sense. The following sections describe four issues about the extensive subject of money as a reinforcer: linking pay to performance, employee stock ownership and options, gainsharing, and problems associated with financial incentives.

Describe how to use financial incentives effectively to motivate others, including the use of employee stock ownership plans, stock options, and gainsharing.

Linking Pay to Performance

Financial incentives are usually more effective when they are linked to (or contingent upon) good performance. Linking pay to performance generally motivates people to work harder because the link acts as a reinforcer. The recommended approach is to tie employee pay to specific performance criteria and link it directly to value-enhancing business results.[22] The variable pay must be earned again each year and does not permanently increase base salary.

A representative example of variable pay is the system at MetLife. The company measures performance of employees and managers by comparing each person to others who are on the same level. Performance is measured on a 1-to-5 scale. The company then calculates which employees are categorized as top, middle, or bottom. Employees in the top category receive about 65% more in bonuses than those in the middle. Employees in the bottom category might receive no bonus.[23] Giving poor performers no salary increase leaves more money in the merit pool to pay to top performers. At the same time, the company that gives no raise for poor results sends a message about the importance of good performance.[24] Clothing retailer Eddie Bauer rewards store associates with an additional 6.5% of their base pay if store goals are met. The company has found that this policy improves retention, and perhaps motivation.[25]

Pay for performance is not based on achieving financial goals exclusively. Other performances factors might include providing good customer service, on-time delivery, ratings from client-satisfaction surveys, being a good team player, and sharing knowledge with other workers. Merit (or variable) pay for both individuals and the team is based on actual results. Merit pay runs from 5% to over 15% of total compensation.

Although many employers believe they link pay to performance, research suggests that merit pay may not be so closely linked to performance. A team of researchers meta-analyzed the results of 39 studies about the relationship between pay and performance. A striking conclusion was that pay had little relationship to the quality of work, but did show a moderately positive relationship with the *quantity* of work. However, managers are not completely to blame. It is often easier to measure how much work employees are performing than how well they are performing. The meta-analysis in question also confirms the obvious: People will produce more work when money is at stake.[26]

Employee Stock Ownership and Stock Options

A widely used method of motivating workers through financial means is to make them part owners of the business through stock purchases. Two variations of the same idea of giving workers equity in the business are stock ownership and stock option plans. Stock ownership can be motivational because employees participate in the financial success of the firm as measured by its stock price. If employees work hard, the company may become more successful and the value of the stock may increase.

Under an employee stock ownership plan (ESOP), employees at all levels in the organization are given stock. The employer either contributes shares of its stock or the money to purchase stock in the open market. Stock shares are usually deposited in employee retirement accounts. Upon retirement, employees can choose to receive company stock instead of cash. Employee stock ownership plans are popular because they are easy to understand, and they contribute to an ownership culture. However, an employee who invests too heavily in company stock may neglect other investments and lack a diversified portfolio.

Employee stock options are more complicated than straightforward stock ownership. **Stock options** give employees the right to purchase a certain number of company shares in the future at a specified price, generally the market price on the day the option is granted. If the stock rises in value, you can purchase it at a discount. If the stock sinks below your designated purchase price, your option is worthless (or "under water"). Exhibit 7-6 shows the mathematics behind a stock option. Stock options also have other goals related to organizational effectiveness, including

Exhibit **7-6**

*How a Stock Option
Works*

*Employee decides to exercise option for 400 shares at $10.57 each when stock reaches
$35 per share.*

Brokerage sells 400 shares of company stock at $35 each (400 shares × $35)	=	$14,000
Brokerage deducts exercise price (400 shares × $10.57)		−4,228
		9,772
Taxes withheld (28% for federal income tax + 7.56% for social security tax)		−3,475
		$6,297
Brokerage deducts fees/commissions/interest		−100
		$6,197
Brokerage pays profit to employee		$6,197

Source: Carrington Nelson, "Exercising Your Stock Options," *Gannett News Service*, 26 July 1998. Copyright 1998, Gannett Co.,
Inc. Reprinted with permission.

attracting and retaining talent, focusing employee attention on organizational performance, and creating a culture of ownership.[27]

A major potential problem with stock options as a motivational tool is that they
become worthless if a stock plunges, because the employee is left with the option to
purchase stock at above the market value! However, some companies attempt to
compensate for fallen stock price by increasing cash compensation or granting additional options at a more favorable price. The employee suffers from disappointed
expectations, and the company looks foolish. Another serious potential source of dissatisfaction with stock options is the tax owed on the gains at the time the employee
exercises the option. If you hold the stock and the price plunges, you pay taxes on
paper profits—an extreme punishment instead of an anticipated reward.

Gainsharing

Many organizations attempt to increase motivation and productivity through a
company-wide bonus plan of linking incentive pay to increases in performance.
Gainsharing is a formal program of allowing employees to participate financially in
the productivity gains they have achieved. Gainsharing Inc. is the institute that helps
promote this motivational method. Gainsharing is based on principles of positive
reinforcement and the motivational impact of money.

The formulas used in gainsharing vary widely, but there are common elements.
Managers begin by comparing what the employees are paid to what they sell or produce. Assume that labor costs make up 50% of production costs. Any reduction below
50% is placed in a bonus pool. The company's share of productivity savings in the pool
can then be distributed to stockholders as increased profits. The savings may allow
managers to lower prices, a move that could make the company more competitive.

The second element of gainsharing is employee involvement. Managers establish a mechanism that actively solicits, reviews, and implements employee suggestions about productivity improvement. A committee of managers and employees
reviews the ideas and then implements the most promising suggestions.[28]

Gainsharing plans have a 67-year history of turning unproductive companies
around and making successful companies even more productive. Gainsharing Inc.
contends that most companies will achieve an increase in their productive output of
10 to 30% within 30 to 90 days after implementing gainsharing. The reason is that it
becomes in the employees' self-interest to maximize company output.[29] Gainsharing

programs began in manufacturing but are also used widely in service firms, such as financial services.

The much-publicized Lincoln Electric gainsharing plan rewards workers for producing high-quality products efficiently while controlling costs. All employees receive a base salary, and production workers also receive piecework pay (money in relation to units produced). A year-end bonus supplements the piecework pay based on increases in profits. Bonus payments are determined by merit ratings based on output, quality, dependability, and personal characteristics (such as cooperativeness).

The Gainsharing Inc. website (http://www.gainsharing.com) points to these four key advantages of this profit-sharing method:

- A dramatic increase in productive capacity, in record time. Most companies will achieve a productivity gain of 10 to 30% within 30 to 90 days after implementing gainsharing.
- The program achieves employee buy-in because employees know exactly what benefit they will gain from performance improvement.
- Employees learn more about business fundamentals. Gainsharing programs illustrate how the different elements in a company must work together to achieve the performance on which bonuses are based.
- Unnecessary overtime is reduced. Because pay is based more on performance than on number of hours worked, employees find ways to get their work accomplished with a minimum of overtime.

Problems Associated with Financial Incentives

Although financial incentives are widely used as motivators, they can create problems. For example, workers may not agree with managers about the value of their contributions. Financial incentives can also pit individuals and groups against each other. The result may be unhealthy competition rather than cooperation and teamwork. A problem noted with pay for performance is that the method typically rewards immediate, short-term actions. Sales representatives may receive bonuses based on the number of contracts they close, but not bonuses for suggesting new products based on customers' changing needs. Also, if employees focus on immediate results to earn bonuses, they will sometimes not invest effort in working on long-range ideas and exploratory tasks that could lead to innovation.[30] When a company moves too much of compensation into variable pay, many workers will feel more insecure about money. They might worry, for example, if they will earn enough to meet all their expenses.[31]

A major concern about pay-for-performance plans is that the ratings assigned to people (such as the high, medium, and low categories at MetLife) are too subjective. Another concern is that individual accomplishment is difficult to measure because most of a worker's contribution in an organization is partially attributed to the work of others or to the organizational system.

The most-researched argument against financial rewards is that they focus the attention of workers too much on rewards such as money or stocks. (This follows the logic of the opposition to extrinsic motivation in general.) In the process, the workers lose out on intrinsic rewards such as joy in accomplishment. Instead of being passionate about the work they are doing, people become overly concerned with the size of their reward. One argument is that external rewards do not create a lasting commitment. Instead, they create temporary compliance, such as working hard in the short run to earn a bonus. A frequent problem with merit pay systems is that a person who does not receive a merit increase one pay period often feels that he or she has been punished. Another argument against financial incentives is that the rewards manipulate people in the same manner as bribes.

In reality, workers at all levels want a combination of internal rewards and financial rewards, along with other external rewards such as praise. The ideal combination is to offer exciting (internally rewarding) work to people and simultaneously pay them enough money so they are not preoccupied with matters such as salary and bonuses. Money is the strongest motivator when people have financial problems. Another reality is that even if a firm offers exciting work, great benefits, and wonderful coworkers, it usually needs to offer financial incentives to attract quality workers.

CHOOSING AN APPROPRIATE MOTIVATIONAL MODEL

Choose an appropriate motivational model for a given situation.

In this and the previous chapter, 13 approaches to understanding and enhancing motivation have been presented. Although these approaches have different labels, most of them have elements in common. In quick review, the 13 approaches are (1) the needs hierarchy, (2) the two-factor theory, (3) the achievement–power–affiliation triad, (4) goal theory, (5) reinforcement theory, (6) expectancy theory, (7) equity theory, (8) social learning theory, (9) intrinsic versus extrinsic motivation, (10) job design, (11) organizational behavior modification, (12) recognition, and (13) financial incentives.

A fruitful approach to choosing an effective motivation theory or program for a given situation is for the manager (or other would-be motivator) to carefully diagnose the situation. Choose a motivational approach that best fits the deficiency or neglected opportunity in a given situation. Observe the people that need motivation, and also interview them about their interests and concerns. Then apply a motivational approach that appears to match the interests, concerns, deficits, or missed opportunity. Four examples will help clarify the diagnostic approach:

1. The manager observes that group members perform their jobs well enough to meet standards, but they are not excited about their work. Introducing job enrichment and intrinsic motivation could be just what the organizational behavior specialist ordered.
2. The manager observes that group members appear interested in their work and that they like the company and their coworkers. Yet they spend too much time grumbling about personal financial problems. The most direct approach to enhancing motivation in this situation would be to introduce a program of financial incentives. To be effective, the financial payouts should be large enough to make a difference in the financial welfare of the workers.
3. The manager attempts to use recognition to motivate workers at different occupational levels. He or she should choose recognition methods that are likely to have the highest valence for the particular level of worker. Symbolic forms of recognition such as company hats, ties, and desk clocks are likely to have the highest valence for people at lower occupational levels, such as clerical and production workers. Professional-level workers are likely to be more motivated by written forms of recognition, including letters added to their personal files documenting their contributions.
4. The manager attempts to motivate members of the contingent workforce such as temporary workers and part-time workers. Recognizing these workers' needs for security, company benefits might prove to have high valence, since many contingent workers lack a good benefits package.

155

IMPLICATIONS FOR MANAGERIAL PRACTICE

1. Although motivation through job design is complex, time consuming, and expensive, it must be given careful consideration in any strategic attempt to enhance motivation and productivity. This is especially true because so many newcomers to the professional workforce seek to grow and develop on the job.

2. A helpful starting point in motivating workers is to ask them to describe in writing what they think would be effective motivators for them, including rewards and type of work. Recognize, however, that not everybody is aware of his or her true motivators. Some workers, for example, will say that the opportunity to make a difference is their biggest motivator, yet they respond better to token rewards such as a gift certificate. Observing what motivates workers should supplement the self-description of motivators.

3. Recognizing workers is an important motivational tool and is usually given only after a task or accomplishment is completed. In situations in which it takes a long time to complete a task or assignment, such as in selling a large commercial truck or developing a system, the worker or team might therefore go without recognition for a long time. A solution is to recognize these workers for progress toward the larger goal. These interim acts of recognition are likely to be motivational for the worker acting diligently to accomplish a long-term goal.[32]

4. No motivational program is a substitute for adequate compensation, including pay and benefits. One of the many reasons that money remains an all-important reinforcer is that most people have financial worries. One problem is that family income has not kept up with the high cost of housing, creating financial pressures for many wage earners.

SUMMARY OF KEY POINTS

 Explain how to enhance motivation through job enrichment, the job characteristics model, and job crafting.

A major strategy for enhancing motivation is to increase the challenge and responsibility in a job. An enriched, and therefore motivational, job includes some of the following characteristics: direct feedback, client relationships, new learning, control over method, control over scheduling, unique experience, control over resources, direct communication authority, and personal accountability. Empowerment is also a form of job enrichment. Job enrichment works best when workers want or need more responsibility, variety, and growth, which is not a given.

Job enrichment has been expanded to create the job characteristics model, which focuses on the task and interpersonal dimensions of a job. Five characteristics of a job can improve employee motivation, satisfaction, and performance: skill variety, task identity, task significance, autonomy, and feedback. These characteristics relate to critical psychological states, which in turn lead to outcomes such as internal motivation, satisfaction, low absenteeism, and high-quality performance.

Workers often enrich their own jobs by modifying their job descriptions themselves through crafting, or adapting their jobs in terms of (1) the number and types of tasks, (2) interactions with others, and (3) their view of the job.

 Summarize the basics of a behavior-modification program in the workplace.

Organizational behavior modification (OB Mod), an application of reinforcement theory, is an elaborate motivational system. A formal program includes steps such as identifying behavior-performance problems, developing a contingency intervention strategy, maintaining desirable behavior, and measuring improvement. OB Mod programs are well documented as a method of enhancing productivity in manufacturing and service settings. Social reinforcers work as well as financial ones.

 Identify rules and suggestions for motivating group members through behavior modification.

Behavior modification can also be applied outside of a formal program by the manager following these rules: Choose an appropriate reward or punishment, reinforce the behaviors you want to encourage, supply ample feedback, make rewards commensurate with the good deed, schedule rewards intermittently, give rewards and punishments promptly, make the rewards visible to the recipient and others, and change the reward periodically.

 Explain why recognition and pride are good motivators, and discuss the nature of reward and recognition programs in the workplace.

Recognition is a strong motivator because it is a normal human need to crave recognition; most workers feel they do not receive enough recognition. To appeal to the recognition need of others, identify a meritorious behavior and then recognize that behavior with an oral, a written, or a material reward. Praise is a powerful form of recognition. Reward and recognition programs should be linked to organizational goals. Employee input into what types of rewards and recognition are valued is useful. Wanting to feel proud motivates many workers, and workers who are proud of their accomplishments are eager to receive recognition for what they have achieved.

 Describe how to use financial incentives effectively to motivate others, including the use of stock options and gainsharing.

Financial incentives are a widely used motivator at all worker levels. Such incentives are more effective when they are linked to performance. Pay for performance is not based on achieving financial goals exclusively, and might include customer service and team player goals.

A widely used way of motivating workers with financial incentives is to make them part owners of the business through stock ownership. Under an employee stock ownership plan (ESOP) employees at all levels are given stock. Stock options give employees the right to purchase a certain number of company shares in the future at a specified price. If the stock price drops, the option is worthless.

Gainsharing is a formal program that enables employees to participate financially in the productivity gains they have achieved, thus enhancing motivation. Bonuses are distributed to employees based on how much they decrease the labor cost involved in producing or selling goods. Employee involvement in increasing productivity is an important part of gainsharing. Financial incentives can create problems such as poor cooperation and focusing too much attention on external rewards such as money or stocks. Instead of being passionate about the work they are doing, people become overly concerned with the size of the reward. In reality, workers at all levels want a combination of internal rewards and financial rewards, along with other external rewards, such as praise.

 Choose an appropriate motivational model for a given situation.

A fruitful approach to choosing an effective motivation theory or program for a given situation is for the manager to carefully diagnose the situation. A motivational approach is then chosen that best fits the deficiency or neglected opportunity in the situation. An example would be to understand that part-time workers might be strongly motivated by good benefits.

KEY TERMS AND PHRASES

Job Enrichment, 139
The process of making a job more motivational and satisfying by adding variety, responsibility, and managerial decision making.

Empowerment, 140
The process of sharing power with group members, thereby enhancing their feelings of self-efficacy.

Job Characteristics Model, 141
A method of job design that focuses on the task and interpersonal demands of a job.

Job Crafting, 143
The physical and mental changes workers make in the task or relationships aspects of their job.

Organizational Behavior Modification (OB Mod), 144
The application of reinforcement theory for motivating people in work settings.

Stock Option, 152
A financial incentive that gives employees the right to purchase a certain number of company shares at a specified price, generally the market price of the stock on the day the option is granted.

Gainsharing, 153
A formal program of allowing employees to participate financially in the productivity gains they have achieved.

157

DISCUSSION QUESTIONS AND ACTIVITIES

1. Give an example of how a technical support representative for an Internet service provider might *craft* his or her job.
2. Give your own example of how rewarding one type of work behavior might result in behavior that the company really does not want to occur.
3. In an effort to eliminate low-performing employees, some large companies fire the 5% of employees who receive the lowest performance evaluations each year. What might be the motivational impact of this method, called "rank and yank"?
4. Which of the motivational programs and methods described in this chapter do you think would be particularly useful in motivating convenience-store cashiers to perform at a high level?
5. What forms of recognition would be the most effective in motivating you? How do you know?
6. Why does gainsharing enhance cooperation rather than competition?
7. Ask a classmate whether he or she would prefer to take a new position that offered (a) below-average pay but some stock options, or (b) above-average pay but no stock options. What might the answer tell you about your classmate's personality?

CASE PROBLEM: We Need More Engagement around Here

Peggy Bates is the CEO of a regional HMO (health-maintenance organization) with 25 local offices serving business and nonprofit organizations. The competition for business has become more intense in recent years as organizations continue to look for ways to reduce costs for medical and dental insurance. A particular concern is that a given company might shift to another HMO if that health care provider can offer lower costs.

Bates expressed her concern at a meeting with the management staff, in these words: "I think our HMO could provide better service and lower costs if our employees put in more effort. A lot of the employees I have seen are so laid back, and almost indifferent. They don't seem to have a sense of urgency.

"I don't think that by simply downsizing the company we will reduce costs. Having fewer workers to accomplish our important work would just make things worse. We would get less work accomplished, and the quality would suffer."

After listening to Bates, Jerry Falcone, the vice president of marketing, commented: "Peggy, you might be right about some of our employees not being totally engaged in our efforts. Yet I cannot understand why. Taking care of people's health is one of the most important responsibilities in the world. I mean, we are often increasing life span as well as saving lives."

Melissa Mitchell, director of human resources, said: "Jerry, from your point of view, you are correct.

Health care is a noble undertaking. Yet when a person is seated at a keyboard and terminal for 8 hours processing claims, he or she might not feel like an angel of mercy.

"We can speculate all we want about how well our employees are engaged and motivated, and what we should do about the situation. I propose that we get some data to work with so we can learn more about the nature of the problem we are working with. I propose we hire a human resources consulting firm to conduct a survey about employee engagement. It could prove to be a good investment."

Bates said with a smile, "Here I am concerned about our costs being too high, and Melissa makes a suggestion for spending money."

Mitchell retorted, "Peggy, I am talking about *investing*, not spending, money. If we could boost our employee level of motivation 10%, we would get a tremendous return on investment."

Bates, Mitchell, and the rest of the executive team agreed to hire a firm to conduct the survey. Four months later, the survey was completed, and the results presented to management. The consultant, Ken Ho, focused on the data presented in the accompanying Exhibit as the key findings of the survey. He said, "Folks, here is the meat of the study. Let's discuss what calls for action are revealed by the data."

CASE PROBLEM (Continued)

Case Exhibit

Data from Employee Attitude Survey

Question	Percent Yes	Percent No
1. Do you know what is expected of you at work?	72	28
2. Do you have the opportunity to do what you do best every day?	55	45
3. Do you put your full effort into the job most days?	44	56
4. Do you think your immediate boss is doing a good job?	85	15
5. Do you expect to be working for this company for at least another 3 years?	34	66
6. Do you ever take work home with you (assuming you have the type of work that can be done off company premises)?	41	59
7. In the past year, have you had opportunities at work to learn and grow?	38	62
8. How satisfied are you with your compensation (salary and benefits combined)?	69	31

Note: 376 employees were polled, representing 89% of the workforce.

Source: Questions 1, 2, and 7 are from an employee attitude survey used by the Gallup Organization, Washington, DC.

Case Questions

1. How bad is employee motivation and engagement, as revealed by the Exhibit?
2. What actions can management take to increase motivation?
3. Should management focus on intrinsic, or extrinsic, motivators in attempting to enhance the motivation and engagement level of these HMO workers?

ENDNOTES

1. Quoted in Steve Bates, "Getting Engaged," *HR Magazine*, February 2004, p. 46.
2. Frederick Herzberg, "The Wise Old Turk," *Harvard Business Review*, September–October 1974, pp. 70–80; Nico W. Van Yperen and Mariët Hagedoom, "Do High Job Demands Increase Motivation or Fatigue or Both?: The Role of Job Control and Social Support," *Academy of Management Journal*, June 2003, pp. 339–348.
3. Bob Nelson, "The Power of the I's: No-Cost Ways to Motivate Employees," *Success in Recruiting and Retaining* (Mclean, VA: National Institute of Business Management, 2000).
4. George B. Graen, Terri A. Scandura, and Michael R. Graen, "A Field Experimental Test of the Moderating Effects of Growth Need Strength on Productivity," *Journal of Applied Psychology*, August 1986, pp. 484–491.
5. John Richard Hackman and Greg R. Oldham, *Work Redesign* (Reading, MA: Addison-Wesley, 1980).
6. "Driving toward Success," *Executive Leadership*, October 2002, p. 3.
7. Marc C. Marchese and Robert P. Delprino, "Do Supervisors and Subordinates See Eye-to-Eye on Job Enrichment?" *Journal of Business and Psychology*, Winter 1998, pp. 179–191.
8. Amy Wrzesniewski and Jane E. Dutton, "Crafting a Job: Revisioning Employees as Active Crafters of Their Work," *The Academy of Management Review*, April 2001, pp. 179–201.
9. Jennifer Daw, "Rep. Osborne is Given Award for Psychology in Management," *Monitor on Psychology*, May 2001, p. 12.
10. Fred Luthans and Alexander D. Stajkovic, "Reinforce for Performance: The Need to Go Beyond Pay and Even Rewards," *Academy of Management Executive*, May 1999, pp. 52–54.
11. Joe Mullich, "Giving Employees Something They Can't Buy with a Bonus Check," *Workforce Management*, July 2004, p. 66.
12. Gregory Smith, "Simple Rewards Are Powerful Motivators," *HRfocus*, August 2001, p. 10.
13. Stephen Kerr, "Practical, Cost-Neutral Alternatives that You May Know, but Don't Practice," *Organizational Dynamics*, Summer 1999, p. 65.
14. Luthans and Stajkovic, "Reinforce for Performance," pp. 54–55.
15. Alexander D. Stajkovic and Fred Luthans, "Differential Effects of Incentive Motivators on Work Performance," *Academy of Management Journal*, June 2001, pp. 580–590.
16. Jennifer Laabs, "Satisfy Them with More Than Money," *Workforce*, November 1998, p. 43; Smith, "Simple Rewards," p. 10.
17. Andrew J. DuBrin, "Self-Perceived Technical Orientation and Attitudes toward Being Flattered," *Psychological Reports*, 96 (2005), pp. 852–854.
18. Gillian Flynn, "Is Your Recognition Program Understood?" *Workforce*, July 1998, p. 30.
19. Diane Cadrain, "Just Desserts: Free Meals Can Create Camaraderie While Thanking Employees for a Job Well Done," *HR Magazine*, March 2005, pp. 97–100.
20. Irwin Speizer, "Incentives Catch on Overseas, but Value of Awards Can Too Easily Get Lost in Translation," *Workforce Management*, November 21, 2005, p. 46.
21. Cited in John A, Byrne, "How to Lead Now," *Fast Company*, August 2003, p. 66.
22. Barbara Davison, "Strategies for Managing Retention," Human Resources Forum (supplement to *Management Review*), November 1997, p. 1.

23. Janet Wiscombe, "Can Pay for Performance Really Work?" *Workforce,* August 2001, p. 29.
24. Susan J. Wells, "No Results, No Raise," *HR Magazine*, May 2005, pp. 76–80.
25. Thomas Nelson, "High Impact for Low-Wage Workers," *Workforce Management*, August 2004, pp. 47–48.
26. G. Douglas Jenkins, Jr., "Are Financial Incentives Related to Performance? A Meta-Analytic Review of Empirical Research," *Journal of Applied Psychology,* October 1998, pp. 777–787.
27. "How Stock Options Are Changing," *HRfocus,* October 2002, p. 7.
28. Larry L. Hatcher and Timothy L. Ross, "Organization Development through Productivity Sharing," *Personnel,* October 1985, p. 44.
29. Cited in "Why Gainsharing Works Even Better Today than in the Past," *HRfocus,* April 2000, p. 3.
30. "Has Usefulness of Pay for Performance Run Its Course?" *Ioma's Report on Salary Surveys*®, January 2003, pp. 1, 14.
31. Fay Hansen, "The New Way to Pay," *Workforce Management*, October 24, 2005, p. 36.
32. "Recognize Staff for Small Achievements," *Manager's Edge*, December 2005, p. 4.

Interpersonal Communication

A study found that for patients undergoing surgery, the biggest risk may be the power structure in the operating room. There is mounting evidence that poor communication between hospital support staff and surgeons is the leading cause of avoidable surgical errors. It can result in a variety of serious problems, from missed signs of blood clots to procedures conducted on the wrong site—or even the wrong patient. Studies show that a big part of the problem is the intense atmosphere of the OR, where surgeons are the captains of the ship, treated with deference because of their unique skills. As a result, nurses, prep technicians, and other aides may be afraid to speak up if they spot a problem.

Now, some hospitals are taking new steps to combat this fearful atmosphere. They are putting programs in place to improve surgeons' attitudes about teamwork, turning to lessons learned over two decades in the aviation industry, where the concept of "crew resource management" empowers anyone on the flight deck to challenge the pilot if they see a potentially deadly error in the making.

VHA, a hospital alliance, launched a program called "Transformation of the Operating Room" to get surgeons to participate in team-building strategies such as formal presurgical and postsurgical briefing sessions for other staffers. The program also includes "safety pauses" and time-outs to encourage anyone in the OR to delay or even suspend surgery if there is a concern. VHA sends facilitators to work with OR teams to air any concerns about speaking up.

Source: Laura Landro, "Making It OK to Challenge Surgeons," *The Wall Street Journal,* November 16, 2005, p. D1. Permission conveyed through Copyright Clearance Center, Inc.

8

OBJECTIVES

After reading and studying this chapter and doing the exercises, you should be able to:

1. Describe the communication process.

2. Describe the impact of information technology on interpersonal communication in organizations.

3. Explain how nonverbal communication can be used to enhance communication.

4. Present details about the various channels of communication in organizations.

5. Summarize barriers to effective communication and how to overcome them.

6. Explain how to overcome potential cross-gender and cross-cultural communication problems.

7. Recognize the basics for becoming a more power-oriented communicator.

Now Ask Yourself: **What does the story concerning improving team-work and communications in the OR illustrate about the potential grave consequences of incomplete or blocked communication in organizations?** Not all communication errors have life-or-death consequences, yet communication errors are still significant. Communication is the basic process by which managers and professionals accomplish their tasks, and people in positions of authority consistently rank communication skills as one of those vital for success. At times, a newsletter distributed in hard copy or electronically can be the communication medium of choice. Yet such communication is enhanced by interacting with employees at all levels about issues large and small. The Nierenberg Group's survey on the top job skills for the 21st century identified interpersonal communication skills as the number one workplace skill. Communication was also rated as a top 5 skill by 95% of Nierenberg survey respondents.[1]

The purpose of this chapter is to explain key aspects of interpersonal communication in organizations and make suggestions for improved communication. To achieve this purpose, we include information about the communication process, the impact of information technology on communication, how to overcome various barriers to communication, and how to develop a more power-oriented communication style.

THE COMMUNICATION PROCESS

162

Describe the communication process.

Interpersonal communication takes place through a series of steps, as illustrated in Exhibit 8-1. For effective communication to take place, six components must be present: a communication source or sender, a message, a channel, a receiver, feedback, and the environment. "Noise" can also have an impact on communication. As you study this model, you will observe that perception and communication are closely linked. To help explain the communication process, assume that a production manager wants to inform a team leader that productivity in his department slipped last month.

1. *Source (the sender).* The source of a communication event is usually a person attempting to send a spoken, written, sign language, or nonverbal message to another person or persons. The perceived authority and experience of the sender are important factors in influencing how much attention the message will receive.

Exhibit **8-1**

The Communication Process

Various sources of interference can prevent a message getting from sender to receiver as intended.

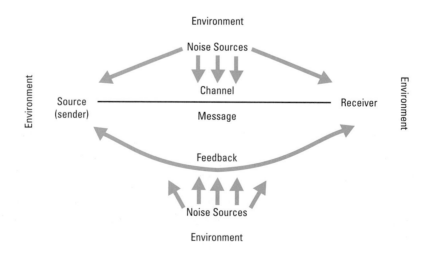

2. *Message.* The heart of a communication event is the **message,** which is a purpose or an idea to be conveyed. Many factors influence how a message is received. Among them are clarity, the alertness of the receiver, the complexity and length of the message, and how the information is organized. The production manager's message will most likely get across if she says directly, "I need to talk to you about last month's below-average productivity figures."

3. *Channel (medium).* Several communication channels, or media, are usually available for sending messages in organizations. Typically, messages are written, spoken, or a combination of written and spoken. Some kind of nonverbal cue, such as a smile or hand gesture, accompanies most spoken messages. Heavy reliance is now placed on electronic transmission of messages. In the production manager's case, she has chosen to drop by the team leader's office and deliver her message in a serious tone.

4. *Receiver.* A communication event can be complete only when another party receives the message and understands it properly. In the example under examination, the team leader is the receiver. Perceptual distortions of various types (as described in Chapter 3) act as filters that can prevent a message from being received as intended by the sender. If the team leader is worried that his job is at stake, he might get defensive when he hears the production manager's message.

5. *Feedback.* Without feedback, it is difficult to know whether a message has been received and understood. The feedback step also includes the reactions of the receiver. If the receiver takes action as intended by the sender, the message has been received satisfactorily. The production manager will know her message got across if the team leader says, "OK, when would you like to review last month's production figures?" Effective interpersonal communication therefore involves an exchange of messages between two people. The two communicators take turns being receiver and sender.

6. *Environment.* A full understanding of communication requires knowledge of the environment in which messages are transmitted and received. The organizational culture is a key environmental factor that influences communication. It is easier to transmit controversial messages when trust and respect are high than when they are low. Also, in some organizations workers hesitate to bring negative results to the attention of management for fear of being reprimanded.

7. *Noise.* Distractions such as noise have a pervasive influence on the components of the communication process. In this context, noise is anything that disrupts communication, including the attitudes and emotions of the receiver. **Noise** includes work stress, fear, ambivalence, and strong advocacy for an opposing position. In a more literal sense, the whir of machinery, piped-in music, and the chatting of coworkers with each other and on cell phones are also examples of noise in the workplace.

COMMUNICATION AND INFORMATION TECHNOLOGY

Advances in information technology have influenced the quantity and quality of interpersonal communications in the workplace. Quite often the influence has been positive, but at other times communication effectiveness has decreased. Four developments that illustrate the impact of information technology on interpersonal communication are e-mail, blogging, slide presentations by computer, and telecommuting.

Describe the impact of information technology on interpersonal communication in organizations.

E-Mail

E-mail has had two major impacts on interpersonal communication. First, written messages have replaced many telephone and in-person interchanges, with the majority of office workers being connected by e-mail networks. Group members often keep in regular contact with one another without having lengthy meetings or telephone conversations. Second, people receive many more messages than they did by paper and telephone. Many managers and professionals process over 100 e-mail messages per day.

E-mail facilitates communication in many ways, including people in various parts of the world exchanging information without worrying about trying to connect through different time zones. A more subtle consequence of e-mail is that it enhances industrial democracy. Ray Maghroori notes: "Ten or 20 years ago, there was no way for average workers to communicate with leaders."[2] Today, messages are no longer filtered through layers of management.

A widespread problem with e-mail is that it encourages the indiscriminate sending of messages, including trivial information, mass distribution of information of interest to a limited number of people, the exchange of jokes and sports news, and requests for seemingly unimportant information. The blitz of messages requires many people to work extra hours just to sort through their mail on matters that do not add value to the organization. According to one estimate, despite filters, more than 60% of corporate e-mail is spam.[3]

Some business firms have counterattacked the problems associated with e-mail by shifting to related technologies. Workers at such well-known organizations as Disney, Eastman Kodak, and the U.S. military are replacing e-mail with other software tools that function in real time. Among them are private workplace wikis, blogs, instant messaging, RSS, and more elaborate forms of groupware that allow workers to create websites for the team's use on a specific project. A *wiki* is a site that allows a group of people to comment on and edit each other's work. *RSS* is the acronym for really simple syndication, which enables people to subscribe to the information they need. E-mail will probably remain strong for one-to-one communication, but the tools just mentioned will be relied on more heavily for collaboration.[4]

Although processing e-mail overwhelms many people, as the technology has matured the situation has been more manageable for many workers. They dedicate certain times of the day to e-mail exchanges to avoid being distracted from other important work. (For some workers, however, responding to e-mail *is* their job, and being away from e-mail is a distraction.) Furthermore, company e-mail systems receive less spam than home systems partially because the company is more likely to use powerful spam filters. Also, the sophisticated e-mail user deletes spam after about a two-second glance.

The most impersonal use of e-mail is for firing people, either for poor performance or as part of a downsizing. A consultant notes, "Most people consider firing by e-mail one of the most heartless things you can do. E-mail is a faceless, cowardly way to fire someone."[5] The distractions associated with e-mail are widely recognized, leading various specialists to suggest ways for more productive use of this mode of communication. Exhibit 8-2 presents representative ideas for the productive use of e-mail.

Company Blogs (Web Logs)

The company blog (or, more precisely, a Web log or journal) is a rapidly growing form of electronic communication, paralleling the surging use of blogs in private

Log on to **www. thomsonedu.com/ infotrac**. Search for articles pertaining to company blogs (Web logs). How can major corporations use such a tool to communicate with the customer?

1. *Check e-mail less often.* Check e-mail only during natural breaks in your workday, such as between tasks, or only at dedicated times during the day. Turn off all automatic notifications regarding incoming messages.
2. *Clear out your inbox.* A cluttered e-mail inbox results in a lot of rereading and worrying about work piling up.
3. *Cancel unnecessary mail.* Unsubscribe to mailing lists of questionable value.
4. *Filter incoming mail.* Use software to move mail to appropriate folders, such as "Urgent" and "Trash."
5. *Use informative subject lines.* The subject line on the e-mail message can be a vital communication tool if it highlights the reason for sending the message, such as "Company truck overturned on highway." Also, the subject line can summarize the message, thereby giving enough information to the busy recipient. For example, "Overturned company truck problem under control."

6. *Delete spam.* The simplest way to deal with unsolicited e-mail is to delete it.
7. *Send to less people.* Watch your list of recipients. Your colleagues are already sagging under a mountain of information. They will thank you for not contributing to it.
8. *Use mailing lists.* Mailing to an address list saves time.
9. *Quote messages.* Include the fragment of the sender's original message for clarification.
10. *Keep replies brief.* With so many e-mail messages requiring a response, you can save a lot of time by responding within several lines if possible.
11. *Use the telephone!* The telephone is preferable to e-mail when dealing with complex issues, emotional discussions, sensitive material, and reprimands.

Source: Gihan Perera, "Ten E-Mail Time Management Tips," **http://www.firststep.com**; "Tips for Taming the E-Mail Monster," *Manager's Edge*, April 2004, p. 7; "5 Tips for Taming E-Mail Overload," *Manager's Edge*, January 2005, p. 7.

Exhibit **8-2**

Ten E-Mail Time-Management Tips

Managers spend about an hour every day processing e-mail. Here are 10 tips for making better use of this time.

165

life. Blogs originated by consumers are often used to complain about products or services, and less often to compliment a company. Blogs were first used by business to communicate with customers in a personal, direct manner, and perhaps form a bond with them.[6] The blog communicates business information, but with a soft, human touch. For example, a product manager for single-use cameras might say, "Just the other day, I heard from an off-the-road bike rider, Lily. She carries a few single-use cameras with her to every rally. Lily says she would rather smash one of our cameras than her $700 digital rig." A company might also use a blog to communicate its side of the story in response to outside criticism, such as the FastLaneBlog launched by GM vice chairman Bob Lutz. At times company employees spread negative information about the company on the blog, such as complaining about product safety or a poor dental insurance plan.

The company blog can also be used to communicate with employees in a relaxed, casual tone. Employees, as well as customers, can interact with the Web log by providing comments that can be a source of valuable feedback to management, and can be communicated directly to other visitors to the site.

Presentation Technology

Virtually every reader of this textbook has witnessed or given a talk using presentation technology. Computer-generated slide software, such as PowerPoint, is currently in vogue, yet overhead projectors are also part of presentation technology. Speakers in all types of organizations supplement their talk with computer slides and often organize their presentation around them. Some speakers sit slumped in a chair, narrating the slides. Many people want presentations reduced to bulleted items and eye-catching graphics. (Have you noticed this tendency among students?) The ability to prepare a slide presentation has become an indispensable corporate survival skill. Audiences have become accustomed to watching an array of impressive graphics during oral presentations.

The communication challenge here is that during an oral presentation, the predominant means of connection between sender and receiver is eye contact. When an audience is constantly distracted from the presenter by movement on the screen, sounds from the computer, or lavish colors, eye contact suffers and so does the message. Another problem is that the speaker who relies on multimedia to the exclusion of person-to-person contact may be communicating the subtle message, "I am not really necessary."[7] The implication for presenters is to find a way to integrate speaking skills with the new technology. One of the biggest challenges is to learn how to handle equipment and maintain frequent eye and voice contact at all times. Jean Mausehund and R. Neil Dortch offer these sensible suggestions:

- *Reveal points only as needed.* Project the overhead transparencies or computer slides only when needed, and use a cursor, laser pointer, or metal pointer for emphasis.
- *Talk to the audience and not the screen.* A major problem with computer slides is that the presenter as well as the audience is likely to focus continually on the slide. If the presenter minimizes looking at the slide and spends considerable time looking at the audience, it will be easier to maintain contact with the audience.
- *Keep the slide in view until the audience gets the point.* A presenter will often flash a slide or transparency without giving the audience enough time to comprehend the meaning of the slide. It is also important for presenters to synchronize the slides with their comments.[8]
- *Project the key points of your presentation as headlines, using a large font.* Most audiences appreciate seeing an outline of your presentation flashed on the screen, a sentence or two (or a small amount of data) at a time using a large font. In this way, the slides become headlines that help the audience follow your oral presentation.

Telecommuting and the Distributed Workforce

A major deviation from the traditional work schedule is having a full-time or part-time schedule working away from company premises. An estimated 22.5 million people in the United States work at home, out of their cars, or from customer premises as corporate employees. Collectively they are referred to as the distributed workforce. Technology companies rely the most heavily on the distributed workforce. For example, at IBM, 40% of employees have no office at the company.[9] The majority of people who work at home do so only a day or two per week at their residence. Concerns about terrorist threats, contagious diseases, and the high cost of gasoline have made working at home appear even more desirable for many workers in recent years.

Telecommuting is an arrangement in which employees use computers to perform their regular work responsibilities at home or in a satellite office. Employees who telecommute usually use computers tied to the company's main office. People who work at home are referred to as telecommuters or teleworkers. The vast majority of people who work at home are either assigned a computer by the company or possess their own computer and related equipment. In addition to using computers to communicate with their employer's office, telecommuters may attend meetings on company premises and stay in contact by telephone and teleconferences. The output of distributed workers is measured frequently by computer.

A major communication challenge to telecommuters is that they rely so heavily on e-mail and groupware and therefore lose out on the social interaction of work, which is so important to many people. Another challenge for distributed workers is that they are expected to respond to company requests outside of typical working hours, partially because there is no standard work week for a professional working away from the office. Teleworkers are also encouraged to spend some time in the traditional office in face-to-face communication with other workers. Avoiding such contact can lead to feelings of isolation, that one is not a part of the office communication network. People who are successful at telecommuting are usually those with relatively low affiliation needs.

The Impact of Computer-Mediated Communication on Behavior

As alluded to previously, computerized communication has had a major impact, both positive and negative, on behavior in organizations. On the positive side, communication can be more widespread and immediate than in making telephone calls, holding meetings, or sending hard-copy memos. With computer-mediated communication, information can be exchanged at a rapid pace, keeping large numbers of people informed and alert. More people have a voice because e-mail, and sometimes instant messaging, is possible with senior managers. For example, it is much easier for an entry-level worker to send an e-mail to the division president than to telephone, send a letter to, or have a meeting with the executive.

Computerized information has also had substantial negative impacts on behavior in organizations. Above all, many workers suffer from the lack of a human touch—they want to relate to a person rather than engage in so many electronic exchanges. It is more difficult to motivate, listen to, or encourage a worker electronically than in person. An emoticon smiley is not as warm as a face-to-face smile. Many workers suffer from substantial productivity losses as they become enticed into excessive Internet surfing during company time. As a result, these workers may suffer from lowered performance evaluations and even job loss. Similarly, reading e-mail messages and searching the Internet becomes so time consuming that the worker neglects the human interaction aspects of the job, such as dealing with coworker and customer problems.

Excessive use of computers often leads to repetitive motion disorder, leaving the worker discouraged and pained. Customer service often deteriorates as a result of information technology. Many banks, for example, force customers with a service problem to call a toll-free number rather than allowing them to deal with a branch representative. A voice-response system instructs the customer to punch in a lengthy account number and make choices from a complicated menu. The process is time consuming and difficult for customers not familiar with information technology. The result can be resentment, frustration, and the loss of a customer.

Computer-mediated communication often results in *wired managerial workers.* Being electronically connected to the office at all times leads many managers and professionals to complain that their employers expect them to be always available for consultation. Wi-Fi–enabled laptops systems enable workers to stay connected to company data even more readily than with the traditional systems.

Finally, computerized communication encourages multitasking to the point that many workers feel they are wasting time unless they are attempting two tasks at once, such as talking on a cell telephone and accessing e-mail at the same time. The problem is that diminished concentration often leads to poorer-quality work and almost precludes the flow experience so necessary for creativity.[10] Multitasking is inherently rude when dealing with another person. Many complaints have been made about customer-contact workers who deal with one customer while talking to another on a cell phone. The opposite problem is also true—some customers talk on their cell phone while being served by a store associate, thereby marginalizing the associate.

To capitalize on the benefits of computer-mediated communication devices, it is important to keep in mind that the human touch is still important. The capability to send and receive messages electronically should not mean that human contact has become undesirable or unnecessary.

 ## NONVERBAL COMMUNICATION

Explain how nonverbal communication can be used to enhance communication.

The most obvious modes of communication are speaking, writing, and sign language. (Many business meetings today include an interpreter who signs for deaf members of the audience.) A substantial amount of interpersonal communication also occurs through **nonverbal communication,** the transmission of messages by means other than words. *Body language* refers to those aspects of nonverbal communication directly related to movements of the body, such as gestures and posture. Nonverbal communication usually supplements rather than substitutes for writing, speaking, and sign language.

The general purpose of nonverbal communication is to express the feeling behind a message. Suppose that a sales representative stands tall when saying, "Our payroll processing service is devoid of bugs and glitches." The representative's posture reveals confidence in making this pitch. The same message delivered in a slouched position with one hand over the mouth would communicate a feeling of limited confidence.

Nonverbal communication incorporates a wide range of behavior. Nevertheless, it can be divided into the following nine categories.[11]

1. *Environment.* The physical setting in which the message takes place communicates meaning. This would include office décor, a type of automobile, and the type of restaurant or hotel chosen for a business meeting. Bigger deals are typically negotiated and consummated in more luxurious restaurants, whereas discussions about work assignments might be held in a family-style restaurant.
2. *Body placement.* The placement of one's body in relation to someone else is widely used to transmit messages. Facing a person in a casual, relaxed style indicates acceptance. Moving close to another person is also a general indicator of acceptance. However, moving too close may be perceived as a violation of personal space, and the message sender will be rejected.
3. *Posture.* Another widely used clue to a person's attitude is his or her posture. Leaning toward another person suggests a favorable attitude toward the message one is trying to communicate. Leaning backward communicates the opposite. Standing up straight is generally interpreted as an indicator of self-confidence, while slouching is usually a sign of low self-confidence.
4. *Hand gestures.* Gestures of the hand, such as frequent movements to express approval and palms spread outward to indicate perplexity, provide meaningful hints in communication. Making a steeple with your hands in the presence of others connotes deep thought and hints at being powerful.
5. *Facial expressions and movement.* The particular look on a person's face and movements of the person's head provide reliable cues as to approval, disapproval, or disbelief.

6. *Voice tone.* Aspects of the voice such as pitch, volume, quality, and speech rate may communicate confidence, nervousness, or enthusiasm. Intelligence is often judged by how people sound. Research suggests that the most annoying voice quality is a whining, complaining, or nagging tone.[12]

7. *Clothing, dress, and appearance.* The image a person conveys communicates such messages as "I feel powerful" and "I think this meeting is important." For example, wearing one's best business attire to a performance appraisal interview would communicate the idea that "I think this meeting is very important."

8. *Mirroring.* To mirror is to build rapport with another person by imitating his or her voice tone, breathing rate, body movement, and language. Mirroring relies 10% on verbal means, 60% on voice tone, and 30% on body physiology. A specific application of mirroring is to conform to the other person's posture, eye movements, and hand movements. The person feels more relaxed with you as a result of your imitation.

9. *Touching.* Touch is a powerful vehicle for conveying such emotions as warmth, comfort, agreement, approval, reassurance, and physical attraction. Yet touching behavior in the workplace is governed by cultural attitudes and status.[13] Touching among people at the approximately the same organizational rank is frequently used to convey agreement and reassurance. Touching between people of different rank often indicates power and status differences, with the higher-ranking person more likely to initiate the touching. Concerns about sexual harassment and sexism have greatly limited the use of touching to emphasize a point in the office. If professional sporting events are considered part of the workplace, then same-sex touching and hugging to express enthusiasm and approval are rampantly practiced!

One of many practical applications of nonverbal communication is to project enthusiasm and confidence with body language. Ron Huff recommends the following:

- *Loosen your facial expression.* A tight, grim look gives the appearance of being unapproachable. Relax your muscles, and look for opportunities to smile and offer encouraging nods.
- *Move closer to message senders.* Work associates feel you are listening intently when you lean slightly toward them when they speak. It is a subtle way of showing that you want to hear every word.
- *Gesture to reinforce a point.* If you are excited or pleased with an idea, do not rely exclusively on words to communicate these feelings. Pump a fist, clap your hands, or point approvingly at the speaker. Use the gesture that feels the most natural to you.[14]

Another workplace application of nonverbal communication is to help combat drug trafficking and terrorism. The art of spotting nervous or threatening behavior has gained respect among airport security officials. Since the terrorist attacks on September 11, 2001, the Federal Bureau of Investigation started teaching nonverbal behavior analysis to all new recruits. Instead of selecting people to be interrogated based on what they look like, custom agents have been trained to observe what people do and to ask pointed questions when suspicious nonverbal behavior surfaces. Among the indicators of suspicious behavior are darting eyes, hand tremors, a fleeting smile, and an enlarged carotid artery (indicating the rapid blood flow associated with anxiety). Failure to make eye contact with the custom official is a strong red flag.[15]

Despite the recommendations and implications of the information about nonverbal communication, keep in mind that many nonverbal signals are ambiguous.

For example, a smile usually indicates agreement and warmth, but can also indicate nervousness.

ORGANIZATIONAL CHANNELS OF COMMUNICATION

Present details about the various channels of communication in organizations.

Messages in organizations travel through many different channels, or paths. Communication channels can be formal or informal and can be categorized by the direction they follow.

Formal Communication Channels

Formal communication channels are the official pathways for sending information inside and outside an organization. The primary source of information about formal channels is the organization chart. It indicates the channels the messages are supposed to follow. By carefully following an organization chart, an entry-level worker would know how to transmit a message to the CEO. Formal communication channels are often bypassed using information technology. Using e-mail, anybody can send a message to anybody else in the organization. During an emergency, workers are also likely to bypass formal channels, such as a technician telephoning the plant manager directly about a chemical spill.

Many companies have developed formal communication channels for managing crises such as fires and explosions, massive product recalls, financial scandals, and terrorist attacks. One of the most crucial parts of a disaster plan is how to communicate with the company's workforce during a crisis. A key part of the challenge is to locate and reestablish contact with employees who may be scattered in the streets or stranded in airports around the world. Aon Corporation, an international insurance, risk-management, and consulting company, improvised to use its website as an official communication channel during the crisis of September 11. A company official said, "With everything else down, we decided to use the company Web site. That seemed like the only option we had."[16] Websites have now become the premier formal crisis communication channel. Formal channels during a crisis are necessary for informing employees about a disaster, work assignments, health services and grief counseling, and assistance in returning to work.

Other formal communication channels during a crisis include the television or radio.

The formal communication channels are precisely specified in a traditional bureaucratic organization with its many layers. Communication channels are more difficult to follow in the modern **network organization,** a spherical structure that can rotate self-managing teams and other resources around a common knowledge base. The key purpose of the network organization is to enter into temporary alliances with other firms in order to capitalize on the combined talents. *Strategic alliance* is the term often used to describe these temporary, multifirm ventures. An example of a strategic alliance is Ford and GM working jointly to develop an SUV based on fuel-cell technology.

Exhibit 8-3 shows the contrast between a bureaucracy (pyramid shape) and a network organization (spherical shape). The connecting lines can be considered formal communication channels.

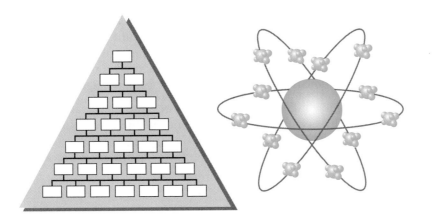

Exhibit **8-3**

Communication Pathways in a Hierarchical Organization and a Spherical Organization

Communication pathways are more complex in a spherical organization than in a hierarchical organization.

Informal Communication Channels

An **informal communication channel** is the unofficial network of channels that supplements the formal channels. Most of these informal channels arise out of necessity. For example, people will sometimes depart from the official communication channels to consult with a person with specialized knowledge. Suppose an administrative professional in the inventory-control department spoke and wrote fluent German. Employees from other department would regularly consult her when they were dealing with a customer from Germany.

Informal communication channels help explain why changes in organizational structure (one that specifies the formal communication channels) sometimes do not change the quantity and quality of work that gets accomplished. The same pattern of networks that workers use to accomplish their tasks may not change despite the changes on the organization chart.[17]

The Grapevine

The **grapevine** is the major informal communication channel in organizations. The *grapevine* refers to the tangled pathways that can distort information. The term referred originally to the snarled telegraph lines on the battlefield during the U.S. Civil War. The grapevine is often thought to be used primarily for passing along negative rumors and negative gossip. Gossips sometimes use the Internet and e-mail as channels for transmitting negative gossip. When left to fester, gossip can cause individuals chagrin, and can lead to turnover, conflict, and lawsuits. Gossip often increases when workers are bored or lack ample information about company events. Managers can often stop negative gossip by confronting the source of the gossip, demanding that he or she stop. Positive gossip, however, makes a contribution to the organization because trading information strengthens ties among workers and humanizes the workplace.[18]

The grapevine is sometimes used purposely to disseminate information along informal lines. For example, top management might want to hint to employees that certain work will be outsourced unless the employees become more productive. Although the plans are still tentative, feeding them into the grapevine may result in improved motivation and productivity.

Rumors

Rumors are an important communication force within organizations, and they tend to thrive in organizations with poor corporate communication, such as a penitentiary.

Furthermore, an active grapevine is correlated with higher levels of stress, threat, and insecurity. Respondents to a worldwide survey agreed that rumors are an important early source of information. Executives from the United Kingdom and the United States agreed most strongly, whereas those from Switzerland and Japan agreed the least. To ensure that rumors are more helpful than harmful, management might do the following:

- Be wary of vague communication, which fosters misinterpretation and anxiety.
- Promote healthy, accurate communication. Encourage employees to discuss rumors with their manager.
- Avoid concealing bad news. Promise employees that they will receive accurate information as soon as it becomes available.
- Correct erroneous communications that relate to organizational policies, practices, and strategic plans.[19]

A problem with inaccurate rumors is that they can distract workers, create anxiety, and decrease productivity. A frequent by-product of false rumors about company relocation or a pending merger is that some of the more talented workers leave in the hopes of more stable employment.

The accompanying Organizational Behavior in Action box describes how one company takes a proactive approach to dealing with rumors.

ORGANIZATIONAL BEHAVIOR *In Action*

Allied Gate & Fence Locks Out Negative Rumors

Managers at Allied Gate & Fence want to keep negative buzz—gossip, innuendos, and rumors—from spiraling out of control. With the help of an IT consultant, the company created a page on the company intranet called "The Rumor Mill," where employees could post any rumor they may have heard about the company. (An intranet is essentially an Internet for company use only.) All types of rumors were encouraged to be reported: negative, positive, or neutral. An example of a negative rumor might be, "Allied Gate & Fence is planning to hire illegal immigrants to do all the basic labor on gate and fence installation. This could result in layoffs of many good employees." An example of a positive rumor might be, "Allied has won a government contract to be a preferred supplier for erecting new gates and fences for any disaster handled by FEMA (Federal Emergency Management Act)." Employees were encouraged to respond to the rumors.

Initially skeptical about allowing unofficial sources to respond to the postings, the managers discovered that employees who typically respond are indeed official sources. That is, they know what they are talking about because they work in the department most involved in the issue. And in the rare instance that someone posts an inaccurate response, there is always someone else who quickly corrects it.

The end result, according to management, is that damaging rumors die a quick and painless death.

Questions

1. What would you offer as a reason that the intranet was a successful method for combating rumors?
2. What do you see as a downside risk for Allied Gate & Fence using an intranet to combat rumors?

Source: Adapted from Shel Holtz, *Corporate Conversations: A Guide to Crafting Effective Appropriate Internal Communications* (New York: AMACOM, 2003).

Chance Encounters and Management by Walking Around

Another informal channel of significance is *chance encounters.* Unscheduled informal contact between managers and employees can be an efficient and effective communication channel. John P. Kotter found that effective managers do not confine their communication to formal meetings.[20] Instead, they collect valuable information during chance encounters. Spontaneous communication events may occur in the cafeteria, near the water fountain, in the halls, and on the elevator. In just 2 minutes, the manager might obtain the information that would typically be solicited in a 30-minute meeting or through a series of e-mail exchanges.

One important communication channel can be classified as either formal or informal. **Management by walking around** involves managers intermingling freely with workers on the shop floor or in the office, as well as with customers. By spending time in personal contact with employees, the manager enhances open communication. During contacts with employees the manager will often ask questions such as, "How are you enjoying your work?" or "What bottlenecks have you encountered today?" Because management by walking around is systematic, it could be considered formal. However, a manager who circulates throughout the company is not following the formal paths prescribed by the organization chart. Management by walking around differs from chance encounters in that the latter are unplanned events; the former occurs intentionally.

Communication Directions

Messages in organizations travel in five directions: downward, upward, horizontally, diagonally, and spherically. *Downward communication* is the flow of messages from one level to a lower level. It is typified by a middle manager giving orders to a lower-level supervisor or by top management sending announcements to employees. Information is sometimes transmitted from a higher level to a lower one without the sender inviting a response. When this occurs, the feedback built into two-way communication is lost.

Upward communication is the transmission of messages from lower to higher levels in an organization. It is the most important channel for keeping management informed about problems within the organization. Management by walking around, chance encounters, and simply talking regularly to employees are factors that improve upward communication. An **open-door policy** is a more formal upward communication channel that allows employees to bring a gripe to top management's attention without first checking with their manager. Upward communication is more widely used in less bureaucratic firms than in highly bureaucratic firms. Almost all executives contend that they value upward communication, whether or not the majority of employees agree.

Horizontal communication is sending messages among people at the same organizational level. It often takes the form of coworkers from the same department talking to one another. Horizontal communication is the basis for cooperation. When coworkers are not sharing information with and responding to one another, they are likely to fall behind schedule. Also, efforts are duplicated and quality suffers. Another type of horizontal communication takes place when managers communicate with other managers at the same level.

Diagonal communication is the transmission of messages to higher or lower organizational levels in different departments. A typical diagonal communication event occurs when a manager from one department contacts a lower-ranking person from a department outside of his or her chain of command.

Spherical communication is communication among members from different teams in the network organization. The communication events take place with team members from the same or different organizations. Visualize a team member from Nike Corporation communicating directly with a team member from Nokia Corporation. He wants to talk about a strategic alliance to develop a basketball shoe with a built-in cell phone!

BARRIERS TO INTERPERSONAL COMMUNICATION

Summarize barriers to effective communication and how to overcome them.

The information presented so far has been helpful in understanding how communication takes place in organizations. Here we explore further why messages sent from one person to another are often not received exactly as intended. As was shown in Exhibit 8-1, barriers (or noises) exist at every step in the communication process. Interference is most likely to occur when a message is complex, arouses emotion, or clashes with a receiver's mental set. An emotionally arousing message may deal with topics such as money or personal inconvenience. A message that clashes with a mental set challenges the receiver to make a radical shift in thinking. For example, a human resources manager had difficulty getting across the message that managers could no longer make a specific request for a woman to fill an administrative assistant position.

Eight communication barriers are described here. The first four relate primarily to the sending of messages; the next three relate more to receiving them, and the last one could relate to sending or receiving. Exhibit 8-4 lists barriers to communication, as well as the means for overcoming them, which will be described in the next section of the chapter.

1. *Semantics.* Many communication problems are created by **semantics,** the varying meanings people attach to words. The symbols (both words and nonverbal behavior) used in communication can take on different meanings for different people. Consequently, it is possible for a person to misinterpret the intended meaning of the sender. One phrase fraught with varying interpretations is "essential personnel." When a CEO announces before a downsizing that only essential personnel will be retained, many people are left wondering about their status. Few people can accept the message that they are "nonessential."

2. *Filtering of negative information.* A formidable upward communication barrier is **filtering,** the coloring and altering of information to make it more acceptable to the receiver. Many managers and individual workers filter information to avoid displeasing their superiors, such as when describing a revenue shortfall. Filtering is most likely to take place when top-level management has a history of punishing the bearer of bad news.

Exhibit 8-4

Barriers to Communication and Means for Overcoming Them

Understanding barriers to communication should be followed up with effective tactics for overcoming them. The techniques for overcoming barriers listed on the right do not necessarily correspond to the barriers listed on the left.

Barriers	Overcoming Barriers
1. Semantics	1. Clarify ideas before sending.
2. Filtering of negative information	2. Motivate the receiver.
3. Lack of credibility of the sender	3. Discuss differences in frames of reference.
4. Mixed signals	4. Foster informal communication.
5. Different frames of reference	5. Communicate feelings behind the facts.
6. Value judgments	6. Be aware of nonverbal communication.
7. Information overload	7. Obtain feedback.
8. Poor communication skills	8. Adapt to the other person's communication style.
	9. Engage in meta-communication.

3. *Lack of credibility of the sender.* The more trustworthy the source or sender of a message, the greater the probability that the message will get through clearly. In contrast, when the sender of the message has low credibility, many times it will be ignored. Credibility in sending messages is so important that it is a major contributor to effective leadership.

4. *Mixed signals.* Communications can break down with a subtle variation of low credibility. The disconnect occurs from **mixed signals**—sending different messages about the same topic to different audiences. For example, a company might brag about the high quality of its products in public statements. Yet on the shop floor and in the office, the company tells its employees to cut corners whenever possible to lower costs. Another type of mixed signal occurs when you send one message to a person about desired behavior, yet behave in another way yourself. A mixed signal of this type would occur when an executive preaches the importance of social responsibility, yet practices blatant job discrimination.

5. *Different frames of reference.* People perceive words and concepts differently depending on their **frame of reference,** a perspective and vantage point based on past experience. (A frame of reference means about the same thing as a *paradigm.*) A typical example of the frame-of-reference problem took place in a financial service company that was instituting work-streamlining teams to improve productivity. The vice president of operations announced the program with great enthusiasm, only to find that the message was received in a distorted, negative fashion. The problem was that the vice president perceived productivity improvement as a vehicle for ensuring increased profits and survival. Lower-ranking employees, however, perceived productivity improvement as a way for the company to maintain output while laying off workers.

6. *Value judgments.* Making value judgments prior to receiving an entire message interferes with the communication of its intended meaning. A **value judgment** is an overall opinion of something based on a quick perception of its merit. When value judgments are made too hastily, the receiver hears only the part of the message that he or she wishes to hear. A manager might begin to read an announcement about a dependent-care center to be sponsored by the company. The manager might make a quick value judgment that this program is "just another human resources initiative to keep people happy." By so doing, the manager will block out the information that dependent-care facilities often increase productivity by reducing absenteeism and turnover. It is also possible that a hasty value judgment will prompt a person to discount a message despite listening to it fully.

7. *Information overload.* Electronic communication has contributed to the problem of too much information being disseminated throughout most private and public firms. **Information (or communication) overload** occurs when people are so overloaded with information that they cannot respond effectively to messages. As a result, they experience work stress. Managers and staff professionals alike are exposed to so much printed, electronic, and spoken information that their capacity to absorb it all is taxed. The human mind is capable of processing only a limited quantity of information at a time.

    The receiver and sender both contribute to communication overload. The receiver's "circuits are jammed," yet many senders contribute to the problem by disseminating too much information to the same person.

8. *Poor communication skills.* A comprehensive communication barrier is a limited ability to send or receive a message clearly. The sender might garble a written or spoken message so severely that the receiver cannot understand it, or the sender

may deliver the message so poorly that the receiver does not take it seriously. The inability or unwillingness to listen is also a poor communication skill.

Overcoming Communication Barriers

An effective strategy for improving communication in organizations is to overcome communication barriers. The following sections provide an overview of tactics and techniques for improving the sending and receiving of messages. In addition, they describe methods of overcoming problems in communicating with people of the opposite sex and from different cultures.

Improving the Sending of Messages

Improving the way messages are sent will help overcome communication barriers. Implementing the following suggestions will improve the chances that messages are received as intended.

1. *Clarify ideas before communicating.* Many communications fail because of inadequate planning and lack of understanding of the true nature of the message to be communicated. To plan effectively, managers and professionals must consider the goals and attitudes of those who will receive the message and those who will be affected by it. Part of clarifying ideas is to present them in a clear, exciting manner, at a level appropriate for the audience. Not presenting ideas clearly, such as in a baffling written performance evaluation, can have legal consequences. If the employee was fired for poor performance, the performance evaluation should have been unambiguous about the poor performance.[21]

2. *Motivate the receiver.* The recipient of the message has to be motivated to attend to the message. This is best accomplished by appealing to the receiver's interests or needs. In sending a message to higher-level management, it is important to frame it in terms of how it contributes to earning money, saving money, or productivity.

3. *Discuss differences in frames of reference or paradigms.* A method for understanding and dealing with differences in frames of reference is to recognize that people have different paradigms that influence how they interpret events. A **paradigm** is a model, framework, viewpoint, perspective, or frame of reference. When two people look at a situation with different paradigms, a communication problem may occur. For instance, a business owner might say, "We should be able to get this order ready for shipment by Monday morning if we work all day Saturday and Sunday." The employee may respond, "How horrible. Nobody works on Saturday and Sunday; those are family days." From the paradigm of the business owner, you work as much as necessary to meet a business goal. But from the standpoint of this worker in particular, a person works a limited number of hours, and reserves other times for personal activities.

   The solution to this communication clash is to discuss the frames of reference or paradigms. The two people live by different rules or guidelines (a major contributor to a paradigm). If they can recognize that they are operating with different paradigms, the chances for agreement are improved. People can change their paradigms when the reasons are convincing. For example, the worker in the preceding situation may never have thought about investing time on weekends to help the employer succeed.

4. *Foster informal communication.* An abundance of informal, open communication enhances trust within an organization. Negative rumors are less likely to appear on the grapevine when talking about sensitive topics comes naturally. Ample casual meeting areas such as lounges and conference rooms also contribute to informal

communication. Management by walking around and chance encounters are other contributors to the flow of informal communication. Informal communication also fosters gossip, yet when the trust level is high, the gossip is more likely to be positive, such as buzzing about who is going to receive a major promotion.

5. *Communicate feelings behind the facts.* The facts in a message should be accompanied by the appropriate feelings. Feelings add power and conviction to the message. The sender of the message should explain his or her personal feelings and encourage the receiver to do the same. For example, a manager who is disappointed with the quality of a finished product might say, "The product has a cheap look. I'm disappointed with the attention you paid to product design. How do you feel about my criticism?" A less-effective approach would be to simply criticize the poor design without mentioning feelings. Expressing feelings is part of *speaking directly.*

6. *Be aware of nonverbal communication.* A speaker's tone of voice, expression, and apparent receptiveness to the responses of others have an impact on the receiver. These subtle nonverbal aspects of communication often affect the listener's reaction to a message even more than the content of the communication. When sending messages to others, it is important to keep in mind all the aspects of nonverbal behavior described previously.

7. *Obtain feedback.* The best efforts at communication may be wasted if feedback on how well the message came across is not received. Asking questions, encouraging the receiver to express reactions, following up on contacts, and subsequently reviewing performance are ways of obtaining feedback. A powerful method of obtaining feedback is to request, "Could you please summarize what you heard me say?"

8. *Adapt to the other person's communication style.* People communicate more freely with those who match their communication style. If you want to assume the burden for decreasing communication barriers with another person, then make some adaptations to his or her style. If your communication target prefers e-mail or text messages to telephone calls, use e-mail or text messages rather than phone calls, except for highly sensitive matters. If your manager prefers brief, bulleted summaries rather than well-developed narrative reports, prepare such brief reports for him or her. If your target responds best to anecdotes, develop anecdotes to support your major points. In contrast, if the receiver prefers statistics to anecdotes, prepare statistics to support major points. It is usually possible to learn the other person's style by careful observation and by posing a question such as, "How do you like your information presented?"

9. *Engage in meta-communication.* When having a difficult time getting through to another person, it helps to talk about your communication difficulty. To **meta-communicate** is to communicate about your communication to help overcome barriers or to resolve a problem. If, as a manager, you are trying to get through to a group member with an angry facial expression, you might say, "You look upset about our conversation. Is this a bad time to talk with you about something important?" The group member might counter, "I think I'm carrying too big a workload, so I'm not very happy." With the air cleared, communication might now flow more smoothly.

Improving the Receiving of Messages

Listening is a basic part of communication, and many communication problems stem from the intended receiver not listening carefully. Reducing communication barriers requires a special type of listening. **Active listening** means listening for full meaning without making premature judgments or interpretations. The active listener listens intently, with the goal of empathizing with the speaker. As a result of listening actively, the listener can feed back to the speaker what he or she thinks the speaker meant. Feeding back the content is referred to as *paraphrasing,* such as "You say you are unhappy with progress in enhancing our customer satisfaction ratings." Too much paraphrasing, however, can be disruptive and annoying. Paraphrasing should focus on key points in the conversation.

Observing nonverbal cues is another facet of active listening. For example, if an employee laughs slightly whenever he mentions a deadline, dig for more information. The laughter may signal that he thinks the deadline is unrealistic.[22]

An active listener also avoids traps such as reacting too quickly to a word or phrase that stirs emotion. Instead he or she carefully interprets the word and analyzes what the word or phrase might mean to the sender. The active listener might hear a speaker say, "People with a weak work ethic have no place in this company." Before getting angry or accepting the entire message, the active listener would wait to find out what the sender really means by a "weak work ethic."

An active listener will postpone presenting his or her viewpoint, particularly in conflict situations. By holding back on presenting your side of the story, the other person will feel fully heard, and then will be more likely to listen to your viewpoint. When people feel shut off, they are unlikely to listen carefully.[23]

A foundational skill for the active listener is to ask open-ended questions because these questions invite an explanation rather than a one-word response. Open-ended questions begin with words such as "Tell me about," "Explain to me," "How are you doing with our project?," and "Where are you headed?" Two examples of closed-end questions are, "Will you make your deadline?" and "Do you like your job?"

Listening can be an important factor in business success. Many companies invest considerable time and energy to better understanding the thinking, values, and behavior patterns of their customers. Quite often the same processes the companies use to gain insights into their customers can be used to learn more about their own employees, such as asking about job satisfaction and morale.

Do the skill-development exercise to build your ability to listen actively.

SKILL-DEVELOPMENT EXERCISE

Actively Listening to a Coworker

Before conducting the following role plays, review the keys to effective listening presented in the text. The suggestion about paraphrasing is particularly important when listening to a person who is talking about an emotional topic.

One student plays the role of a coworker who has just been offered the position of manager of another department. He or she will be receiving 10% higher pay and be able to travel overseas twice a year for the company. He or she is eager to describe full details of this good fortune to a coworker. At the same time, the person has some concerns about the promotion. The person is concerned that his or her spouse might not appreciate the idea of overseas travel.

Another student plays the role of the coworker to whom the first worker wants to describe his or her good fortune. The second worker wants to listen intently to the first worker. At the same time, the listener is facing some urgent work problems and therefore may have to fight being distracted.

Other class members will rate the second person on his or her listening ability.

Collaboration

DEALING WITH GENDER DIFFERENCES IN COMMUNICATION STYLE

Despite the trend toward equality in organizations, substantial interest has arisen in identifying differences in communication styles between men and women. People who are aware of these differences will face fewer communication barriers between themselves and members of the opposite sex. As we describe these differences, recognize them as group stereotypes, reflecting how the average man or woman is likely to behave. Individual differences in communication style are usually more important than group (men versus women) differences. Key differences in sex-related communication styles are as follows:

- Women prefer to use communication for rapport building and building social connections.
- Men prefer to use talk primarily as a means of preserving independence and status by displaying knowledge and skill, and women tend to downplay their status.
- Men prefer to work out their problems by themselves, whereas women prefer to talk out solutions with another person.
- Women want empathy, not solutions. When women share feelings of being stressed out, they seek empathy and understanding.
- Women are more likely to compliment the work of a coworker, whereas men are more likely to be critical.
- Men tend to be more direct in their conversation, whereas women emphasize politeness.
- Women tend to be more conciliatory when facing differences, whereas men become more intimidating.
- Men are more interested than women in calling attention to their accomplishments or hogging recognition.
- Men tend to dominate discussions during meetings.
- Women tend to downplay their certainty about a subject, whereas men are more likely to minimize their doubts. As a result, women tend to appear less confident than men, even when their confidence levels are equal.
- Women are more likely to use a gentle expletive, whereas men tend to be harsher. (Do you think this difference really exists?)[24]

Understanding these differences can help you interpret the behavior of people, thus avoiding a communication block. For example, if a male team member is not as effusive with praise as you would like, remember that he is simply engaging in gender-typical behavior. (Again, this is a gender stereotype that is not universally applicable.) Factor in this gender difference before taking the shortfall personally.

A potential dysfunction of stereotypes about gender differences in communication is that it can lead to a disconnect between men and women in the workplace. Men might talk over women, not giving them a chance to speak or ignoring them.[25] Women, in contrast, might think men are being needlessly aggressive, and not take them seriously.

OVERCOMING CROSS-CULTURAL COMMUNICATION BARRIERS

The modern workforce has become more culturally diverse in two major ways. Many subgroups within our own culture have been assimilated into the workforce, and there is increasing interaction with people from other countries. Cultural

Explain how to overcome potential cross-gender and cross-cultural communication problems.

179

differences within a diverse country, such as the United States or Canada, can be as pronounced as differences between two countries. Managers therefore face the challenge of preventing and overcoming communication barriers created by differences in language and customs. Sensitivity to cultural differences goes a long way toward overcoming these potential communication barriers. If you are aware that these barriers exist, you will be ready to deal with them. In addition, communicators should keep in mind several suggestions:

1. *Show respect for all workers.* The same behavior that promotes good cross-cultural relations in general helps overcome communication barriers. A widely used comment that implies disrespect is to say to a person from another culture, "You have an accent." If you were in that person's culture, you, too, might have an accent.

2. *Use straightforward language and speak slowly and clearly.* When working with people who do not speak your language fluently, speak in an easy-to-understand manner. Face-to-face communication is particularly helpful to check for comprehension. Minimize the use of idioms and analogies specific to your language. Particularly difficult for foreigners to interpret are sports analogies such as "This should be a slam dunk." Also perplexing are general idioms such as "My manager passed the buck," or "Our competitor is over the hill."

3. *Be alert to cultural differences in customs and behavior.* To minimize cross-cultural communication barriers, recognize that many subtle job-related differences in customs and behavior may exist. For example, Asians may feel uncomfortable when asked to brag about themselves in the presence of others. From their perspective, calling attention to oneself at the expense of another person is rude and unprofessional. Exhibit 8-5 presents a sampling of cross-cultural differences in customs and behavior that relate to communications.

4. *Be sensitive to differences in nonverbal communication.* All cultures use nonverbal communication, but the specific cues differ across cultures. To receive messages accurately when working with people from diverse cultures, one must be sensitive to these differences. When visiting another country, take caution in using the popular thumbs–up signal accompanied by a smile to indicate acceptance

180

Exhibit 8-5

Cross-Cultural Differences in Communication

- Members of Asian and some Middle-Eastern cultures consider direct eye contact rude.
- Japanese people rarely use the word "no." When they say "yes" ("hai"), it acknowledges only that they have heard what was said.
- When Japanese people nod, they are indicating that you have been heard and understood, not necessarily that they agree with you.
- Korean people are hesitant to say "no," even when they have rejected a proposal. Koreans feel it is important to have visitors leave with good feelings.
- British people understate their feelings. If a British person says "Your report does raise a few questions," the real meaning is probably "Your report is atrocious."
- People from Latin America are very conscious of rank, and they expect the manager to be the voice of authority. Consequently, Latin Americans may be hesitant to make suggestions to a superior.
- Americans are eager to get down to business quickly and will therefore spend less time than people from other cultures in building a relationship.
- Americans value time much more than do people from other cultures. They are therefore more likely than people from other cultures to appear perturbed when a person shows up late for a meeting.
- French-speaking people tend to use polite forms of greeting, particularly in business settings, while Americans are less formal. When greeting a business contact in a French-speaking country, it is therefore important to include prefixes such as *Sir, Monsieur, Madame, Ms., Mademoiselle,* or *Miss.* (Note, however, that the entire world is becoming increasingly informal and first-name greetings have become more popular.)

SKILL-DEVELOPMENT EXERCISE

Cross-Cultural Skills

The information presented in the accompanying list will lead to cross-cultural skill development if practiced in the right setting. During the next 30 days, look for an opportunity to relate to a person from a given culture in the way described in the list. Observe the reaction of the other person to provide feedback on your cross-cultural effectiveness.

and contentment. The signal connotes acceptance and agreement in many cultures, but could be interpreted as a vulgarity in others. As with other nonverbal indicators, check out the possible interpretation of nonverbal gestures before using them in a business or social setting. (It could be argued that the agreement signal is really verbal communication because it is a symbol.)

5. *Do not be diverted by style, accent, grammar, or personal appearance.* Although these superficial factors all relate to business success, they are difficult to interpret when judging a person from another culture. It is therefore better to judge the merits of the behavior.[26] (This is also good advice in dealing with people from your own culture.) A brilliant individual from another culture may be still learning your language and thus make basic mistakes when speaking in your tongue. Or he or she might also not have yet developed a sensitivity to dress style in your culture.

6. *Listen for understanding, not agreement.* When working with diverse teammates, the differences in viewpoints can lead to conflict. If you listen for understanding, you prepare yourself to consider the viewpoints of others as a first resort. If everyone listens to understand, they can begin to appreciate one another's paradigms and accept differences of opinion.[27]

7. *Be attentive to individual differences in appearance.* A major cross–cultural insult is to confuse the identity of people because they are members of the same race or ethnic group. Research experiments suggest that people have difficulty seeing individual differences among people of another race because they react to race first, such as thinking, "He has the lips of an African American." However, people can learn to search for more distinguishing features, such as a dimple or eye color.[28]

THE POWER-ORIENTED LINGUISTIC STYLE

A major part of being persuasive involves choosing the right linguistic style, which is a person's characteristic speaking pattern. According to Deborah Tannen, **linguistic style** involves such behaviors as the amount of directness used, pacing and pausing, word choice, and the use of such communication devices as jokes, figures of speech, anecdotes, questions, and apologies.[29] A linguistic style is complex because it includes the culturally learned signals by which people communicate what they mean, along with how they interpret what others say and how they evaluate others. The complexity of linguistic style makes it difficult to offer specific prescriptions for using a power-oriented style. Nevertheless, here are many components of a linguistic style that would give power and authority to the message sender:[30]

Recognize the basics for becoming a more power-oriented communicator.

- Choose words that show conviction, such as "I'm convinced," or "I'm confident that. . . ." Similarly, avoid expressions that convey doubt or hesitancy, such as "I think," or "I hope." Be bold in expressing ideas, yet do not attack people. Intensify your writing with action verbs such as "spearheaded," "expanded," "innovated," and "decimated."
- Use the pronoun "I" to receive more credit for your ideas. (Of course, this could backfire in a team-based organization.)
- Emphasize direct rather than indirect talk, such as saying, "I need your report by 3 tomorrow afternoon," rather than, "I'm wondering if your report will be available by noon tomorrow."
- Frame your comments in a way that increases your listener's receptivity. The frame is built around the best context for responding to the needs of others. An example would be to use the frame "Let's dig a little deeper" when the other people in the room know something is wrong, but find pinpointing the problem to be elusive. Your purpose is to enlist the help of others in finding the underlying nature of the problem.
- Speak at length, set the agenda for a conversation, make jokes, and laugh. Be ready to offer solutions to problems, as well as suggest a program or plan. All of these points are more likely to create a sense of confidence in listeners.
- Minimize the number of questions you ask that imply you lack information on a topic, such as, "What do mean that most dot-com companies are burning cash?"
- Apologize infrequently, and particularly minimize saying, "I'm sorry."
- Take deep breaths to project a firm voice. People associate a firm voice with power and conviction.
- Occupy as much space as possible when speaking before a group. Stand with your feet approximately 18 inches apart, and place your hands on the top of your hips occasionally. The triangles you create with arms occupy space, and the hand-on-hip gesture symbolizes power to most people.
- Let others know of your expertise because people tend to defer to experts. Mention how much experience you have had in a particular phase of the business to get people to take your message more seriously. An executive might say, "I've brought two companies out of crises before, and I can do it for us right now."

Despite these suggestions for developing a power-oriented linguistic style, Tannen cautions that there is no one best way to communicate. How to project your power and authority is often dependent on the people involved, the organizational culture, the relative rank of the speakers, and other situational factors. The power-oriented linguistic style should be interpreted as a general guideline. Another consideration is that you may not want to project a powerful, imposing image. Some managers and professionals prefer to play a more laid-back, behind-the-scenes role.

IMPLICATIONS FOR MANAGERIAL PRACTICE

1. *Interpersonal communication is the basic process by which managers and professionals carry out their functions.* It is therefore critical to work toward unclogging communication channels in all directions. Part of unclogging these channels is to overcome communication barriers following some of the guidelines presented in this chapter. It is particularly important to be aware of communication barriers and to recognize the receiver's frame of reference.

2. *Two-way communication is usually superior to one-way communication.* Interact with the receiver to foster understanding. While delivering your message, ask for verbal feedback and be sensitive to nonverbal signals about how your message is getting across. Look for signs of agreement such as smiling or nodding, or signs of disagreement such as sideways shaking of the head or a frown. By so doing, many communication barriers (such as value judgments) will be overcome.

3. *Managers and professionals are well advised to pay attention to the nonverbal messages they send and receive.* A starting point is to become more conscious of one's facial expressions and those of other people. Managerial workers can also listen more carefully to vocal inflections, look closer to see what other people's eyes show about their true feelings, and pay attention to what they wear to transmit the desired messages about themselves. By paying close attention to nonverbal communication, managerial workers can improve communication and consequently improve productivity.

4. *Spoken and written communication in organizations,* as well as in the world outside, has become increasingly informal, and even managers and professionals make grammatical errors and overuse abbreviations in e-mail. Nevertheless, committing too many language errors can hold a person back from being promoted into higher-level positions. Executives tend to use language more formally and commit fewer major errors in grammar, such as double negatives and the confusion of plural and singular.

Communication Is Paramount at Le Meridien Visit **www.thomsonedu.com/management/dubrin** and watch the video for this chapter. How important is nonverbal communication to a hotel manager such as Bon van den Oord or Michiel Lugt?

183

SUMMARY OF KEY POINTS

 Describe the communication process.

Interpersonal communication takes place through the following steps: source (the sender), message, channel (medium), receiver, and feedback. The environment in which the message is sent and noise are also part of the communication process.

 Describe the impact of information technology on interpersonal communication in organizations.

Advances in information technology have influenced the quantity and quality of interpersonal communications in the workplace. Four such advances are e-mail, telecommuting, blogging, and presentation technology. E-mail facilitates communication but contributes to information overload. Some business firms have counterattacked the problems associated with e-mail by shifting to related technologies such as wikis and instant messaging. The company blog communicates business information with a soft, human touch, and can also be used to communicate similarly with employees. Telecommuters can lose out on face-to-face human interaction. People who make extensive use of presentation technology sometimes neglect to connect with the audience.

Computer-mediated communication can enhance communication by being more widespread and rapid. Yet many negative impacts are possible, including communication without the human touch, stress from repetitive motion disorder, the existence of wired managerial workers, and the encouragement of multitasking that leads to errors.

 Explain how nonverbal communication can be used to enhance communication.

Nonverbal communication helps express the feeling behind a message and includes the following forms: environment (physical setting), body placement, posture, hand gestures, facial expressions and movements, voice tone, dress and appearance, mirroring (to establish rapport), and touching. One of the many practical applications of nonverbal communication is to project enthusiasm and confidence with body language, such as when a person loosens his or her facial expression.

 Present details about the various channels of communication in organizations.

Formal communication channels are specified precisely in bureaucratic organizations. These channels are more difficult to follow in a network organization because of its spherical structure of self-directed teams. Informal communication channels supplement the formal channels, with the grapevine being the major informal communication channel. Rumors are an important communication force within organizations and provide information early. Management by walking around can be classified as both a formal and an informal channel.

Messages in organizations travel in five directions: downward, upward, horizontally, diagonally, and spherically (in the network organization). An open-door policy is an example of a formal upward communication channel.

 Summarize barriers to effective communication and how to overcome them.
Key barriers to communication include semantics, filtering of negative information, lack of credibility of the sender, mixed signals, different frames of reference, value judgments, information overload, and poor communication skills. Overcoming these barriers can involve activities such as clarifying ideas before sending, motivating the receiver, discussing differences in frames of reference, fostering informal communication, communicating feelings behind the facts, being aware of nonverbal behavior, obtaining feedback, adapting to the other person's communication style, and engaging in meta-communications. Active listening facilitates receiving messages more accurately.

 Explain how to overcome potential cross-gender and cross-cultural communication problems.
Sensitivity to gender differences in style is important for overcoming communication barriers. For example, men tend to be more direct in their conversation, whereas women emphasize politeness. Cross-cultural communication barriers can be overcome in general by sensitivity to cultural differences. Two specific tactics are to show respect for all workers and to use straightforward language and speak slowly and clearly.

 Recognize the basics for becoming a more power-oriented communicator.
To become a more power-oriented communicator, it is important to choose the right linguistic style. Among the features of a power-oriented linguistic style are choosing words that show conviction, emphasizing direct talk, and apologizing infrequently.

KEY TERMS AND PHRASES

Message, 163
A purpose or an idea to be conveyed in a communication event.

Noise, 163
Anything that disrupts communication, including the attitude and emotions of the receiver.

Telecommuting, 166
Working at home and sending output to the office electronically.

Nonverbal Communication, 168
The transmission of messages by means other than words.

Formal Communication Channels, 170
The official pathways for sending information inside and outside an organization.

Network Organization, 170
A spherical structure that can rotate self-managing teams and other resources around a common knowledge base.

Informal Communication Channels, 171
The unofficial network of channels that supplements the formal channels.

Grapevine, 171
The major informal communication channel in organizations.

Management by Walking Around, 173
The process of managers intermingling freely with workers on the shop floor and in the office, and with customers.

Open-Door Policy, 173
An understanding in which any employee can bring a gripe to the attention of upper-level management without checking with his or her immediate manager.

Semantics, 174
The varying meanings people attach to words.

Filtering, 174
The coloring and altering of information to make it more acceptable to the receiver.

Mixed Signals, 175
Communication breakdown resulting from the sending of different messages about the same topic to different audiences.

Frame of Reference, 175
A perspective and vantage point based on past experience.

Value Judgment, 175
An overall opinion of something based on a quick perception of its merit.

Information (or Communication) Overload, 175
A situation that occurs when people are so overloaded with information that they cannot respond effectively to messages, resulting in stress.

Paradigm, 176
A model, framework, viewpoint, perspective, or frame of reference.

Meta-Communicate, 177
To communicate about your communication to help overcome barriers or resolve a problem.

Active Listening, 177
Listening for full meaning without making premature judgments or interpretations.

Linguistic Style, 181
A person's characteristic speaking pattern, involving the amount of directness used, pacing and pausing, word choice, and the use of jokes, figures of speech, questions, and apologies.

DISCUSSION QUESTIONS AND ACTIVITIES

1. When a large number of job applicants are available to fill technical positions, hiring managers and human resource professionals are even more insistent about finding technical workers who have good communication skills. What might be the reasoning of these people hiring the technical workers?

2. Watch a business executive on television and evaluate how effectively the person uses nonverbal communication. Be ready to report your findings to your class.

3. We have all heard complaints about e-mail overuse on the job, yet how can the use of e-mail contribute to your effectiveness as a communicator?

4. If you are, or were, a full-time professional employee in a large business firm, would you establish your own blog to chat about the company with the public? Why or why not?

5. How can an organization benefit from good upward communication?

6. A business analyst from the Dominican Republic, working in the United States, said to her manager, "I am having a problem in meetings. When my coworkers are laughing, I do not know what they are laughing about. They all speak English too fast for me." What should the manager do in this situation?

7. Ask a successful person his or her impression of the importance of being a power-oriented communicator. Be prepared to share your observations with classmates.

CASE PROBLEM: Do We Need This Blogger?

Genève Ltd. is a manufacturer of upscale clothing and accessories for men and women. The company is headquartered in New York and has worldwide distribution. Manufacturing is carried out in the United States, Italy, Spain, Lithuania, and, most recently, China. Genève was founded in 1925, and has remained in business as an independent company.

As the demand for formal business attire diminished during the 1990s, Genève suffered a 35% decrease in sales. However, as the demand for formal attire on the job rebounded from 2002 forward, Genève has reestablished its sales volume. A few late-night shows featured guests who mentioned they were wearing suits with the Genève label, resulting in a surge in sales.

CEO Pauline Matthieu holds a 10 A.M. staff meeting most Monday mornings. Although she would like to have the meetings at 8 A.M., Matthieu recognizes that the commuters on the top executive team can rarely get to the office before 9:30 A.M. On this particular Monday, Matthieu is visibly upset. She tells her staff:

"It's not my pattern to dig too deeply into operational matters. As you know, I'm interested primarily in strategy and merchandising. Yet, I'm ticked off today. You probably all know about Jimmy Kincaid, the production planner from our Vermont plant who has set up a blog on Blogger.com to hold his personal forum about Genève. What he has to say about our fashions and our company usually isn't too negative, but he has become an embarrassment.

(continued)

CASE PROBLEM (Continued)

"In his latest blog, Jimmy has superimposed the faces of apes on the models featured in a current ad. The male ape says that Genève fashions will never be sold at Wal-Mart or Target, and the female ape responds, 'Are you sure?'"

"I guess that is a little edgy," said Harry Overstreet, vice president of operations. "Can you give us another recent example of Jimmy's blogs that should be a concern to the company?"

"I have a print copy in my briefcase," replied Matthieu. "Here, I will read it to you:"

The Genève label is still tops, but we're are slipping into some of the offshoring excesses of other companies. I saw a few undercover photos taken in one of our China factories, and the image does not do us proud. There are loads of Chinese women working in cramped quarters, the lighting is poor, and some of the girls working the cutting tools look to be adolescents.

Maybe the cool Genève image has an ugly underbelly at times.

Georgia Santelli, vice president of merchandising, commented, "Has any manager in our Vermont operation attempted to shut down this clown? I mean, he is a corporate menace."

Overstreet chimed in, "Wait a minute. Jimmy Kincaid may be a clown at times, yet he also says a lot of good things about Genève. He drops a lot of hints that create a buzz for our next season's offerings. One time he mentioned something about seeing a new handbag in the design stages that will make thousands of women switch from the Coach bags."

Sam Cohen, the director of marketing, said the company is contemplating a policy on blogging, and that it has been discussed internally. He said, "Here, let me dredge up the preliminary policy from my laptop.

Pauline was in on one of the preliminary discussions, but we didn't do much with it."

Cohen projected the slides, containing some bulleted points on the conference room screen:

- At work, employees can only use their blogs for work-related matters.
- Employees cannot disclose confidential or proprietary information.
- Private issues must be kept private.
- Public statements cannot be defamatory, profane, libelous, harassing, or abusive.
- Employees can only form links for their blogs to Genève with permission from executive-level management.
- An employee's blog must contain the following disclaimer: "The views expressed on this blog are mine alone and do not necessarily reflect the views of Genève Ltd."
- A breach of the above blogging policy could result in discipline up to and including termination.

Cohen said, "I'm still ticked off at Jimmy, but before we take action, let's think through whether he has done something drastically wrong. We have to protect Genève brand equity, but we must be fair. Let's talk."

Case Questions

1. Even though the blogging policy has not yet been implemented, how well have Kincaid's actions conformed to the tentative policy?
2. What steps, if any, do you think top management should take to control Kincaid's blogs?
3. What relevance does this case have for the subject of interpersonal communication?

Source: The blogging policy ideas are adapted from "Myemployersucks.com: Why You Need a Blogging Policy," *Virginia Employment Law Letter*, www.HRhero.com.

ENDNOTES

1. Cited in "The Top Job Skills for the 21st Century," *People@work*, May 1999, Professional Training Associates Inc.
2. Quoted in "Like It or Not, You've Got Mail," *Business Week*, October 4, 1999, p. 178.
3. Michelle Conlin, "E-Mail Is So Five Minutes Ago: It's Being Replaced by Software that Promotes Real-Time Collaboration," *Business Week*, November 28, 2005, p. 111.
4. Conlin, "E-Mail is So Five Minutes Ago," pp. 111–112.
5. Quoted in Todd Raphael, "E-mailing Your Way to Disaster," *Workforce*, July 2002, p. 88.
6. Michelle Conlin and Andrew Park, "Blogging with the Boss's Blessing," *Business Week*, June 28, 2004, p.102.
7. Jean Mausehund and R. Neil Dortch, "Presentation Skills in the Digital Age," *Business Education Forum*, April 1999, pp. 30–32.
8. Mausehund and Dortch, "Presentation Skills," pp. 31–32.
9. Based on U.S. Bureau of Labor statistics and data reported in Michelle Conlin, "The Easiest Commute of All," *Business Week*, December 12, 2005, p. 79.
10. Megan Santosus, "Why More Is Less," *CIO Magazine*, September 15, 2003.

11. Many of these ideas were first synthesized by Michael Argyle, *Bodily Communication,* 2nd ed. (Madison, CT: International Universities Press, 1990).

12. Jeffrey Jacobi, *The Vocal Advantage* (Upper Saddle River, NJ: Prentice Hall, 1996).

13. John V. Thill and Courtland L. Bovée, *Excellence in Business Communication*, 5th ed. (Upper Saddle River, NJ: Prentice Hall, 2002), p. 38.

14. Research cited in "Use Body Language to Gain Their Trust," *Managers Edge,* April 2000, p. 5.

15. Ann Davis, Joseph Pereira, and William M. Bulkeley, "Silent Signals: Security Concerns Bring New Focus on Body Language," *The Wall Street Journal,* August 15, 2002, pp. A1, A6.

16. Patrick Kiger, "Lessons from a Crisis: How Communication Kept a Company Together," *Workforce,* November 2001, p. 28.

17. Interview by Bob Rosner, "Studying the World beneath the Org Chart," *Workforce,* September 2001, p. 65.

18. Samuel Greengard, "Gossip Poisons Business: HR Can Stop It," *Workforce,* July 2001, pp. 26–27.

19. Cited in Mildred L. Culp, "Rumor Important, Say Managers Worldwide," WorkWise® syndicated column, March 28, 1999; "Make the Rumor Mill Work for You," *Executive Leadership,* May 2003, p. 7.

20. John P. Kotter, *The General Managers* (New York: Free Press, 1991).

21. Carroll Lachnit, "Tongue-Tied," *Workforce Management*, August 2003, p. 10.

22. The comment about nonverbal cues is from "See How Much You're Missing? How to Listen When You'd Rather Talk," *Working Smart,* April 2000, p. 7.

23. "5 Keys to Effective Listening," *Black Enterprise,* March 2005, p. 113.

24. Deborah Tannen, *Talking from 9 to 5* (New York: William Morrow, 1994); Tannen, "The Power of Talk: Who Gets Heard and Why?", *Harvard Business Review,* September–October 1995, pp. 138–148; Daniel J. Canary and Kathryn Dindia, *Sex Differences and Similarities in Communication* (Mahwah, NJ: Erlbaum, 1998), p. 318; John Gray, *Men Are from Mars, Women Are from Venus* (New York: HarperCollins, 1992).

25. "Cracking the Communication Code between Men and Women in the Workplace," http://www.advancingwomen.com/workplace/crack_communcode.html.

26. Roger E. Axtell, *Gestures: The Do's and Taboos of Body Language Around the World* (New York: Wiley, 1990).

27. "Use Team's Diversity to Best Advantage," *ExecutiveSTRATEGIES,* April 2000, p. 2.

28. Siri Carpenter, "Why Do they All Look Alike?", *Monitor on Psychology*, December 2000, p. 44.

29. Deborah Tannen, "The Power of Talk: Who Gets Heard and Why?", *Harvard Business Review,* September–October 1995, pp. 138–148.

30. Tannen, "The Power of Talk," pp. 138–158; "How You Speak Shows Where You Rank," *Fortune,* February 2, 1998, p. 156; "Proven Strategies for Gaining Cooperation," *Manager's Edge*, April 2000, p. 4; Robert B. Ciadini, "Harnessing the Science of Persuasion," *Harvard Business Review,* October 2001, p. 77; "Leadership Tips," *Executive Leadership*, June 2004, p. 8.

9

Group Dynamics

Ray Ogelthorpe, president of AOL Technologies, America Online Inc., was asked "What's the secret to a great team?" "Think small," he replied. "Ideally your team should have 7 to 9 people. If you have more than 15 or 20, you're dead. The connections between team members are hard to make.

"Two and one-half years ago, AOL was feeling hamstrung at the technologies level. There was a bottleneck at the top. We decided to make that division team-based, and created core teams that were empowered to make decision about products.

"It was the best thing we could have done. The core teams spun off satellite teams (also made up of small groups of people) that focused on specific projects, with specific goals and expectations.

"The management challenge is to understand that the people who report to you may get most of their direction from another person or from several other people: their team leaders. And people can be on more than one team, of course. It's the manager's job to think about whether *this* person is being stretched too thin, or whether *that* person needs some special training.

"Size is the key. Have the smallest number of people possible on each team."

Source: Regina Fazio Maruca, "Unit of One: What Makes Teams Work?" *Fast Company*, November 2000, p. 110. Permission conveyed through Copyright Clearance Center, Inc.

Now Ask Yourself: **What does this story about teams at AOL tell us about how group size can contribute to group effectiveness?** Understanding the characteristics of an effective work group, including size, is one of the major topics about group and teams discussed in this chapter. The heavy emphasis on teams and group decision making in today's organizations only increases the importance of understanding teams and groups for tomorrow's managers. In modern organizations, standard practice is to organize all sorts of work around groups and teams. Groups are vital to the understanding of organizational behavior because they are the building blocks of the larger organization.

TYPES OF GROUPS AND TEAMS

A **group** is a collection of people who interact with one another, work toward some common purpose, and perceive themselves as a group. The head of a customer service team and her staff would be a group. In contrast, 12 people in an office elevator would not be a group because they are not engaged in collective effort. According to Jon R. Katzenbach and Douglas K. Smith, groups and teams function differently.[1] A **team** is a special type of group. Team members have complementary skills and are committed to a common purpose, a set of performance goals, and an approach to the task. An important part of team functioning is **teamwork**—an understanding of and commitment to group goals on the part of all team members.

Describe the various types of groups and teams in organizations.

Groups and teams can also be differentiated in other ways. A working group has a strong, clearly focused leader, while a team leader shares leadership roles. A group is characterized by individual accountability, while a team has individual and mutual accountability. Another distinction is that the team delivers actual joint work products. Also, a group strives to run efficient meetings, while a team encourages open-ended discussion and full participation in problem solving. Speaking informally, a team might be regarded as a supergroup.

A major factor in understanding both groups and teams is that they are governed to some extent by **group norms,** the guidelines for acceptable and unacceptable behaviors that are informally agreed on by group members. Norms include behaviors such as (a) praising a group member who has just given a presentation at a meeting, (b) not flaunting the use of a competitive product or service, (c) assisting a coworker who needs your expertise, and (d) working on weekends to finish a project if necessary. Any punishment for not complying with norms comes from the group rather than formal systems established by the organization.[2] For example, the offender might be excluded from a group lunch or not consulted on a work problem.

Evidence suggests that being a good organizational citizen stems from both individual attitudes and group norms. One of the ways in which organizational citizenship behavior (OCB) and group norms are related is that when enough individuals in the group demonstrate OCB, the behavior becomes normative.[3] In one company, several members of the group took the initiative to welcome student interns and share work experiences with them, even when the interns worked in another department. Within a few years, helping interns became a group norm.

Groups and teams have been classified in many different ways. Here we describe the distinctions between formal and informal groups and among four different types of work teams. In Chapter 10, more information is presented about work teams.

Formal versus Informal Groups

Some groups are formally sanctioned by management and the organization itself, while others are not. A **formal group** is one deliberately formed by the organization to accomplish specific tasks and achieve goals. Examples of formal or work groups include departments, projects, task forces, committees, and search teams to find a new executive. In contrast, **informal groups** emerge over time through the interaction of workers. Although the goals of these groups are not explicitly stated, informal groups typically satisfy a social or recreational purpose. Members of a department who dine together occasionally would constitute an informal group. Yet the same group might also meet an important work purpose of discussing technical problems of mutual interest.

Types of Work Teams

All workplace teams have the common elements of people who possess a mix of skills working together cooperatively. Four representative work teams are cross-functional teams, top management teams, crews, and virtual teams. Self-managing work teams are described in Chapter 10. Projects, task forces, and committees are quite similar in design to cross-functional teams, so they do not receive separate mention here. No matter what label the team carries, its broad purpose is to contribute to a collaborative workplace in which people help one another achieve constructive goals. The idea is for workers to collaborate (a high level of cooperation) rather than compete with or prevent others from getting their work done.

As teams have become an integral part of the workplace, much effort has been directed toward specifying the skills and knowledge needed to function effectively on a team. The accompanying self-assessment quiz presents a representative listing of team skills perceived as necessary by employers. How many team skills do you possess?

Cross-Functional Teams

It is common practice for teams to be composed of workers from different specialties. A **cross-functional team** is a work group composed of workers from different specialties, but at about the same organizational level, coming together to accomplish a task. The purpose of the cross-functional team is to get workers from different specialties to blend their talents toward a task that requires such a mix. Product development is the most frequent purpose of a cross-functional team. In addition, cross-functional teams are used for purposes such as improving quality, reducing costs, and engaging in systems development.

A key success factor for cross-functional teams is that the team leader has both technical and process skills. The leader needs the technical background to understand the group task and to recognize the potential contribution of members from diverse specialties. At the same time the leader must have the interpersonal skills to facilitate a diverse group of people with limited, zero, or even negative experiences in working collectively.[4]

A major advantage of cross-functional teams is that they enhance communication across groups, thereby saving time. The cross-functional team also offers the advantage of a strong customer focus because the team orients itself toward satisfying a specific internal or external customer or group of customers. A challenge with these teams, however, is that they often breed conflict because of the different points of view. Also, the members may lack the teamwork skills to bring about a strong collaboration.[5]

190

SELF-ASSESSMENT

Team Skills

A variety of skills are required to be an effective member of various types of teams. Several different business firms use this skill inventory to help guide team members toward the competencies they need to become high-performing team members. Review each team skill listed and rate your skill level for each one, using the following classification:

S = strong (capable and comfortable with effectively implementing the skill)
M = moderate (demonstrated skill in the past)
B = basic (minimum ability in this area)
N = not applicable (not relevant to the type of work I do)

	Skill Level (S, M, B, or N)		Skill Level (S, M, B, or N)
Communication Skills		**Thought Process Skills**	
Speak effectively	_____	Innovate solutions to problems	_____
Foster open communications	_____	Use sound judgment	_____
Listen to others	_____	Analyze issues	_____
Deliver presentations	_____	Think "outside the box"	_____
Prepare written communication (including e-mail, intranet, and hard copy)	_____	**Organizational Skills**	
		Know the business	_____
		Use technical/functional expertise	_____
Self-Management Skills		Use financial/quantitative data	_____
Act with integrity	_____	**Strategic Skills**	
Demonstrate adaptability	_____	Recognize big-picture impact	_____
Engage in personal development	_____	Promote corporate citizenship	_____
Strive for results	_____	Focus on customer needs	_____
Show commitment to work	_____	Commit to quality	_____
		Manage profitability	_____

191

To perform well on a cross-functional team, a person has to think in terms of the good of the larger organization rather than in terms of his or her own specialty. For example, a manufacturing technician might say, "If I propose using expensive components for the plasma screen for television sets, would the product cost too much for its intended market?"

Virtual Teams

Some teams conduct most of their work by sending electronic messages to one another rather than conducting face-to-face meetings. A **virtual team** is a small group of people who conduct almost all of their collaborative work by electronic communication rather than face-to-face meetings. The team members are typically dispersed physically, but could also work in the same organization and contribute input at different times. Teleworkers are often part of a virtual team. E-mail is the usual medium for sharing information and conducting meetings. Groupware is another widely used approach to conducting a virtual meeting. Using groupware, several people can edit a document at the same time or in sequence. Videoconferencing is another technological advance that facilitates the workings of virtual team. Electronic brainstorming, as described in Chapter 5, is also well suited for a virtual team.

Most high-tech companies make some use of virtual teams. Strategic alliances, in which geographically dispersed companies work with one another, are a natural fit for virtual teams. It's less expensive for the field technician in Iceland to hold a virtual meeting with her counterparts in South Africa, Mexico, and California than to bring them all together in one physical location. If simultaneous input is desired, finding a time that fits all time zones can be a struggle. IBM makes some use of virtual teams in selling information technology systems, partially because so many IBM field personnel work from their homes and vehicles. Virtual teams are also an effective way of responding to new workforce demographics, in which the most talented employees may be located anywhere in the world, and may demand personal flexibility in terms of when and where to perform work.[6]

Global virtual teams face some unique opportunities and challenges. One advantage of team members from different time zones working together is that a project can be worked on 24 hours per day without anybody working an extended day. For example, workers in India can provide input to a project, pass it along to workers in England, who in turn pass it along to workers in New York. Yet global virtual teams also face the challenge of differences in perception of time, and different non-work days. July 4 might be a holiday for Americans, but not for Europeans. A project manager in Japan might need input from her counterparts in the United States and Europe on December 25, only to realize that most Americans and Europeans have a day off from work on Christmas Day. Another challenge is that some members of the global virtual team might regard time as a precious commodity, while others might not be concerned about deadlines. The lead member of the global virtual team has to be aware of different perceptions of time, and take actions such as building time-related norms.[7] For example, "Responding to client time demands transcends our personal convenience or cultural beliefs about time."

Mutual trust is a major factor for the success of most teams, and even more critical for a virtual team. Wayne F. Cascio and Stan Shurygailo observe that in a virtual team trust is established by repeatedly setting expectations and then delivering results that meet or surpass those expectations. An analysis of the development of trust in 29 global virtual teams that communicated exclusively by e-mail over a 6-week period found that three characteristics were associated with the highest level of trust. First, the interactions began with warm-up introductions about members, including the exchange of personal information. Second, clear roles were established for each member. Third, all team members demonstrated positive attitudes such as by showing enthusiasm and giving quick responses to all e-mail messages. The researchers also noted that the presence of just one pessimist in the group might undermine trust in the entire virtual team. Lack of trust, in turn, often lowers overall group productivity.[8]

Although members of a virtual team have limited or minimum face-to-face contact with each other, they still need guidance and direction. In many firms, members of the virtual team participate in face-to-face team training before beginning the formal work of the team. Exhibit 9-1 provides a variety of useful suggestions for managing a virtual team and enhancing teamwork.

Despite the efficiency of virtual teams, there are times when face-to-face interaction is necessary to deal with complex and emotional issues. Negotiating a new contract between management and a labor union, for example, is not well suited to a virtual meeting.

Establishing trust and commitment, encouraging communication, and assessing team members poses tremendous challenges for virtual team managers. Here are a few tips to make the process easier:

- Establish regular times for group interaction.
- Set up rules for communication.
- Use visual forms of communication when possible.
- Emulate the attributes of colocated teams. For example, allow time for informal chit-chat and socializing, and celebrate achievements.
- Give and receive feedback and offer assistance on a regular basis. Be persistent with people who aren't communicating with you or each other.
- Agree on standard technology so all team members can work together.
- Consider using 360-degree feedback (feedback from several different raters) to better understand and evaluate team members.
- Provide a virtual meeting room via intranet, website, or bulleting board.
- Note which employees effectively use e-mail to build team rapport.
- Smooth the way for an employee's next assignment if membership on the team, or the team itself, is not permanent.
- Be available to employees, but don't wait for them to seek you out.
- Encourage informal, off-line conversation among team members.

Source: Carla Johnson, "Virtual Teamwork," *HR Magazine*, June 2002, p. 71. Reprinted with the permission of *HR Magazine*, published by the Society for Human Resource Management, Alexandria, VA.

Exhibit 9-1

How to Achieve Virtual Teamwork

193

Crews

We are all familiar with the common usage of the term *crew* in relation to such groups as those who operate airplanes, boats, and firefighting equipment. The technical definition of the term means virtually the same thing. A **crew** is a group of specialists each of whom has specific roles, performs brief events that are closely synchronized with the work of other specialists, and repeats these events under different environmental conditions. A crew is identified by the technology it handles, such as an aircraft crew or a deep-sea salvage operation. The crew members rarely rotate specialties, such as the flight attendant taking over for the chief pilot. (Special training and licensing would be required.) The following are several criteria of a group qualifying as a crew[9]:

- There are clear roles and responsibilities.
- The workflow is well established before anyone joins the team.
- Careful coordination is required with other members in order to perform the task.
- The group needs to be in a specific environment to complete its task.
- Different people can join the group without interfering with its operation or mission.

Because of the specialized roles they play, and the essential tasks they perform, much is expected of crews. The future of crews is promising. For example, computer-virus-fighting crews would be a welcome addition to business and society.

Top Management Teams

The group of managers at the top of most organizations is referred to as a team—the management team, or the top management team. Yet as team expert Jon R. Katzenbach observes, few groups of top managers function as a team in the sense of the definition presented in this chapter.[10] The CEO gets most of the publicity, along with credit and blame for what goes wrong. Nevertheless, groups of top

ORGANIZATIONAL BEHAVIOR *In Action*

Top Management Team to the Rescue at Corning, Inc.

Corning, Inc. is prospering these days, particularly because of its booming LCD (liquid crystal display) business. Yet in 2002, the company faced difficult times. James J. O'Connor, the lead outside director, quietly began a campaign to replace CEO John W. Loose. Such unrest was unheard of at Corning, which for most of its 150 years had been governed by the descendants of founder Amory Houghton, Sr. "But I felt the business was in a meltdown, and time was running out," says O'Connor.

Just 2 years earlier, Corning had been a high-tech star, with $7 billon in sales and a market value of $100 billion. But now tornado-force winds were whipping through the telecom industry, slicing sales by more than half, sending the stock down 95%, and raising fears that Corning—one of America's oldest and most innovative companies—might not survive. To have a chance, "we needed someone at the top whom everyone could rally around," says O'Connor. In the board's view, there was only one credible candidate: retired CEO James R. Houghton, 68, who had turned Corning over to an outsider in 1996 after 13 years at the top.

Sure enough, Houghton electrified the company and its hometown in his maiden speech at a company annual meeting. He compared Corning's predicament to the darkest days of World War II and his role to that of Winston Churchill's. He vowed that Corning would reinvent itself just as previous generations had reinvented the technology for mass producing Thomas Edison's light bulb, the glass tubes that fueled the explosive rise of TV, and optical fiber, which ultimately made the Internet possible. "I am confident of victory," he concluded. "We will succeed." Within days, "We Will Succeed" posters, banners, and buttons had popped up everywhere.

After analyzing the problems facing Corning, Houghton recalls thinking that "Someone really screwed up. So let's line up everyone against the wall and figure out which one you shoot." He was especially enraged at the damage to Corning's culture. "The company had been ripped apart in a lot of ways, and there was a lot of backbiting and very little teamwork," he says. And the arrogance of the telecom group had become insufferable. "They felt they were king of the hill."

Houghton's answer was to return to a team style of management. He immediately reconstituted the management committee structure he had used to govern Corning in his first term, composed of the top seven execs. "I told them we are going to be together all the time, and that 95% of what we decide, we decide together."

Problem was, Houghton would have to achieve this change with the same executives who had served under Loose. With Corning in such dire straits, recruiting stellar outsiders would have been difficult, if not impossible. Houghton also knew that in a company dominated by lifers, ax-wielding outsiders would have quickly alienated the workforce and caused some of his best people to leave. Houghton promoted Weeks to president. "I need you to lead us out of this dilemma that you helped lead us into," he told the stunned executive. Similarly, he vaulted James B. Flaws, the CFO who had helped negotiate and arrange financing for billions of now nearly worthless photonic deals, to vice chairman.

Questions

1. Why might a top management team approach have helped Houghton turn around the company?
2. Why might have retaining executives who had failed the company helped build group (or team) spirit?
3. What do you think of the motivational value of "We Will Succeed" banners, posters, and buttons?

Source: Adapted from William C. Symonds, "Corning: Back from the Brink," *Business Week*, October 18, 2004, pp. 96, 100; http://www.corning.com.

managers are teams in the sense that most major decisions are made collaboratively with all members of the top management group included. Reuben Marks (Colgate-Palmolive) and Michael Dell (Dell, Inc.) are examples of highly visible and intelligent CEOs who regularly consult with their trusted advisors before making major decisions.

The term *top management team* has another, less frequent meaning. A handful of companies are actually run by a committee of two or more top executives who claim to share power equally. The executives agree between themselves as to which type of decisions each one makes independently and which decisions they make collaboratively. In this way, they are like a husband-and-wife team running a household. An example of a two-person team sharing power at the top comes from the merger of Exxon and Mobil. Some observers, however, are skeptical that a company can really be run well without one key executive having the final decision. Can you imagine your favorite athletic team having two head coaches?

The accompanying Organizational Behavior in Action illustrates how a company in trouble reverted to the top management team structure in order to rebound.

STAGES OF GROUP DEVELOPMENT

Key to understanding the nature of work groups is to know what the group does (the content) and how it proceeds (the process). A key group process is the group's development over time. To make this information more meaningful, relate it to any group to which you have belonged for at least one month. Understanding the stages of group development can lead to more effective group leadership or membership. The five group stages are shown in Exhibit 9-2 and described next[11]:

Stage 1: Forming. At the outset, members are eager to learn what tasks they will be performing, how they can benefit from group membership, and what constitutes acceptable behavior. Members often inquire about rules they must follow. Confusion, caution, and communality are typical during the initial phase of group development.

Stage 2: Storming. During this "shakedown" period, individual styles often come into conflict. Hostility, infighting, tension, and confrontation are typical. Members may argue to clarify expectations of their contributions. Coalitions and cliques may form within the group, and one or two members may be targeted for exclusion. Subgroups may form to push for an agenda of interest to them. (Despite the frequency of storming, many workplace groups work willingly with one another from the outset, thus skipping stage 2.)

Stage 3: Norming. After storming comes the quieter stage of overcoming resistance and establishing group standards of conduct (norms). Cohesiveness and commitment begin to develop. The group starts to come together as a

Summarize the stages of group development and key roles members occupy within a work group.

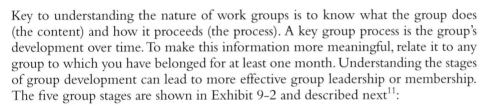
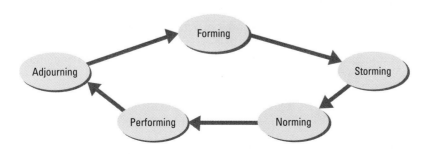

Exhibit **9-2**

The Stages of Group Development

Most groups follow a predictable sequence of stages.

coordinated unit, and harmony prevails. Norms stem from three sources. The group itself quickly establishes limits for members, often by the effective use of glares and nods. For example, the team member who swears at the leader might receive angry glances from other members. Norms may also be imposed that are derived from the larger organization and from professional codes of conduct. A third source of norms might be an influential team member who inspires the group to elevate its performance or behavior. The head of an audit team might say, "Let's develop the reputation of an audit team that is the most professional and objective in the industry."

Stage 4: Performing. When the group reaches the performing stage, it is ready to focus on accomplishing its key tasks. Issues concerning interpersonal relations and task assignment are put aside as the group becomes a well-functioning unit. Intrinsic motivation and creativity are likely to emerge as the group performs. At their best, members feel they are working "for the cause," much like a political campaign team or a team bringing a breakthrough product to market.

Stage 5: Adjourning. Temporary work groups are abandoned after their task has been accomplished, much like a project team formed to erect an office tower. The same group members, however, have developed important relationships and understandings they can bring with them should they be part of the same team in the future. The link between adjourning and forming shown in Exhibit 9-2 is that many groups do reassemble after one project is completed. The link between stages 1 and 5 would not apply for a group that disbanded and never worked together again.

A key managerial challenge is to help the group move past the first three stages into performing. At times, group members may have to be confronted about the fact that they are spending too much time on process issues and not enough on the task at hand.

Roles within Groups

Another perspective on group process is to identify team members' roles.[12] Positive roles are described here to help you identify areas of possible contribution in group efforts:

1. *Knowledge contributor.* Being technically proficient, the knowledge contributor provides the group with useful and valid information. He or she is intent on helping with task accomplishment and values sharing technical expertise with team members.

2. *Process observer.* A person occupying this role forces the group to look at how it functions, with statements such as, "We've been at it for two and a half hours, and we have only taken care of one agenda item. Shouldn't we be doing better?" The process observer might also point to excellent team progress.

3. *People supporter.* A person occupying this role assumes some of the leader's responsibility for providing emotional support to teammates and resolving conflict. He or she serves as a model of active listening while others make presentations. The people supporter helps others relax by smiling, making humorous comments, and appearing relaxed. He or she supports and encourages team members even when disagreeing with them.

4. *Challenger.* To prevent complacency and noncritical thinking, a team needs one or more members who confront and challenge bad ideas. A challenger will criticize any decision or preliminary thinking that is deficient in any way,

including being ethically unsound. Effective interpersonal skills are required to be a challenger. Antagonistic, attack-oriented people who attempt the challenger role lose their credibility quickly because they appear more interested in attacking than solving problems.

5. *Listener.* Listening contributes so substantially to team success that it comprises a separate role, even though other roles involve listening. If other people are not heard, the full contribution of team effort cannot be realized. As a result of being a listener, a team member or team leader is able to summarize discussion and progress for the team.

6. *Mediator.* Disputes within the group may become so intense and prolonged that two people no longer listen or respond to each other. The two antagonists develop such polarized viewpoints that they are unwilling to move toward each other's point of view. Furthermore, they have moved beyond the point at which conciliation is possible. At this point, the team leader or a team member must mediate the dispute.

7. *Gatekeeper.* A recurring problem in group effort is that some members may fail to contribute because other team members dominate the discussion. Even when the viewpoints of the timid team members have been expressed, they may not be remembered because one or two other members contribute so frequently to discussion. When the opportunity gate is closed to several members, the gatekeeper pries it open. He or she requests that a specific team member be allowed to contribute or that the member's past contribution be recognized.

8. *Take-charge leader.* Some teams cry out for direction because either a formal leader has not been appointed or the appointed leader is unusually laid back. In such situations, a team member can assume the role of the take-charge leader. The problem could be that team members are hesitant to make even simple decisions or take a stand on controversial matters. A starting point for the take-charge leader is to encourage the team to define its mission and list its three main objectives.

According to the team-role theory developed by R. Meredith Belbin, it is important for group members to understand the roles that others play, when and how to let another group member take over, and how to compensate for the shortcomings of others in the group. Roles tend to be based on the psychological makeup of individuals, who adopt them naturally.[13] For example, a person who has developed good listening skills will gravitate toward the listener role, and a knowledgeable, bright person will naturally assume the knowledge-contributor role.

The accompanying skill-development exercise gives you an opportunity to identify and observe the roles just described. Recognize, however, that these roles may overlap; they are not entirely independent of each other.

CHARACTERISTICS OF EFFECTIVE WORK GROUPS

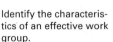

Identify the characteristics of an effective work group.

Groups, like individuals, have characteristics that contribute to their uniqueness and effectiveness. As shown in Exhibit 9-3, these characteristics can be grouped into 10 categories. Our description of work-group effectiveness follows this framework.[14]

Job Design

Effective work groups follow the principles of job design embodied in job enrichment and the job characteristics model described in Chapter 7. For example, both

SKILL-DEVELOPMENT EXERCISE

Team Member Roles

Form small teams to conduct a 20-minute meeting on a significant topic. Possibilities include (1) a management team deciding whether to lay off one-third of the workforce in order to increase profits, and (2) a group of fans who have volunteered to find a new team mascot name to replace "Redskins." While team members conduct their heated discussions, other class members should make notes of which team members carry out which roles. Watching for the eight different roles can be divided among class members, such as people in the first row looking for examples of a knowledge contributor. Use the following role worksheet to help you make your observations. Summarize the comments indicative of the role.

Knowledge contributor: _____
_____
_____

Process observer: _____
_____
_____

People supporter: _____
_____
_____

Challenger: _____
_____
_____

Listener: _____
_____
_____

Mediator: _____
_____
_____

Gatekeeper: _____
_____
_____

Take-charge leader: _____
_____
_____

Collaboration

task significance and task identity should be strong. Group members therefore perceive their work as having high intrinsic motivation.

A Feeling of Empowerment

An effective group or team believes that it has the authority to solve a variety of problems without first obtaining approval from management. Empowered teams share four experiences: potency, meaningfulness, autonomy, and impact. *Potency* refers to team members believing in themselves and exhibiting a confident, can–do attitude. Teams with a sense of *meaningfulness* have a strong collective commitment to their mission and see their goals as valuable and worthwhile. *Autonomy* refers to the freedom, discretion, and control the teams experience (the same as in job enrichment). A team experiences impact when members see the effect of their work on other interested parties such as customers and coworkers.[15]

Interdependence

Several types of interdependence characterize effective work groups. Such groups show task interdependence in the sense that members interact and depend on one another to accomplish work. *Task interdependence* is valuable because it increases motivation and enhances the sense of responsibility for the work of other group members. *Goal interdependence* refers to the linking of individual goals to the group's goals. For example, a member of a sales team might establish a compensation goal for

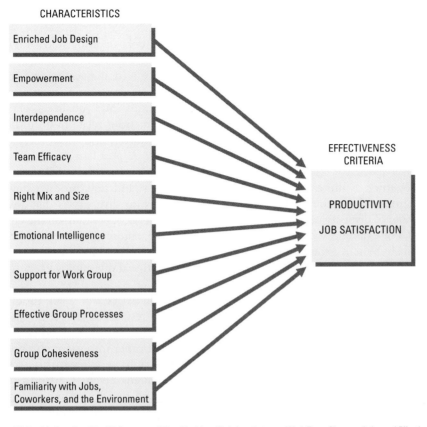

CHARACTERISTICS

Enriched Job Design

Empowerment

Interdependence

Team Efficacy

Right Mix and Size

Emotional Intelligence

Support for Work Group

Effective Group Processes

Group Cohesiveness

Familiarity with Jobs,
Coworkers, and the Environment

EFFECTIVENESS
CRITERIA

PRODUCTIVITY

JOB SATISFACTION

Exhibit **9-3**

Work-Group Characteristics Related to Effectiveness

All of the characteristics to the left contribute to group effectiveness in terms of productivity and satisfaction.

199

Sources: Michael A. Campion, Ellen M. Papper, and Gina Medsker, "Relations between Work Team Characteristics and Effectiveness: A Replication and Extension," *Personnel Psychology*, Summer 1996, p. 431; Bradley L. Kirkman and Benson Rosen, "Powering Up Teams," *Organizational Dynamics*, Winter 2000, pp. 48–52; Stanley M. Gulley, Kara A. Incalcaterra, Aparna Joshi, and J. Matthew Beaubien, "A Meta-Analysis of Team Efficacy, Potency, and Performance: Interdependence and Level of Analysis as Moderators of Observed Relationships," *Journal of Applied Psychology*, October 2002, pp. 819–832; Scott W. Lester, Bruce M. Meglino, and M. Audrey Korsgaard, "The Antecedents and Consequences of Group Potency: Longitudinal Investigation of Newly Formed Work Groups," *The Academy of Management Journal*, April 2002, pp. 352–368; Vanessa Urch Druskat and Steven B. Wolff, "Building the Emotional Intelligence of Groups," *Harvard Business Review*, March 2001, pp. 80–90; Claus W. Langred, "Too Much of a Good Thing? Negative Effects of High Trust and Individual Autonomy in Self-Managing Work Teams," *Academy of Management Journal*, June 2004, pp. 385–399.

herself, but she can realize this goal only if the other team members achieve similar success. Aside from the reality of interdependence, clearly defined goals are a major requirement for group effectiveness. Interdependent feedback and rewards also contribute to group effectiveness. Individual feedback and rewards should be linked to group performance to encourage good team play.

Team Efficacy

As with self-efficacy at the individual level, a productive group believes in itself. **Team efficacy** refers to a team's belief that it can successfully perform a specific task. A meta-analysis of 259 different samples indicated that team efficacy had a statistically significant relationship with job performance of teams. The relationship between team efficacy and performance was stronger when task interdependence was high rather than low. In other words, when group cohesiveness was more important, group self-confidence made a bigger contribution.[16]

Right Mix and Size

A variety of factors relating to the mix of group members are associated with effective work groups. A diverse group of members—in terms of experience, knowledge, and education—generally improves problem solving. Cultural diversity tends to enhance creativity because various viewpoints are brought into play. A study cautions, however, that only when each member of the group enjoys high-quality interactions can the full benefits of diversity be realized. The interactions relate to both the task itself (such as talking about improving a motorcycle starter) and social interactions (such as chatting about children during a break).[17] A problem with functional (technical specialty) diversity is that it can decrease the tendency of the group to stick together, as illustrated in a study of 93 research and new product development groups.[18] A general statement about work-group diversity is that any one dimension of diversity can have positive or negative effects, depending on the circumstances. For example, when group motivation and task ability are high, diversity will most likely benefit group performance. Imagine an auto design team composed of motivated and talented members. Cultural and educational diversity is likely to help the team produce a winning auto design.[19]

Groups should be large enough to accomplish the work, but when groups become too large, confusion and poor coordination may result. Also, larger groups tend to be less cohesive. Cross-functional teams, work teams, committees, and task forces tend to be most productive with 7 to 10 members. Another important composition factor is the quality of the group or team members. Bright people with constructive personality characteristics contribute the most to team effectiveness. A study involving 652 employees composing 51 work teams found that teams with members higher in mental ability, conscientiousness, extraversion, and emotional stability received higher supervisor ratings for team performance.[20] (In other words, put winners on your team, and you are more likely to have a winning team.)

Emotional Intelligence

As described in Chapter 2, emotional intelligence makes a major contribution to individual effectiveness. Teams also benefit from having members with high emotional intelligence in such ways as building relationships both inside and outside the team, and understanding the subtle human aspects of their environment. An emotionally intelligent group, for example, would not propose a costly, elaborate program during a period of corporate downsizing. For a group to be emotionally intelligent, it must do more than assemble a handful of emotionally intelligent members. High group emotional intelligence requires creating norms that establish mutual trust among members, a sense of group identity, and team efficacy. A potential problem, however, is that when group members trust one another too much, they neglect to monitor one another's work and may not catch errors and unethical behavior. The emotionally intelligent group deals constructively with emotion within the group, such as recognizing that the group is sad because a likeable member has been downsized out of a job, or that the group is ecstatic because it has surpassed its annual productivity goal.[21]

Support for the Work Group

The resources available to support the group and the context (environment) influence effectiveness. Key support factors include giving the group the information it needs, coaching group members, providing the right technology, and receiving recognition and other rewards. Training quite often facilitates work-group effectiveness. The training content typically includes group decision making, interpersonal skills, technical knowledge, and the team philosophy. Managerial support in the form of investing resources and believing in group effort fosters effectiveness. Communication and cooperation between groups improves group effectiveness, although management must help create an environment in which communication and cooperation can occur.

A representative example of how company-sponsored training improves group effectiveness took place at Centria, a manufacturer of wall and roof systems. One aspect of the training was to teach supervisors the STAR (Specific Task Action Result) system, a tool for positive feedback, as explained by the HR director:

> When you give somebody positive feedback, you say, "Today when you were running the line and set the new record, I was really impressed with the way you worked with all the team members and kept them focused on what they needed to do. By doing that, you were able to set a record that was 10% higher than anytime before."

That would be a positive STAR. The theory is if you give enough feedback and reward and recognize people for when they do it right, they're going to it right all the time.[22]

Effective Processes within the Group

Many processes (activities) that influence effectiveness take place within the group. One is the belief that the group can do the job (team efficacy), reflecting high team spirit. Effectiveness is also enhanced when workers provide *social support* to one another through such means as helping one another have positive interactions. *Workload sharing* is another process characteristic related to effectiveness. *Communication and cooperation* within the work group also contribute to effectiveness.

Interpersonal processes are important, and so are work processes. Teams that can be trusted to follow work processes and procedures tend to perform better. Adhering to such processes and procedures is also associated with high-quality output. Although following processes and procedures might appear to be a routine expectation, many problems are created by workers who fail to do so. For example, a group might show a dip in productivity if workers on a project fail to back up computer files and a computer virus attacks.

Group Cohesiveness

Group cohesiveness takes place when members work closely with each other, in a unified, cooperative manner. A cohesive group is likely to be effective. Cohesiveness is closely linked to several other dimensions of an effective work group. Collectively, the process characteristics described previously contribute to a group that pulls together. Without cohesiveness, a group will fail to achieve synergy. The right size and mix within a group will also foster group cohesiveness.

As with many organizational behavior concepts, group cohesiveness is composed of several components. *Interpersonal attraction* is a shared liking or emotional attachment to other members of the group. *Task commitment* is the extent to which there is a shared commitment to the group task. *Group pride* is the shared importance of being a member of the group. All three components are related to group efficiency in terms of making good use of resources, such as producing a website in a short period of time at a low cost. The components are also related to constructive behaviors, such as putting in the time required to produce the website.[23]

Familiarity with Jobs, Coworkers, and the Environment

Another important factor related to work-group effectiveness is familiarity. *Familiarity* refers to the specific knowledge group members have of their jobs, coworkers, and the environment. If you are familiar with your job, such as being an experienced market analyst, you have the knowledge base to make a better contribution to the group. If you know your group members well, there is more likely to be mutual trust, which facilitates group accomplishment. Knowing your coworkers also makes it easier to know who to ask for certain types of assistance, which leads to higher productivity. Knowing the environment, or culture, contributes to group effectiveness in ways such as knowing the kind of initiatives management will or will not accept. For example, in some companies suggesting that more money should be invested in the manufacture of a product is doomed to failure.

Familiarity, as it ties in to experience, is an asset for many types of jobs—at least if one has a certain level of proficiency. The contribution of familiarity is evident when new members join an athletic team. Quite often the team loses momentum during the adjustment period. The characteristics of an effective work group or team should be supplemented by effective leadership. Team leaders must emphasize coaching more than controlling. Instead of being a supervisor, the leader should become a team developer.

④

GROUP PROBLEM SOLVING AND DECISION MAKING

The majority of organizations use some types of groups. A major activity of many of these groups, including teams, is to make decisions. Furthermore, groups make most major decisions in organizations. In general, decision making by groups has proven superior to individual decision making. An exception is that people working alone generate a larger number of creative alternative solutions to a problem than they do during group brainstorming.[24] One reason might be that if you spend your time thinking of solutions rather than listening to other group members, you produce more ideas.

One method of group problem solving, brainstorming, was described in Chapter 5. Here we describe group decision-making styles, along with two other methods of group decision making and problem solving—the nominal group and Delphi techniques.

Group Decision-Making Styles

The term *group decision making* refers to a group playing a role in making a decision. Group decision making takes place in different degrees. One extreme is *consultative* decision making, in which the group leader consults with members before making a decision. The other extreme is *democratic* decision making, in which the problem at hand is turned over to the group, and group members are empowered to make the decision themselves.

Midway between the two is *consensus* decision making, in which the manager shares the problem with group members. Together they generate and evaluate alternatives and attempt to reach agreement on a solution. Consensus is achieved when every member can say, "I have had an opportunity to express my views fully, and they have been thoughtfully considered by the group. Even though this solution is not the one I believe is optimal, it is acceptable and I will support it. I endorse the validity of the process we have undertaken."[25]

The Nominal Group Technique

The opposite of an interacting group is a nominal group whose distinguishing characteristic is silent effort during part of group problem solving. Brainstorming by computer allows for the same noninteractive input by group members. The steps in the **nominal group technique (NGT)** proceed as follows:

1. Members of the target group are chosen and brought together.
2. If the group is too large, it is divided into subgroups of eight or fewer.
3. The group leader presents a specific question.
4. Individual members silently and independently record their ideas in writing.
5. Each group member (one at a time, in turn, around the table) presents one idea to the group without discussion. The ideas are summarized and recorded on a chalkboard, flipchart, or sheet of paper on the wall. If computers are used, the output can be displayed on a large monitor.
6. After all members have presented their ideas, a discussion takes place to clarify and evaluate the ideas.
7. The meeting terminates with silent, and independent, voting by individuals through a rank-ordering system (such as using a 1-to-10 scale). The nominal group decision is the pooled outcome of the individual rankings.[26]

The NGT has met with acceptance because it results in a disciplined decision. An advantage of this technique is that it combines the merits of individual reflection with the scrutiny of collective thought. One study demonstrated that the NGT overwhelmingly outperformed a standard brainstorming group.[27] Also, the NGT helps introverted people become actively involved in group activity.

The Delphi Technique

In some decision-making situations, group input is needed, yet it is difficult to bring people together because of the cost or time away from the office. Another problem is that some groups conflict so much in face-to-face meetings that it is difficult to solve problems and reach decisions. Managers might also believe that teleconferencing is not appropriate for decision making. The **Delphi technique** is well suited for these situations. (You will observe that this technique is a variant of the nominal group technique.) It is a group decision-making technique designed to provide group members with one another's ideas and feedback, while avoiding some of the problems associated with interacting groups.[28]

The Delphi technique incorporates a carefully structured sequence of questionnaires distributed to each group member, usually by e-mail. Each person answers the questionnaire about the problem at hand and transmits his or her responses and thoughts to the coordinator in an attached file or directly in the e-mail message. The leader aggregates the responses, and then sends them back to the team, and asks for feedback. Group members must trust the leader to aggregate and integrate the responses honestly. In some community groups, for example, the coordinator of the Delphi technique has been accused of using the technique to manipulate group opinion with no real intent of being objective about the decision reached by the group.[29]

Problem solving ordinarily improves with each successive input. In the last round of the questionnaire, group members are asked to vote for their choice of solutions. The coordinator edits the final version containing successive input from all the participants. The Delphi technique becomes a type of chain letter, and might be classified as a virtual group. Responses are sometimes averaged if the questionnaire calls for quantitative data. At other times, some people's choices and decisions are given more weight than those of other group members.

One problem with the Delphi technique is that it is more time consuming than group brainstorming or the nominal group technique. Delphi-technique sessions can last several days or even weeks.

POTENTIAL PROBLEMS WITHIN GROUPS

Pinpoint several potential problems with group effort and know how to prevent them.

204

Group activity, including group decision making, does not always lead to superior results. Failure to attain outstanding results typically stems from lacking the characteristics of effective work groups, as summarized in Exhibit 9-3. For example, a work group might fail if it was not empowered, the group was low on emotional intelligence, and the members were poorly trained. Furthermore, similar results would occur if the group lacked the support of management, members did not support one another, and members were quite unfamiliar with the task and with one another. Work-group failures also stem from dysfunctional processes. Here we look at three major processes within groups that can hamper their effectiveness: group polarization, social loafing, and groupthink.

Group Polarization

During group problem solving, or group discussion in general, members often shift their attitudes. Sometimes the group moves toward taking greater risks; this is called the *risky shift*. At other times the group moves toward a more conservative position. The general term for moving in either direction is **group polarization,** a situation in which postdiscussion attitudes tend to be more extreme than prediscussion attitudes.[30] For example, as a result of group discussion, members of an executive team become more cautious about entering a new market.

Group discussion facilitates polarization for several reasons. Discovering that others share our opinions may reinforce and strengthen our position. Listening to persuasive arguments may also strengthen our convictions. The "it's not my fault" attitude is another contributor to polarization. If responsibility is diffused, a person will feel less responsible—and guilty—about taking an extreme position.

Group polarization has a practical implication for managers who rely on group decision making. Workers who enter into group decision making with a stand on an issue may develop more extreme postdecision positions. For example, a group of employees who were seeking more generous benefits may decide as a group that the company should become an industry leader in employee benefits even in a era when benefits are being reduced.

Social Loafing

An unfortunate by-product of group effort is that an undermotivated person can often squeeze by without contributing a fair share. **Social loafing** is freeloading, or shirking individual responsibility, when a person is placed in a group setting and removed from individual accountability. If you have worked on group projects for courses, you may have encountered this widely observed dysfunction of collective effort.

Two motivational explanations of social loafing have been offered. First, some people believe that because they are part of a team, they can "hide in the crowd." Second, group members typically believe that others are likely to withhold effort when working in a group. As a consequence, they withhold effort themselves to avoid being taken advantage of. Their attitude is, "Why should I work so hard when the others are goofing off?" In contrast, a good organizational citizen would not succumb to social loafing.

Groupthink

A potential disadvantage of group decision making is **groupthink,** a deterioration of mental efficiency, reality testing, and moral judgment in the interest of group cohesiveness. Simply put, groupthink is an extreme form of consensus. Those in this group atmosphere value getting along more than getting things done.[31] The group thinks as a unit, believes it is impervious to outside criticism, and begins to have illusions about its own invincibility. As a consequence, the group loses its powers of critical analysis. Here is a relatively recent business decision that appears to have been the product of groupthink[32]:

> In January 2005, Microsoft Corp. threatened to sue Canadian teenager Mike Rowe for registering the domain name Mikerowesoft.com. After an online hue and cry, the company backed down and offered Rowe free software. "We take our trademark seriously," said spokesperson Jim Desler, "but in this case a little too seriously." [Note that Microsoft executives recognized that perhaps they made a poor decision, and proceeded to reverse the decision.]

Groupthink is most likely to take place under certain conditions. A highly cohesive group favors groupthink because members identify strongly with the group. Other contributing factors include directive leadership, high stress, group insulation, and a lack of built-in mechanisms for evaluating decisions. Having to choose between two unfavorable alternatives can lead to groupthink. An example would be an executive group deciding whether to recall a potentially unsafe product (and taking a huge loss) or leaving the product in distribution (and risking human suffering and negative publicity). Having limited time to make a major decision is another contributor to groupthink because the contributors may rush through the decision-making process.

A negative implication of groupthink is that it interferes with effective decision making. The emotional factors of wanting to achieve consensus and not wanting to be perceived as an irritant by other group members interferes with a person making an optimal decision. You might think that the alternative chosen by the group is terrible, yet you suppress your dissent to avoid being perceived as a dissident.

Groupthink can often be prevented if the group leader or member encourages all group members to express doubts and criticism of proposed solutions to the problem. It is also helpful to periodically invite qualified outsiders to meet with the group and provide suggestions. A specific technique proposed for combating groupthink is for the group leader in advance of the meeting to ask group members to write down their views anonymously on the decision in question. The leader then aggregates the individual statements into one list and distributes it to the group before the meeting. This kind of precommitment decreases group members' tendency to conform, even though the views remain anonymous.[33]

IMPLICATIONS FOR MANAGERIAL PRACTICE

Log on to **www.thomsonedu.com/infotrac**. Look for articles that highlight team building. Can you find examples of groupthink? What could be done to combat this mentality?

1. Be aware of group norms and the extent to which they facilitate or inhibit reaching organizational objectives. Reward systems must be developed that encourage high group performance. For example, if a group performs well on a given task and management then elevates performance standards, a norm toward lowered productivity may result.

2. When forming a new work group or team, recognize that time is needed before the group will be able to achieve maximum performance. Be alert to somewhat predictable stages of group formation and development: forming, storming, norming, and performing.

3. Be aware that group effectiveness is not a random occurrence. Strive to incorporate into the group many of the characteristics associated with work–group effectiveness, such as proper job design, the right composition, and workload sharing. At the same time, if the task to be performed does not really require interdependent work, a group is not likely to make a better contribution than individuals working independently.

SUMMARY OF KEY POINTS

 Describe the various types of groups and teams in organizations.

Groups and teams can be classified in various ways. They are governed to some extent by group norms, and organizational citizenship behavior stems from both individual attitudes and group norms. Formal groups are deliberately formed by the organization, whereas informal groups emerge over time through worker interaction. Four types of work teams described here are cross-functional teams, virtual teams (ones that meet electronically), crews, and top management teams.

 Summarize the stages of group development and key roles members occupy within a work group.

Groups are thought to go through five predictable stages of development: forming, storming, norming, performing, and adjourning. Group member roles include knowledge contributor, process observer, people supporter, challenger, listener, mediator, gatekeeper (letting others into the discussion), and take-charge leader.

Identify the characteristics of an effective work group.

Effective work-group characteristics are well documented. The jobs should be enriched, and the members should have a feeling of empowerment. Group members should be interdependent in terms of tasks, goals, and feedback and rewards. Team efficacy, the feeling of being able to accomplish the task, is important. The group should be a heterogeneous mix of members who are flexible and have a preference for group work. Group emotional intelligence—especially in terms of developing trust—is useful. The group should have support, including giving the group the information it needs, coaching group members, providing the right technology, and receiving recognition and other rewards. The group process should include team spirit, social support, and workload sharing, and following work processes and procedures enhances performance. Group cohesiveness contributes to performance and satisfaction and is composed of interpersonal attraction, task commitment, and group pride. Group members should be familiar with their jobs, coworkers, and the work environment.

 Implement two different methods of group problem solving and decision making.

Group decision-making styles follow a continuum from being consultative, through being based on consensus, to being democratic. When consensus is reached, all group members are at least willing to support the decision. The nominal group and Delphi techniques capitalize on the value of collective thought, yet minimize some of the problems that occur in interacting groups. Using the NGT, each person writes down ideas separately and later shares ideas with the group before all the ideas are ranked by group members. With the Delphi technique, each member responds to a questionnaire about the problem, passing along his or her input to the team leader, who aggregates the information and redistributes it as often as necessary. Finally, group members vote on the best solution.

 Pinpoint several potential problems with group effort and know how to prevent them.

Group effectiveness can be hampered in several ways. Polarization, or taking extreme positions, can result. Members may engage in social loafing, or freeloading. Groupthink, an extreme form of consensus and lack of critical reasoning, may occur as members strive for solidarity.

KEY TERMS AND PHRASES

Group, 189
A collection of people who interact with one another, work toward some common purpose, and perceive themselves as a group.

Team, 189
A special type of group in which the members have complementary skills, and are committed to a common purpose, a set of performance goals, and an approach to the task.

Teamwork, 189
A situation in which there is understanding and commitment to group goals on the part of all team members.

Group Norm, 189
The guidelines for acceptable and unacceptable behaviors that are informally agreed on by group members.

Formal Group, 190
A group deliberately formed by the organization to accomplish specific tasks and achieve goals.

Informal Group, 190
A group that emerges over time through the interaction of workers, typically to satisfy a social or recreational purpose.

Cross-Functional Team, 190
A work group, composed of workers with different specialties but from about the same organizational level, who come together to accomplish a task.

Virtual Team, 191
A group that conducts almost all of its collaborative work via electronic communication rather than face-to-face meetings.

Crew, 193
A group of specialists each of whom has specific roles, performs brief events that are closely synchronized with the work of other specialists, and repeats these events under different environmental conditions.

Team Efficacy, 199
A team's belief that it can successfully perform a specific task.

Group Cohesiveness, 201
A situation that takes place when members work closely with each other, in a unified, cooperative manner.

Nominal Group Technique (NGT), 203
An approach to developing creative alternatives that requires group members to generate different solutions independently.

Delphi Technique, 203
A group decision-making technique designed to provide group members with one another's ideas and feedback, while avoiding some of the problems associated with interacting groups.

Group Polarization, 204
A situation in which postdiscussion attitudes tend to be more extreme than prediscussion attitudes.

Social Loafing, 204
Freeloading, or shirking individual responsibility when placed in a group setting and removed from individual accountability.

Groupthink, 205
A deterioration of mental efficiency, reality testing, and moral judgment in the interest of group cohesiveness.

DISCUSSION QUESTIONS AND ACTIVITIES

1. Explain the meaning of this sentence: "All teams are groups, but not all groups are teams."
2. As you join a new work group, how will you learn the norms in order to fit in well with the group?
3. Why is membership on a cross-functional team such good experience for becoming an executive?
4. What relevance do the activities of a crew, such as a firefighting team, have for a professional group in the office?

5. Critics of the group and team movement in organizations often make a quip like "Have you ever seen a statue of a committee in a park?" What is their point?

6. How might you use the Delphi technique to help you prepare a more effective job résumé?

7. What is the difference between group decision making and groupthink?

Case Problem: The Adam Aircraft Work Group/Team

Joe Wilding scanned the skies over Oshkosh, Wisconsin, looking for the A700 jet aircraft he helped build. Wilding and his colleagues at Adam Aircraft had decided just 6 weeks earlier to sprint and finish their plan in time for Oshkosh's big summer air show.

In the aviation world, the A700's appearance would be one of the biggest surprise debuts ever. No one at the Oshkosh show expected Adam Aircraft Industry, a Colorado startup, to arrive with its jet. The company had announced the aircraft—its second product—only a year ago.

The plane had taken to the skies for its inaugural test flight just 4 days before. It had flown for a grand total of 15 hours since then, and was still a work in progress. The cabin wasn't pressurized, so the pilots had to wear oxygen masks in the cockpit. There were no seats or carpeting in the cabin. The landing gear stayed down, since the hydraulic system to retract it hadn't been installed yet.

Adam Aircraft's A700 was just one entrant in a race to build the first of a new generation of small jets. Also called "light business jets" or "personal jets," these planes hold fewer than eight passengers. They use newer, more fuel-efficient turbofan engines to slash the operating costs of the current generation of gas-guzzling private planes. The A700 costs about $2.25 million, less than half the price of many planes bought for personal use.

At a banquet, Rick Adam had batted the idea around with a few of his employees: What if they tried to finish the A700 in time for a cameo at the air show at Oshkosh? Adam felt good about the company's momentum. Earlier in his career, he had been chief information officer at Goldman Sachs, and then started a software company, New Era of Networks. As a Captain in the U.S. Air Force, Adam had worked on the mission-control computers for lunar missions 8 through 14.

When Adam returned to his office the day after the banquet, he called a meeting. "There were about 10 of us," recalled Dennis Olcott, the vice president of design engineering. The question was the feasibility of getting the A700 flying in time for Oshkosh. What would it take? Would it be a distraction from getting the A500 (the company's other plane) certified by the FAA?

The conceptual design for the A700 had been completed earlier in the year. In the spring, the team had started building a few random parts for the new plane. But the only pieces that were done by June, says Olcott, were "a lot of wing, most of the pieces for the tail, the landing gear, and one-half the fuselage shell." Only about 15% of the plan's exterior was finished.

The group gave the A700 a green light, and work started immediately. The plane would look like an elongated version of the A500, with twin turbofans on the back of the fuselage, instead of at the front and back of the cabin.

The team was able to move fast because team members did almost everything in-house. The engineers and the quality assurance manager sit in one big room at headquarters, with Rick Adam in the middle. In addition, the A700 shared more than 80% of its components with its predecessor. The manufacturing department already had experience assembling those parts on the three A500s they had put together.

The carbon composite construction would make the A700 lighter than jets made from aluminum, but more important, Olcott said, it let the team work faster. "We can build our own tools for making exterior panels extremely fast, and change them quickly. Our process takes a week and a half to build a tool. Aluminum tooling is bigger and heavier, and it can take months to have it made. You also wind up with more parts, which have to be riveted together, which takes a long time."

The streamlined process also meant the plan was a vivid presence for the team. "There was visible progress every day, and it was just incredible," Olcott said. "Parts would be glued together, or the plane would be painted, or the engines put on. One day it was standing on its own landing gear."

"Everyone in the whole company knew what out goal was, and everyone chipped in," says Wilding. In the engineering department, there's a large window that

CASE PROBLEM (Continued)

overlooks the shop floor. "We could see in an instant what the status was. The airplane itself became the motivator."

A month after the initial A700 meeting, the company's chief test pilot began conducting slow-speed taxi tests. "We've never built an airplane that fast before," says Wilding. "I don't know if anybody's built an airplane that fast before." During the first airborne test of the plane, the electrical generators did not function and had to be fixed the next morning.

The A700's presence so surprised the crowd at the Oshkosh show that Adam put a sign on the nose asserting that, yes, the airplane really did fly to the show from Denver. After the show, the team continued its work, treating the first A700 as a kind of airborne proof-of-concept, using it to make small adjustments to the design before the team began building planes for customers. The A700 received FAA certification in May 2005. Mike Leahy, a chiropractor from Colorado whose patients include the Denver Broncos, bought the first plane in November 2005.

Management is proud of the finished product, as stated on http://www.adamaircraft.com: "The A700 AdamJet is revolutionizing the value proposition in the Very Light Jet (VLJ) business jet class by delivering exceptional performance and comfort at a fraction of the ownership cost. Modern airframe design and materials, coupled with highly efficient turbofan engines, usher in a new era of business jet travel."

Case Questions

1. In what way did the speed factor enhance group performance?

2. Which characteristics of an effective work group does the Adam Aircraft team display?

3. In what way might the task of building a personal jet have contributed to the A700 team being a high-performing work group?

Sources: Scott Kirsner, "Some Magnificent Me and Their Flying Machines," *Fast Company*, November 2003, pp. 100–108; Kelly Yamanouchi, "Pops Go to Company, Pilot," *DenverPost.com*, November 15, 2005; "Ramping Up," http://www.redcoatpublishing.com/features/f_09_05_Cover.asp.

ENDNOTES

1. Jon R. Katzenbach and Douglas K. Smith, "The Discipline of Teams," *Harvard Business Review*, March–April 1993, p. 113.

2. Mark G. Ehrhart and Stefanie E. Naumann, "Organizational Citizenship Behavior in Work Groups: A Group Norm Approach," *Journal of Applied Psychology*, December 2004, p. 961.

3. Ehrhart and Naumann, "Organizational Citizenship Behavior," p. 964.

4. Glenn Parker, "Team with Strangers: Success Strategies for Cross-Functional Teams,"http://www.glennparker.com/Freebees/teaming-with-strangers.html. Material copyright © 1998 Glen Parker.

5. Avan R. Jassawalla and Hemant C. Sashittal, "Building Collaborative Cross-Functional New Product Teams," *Academy of Management Executive*, August 1999, pp. 50–63.

6. Anthony M. Townsend, Samuel M. DeMarie, and Anthony R. Hendrickson, "Virtual Teams: Technology and the Workplace of the Future," *Academy of Management Executive*, August 1998, p. 17.

7. Carol Saunders, Craig Van Slyke, and Douglas R. Vogel, "My Time or Yours? Managing Time Visions in Global Virtual Teams," *Academy of Management Executive*, February 2004, pp. 19–31.

8. Wayne F. Cascio and Stan Shurgailo, "E-Leadership and Virtual Teams," *Organizational Dynamics*, 4(2003), pp. 362–376.

9. Shelia Simsarian Webber and Richard J. Kimoski, "Crews: A Distinct Type of Work Team," *Journal of Business and Psychology*, Spring 2004, pp. 261–279.

10. Jon R. Katzenbach, "The Myth of the Top Management Team," *Harvard Business Review*, November–December 1997, pp. 82–99.

11. J. Steven Heinen and Eugene Jacobsen, "A Model of Task Group Development in Complex Organizations and a Strategy of Implementation," *Academy of Management Review*, October 1976, pp. 98–111; Bruce W. Tuckman and Mary Ann C. Jensen, "Stages of Small Group Development Revisited," *Group & Organization Studies*, 2(1977), pp. 419–427.

12. Glen M. Parker, *Team Players and Teamwork: The New Competitive Business Strategy* (San Francisco: Jossey-Bass, 1990); Thomas L. Quick, *Successful Team Building* (New York: AMACOM, 1992), pp. 40–52; "Lead or Lay Back? How to Play the Right Role on a Team," *Executive Strategies*, November 1999, p. 2.

13. R. Meredith Belbin, "Team Builder," in *Business: The Ultimate Resource Business* (Cambridge, MA: Perseus Books, 2002), p. 966.

14. Based on literature reviews and original material in Michael A. Campion, Ellen M. Papper, and Gina Medsker, "Relations between Work Team Characteristics and Effectiveness: A Replication and Extension," *Personnel Psychology*, Summer 1996, p. 431; Scott W. Lester, Bruce M. Meglino, and M. Audrey Korsgaard, "The Antecedents and Consequences of Group Potency: A Longitudinal Investigation of Newly Formed Work Groups," *Academy of Management Journal*, April 2002, pp. 352–368; Claus W. Langred, "Too Much of a Good Thing? Negative Effects of High Trust and Individual Autonomy in Self-Managing Work Teams," *Academy of Management Journal*, June 2004, pp. 385–399.

15. Bradley L. Kirkman and Benson Rosen, "Powering Up Teams," *Organizational Dynamics*, Winter 2000, pp. 48–52.

16. Stanley M. Gulley, Kara A. Incalcaterra, Aparna Joshi, and J. Matthew Beaubien, "A Meta-Analysis of Team Efficacy, Potency, and Performance: Interdependence and Level of Analysis as Moderators of Observed Relationships," *Journal of Applied Psychology*, October 2002, pp. 819–832.

17. Priscilla M. Elsass and Laura M. Graves, "Demographic Diversity in Decision-Making Groups: The Experiences of Women and People of Color," *Academy of Management Review*, October 1997, p. 968.

18. Robert T. Keller, "Cross-Functional Project Groups in Research and New Product Development: Diversity, Communications, Job Stress, and Outcomes," *Academy of Management Journal*, June 2001, pp. 547–555.

19. Daan van Knippenberg, Carsten K. W. De Dreu, and Astrid C. Homan, "Work Group Diversity and Group Performance: An Integrative Model and Research Agenda," *Journal of Applied Psychology*, December 2004, p. 1012.

20. Murray R. Barrick, Greg L. Stewart, Mitchell J. Neubert, and Michael K. Mount, "Relating Member Ability and Personality to Work-Team Processes and Team Effectiveness," *Journal of Applied Psychology*, June 1998, pp. 377–391.

21. Vanessa Urch Druskat and Steven B. Wolff, "Building the Emotional Intelligence of Groups," *Harvard Business Review*, March 2001, pp. 80–90; Claus W. Langred, "Too Much of a Good Thing? Negative Effects of High Trust and Individual Autonomy in Self-Managing Work Teams," *Academy of Management Journal*, June 2004, pp. 385–399.

22. "Centria's Hybrid Approach Trains Promoted-from-Within Plant Supervisors," *IOMA Report on Training Programs*, January 2003, p. 11.

23. Daniel J. Beal, Robin R. Cohen, Michael J. Burke, and Christy L. McLendon, "Cohesion and Performance in Groups: A Meta-Analytic Clarification of Construct Relations," *Journal of Applied Psychology*, December 2003, pp. 989–1004.

24. Larry K. Michaelsen, Warren E. Watson, and Robert H. Black, "A Realistic Test of Individual versus Group Decision Making," *Journal of Applied Psychology*, October 1989, pp. 834–839; Leigh Thompson, "Improving the Creativity of Organizational Work Groups," *Academy of Management Executive*, February 2003, p. 99.

25. William B. Eddy, *The Manager and the Working Group* (New York: Praeger, 1985), pp. 150–151.

26. Andrew J. Van de Ven and André L. Delberq, "The Effectiveness of Nominal, Delphi, and Interacting Group Decision-Making Processes," *Academy of Management Journal*, December 1974, p. 606.

27. The evidence is reviewed in Thompson, "Improving the Creativity of Organizational Work Groups," p. 104.

28. Normal Dalkey, *The Delphi Method: An Experimental Study of Group Opinions* (Santa Monica, CA: Rand Corporation, 1969); Thomson, "Improving the Creativity of Organizational Work Groups," p. 104.

29. For example, see "The Delphi Technique," **http://home. hiwaay.net/~becraft/Delphi.htm.**

30. Our discussion is based on Gregory Moorhead and Ricky W. Griffin, *Organizational Behavior: Managing People and Organizations*, 4th ed. (Boston: Houghton Mifflin, 1995), pp. 278–279.

31. Irving L. Janis, *Victims of Groupthink: A Study of Foreign Policy Decisions and Fiascoes* (Boston: Houghton Mifflin, 1972), pp. 39–40; Glenn Whyte, "Groupthink Reconsidered," *Academy of Management Review*, January 1989, pp. 40–56.

32. Adam Horowitz, Mark Athitakis, Mark Lasswell, and Owen Thomas, "101 Dumbest Moments in Business," *Business 2.0*, January/February 2005, p. 110.

33. Research reported in "Avoid 'Groupthink,'" *Manager's Edge*, March 2003, p. 2.

Teams and Teamwork

A while back, Julie Anderson was a manager in the Hewlett Packard distribution group. She volunteered to take on the challenge of redesigning the order-fulfillment system for a major client. Part of the challenge was that several teams had failed to accomplish the redesign goal despite the availability of considerable resources.

Anderson's new team—which included employees from each of the key HP business units plus two outside suppliers—had to operate at peak performance. The project was labeled the da Vinci Program, partly because of its importance and the creativity required. Anderson took several steps to guarantee the success of the program. First, she eliminated hierarchy. Anderson removed titles and rank and steadfastly refused to tell anyone what to do. Team members soon realized that they would have to fill that vacuum themselves. Second, she redefined the leader's role. Anderson describes her role as keeping everyone focused on the problem and reminding them of constraints.

Third, she challenged team members. Anderson encouraged everyone to ask "How am I contributing?" versus "How do you like the work I'm doing?" Fourth, she maintained momentum. Once a week, the team met to identify barriers and generate solutions.

As a result of these steps, the Da Vinci team completed the nearly impossible project under budget and ahead of schedule.

Source: Adapted from I. Barry Goldberg, "Teams Need More than Labels," http://www.arkansasbusiness.com, March 2005.

OBJECTIVES

After reading and studying this chapter and doing the exercises, you should be able to:

1. Explain the nature of a self-managing work team, and characteristics associated with team-member success.

2. Explain several mechanisms by which continuous learning takes place in teams.

3. Explain how to foster teamwork.

4. Develop insight into managing on-site teams as well as virtual teams.

Now Ask Yourself: **What does this anecdote from HP tell us about teamwork in business?** A major point is that the manager must sometimes take deliberate steps to enhance teamwork in order to accomplish a difficult goal. In this chapter we extend the discussion of workplace groups by focusing on teams. Teams, as a special type of group, are part of the collaborative organization. Workers within teams collaborate with each other, and teams also collaborate with other groups and teams throughout the organization. In a collaborative workplace, workers pay attention to superordinate goals, in which the needs of customers, investors, and other stakeholders (parties at interest) are as important as the self-interest of the teams and its members.[1] Our study of teams encompasses self-managing work teams, the selection of members for teams, how teams emphasize continuous learning, how teamwork is foster, and ideas about managing on-site (physical) teams and virtual teams.

SELF-MANAGING WORK TEAMS

Explain the nature of a self-managing work team, and characteristics associated with team-member success.

A dominant trend in job design is to organize workers into teams with considerable authority to direct and supervise themselves. A majority of U.S. corporations incorporate team structures, using some form of self-management, in their organizations. Team structures are also prevalent in European and Asian industry, particularly in manufacturing. A **self-managed work team** is a formally recognized group of employees responsible for an entire work process or segment that delivers a product or service to an internal or external customer.[2] Other terms for self-managed work teams include *self-directed work teams, production work team,* and *work team.* The difference in title sometimes refers to varying amounts of authority held by the group. Self-managed work groups originated as an outgrowth of job enrichment. Working in teams broadens the responsibility of team members. Implementing self-managed work teams requires that managers focus on empowering and motivating, rather than on controlling. A manager who uses a command-and-control style would not be comfortable with self-managed teams.[3]

Small as well as large companies make use of this form of job design. The key purposes for establishing self-managed teams are to increase productivity, enhance quality, reduce cycle time (the amount of time required to complete a transaction), and respond more rapidly to a changing workplace. Next we describe the method of operation of these teams and take a brief look at the results.

Method of Operation

Members of a self-managed work team typically work together on an ongoing, day-by-day basis, thus differentiating a work team from a task force or committee. The work team is often given total responsibility or "ownership" of a product or service. A work team might be assigned the responsibility for preparing a merchandise catalog. At other times, the team is given responsibility for a major chunk of a job, such as building a truck engine (but not the entire truck). The self-managed work team is taught to think in terms of customer requirements. The team members might ask, "How easy would it be for a left-handed person to use this can opener?"

To promote the sense of ownership, workers are taught to become generalists rather than specialists. Each team member learns a broad range of skills and switches job assignments periodically. Members of the self-directed work team also receive training in team skills. Cross-training in different organizational functions is also important to help members develop an overall perspective of how the firm operates.

212

1. Team members are empowered to share many management and leadership functions, such as making job assignments and giving pep talks.	6. Members typically order materials, keep inventories, and deal with suppliers.
2. Members plan, control, and improve their own work processes.	7. Members are sometimes responsible for obtaining any new training they might need. (The organization, however, usually mandates the start-up training.)
3. Members set their own goals and inspect their own work.	8. Members are authorized to hire their own replacements or assume responsibility for disciplining their own members.
4. Members create their own schedules and review their group performance.	9. Members assume responsibility for the quality of their products and services, whether provided to internal or external customers.
5. Members often prepare their own budgets and coordinate their work with other departments.	

As compiled by a team of experts,[4] the distinguishing characteristics of a self-directed work team are presented in Exhibit 10-1. Studying these characteristics will provide insight into work teams.

As a result of having so much responsibility for a product or service, team members usually develop pride in their work and team. At best, the team members feel as if they are operating a small business, with the profits (or losses) directly attributable to their efforts. An entry-level worker, such as a data-entry specialist in a market research firm, is less likely to have such feelings.

Although self-managing work teams may have an internal team leader, or work without one member being appointed as a leader, an external leader, such as a middle manager, still makes a contribution. One study showed that self-managing work teams were more effective when the external leader coached the team and prepared the team for challenges. One such challenge would be a heavy workload in the near future. To prepare the team, the leader could analyze what resources would be needed to cope with the workload, and provide these resources, such as hiring a new team member.[5]

Exhibit **10-1**

Characteristics of a Self-Managed Work Team

213

Research about Team-Member Characteristics

The previous discussion pointed to the importance of personal characteristics to be an effective member of a self-managing work team. The general idea is that to be a successful team member you need the right personality and cognitive characteristics. For example, an effective team member in most settings would need to be extraverted, conscientious, and mentally quick enough to adapt to changing circumstances. Here we summarize research about desirable characteristics of work team members.[6]

The data for the study were collected in a Midwest mill of a national steel corporation that emphasized human resource practices that facilitated employee commitment. The company is decentralized, has a flat organizational structure, and emphasizes employee involvement and empowerment. All hiring was done at the entry, individual level without a specific team in mind for the job candidate. Employees were placed (assigned to) specific teams after hiring. Teams of 5 to 10 workers were used to perform all production-oriented tasks, with most day-to-day decisions made at the team level. Team members were interdependent, and the teams in the mill were also interdependent—each department depended on the preceding department to complete its task. Visualize a band of steel going through different phases before being completed.

A *job analysis* was conducted to identify the skills, abilities, work styles, and other attributes needed for successful performance. Team members performed a range of activities in the departments; for example, teams in material handling delivered and distributed scrap metal to the melting and casting department and shipped finished product to customers.

Interview questions were then developed to assess the social skills needed for successful performance as identified in the job analysis. Among these skills were active listening, and a service orientation of looking for ways to help people. A sample interview question used was, "Suppose you thought you were being given more than your share of unpleasant tasks. What would you do?"

Personality characteristics were assessed through an instrument measuring conscientiousness, extraversion, agreeableness, and emotional stability (all part of the Five Factor Model described in Chapter 2). *Teamwork knowledge* was assessed through a test that measures how well a person responds to certain scenarios, such as those involving conflict resolution and goal setting.

For the *dependent variables,* department managers rated individual team members on their contextual performance (or behavior) in matters such as helping other workers and taking the initiative. Ratings were also made of how well workers performed on tasks.

Results of the study showed that workers who have good contextual performance tend to have good social skills and teamwork knowledge, along with relatively high standing on extraversion, agreeableness, and emotional stability. In this team setting, contextual performance was closely related to task performance, to the point that there is little difference between the two measures of performance. This information is useful in hiring people for work teams. A possible reason that conscientiousness did not differentiate between high and low performers in this study is that workers who did not appear to be conscientious were not hired. As a consequence, the workers in the study did not show large variation in conscientiousness.

Self-Managed Work Team Effectiveness

Self-managed work teams demonstrate a reasonably good record of improving productivity, quality, and customer service. Corporate executives and small-business owners have found that self-managed work teams are a highly effective form of work-group design. About 50% of the time, they result in at least some productivity gains, and effective teams can produce remarkable results. When self-management works, productivity gains of 10 to 20% are typical.[7] A representative example of the potential productivity gains from a self-managed work team took place at Monarch Marking Systems, based in Dayton, Ohio. The company manufactures labeling, identification, and tracking equipment. The teams trimmed the square footage needed in the assembly area by 70%, reduced past-due shipments by 90%, and increased productivity by 100%.[8]

A major contributor to work team effectiveness is the suitability of its members to a team operation. The accompanying self-assessment quiz gives you a chance to think about your mental readiness to work on a team.

Despite their potential contribution, self-managed work teams create challenges for managers. High-caliber employees are required for the team because they must be able to solve problems on their own and rely less on a supervisor. Many of the personal qualities required for team effectiveness are outlined in Exhibit 10-1. Effective contributors to a self-managed team must be multiskilled, and not all employees are willing or able to develop new skills. Another challenge for the manager, particularly the team leader, is being left with relatively little to do because the team is self-managing. In some firms, however, a middle-level manager might have overall responsibility for several teams. The team leaders become the direct reports, and the manager acts as a facilitator.

SELF-ASSESSMENT

Mental Readiness for Assignment to a Work Team

Directions: Respond to each statement using the following scale: SD, strongly disagree; D, disagree; N, neutral; A, agree; SA, strongly agree.

Amount of Agreement

1. Employees should make the majority of decisions related to their work.   SD   D   N   A   SA
2. It is possible for corporate employees to take as much pride in their work as   SD   D   N   A   SA
   if it were their own business.
3. Workers who lack advanced training and education are capable of making   SD   D   N   A   SA
   useful work improvements.
4. Groups can work effectively without a clear-cut center of authority.   SD   D   N   A   SA
5. It is worth sacrificing some specialization of labor to give workers a chance   SD   D   N   A   SA
   to develop multiple skills.
6. Competent workers do not require too much supervision.   SD   D   N   A   SA
7. Having authority over people is not as important as being part of a   SD   D   N   A   SA
   smoothly working team.
8. Given the opportunity, many workers could manage themselves without   SD   D   N   A   SA
   much supervision.
9. Cordial relationships are important even in a factory setting.   SD   D   N   A   SA
10. The more power workers are given, the more likely they are to   SD   D   N   A   SA
    behave responsibly.

Scoring and Interpretation: Score the answers 1 through 5, with SD being 1 and SA being 5. Add the numerical value you assigned to each statement and total your scores. The closer your score is to 50, the higher is your degree of mental readiness to lead or participate on a work team. If your score is 30 or less, attempt to develop a more optimistic view of the capabilities and attitudes of workers. Start by looking for evidence of good accomplishments by skilled and semiskilled workers.

CONTINUOUS LEARNING BY TEAMS

As teams of various types have evolved in recent years, increasing emphasis has been placed on continuous learning by members and the team as an entity itself. The general belief is that continuous learning leads to individual development and higher team performance. Here we look at four important factors related to continuous learning by teams: team learning orientation, unusual problems and crises leading to rapid learning, collective problem solving, and team coaching, as depicted in Exhibit 10-2.

Explain several mechanisms by which continuous learning takes place in teams.

KEY MECHANISMS

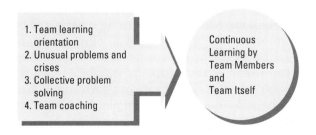

1. Team learning orientation
2. Unusual problems and crises
3. Collective problem solving
4. Team coaching

Continuous Learning by Team Members and Team Itself

Exhibit **10-2**

Key Mechanisms for Continuous Learning by Teams

Certain external factors as well as processes can foster continuous learning by teams.

Team Learning Orientation

Research has suggested that an appropriate emphasis on team learning will enhance performance, but too much emphasis on learning might lower performance. Data for the study were collected from the management team members of business units in a *Fortune* 100 consumer products company. Each business unit is responsible for marketing, producing, selling, and distributing the company's product line in the business unit's geographic market area. Performance was measured in terms of profitability relative to plan (or goals), and profitability relative to the number of units sold. The strength of team learning orientation was measured by a questionnaire. Team members were asked to assess, on a 7-point scale, the extent to which their team: (a) looks for opportunities to develop new skills and knowledge, (b) likes challenging and difficult assignments, (c) is willing to take risks on new ideas in order to find out what works, (d) likes to work on things that require a lot of skill and ability, and (e) sees learning and developing skills as very important.

Performance data were collected 1 year after the measurement of team learning, to provide a more precise understanding of how learning orientation is related to performance. For control purposes, factors such as team size, experience, and the functional (or professional discipline) composition of the teams were taken into account when investigating the relationship between team learning orientation and performance. Controls were important for the experiment because a factor such as team experience might influence how much attention is paid to learning, with more experienced teams emphasizing learning.

A major conclusion was that a team learning orientation did help groups improve business unit performance up to a point, particularly when the team has been performing well. Another conclusion reached is that if the organizational climate encourages learning, the team is more likely to engage in continuous learning.[9]

Unusual Problems and Crises Facing the Team

A workplace team can learn in a hurry when faced with an unusual problem or a crisis. D. Christopher Kayes describes the extreme example of September 11, 2001, when two pilots, five flight attendants, and 33 passengers responded to armed hijackers in midflight. In slightly over 30 minutes, a collection of passengers and crew formed a team, quickly analyzed the situation, asked around for additional information, wrote down a plan, and then took decisive action. The temporary team did not prevent the hijacking or a crash, but the plane was diverted from attacking a highly populated area by the team physically combating the hijackers.[10]

The relevance of fighting the hijackers to continuous team learning is that a team can learn from dealing with the unexpected. Faced with a crisis a team will skip the usual stages of group development described in Chapter 9. Instead, the team will learn immediately how to deal with the unexpected, including a crisis. Team members learn from each other and perform at levels that go beyond the capacity of the individual learning alone. Much of the learning is prompted by the complexity of the problem. A recurring example is that of an office totally damaged by a fire, explosion, hurricane, or flood. The team assigned to the project gets the company, or unit, back up and running faster than anybody believed possible. Among the complex tasks is to retrieve customer or patient information when both paper and computer files have been destroyed. (One team pleaded with customers to provide any records of transactions with the firm they might have.)

According to Kayes, much of team learning under unusual conditions stems from conversations among team members about specific and pressing problems. Conversation becomes the mechanism to shift individual knowledge into team learning. In the example of destroyed files, one team member said, "My aunt had a hardware store that catered to contractors. Her files were destroyed by a fire. She asked her customers to search their files to tell her what they owed. However crude it was, the system worked, and we can learn from her story."

Team learning from conversation has four elements. First is the generation phase—the team talks through the problem. Second is the gathering phase, consisting of asking around about ways of dealing with the problem. Third is the organizing phase—writing it down. Fourth is the acting phase—trying it out.[11] For example, in 2005 a recreational vehicle (RV) marketing team was dealing with the unusual problem of declining sales as gas prices surged. A conversation led to the idea that minority-group members seemed to have an affinity for luxury RVs. So the team decided to give the idea a try by drawing up plans to advertise in the magazines *Black Enterprise* and *Hispanic Business.*

Collective Problem Solving

One of the mechanisms for team learning is collective problem solving. Members freely share information and opinions with one another to facilitate problem solving.[12] The team learning can take place in several ways. The basic approach is to use group problem solving throughout the firm. As members solve problems together, they continue to learn. A clothing firm in the United States struggled with the challenge of exporting goods to China, as Chinese-made clothing was dominating the market. A team assigned to the project learned to find a few high-end niches in the market not now being served by Chinese manufacturers in China. The solution was profitable, leading to new team learning about exports and imports.

Another collective-problem-solving approach to team learning is to bring people together at a retreat, where they work in teams to reflect on ways of improving the organization. At one manufacturing company, a team-based revelation was that too many employee suggestions were too superficial, resulting in minor modifications of procedures or products. Supervisors were instructed to encourage workers to make suggestions that made dramatic improvements in how a product was manufactured, such as skipping a step or even questioning whether a part was needed at all. The continuous learning here is that the team learned how to bring about organizational improvement. In addition, many individual employees learned to make suggestions of greater substance.

Team Coaching

A direct way for a team to engage in continuous learning is to be coached as a team, in contrast to individual members being coached. As it relates to assisting teams, **coaching** is a direct interaction with the team with the intention of improving team processes to enhance performance. Both managers and professional coaches engage in coaching. A manager might coach a product-development team toward becoming more adventuresome and risk prone by asking the question, "Have you folks ever thought of going beyond the state of the art? What blocks you from thinking of a revolutionary product?" The team as a whole might then reflect on the level of its creativity. Individual coaching on this issue would take the form of asking team members one at a time the same questions.

217

Here, we briefly describe three aspects of team coaching: negative versus positive coaching, coaching functions, and leadership team coaching by an outside professional.

Negative versus Positive Coaching

The manager/coach can emphasize the positive or the negative. Positive coaching involves being supportive and reinforcing, such as pointing out where the product-development team has approached being revolutionary. In the process, the coach encourages self-management. Negative coaching emphasizes active intervention in the team instead of encouraging self-management by the team. An intervention in the product-development situation would be for the manager/coach to join the team for a few product-development brainstorming sessions so he or she could contribute a couple of revolutionary ideas.

Frederick P. Morgeson, in a study conducted in three organizations, found that supportive coaching was associated with being perceived as effective by team members. However, negative coaching in the form of the manager intervening was associated with effectiveness when the team was facing disruptive events.[13] (An axiom of leadership is that being direct with the group is important during an urgent problem.)

Coaching Functions

Another perspective on team coaching is that it consists of three primary functions, and each function works best at a particular point in the life cycle of the team.[14] *Motivational coaching* focuses on effort, and its functions are to minimize social loafing and to build shared commitment to the group and its tasks. Coaching aimed at motivation tends to be the most helpful when provided at the beginning of a performance period.

Consultative coaching focuses on performance strategy, and its functions are to point the way toward avoiding the wrong approach to the task, and to encourage proceeding with the task in ways that are aligned with task requirements. For example, a market research team might be encouraged to avoid using face-to-face focus groups to study whether a new method of storing image (photos and drawings) memories through an Internet service would have much of a market. Instead, the group might be coached to use an Internet survey technique because the respondents are the people who would most likely use the memory-storage service. Consultative coaching is most helpful when provided at the midpoint of a performance period, most likely because the team becomes aware of what type of task assistance it needs.

Educational coaching addresses knowledge and skills, and its main function is to encourage the best use of team-member talents, and to foster the development of members' knowledge and skill. A problem that sometimes arises in a team is that the ideas of an outspoken member are given more weight than his or her talent merits. Educational coaching is most helpful when provided after performance activities have been completed, so the team can perform even better in the future.

The time at which these coaching interventions are made influences their effectiveness, yet two other conditions are also influential. The first of these conditions is the extent to which key performance processes are constrained by external forces. With fewer constraints, coaching will have a more positive effect. For example, a cockpit-assembly team at Adam Aircraft can enhance its effectiveness in response to coaching only if there is an airplane awaiting construction.

The second of these conditions is the degree to which the group is a well-designed performing unit, following the characteristics of an effective work group described in Chapter 9. For example, if the mix of the team includes members who have considerable task-relevant knowledge and are conscientious, coaching will be more effective. As is generally recognized, it is much easier to coach talented people or groups!

Leadership Team Coaching by an Outside Professional

The team of organizational leaders is sometimes coached as an entity by an outside coach, often referred to as an *executive coach*. The subjects for coaching might include interpersonal or task issues. Interpersonal issues could include the executives having too much conflict among themselves, or having poor relationships with company insiders and outsiders. Task issues could include making hasty decisions, stonewalling against criticism, procrastinating, and behaving unethically. The role of the coach would not be to tell the leadership what to do, but to help leaders examine their own behavior and understand where improvement is needed. Often the focus is on individual members of the team, but the coaching is done with other team members present.

According to Manfred F. R. Ket de Vries, executive team coaching has become more in demand because managers realize that managing interpersonal relationships differentiates mediocre from high-performing organizations. The reason is that good interpersonal relationships help capitalize on talent and human capital. Many executives also realize that without continuous learning about dealing with people and making decisions, they will be left behind in an ever-changing global environment.[15]

The coaching session with the top-management team might take different forms, but a basic approach would be to frame the activity as team building (improvement in working as a team). The session might include team members completing questionnaires about their own leadership effectiveness and that of the other team members. Some of the feedback is personal, and some is shared with other members of the group. For sharing, each member of the team receives feedback on how others perceived him or her, such as "Janet makes some creative decisions, but she sometimes makes bad decisions because she doesn't listen to other members of the team." The written feedback is supposed to be a starting point for discussions about how the team members work with each other, and how interpersonal relationships and decision making might be improved. During a coaching session, the coach might ask the participants to share the feedback they received.

In one session, the coach read feedback to the group about John, one of the executives present. The coach talked about John's need for details, his problems in delegation because of being a micromanager, his inclination to take over for less-capable subordinates, his occasional moodiness, and his tendency to work too hard and to become overstressed. Being confronted with such feedback can sometimes lead to change, but may require a few individual coaching sessions to supplement the team coaching. During the session, the coach brought John's strengths to the attention of the other team members, to help boost the executive's confidence.

Team members were also asked what advice they could give John to help him become even more effective. One member said John should stop protecting the incompetents in his department, and avoid doing their work in addition to his own. Another participant complained how difficult it is to approach John and the people who report to him.

The expectation of team coaching is that interactions like those just described will lead to changes in behavior and style that will enable the team to be more productive. As you have probably observed in working in teams, it is often people problems that prevent the group from excelling. The same is true of the executive suite.

BUILDING TEAMWORK

Explain how to foster teamwork.

The team player roles described in Chapter 9 point to actions the individual can take to become a team player. The accompanying self-assessment quiz gives you the opportunity to gauge your current mental readiness to be a contributing team member. Here we highlight managerial actions and organizational practices that facilitate teamwork.[16] Good teamwork enhances, but does not guarantee, a successful team. Most executives, including CEO Jeffrey R. Immelt of GE, believe that teamwork is fundamental to the success of their organizations. Immelt often plays on the guilt of poor performers by telling them they are letting the team down.[17]

A robust strategy for building teamwork is to *share leadership among team members*, rather than the traditional practice of one person being in charge of leading his or her subordinates. In some teams, for example, the position is team leader is rotated among team members for a 1-year term. Leadership sharing can help develop the abilities of other team members, resulting in higher performance of the team as a whole.

The manager can begin by helping team members believe that they have an *urgent constructive purpose*. A demanding performance challenge helps create and sustain the team. Early in the history of the group, the manager should establish trust by *empowering the group to determine how to meet the objectives*. Teamwork is fostered when the team leader establishes the direction, then steps aside to allow the group to work out the details of getting the job done. A major strategy for teamwork is to promote the attitude that *working together effectively is the established norm*. Developing such a culture of teamwork will be difficult when a strong culture of individualism exists within the firm. The team leader can communicate the norm of teamwork by *making frequent use of words and phrases that support teamwork*. Emphasizing the words *team members* or *teammates* and de-emphasizing the words *subordinates* and *employees* helps communicate the teamwork norm.

A comprehensive tactic for building teamwork is to create a code of conduct for teamwork that functions much like a norm of teamwork, except that the code is written. The team creates a code that achieves consensus, and all members sign a copy of the code. To build the code, the manager or team leader identifies recurring issues that inhibit team performance and sets rules to govern that behavior. A few examples follow:

- Never abandon a teammate.
- Be on time.
- Keep all agreements. When necessary, clarify and commit to new agreements.
- Deal directly. If you have a problem with someone, go directly to that person with it or let it go.
- Be responsible. No laying blame on others, no justifications.
- Never humiliate anyone. No yelling or name-calling.
- Be loyal.

To enforce the code, thereby enhancing teamwork, if someone breaks the code, the manager or team leader says something such as, "This is what the code says and we all agreed to follow it."[18] A code of conduct also helps improve teamwork because the code facilitates *mutual trust among team members*. For example, if team members believe that their teammates will be responsible, deal directly with problems, and be loyal, mutual trust is enhanced.

SELF-ASSESSMENT

Team Player Attitudes

Directions: Describe how well you agree with each of the following statements, using this scale: Disagree Strongly (DS); Disagree (D); Neutral (N); Agree (A); Agree Strongly (AS).

	DS	D	N	A	AS
1. I am at my best working alone.	5	4	3	2	1
2. I have belonged to clubs and teams ever since I was a child.	1	2	3	4	5
3. It takes far too long to get work accomplished with a group.	5	4	3	2	1
4. I like the friendship of working in a group.	1	2	3	4	5
5. I would prefer to run a one-person business than to be a member of a large firm.	5	4	3	2	1
6. It's difficult to trust others in the group on key assignments.	5	4	3	2	1
7. Encouraging others comes naturally to me.	1	2	3	4	5
8. I like the give and take of ideas that is possible in a group.	1	2	3	4	5
9. It is fun for me to share responsibility with other group members.	1	2	3	4	5
10. Much more can be accomplished by a team than by the same number of people working alone.	1	2	3	4	5

Total Score _____

Scoring and interpretation: Add the numbers you have circled to obtain your total score.

41–50   You have strong positive attitudes toward being a team member and working cooperatively with other members.

30–40   You have moderately favorable attitudes toward being a team member and working cooperatively with other members.

10–29   You much prefer working by yourself than being a team member. To work effectively in a company that emphasizes teamwork, you may need to develop more positive attitudes toward working jointly with others.

Using the *consensus decision-making style* is another way to reinforce teamwork. By sharing in decision making, the leader communicates a sense of trust. As members collaborate in decision making, they are likely to develop more trust in each others' judgment. A sophisticated approach to enhancing teamwork is to *feed team members valid facts and information that motivate them to work together.* New information prompts the team to redefine and enrich its understanding of the challenge it is facing, thereby allowing team members to focus on a common purpose. A subtle yet potent method of building teamwork is for the team to *use language that fosters cohesion and commitment.* In-group jargon bonds a team and sets the group apart from others. An example is a team of information technology specialists saying "Send me a deck" to mean "Send me a PowerPoint presentation."

To foster teamwork, the manager should avoid **micromanagement,** or supervising group members too closely and second-guessing their decisions. Micromanagement can hamper a spirit of teamwork because team members do not feel in control of their own work. Yet, the team leader should also avoid a style of management so laid back that team members receive too little feedback and guidance (often referred to as macromanagement). A practical initiative that gets at the heart of teamwork is for team members to *learn what other members of the team are working on.* In this way, team members can fill in for each other, thereby fostering a spirit of teamwork.

Creating physical structures suited for teams is an effective organizational intervention to support teamwork. Group cohesiveness, and therefore teamwork, is enhanced when teammates are located close together and can interact frequently and easily. Frequent interaction often leads to camaraderie and a feeling of belonging. A useful method for getting people to exchange ideas is to establish a shared physical facility, such as a conference room, research library, or break lounge. Recognize, however, that workers still need private space so they can concentrate on work without interruption. The accompanying Organizational Behavior in Action box illustrates the use of both a cross-functional structure and physical structures to facilitate teamwork.

ORGANIZATIONAL BEHAVIOR *In Action*

Hypertherm Chief Executive Organizes for Teamwork

Richard Couch is the chief executive of Hypertherm Inc., a closely held maker of metal-cutting equipment in Hanover, New Hampshire, with annual revenues of roughly $200 million. For example, he has long promoted cooperation, with a company-wide profit-sharing plan that pays the same percent of salary to each employee.

As Hypertherm grew in the 1990s, Couch saw increasing friction between departments, such as engineering and marketing. So in 1997, he reorganized the company into cross-functional teams based on Hypertherm's five product lines. He forced the teams of researchers, engineers, marketers, and salespeople to sit together in closely bunched circles. He wanted the teams close to the shop floor, but retreated in face of safety rules requiring that manufacturing be shielded by a wall.

"The plan met resistance at first. One engineer complained about 'sitting next to this marketing guy. I don't have anything to say to him,'" Couch recalls. "I thought, precisely my point. Maybe you will actually say something to him." Some employees quit, he says, although the once-unhappy engineer is still at Hypertherm.

Today, Couch credits the reorganization with helping Hypertherm grow faster and more profitably. Instead of one product-development team, Hypertherm has five, which helps the company introduce new products faster. Couch says the new organization is also more efficient, because salespeople and marketers, who know customers best, are more involved in product development. The company recently paid $6.7 million in profit-sharing, equivalent to 26% of salaries, to its 612 employees.

Couch acknowledges that the team approach doesn't appeal to everyone. "The star can make more money going somewhere else," he says. But with attrition below 5% annually, Couch believes Hypertherm is doing a good job screening out nonteam players before they are hired.

Questions

1. In what way did cross-functional teams fit the purposes of Hypertherm?
2. How do you think the company screens out nonteam players before they are hired?
3. What is the difference between a star and a team player?

Source: Scott Thurm, "Teamwork Raises Everyone's Game," *The Wall Street Journal,* November 7, 2005, p. B8.

A key strategy for encouraging teamwork is to *reward the team as well as individuals.* The most convincing team incentive is to calculate compensation partially on the basis of team results. Team-based pay is useful for motivating employees to work more cooperatively, as long as the corporate culture emphasizes collaboration rather than individualism. Pal's Sudden Service, a chain of 19 fast-food restaurants in the southeastern United States, has a points-based reward program that is team oriented. The program is call "Feed the GATOR," an acronym for Get All the Orders Right. When there are no customer complaints after a shift, the manager "feeds the gator" with Pal's Bucks, which can be redeemed for high-end gifts from a company catalog, and distributes the Bucks equally to that shift's employees each month. The CEO says, "The only way to get Pal's Bucks is to build teamwork. The whole team has to be on."[19]

Another option available to organizations for enhancing teamwork is to *send members to outdoor (or off-site) training,* a form of experiential learning. Participants acquire leadership and teamwork skills by confronting physical challenges and exceeding their self-imposed limitations. Rope activities are typical of outdoor training. Participants attached to a secure pulley with ropes will climb up a ladder and jump off to another spot. Walking over white-hot coals to promote bonding is another team-building activity. (Yes, some participants have been hospitalized.) All of these challenges are faced in teams rather than individually, which fosters the development of teamwork. Outdoor training is likely to have the most favorable outcomes when the trainer helps the team members comprehend the link between such training and on-the-job behavior.

Some companies use off-site style team-building exercises on their own, without going to the time and expense of consultant-directed team building. Robert Grainger, associate marketing director for Kellogg Co., organized an afternoon scavenger hunt with the purpose of building teamwork. He divided his group into teams, giving each team 50 clues to find specific objects in the Chicago area. Among the objects were Kellogg and Keebler (now a division of Kellogg) products and photos of team members. Participants shared ideas and rotated leadership roles. Grainger believes that the team members developed mutual respect and gained new perspectives on problem solving and creativity.[20]

A modest technique for developing teamwork is for the manager or team leader to *publish a team book.* Each member prepares a one-page biography that might include a photo, a list of hobbies, personal interests, and family information. The responses are assembled in a volume that is distributed to other team members. If the book is published electronically, it can readily be updated as team members have worthwhile new entries. As coworkers scan the team book, they will become better acquainted with each other, and perhaps form stronger bonds.[21]

The accompanying skill-development exercise will give you additional experience in developing team skills. (We assume that most readers have had many opportunities to build team skills, in or outside of school.)

MANAGING ON-SITE TEAMS AND VIRTUAL TEAMS

Many other topics in this textbook deal with managing people, including motivation, communication, leadership, encouraging creativity, and resolving conflict. Building teamwork, as just described, is also an essential part of team management. Managing teams involves a few considerations additional to those of managing people in general. Here we describe a few special considerations about managing both on-site (or physical) teams and virtual teams.

Develop insight into managing on-site teams as well as virtual teams.

223

SKILL-DEVELOPMENT EXERCISE

Housing for the Homeless

Organize the class into teams of about six people. Each team takes on the assignment of formulating plans for building temporary shelters for the homeless. The task will take about 1 hour and can be done inside or outside of class. The dwellings you plan to build, for example, might be two-room cottages with electricity and indoor plumbing.

During the time allotted to the task, formulate plans for going ahead with Housing for the Homeless. Consider dividing up work by assigning certain roles to each team member. Sketch out tentative answers to the following questions:

1. How will you obtain funding for your venture?
2. Which homeless people will you help?
3. Where will your shelters be located?
4. Who will do the actual construction?

After your plan is completed, evaluate the quality of the teamwork that took place within the group. Specify which teamwork skills were evident and which ones did not surface. Search the chapter for techniques you might use to improve teamwork. The skills used to accomplish the house-for-the-homeless task could relate to the team skills presented in the self-assessment on page 191 of team skills presented in Chapter 9 or some team skill not mentioned in this chapter. Here is a sampling of the many different skills that might be relevant in this exercise:

- Speaks effectively
- Listens to others
- Innovates solutions to problems
- Thinks outside the box
- Displays a high level of cooperation and collaboration
- Provides knowledge of the task
- Sees the big picture
- Focuses on deadlines

Collaboration

On-Site Teams

The long-term research of J. R. Hackman suggests there are five conditions that foster a team's effectiveness.[22] An *effective* team according to Hackman meets or exceeds the expectations of the user of its output (the client). Also, the group works well interdependently, and the group experience contributes to the learning and personal well-being of its members.

The first condition for fostering effectiveness is that the team be a real team in terms of working together interdependently and understanding what authority it has in managing its work processes. Stability of membership is also important. A team that met the definition of a team presented at the beginning of this chapter would constitute a real team. The second condition is that the team has a compelling direction. Without giving the team clear direction of where it is headed, the team could flounder. One recommendation is to express the overall team task as a single short statement. Subtasks can be assigned later.[23] A compelling direction for a team of financial planners might be, "Our portfolio of investments must have a return 4 percentage points better than the S&P 500 this year."

The third condition is for the team manager to provide an enabling structure, including the design of the work, the norms of conduct, and the mix of people in the team. The characteristics of an effective work group presented in Chapter 9 could be interpreted as factors that lead to an enabling structure. The fourth condition is a supportive organizational environment. Included here would be reward systems, information systems, and education systems to handle the complexity of teamwork. Few managers would have the authority to modify the total organization to provide support, but at least the manager can make organizational executives aware of this condition. The fifth condition is that to manage a team toward effectiveness, the leader needs to be an expert coach. Keep in mind the previous discussion of team coaching. In addition, recognize that an effective coach listens, gives encouragement, and rewards good performance.

Attaining Collaboration in Virtual Teams

A major challenge in managing virtual teams is to ensure that collaboration and a spirit of teamwork exists among the geographically dispersed members. Virtual team members may work in different time zones, and even different companies. The suggestions for achieving virtual teamwork presented in Exhibit 9-1 are aimed at the successful management of virtual teams. Here are some additional suggestions for enhancing collaboration, communication, and group cohesion.[24]

To begin, work agreements should be formal and signed. A written pact should outline the team's job responsibilities, expectations, and deadlines. The role of the team leader or facilitator should also be made clear, such as indicating that the leader will carefully review all output and make suggestions for revision. Agreement should also be reached about which network technology will be used for the group members to communicate with each other. The technology could be as basic as e-mail or as advanced as online workspace, where team members can store and edit documents and have access to a shared database. The shared document is helpful in making sure that team members are working on the latest version of the project.

The leader should provide an organization chart that specifies who to contact for every part of a project. In this way each team member knows who is responsible for which phase of the project, thereby minimizing communicating to everyone on the team in search of information.

Although some virtual teams are far-flung, it is helpful to supplement virtual interaction with an occasional face-to-face meeting. Face-to-face meetings bring energy to collaboration that is difficult to attain electronically. The face-to-face meetings should focus on big issues facing the group, including major plans, and brainstorming. If the entire group cannot meet together face to face, the manager or a delegate should make an occasional visit to team members in their various locations. A caution is that if meetings are too frequent, the advantages of being a virtual team disappear. Team members can work faster when they do not have to wait for meetings to make decisions. Also, timid members of the group are more likely to offer criticisms when done online rather than face to face.

IMPLICATIONS FOR MANAGERIAL PRACTICE

1. Employees chosen for self-managed work teams should be those who show pride in their work and enjoy working cooperatively with others. Self-nomination or asking for volunteers for the self-directed work team will decrease selection errors. After employees are selected, they must be trained thoroughly to become productive members of work teams. Essential training areas include problem-solving techniques, technical skills, and interpersonal and leadership skills.
2. Managers can remove themselves as impediments to self-management of teams, while retaining the role of adviser and resource person, by asking these

225

Log on to **www. thomsonedu.com/ infotrac**. Search for articles related to team building activities in major corporations. What is the most productive example? The most outlandish? Do these sorts of team-building exercises translate into results back at the office?

Cannondale: Teams
Perform in the Race for
the Perfect Bicycle

Visit **www.
thomsonedu.com/
management/dubrin**
and watch the video for
this chapter. How does
Cannondale make use
of virtual teamwork to
produce its products?

questions of team members: (a) What is the cause of the problem?, (b) What are you doing to fix it?, (c) How will you know when it is accomplished?, and (d) How can I help?[25]

3. Even well-motivated teams tend to function best when given deadlines for certain tasks. To help build commitment to the deadline, it is helpful to discuss the feasibility of when the team receives the assignment. The discussion will sometimes point to impediments to reaching the deadline, such as needing another team member to carry out a specialized task. For example, a manufacturing team might need a robotics specialist part time to accomplish its mission.

4. Keep in mind the *team halo effect*, the curious phenomenon that teams are rarely blamed for their failures. Instead, the finger points to individual team members when the team does not accomplish its mission. Two studies conducted with business graduate students found that individuals were more likely to be identified as the cause of failure than the team as a whole.[26] It might therefore be valuable to recognize that the team as an entity could have problems that contribute to failure rather than immediately blaming one or two individuals for poor performance.

SUMMARY OF KEY POINTS

 Explain the nature of a self-managing work team, and characteristics associated with team-member success.

A dominant trend in job design is to organize workers into self-managed work teams in order to increase productivity and quality and reduce cycle time. The team is given total responsibility for a product or service in dealing with an external or internal customer. Each team member learns a broad range of skills and switches job assignments periodically. Team members plan, control, and improve their own work processes. They usually order materials, keep inventories, and deal with suppliers. Self-managed work team members have to be mentally flexible and alert and possess at least average interpersonal skills. They must take pride in their work and enjoy working cooperatively.

 Explain several mechanisms by which continuous learning takes place in teams.

Continuous learning in teams is most likely to take place when the team has a moderate learning orientation, is faced with an unusual problem or crisis, engages in collective problem solving, and receives coaching as a team from the team leader or an outside professional coach.

 Explain how to foster teamwork.

Managers and leaders can enhance teamwork through many behaviors, attitudes, and organizational actions, including the following: Share leadership among members; give the team an urgent, constructive purpose; develop a norm for teamwork; create a code of conduct for teamwork that facilitates mutual trust; use a consensus decision-making style; and feed team members valid facts and information that motivate them to work together. In addition, refrain from micromanagement; create physical structures suited for teams; reward the team as well as individuals; support outdoor (or off-site) training; and publish a team book.

 Develop insight into managing on-site teams as well as virtual teams.

Building teamwork is a key part of managing teams. In managing on-site, or physical teams, keep these conditions in mind: Make sure the group is a real team; give the team a compelling direction; provide an enabling structure for the team, such as the right size; provide a supportive organizational environment; and be an expert coach. To better attain collaboration, good communication, and group cohesion in virtual teams, follow these points: Have formal work agreements; clarify the team leader's role; agree on the network technology to be used; use an organization chart to specify who is responsible for what; and have occasional face-to-face interaction.

KEY TERMS AND PHRASES

Self-Managed Work Team, 212
A formally recognized group of employees responsible for an entire work process or segment that delivers a product or service to an internal or external customer.

Coaching (in relation to teams), **217**
A direct interaction with the team with the intention of improving team processes to enhance performance.

Micromanagement, 221
Supervising group members too closely and second-guessing their decisions.

DISCUSSION QUESTIONS AND ACTIVITIES

1. Many managers believe that experience on a sports team is good preparation for performing well as a member of a workplace team. As a result, these managers often give preference in hiring to people with experience in team sports. What is your reaction to the thinking and behavior of these managers?
2. Visualize a work team manufacturing a luxury sports car. What would be the alternative way of manufacturing such a vehicle?
3. How appropriate for working professionals are the teamwork code-of-conduct examples presented on page 220?
4. Imagine yourself as a virtual team member, working with teammates geographically dispersed who you have never met in person. Explain whether you would feel like you were really working on a team.
5. Outdoor (or off-site) training has achieved enormous popularity as a method of developing teamwork, even without research substantiation. What factors do you think account for its popularity?
6. If you were the executive in charge of an organization, would you authorize key members of management to participate in a scavenger hunt during working hours? Explain your reasoning.
7. Speak to a manager in a retail setting such as a supermarket or restaurant. Get his or her impression of the importance of teamwork in that work setting. Be prepared to share your findings with classmates.

CASE PROBLEM: Home Rehab Day at Tymco

Fifteen years ago, Maria Cortez was working as a freelance writer of technical manuals for a variety of companies. The manuals supported a number of products, including household appliances, alarm systems, lawnmowers, and tractors. Soon Cortez's freelance activity became more than she could handle, so she subcontracted work to one other freelancer, and then another, and then another. Two years later, Cortez founded Tymco, and the firm has grown steadily. The company now provides technical manuals, training and development, and foreign-language translation and interpreting.

Tymco now employs 75 full-time employees, as well as about 45 freelancers who help the company with peak loads as well as specialized services. For example, one freelancer translates software into Japanese. Another specializes in preparing user guides for digital cameras and digital video cameras.

Cortez recently became concerned that the unit heads and other key personnel in the company were not working particularly well as a team. She explained to Tim Atkins, a training specialist on the staff, "We all work for a company called Tymco, yet we function like independent units and freelancers. I notice that our staff members hardly even have lunch together. I've arranged a couple of group dinners, but other than having a nice meal, no team spirit seems to develop.

"I think that if we had better teamwork, our units could help each other. We might even be able to cross-sell better. I'll give you an example. A person in the technical manual group might have an assignment to prepare a manual for an appliance. He or she should immediately mention that Tymco has another group that could do the foreign-language translations for the manual. A lot of manuals for U.S. distribution are written in English, Spanish, and French."

(continued)

CASE PROBLEM (Continued)

Atkins replied, "Look, I've been eager to run a team-development activity that has worked well for dozens of companies, and it is so simple. We first designate who you think should be included in the group that requires the most development as a team. You choose one work day for the team-building activity. It involves targeting an old house badly in need of repair in a poor neighborhood. Abandoned houses don't count. We need a house with a family living in it. Working with churches in the neighborhood, it's easy to find a suitable house and a family willing to be helped.

"About a week before the team-building date, a handyperson and I visit the house to get some idea of the type of work that needs to be done. We then purchase all the needed supplies such as paint, roofing shingles, and wood. We also round up the ladders, paint brushes, and tools.

"On team-building day, the group descends on the house and starts the rehab process. Two days is usually needed. If we start the job on Friday, it could be finished on Saturday. In this way the group would receive 1 day off from work, and the members would contribute 1 day of their time."

Cortez was so enthused about Atkins's idea that she agreed on the spot on Friday, May 19, as the team-building day. She suggested that the day be called Tymco Home Rehab. Cortez made up a list of 10 key employees, including her, to participate in the team-building activity.

Friday morning at 7, the first of five different cars and trucks filled with Tymco staff members, ladders, tools, and home building supplies arrived at 47 Blodgett Street. Teena Jones, supervisor of technical manuals, shouted to the group, "We can't get anywhere until we start getting rid of the debris around the house and in the hallway. So let's get shoveling. The dumpster is on the way."

"Grab a few people and do what you want," responded Larry Boudreau, supervisor of technical documentation. "If we don't patch up that torn apart roof first, nothing else will matter. I need two warm bodies that aren't acrophobic [afraid of heights] to help me." Two other staffers agreed to agreed to work with Boudreau, while the seven other staff members, including Cortez, formed the clean-up brigade.

"Carpentry is my thing," said Mary Benito from translations services. "Let's get out the hammers, saws,

nails, and screws and start repairing this broken porch first. I want us to be ready for painting the house by noon tomorrow."

"Do what you want, Mary," said Dale Jenkins, a technical training team leader. "I'm good at home plumbing, and the toilets and sinks here are leaking more than the Titanic. I need a skilled pair of hands to help me. Any volunteer?"

Cortez said, "While you folks are shoveling debris and fixing, I'll run out and get us the food for snacks and lunch, and I'll order pizza for a supper break."

"That's the most sensible idea I've heard today," commented Larry Boudreau.

The Tymco team-building participants had supper together at 5 that evening, and went home at 8 to return at 7 the next morning. By 1 P.M., painting the house began, with all 10 people on the team participating. By 7:30, the house at 47 Blodgett Street was painted. The family, that was staying with neighbors, came by to cheer and weep with joy.

The Tymco team members exchanged smiles, high-fives, and hugs. "We can all go home now feeling that we've accomplished something really important as a team. And we can come back to the office on Monday morning knowing that we can work well as a team despite a few bumps and bruises."

"Good comment, Mary," said Ian Graham from the technical manual group. "Yet, I'm not so sure that replacing shingles on an old roof has made me a better team player."

Case Questions

1. What evidence was presented in this case that the staff members from different units at Tymco might have become better acquainted with each other?

2. What should Maria Cortez do next to improve the chances that the home-rehab day results in genuine team development?

3. What evidence is presented in this case that the home-rehab day did give a boost to team spirit?

4. How valid is Graham's comment about replacing shingles having no particular impact on becoming a better team player?

Source: The company described in this case has chosen to remain anonymous.

ENDNOTES

1. Michael M. Beyerlein, Sue Freedman, Craig McGee, and Linda Moran, *Beyond Teams: Building the Collaborative Organization* (San Francisco: Jossey-Bass/Pfeiffer, 2003).

2. Richard S. Wellings, William C. Byham, and Jeanne M. Wilson, *Empowered Teams: Creating Self-Directed Work Groups that Improve Quality, Productivity, and Participation* (San Francisco: Jossey-Bass, 1991), p. 3.

3. Andrew Leigh and Michael Maynard, "Self-Managed Teams: How They Succeed or Fail," in *Business: The Ultimate Resource Business* (Cambridge, MA: Perseus Books, 2002), p. 202.

4. This list is paraphrased from Wellings, Byham, and Wilson, *Empowered Teams,* p. 4.

5. Frederick P. Morgeson, "The External Leadership of Self-Managing Teams: Intervening in the Context of Novel and Disruptive Events," *Journal of Applied Psychology,* May 2005, pp. 497–508.

6. Frederick P. Morgeson, Matthew H. Reider, and Michael A. Campion, "Selecting Individuals in Team Settings: The Importance of Social Skills, Personality Characteristics, and Teamwork Knowledge," *Personnel Psychology,* Autumn 2005, pp. 583–611.

7. The evidence is reviewed in Roy A. Cook and J. Larry Goff, "Coming of Age with Self-Managed Teams: Dealing with a Problem Employee," *Journal of Business and Psychology,* Spring 2002, pp. 487–488; Leigh and Maynard, "Self-Managed Teams," p. 202.

8. Data in this paragraph are from Carla Johnson, "Teams at Work," *HR Magazine,* May 1999, p. 32.

9. J. Stuart Bunderson and Kathleen M. Sutcliffe, "Management Team Learning Orientation and Business Unit performance," *Journal of Applied Psychology,* June 2003, pp. 552–560.

10. D. Christopher Kayes, "Proximal Team Learning: Lessons from United Flight 93 on 9/11," *Organizational Dynamics,* 1(2003), pp. 80–91.

11. Kayes, "Proximal Team Learning," p. 84.

12. Ruth Wageman, "How Leaders Foster Self-Managing Team Effectiveness: Design Choices versus Hands-On Coaching," *Organization Science, 12* (2001), p. 561.

13. Morgeson, "The External Leadership of Self-Managing Teams," p. 505.

14. J. Richard Hackman and Ruth Wageman, "A Theory of Team Coaching," *Academy of Management Review,* April 2005, pp. 269–287.

15. Manfred F. R. Ket de Vries, "Leadership Group Coaching in Action: The Zen of Creating High Performance Teams," *Academy of Management Executive,* February 2005, pp. 61–76.

16. Many of the ideas in this section come from "Teamwork in a Shock Trauma Unit: New Lessons in Leadership," *Leadership and Change,* http://www.Knowledge@Wharton.com; Ruth Wageman, "Critical Success Factors for Creating Superb Self-Managing Teams," *Organizational Dynamics,* Summer 1997, p. 57; "What Makes Teams Work?" *HRfocus* (Special Report on Teams), April 2002, S1, S3–S4; Jon R. Katzenbach and Douglas K. Smith, "The Discipline of Teams," *Harvard Business Review,* March-April 1993, pp. 118–119; Rebecca Winters, "Extreme Offsites," *Time,* August 9, 1999, pp. 75A–76A; Charlotte Garvey, "Steer Teams with the Right Pay," *HR Magazine,* May 2002, pp. 70–78.

17. Matt Murray, "GE's Immelt Starts Renovations in the House that Jack Built," *The Wall Street Journal,* February 6, 2003, p. A6.

18. "Improve Teamwork with a 'Code of Conduct,'" *Manager's Edge,* February 2005, p. 1; Blair Singer, *Rich Dad's Advisor: The ABC's of Building a Business Team That Wins,* Warner Business Books, http://www.twbookmark.com. (Audio book, 2005.)

19. "Teamwork that Builds Happiness," *Manager's Edge,* March 2005; "Fast and Happy," Leo Jakobson, *Incentives,* http://www.incentivemag.com.

20. "'Do-It Yourself' Team Retreats," *Manager's Edge,* June 2005, p. 2; "Goodwill Hunting," *Training Magazine,* http://www.trainingmag.com.

21. "Easy Ways to Build Team Spirit," *Executive Leadership,* August 2003, p. 5.

22. J.R. Hackman, *Leading Teams: Setting the Stage for Great Performances* (Boston: Harvard Business School Press, 2002).

23. "Clarify Team Roles to Ensure Success," *Manager's Edge,* August 2005, p. 6.

24. "Seven Tactics to Build Cohesion," *Flexible Workplace Management,* sample issue, 2001 (Chicago: Lawrence Ragan Communications); Rachael King, "All Together Now: How Collaboration Software Can Make Your Company More Efficient," *Business Week SmallBiz,* Winter 2005, pp. 68–70.

25. Ann Majchrzak, Arvind Malhotra, Jeffery Stamps, and Jessica Lipnack, "Can Absence Make a Team Grow Stronger?" *Harvard Business Review,* May 2004, pp. 131–137.

26. Charles E. Naquin and Renee O. Tynan, "The Team Halo Effect: Why Teams Are Not Blamed for Their Failures," *Journal of Applied Psychology,* April 2003, pp. 332–340.

229

11

OBJECTIVES

After reading and studying this chapter and doing the exercises, you should be able to:

1. Differentiate between leadership and management.

2. Describe key leadership traits, styles, and behaviors.

3. Explain the basics of four contingency theories of leadership.

4. Present an overview of transformational and charismatic leadership.

5. Identify forces that can sometimes decrease the importance of leadership.

Leadership in Organizations

At one point in the history of his company, Linus Torvalds faced a mutiny. The reclusive Finn had taken the lead in creating the Linux computer operating system, with the help of thousands of volunteer programmers, and the open-source software had become wildly popular for running websites during the dot-com boom. But just as Linux was taking off, some programmers rebelled. Torvalds's insistence on manually reviewing everything that went into the software was creating a logjam, they warned. Unless he changed his ways, they might concoct a rival software package—a threat that could have crippled Linux. "Everybody knew things were falling apart," recalls Larry McVoy, a programmer who played peacemaker. "Something had to be done."

The crisis came to a head during a tense meeting at McVoy's house, on San Francisco's Twin Peaks. A handful of Linux's top contributors took turns urging Torvalds to change. After an awkward dinner of quiche and croissants, they sat on the living room floor and hashed things out. Four hours later, Torvalds relented. He agreed to delegate more and to use a software program for automating the handling of code. When the program was ready in 2002, Torvalds was able to process contributions five times as fast as he had in the past.

Source: Steve Hamm, "Linux Inc.," *Business Week*, January 31, 2005, p. 60.

Now Ask Yourself: **What does this Linux story tell us about leadership?**
For a leader to enable the company to move forward, it may be necessary for him or her to adapt his or her leadership approach in response to the demands of the situation—particularly the requests of subordinates. The effective leader is flexible enough to tweak his or her approach to leading as circumstances arise, and trusts the group members enough to listen to their suggestions. In this chapter we describe a variety of leadership theories and practices. Many of them involve some type of participation of group members in decision making.

Leadership has always been a topic of major importance to scholars and practitioners, and current interest is intense as organizations struggle to survive in a hypercompetitive world. Executives themselves think that knowledge of leadership is important for organizational success. Samuel J. Palmisano, the CEO of IBM, invested $100 million of company funds in 1 year into teaching 30,000 employees to lead, rather than control, their staffs so that employees would not feel like cogs in a machine.[1] He continues to invest heavily in leadership development and training.

Leadership is not the domain of just a few members of top management. Today, leadership is often thought of as being distributed among all group members, so one person is not responsible for all the leadership activities.[2] The ability to take charge is important at all levels of management. Employees who are in direct contact with customers and clients often require stronger leadership than do higher-level workers. Entry-level workers often lack experience, direction, and a strong work ethic. Furthermore, the emphasis on teams means that effective team leaders are needed throughout the organization.

The discussion of leadership in this chapter centers on several topics of interest to managers and professionals: leadership traits, styles, and behaviors; contingency theories of leadership; transformational and charismatic leadership; and substitutes for leadership. Chapter 12 deals with other topics closely associated with leaders, such as power and influence. First, however, let us look at the nature of leadership.

THE NATURE OF LEADERSHIP

Leadership involves influencing others to achieve objectives important to them and the organization. With effective leadership, people want to contribute to the organization's success. A representative definition is that **leadership** is the ability to inspire confidence and support among the people on whose competence and commitment performance depends.[3] The term *leadership* generally refers to leadership exercised at any organizational level, whereas *strategic leadership* refers to leadership activity among the top-level executives.

Differentiate between leadership and management.

Although leadership is a major function of management, it is not the same thing *as* management. Management copes with complexity, which requires preserving order and consistency. Leadership, in comparison, copes with change in a competitive, rapidly evolving world. Effective leaders deal with change by formulating a vision of the future and setting a direction for that vision. Leaders focus on inspiration, vision, and human passion.[4] Leaders are also heavily involved in persuading and motivating others and spearheading useful changes.

Exhibit 11-1 presents a broad view of the difference between leadership and management. The same information provides more insight into the nature of leadership. Effective leadership and management are both required in the modern workplace. Managers must be leaders, but leaders must also be good managers.

Exhibit **11-1**

Leaders versus Managers

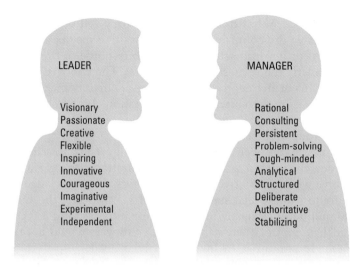

LEADER	MANAGER
Visionary	Rational
Passionate	Consulting
Creative	Persistent
Flexible	Problem-solving
Inspiring	Tough-minded
Innovative	Analytical
Courageous	Structured
Imaginative	Deliberate
Experimental	Authoritative
Independent	Stabilizing

Source: Genevieve Capowski, "Anatomy of a Leader: Where Are the Leaders of Tomorrow?" *Management Review* (March 1994): 12. Copyright ©1994 American Management Association International. Reprinted by permission of American Management Association International, New York. All rights reserved. http://www.amanet.org.

Workers need to be inspired and persuaded, but they also need assistance in developing and maintaining a smoothly functioning workplace.

A growing body of evidence supports the common-sense belief that leadership contributes to organizational effectiveness. For example, a comprehensive study of many organizations concluded that incompetent managers are responsible for billions of dollars of lost productivity each year.[5] A later study with 48 Fortune 500 firms found that the presence of a charismatic leader contributed to a firm's net profit margin, particularly in an uncertain environment.[6] (One explanation for this is that a leader with a strong personality helps people focus on their work.) The argument that leaders do not contribute to organizational effectiveness is presented later.

LEADERSHIP TRAITS AND CHARACTERISTICS

Describe key leadership traits, styles, and behaviors.

A logical approach to understanding leadership is to study the traits and characteristics of effective leaders. For many years, scholars downplayed the study of leadership characteristics, but an interest in the inner qualities of leaders has reawakened, particularly with respect to ethical qualities and charisma, including vision. The traits of leaders relate closely to the degree to which others perceive these people to be leaders. For example, a person who exudes self-confidence would generally be perceived as having leadership qualities. Research evidence confirms that effective leaders are different from other people—they have the "right stuff." The differences relate to the traits and characteristics described in this section.[7] The current interest in leadership traits is also reflected in a demand for leaders with vision and charisma.

Hundreds of traits and personal characteristics of leaders have been researched over the years, dating back to the early 1900s. Here we discuss illustrative leadership qualities, under the categories of cognitive skills and personality traits and motives supported by research and careful observation.

Cognitive Skills

An effective leader must have appropriate **cognitive skills,** or mental ability and knowledge. Organizational leaders possess effective problem-solving ability. They anticipate problems before they occur, and persevere until the problems are solved. In the process, they demonstrate imagination, creativity, and a willingness to experiment with unproven methods. Leadership positions place a continuously increasing demand on problem-solving ability. For example, managers are pressured to perform tasks in a shorter time with a smaller staff, and contribute to developing a business strategy that will point the firm in the right direction. A meta-analysis of the relationship between leadership and intelligence concluded that intelligence contributes more to leadership performance when the leader is more directive (makes decisions on his or her own).[8] In such situations, the leader can use his or her problem-solving ability to good advantage instead of relying heavily on the input of others.

A high-level cognitive skill is for an executive to be able to understand changing business conditions that could affect the organization, and then make appropriate adjustments.[9] An example would be Bill Gates of Microsoft focusing the company on the Internet in 1995, making software security a top priority in 2002, and encouraging employees to do a better job of selling software on the Internet as a service in 2005 and forward.[10] (Microsoft classifies software sold on the Internet to be a service.)

Technical and professional competence, or knowledge of a particular business, is another cognitive requirement for effective leadership. When outsiders are brought into a company to fill senior management positions, they usually need a specialty to complement their leadership and administrative skills. In lesser leadership positions, technical competence is important because it is difficult to establish rapport with group members when the leader does not understand the technical details of the work. The accompanying Organizational Behavior in Action box illustrate how technical expertise can be an important part of a business leader's qualifications.

Personality Traits

Personality traits and characteristics have an important influence on leadership effectiveness. Which traits and characteristics are the most relevant varies with the situation. For example, enthusiasm may be more important for a sales manager for mortgage refinancing than for an inventory-control manager. The sales manager's enthusiasm may be needed to help sales representatives cope with rejection by customers, particularly when telemarketing the refinancing of homes.

A foundation trait for leadership effectiveness is **self-awareness,** insightfully processing feedback about oneself to improve personal effectiveness. Other aspects of self-awareness can be categorized as emotional intelligence, as described in Chapter 2. The leader must be able to benefit from feedback that is sometimes obvious and at other times subtle. For example, a leader might notice a blank stare (a form of nonverbal feedback) while explaining a new initiative to group members. The leader could profitably use this feedback and take another approach to describing the initiative.

A realistic degree of *self-confidence* is frequently associated with leadership effectiveness. A leader who is self-confident without being overbearing instills confidence among group members. The concept of self-confidence is useful in studying

ORGANIZATIONAL BEHAVIOR *In Action*

Corporate Turnaround Artist Heads Effort to Revitalize New Orleans Schools

Just one look at Bill Roberti's face tells you all you need to know. When it comes to business, he's brusque and focused, not much for small talk or a joke. Even as he folds his tree trunk of a body into the elementary school desk that has become his makeshift office space, he oozes steely resolve, honed through a dual career as a U.S. Army Reserve colonel and corporate turnaround artist. If the commanding 59-year-old is more indelicate than ever these days, it's because he's knee deep in the most daunting challenge of his professional life: reconstituting the entire New Orleans public school system.

Roberti is a managing director at Alvarez & Marsal LLC, the New York turnaround consultant renowned for whipping Timex, Interstate Bakeries, and HealthSouth into shape. In June 2005, the firm was awarded a modest contract to help straighten out the crooked finances of the New Orleans system's 117 schools and its administration. After Hurricane Katrina the job ballooned into something unimaginably more important.

Even before Katrina flooded 80% of the city and emptied it of almost all of its residents, the New Orleans public school system was the worst of all major U.S. cities and faced intractable corruption, infighting, and racial tension. No one knows the odds against the schools better than Roberti, who did similar financial work at A&M for the St. Louis School system.

Largely because of him and his staff, 10,165 students are back in the 20 public schools that are up and running.

Despite all the political in-fighting, Roberti and his staff have managed to earn the respect of many locals because of their undeniable drive to get the job done. One of Roberti's initiatives after Katrina was to rescue computer tapes so workers could get their paychecks.

In St. Louis as well as in New Orleans, Roberti was known for his in-your-face style of leadership. If Roberti saw something he didn't like, he confronted bureaucrats, bus drivers, janitors, teachers—anybody—in the same direct way. Once he scolded a school's principal for having a photocopier in her office that the teachers could not use. Roberti had earlier sent memos ordering the machines out of administrative offices in response to teacher complaints that they couldn't make copies.

Questions

1. What specifically is Roberti's "knowledge of the business" or technical expertise?
2. What fit might be between Roberti's in-your-face leadership approach and helping to rescue troubled enterprises?

Source: "A Turnaround for New Orleans," Business Week, April 3, 2006, pp. 108–109; Brian Thevenot, "Rough Roberti's All About Business: Executive Is Known for Brash Demeanor," New Orleans, Louisiana, The Times-Picayune, June 26, 2005.

leadership because it illustrates the relationship between traits and behavior. A manager who is inwardly self-confident will behave confidently and will be perceived as acting cool under pressure. George P. Hollenbeck and Douglas T. Hall propose that leaders with high self-confidence are likely to stay motivated. They will work harder in approaching a task and exert more effort. The motivation propelled by self-confidence will also facilitate the leader staying with the task longer without positive feedback, and not becoming discouraged when faced with problems and difficulties.[11]

Self-confidence is also important because it contributes to being courageous. The leader must sometimes have the courage to make a decision even though others may think he or she is wrong, foolish, or both. It is easy to find advisors who recommend that you not take action, so courage is required to make a bold decision. Howard Shultz, the CEO of Starbucks, was advised not to enter a particular international market, yet he persisted and the company is beginning to show a profit in the country in question.[12]

Projecting self-confidence is especially important when leading an organization or a group out of a crisis, because most people need to rely on a strong person when faced with turmoil. A financial executive observed that a confident boss finds the right balance between micromanaging (looking over every possible detail) versus delegating so much that his or her authority is diluted.[13] A leader with low self-confidence will exhibit behavior at one of two extremes. At one extreme, an insecure boss will obsessively check on every detail to avoid mistakes that reflect poorly on his or her leadership. At the other extreme, a leader who lacks confidence in his or her own abilities will rely too much on others to accomplish tasks.

Trustworthiness contributes to leadership effectiveness in most situations. Being perceived as trustworthy involves many different behaviors. At the top of the list, however, are behavioral consistency and integrity. *Consistency* refers to reliability and predictability, such as when a manager conducts performance evaluations and reimburses for expenses as agreed. *Integrity* centers on telling the truth and keeping promises.[14] *Authenticity* is a cluster of traits, related to trustworthiness. Authentic leadership is defined as being self-aware, confident, open, optimistic, resilient, and honest, and being more concerned about the welfare of others than about personal welfare. For leaders to display authentic moral behavior they must perceive their roles as including an ethical responsibility to all of their stakeholders, such as employees, subcontractors, and customers.[15] An example of such behavior would be establishing a scholarship fund for the teenage workers in an overseas clothing factory operated by a subcontractor.

To become more authentic, the leader has to consistently match words and deeds, as with being trustworthy. At the same time, the leader must establish good relationships with others, which could mean emphasizing different aspects of the self with different groups.[16] An example would be a financial manager acting reserved among bosses and colleagues, yet quite jovial and outgoing when collecting data in the factory. As long as being reserved and jovial are true parts of the manager's self, he or she would be authentic.

A study about the consequences of trust was conducted in a small nonunion manufacturing firm that produced tools used by other manufacturers. The study participants responded to questionnaires about how much trust they had in management, and supervisors rated employees in terms of how well they performed their roles as employees. A sample item would be "Conserves and protects organizational property." The results of the study indicated that employees who trusted plant management and top management were more likely to focus on value-producing activities and organizational citizenship behavior.[17] So, trust pays!

The accompanying self-assessment quiz pinpoints the type of behaviors that prompt people to trust a leader.

Emotional intelligence is a major contributor to leadership effectiveness. As described in Chapter 2, the concept refers to managing ourselves and our relationships effectively. A newer conception of emotional intelligence is so broad that it

235

SELF-ASSESSMENT

Behaviors and Attitudes of a Trustworthy Leader

Listed here are behaviors and attitudes of leaders who are generally trusted by their group members and other constituents. After you read each characteristic, check to the right whether this is a behavior or attitude that you appear to have developed already, or does not fit you at present.

	Fits Me	Does Not Fit Me
1. Tells people he or she is going to do something, and then always follows through and gets it done	☐	☐
2. Described by others as being reliable	☐	☐
3. Good at keeping secrets and confidences	☐	☐
4. Tells the truth consistently	☐	☐
5. Minimizes telling people what they want to hear	☐	☐
6. Described by others as "walking the talk"	☐	☐
7. Delivers consistent messages to others in terms of matching words and deeds	☐	☐
8. Does what he or she expects others to do	☐	☐
9. Minimizes hypocrisy by not engaging in activities he or she tells others are wrong	☐	☐
10. Readily accepts feedback on behavior from others	☐	☐
11. Maintains eye contact with people when talking to them	☐	☐
12. Appears relaxed and confident when explaining his or her side of a story	☐	☐
13. Individualizes compliments to others rather than saying something like "You look great" to a large number of people	☐	☐
14. Doesn't expect lavish perks for himself or herself while expecting others to go on an austerity diet	☐	☐
15. Does not pretend that a crisis is pending just to gain the group's cooperation	☐	☐
16. Collaborates with others to make creative decisions	☐	☐
17. Communicates information to people at all organizational levels	☐	☐
18. Readily shares financial information with others	☐	☐
19. Listens to people and then acts on many of their suggestions	☐	☐
20. Generally engages in predictable behavior	☐	☐

Scoring and Interpretation: These statements are mostly for self-reflection, so no specific scoring key exists. However, the more statements that fit you, the more trustworthy you are—assuming you are answering truthfully. The usefulness of this self-quiz increases if somebody who knows you well answers it for you to supplement your self-perceptions. Your ability and willingness to carry out some of the behaviors specified in this quiz could have an enormous impact on your career because so many business leaders in recent years have not been perceived as trustworthy. Being trustworthy is therefore a career asset.

Question

Suppose you think you are not as trustworthy as you could be to advance your leadership ability. What could you do about your too-low level of trustworthiness?

encompasses many traits and behaviors related to leadership effectiveness, including self-confidence, empathy, and visionary leadership.[18] Passion for the work and the people is a particularly important aspect of emotional intelligence for leadership effectiveness. It is difficult to inspire others if you are not passionate about your major work activities. Making connections with people is another aspect of emotional intelligence that is vital for effective leadership. David Neeleman, JetBlue founder and CEO, is highly regarded for his ability to connect with people, as illustrated in an anecdote:

> Neeleman often works alongside of his employees—loading baggage, serving snacks, cleaning aircraft after a flight, and similar tasks. When asked about this, Neeleman commented that his primary reason for going on flights is to communicate to his crew members that what they are doing is important to accomplishing the company's mission. He also mentioned that it is an excellent opportunity to see his company from multiple perspectives as well as to hear the concerns of crewmembers at all levels.[19]

Continuing research into emotional intelligence suggests another reason for its contribution to effective leadership. When a company faces a sudden crisis, how leaders handle their emotions can determine whether the company survives. The emotionally intelligent leader is able to articulate a group's shared yet unexpressed feelings, and develop a mission that inspires others. An example of a sudden crisis facing a company would be if it did not win a major government contract that could ensure its short-term survival.[20] A leader would talk about the grief the group was feeling and then point toward other areas of profitable activity for the group.

Many leaders have failed because of glaring deficits in emotional intelligence. When Frank Lorenzo took over Eastern Air Lines (which he later led into bankruptcy), the animosity that developed between him and union bosses grew so great that it hastened the airline's demise. Leona Helmsley played evil stepmother to all the employees of her real-estate mogul husband. She fired employees at whim (one for taking an apple while she worked through lunch). Eventually Helmsley was convicted of tax evasion and sent to prison.[21]

More evidence for the contribution of personality to leadership effectiveness stems from research with the Five Factor Model of personality, combining the results of 73 samples. The four factors with the highest correlations with leadership effectiveness were neuroticism (lower was better), extraversion, openness, and conscientiousness. Extraversion was related to leadership effectiveness most consistently across different studies and different criteria of leadership effectiveness. When the five factors were combined, the relationship with leadership effectiveness was quite high (a correlation coefficient of .48).[22] Personality, therefore, does matter for leadership, at least to some degree.

Motives

The power and achievement motives, described in Chapter 6, are closely associated with leadership effectiveness. A strong power motive propels the leader to be interested in influencing others. When a power motive is too intense, it can manifest itself in ruthless leadership behavior. The two leaders just cited for having low emotional intelligence fit here.

A need for achievement often facilitates leadership effectiveness. As a leader, a person with a strong need for achievement will typically have a strong sense of time urgency, which can be a positive force for innovation.[23] For example, a leader desiring to be the first mover on a product exhibits this sense of urgency.

Even if one understands the disposition of the leader, however, the situation in which the leader functions is also enormously important. Consultant Larraine Segil explains: "My research revealed that you can be a wonderful manager or leader, but if you have an organization that doesn't support or enable you, you're either going to leave the company or put on the cloaks and clothes of a non-dynamic leader to protect your position.[24]

LEADERSHIP BEHAVIORS AND STYLES

Explain the basics of four contingency theories of leadership.

A focus on the activities carried out by leaders to enhance productivity and morale followed the trait approach. The **behavioral approach to leadership** attempts to specify how the behavior of effective leaders differs from their less-effective counterparts. Dozens of leadership behaviors are mentioned in this chapter and throughout the book. A key concept here is **leadership style,** which is the relatively consistent pattern of behavior that characterizes a leader. Much of this consistency occurs because a leadership style is based somewhat on an individual's personality. Despite this consistency, some managers can modify their style as the situation requires.

Our presentation of leadership styles and behaviors consists of three parts: the pioneering Ohio State University and University of Michigan studies, the Leadership Grid®, and the leader–member exchange model. Before reading ahead, use the accompanying self-assessment quiz to assess your leadership style.

SELF-ASSESSMENT

What Style of Leader Are You or Would You Be?

Directions: Answer the following questions, keeping in mind what you have done, or think you would do, in the scenarios and attitudes described.

	Mostly True	Mostly False
1. I am more likely to take care of a high-impact assignment myself than turn it over to a group member.	☐	☐
2. I would prefer the analytical aspects of a manager's job rather than working directly with group members.	☐	☐
3. An important part of my approach to managing a group is to keep the members informed almost daily of any information that could affect their work.	☐	☐
4. It's a good idea to give two people in the group the same problem, and then choose what appears to be the best solution.	☐	☐
5. It makes good sense for a leader or manager to stay somewhat aloof from a group, so he or she can make a tough decision when necessary.	☐	☐
6. I look for opportunities to obtain group input before making a decision, even on straightforward issues.	☐	☐
7. I would reverse a decision if several of the group members presented evidence that I was wrong.	☐	☐
8. Differences of opinion in the work group are healthy.	☐	☐

SELF-ASSESSMENT

(Continued)

	Mostly True	Mostly False
9. I think that activities to build team spirit, like a team fixing up a poor family's house on a Saturday, are an excellent investment of time.	☐	☐
10. If my group were hiring a new member, I would like the person to be interviewed by the entire group.	☐	☐
11. An effective team leader today uses e-mail for about 98% of communication with team members.	☐	☐
12. Some of the best ideas are likely to come from the group members rather than the manager.	☐	☐
13. If our group were going to have a banquet, I would get input from each member on what type of food should be served.	☐	☐
14. I have never seen a statue of a committee in a museum or park, so why bother making decisions by a committee if you want to be recognized?	☐	☐
15. I dislike it intensely when a group member challenges my position on an issue.	☐	☐
16. I typically explain to group members how (which method they should use) to accomplish an assigned task.	☐	☐
17. If I were out of the office for a week, most of the important work in the department would get accomplished anyway.	☐	☐
18. Delegation of important tasks is something that would be (or is) very difficult for me.	☐	☐
19. When a group member comes to me with a problem, I tend to jump right in with a proposed solution.	☐	☐
20. When a group member comes to me with a problem, I typically ask that person something like, "What alternative solutions have you thought of so far?"	☐	☐

Scoring and Interpretation: The answers in the participative/team-style leader direction are as follows:

1. Mostly False	8. Mostly True	15. Mostly False
2. Mostly False	9. Mostly True	16. Mostly False
3. Mostly True	10. Mostly True	17. Mostly True
4. Mostly False	11. Mostly False	18. Mostly False
5. Mostly False	12. Mostly True	19. Mostly False
6. Mostly True	13. Mostly True	20. Mostly True
7. Mostly True	14. Mostly False	

You receive one point for each answer that agrees with the scoring key. If your score is 15 or higher, you are most likely (or would be) a participative (or team-style) leader. If your score is 5 or lower, you are most likely (or would be) an authoritarian leader.

Skill Development: The quiz you just completed is also an opportunity for skill development. Review the 20 questions and look for implied suggestions for engaging in participative or team leadership. For example, question 20 suggests that you encourage group members to work through their own solutions to problems. If your goal is to become an authoritarian leader, the questions can also serve as useful guidelines. For example, question 19 suggests that an authoritarian leader looks first to solve problems for group members.

Pioneering Studies on Leadership Dimensions

Much of the theory underlying leadership styles can be traced back to studies conducted at Ohio State University and the University of Michigan beginning in the late 1940s. A major output of the Ohio State studies was the emphasis placed on two leadership dimensions, initiating structure and consideration.

Initiating structure describes the degree to which the leader establishes structure for group members. Structure is initiated by activities such as assigning specific tasks, specifying procedures to be followed, scheduling work, and clarifying expectations. **Consideration** describes the degree to which the leader creates an environment of emotional support, warmth, friendliness, and trust. He or she does so by engaging in behaviors such as being friendly and approachable, looking out for the personal welfare of the group, keeping the group informed about new developments, and doing small favors for group members.[25] Exhibit 11-2 shows how leadership style can be based on a combination of these two key dimensions.

Many of the Ohio State studies were conducted with first-level supervisors and therefore may not apply well to executive leadership. It was discovered that employee turnover was lowest and job satisfaction highest under leaders who were rated highest in consideration. Research also indicated that leaders high on initiating structure were generally rated highly by superiors and had higher-producing work groups.

Researchers at the University of Michigan also investigated the differences in results obtained by production-centered and employee-centered managers (about the same idea as initiating structure versus consideration). Production-centered managers set tight work standards, organized tasks carefully, prescribed the work methods to be followed, and supervised closely. Employee-centered managers encouraged group members to participate in goal setting and other work

Exhibit **11-2**

Leadership Styles Based on a Combination of Initiating Structure and Consideration

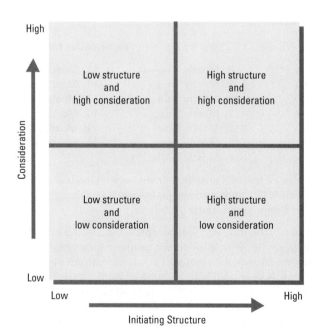

decisions, and helped to ensure high performance by engendering trust and mutual respect.

A dominant finding of the Michigan studies was that the most productive work groups tended to have leaders who were employee centered rather than production centered. Also, the most effective leaders were those who had supportive relationships with group members. They also tended to use group rather than individual decision making and encouraged subordinates to set and achieve high performance goals. Despite this dominant finding, exceptions were found. A study conducted with 20,000 employees at a heavy-equipment manufacturer indicated that supervisors with the best production records were both production- and employee centered.[26]

One meta-analysis has indicated that the pioneering studies under discussion are still relevant to understanding leadership. The results revealed that both consideration and initiating structure are related to leadership outcomes. Consideration is more strongly related to satisfaction with the leader and job satisfaction in general. Initiating structure is slightly more strongly related to the job performance of leaders, as well as group and organization performance. An implication for leaders and managers is that to attain job satisfaction and production, attention must be paid to consideration and initiating structure.[27]

In practice, effective leaders exhibit a wide range of behaviors in addition to the key behaviors mentioned here. The behaviors associated with trustworthiness are relevant here. A key leadership behavior capturing attention in recent times is to understand the strengths and weaknesses of group members, and capitalize on each person's strengths. Rather than encourage employees to follow tight job descriptions that may include tasks they dislike or are not good at, the leader develops positions for group members based on their unique abilities. For example, if a store clerk is good at stocking and organizing shelves, yet poor in dealing with customers, he or she is assigned full time to maintaining and replenishing shelves.[28] (Marcus Buckingham, who publicized this concept of understanding individual differences, claims it is part of management, not leadership. However, effective leaders also get involved in assigning work for group members.)

The Leadership Grid®

The **Leadership Grid®** is a framework for classifying leadership styles that simultaneously examines a leader's concerns for production (task accomplishment) and for people. With roots in the Ohio State leadership dimensions, the Grid is the nucleus of a system of leadership training and organization development. No history of the formal study of leadership is complete without some mention of the once-famous Grid. The concerns about production and people reflect attitudes rather than actual behavior. However, attitudes *often* translate into behavior.

Concern for production includes results, the bottom line, performance, profits, and mission. Concern for people includes group members and coworkers. Each of these concerns (or dimensions) exists in varying degrees along a continuum from 1 to 9. A manager's standing on one concern is not supposed to influence his or her standing on the other. Mark V. Hurd, the CEO of Hewlett Packard, exemplifies a leader with a strong concern for production because of his reputation for number-crunching operations efficiency.[29] His reputation for being affable and approachable at the same time would suggest he also has at least moderate concern for people.

According to the Grid, a 9,9 style (team management) is the best because it leads to positive consequences such as high productivity, satisfaction, and creativity. The 9,9 style has built-in flexibility, rather than a "one size fits all" philosophy. With it, the manager can evaluate a situation and then use principles of human behavior to handle problems.[30]

The Leader–Member Exchange Model

The behavioral models presented so far assume that the leader relates in approximately the same manner toward all group members. George Graen and his associates have developed a leadership model that challenges the reality of such consistency in behavior. The **leader–member exchange model (LMX)** recognizes that leaders develop unique working relationships with each group member.[31] A leader might be considerate and compassionate toward one team member yet rigid and unfeeling toward another.

Each relationship between the leader/manager and the group members differs in quality. One subset of employees, the in-group, is given additional rewards, responsibility, and trust in exchange for its loyalty and performance. In contrast, another subset of employees (the out-group) is treated in accordance with a more formal understanding of supervisor–subordinate relations. The leader's first impression of a group member's competency heavily influences whether he or she becomes a member of the in-group or out-group.

In-group members have attitudes and values similar to those of the leader and interact frequently with the leader. Out-group members have less in common with the leader and operate in a way that is somewhat detached from the leader. The one-to-one relationships have a major influence on the subordinate's behavior in the group. Members of the in-group become part of a smoothly functioning team headed by the formal leader. Out-group members are less likely to experience good teamwork.

A contributing factor to the current stream of research about LMX is that it is sensible: The quality of your relationship with your manager has a big impact on your job behavior and performance. Here we highlight research findings with the most direct implications for organizational behavior:

1. Being a member of the in-group facilitates achieving high productivity and satisfaction. Out-group members receive less challenging assignments and are more likely to quit because of job dissatisfaction.[32]
2. High-quality leader–member exchanges lead to more effective delegation, in addition to higher productivity and satisfaction. The study in question showed that the quality of exchanges from the standpoints of both supervisors and group members was associated with improved delegation, which in turn enhanced performance and satisfaction.[33]
3. Despite the many consequences of positive leader–member exchanges, most supervisors are not overly influenced by them in making performance evaluations. Supervisors may have their "pets," but research has shown that supervisors can overcome these biases to make objective performance evaluations.[34]
4. Communication frequency between the leader and group member moderates (influences) the relationship between leader–member exchanges and performance evaluations. In a study of 188 private-sector workers, it was found that LMX was more strongly related to performance evaluation results when the group members communicated more frequently with the manager. A second

study with 153 public-sector workers attained similar results. One implication of these studies is that the importance of LMX depends on how frequently supervisors and subordinates interact. LMX has the biggest impact when interactions are frequent.[35] Frequent interaction with the supervisor is probably important even to develop and maintain a positive leader-member exchange.

5. A study conducted with 146 supervisor–subordinate pairs in a hospital laboratory suggested that the link between LMX and performance, as measured by supervisory ratings, is strongest when job conflict is low, task ambiguity is high, and intrinsic job satisfaction is high.[36]

6. A study with Turkish high-school teachers suggested that high-quality exchanges with group members can help overcome the problem of the group members not having a good value fit with the organization. When teachers perceived that the organization was a poor fit for their values, their job and career satisfaction tended to be low. However, with high-quality leader–member exchanges, this problem was softened.[37]

An important implication of the leader–member exchange is that the quality of the relationship between the leader/manager and each group member has important job consequences. Favorable exchanges can lead to important effects such as higher productivity and satisfaction, improved motivation, and smoother delegation.

Servant Leadership

Some effective leaders believe that their primary mission is to serve the needs of their constituents. They measure their effectiveness in terms of their ability to help others. Instead of seeking individual recognition, servant leaders see themselves as working for the group members. A **servant leader** is one who serves constituents by working on their behalf to help them achieve their goals, not the leader's own goals. Such a leader is self-sacrificing and humble. A servant leader, for example, might take over the responsibilities of a team member on a given day so the team member can be home with an ailing spouse. Servant leaders also focus on helping people to develop, such as giving them an opportunity to acquire new skills. The humanistic approach of the servant leader also helps build community, or a sense of togetherness among the stakeholders.

Servant leadership is more accurately categorized as a related set of behaviors than a style. The servant leader uses his or her talents to help group members. For example, if the leader happens to be a good planner, he or she engages in planning because it will help the group attain its goals. Servant leadership is gaining in popularity as companies attempt to establish harmony between executives and workforce members who dislike all-knowing and powerful leaders.[38]

Many academic administrators see themselves as servant leaders; they take care of administrative work so instructors can devote more time to teaching and scholarship. To be an effective servant leader, a person needs the many leadership traits and behaviors described in this chapter.

CONTINGENCY THEORIES OF LEADERSHIP

The behavioral theories of leadership provide general guidelines for leadership effectiveness, emphasizing both production and people. After development of behavioral theories came an attempt to specify the conditions under which various

243

leadership styles would lead to the best results. The intent was to make explanations of leadership precise and scientific. According to the **contingency theory of leadership,** the best style of leadership depends on factors relating to group members and the work setting. Contingent, or flexible, leadership can be thought of in terms of doing the right thing at the right time.[39]

A major contingency factor, for example, involves the needs of the group.[40] For example, a leader might want to push ahead immediately with the implementation of a new technology, but if the group needs more training before implementation, the leader must first help the group develop the necessary skills. Here we present four contingency theories, or explanations, of leadership: Fiedler's contingency theory, the path–goal theory, the situational leadership model, and the normative decision model.

Fiedler's Contingency Theory of Leadership

Fred E. Fiedler developed an elaborate contingency model, which holds that the best style of leadership is determined by the leader's work situation. Although historically important, studies related to Fiedler's contingency theory are rarely published. Fiedler's model specifies the conditions under which leaders should use task- and relationship-motivated styles.[41] (Observe again the two key leadership dimensions of initiating structure and consideration.) To implement Fiedler's theory, leadership style and the situation are measured through questionnaires.

Fiedler measures the leader's style by means of the least-preferred coworker (LPC) scale. Whether the leader is primarily task- or relationship-motivated is measured by how favorably the leader describes his or her least-preferred coworker. The LPC is defined as the past coworker with whom he or she would least like to work. Ratings of coworkers are made on a scale of polar-opposite adjectives such as *pleasant* versus *unpleasant*. The logic is that people who describe their least-preferred coworker in relatively positive terms are relationship-oriented. In contrast, people who describe their least-preferred coworker in very negative terms are task-motivated.

Situational control is the degree to which the leader can control and influence the outcomes of group effort. Measurements of situational control (or favorableness to the leader) are based on three factors, listed here in order of importance:

1. *Leader–member relations.* The extent to which group members accept and support their leader
2. *Task structure.* The extent to which the leader knows exactly what to do, and how well and in what detail the tasks to be completed are defined
3. *Position power.* The extent to which the organization provides the leader with (a) the means of rewarding and punishing group members, and (b) appropriate formal authority to get the job done

Numerous studies have investigated the relationship among leadership-style situational control by the leader and leadership effectiveness. Exhibit 11-3 summarizes the major findings of these studies with over 800 groups in various settings. The task-motivated style generally produces the best results when the leader has very high or very low control of the situation. The relationship-motivated style is best when the situation is under moderate or intermediate control.

A practical implication of Fiedler's theory would be for the leader to understand how to make the situation more favorable by (a) improving relationships with group

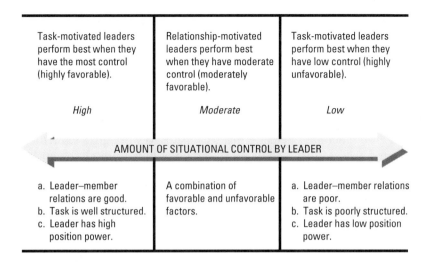

Exhibit **11-3**

Summary of Findings from Fiedler's Contingency Theory

members, (b) enhancing task structure by providing more guidelines and instructions, and (c) requesting more position power from the organization.

The Path–Goal Theory of Leadership

The **path–goal theory of leadership** specifies what the leader must do to achieve high morale and productivity in a given situation.[42] *Path–goal* refers to a focus on helping employees find the correct path to goal attainment. Exhibit 11-4 presents a model of the theory. It indicates that the leader should choose the right leadership style to match the contingency factors in order to achieve results.

An important contribution of the path–goal theory is that it both specifies what leaders need to do in different situations and explains the reasoning behind such

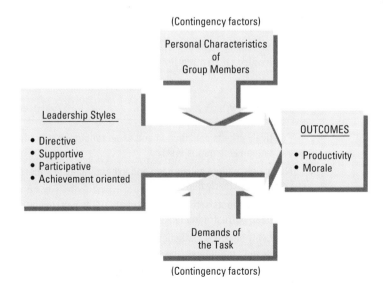

Exhibit **11-4**

The Path–Goal Theory of Leadership

The leader chooses the right leadership style to match the contingency factors in order to achieve outcomes.

behavior. The key propositions relate to motivation, satisfaction, and performance. (Path–goal theory is based on the expectancy theory of motivation.)

1. Leaders perform a motivational function by increasing personal payoffs (rewards) to group members for achieving work objectives and making the path to payoffs smoother. Clarifying the path, reducing roadblocks and pitfalls, and increasing opportunities for satisfaction on the way to the goal are behaviors that make the path smoother.
2. When group members perceive that clear paths to work goals exist, they will be motivated because they will be more certain of how to reach the goals.
3. Attempts by the leader to clarify path–goal relationships will be seen as redundant by group members if the work system already carefully defines the path to the goal. Under these conditions, control may increase performance, but it will also decrease satisfaction.

According to path–goal theory, the leader needs to choose among four leadership styles to handle the contingency demands of a given situation. *Directive leadership* involves initiating structure, setting guidelines on standards, and conveying expectations. *Supportive leadership* emphasizes showing concern for the well-being of group members and developing mutually satisfying relationships.

Participative leadership involves consulting with group members to solicit their suggestions, and then using this input for decision making. As technology continues to change and organizations decentralize, workers on the front line have more independence and responsibility. Consequently, these workers have valuable inputs for leaders. In *achievement-oriented leadership,* the leader sets challenging goals, promotes work improvement, sets high expectations, and expects group members to assume responsibility.

Each of these leadership styles works well in some situations but not in others. As shown in Exhibit 11-4, one set of contingency factors involves personal characteristics of group members, such as personality traits and abilities. Another set of contingency factors involves the demands of the task, such as the degree of ambiguity, repetitiveness, and the amount of structure. Exhibit 11-5 presents a statement of the circumstances, or contingency factors, appropriate to each of the four leadership styles.

Situational Leadership® II (SLII)

The two contingency approaches to leadership presented so far take into account collectively the task, the authority of the leader, and the nature of the subordinates.

Exhibit **11-5**

Contingency Relationships in Path–Goal Leadership

Leadership Style	Situation in Which Appropriate
Directive	Positively affects satisfaction and expectancies of subordinates working on ambiguous tasks.
	Negatively affects satisfaction and expectancies of subordinates working on clearly defined tasks.
Supportive	Positively affects satisfaction of subordinates working on dissatisfying, stressful, or frustrating tasks.
Participative	Positively affects satisfaction of subordinates who are ego involved and have nonrepetitive tasks.
Achievement oriented	Positively affects confidence that effort will lead to effective performance of subordinates working on ambiguous and nonrepetitive tasks.

Another explanation of contingency leadership places its primary emphasis on the characteristics of group members. The **Situational Leadership® II (SLII) theory** of Kenneth H. Blanchard and his colleagues explains how to match the leadership style to capabilities of group members on a given task.[43] For example, you might need less guidance from a supervisor when you are skilled in a task than when you are performing a new task.

SLII is designed to increase the frequency and quality of conversations about performance and professional development between managers and group members so that competence is developed, commitment takes place, and turnover among talented workers is reduced. Leaders are taught to use the leadership style that matches or responds to the needs of the situation.

SLII stems from the original situational model that has been widely studied in leadership and used in training programs. The major premise of SLII is that the basis for effective leadership is managing the relationship between a leader and a subordinate on a given task. The major concepts of the SLII model are presented in Exhibit 11-6. According to SLII, effective leaders adapt their behavior to the level of *commitment* and *competence* of a particular subordinate to complete a given task. For example, team member Russ might be committed to renting some empty office space by year's end, and also highly skilled at such an activity. Or he might feel that the task is drudgery, and not have much skill in selling office space. The combination of the subordinate's commitment and competence determines his or her *developmental level*, as follows:

- **D1**—Enthusiastic Beginner. The learner has low competence but high commitment.
- **D2**—Disillusioned Learner. The individual has gained some competence but has been disappointed after having experienced several setbacks. Commitment at this stage is low.
- **D3**—Capable but Cautious Performer. The learner has growing competence, yet commitment is variable.
- **D4**—Self-Reliant Achiever. The learner has high competence and commitment.

SLII explains that effective leadership depends on two independent behaviors: *supporting* and *directing*. (By now, you have read about this dichotomy at several places

Supporting (relationship behaviors) ↑	**Style 3** **Supporting:** Low on directing behavior and high on supporting behavior **Developmental level 3** **Capable but Cautious Performer:** Growing competence and variable commitment	**Style 2** **Coaching:** High on directing behavior and high on supporting behavior **Developmental level 2** **Disillusioned Learner:** Some competence but low commitment
	Style 4 **Delegating:** Low on directing behavior and low on supporting behavior **Developmental level 4** **Self-Reliant Achiever:** Highest level of commitment and competence	**Style 1** **Directing:** High on directing behavior and low on supporting behavior **Developmental level 1** **Enthusiastic Beginner:** Low competence but high commitment

←——Directing (task-related behaviors)——→

Exhibit **11-6**

Situational Leadership II (SLII)

For best results on a given task, the leader is required to match style to the developmental level of the group member. Each quadrant indicates the desired match between leader style and subordinate development level.

in this chapter.) *Supporting* refers to relationship behaviors such as the leader listening, giving recognition, communicating, and encouraging. *Directing* refers to task-related behaviors, such as the leader giving careful directions and controlling.

As shown in Exhibit 11-6, the four basic styles are as follows:

- **S1**—Directing. High directive behavior/low supportive behavior
- **S2**—Coaching. High directive behavior/high supportive behavior
- **S3**—Supporting. Low directive behavior/high supportive behavior
- **S4**—Delegating. Low directive behavior/low supportive behavior

A key point of SLII is that no one style is best: An effective leader uses all four styles depending on the subordinate's developmental level on a given task. The most appropriate leadership style among S1 to S4 corresponds to the subordinate developmental levels of D1 to D4, respectively. Specifically, Enthusiastic Beginners (D1) require a directing (S1) leader; Disillusioned Learners (D2) need a coaching (S2) leader; Capable but Cautious Workers (D3) need a supporting (S3) leader; and Self-Reliant Achievers (D4) need a delegating (S4) of leader.

Situational leadership represents a consensus of thinking about leadership behavior in relation to group members: Competent people require less specific direction than do less competent people. The model is also useful because it builds on other explanations of leadership that emphasize the role of task and relationship behaviors. As a result, it has proved to be useful as the basis for leadership training. At least 3 million managers have been trained in situational leadership, covering various stages of the model, so we can assume that situational leadership makes sense to managers and companies. The situational model also corroborates common sense and is therefore intuitively appealing. You can benefit from this model by attempting to diagnose the readiness of group members before choosing the right leadership style.

A challenge in applying SLII is that the leader has to stay tuned into which task a group member is performing at a given time, and then implement the correct style. Given that assignments change rapidly, and group members are often working on more than one task in a day, the leader would have to keep shifting styles. SLII presents categories and guidelines so precisely that it gives the impression of infallibility. In reality, leadership situations are less clear cut than the four quadrants suggest. Also, the prescriptions for leadership will work only some of the time. For example, many supervisors use a coaching style (S2) with a Disillusioned Learner (D2) and still achieve poor results.

The Normative Decision Model

Another contingency viewpoint is that leaders must choose a style that elicits the correct degree of group participation when making decisions. Given that much of a leader's interactions with group members involves decision making, this perspective is sensible. The **normative decision model** views leadership as a decision-making process in which the leader examines certain factors within the situation to determine which decision-making style will be the most effective. Here we present the latest version of the model, built by Victor Vroom and his associates.[44]

The normative model (formerly known as the leader-participation model) identifies five decision-making styles, each reflecting a different degree of participation by group members:

Decide. The leader makes the decision alone and either announces or sells it to the group. The leader might use expertise in collecting information from the group or others who appear to have information relevant to the problem.

Consult (Individually). The leader presents the problem to group members individually, gathers their suggestions, and then makes the decision.

Consult (Group). The leader presents the problem to group members in a meeting, gathers their suggestions, and then makes the decision.

Facilitate. The leader presents the problem, then acts as a facilitator, defining the problem to be solved and the boundaries in which the decision must be made. The leader wants concurrence and avoids having his or her ideas receive more weight based on position power.

Delegate. The leader permits the group to make the decision within prescribed limits. Although the leader does not directly intervene in the group's deliberations unless explicitly asked, he or she works behind the scenes, providing resources and encouragement.

The leader diagnoses the situation in terms of seven variables. Based on answers to those variables, the leader/manager follows the path through decision matrices to choose one of the five decision-making styles. The model includes two versions: one when time is critical and one when a more important consideration is the development of the decision-making capabilities of group members. Specifying the situational factors makes the model a contingency approach. The decision-making style chosen depends on these factors:

Decision significance. The significance of the decision to the success of the project or the organization

Importance of commitment. The importance of team members' commitment to the decision

Leader's expertise. Your knowledge or expertise in relation to the problem

Likelihood of commitment. The likelihood that the team would commit itself to a decision that you might make on your own

Group support for objectives. The degree to which the team supports the organization's objectives at stake in the problem

Group expertise. Team members' knowledge or expertise in relation to the problem

Team competence. The ability of the team members to work together in solving problems

Accurate answers to these seven situational factors are not always easy to obtain. The leader may have to rely heavily on intuition and minimize distorted thinking; for example, in believing he or she has expertise when it might be lacking. To use the model, the decision maker answers whether each of the variables in the preceding list is high or low, such as high team competence. In general, the more significant decisions, and those requiring commitment from the group, are likely to prompt the leader to use the decision-making style, Consult (Individually) or Consult (Group).

The normative model provides a valuable service to practicing managers and leaders. It prompts them to ask questions about important contingency variables in decision-making situations. Based on research with previous versions of the model, managers who follow its procedures are likely to increase their decision-making effectiveness.

TRANSFORMATIONAL AND CHARISMATIC LEADERSHIP

Present an overview of transformational and charismatic leadership.

Log on to **www.thomsonedu .com/infotrac.** Search for articles pertaining to transformational leadership. What characteristics are most important for these people? Are there individuals at your college or university that you consider to be transformational and charismatic leaders?

Considerable attention is paid to the type of leader who goes beyond merely conducting transactions with people, such as rewarding and disciplining them. The **transformational leader** is one who helps organizations and people make positive changes in the way they conduct their activities. Transformational leadership is closely linked to strategic leadership, which provides direction and inspiration to an organization. However, the emphasis in transformational leadership is on sweeping, positive changes. A major contributing factor to transformational leadership is **charisma,** the ability to lead others based on personal charm, magnetism, inspiration, and emotion. The study of transformational leadership and charismatic leadership is based on trait theory, because the focus of analysis is the leader's personal characteristics.

Transformational Leadership

James McGregor Burns originated the idea of transformational leadership, stating that it occurs when one or more persons engage with others in such a way that leaders and followers raise one another to higher levels of motivation and morality. The purposes of leaders and followers become fused, and the power bases are linked as mutual support for a common purpose.[45] In its pure form, transformational leadership is moral and uplifting and is concerned with engaging the hearts and minds of many people. The responsibility for leadership is thereby shared with many people. A leader with good moral reasoning is more likely to be perceived as transformational by group members. Managers with the highest moral reasoning scores on a questionnaire exhibited more transformational leadership behaviors than leaders with lower scores, as rated by subordinates on a questionnaire about transformational leadership.[46]

Burns contrasted the transformational leader with a transactional leader. The transformational leader exerts a higher level of influence than does a transactional (routine) leader, and thereby motivates people to do more than expected. Transformational leadership is key to revitalizing large organizations of many types. A transformational leader can develop new visions for a firm and mobilize employees to accept and work toward attaining these visions. At their best, transformational leaders make a difference in the lives of others, such as by creating jobs, saving jobs, giving people an opportunity for personal development, or engaging in philanthropy.[47]

Transformations take place in one or more of the following ways, with not every transformational leader accomplishing all of the below:

1. By raising people's level of consciousness about the importance and value of designated rewards and ways to achieve them.
2. By getting people to transcend their self-interests for the sake of the work group and the firm.
3. By raising people's focus on minor satisfactions to a quest for self-fulfillment. At the same time, group members are encouraged to seek satisfaction of higher-level needs. Group members are shown that attaining organizational goals also leads to self-fulfillment.
4. By helping workers to adopt a long-range, broad perspective and focus less on day-to-day concerns.

5. By helping people understand the need for change. The transformational leader must help group members understand the need for change both emotionally and intellectually. A transformational leader recognizes this emotional component to resisting change and deals with it openly.

6. By investing managers with a sense of urgency. If managers throughout the organization do not perceive a vital need for change, the leader's vision will not be realized.

7. By committing to greatness. Greatness encompasses striving for business effectiveness such as profits and high stock value, as well as impeccable ethics.[48]

8. By enhancing intrinsic motivation, workers become more creative, contributing to a transformed organization—as revealed in a study with Korean workers.[49]

9. By engaging in worthwhile exchanges with group members, the transformational leader encourages high performance. A high-quality LMX relationship leads to an unstated emotional bonding that facilitates subordinates wanting to perform better.[50]

Several different concepts of the characteristics and qualities of transformational leaders have been developed. An analysis of the components of transformational leaders was based on 1440 subordinates who assessed the leadership behavior of 695 branch managers in a large Australian financial institution.[51] You will observe that these components overlap a little with the methods of bringing about transformations just listed. As summarized in Exhibit 11-7, the results are useful because they reinforce other understandings of transformational leadership. The statements accompanying each leadership dimension are essentially behavioral descriptions as expressed in survey statements about transformational leadership. For example, empowerment is operationally defined as "My manager fosters trust, involvement, and cooperation among team members."

Few leaders can qualify as meeting all the behavioral and moral criteria of transformational leadership; yet, if we focus on achieving a business turnaround while still treating workers humanely, many executives qualify. One example is Bob Nardelli, the CEO of Home Depot, who turned a massive, unwieldy company into one that became much more profitable and innovative. One such innovation is a closed-circuit television system that enables Home Depot executives to do a

Exhibit **11-7**

251

Dimensions and Corresponding Behaviors of Transformational Leadership

1. **Vision**
   Communicates a clear and positive vision of the future
2. **Staff Development**
   Treats staff as individuals; supports and encourages their development
3. **Supportive Leadership**
   Gives encouragement and recognition to staff
4. **Empowerment**
   Fosters trust, involvement, and cooperation among team members
5. **Innovative Thinking**
   Encourages thinking about problems in new ways and questions assumptions

6. **Lead by Example**
   Is clear about his or her values, and practices what he or she preaches
7. **Charisma**
   Instills pride and respect in others and inspires by being highly competent

Source: Sally A. Carless, Alexander J. Wearing, and Leon Mann, "A Short Measure of Transformational Leadership," *Journal of Business and Psychology,* Spring 2000, p. 396.

virtual inspection of each of the 2000 stores using a desktop computer. Nardelli imposed the discipline of his former employer, GE, onto an entrepreneurial-style company.[52]

Turnarounds of the type engineered by Bob Nardelli reflect the actions of a transformational leader. Some turnaround leaders, however, use brutal tactics to restore profitability to a firm, including slashing the payroll by as much as 50%, selling off assets, and delaying payments to suppliers. The positive turnaround artist works closely with people to restore a healthy psychological climate. According to Rosabeth Moss Kanter, these leaders replace secrecy and denial of problems with dialogue, and blame and scorn with respect. The transformational leader also rewards initiative, and encourages people to stop protecting their turf and begin collaborating.[53]

Charismatic Leadership

Charisma in a leader generally inspires group members and facilitates transformations. Charisma, to a large extent, lies in the eye of the beholder and involves a relationship between the leader and the follower. A good example is Steve Jobs, considered by many to be the number-one visionary of Silicon Valley. One of his current visions has been to make his Pixar Animation Studios as successful as Disney Studios. His earlier visions for Apple Computer may have changed personal computing. Despite Jobs's wide popularity, for many people he is too arrogant, sarcastic, and impatient to be charismatic and inspirational. When a charismatic leader has good ethics, the transformations will be beneficial to society. An immoral charismatic leader, in contrast, can lead people toward evil ends. Who in your mind is an *evil charismatic*?

A key characteristic of charismatic leaders is their *vision*. They offer a vision (or lofty goal) of where the organization is headed and how it can get there (a plan). A vision is multifaceted, extending beyond organizational goals. It also involves a way of identifying with the organization, aligning with the organization's actions and strategies, and even building a collective identity for the firm.[54] A sense of vision inspires employees to perform well. Charismatic leaders often use input from workers to craft their visions so that the vision will appear more realistic.

Charismatic leaders are *masterful communicators.* They formulate believable dreams and portray their vision of the future as the only path to follow. Charismatics also use metaphors to inspire people. An example is a favorite aphorism of Richard Marcus, the president of Neiman-Marcus stores: "If you follow in someone else's footsteps, you never get ahead." Almost by definition, leaders perceived as charismatic by group members score high on *extraversion*.[55] Quite often leaders, as well as others, are labeled as charismatic because they are friendly and outgoing.

Charismatic leaders at their best *inspire trust*. Quite often their followers are willing to gamble with their careers to follow their chief's vision, such as accepting a low starting salary with stock options based on the start-up's vision of great success. Charismatic leaders are *energetic* and use an action-oriented leadership style. They exude energy, serving as a model for getting things done well and on time.

Charismatic leaders are adept at *managing their impression well,* which helps them be perceived as charismatic.[56] Impression management can take place at the physical level, such as an appealing appearance, yet can also take place at an intellectual level.

An intellectual example would be if the person indicates he or she has powerful contacts, such as by saying, "Bill Gates and I were discussing the future of the PC just last week."

Charisma is not necessarily a mystical, in-born set of characteristics and behaviors. As the accompanying skill-development exercise shows, charisma is an attainable skill if you have the discipline to practice the techniques the exercise outlines. Observe that several of the suggestions are geared toward impression management.

A major concern about the heavy emphasis on charisma for leadership is that too many CEOs are evil charismatics, who win the support of thousands and then plunder the organization for personal gain.[57] Former key executives at Enron Corporation and Global Crossing serve as prominent examples. As a backlash to relying so heavily on charismatic executives, in recent years major corporations have sought hard-working, ethical individuals as CEOs, even if they are less flamboyant. Carly Fiorina was pushed out as CEO of Hewlett Packard partially because she was

SKILL-DEVELOPMENT EXERCISE

Developing Charisma

Establishing the goal of becoming more charismatic is the starting point for developing charisma. In addition, you can then discipline yourself to develop some of the traits and characteristics described in the text. Here are 11 specific suggestions for skill development:

1. *Use visioning.* If you are the leader of an organizational unit, develop a dream about its future. Discuss your vision with others in the unit and your immediate superior.

2. *Make frequent use of metaphors.* Develop metaphors to inspire people around you. A commonly used one after a group has suffered a substantial setback is, "Like the phoenix, we will rise from the ashes of defeat."

3. *Inspire trust and confidence.* Make your deeds consistent with your promises. Get people to believe in your competence by making your accomplishments known in a polite, tactful way.

4. *Make others feel capable.* Give out assignments on which others can succeed, and lavishly praise their success.

5. *Be highly energetic and goal oriented.* Impress others with your energy and resourcefulness. To increase your energy level, exercise frequently, eat well, and get ample rest.

6. *Express your emotions frequently.* Freely express warmth, joy, happiness, and enthusiasm.

7. *Develop and display a sense of humor.* Appropriate use of humor helps build workplace relationships because people feel more comfortable with people who make them feel good, and humor often puts people in a good mood. Self-effacing humor is often effective, whereas humor that pokes fun at others is usually highly ineffective.

8. *Smile frequently, even if you are not in a happy mood.* A warm smile seems to indicate a confident, caring person, which contributes to a perception of charisma.

9. *Make everybody you meet feel that he or she is quite important.* For example, at a company meeting, shake the hand of every person you meet.

10. *Focus on the positive.* Charismatic people are optimists, who minimize complaints and emphasize the positive steps that can be taken to overcome a problem.

11. *Maintain positive body language.* To radiate authenticity and confidence, stand and sit up straight. When standing, keep your feet about 12 inches apart. When sitting, do not tap your feet nervously.[58]

seen as too much of a publicity seeker and made too many extravagant promises she could not deliver. She was replaced by Mark Hurd, who is more laid back and focuses more on operational efficiency with the company. The ideal executive leader would be an ethical, hard-working, and charismatic person. One of many possible examples is CEO Andrea Jung of Avon Corporation.

SUBSTITUTES FOR LEADERSHIP

Identify forces that can sometimes decrease the importance of leadership.

An implicit theme of this chapter has been that leadership is important because it affects outcomes such as productivity and satisfaction. At times, however, competent leadership is not necessary, and incompetent leadership can be counterbalanced by certain factors in the work situation. Under these circumstances, leadership is of little consequence to the performance and satisfaction of team members. According to this viewpoint, many organizations have **substitutes for leadership.** Such substitutes are factors in the work environment that provide guidance and incentives to perform well, making the leader's role almost superfluous.[59] Leadership substitutes, in effect, neutralize the effects of leadership.

Group-member characteristics that can substitute for leadership include ability, experience, training, and professional orientation. For example, a highly capable employee with strong professional values will accomplish the job with *any* plausible person acting as the formal leader. Task characteristics that can substitute for leadership include standardized methods, jobs with built-in feedback, and intrinsically satisfying work. Information technology can also substitute for leadership (or at least supervision) when instructions for tasks are entered into the computer. In the example of the electronic monitoring of store managers and employees at Home Depot, both sets of workers are being influenced to do a good job from afar. (One could argue that this type of monitoring is more management than leadership.)

Organizational factors that can substitute for leadership include explicit plans and goals and cohesive work groups. The cohesive work group, for example, will exert its own influence over group members.

CHOOSING AN APPROPRIATE LEADERSHIP MODEL

Twelve different leadership theories, models, and explanations have been presented. Although these approaches have different labels, there are many common elements. Furthermore, all the different theories, models, and explanations are useful for guiding and influencing group members. In quick review, the 12 approaches are (1) developing the right traits, (2) the initiating structure and consideration dimensions of leadership, (3) the Leadership Grid, (4) the leader–member exchange model, (5) Fiedler's contingency theory of leadership, (6) the path–goal theory of leadership, (7) the situational leadership model, (8) the normative decision model, (9) transformational leadership, (10) charismatic leadership, and (12) substitutes for leadership.

A fruitful approach to choosing an effective leadership theory, model, or explanation is for the manager to carefully diagnose the situation. Choose a leadership approach that best fits the deficiency or neglected opportunity in a given situation. Observe the people to be led, and interview them about their interests, goals, and concerns. Then apply a leadership approach that appears to match the interests,

SKILL-DEVELOPMENT EXERCISE

My Leadership Journal

A potentially important aid in your development as a leader is to maintain a journal or diary of your experiences. Make a journal entry within 24 hours after you have carried out a significant leadership action, or failed to do so when the opportunity arose. You therefore will have entries dealing with leadership opportunities both capitalized on and missed. For example, "A few of my neighbors were complaining about all the vandalism in the neighborhood. Cars were getting dented and scratched, and lamplights were being smashed. A few bricks were thrown into home windows. I volunteered to organize a neighborhood patrol. The patrol actually helped cut back on the vandalism." Or, in contrast:

"A few of my neighbors. . . . windows. I thought to myself that someone else should take care of the problem. My time is too valuable."

Also include in your journal entries such as feedback you receive on your leadership ability, leadership traits you appear to be developing, and key leadership ideas you read about.

Review your journal monthly, and make note of any progress you think you have made in developing your leadership skills. Also consider preparing a graph of your leadership skill development. The vertical axis can represent skill level on a 1-to-100 scale, and the horizontal axis might be divided into time intervals, such as calendar quarters.

concerns, deficits, or missed opportunities. The following two examples will help clarify this diagnostic approach:

1. A manager observes that many important decisions are being made and that group members are eager to get involved. Nevertheless, the group members are overworked and pressed for time. The leader would be advised to use the normative decision model to help decide how important it is to involve the group in a particular decision. (The leader wants to involve group members, but needless involvement will intensify the overwork problem.)
2. A manager observes that the group is accomplishing its job, and morale is satisfactory. Yet something is missing; a sense of urgency and excitement does not pervade the atmosphere. In this situation, the leader is advised to take the steps in his or her power to behave like a transformational and charismatic leader.

The accompanying skill-development exercise will give you the opportunity now and in the future to further develop your leadership skills.

IMPLICATIONS FOR MANAGERIAL PRACTICE

1. Technically competent and well-motivated employees require less guidance and control than their less competent and poorly motivated counterparts.
2. Exhibiting charisma can benefit the vast majority of leaders. Although charisma is somewhat dependent on long-standing personality characteristics, it can be enhanced through such means as suggested in the skill-development exercise on page 253.
3. Although the modern organization emphasizes team-oriented, collaborative leadership, organizations still need decisive, creative, and independent-thinking leaders.

Donna Fernandes: She's
the Leader of the Pack

Visit www.thomsonedu
.com/management/dubrin
and watch the video for
this chapter. Would you
characterize Fernan-
des's leadership style
as appropriate for
building a learning
organization? Why or
why not?

4. Transformational leadership is sometimes not necessary. The transformational leader might attempt to make sweeping changes in a system that needs modification only. In many situations, practicing small acts of leadership, such as listening to workers, is all that is needed. Michael E. McGill and John W. Slocum, Jr. observe, "A little leadership is what followers want and what leaders can do. Moreover, it can be learned. No less important, it is exactly the amount and kind of leadership that most organizations need."[60] (An example of a little act of leadership would be to set a realistic weekly goal, or give encouragement and support to a group member.)

SUMMARY OF KEY POINTS

 Differentiate between leadership and management. Leadership involves influencing others to achieve important objectives. Leaders are heavily involved in persuading, inspiring, and motivating others and spearheading change. Managers are more involved with stability and control.

 Describe key leadership traits, styles, and behaviors. Certain traits and characteristics contribute to leadership effectiveness in many situations. These personal attributes fall into the general categories of cognitive skills and personality characteristics, including emotional intelligence. Self-confidence, trustworthiness, and good problem-solving ability are three examples of key traits.

A foundation concept of the behavioral approach to leadership includes the two dimensions of initiating structure and consideration, and similarly, production-centered and employee-centered leadership. The Leadership Grid describes a manager's leadership style along the dimensions of concern for production and concern for people. Each of these concerns exists in varying degrees. The leader–member exchange model emphasizes that leaders have unique relationships with group members. In-group members have good relationships with the leader, whereas out-group members have poor relationships. Being part of the in-group enhances productivity and satisfaction.

 Explain the basics of four contingency theories of leadership.
Fiedler's contingency theory specifies the conditions under which leaders need to use task-motivated and relationship-motivated styles. In situations of high control and low control, the task-motivated style is better. Relationship-motivated leaders have the highest-producing groups under situations of moderate control.

According to the path–goal theory, leaders can enhance motivation by increasing personal payoffs to group members for achieving work objectives and by making the paths to payoffs smoother. The effective leader will choose among leadership styles according to two sets of contingency factors: characteristics of subordinates and task demands.

Situational Leadership II (SLII) explains how to match leadership style to the capabilities of group members on a given task. The combination of the subordinate's commitment and competence determines the four developmental levels: Enthusiastic Beginner, Disillusioned Learner, Capable but Cautious Performer, and Self-Reliant Achiever. The model classifies leadership style according to the relative amounts of supporting and directing in which the leader engages. The four styles are different combinations of task and relationship behavior, both rated as high versus low: directing, coaching, supporting, and delegating. The most appropriate leadership style corresponds to the subordinate developmental levels.

The normative decision model explains that leadership is a decision-making process. A leader examines certain contingency factors in the situation to determine which decision-making style will be the most effective, in either a time-driven or a developmental situation. The model identifies five decision-making styles: two based on individuals and three on groups. By answering a series of seven diagnostic questions in a matrix, the manager follows the path to a recommended decision style.

Present an overview of transformational and charismatic leadership.

The transformational leader is a charismatic person who helps bring about profound changes in people and the organization, often transforming the culture. Charismatic leaders are known to have vision, be masterful communicators, and inspire trust. They are also adept at managing their impression well. Charisma can be developed to some extent.

 Identify forces that can sometimes decrease the importance of leadership.

Although leadership is important, in certain situations, other factors may function as substitutes for leadership. These factors can be found within group members, the task, or the organization. Effective followers also decrease the need for leadership.

KEY TERMS AND PHRASES

Leadership, 231
The ability to inspire confidence and support among the people on whose competence and commitment performance depends.

Cognitive Skills, 233
Mental ability and knowledge.

Self-Awareness, 233
Insightfully processing feedback about oneself to improve personal effectiveness.

Behavioral Approach to Leadership, 238
An attempt to specify how the behavior of effective leaders differs from their less effective counterparts.

Leadership Style, 238
The relatively consistent pattern of behavior that characterizes a leader.

Initiating Structure, 240
The degree to which a leader establishes structure for group members.

Consideration, 240
The degree to which the leader creates an environment of emotional support, warmth, friendliness, and trust.

Leadership Grid, 241
A framework for classifying leadership styles that simultaneously examines a leader's concerns for task accomplishment and for people.

Leader–Member Exchange Model, 242
The model that recognizes that leaders develop a unique working relationship with each group member.

Servant Leader, 243
A leader who serves constituents by working on their behalf to help them achieve their goals, not the leader's own goals.

Contingency Theory of Leadership, 244
The position that the best style of leadership depends on factors relating to group members and the work setting.

Situational Control, 244
The degree to which the leader can control and influence the outcomes of group effort.

Path–Goal Theory of Leadership, 245
An explanation of leadership that specifies what the leader must do to achieve high morale and productivity in a given situation.

Situational Leadership II (SLII), 247
A model of leadership explaining how to match the leadership style to the capabilities of group members on a given task.

Normative Decision Model, 248
A contingency viewpoint of leadership that views leadership as a decision-making process in which the leader examines certain situational factors to determine which decision-making style will be most effective.

Transformational Leader, 250
One who helps organizations and people make positive changes in the way they conduct their activities.

Charisma, 250
The ability to lead others based on personal charm, magnetism, inspiration, and emotion.

Substitutes for Leadership, 254
Factors in the work environment that provide guidance and incentives to perform, making the leader's role almost superfluous.

257

DISCUSSION QUESTIONS AND ACTIVITIES

1. Describe how a person might be a good leader but a poor manager.
2. Describe how a person might be a good manager but a poor leader.
3. What would a manager of yours have to do before you considered him or her to be trustworthy?
4. Assuming you believe that the leader–member exchange theory is valid, how would you go about becoming part of a leader's in-group?
5. How would the Situational Leadership II model help you do a better job of managing or leading poorly motivated workers?
6. What do you perceive to be a major difference between a contingency leader and a charismatic leader?
7. Describe a scenario in which a team leader or first-level supervisor can be a transformational leader.

CASE PROBLEM: Russell Simmons, the CEO of Hip Hop

Russell Simmons is regarded as the most important businessperson in the history of rap music. He lives at a curious intersection: Simmons is in Corporate America but not quite of it. He is widely regarded as the impresario of hip-hop, a self-taught, self-made, 46-year-old entrepreneur who in the past two decades started two of the most successful enterprises of their kind: the hip-hop label Def Jam and clothing line Phat Farm. Simmons, more than anyone else, has helped bring an urban sensibility, with its bravado, its exaggerated desires, it urgent longing for the good life, to popular culture: The godfather of hip-hop has combined street smarts, yoga teachings, and a platinum Rolodex to create a $300 million empire.

Phat Farm sells itself as "classic American flava with a twist" and its slogan is an upside-down American flag. Phat Farm does its best business in a chain of stores called d.e.m.o. located almost entirely in suburban malls. The word *phat,* meaning highly attractive or gratifying, has been added to several English dictionaries.

Hip-hop music, and its signature style, rap, emerged from mostly impoverished, largely African-American urban neighborhoods, grew into an entire way of life, and today dominates youth culture. Marketing experts estimate that one-quarter of all discretionary spending in America today is influenced by hip-hop.

Simmons's Management and Business Approach
Simmons has created a new kind of empire, one that is organic (he operates more on instinct than anything else), fluid (businesses come and go), and frugal (he usually doesn't risk much of his own money). "Any company that wants to tap into the youth market today has to pay attention to Russell," says Frank Cooper, the head of multicultural market development at Pepsi. "He is one of the principal architects of hip-hop culture. It's a market that is massive, and that is global."

Simmons prefers to call himself a pioneer, and a generation of young, brash entrepreneurs has come to regard him as such. "Here's what other people's business plan is: Let Russell bash his head," he jokes, "and then we'll follow." Rush Communications has ventured into nearly every haunt of popular culture.

The entertainment group has produced two popular programs for HBO and a Tony Award–winning Broadway show. The Rush Visa Card is a prepaid debit card for people who may or may not have a bank account. There's even a vitamin-fortified energy drink, DefCon3, that sells in 5000 7-Eleven stores. Over the years Simmons has also opened and closed or sold a variety of ventures. He has started the Rush Philanthropic Arts Foundation, which in 1 year gave away about $350,000 to groups that introduce underprivileged kids to the arts.

Simmons has developed partnerships with well-established business firms. He was the first person to design a series of limited-edition Motorola Inc. cell phones with his name on them. He also advises Motorola on how to insinuate itself further into the hip-hop community, where a cell phone has become a fashion statement. The director of strategic planning and new business development for Motorola's iDen subscriber group says, "We want to intertwine our brands."

Simmons conducts his business day at a maddening pace. The door to his executive suite is wide open,

CASE PROBLEM *(Continued)*

which facilitates a stream of designers, friends, and employees trickling in and out without advance notice, asking Simmons to sign this or approve that. The phone is either ringing or Simmons is using it, all the while thumbing messages on his Motorola two-way like a madman, or talking a blue streak to a reporter.

Simmons surrounds himself with people he trusts to handle the day-to-day aspects of his business. He functions as a grand pooh-bah of marketing, a master brander and hype creator who leverages his reputation as the granddaddy of hip-hop to bring people together and let people combust. "Not only does he have a finger on the pulse of the popular culture," says Tommy Hilfiger, a friend and rival, "but he truly recognizes raw material and understands how to turn that potential into a marketable product."

Although other workers handle the day-to-day aspects of the business, Simmons is a hive of activity in tiny matters such as the number of buttons that should be placed on a Phat Farm suit. He is always in action, checking up, checking in, and connecting with everybody.

The Hip-Hop Niche

Simmons has built a career—and incubated a vast array of businesses—on the simple premise that the music and culture of today's urban youth have broad commercial appeal across the United States and around the world. As hip-hop has blossomed in Iowa, Connecticut, and Paris, so too have Simmons's wealth, power, and influence. "I consider him one of the great entrepreneurs out there today," says his pal Donald Trump. "He's a fabulous guy with a tremendous understanding of business. Russell has a great ability to see where the world is going and to take advantage of it."

The seamy side of hip-hop is what makes Simmons so valuable to mainstream marketers who want to adopt what's fresh about hip-hop without appearing to condone what's dangerous. They trust Simmons to navigate the fine line between edgy and appalling, authentic and offensive.

For Simmons, as much as the artists, these deals with mainstream business corporations are the ultimate status symbol, a sign that hip-hop can feed off the corporate world and not just the other way around. "To us it's not selling out," he says. "We want what represents success."

Simmons unashamedly promotes his products and political concerns, often at the same time. He promotes them at store appearances during dozens of television and radio interviews, at the regular talks he has with school kids in his Manhattan office, at his hip-hop summits around the country, at his annual Hamptons fundraiser for his foundation, and during protest rallies about the harsh penalties for nonviolent drug crimes in New York State. The ads for a line of sneakers include calls for reparations for African Americans. The label on DefCon3 reads: "Energize yourself and empower your community by drinking a healthier smart energy soda that gives back."

Simmons expresses his reason for promoting social causes in these words: "I want to contribute more to earth than I take from it." He also likes to say that it is difficult to help the poor if you are one of them.

Simmons's Concerns about Corporate America

Simmons is ambivalent about the relationship between his hip-hop nation and Corporate America. He has seen how some companies try to take advantage of the urban community's ability to detect and set cultural trends without bankrolling its entrepreneurs. However, he has benefited greatly from not being taken seriously at first. "I could complain about the lack of cultural sensitivity," he says, "but I also say that because of the old guy's stupidity I'm here in the first place. If the music business understood hip-hop in the beginning, I wouldn't have build Def Jam. If the banks served these (urban) folks, I wouldn't be here with the Rush Card."

Case Questions

1. In what way does Russell Simmons qualify as an innovative leader?
2. Which style or styles of leadership does Simmons emphasize?
3. Identify several of Simmons's leadership characteristics.
4. Any advice for Simmons? Do you detect an Achilles' heel?

Sources: Diane Brady and Tom Lowery, "The CEO of Hip Hop," *Business Week*, October 23, 2003, pp. 90–98; Jennifer Reingold, "Rush Hour," "*The Godfather of Hip-Hop*," *Fast Company*, November 2003, pp. 68-80; "Russell Simmons," http://www.vh1.com/artists/az/simmons_russel/bio.html.

ENDNOTES

1. Spencer E. Ante, "The New Blue," *Business Week,* March 17, 2003, p. 83.
2. Joseph A. Raelin, *Creating Leaderful Organizations: How to Bring Out Leadership in Everyone* (San Francisco: Berrett-Koehler, 2003).
3. W. Chan Kim and Renee A. Mauborgne, "Parables of Leadership," *Harvard Business Review,* July–August 1992, p. 123.
4. John P. Kotter, "What Leaders Really Do," *Harvard Business Review,* May–June 1990, pp. 103–111; Abraham Zaleznik, "Managers and Leaders: Are they Different?" *Harvard Business Review,* January 2004, p. 74 (Best of *HBR,* 1977).
5. Robert Hogan, Gordon J. Curphy, and Joyce Hogan, "What We Know about Leadership Effectiveness and Personality," *American Psychologist,* June 1994, p. 494.
6. David A. Waldman, Gabriel G. Ramírez, Robert J. House, and Phanish Puranam, "Does Leadership Matter? CEO Leadership Attributes and Profitability under Conditions of Perceived Environmental Uncertainty," *Academy of Management Journal,* February 2001, pp. 134–143.
7. Shelly A. Kirkpatrick and Edwin A. Locke, "Leadership: Do Traits Matter?" *Academy of Management Executive,* May 1991, pp. 48–60; Edwin A. Locke and Associates, *The Essence of Leadership: The Four Keys to Leading Successfully* (New York: Lexington/Macmillan, 1991), pp. 13–34.
8. Timothy A. Judge, Amy E. Colbert, and Remus Ilies, "Intelligence and Leadership: A Quantitative Review and Test of Theoretical Propositions," *Journal of Applied Psychology,* June 2004, p. 548.
9. Anthony J. Mayo and Nitin Nohria, "Zeitgeist Leadership," *Harvard Business Review,* October 2005, pp. 45–60.
10. "Gates Rallies Microsoft Troops to Set New Course," *USA Today,* November 10, 2005, p. 3B.
11. George P. Hollenbeck and Douglas T. Hall, "Self-Confidence and Leadership Performance," *Organizational Dynamics,* Issue 3, 2004, pp. 259.
12. Carol Hymowitz, "The Confident Boss Doesn't Micromanage or Delegate Too Much," *The Wall Street Journal,* March 11, 2003, p. B1.
13. "What Is Courage?" (Interview with Warren Bennis), *Fast Company,* September 2004, p. 99.
14. Ellen M. Whitener, Susan E. Brodt, M. Audrey Korsgaard, and Jon M. Werner, "Managers as Initiators of Trust: An Exchange Relationship Framework for Understanding Managerial Trustworthy Behavior," *Academy of Management Review,* July 1998, p. 516.
15. Douglas R. May, Adrian Y. L. Chan, Timothy D. Hodges, and Bruce J. Avolio, "Developing the Moral Component of Authentic Leadership," *Organizational Dynamics,* 3(2003), p. 248.
16. Rob Goffee and Gareth Jones, "Managing Authenticity: The Paradox of Great Leadership," *Harvard Business Review,* December 2005, pp. 86–94.
17. Roger C. Mayer and Mark B. Gavin, "Trust in Management and Performance: Who Minds the Shop While the Employees Watch the Boss?" *Academy of Management Journal,* October 2005, pp. 874–888.
18. Daniel Goleman, "Leadership that Gets Results," *Harvard Business Review,* March–April 2000, p. 80.
19. Brian Tribus, "Making Personal Connections with Your People," *Leader to Leader: Breakthroughs from West Point,* 2005, pp. 26–27.
20. Loren Gray, "Becoming a Resonant Leader," *Harvard Management Update,* July 2002, pp. 4–5.
21. Joel Stein, "Bosses from Hell," *Time,* December 7, 1998, p. 181.
22. Timothy A. Judge, Joyce E. Bono, Remus Ilies, and Megan W. Gerhardt, "Personality and Leadership: A Qualitative and Quantitative Review," *Journal of Applied Psychology,* August 2002, pp. 765–780.
23. Martin L. Maher and Douglas A. Klieber, "The Greying of Achievement Motivation," *American Psychologist,* July 1981, pp. 787–793.
24. Quoted in Shari Caudron, "Where Have All The Leaders Gone?" *Workforce,* December 2002, p. 31.
25. Ralph M. Stogdill and Alvin E. Coons (eds.), *Leader Behavior: Its Description and Measurement* (Columbus: Ohio State University Bureau of Business Research, 1957); Carroll L. Shartle, *Executive Performance and Leadership* (Upper Saddle River, NJ: Prentice Hall, 1956).
26. Arnold S. Tannenbaum, *Social Psychology of the Work Organization* (Monterey, CA: Wadsworth, 166), p. 74; Robert Dubin, "Supervision and Productivity: Empirical Findings and Theoretical Considerations," in Walter Nord (ed.), *Concepts and Controversies in Organizational Behavior* (Glenview, IL: Scott, Foresman, 1972), pp. 524–525.
27. Timothy A. Judge, Ronald F. Piccolo, and Remus Ilies, "The Forgotten Ones? The Validity of Consideration and Initiating Structure in Leadership Research," *Journal of Applied Psychology,* February 2004, pp. 36–51.
28. Marcus Buckingham, "What Great Managers Do," *Harvard Business Review,* March 2005, pp. 70–79.
29. Peter Burrows, "HP Says Goodbye to Drama," *Business Week,* September 12, 2005, pp. 83–86.
30. Robert R. Blake and Anne Adams McCanse, *Leadership Dilemmas—Grid Solutions* (Houston: Gulf Publishing, 1991).
31. George Graen and J. F. Cashman, "A Role-Making Model of Leadership in Formal Organizations: A Developmental Approach," in J. G. Hunt and L. I. Larson (eds.), *Leadership Frontiers* (Kent, OH: Kent State University Press, 1975), pp. 143–165; Robert P. Vecchio, "Leader-Member Exchange, Objective Performance, Employment Duration, and Supervisor Ratings: Testing for Moderation and Mediation," *Journal of Business and Psychology,* Spring 1998, pp. 327–341.
32. Robert P. Vecchio, "Are You In or OUT with Your Boss?" *Business Horizons, 29* (1987), pp. 76–78.
33. Chester A. Schriesheim, Linda L. Neider, and Terri A. Scandura, "Delegation and Leader-Member Exchange: Main Effects, Moderators, and Measurement Issues," *Academy of Management Journal,* June 1998, pp. 298–318.
34. Vecchio, "Leader-Member Exchange," p. 340.
35. K. Michele Kacmar, L. A. Witt, Suzanne Zivnuska, and Stanley M. Gulley, "The Interactive Effect of Leader-Member Exchange and Communication Frequency on Performance Ratings," *Journal of Applied Psychology,* August 2003, pp. 764–772.
36. Kenneth J. Dunnegan, Mary Uhl-Bien, and Dennis Duchon, "LMX and Subordinate Performance: The Moderating Effects of Task Characteristics," *Journal of Business and Psychology,* Winter 2002, pp. 275–285.
37. Berrin Erdogan, Maria L. Kraimer, and Robert C. Liden, "Work Value Congruence and Intrinsic Career Success: The Compensatory Roles of Leader-Member Exchange and Perceived Organizational Support," *Personnel Psychology,* Summer 2004, pp. 305–332.
38. Robert K. Greenleaf, *The Power of Servant Leadership* (San Francisco: Berrett-Koehler, 1998); James C. Hunter, *The World's Most Powerful Leadership Principle: How to Become a Servant Leader* (New York: Crown Business, 2004).
39. Gary Yukl and Richard Lepsinger, *Flexible Leadership: Creating Value by Balancing Multiple Challenges and Choices* (San Francisco: Jossey-Bass, 2004).
40. Michael Useem, "The Leadership Lessons of Mount Everest," *Harvard Business Review,* October 2001, p. 53.

41. Fred E. Fiedler, Martin M. Chemers, and Linda Mahar, *Improving Leadership Effectiveness: The Leader-Match Concept*, 2nd ed. (New York: Wiley, 1984); Martin M. Chemers, *An Integrative Theory of Leadership* (Mahwah, NJ: Lawrence Erlbaum Associates, 1997), pp. 28–38.

42. Robert J. House and Terence R. Mitchell, "Path-Goal Theory of Leadership," *Journal of Contemporary Business* (Fall 1974), p. 83.

43. Kenneth H. Blanchard, David Zigarmi, and Robert Nelson, "Situational Leadership after 25 Years: A Retrospective," *Journal of Leadership Studies, 1* (1993), pp. 22–26; Blanchard and Robert Nelson, "Recognition and Reward," *Executive Excellence*, 4(1997), p. 15; "Building Materials Leader Builds Better Leaders," http://www.kenblanchard.com.

44. Victor H. Vroom, "Leadership and the Decision-Making Process," *Organizational Dynamics,* Spring 2000, pp. 82–93.

45. Quoted in "Leadership," in *Business: The Ultimate Resource Business* (Cambridge, MA: Perseus Books Group, 2002), p. 916; James McGregor Burns, *Leadership* (New York: Harper & Row, 1978).

46. Nick Turner, et al., "Transformational Leadership and Moral Reasoning," *Journal of Applied Psychology,* April 2002, pp. 304–311.

47. Marshall Sashkin and Molly G. Sashkin, *Leadership that Matters* (San Francisco: Berrett-Koehler, 2003).

48. John J. Hater and Bernard M. Bass, "Supervisors' Evaluations and Subordinates' Perceptions of Transformational and Transactional Leadership," *Journal of Applied Psychology,* November 1988, p. 695; Noel M. Tichy and May Anne Devanna, *The Transformational Leader* (New York: Wiley, 1990).

49. Shun Jase Shin and Jing Zhou, "Transformational Leadership, Conservation, and Creativity: Evidence from Korea," *Academy of Management Journal*, December 2003, pp. 707–714.

50. Hui Wang, Kenneth S. Law, Rick D. Hackett, Duanxu Wang, and Zhen Xiong Chen, "Leader-Member Exchange as Mediator of the Relationship between Transformational Leadership and Followers' Performance and Organizational Citizenship Behavior," *Academy of Management Journal*, June 2005, p. 430.

51. Sally A. Carless, Alexander J. Wearing, and Leon Mann, "A Short Measure of Transformational Leadership," *Journal of Business and Psychology,* Spring 2000, pp. 389–405.

52. Jennifer Reingold, "Bob Nardelli is Watching," *Fast Company*, December 2005, pp. 76–78.

53. Rosabeth Moss Kanter, "Leadership and the Psychology of Turnarounds," *Harvard Business Review,* June 2003, pp. 58–67.

54. Jay A. Conger and Rabindra N. Kanungo, *Charismatic Leadership in Organizations* (Thousand Oaks, CA: Sage, 1998).

55. Joyce E. Bono and Timothy A. Judge, "Personality and Transformational and Transactional Leadership: A Meta-Analysis," *Journal of Applied Psychology*, October 2004, pp. 901–910.

56. William L. Gardner and Bruce J. Avolio, "The Charismatic Relationship: A Dramaturgical Perspective," *Academy of Management Review,* January 1998, p. 33.

57. Rakesh Khurana, *Searching for a Corporate Savior* (Princeton, NJ: Princeton University Press, 2002).

58. Several of the suggestions are from Roger Dawson, *Secrets of Power Persuasion: Everything You'll Need to Get Anything You'll Ever Want* (Upper Saddle River, NJ: Prentice Hall, 1992), pp. 179–194: "Secrets of Charismatic Leadership," *WorkingSMART,* February 1998, p. 1.

59. Jon P. Howell, David E. Bowen, Peter W. Dorfman, Steven Kerr, and Philip Podsakoff, "Substitutes for Leadership: Effective Alternatives to Ineffective Leadership," *Organizational Dynamics,* Summer 1990, p. 23.

60. Michael E. McGill and John W. Slocum, Jr., "A Little Leadership, Please?" *Organizational Dynamics,* Winter 1998, p. 48.

12

Power, Politics, and Influence

At Planar Systems, an electronic-display system maker, Chairman and CEO Balaji Krishnamurthy seeks a culture in which employees routinely ask questions and debate strategies. In addition to town-hall meetings, he holds monthly meetings with 50 to 60 middle managers in an amphitheater-style room where everyone can see each other. He gauges their integrity partly on whether they say what they think—in a constructive way.

Planar employees can also question Krishnamurthy and other top executives privately through an internal e-mail system called "ask the expert." Recently, a manager overseas questioned whether a certain financial goal was realistic. When responding, Krishnamurthy didn't insist he was absolutely certain the goals could be achieved. Instead he wrote that he "had certain convictions about how some markets would likely grow." He subsequently met the manager and was pleased to hear him say, "Well, even though I may not share your convictions, I know what I can do to further the company's cause."

Source: Excerpted from Carol Hymowitz, "Like Rumsfeld, CEOs Who Seek Questions May Not Like Them," *The Wall Street Journal,* December 14, 2004, p. B1.

Now Ask Yourself: **What does this story about an electronics–display company tell us about power, politics, and influence?** One point is that in some organizations employees are empowered to make constructive suggestions for improving the company. Similarly, in some political climates being a yes-person is *not* the way to impress top management. Power, politics, and influence are such major parts of the workplace that they have become standard topics of organizational behavior.

In this chapter, we approach power, politics, and influence from multiple perspectives. We describe the meaning of these concepts, how power is obtained, and how it is shared (empowerment). We examine why organizational politics is so prevalent, and then describe the tactics of politics and influence. In addition, we describe the control of dysfunctional politics, and ethical considerations about the use of power, politics, and influence. As you read the chapter, you will learn that some tactics of power, politics, and influence violate ethical codes and therefore should be avoided.

THE MEANING OF POWER, POLITICS, AND INFLUENCE

A challenge in understanding power, politics, and influence in organizations is that the terms appear close in meaning. Here we present meanings of these terms aimed at providing useful distinctions. **Power** is the potential or ability to influence decisions and control resources. The predominant view of power is that it is the influence over others' actions, thoughts, and outcomes.[1] Realize that, like gravity, power cannot be observed directly. Yet you can observe its effects, such as when the corporate name is used as a verb.[2] For example, "Have you "Googled" that job applicant yet?

Many definitions of *power* center on the ability of a person to overcome resistance in achieving a result. Some researchers suggest that power lies in the potential, while others focus on use.[3] As a hedge, our definition includes both potential and use. If you have a powerful battery in your car, isn't it still powerful whether or not it is in use?

Politics is a way of achieving power. As used here, **organizational politics** refers to informal approaches to gaining power through means other than merit or luck. *Influence* is close in meaning to *power. Influence* is also the ability to change behavior, but it tends to be more subtle and indirect than *power. Power* indicates the ability to affect outcomes with greater facility and ease than *influence.*[4] A person who has political skill is able to use influence behaviors in organizations, such as building strong relationships with key people. John Chambers, the CEO and chairman of Cisco Systems, is widely recognized for his ability to build alliances with key people in the Internet industry, contributing to the success of his company.

Managers and professionals often need to use political tactics to achieve the power and influence they need to accomplish their work. An example would be a human resources manager cultivating the support of a top executive so she can proceed with a program of employee wellness. Cultivating support is a political tactic.

SOURCES OF INDIVIDUAL AND SUBUNIT POWER

The sources or bases of power in organizations can be classified in different ways. A useful starting point is to recognize that power can be used to forward either the interests of the organization or personal interests. **Socialized power** is the use of power to achieve constructive ends. An example would be the manager who attempted to gain power to spearhead a program of employee wellness. **Personalized power** is the use of power primarily for the sake of personal aggrandizement and gain.[5] An example would be a new CEO using his power to insist that company

Identify sources of power for individuals and subunits within organization.

263

headquarters be moved to a location near his home or that his family members be allowed to use a company jet.

Here we classify the sources (and also the bases and origins) of power, which stem from the organization, from the individual, and from providing resources.[6]

Power Granted by the Organization (Position Power)

Managers and professionals often have power because of the authority, or right, granted by their positions. The power of a manager's position stems from three sources: legitimate power, coercive power, and reward power. **Legitimate power** is based on the manager's formal position within the hierarchy. A government agency head, for example, has much more position power than a unit supervisor in the same agency. Managers can enhance their position power by formulating policies and procedures. For example, a manager might establish a requirement that she must approve all new hires, thus exercising authority over hiring.

Coercive power comes from controlling others through fear or threat of punishment. Typical organizational punishments include bypassing an employee for promotion, terminating employment, and giving damaging performance evaluations to people who do not support your initiatives, even if the initiatives are unethical or illegal. The threat of a lawsuit by an employee who is treated unjustly serves as a constraint on legitimate power, and is referred to as *subordinate power*. **Reward power** involves controlling others through rewards or the promise of rewards. Examples of this include promotions, challenging assignments, and recognition given to employees.

The effectiveness of coercive power and reward power depends on the perceptions and needs of group members. For coercive power to be effective, the employee must fear punishment and care about being a member of the firm. Conversely, an employee who did not care much for recognition or power would not be strongly influenced by the prospects of a promotion.

Executives who abuse power by voting themselves extraordinary compensation during a business downturn have been under attack from many observers of business. At American Airlines, the labor union was able to constrain executive abuse of legitimate power as follows:

> In 2003, after sharp criticism from angry employees, the head of American Airlines apologized as the company dropped a plan to give bonuses to six top executives if they stayed with the airline for two more years. The bonuses were equal to twice the executives' salaries. The employees learned of the perks after agreeing to cut their own benefits by $10 billion over six years, to help save the company. American Airlines did not tell the workers about the executive perks until workers agreed to pay cuts of 15.6 percent to 23 percent.
>
> Chairman and CEO Donald J. Carty, who would have received a $1.6 million bonus, said, "I have apologized to our union leaders for this and for the concern it has caused our employees."[7]

Power Stemming from the Individual (Personal Power)

Managers and other categories of workers also derive power from two separate personal characteristics: knowledge and personality. **Expert power** is the ability to influence others because of one's specialized knowledge, skills, or abilities. For expertise to be an effective source of power, group members must respect that expertise.

Exercising expert power is the logical starting point for building one's power base. Powerful people in business, government, and education almost invariably launched their careers by developing expertise in a specialty of value to their employers. Furthermore, expert power also keeps a person in demand for executive positions. Fritz Henderson, chairman of GE Europe, illustrates the exercise of expert power. He has spent much of his 20-year career jumping into troubled GM operations, usually spending just enough time to take decisive, and often painful, action. After that he moves on to the next turnaround assignment. Known as a master financial analyst, he brought GM further into the profitable residential mortgage business. Anderson also makes major marketing decisions, such as moving the Latin American operations into more small, inexpensive vehicles. (Anderson has three sources of expert power: making operations, finance, and marketing.)[8]

Referent power is the ability to influence others that stems from one's desirable traits and characteristics. It is based on the desire of others to be led by or to identify with an inspiring person. Having referent power contributes to a perception of being charismatic, but expert power also makes a contribution.[9]

Power from Providing Resources

Another way of understanding the sources of power is through the **resource dependence perspective.** According to this perspective, the organization requires a continuing flow of human resources, money, customers, technological inputs, and material to continue to function. Subunits or individuals within the organization who can provide these resources derive power from this ability.[10]

A variation on power from providing resources is the derivation of power from gossip, which is an important resource in many organizations. Most people know that an influential member of the grapevine can accrue a small degree of power, and a scientific analysis supports this idea. The authors of the analysis define *gossip* as "informal and evaluative talk in an organization, usually among no more than a few individuals, about another member of that organization who is not present."[11] According to the model developed, a supplier of gossip will develop the sources of power already described, such as reward, expert, and coercive power. However, if the person provides mostly negative gossip, his or her referent power will decrease. Another problem is that negative gossip can be perceived as a form of harassment that creates an unsafe workplace for employees.[12]

Power from Meeting the Expectations of Group Members: Implicit Leadership Theory

Another perspective on leadership power is that a leader can accrue power by behaving and acting in the way group members expect. For example, a team leader who is intelligent and dedicated when team members want an intelligent and dedicated leader will have some power based on meeting these expectations. According to **implicit leadership theory**, group members develop prototypes specifying the traits and abilities that characterize an ideal business leader. People are characterized as true leaders on the basis of the perceived match between their behavior and character and the leader category they have in their minds. Implicit leadership theories (or expectations) are the benchmarks group members use to form an impression of their leader/manager. Group members have both prototypes and antiprototypes (what they want the leader not to be).

In organizational settings the leadership prototypes (desirable characteristics and traits) are as follows: sensitivity, intelligence, dedication, charisma, strength, and attractiveness. The antiprototypes are tyranny and masculinity (a sexist term for being cold and non–relationship oriented). A study of 439 employees indicated that the closer the employees perceived their manager's profile to fit the implicit

ORGANIZATIONAL BEHAVIOR *In Action*

Laura Wright Climbs to Power at Southwest Airlines

Despite a small-town background, Laura Wright, chief financial officer of Southwest Airlines, has always thought big. Off to college after growing up in western Nebraska and east Texas, she decided not to waste any time and earned her bachelor's and master's degree simultaneously, in a little over 4 years.

And when Southwest recruited her to handle its company taxes in 1988, her main concern was whether she would have enough room to advance at the small discount airline. She liked her job at Arthur Young & Co., then one of the world's top accounting firms. While Southwest seemed like a fun place to work, "I was worried about long-term opportunity," she said, a thought that now makes her laugh.

But Wright jumped on board Southwest as the tiny airline rocketed to the top tier of the industry. Her small-town roots fit right in with Southwest's casual culture, and she quickly broadened her résumé as director of corporate finance in 1990. Wright assumed the duty of negotiating the purchase of airplanes dumped on the market by other downsizing and bankrupt carriers. Her experience debating arcane business details with government tax auditors had turned her into a painstaking negotiator. Her hard-nosed deal-making contrasts with a mild nature that prompts Southwest's chief executive to describe her as "the sweetest tough lady you will ever meet."

Even as she's risen through the executive ranks, Wright, 45 years old, likes to stay involved at every level of the business. When Southwest was in secret negotiations to buy Morris Air in 1993, she flew to Salt Lake City for a middle-of-the-night, flashlight inspection of its airplane fleet parked on the tarmac. "I'm really not just a paper pusher," Wright says. "I've always been a roll-up-your-shirt-sleeves type."

Wright succeeded Kelly as CFO when he moved to the chief executive suite in July 2004. As CFO, she's involved in approving capital projects and helping decide what makes sense for the company strategically. She also cohosts the earnings conference calls with analysts and Kelly.

But Wright gets the most attention these days for steering the company's lauded fuel-hedging program, which has secured Southwest a supply of cheaper fuel at a time when energy costs are putting a huge strain on the industry. That program could prove crucial to Southwest's future success, giving the carrier the resources to continue growing while other airlines struggle to remain solvent.

As energy prices stay high and opportunities for cheaper fuel contracts evaporate, it's becoming more difficult to maintain that edge. "Clearly the decisions are much, much harder today, but they've always been hard," says Wright. Making tough decisions is a hallmark of leadership, she adds. "You have to be able to make a hard decision, and you can't procrastinate," she says. "Because if you do, that decision will be made for you."

Questions

1. Which types of power does Wright display?
2. What career advice might a student of organizational behavior glean from this story?

Source: Susan Warren, "In Line to Lead: Laura Wright: Chief Financial Officer, Southwest Airlines," *The Wall Street Journal*, October 31, 2005, p. R7.

leadership theory they endorsed, the better the quality of the leader–member exchange.[13] It can be inferred that as a result of these high-quality exchanges the leader has a little more power.

The accompanying Organizational Behavior in Action box describes an executive who has made intelligent use a variety of types of power.

EMPOWERMENT OF GROUP MEMBERS

Distributing power throughout the organization has become a major strategy for improving productivity, quality, satisfaction, and motivation. Employees experience a greater sense of self-efficacy (self-confidence for a particular task) and ownership in their jobs when they share power. **Empowerment** is the process of sharing power with group members, thereby enhancing their feelings of self-efficacy.[14] You can begin to personalize the meaning of *empowerment* by doing the accompanying skill-development exercise.

Exhibit 12-1 shows a model of the empowerment process. According to this model, managers must act in specific ways to empower employees, such as those mentioned in stage 2. Participative management is the general strategy for empowering workers. The techniques of participative management listed in stage 2, such as goal setting, modeling, and job enrichment, have been described in previous chapters. The information about empowering teams presented in Chapter 10 is also relevant here. To link empowerment directly to leadership, empowerment can be regarded as shared leadership as opposed to vertical leadership. Such shared leadership is particularly necessary when the work within the group is interdependent, creative, and complex. The typical work of cross-functional teams and virtual teams calls for shared leadership or empowerment.[15]

Describe the essence of empowerment.

Log on to **www.thomsonedu.com/infotrac**. Perform a keyword search on *workplace bullies.* Come up with tactics for dealing with verbal assaults, intimidation, and other bullying behavior.

SKILL-DEVELOPMENT EXERCISE

Becoming an Empowering Leader

To empower employees, leaders and managers must convey appropriate attitudes and develop the right interpersonal skills. The following list of attitudes and skills will help you become an empowering manager and leader. To the best of your self-evaluation, indicate which skills and attitudes you have and which ones require development.

Empowering Attitude or Behavior	Can Do Now	Would Need to Develop
1. Believe in the ability of team members to be successful.	_____	_____
2. Be patient with people and give them time to learn.	_____	_____
3. Provide group members with direction and structure.	_____	_____
4. Teach group members new skills in small, incremental steps so they can easily learn those skills.	_____	_____
5. Ask group members questions that challenge them to think in new ways.	_____	_____
6. Share information with team members, sometimes just to build rapport.	_____	_____
7. Give group members timely feedback and encourage them throughout the learning process.	_____	_____
8. Offer group members alternative ways of doing things.	_____	_____
9. Exhibit a sense of humor and demonstrate caring for workers as people.	_____	_____
10. Focus on group members' results and acknowledge their personal improvement.	_____	_____

Source: Republished with permission of Supervisory Management from Richard Hamlin, "A Practical Guide to Empowering Your Employees," *Supervisory Management* (April 1991), p. 8. Permission conveyed through Copyright Clearance Center, Inc.

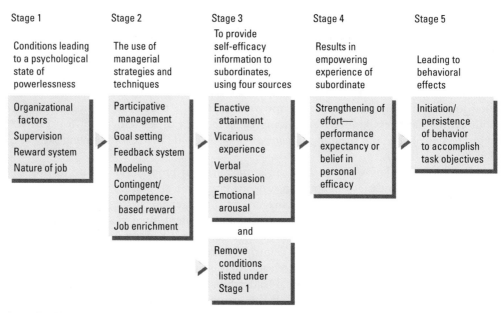

Stage 1	Stage 2	Stage 3	Stage 4	Stage 5
Conditions leading to a psychological state of powerlessness	The use of managerial strategies and techniques	To provide self-efficacy information to subordinates, using four sources	Results in empowering experience of subordinate	Leading to behavioral effects
Organizational factors Supervision Reward system Nature of job	Participative management Goal setting Feedback system Modeling Contingent/competence-based reward Job enrichment	Enactive attainment Vicarious experience Verbal persuasion Emotional arousal and Remove conditions listed under Stage 1	Strengthening of effort—performance expectancy or belief in personal efficacy	Initiation/persistence of behavior to accomplish task objectives

Source: Republished with permission of the Academy of Management Review from Jay A. Conger and Rabindra N. Kanungo, "The Empowerment Process: Integrating Theory and Practice," *Academy of Management Review* (July 1988): p. 475. Permission conveyed through Copyright Clearance Center, Inc.

Exhibit **12-1**

Five Stages in the Process of Empowerment

A study of 35 sales and service virtual teams showed that team empowerment was related to two measures of team performance—process improvement and customer satisfaction. Empowerment was measured by a questionnaire with statements such as, "My team makes its own choices without being told by management." Empowerment was even more effective for the virtual teams with fewer face-to-face meetings, suggesting that the less you meet with a manager, the more empowerment virtual team members need.[16]

To bring about empowerment, managers must remove conditions that keep employees powerless, such as authoritarian supervision or a job over which they have little control. An example of a person in a low-control job would be a manager who cannot shut off interruptions even to prepare budgets or to plan. Employees must also receive information that increases their feelings of self-efficacy. As shown in Exhibit 12-1, when employees are empowered, they will take the initiative to solve problems and strive hard to reach objectives.

Empowerment may not proceed smoothly unless certain conditions are met. A major consideration is that the potentially empowered workers must be competent and interested in assuming more responsibility. Otherwise the work will not get accomplished. W. Alan Randolph observed 10 companies that made the transition to empowerment.[17] The first key to effective empowerment is *information sharing*. Lacking information, it is difficult for workers to act with responsibility.

Another critical factor for successful empowerment is for management to *provide more structure* as teams move into self-management. To initiate empowerment, managers must teach people new skills and make the parameters clear. Workers need to know, for example, "What are the limits to my empowerment?" The third critical factor Randolph observed was that *teams must gradually replace the traditional organizational hierarchy*. Empowered teams do not only make recommendations, they make and implement decisions and are held accountable. A major contributor to successful empowerment at a large food company studied was that teams acted as managers. They hired and fired people, appraised performance, scheduled work, and managed a budget.

Empowerment is also more effective when the empowered individuals and teams are told what needs to be done but are *free to determine how to achieve the objectives.* Consultant Norman Bodek says, "Allowing people to determine the most efficient work techniques is the essence of empowerment."[18] A final consideration for successful empowerment is implied in the other conditions. *Unless managers trust employees,* empowerment will not be effective or even take place. For example, when employees are trusted, they are more likely to be given the information they need and be granted the freedom to choose an appropriate method.

Meg Whitman, the CEO of eBay, is an example of a prominent business leader who believes that sharing power improves organizational effectiveness. She claims, "I don't actually think of myself as powerful" and endorses the statement, "To have power, you must be willing to not have any of it."[19] In practice this means that Whitman relies on consensus leadership, and believes that the eBay community is the true source of the company's greatness.

Exhibit 12-2 provides additional insight into empowerment by listing indicators of whether group members show signs of empowerment or disempowerment.

Now that we have described the sources of power and empowerment, we shift focus to more details about political behavior and influence tactics.

Exhibit **12-2**

Signs of Empowerment and Disempowerment

One valuable way to track progress in empowerment is to look for the behaviors exhibited by employees who are moving toward effective empowerment. Compare those behaviors with the behaviors you might see from disempowered employees.

Empowered Employees:

- Take initiative in ambiguous situations and define problems in a way that enables further analysis of decisions.
- Identify opportunities in ambiguous situations, such as when customers complain or competitive threats arise.
- Apply critical thinking skills, such as surfacing and testing assumptions or evaluating arguments.
- Offer judgments about how and why specific decisions or actions support the shared purpose.
- Build consensus for decisions and actions both within and across functional groups.
- Identify and act on opportunities to systematize activities, document and communicate system information, identify and resolve systemic problems, and adapt or dismantle systems that no longer add value.
- Optimize resources by reducing expenses and finding opportunities to invest new resources (process improvements, technology upgrades, etc.).

Disempowered Employees:

- Wait for a designated authority to define the problem and assign responsibilities.
- Address a problem effectively but fail to notice the possible opportunity.
- Accept information, reasoning, or conclusions without testing (especially when presented by an authority).
- Discuss but may not be able to apply the available information about shared purpose.
- Expect to attempt consensus building, but appeal to hierarchical authority if the attempt fails.
- Focus on improving individual or team effectiveness yet fail to notice problems that extend beyond the group, create good one-time solutions yet fail to systematize them, and rely on existing systems even if they are less valuable.
- Focus on the resources question only when and as directed by a designated authority.

ORGANIZATIONAL POLITICS

Pinpoint factors contributing to, and examples of, organizational politics.

Our study of organizational politics includes the reasons behind political behavior in the workplace, ethical and unethical tactics, and gender differences in the use of politics.

Factors Contributing to Political Behavior

The most fundamental reason for organizational politics is the political nature of organizations. Coalitions of interests and demands arise both within and outside organizations. Similarly, organizations can be viewed as loose structures of interests and demands in competition with one another for attention and resources. The interaction among different coalitions results in an undercurrent of political tactics, such as when one group tries to promote itself and discredit another.

Another contributor to political activity is the pyramid structure of organizations. The people at the top of the organization hold most of the power, while people at each successive level down the hierarchy hold less power. The amount of power that can be distributed in a hierarchy is limited. Power-oriented managers sometimes cope with the limited amount of power available by expanding their sphere of influence sideways. For example, the director of the food-stamp program in a government agency might attempt to gain control over the housing assistance program, which is at the same level.

Executive coach Marshall Goldsmith observes a major reason for kissing up (a form of organizational politics) to people in power. Without meaning to, many managers create an environment in which people learn to reward others with accolades that are not really warranted. People who are kind, courteous, and complimentary toward their managers are most likely to receive the most recognition—assuming their job performance is at least in the acceptable range.[20]

Downsizing and team structures create even less opportunity for climbing the hierarchy, thus intensifying political behavior for the few remaining powerful positions. Worried about layoffs themselves, many workers attempt to discredit others so that the latter would be the first to go. Internal politics generally increase as good jobs, promotions, and bonuses become scarcer. A business columnist made an observation a few years back that continues to be true: "The art of fawning over a boss may be more important now because of the stagnant economy and shortage of well-paying, full-time jobs."[21]

Organizational politics is also fostered by the need for power. Executives have much stronger power needs than others, and thus propel themselves toward frequent episodes of political behavior. Because executives are responsible for controlling resources, their inner desire to do so helps them in their jobs. A personalized power need is more likely to trigger political behavior than a socialized power need.

Finally, a devious reason for the existence of politicking is **Machiavellianism,** a tendency to manipulate others for personal gain. (Niccolo Machiavelli was a 15th-century political philosopher whose book, *The Prince,* describes how leaders may acquire and maintain power by placing expediency above morality.) One analysis suggests that many ambitious and successful corporate executives have strong Machiavellian tendencies, such as acquiring other companies just to give the appearance of true corporate growth.[22]

To make effective use of organizational politics, managerial workers must be aware of specific political strategies and tactics. To identify and explain the majority of political behaviors would require years of study and observation. Managers so frequently need support for their programs that they search for innovative political maneuvers. Furthermore, new tactics continue to emerge as the workplace becomes increasingly competitive.

The accompanying self-assessment quiz gives you an opportunity to think through your tendencies to engage in organizational politics. In the two following sections we first describe mostly ethical, followed by unethical, political tactics.

Mostly Ethical and Positive Political Tactics

Here we describe political tactics that many people would consider to be ethical and positive. Nevertheless, some managers and management scholars regard all political tactics as being ethically tainted.

1. *Develop power contacts through networking.* A fundamental principle of success is to identify powerful people and then establish alliances with them. Cultivating friendly, cooperative relationships with powerful organizational members and outsiders can make the managerial worker's cause much easier to advance. These contacts can support a person's ideas and recommend him or her for promotions and visible temporary assignments. A challenge in the era of electronic communications is that face time, or in-person contact, is helpful for building contacts. It is important to converse with powerful people in person in addition to sending them electronic messages. Although still electronic, an occasional telephone call is a useful supplement to e-mail for purposes of building a network.

2. *Manage your impression.* You will recall that charismatic leaders rely heavily on impression management, and the same technique is important for other success-oriented people. An example of an ethical impression-management tactic would be to contribute outstanding performance and then make sure key people know of your accomplishments. Making others aware of what you accomplish is often referred to as *achieving visibility.* When tactics of impression management appear insincere, they are likely to create a negative impression and thus be self-defeating. A key person to impress is your immediate superior. Many firms send professionals to etiquette training, because displaying proper etiquette makes a positive impression on customers and clients.[23]

3. *Control vital information.* Power accrues to those who control vital information, such as knowing how to maneuver contracts through private and governmental bureaucracies. Here, *control* generally refers to keeping the information covert until it serves one's purpose. If the information is made public, the person loses control.

4. *Keep informed.* In addition to controlling vital information, it is politically important to keep informed. Successful managers and professionals develop a pipeline to help them keep abreast, or even ahead, of developments within the firm. For example, a politically astute individual might befriend a major executive's assistant.

5. *Be courteous, pleasant, and positive.* Courteous, pleasant, and positive people are the first to be hired and the last to be fired (assuming they are also technically qualified).[24] A key part of being courteous, pleasant, and positive to is socialize with coworkers, including having meals and drinks with them. Executive coach Leslie Williams observes that "Socialization has everything to do with influence. It's not enough to just be good at your job." In addition to doing a good job you have to be somebody who people know and know well enough to trust.[25]

6. *Ask satisfied customers to contact your manager.* A favorable comment by a customer receives considerable weight because customer satisfaction is a top corporate priority. If a customer says something nice, the comment will carry more weight

SELF-ASSESSMENT

The Positive Organizational Politics Questionnaire

Answer each question "mostly agree" or "mostly disagree," even if it is difficult for you to decide which alternative best describes your opinion.

		Mostly Agree	Mostly Disagree
1.	Pleasing my boss is a major goal of mine.	___	___
2.	I go out of my way to flatter important people.	___	___
3.	I am most likely to do favors for people who can help me in return.	___	___
4.	Given the opportunity, I would cultivate friendships with powerful people.	___	___
5.	I will compliment a coworker even if I have to think hard about what might be praiseworthy.	___	___
6.	If I thought my boss needed the help, and I had the expertise, I would show him or her how to use an electronic gadget for personal life.	___	___
7.	I laugh heartily at my boss's humor, so long as I think he or she is at least a little funny.	___	___
8.	I would not be too concerned about following a company dress code, so long as I looked neat.	___	___
9.	If a customer sent me a compliment through e-mail, I would forward a copy to my boss and another influential person.	___	___
10.	I smile only at people in the workplace whom I genuinely like.	___	___
11.	An effective way to impress people is to tell them what they want to hear.	___	___
12.	I would never publicly correct mistakes made by the boss.	___	___
13.	I would be willing to use my personal contacts to gain a promotion or desirable transfer.	___	___
14.	I think it is a good idea to send a congratulatory note to someone in the company who receives a promotion to an executive position.	___	___
15.	I think "office politics" is only for losers.	___	___

Scoring and interpretation: Give yourself a plus 1 for each answer that agrees with the keyed answer. Each question that receives a score of plus 1 shows a tendency toward playing positive organizational politics. The scoring key is as follows:

1. Mostly agree
2. Mostly agree
3. Mostly agree
4. Mostly agree
5. Mostly agree
6. Mostly agree
7. Mostly agree
8. Mostly disagree
9. Mostly agree
10. Mostly disagree
11. Mostly agree
12. Mostly agree
13. Mostly agree
14. Mostly agree
15. Mostly disagree

1–6, Below-average tendency to play office politics
7–11, Average tendency to play office politics
12 and above, Above-average tendency to play office politics; strong need for power

Thinking about your political tendencies in the workplace is important for your career because most successful leaders are moderately political. The ability to use politics effectively and ethically increases with importance in the executive suite. Most top players are effective office politicians. Yet being overly and blatantly political can lead to distrust, thereby damaging your career.

than one from a coworker or subordinate. The reason is that insiders might praise you for political reasons, whereas a customer's motivation is thought to be pure.

7. *Avoid political blunders.* A strategy for retaining power is to refrain from making power-eroding blunders. Committing these politically insensitive acts can also prevent you from attaining power. Leading blunders include strong criticism of a superior in a public forum and going around your manager with a complaint. Another blunder is burning your bridges by creating ill will with former employees.

8. *Sincere flattery.* A powerful tactic for ingratiating yourself to others is to flatter them honestly and sincerely. Although one meaning of the term *flattery* is insincere praise, another meaning refers to a legitimate compliment. Charismatic people use flattery regularly. The accompanying skill-development exercise

SKILL-DEVELOPMENT EXERCISE

A Short Course in Effective Flattery

Flattering others is an effective way of building personal relationships (or engaging in organizational politics), if done properly. Suggestions for effective flattery are presented here. *Flattery* here refers to pleasing others through complimentary remarks or attention; we are not referring to *flattery* in the sense of giving insincere or excessive compliments. To build your skills in flattering others, practice these suggestions as the opportunity presents itself. Rehearse your flattery approaches until they feel natural. If your first attempt at flattery does not work well, analyze what went wrong the best you can.

- *Use sensible flattery.* Effective flattery has at least a spoonful of credibility, implying that you say something positive about the target person that is quite plausible. Credibility is also increased when you point to a person's tangible accomplishment. Technical people in particular expect flattery to be specific and aimed at genuine accomplishment.
- *Compliment what is of major importance to the flattery target.* You might find out what is important to the person by observing what he or she talks about with the most enthusiasm.
- *Flatter others by listening intently.* Listening intently to another person is a powerful form of flattery. Use active listening (see Chapter 8) for best results.
- *Flatter by referring to or quoting the other person.* By referring to or quoting (including paraphrasing) another person, you are paying that person a substantial compliment.
- *Use confirmation behaviors.* Use behaviors that have a positive or therapeutic effect on other

people, such as praise and courtesy. Because confirmation behaviors have such a positive effect on others, they are likely to be perceived as a form of flattery.
- *Give positive feedback.* A mild form of flattering others is to give them positive feedback about their statements, actions, and results. The type of feedback referred to here is a straightforward and specific declaration of what the person did right.
- *Remember names.* Remembering the names of people with whom you have infrequent contact makes them feel important. To help remember the person's name, study the name carefully when you first hear it and repeat it immediately.
- *Avoid flattery that has a built-in insult or barb.* The positive effect of flattery is eradicated when it is accompanied by a hurtful comment, such as "You have good people skills for an engineer" or "You look good. I bet you were really beautiful when you were younger."

To build your skills in flattering others, you must try some of the above techniques. For starters, within the next few days flatter a classmate, coworker, boss, or friend for something laudable the person accomplished. Or, flatter a customer-contact worker for a service well delivered. Observe carefully the results of your flattery.

Sources: Andrew J. DuBrin, *Personal Magnetism: Discover Your Own Charisma and Learn to Charm, Inspire, and Influence Others* (New York: AMACOM, 1997), pp. 75–92; Karen Judson, "The Fine Art of Flattery," *Kiwanis*, March 1998, pp. 34–36, 43; DuBrin, "Self-Perceived Technical Orientation and Attitudes toward Being Flattered," *Psychological Reports, 96* (2005), pp. 852–854.

Collaboration

273

will help you develop flattery skills. Such development should come easy to you because organizational behavior students typically have great potential interpersonal skills, along with high cognitive and emotional intelligence.

Mostly Unethical and Negative Political Tactics

In this section we describe tactics of organizational politics that most people would consider to be unethical and negative. The majority of people who use these tactics would not admit to their use.

1. *Backstabbing.* The ubiquitous backstab requires that you pretend to be nice but all the while plan someone's demise. A frequent form of backstabbing is to inform your rival's immediate superior that he or she is faltering under the pressure of job responsibilities. The recommended approach to dealing with a backstabber is to confront the person directly, ask for an explanation of his or her behavior, and demand that he or she stop. Threaten to complain to the person's superior.[26]

2. *Embrace-or-demolish.* The ancient strategy of embrace-or-demolish suggests that you remove from the premises rivals who suffered past hurts through your efforts. (The same tactic is called "take no prisoners.") Otherwise the wounded rivals might retaliate at a vulnerable moment. An illustration of embrace-or-demolish is when, after a hostile takeover, many executives lose their jobs because they opposed the takeover.

3. *Stealing credit.* For many workers, the most detestable form of office politics is for their boss, or other worker, to take credit for their ideas without acknowledging the source of the idea. Paul Lapides estimates that up to 80% of workers suffer this indignity at some time in their careers. The credit stealing breeds distrust, damages motivation, and is sometimes misperceived as a perk of power.[27] A good starting point in stopping idea thieves is to hold a one-on-one session with the thief, and confront the issue. If the issue is not resolved, tell key decision makers about the idea theft.[28]

4. *Territorial games.* Also referred to as *turf wars,* **territorial games** involve protecting and hoarding resources that give a person power, such as information, relationships, and decision-making authority. The purpose of territorial games is to compete for three kinds of territory in the modern corporate survival game: information, relationships, and authority. A relationship is "hoarded" in such ways as not encouraging others to visit a key customer, or blocking a higher performer from getting a promotion or transfer by informing other managers that he or she is mediocre.[29] Other examples of territorial games include monopolizing time with clients, scheduling meetings so someone cannot attend, and shutting out coworkers on an important assignment.

5. *Good-mouthing an incompetent to make him or her transferable.* A long-entrenched devious political maneuver in large firms is for a manager to giving outstanding performance evaluations to an incompetent worker or trouble maker within the group. By good-mouthing the undesired worker, he or she becomes more marketable within the company. Although this technique can sometimes work, most experienced human resource professionals are aware of this tactic. An HR director noted, "We look for a certain pattern when a manager is puffing up a worker for transfer. Typically the problem worker received low evaluations for a long time, then starts getting outstanding evaluations. When this happens, we really grill the manager about the worker who has been offered for transfer."

6. *Placing a weak manager under you to help secure your position.* A negative political tactic practiced mostly in the executive suite is for a high-level manager to

recruit a lame person to a managerial position reporting to him or her. The lame person is valued because he or she is unlikely to become a candidate as a successor to the first executive—who would not have pulled this stunt if he or she were highly competent and secure. As a financial executive describes the situation, "Normally a boob has a boob for a boss."[30]

E-mail, including instant messaging, has become a major vehicle for conducting both ethical and unethical organizational politics. To help manage their impressions, many people distribute e-mails regarding their positive contribution to a project to many key people. E-networking is a convenient way to maintain minimum contact with many people, until the in-person meeting can be arranged. People flatter their target person via e-mail, and send copies to key people. On the downside, some people reprimand others by e-mail and let others know of the target's mistakes. Sometimes managers who are haggling with each other will send a copy to a common boss, hoping that the boss will intervene in the dispute.[31] A productivity problem with so many people being copied for political purposes is that in-boxes can become overloaded.

Gender Differences in Political Skill

A major message from this section of the chapter is that positive political skills are necessary to succeed in the workplace. Pamela L. Perrewé and Debra L. Nelson argue that because of barriers hampering their success, such as job discrimination, women need to develop even greater political astuteness than men. Political skills will not only increase the performance of women but will also decrease stress and increase well-being. For example, if a woman fails to network with men in power she will experience job stress and lower well-being as a result of being excluded from consideration for a promotion or important work assignment.

The authors in question contend that women are more reluctant than men to use politics because they are less political skill than men, may not see the relevance of politics, and often find politics distasteful. Instead, women are more likely to rely on merit and traditional values to advance in their careers. Women tend to be excluded from the inside power group in organizations, so they do not know the informal rules for getting ahead. Perrewé and Nelson propose that women in organizations obtain the right coaching and mentoring to obtain the political skills they need to level the playing field in competing with men.[32]

The argument that there are large gender differences in political skill can be challenged. Women leaders are often cited as being more effective at relationship building than are men, and relationship building is a primary political skill. Furthermore, the number of businesswomen playing golf has surged, and golf is important because of its networking potential. Women also tend to score as high as men on the traits within the implicit leadership theory described previously. An example of support for this argument comes from a study conducted by the research firm Caliper. The researchers administered personality test results and conducted interviews with 59 women leaders in 19 different business sectors from major companies in the United Kingdom and the United States. Among the findings were that (a) women leaders are more persuasive than their male counterparts, and (b) women leaders have an inclusive, team building style of problem solving and decision making. These results suggest strongly that women leaders have good political skill.[33] (Of course, these highly placed women may not be a representative sample of women in organizations.)

ORGANIZATIONAL INFLUENCE TACTICS

Identify and describe a variety of influence tactics.

In addition to using power and political tactics to win people over to their way of thinking, managerial workers use a variety of influence tactics. Extensive research has been conducted on social influence tactics aimed at upward, horizontal, and downward relations.[34] The person doing the influencing chooses which tactic seems most appropriate for a given situation. Seven of the most frequently used influence tactics are described here.

1. *Leading by example* means that the manager influences group members by serving as a positive model of desirable behavior. A manager who leads by example shows consistency between actions and words. For example, suppose a firm has a strict policy on punctuality. The manager explains the policy and is always punctual. The manager's words and actions provide a consistent model.

2. *Assertiveness* refers to being forthright in your demands without violating the rights of others. It involves a person expressing what he or she wants done and how he or she feels about it. A manager might say, for example, "Your report is late, and that makes me angry. I want you to get it done by noon tomorrow." Assertiveness, as this example shows, also refers to making orders clear.

3. *Rationality* means appealing to reason and logic. Strong managers and leaders frequently use this influence tactic. Pointing out the facts of a situation to group members to get them to do something exemplifies rationality. Intelligent people respond the best to rational appeals.

4. *Ingratiation* refers to getting someone else to like you, often through the use of flattery and doing favors. A typical ingratiating tactic would be to act in a friendly manner just before making a demand. Effective managerial workers treat people well consistently to get cooperation when it is needed. A theoretical analysis of the subject concluded that humor is an effective type of ingratiatory behavior. One reason humor leads to ingratiation is because it makes the person with the sense of humor more attractive to the target. Humor may also be seen as more acceptable than an ingratiation tactic such as doing a favor for another person.[35]

5. *Exchange* is a method of influencing others by offering to reciprocate if they meet your demands. When asking favors in a busy workplace, it is best to specify the amount of time the task will take, such as by saying "I will need 10 minutes of your time sometime between now and next Wednesday." Be aware of what skills or capabilities you have that you can barter with others. Perhaps you are good at retrieving crashed computer files or explaining the tax code. You can then offer to perform these tasks in exchange for favors granted to you.[36] An example of exchange among two of the mostly highly compensated people in business was alleged to have taken place at Citigroup several years ago. The story has since become a widely repeated tale about the abuse of power.

   Sanford Weill, at the time co-CEO of Citigroup, asked star analyst Jack Grubman to "take a fresh look" at his rating for AT&T. Grubman informed Weill of "his progress with AT&T" and asked his boss (Weill) for help in getting his twin daughters accepted at an elite nursery school in New York City. Grubman upgraded AT&T to "buy" from neutral, and Grubman's unit of Citigroup later received $45 million in fees from AT&T for underwriting new stock. Citigroup began donating $1 million a year for 5 years to the nursery school (the 92nd Street Y). A reporter uncovered a Grubman e-mail that read,

"I used Sandy to get my kids in 92nd St. Y preschool (which is harder than Harvard) and Sandy needed Armstrong's vote on our board to nuke Reed [the co-CEO at Citigroup] in showdown." Grubman says his e-mail was baseless and simply a lie to inflate his importance.[37]

6. *Inspirational appeal and emotional display* is an influence method centering on the affective (as opposed to the cognitive) domain. Given that leaders are supposed to inspire others, such an influence tactic is important. As Jeffrey Pfeffer observes, "Executives and others seeking to exercise influence in organizations often develop skill in displaying, or not displaying, their feelings in a strategic fashion."[38] An inspirational appeal usually involves an emotional display by the person seeking to influence. It also involves appealing to group members' emotions.

7. *Joking and kidding,* according to one survey, are widely used to influence others on the job.[39] Good-natured ribbing is especially effective when a straightforward statement might be interpreted as harsh criticism. A manager concerned about the number of errors in a group member's report might say, "Now I know what you are up to. You planted all those errors just to see if I really read your reports."

Which influence tactic should you choose? Managers are unlikely to use all the influence tactics in a given situation. Instead, they tend to choose an influence tactic that fits the demands of the circumstance. Researchers found support for this conclusion in a study with 120 managers, along with about 1200 subordinates, peers, and superiors. (The tactics studied were similar to many of those mentioned in this chapter.) An effective tactic was one that led to task commitment, used by managers who were perceived to be effective by the various raters.

The results suggested that the most effective tactics were rational persuasion, inspirational appeal, and consultation. In contrast, the least effective influence tactics were pressure, coalition formation, and appealing to legitimate authority. The researchers cautioned that the outcome of a specific influence attempt is also determined by factors such as the target's motivation and organizational culture.[40] Also, any influence tactic can trigger target resistance if it is inappropriate for the situation or is applied unskillfully. Tact, diplomacy, and insight are required for effective application of influence (and political) tactics.

THE CONTROL OF DYSFUNCTIONAL POLITICS, AND ETHICAL CONSIDERATIONS

Explain how managers can control dysfunctional politics.

Carried to excess, organizational politics and influence tactics can hurt an organization and its members. One consequence is that when political factors far outweigh merit, competent employees may become unhappy and quit. Another problem is that politicking takes time away from tasks that could contribute directly to achieving the firm's goals. Many managers spend more time developing political allies (including "kissing up") than coaching group members or doing analytical work.

The most comprehensive antidote to improper, excessive, and unethical organizational politics is to rely on objective measures of performance. This is true because people have less need to behave politically when their contributions can be measured directly. With a formal system of goal setting and review, the results a person attains should be much more important than the impression the person creates. However, even a goal-setting program is not immune from politics. Sometimes the goals are designed to impress key people in the organization. As such, they may not

277

be the most important goals for getting work accomplished. Another political problem with goal setting is that some people will set relatively easy goals so they can look good by attaining all their goals.

Meshing individual and organizational objectives would be the ideal method of controlling excessive, negative political behavior. If their objectives, needs, and interests can be met through their jobs, employees will tend to engage in behavior that fosters the growth, longevity, and productivity of the firm. L. A. Witt investigated how goal congruence between the individual and the organization affected political behavior. When employees perceived considerable politics in the workplace, their commitment to the organization and job performance both suffered. However, when employees and their superiors shared the same goals, commitment and performance were less negatively affected by politics. Witt concluded that one way to reduce the negative impact of organizational politics is for the manager to ensure that his or her subordinates hold the appropriate goal priorities. In this way, group members will have a greater sense of control over, and understanding of, the workplace and thus be less affected by the presence of organizational politics.[41]

Differentiate between the ethical and unethical use of power, politics, and influence.

Finally, open communications can also constrain the impact of political behavior. For instance, open communication can let everyone know the basis for allocating resources, thus reducing the amount of politicking. Organizational politics can also be curtailed by threatening to discuss questionable information in a public forum. If one employee engages in backstabbing of another, the manager might ask her or him to repeat the anecdote in a staff meeting. It has been said that sunlight is the best disinfectant to deviousness.

Our discussion of sources of power, political tactics, and influence tactics should not imply an endorsement of all of these methods to gain an advantage in the workplace. Each strategy and tactic must be evaluated on its merit by an ethical test, such as those described in Chapter 4. One guiding principle is to turn the strategy or tactic inward. Assume that you believe that a particular tactic (for example, ingratiation) would be ethical in working against you. It would then be fair and ethical for you to use this tactic in attempting to influence others.

Another guiding principle is that it is generally ethical to use power and influence to help attain organizational goals. In contrast, it is generally unethical to use the same tactics to achieve a personal agenda and goals not sanctioned by the organization. Yet even this guideline involves enough "grayness" to be open for interpretation. The accompanying skill-development exercise provides an opportunity to evaluate the ethics of behavior.

Another perspective on organizational politics is to recognize that both the means and the ends of political behavior must be considered. A study of the subject cautioned, "Instead of determining whether human rights or standards of justice are violated, we are often content to judge political behavior according to its outcomes."[42] The authors of the study suggest that when it comes to the ethics of organizational politics, respect for justice and human rights should prevail for its own sake.

IMPLICATIONS FOR MANAGERIAL PRACTICE

1. Recognize that a significant portion of the efforts of organizational members will be directed toward gaining power for themselves or their group. At times, some of this behavior will be directed more toward self-interest than organizational interest. It is therefore often necessary to ask, "Is this action being taken to help this person or is it being done to help the organization?" Your answer to this question should influence your willingness to submit to that person's demands.

SKILL-DEVELOPMENT EXERCISE

The Ethics of Influence Tactics

You decide if the following manager made ethical use of influence tactics.

Sara Nelson is a marketing manager for a finance company that lends money to companies as well as individuals. She comes up with the idea of forming a division in the company that would collect delinquent student loans, strictly on commission. Her company would retain about one-third of the money collected. The clients would be banks having difficulty collecting loans after students graduate. Nelson brings her idea to the CEO, and he grants her the opportunity to make a presentation about the new idea to top management within 1 month. The CEO states that he sees some merit in the idea, but that the opinion of the rest of the committee will be given considerable weight.

With 29 days to go before the meeting, Sara invites all five members of the executive committee to join her for lunch or breakfast individually.

All five finally agree on a date for the lunch or breakfast meeting. During the meals, Sara makes a strong pitch for her idea, and explains that she will need the person's support to sell the idea to the rest of the committee. She also promises, "If you can help me get this collection division launched, you will have one big IOU to cash." Sara stays in touch with the CEO about the upcoming meeting, but does not mention her "pre-selling" lunches.

During the new-initiative review meeting, the five members of the committee support Sara's idea, and the CEO says that he is encouraged, and will now warmly consider the idea of a student loan collection division.

Questions

1. Was Sara Nelson behaving ethically?
2. Which influence tactic did she use in attempting to achieve her goals?

---

2. If you want to establish a power base for yourself, a good starting point is to develop expert power. Most powerful people began their climb to power by demonstrating their expertise in a particular area, such as being outstanding in sales or a niche within information technology. (This tactic is referred to as becoming a subject–matter expert.)

3. In determining if a particular behavior is motivated by political or merit considerations, evaluate the intent of the actor. The same action might be based on self-interest or concern for others. For instance, a team member might praise you because he believed that you accomplished something of merit. On the other hand, that same individual might praise you to attain a favorable work assignment or salary increase.

SUMMARY OF KEY POINTS

 Identify sources of power for individuals and subunits within organizations.

Power, politics, and influence are needed by managers to accomplish their work. In the model presented here, managers and professionals use organizational politics to achieve power and influence, thus attaining desired outcomes.

Socialized power is used to forward organizational interests, whereas personalized power is used to forward personal interests. Power granted by the organization consists of legitimate power, coercive power, and reward power. Power stemming from the individual consists of expert power and referent power (the basis for charisma). According to the resource dependence perspective, subunits or individuals who can provide key resources to the organization accrue power. At times, gossip can be a power-giving source. Power can also be derived from meeting the group members' expectations of how a leader should behave (implicit leadership theory).

Describe the essence of empowerment.

Managers must act in specific ways to empower employees, including removing conditions that keep employees powerless and giving information that enhances employee feelings of self-efficacy. Five critical conditions for empowerment are for an organization to share information with employees, provide them with structure, use teams to replace the traditional hierarchy, grant employees the freedom to determine how to achieve objectives, and trust employees.

 Pinpoint factors contributing to, and examples of, organizational politics.

Contributors to organizational politics include the political nature of organizations, the pyramid structure of organizations, encouragement of unwarranted accolades from subordinates, less opportunity for vertical advancement, the need for power, and Machiavellianism.

Among the ethical tactics of organizational politics are developing power contacts; managing your impression; controlling vital information; keeping informed; being courteous, pleasant, and positive; asking satisfied customers to contact your manager; avoiding political blunders; and using sincere flattery. Among the unethical tactics are backstabbing, embracing-or-demolishing, stealing credit, playing territorial games, good-mouthing incompetents, and choosing a weak manager as an underling.

According to one analysis, women need to develop greater political skill because of barriers hampering their success. However, it can be argued that many women have exceptional political skills, such as relationship building.

 Identify and describe a variety of influence tactics.

Influence tactics frequently used by managerial workers include leadership by example, assertiveness, rationality, ingratiation, exchange, inspirational appeal and emotional display, and the use of joking and kidding.

 Explain how managers can control dysfunctional politics.

Approaches to controlling dysfunctional politics include relying on objective performance measures, meshing individual and organizational objectives, minimizing political behavior by top management, and implementing open communications, including threatening to discuss politicking publicly.

 Differentiate between the ethical and unethical use of power, politics, and influence.

Political behaviors chosen by an individual or organizational unit must rest on ethical considerations. A guiding principle is to use only those tactics you would consider fair and ethical if used against you. Also recognize that both the means and the ends of political behavior must be considered.

KEY TERMS AND PHRASES

Power, 263
The potential or ability to influence decisions and control resources.

Organizational Politics, 263
Informal approaches to gaining power through means other than merit or luck.

Socialized Power, 263
The use of power to achieve constructive ends.

Personalized Power, 263
The use of power primarily for the sake of personal aggrandizement and gain.

Legitimate Power, 264
Power based on one's formal position within the hierarchy of the organization.

Coercive Power, 264
Controlling others through fear or threat of punishment.

Reward Power, 264
Controlling others through rewards or the promise of rewards.

Expert Power, 264
The ability to influence others because of one's specialized knowledge, skills, or abilities.

Referent Power, 265
The ability to influence others that stems from one's desirable traits and characteristics; it is the basis for charisma.

Resource Dependence Perspective, 265
The need of the organization for a continuing flow of human resources, money, customers, technological inputs, and material to continue to function.

Implicit Leadership Theory, 265
An explanation of leadership contending that group members develop prototypes specifying the traits and abilities that characterize an ideal business leader.

Empowerment, 267
The process of sharing power with group members, thereby enhancing their feelings of self-efficacy.

Machiavellianism, 270
A tendency to manipulate others for personal gain.

Territorial Games, 274
Also known as turf wars, territorial games refer to behaviors involving the hoarding of information and other resources.

DISCUSSION QUESTIONS AND ACTIVITIES

1. What might be the negative consequences to a manager if he or she ignored power, politics, and influence tactics?
2. How might having a lot of power help a person achieve ethical ends within an organization?
3. What type of power might a worker acquire to help prevent his or her job being outsourced?
4. Why does empowering workers often motivate them to work harder?
5. Job hunters are advised to "size up the political climate" before accepting a job at a company. How might the candidate go about sizing up the political climate?
6. What is your take on humor as an ingratiating tactic? To what extent do you like people better who are humorous in their conversations with you?
7. What can you do today to start increasing your power? Compare your observations with those of your classmates.

CASE PROBLEM: Infighting at DaimlerChrysler

A few months before Dieter Zetsche became CEO of DaimlerChrysler AG in 2006, he had already started work on a vital task: softening the caustic corporate culture that marked the tenure of outgoing CEO Jürgen Schrempp.

In July 2005, Schrempp, 61 years old, unexpectedly announced he would retire after 11 tumultuous years running the automaker. As his successor he named Zetsche, an occasional boardroom rival who engineered the dramatic turnaround of the company's U.S. arm, Chrysler Group. In September 2005, Zetsche, 52 years old, moved from Chrysler to the company's Stuttgart headquarters and took control of the Mercedes division. After only a few days as Mercedes chief he signaled a big change, telling the unit's entire management staff in a memo that he "won't tolerate any infighting, intrigue or political games."

The missive, Zetsche said in an interview during a gathering of Chrysler dealers in Las Vegas, was "a great chance to set the tone right from the beginning" and to make clear that under his leadership "what counts is performance," not internal alliances.

Such wasn't always the case under Schrempp. The prime mover behind the 1998 merger that created the German-American car maker, Schrempp epitomized the jet-setting, deal-making celebrity CEO of the 1990s. But when his strategy floundered and DaimlerChrysler's market value plunged, he came under sharp criticism from investors. At an annual company meeting in April 2005, he faced hours of withering attacks on his strategy and leadership. That spectacle, people familiar with the matter said, contributed to his decision to retire with more than 2 years remaining on his contract.

In January 2006, all eyes were on the consensus-building Zetsche as he attempted to reverse several problems. At Mercedes, quality and profitability were both sliding. Chrysler was profitable but was earning far less than Japanese car makers and faced bitter competition from General Motors Corp. and Ford Motor Co. And the company's German and American halves did not did not work together as closely as Zetsche would have liked.

DaimlerChrysler's problems were nothing like the troubles at General Motors and Ford Motor, in part because of Zetsche's work at Chrysler during a 5-year period when he closed plants, slashed thousands of jobs, and revitalized product development. Both GM and Ford started tackling those issues in 2005.

Zetsche's 5 years at Chrysler showed him to be a hands-on, straight-talking manager willing to suffer

(continued)

CASE PROBLEM (Continued)

a short-term setback for long-term benefit. In contrast to Schrempp, who distanced himself from operational matters and rarely mixed with ordinary employees, Zetsche has spent time before assuming the CEO position with Mercedes designers, offering suggestions to improve the styling of several models in development. He also spoke at a gathering of Chrysler dealers—an audience Schrempp never addressed—and vowed to return to speak to the group as CEO.

Zetsche said he wasn't planning to replace the outgoing CEO's confidantes who continue to hold powerful posts at headquarters. These included Schrempp's wife, Lydia, who has a highly paid job in the office of the CEO. Zetsche said she will stay with the company, although she won't be part of the management team.

In September 2005, after the company's supervisory board agreed to cut 8500 jobs in Germany, Zetsche decided to be the one to deliver the bad news to workers at the Mercedes plant that would take the brunt of the cuts. Officials at corporate headquarters in Stuttgart advised Zetsche not to do it. The executive went anyway, and despite the dour news he was "favorably received,"

said Rolf Weber, a union leader who represents the German workers and attended the meeting. Any booing was too scattered to be heard and on a few occasions, according to Weber and others who were present, Zetsche even received polite applause.

Case Questions

1. What should Zetsche do to get rid of infighting, intrigue, and political games?

2. How will Zetsche's leadership and management style help him combat excessive organizational politics?

3. From the standpoint of power and politics, how smart was Zetsche to transfer Lynda Schrempp from his management team to another position in the company?

4. How is the current status of the demand for automobiles likely to influence the amount of negative organizational politics at DaimlerChrysler?

Source: Neal E. Boudette and Stephen Power, "New DaimlerChrysler CEO Targets 'Infighting, Intrigues,'" *The Wall Street Journal*, November 28, 2005, pp. B1, B4.

ENDNOTES

1. Book review in *Personnel Psychology,* Summer 2002, p. 502.
2. Jerry Useem, "Power," *Fortune*, August 11, 2003, p. 58.
3. Daniel J. Brass and Marlene E. Burkhardt, "Potential Power and Power Use: An Integration of Structure and Behavior," *Academy of Management Journal,* June 1993, pp. 441–442.
4. Robert P. Vecchio, *Organizational Behavior: Core Concepts,* 4th ed. (Mason, OH: South-Western/Thomson Learning, 2000), p. 126.
5. Leonard H. Chusmir, "Personalized vs. Socialized Power Needs among Working Men and Women," *Human Relations,* February 1986, p. 149.
6. John R. P. French and Bertram Raven, "The Basis of Social Power," in Dorwin Cartwright and Alvin Zander, eds., *Group Dynamics: Research and Theory* (Evanston, IL: Row, Peterson and Company, 1962), pp. 607–623.
7. David Koenig, "American Airlines Dumps Executive Bonuses after Criticism from Unions," Associated Press, April 19, 2003. Reprinted with permission of the Associated Press.
8. David Welch, "Toughest Job Yet for this Mr. Fixit," *Business Week,* November 15, 2004, pp. 72–73.
9. Jeffrey D. Kudisch, Mark L. Poteet, Gregory H. Dobbins, Michael C. Rush, and Joyce E. A. Russell, "Expert Power, Referent Power, and Charisma: Toward the Resolution of a Theoretical Debate," *Journal of Business and Psychology,* Winter 1995, p. 189.
10. Jeffrey Pfeffer, *Managing with Power* (Boston: Harvard Business Review Publications, 1990), pp. 100–101.
11. Nancy B. Kurland and Lisa Hope Pelled, "Passing the Word: Toward a Model of Gossip and Power in the Workplace," *Academy of Management Review,* April 2000, p. 429.
12. Anita Bruzzese, "Office Gossip Really Harassment," Gannett News Service, June 2, 2003.
13. Olga Epitropaki and Robin Martin, "Implicit Leadership Theories in Applied Settings: Factor Structure, Generalizability, and Stability Over Time," *Journal of Applied Psychology*, April 2004, pp. 293–310; Epitropaki and Martin, "From Ideal to Real: A Longitudinal Study of the Role of Implicit Leadership Theories on Leader-Member Exchanges and Employee Outcomes," *Journal of Applied Psychology*, July 2005, pp. 659–676.
14. Jay A. Conger and Rabindra N. Kanungo, "The Empowerment Process: Integrating Theory and Practice," *Academy of Management Review,* July 1988, pp. 473–474.
15. Craig L. Pearce, "The Future of Leadership: Combining Vertical and Shared Leadership to Transform Knowledge Work," *Academy of Management Executive*, February 2004, pp. 47–57.
16. Braley L. Kirkman, Benson Rosen, Paul E. Tesluk, and Cristina B. Gibson, "The Impact of Team Empowerment on Virtual Team performance: The Moderating Role of Face-to-Face Interaction, *Academy of Management Journal*, April 2004, pp. 175–192.
17. W. Alan Randolph, "Navigating the Journey to Empowerment," *Organizational Dynamics,* Spring 1995, pp. 19–31.
18. Quoted in Phillip M. Perry, "Seven Errors to Avoid When Empowering Your Staff," *Success Workshop,* A supplement *to Manager's Edge,* 1999, p. 4.
19. Patricia Sellers, "eBay's Secret," *Fortune*, October 18, 2004, p. 161.
20. Marshall Goldsmith, "All of Us Are Stuck on Suck-Ups," *Fast Company*, December 2003, p. 117.
21. Chad Graham and Dawn Sagario, " 'Good Fawning' Over Boss Can Help in Tough Times," *The Des Moines Register* syndicated story, April 20, 2003.

22. Stanley Bing, *What Would Machiavelli Do?* (New York: Harper-Collins, 2000).
23. "Etiquette for the Young—with Bite," The Associated Press, June 8, 2002.
24. "'Career Insurance' Protects DP Professionals from Setbacks, Encourages Growth," *Data Management,* June 1986, p. 33. The same principle is equally valid today.
25. Quoted in Amy Joyce, "Schmoozing on the Job Pays Dividends," *The Washington Post*, November 13, 2005.
26. "Face Cowardly Backstabbers in the Workplace," Knight Ridder story, February 13, 2000.
27. Jared Sandberg, "Some Bosses Never Meet a Success That Isn't Theirs," *The Wall Street Journal,* April 23, 2003, p. B1.
28. "Stopping Idea Thieves: Strike Back When Rivals Steal Credit," *Executive LeadershipExtra!* April 2003, p. 3.
29. Annette Simmons, *Territorial Games: Understanding & Ending Turf Wars at Work* (New York: AMACOM, 1998).
30. Quoted in Jared Sandberg, "When Affixing Blame for Inept Managers, Go Over Their Heads," *The Wall Street Journal*, April 20, 2005, p. B1.
31. Jeffrey Zaslow, "The Politics of the 'CC' Line," *The Wall Street Journal,* May 28, 2003, p. D2.
32. Pamela L. Perrewé and Debra L. Nelson, "Gender and Career Success: The Facilitative Role of Political Skill," *Organizational Dynamics, 4* (2004), p. 366.
33. "Women Leaders Study: The Qualities that Distinguish Women Leaders," http://www.calipercorp.com/womenstudy/index.shtml.
34. Several of the tactics are from Gary Yukl and Cecilia M. Falbe, "Influence Tactics and Objectives in Upward, Downward, and Lateral Influence Attempts," *Journal of Applied Psychology,* April 1990, pp. 132–140. Part of the definitions of assertiveness and ingratiation stem from Perrewé and Nelson, "Gender and Career Success," pp. 372–373.
35. Cecily D. Cooper, "Just Joking Around? Employee Humor Expression as Ingratiatory Behavior," *Academy of Management Review*, October 2005, pp. 765–776.
36. "Aloofness Doesn't Pay," *Executive Strategies,* April 2000, p. 1.
37. Daniel Kadlec, "Did Sandy Play Dirty?" *Time,* November 25, 2002, pp. 21–22.
38. Pfeffer, *Managing with Power,* p. 224.
39. Andrew J. DuBrin, "Sex Differences in the Use and Effectiveness of Tactics of Impression Management," *Psychological Reports, 74* (1994), pp. 531–544.
40. Gary Yukl and J. Bruce Tracey, "Consequences of Influence Tactics Used with Subordinates, Peers, and the Boss," *Journal of Applied Psychology,* August 1992, pp. 525–535.
41. L. A. Witt, "Enhancing Organizational Goal Congruence: A Solution to Organizational Politics," *Journal of Applied Psychology,* August 1998, pp. 666–674.
42. Gerald F. Cavanagh, Dennis J. Moberg, and Manuel Velasquez, "The Ethics of Organizational Politics," *Academy of Management Review,* July 1981, p. 372.

13

OBJECTIVES

After reading and studying this chapter and doing the exercises, you should be able to:

1. Understand the nature of conflict in organizations and its leading causes.

2. Have the necessary information to resolve many workplace conflicts, including dealing with difficult people.

3. Be aware of basic negotiating and bargaining techniques to resolve conflict.

4. Understand the nature, causes, and consequences of work stress.

5. Explain what organizations can do to manage and reduce stress.

6. Do a more effective job of managing your own stress.

Conflict and Stress

Penelope Trunk wrote the following comments on http://www.Bankrate.com: "My favorite example of a bad boss is one I had at a software company who refused to learn how to use a computer. I conducted most communication with him via phone, and when other people didn't, I often played the role of secretary, even though I was a vice president. He once said to me, 'You're such a fast typist!' And I thought, 'You are such an incompetent, lazy idiot.'

"But in truth, he was not. He was a top negotiator of government contracts. I stepped back and recognized he was overwhelmed with the prospect of changing the way he had been working for 20 years, and I was in a position to help him. I found that the more dependent he was on me for e-mail, the more I was able to insert myself into high-level deals that he would not otherwise have let me in on. I helped him avoid having to change, and he taught me how to be a deal maker."

Source: Penelope Trunk, "Learn How to Manage Your Boss Productively," http://www.Bankrate.com, August 2, 2004.

Now Ask Yourself: **In what way does the story about a business writer whose manager did not use e-mail indicate that conflict and stress on the job can sometimes be minimized by taking a different perspective?** (The same story also illustrates good political skills by finding a way to maintain a constructive relationship with the boss.) At the same time, stress and conflict can sometimes be converted into positive forces to enhance productivity, such as learning a valuable new skill. The purpose of this chapter is to present information that will help the reader better understand two closely related processes: conflict and stress.

CONFLICT IN ORGANIZATIONS

Conflict refers to the opposition of persons or forces giving rise to some tension, or to a disagreement between two or more parties who are interdependent.[1] A conflict occurs when two or more parties perceive mutually exclusive goals, values, or events. Each side believes that what it wants is incompatible with what the other wants. Conflict can also take place at the individual level when a person has to decide between two incompatible choices. For example, a person might have to choose between accepting a job transfer and remaining in town with family and friends. Refusing to transfer could mean a job loss, whereas accepting the transfer would mean less contact with family and friends. Conflict has enough emotional content to lead to stress for the individuals involved. Conflict and stress can be studied as part of group behavior because so much conflict and stress is generated by interactions among two or more people.

Our study of conflict concentrates on sources of conflict, task versus relationship conflict, the consequences of conflict, and various methods, including negotiation, for resolving conflict.

Understand the nature of conflict in organizations and its leading causes.

Sources and Antecedents of Conflict

Conflict is pervasive in organizations. Managers allegedly spend between 20 and 30% of their work activities directly or indirectly resolving conflict. The sources, antecedents, or outright causes of conflict are numerous, and the list is dynamic. At any given time, a new and potent source of conflict might emerge, such as management's current emphasis on hiring temporary workers rather than offering full-time employment, and outsourcing jobs. Here we describe six illustrative sources of workplace conflict.

Perceived Adverse Changes

A high-impact source of conflict is a change in work methods, conditions of work, or employment opportunities that the people involved perceive negatively. **Downsizing,** the laying off of workers to reduce costs and increase efficiency, is one such change. The people eliminated from the payroll do not remain in conflict with the organization. Survivors, however, suffer from guilt, anger, and bereavement as they feel sorry for the departed coworkers.[2] Continuous downsizing, even when business conditions improve, can precipitate labor versus management conflict. Management wants to eliminate as many jobs as possible, whereas the labor union values job security for its members. Despite these conditions, all parties do not perceive downsizing as an adverse change. Company executives may believe that downsizing is rightsizing, leading to an efficient, competitive firm that will attract investors.

Another example of a perceived adverse change is company management freezing wages or pension payments. For example, several years ago the CEO of Volkswagen wanted to freeze the wages of 103,000 workers and make its factories more efficient by loosening its work rules. Labor and management finally reached a compromise without a strike.

Line versus Staff Differentiation

A major form of conflict takes place between line and staff units. Line units deal with the primary purposes of the firm, such as the sales group in a business firm. Staff units deal with the secondary purposes of the firm, such as the environmental protection unit in a business firm. They also deal with the activities necessary to make the line activities more efficient and effective. Staff units might do the hiring and the labor-contract interpretations, and verify that the line group complies with environmental laws. Yet they would not manufacture or sell the product or service. Although some people regard the line versus staff dichotomy as outdated, most managers and professionals in organizations still find this distinction useful.

Staff managers and professionals advise managers but cannot make certain decisions about themselves. A human resources professional, for example, might advise top management about the adverse consequences of downsizing following a merger. Nevertheless, this professional does not have the authority to halt the downsizing. Line and staff workers may conflict when the line manager perceives that the staff professional is attempting to heavily influence his or her decisions. Another source of conflict is that staff professionals are often more loyal to their own discipline than to the organization. An organizational behavior specialist working for a large firm might feel that attending professional meetings is her right. In contrast, her manager feels she should attend such meetings only while on vacation.

Sexual Harassment

Some employees experience conflict because of sexual harassment by a manager, coworker, customer, or vendor. **Sexual harassment** is unwanted sexually oriented behavior in the workplace that results in discomfort and/or interference with the job. Sexual harassment is divided into two types. In *quid pro quo* harassment, the employee's submission to or rejection of unwelcome sexual advances is used as the basis for a tangible employment action about the employee. (A tangible employment action is defined by the Supreme Court as "hiring, firing, failing to promote, reassignment with significantly different responsibilities, or a decision causing a significant change in benefits," *Faragher v. City of Boca Raton.*) The demands of a harasser can be explicit or implied.

Hostile working environment harassment occurs when someone in the workplace creates an intimidating, hostile, or offensive working environment. A tangible employment advantage or adverse economic consequence does not have to exist. The hostile-environment type of harassment is subject to considerable variation in perception and interpretation. A company executive might decide to hang a French impressionist painting of a partially nude woman in the lobby. Some people would find this offensive and intimidating, and complain that they were harassed. Others might compliment the executive for being a patron of the arts.

A group of researchers provided useful insights into the role of perception in deciding which behaviors of supervisors and coworkers constituted either type of harassment.[3] Typical harassment behaviors include physical contact, inappropriate remarks, a sexual proposition, a threat or promise associated with a job, comments on the other person's physical appearance, or a glaring stare at the person being harassed. The setting for the survey was a manufacturing plant that had a strict policy

Exhibit **13-1**

*Accuracy in Identifying
Sexually Harassing
Behavior*

Supervisory Behaviors	Correspondence with U.S. Federal Guidelines	
If your supervisor did this, would you consider this sexual harassment?	Inaccurate	Accurate
1. Asks you to have sex with the promise that it will help you on the job.	18	96
2. Asks you to have sex with the threat that refusing to have sex will hurt you on the job.	17	97
3. Asks you to go out on a date with the promise that it will help you on the job.	18	96
4. Asks you to go out on a date with the promise that it will hurt you if you do not go.	16	98
5. Touches you on private parts of the body; for example, breasts, buttocks, etc.	22	92
6. Touches you on parts of the body not considered private; for example, shoulder, hand, arm, etc.	77	37
7. Looks at you in a flattering way.	75	39
8. Makes gestures (signs) of a flattering nature.	51	63
9. Makes comments about your dress or appearance that are meant to be complimentary.	96	18
10. Makes comments about your appearance meant to be insulting.	91	23
11. Makes sexually offensive comments.	49	65
12. Tells sexually oriented jokes.	75	39

Source: Marjorie L. Icenogle, Bruce W. Eagle, Sohel Ahman, and Lisa A. Hanks, "Assessing Perceptions of Sexual Harassment Behaviors in a Manufacturing Environment," *Journal of Business and Psychology,* Summer 2002, p. 607. Used with permission.

against sexual harassment. Furthermore, the supervisory and professional personnel had had training in dealing with sexual harassment. Employee perceptions were compared with U.S. federal guidelines of sexual harassment—the basis for a "correct" response.

Exhibit 13-1 presents the responses of the 114 participants in the survey with regard to supervisory behavior. The accuracy versus inaccuracy tabulations for perceptions of coworker behavior were essentially the same as the perceptions of supervisory behavior. The responses indicated that the majority of workers can accurately identify behaviors frequently associated with quid pro quo harassment. However, the same workers had difficulty identifying behaviors used to establish evidence of a hostile work environment. Male workers had a slight edge in the accuracy of their perceptions about what constitutes harassment, and women in white-collar jobs were more accurate than women in blue-collar jobs.

The meanings and interpretations of what constitutes sexual harassment continue to evolve with judicial rulings. Three U.S. Supreme Court decisions in 1998 are now given considerable weight by lower courts and employers:

- In *Oncale v. Sundowner Offshore Services Inc.,* the Court unanimously declared that sexual harassment is actionable, even when the people involved are of the same sex. What matters is the conduct at issue, not the sex of the people involved, or the presence or absence of sexual desire. The case involved a roustabout (a waterfront laborer) who was forcibly subjected on numerous occasions to humiliating sex-related actions. His harassers were three crew members, including two supervisors.

- In *Burlington Industries, Inc. v. Ellerth,* the Court ruled that an employer can be liable for sexual harassment and can be sued regardless of whether a supervisor's threats against an employee are carried out. However, employers can assert an affirmative defense. This means that the employer may be relieved of liability if it genuinely tried to prohibit and remedy sexual harassment and the employee did not take advantage of corrective opportunities offered by the employer. The case involved a marketing assistant who claimed that her boss made repeated passes at her and advised her to wear short skirts. The assistant never informed management about her supervisor's misconduct.

- In *Faragher v. City of Boca Raton, Florida,* the Court ruled that an employer is liable for a pervasive, hostile atmosphere of harassment and is potentially liable for its supervisors' misconduct whether the company was aware of the harassment or not. The case involved an ocean lifeguard who claimed she endured repeated sexual harassment from two male supervisors during 5 years of employment.[4]

At least 50% of women perceive that they have been harassed at some point in their career. Sexual harassment is widely considered an ethical and legal problem, and harassment also has negative effects on the well-being of its victims. The harassed person may experience job stress, lowered morale, severe conflict, and lowered productivity. A study with both business and university workers documented some of the problems associated with sexual harassment. It was found that even at low levels of frequency, harassment exerts a significant impact on women's psychological well-being, job attitudes, and work behaviors. For both business and university workers, women who had experienced high levels of harassment reported the worst job-related and psychological effects. The study also found that women who had experienced only a moderate level of harassment also suffered from negative outcomes.[5]

Unwanted turnover is a negative consequence of harassment for both the organization and the individual. A sample of 11,521 military servicewomen studied over 4 years found that experiences of harassment lead to increased turnover. At higher pay grades, however, the turnover risk due to harassment was lower. (Some servicewomen may have reasoned that being lowly paid makes sexual harassment even more insufferable.) The same study also found that experiencing sexual harassment lowered satisfaction with coworkers, supervisors, and work.[6] A study of 35 teams in the food-service industry found that when sexual harassment is frequent within a team, cohesiveness and financial performance tended to be lower.[7]

Company policy that emphasizes the illegality of sexual harassment is helpful in minimizing harassment on the job. The policy should be supported by an organizational culture that promotes just treatment of employees by managers and coworkers. A highly effective preventive measure is for individual workers to assert their rights at the first instance or hint of harassment. An example would be a woman explaining to a supervisor who hugged her suggestively that she will not tolerate such behavior, and that she will file a report to upper management should the incident be repeated. A woman who curtails harassment on her own before it is necessary to file a formal complaint may experience the career problems typical of whistle-blowers reported in Chapter 4. Women who quit a job after filing a complaint about sexual harassment may sometimes find it difficult to find a new job—however unjust such a practice may be.[8]

Factional Groups

Interpersonal conflict often takes place because there are different factions (subgroups) within groups with different points of view and different loyalties. The factions often take place because of a merger, and groups are formed to balance the representatives from the two merged companies, such as two merged banks. Factional groups may also arise when a joint venture takes place, such as two companies working together to produce top-of-the line home-entertainment centers. Each of the two parent companies assigns a few of its own managers to be on the new joint venture's management team. Often the factional group consists of two subgroups, each with several representatives, such as a cost-cutting task force consisting of three representatives each from marketing, operations, and finance. The potential for conflict within factional groups increases when the subgroups differ substantially in demographic characteristics such as age, gender, and educational level.

Researchers Jiatao Li and Donald C. Hambrick studied factional groups at 71 Sino-foreign ventures in China, with 535 managers completing surveys in either English or Chinese. Among the findings were that when there were large demographic differences between the members of the joint venture teams, stereotyping, distrust, and discord mounted. These negative emotions in turn led to emotional conflict, task conflict, and behavior disintegration such as less information sharing and collaboration. As a result of all these problems, performance suffered.[9] In short, factional groups can have so much conflict that they fail to live up to the characteristics of an effective work group described in Chapter 9.

Competing Work and Family Demands

Balancing the demands of career and family has become a major challenge facing today's workforce. The challenge is particularly intense for employees who are part of a two-wage-earning family. **Work–family conflict** occurs when the individual has to perform multiple roles: worker; spouse; and, often, parent.[10] This type of conflict is frequent because the multiple roles are often incompatible. Imagine having planned to attend your child's championship soccer game and then being ordered at the last minute to attend a late-afternoon meeting. A survey revealed the following evidence of work–family conflict and the potential of such conflict:

- About 45% of college students say their top consideration in selecting a first employer is the opportunity to achieve a balance between work and life outside of work.
- Approximately 80% of workers consider their effort to balance work and personal life as their first priority.
- More than one-third of employed Americans are working 10 or more hours a day, and 39% work on weekends.
- One-third of employees say they are forced to choose between advancing in their jobs or devoting attention to their family or personal lives.[11]

Work–family conflict is significant for the individual. A survey conducted with 513 employees in a Fortune 500 company supports the plausible finding that working long hours interferes with family life. The long hours, in turn, lead to depression for some individuals, and stress-related health problems, such as ulcers.[12] The study supports the well-accepted proposition that conflict leads to stress. Work–family conflict is also a problem for employers because stressed-out workers are often less productive because of a reduced ability to concentrate on work. Furthermore, a study revealed that dual-earner couples who experienced work–family conflict were more likely to engage in family interruptions at work, tardiness, and absenteeism.[13]

Organizational programs to help reduce work–family conflict include flexible working hours, work-at-home programs, dependent-care centers, and parental leave programs. Related to these specific observations, a study conducted with over 212 faculty members at 23 universities suggests that work–family conflict is likely to be reduced when working for a just (fair) employer. Organizations can promote justice through means such as ensuring that employee viewpoints are heard on controversial matters, that people are fairly compensated, and that their individual problems are given reasonable consideration. At the work–family level, supervisors would listen to concerns about balancing work and family and would be supportive of workers taking care of emergency situations during working hours. The study in question found that the presence of organizational justice, as perceived by the faculty members, was associated with lower levels of work–family conflict and stress.[14]

A note of caution for career-minded people is that a conflict-free balance between work and home life may be difficult to attain because significant career accomplishments require so much commitment. In the words of business writer Keith H. Hammonds, "Simply cutting back on work inevitably fails, because in real life, success in work is predicated on achievement. In a competitive business environment—which is to say, every business environment—leadership requires commitment, passion, and to be blunt, a lot of time."[15]

Incivility, Personality Clashes, and Workplace Bullies

Many instances of workplace conflict stem from individuals' dispositions as well as personality clashes. (A *disposition* is a characteristic attitude, similar to a personality trait.) People who are rude and uncivil or bullying readily enter into conflict. Incivility (or employees' lack of regard for one another) has gained attention as a cause of workplace conflict. A poll of nearly 800 workers in the United States found that 10% witnessed incivility each day on the job, and 20% said they were the direct targets of incivility at least once a week. Examples of incivility include the following:

- A salesperson makes a sarcastic comments about another employee in front of a customer.
- A coworker receives and initiates cell phone messages while listening to a presentation at a meeting.
- One worker continues responding to e-mail messages while another is talking to him in person.

Incivility has negative consequences for the individual and the organization. Employees who feel they have been treated uncivilly may decrease work effort, lose time from work, become less productive, or leave the organization. Job satisfaction may also suffer. Another problem is that workplace incivility can spiral downward because the offended party might reciprocate with a counter-incivility. More rudeness results, and the interpersonal conflict becomes intense. An organizational climate characterized by rudeness can result in aggressive behavior, high turnover, and lost customers.[16]

Many other workplace conflicts arise because of people simply disliking each other. A **personality clash** is an antagonistic relationship between two people based on differences in personal attributes, preferences, interests, values, and styles. People involved in personality clashes often have difficulty in specifying why they dislike each other. Generational differences can result in personality clashes based on differences in values. As described in Chapter 4, members of different generations often have different values, and these differences can lead to workplace conflict.

Bullying behavior contributes to substantial interpersonal conflict in the workplace. An example of such a bully is one who tries to control his or her victim through fear and intimidation. According to bullying specialist Gary Namie, "The vast majorities of bullies are bosses because they can make good on their threats."[17] As with sexual harassment, bullying behavior leads to conflict because a worker's demands for tranquility on the job are incompatible with the demands of the harasser or bully. The verbal abuse aspect of bullying leads to a hostile environment and can drive many people to leave an employer.[18] Bullying is also associated with job discrimination because the bully will often insult another worker based on his or her race or ethnicity.

Task versus Relationship Conflict

In addition to their antecedents, another way to understand conflict is whether it is aimed at work or personal issues. Some conflicts within the group deal mostly with disagreements over how work should be done. They are referred to as task or *cognitive* conflicts because they deal mostly with the work itself rather than with emotions and relationships. Two group members, for example, might argue over whether it is better to use their limited advertising budget to buy space on the outside of a bus versus on the radio air time. **Task conflict** focuses on substantive, issue-related differences, related to the work itself. These issues are tangible and concrete and can be dealt with more intellectually than emotionally.

Other conflicts within the group are more people oriented. They occur because people have personality clashes, are rude to each other, or simply view many problems and situations from a different frame of reference. **Relationship conflict** focuses on personalized, individually oriented issues. The conflict relates to subjective issues that are dealt with more emotionally than intellectually.[19] One symptom that relationship conflict exists within the group is when, during a meeting, two people say to each other frequently, "Please let me finish. I'm still speaking."

Task conflict in moderate doses can be functional because it requires teams to engage in activities that foster team effectiveness. Team members engaged in moderate task conflict would critically examine alternative solutions and incorporate different points of view into their goals or mission statement. Because frank communication and different points of view are encouraged, task conflict can encourage innovative thinking. In contrast, relationship (or affective) conflict undermines group effectiveness by blocking constructive activities and processes. By means such as directing anger toward individuals and blaming each other for mistakes, affective conflict leads to cynicism and distrust.

An analysis of many studies cautions that task conflict and relationship conflict can be equally disruptive. A little conflict may be beneficial, but this advantage quickly breaks down as conflict intensifies.[20] The underlying explanation is that most people take differences of opinion personally whether the issue is strictly the task or their personal characteristics.

Consequences of Conflict

Conflict results in both positive and negative consequences. The right amount of conflict may enhance job performance, but too much or too little conflict lowers performance. If the manager observes that job performance is suffering because of

Log on to **www.thomsonedu. com/infotrac.** Search for articles on conflict and stress. Can conflict become advantageous in some situations?

291

too much conflict, he or she should reduce it. If performance is low because employees are too placid, the manager might profitably increase conflict. For example, the manager might establish a prize for top performance in the group.

Positive Consequences of Conflict

Many managers and scholars believe that job conflict can have positive consequences. As described previously, the new evidence indicates that the right amount of conflict is usually quite low—somewhat like fat in your diet. When the right amount of conflict is present in the workplace, one or more of the following outcomes can be anticipated.

1. *Increased creativity.* Talents and abilities surface in response to conflict. People become inventive when they are placed in intense competition with others.
2. *Increased effort.* Constructive amounts of conflict spur people to new heights of performance. People become so motivated to win the conflict that they may surprise themselves and their superiors with their work output.
3. *Increased diagnostic information.* Conflict can provide valuable information about problem areas in the department or organization. When leaders learn of conflict, they may conduct investigations that will lead to the prevention of similar problems.
4. *Increased group cohesion.* When one group in a firm is in conflict with another, group members may become more cohesive. They perceive themselves to be facing a common enemy.

Negative Consequences of Conflict

When the wrong amount or type of conflict exists, job performance may suffer. Some types of conflict have worse consequences than others. A particularly bad form of conflict is one that forces a person to choose between two undesirable alternatives. Negative consequences of conflict include the following:

1. *Poor physical and mental health.* Intense conflict is a source of stress. A person under prolonged and intense conflict may suffer stress-related disorders. Many acts of workplace violence stem from highly stressed employees or ex-employees who experienced conflict with supervisors or coworkers.
2. *Wasted resources.* Employees and groups in conflict frequently waste time, money, and other resources while fighting their battles. One executive took a personal dislike to one of his managers and therefore ignored his cost-saving recommendations.
3. *Poor performance and sidetracked goals.* When emotional conflict is too strong, the team performance may suffer because not enough attention is paid to the task. Emotions may run so high in the group that the members may be unable to discuss their differences in a rational way. This problem has been found prevalent in multicultural groups.[21] In extreme forms of conflict, the parties involved may neglect the pursuit of important goals. Instead, they focus on winning their conflicts. A goal displacement of this type took place within an information systems group. The rival factions spent so much time squabbling over which new hardware and software to purchase that they neglected some of their tasks.
4. *Heightened self-interest.* Conflict within the group often results in extreme demonstrations of self-interest at the expense of the group and the larger organization. Individuals or groups place their personal interests over those of the rest of the firm or customers. One common result of this type of self-interest is hogging resources. A team member might attempt to convince the team leader to place him on an important customer troubleshooting assignment even though he knows his rival on the team is better qualified.

CONFLICT MANAGEMENT STYLES

Before describing specific methods of resolving conflict, it is useful to understand five styles of handling conflict. As shown in Exhibit 13-2, the five styles are based on a combination of satisfying one's own concerns (assertiveness) and satisfying the concerns of others (cooperativeness).[22]

1. *Competitive.* The competitive style is a desire to achieve one's own concerns or goals at the expense of the other party, or to dominate. A person with a competitive orientation is likely to engage in win–lose power struggles.
2. *Accommodative.* The accommodative style favors appeasement, or satisfying the other's concerns without taking care of one's own. People with this orientation may be generous or self-sacrificing just to maintain a relationship. A dissatisfied employee might be accommodated with a larger-than-average pay raise just to calm down the person and obtain his or her loyalty.
3. *Sharing.* The sharing style is halfway between domination and appeasement. Sharers prefer moderate but incomplete satisfaction for both parties, which results in a compromise. The phrase *splitting the difference* reflects this orientation and is commonly used in activities such as negotiating a budget or purchasing equipment.
4. *Collaborative.* In contrast to the other styles, the collaborative style reflects a desire to fully satisfy the desires of both parties. It is based on an underlying philosophy of **win–win,** the belief that after conflict has been resolved, both sides should gain something of value. A win–win approach is genuinely concerned with arriving at a settlement that meets the needs of both parties, or at least one that does not badly damage the welfare of either side. When a collaborative approach is used, the relationship between the parties improves. An example of a win–win approach would be for a manager to permit a call-center employee to work

Have the necessary information to resolve many workplace conflicts, including dealing with difficult people.

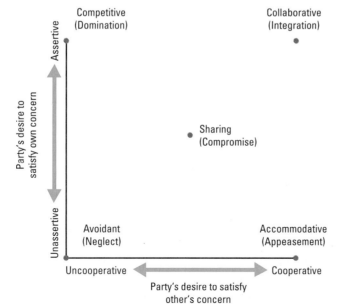

Exhibit 1**3-2**

*Conflict-Handling Styles
According to Degree of
Cooperation and
Assertiveness*

Source: Kenneth W. Thomas, "Organizational Conflict," in Steven Kerr (ed.), *Organizational Behavior* (Columbus, Ohio: Grid Publishing, 1979), p. 156.

from home provided that her productivity increased enough to pay for the equipment needed to set up a work station in her home.

5. *Avoidant.* The avoider is both uncooperative and unassertive. He or she is indifferent to the concerns of either party. The person may actually withdraw from the conflict or rely on fate. A manager sometimes uses the avoidant style to stay out of a conflict between two team members, who are left to resolve their own differences.

Conflict-Resolution Methods

Styles of dealing with conflict are closely related to methods of resolving conflict. For example, a collaborative style is a way of managing and resolving conflict. Here we present a sampling of conflict-resolution methods by describing confrontation and problem solving, as well as several structural methods.

Confrontation and Problem Solving

A widely applicable approach to resolving conflict is **confrontation and problem solving,** a method of identifying the true source of conflict and resolving it systematically. The confrontation approach is gentle and tactful rather than combative and abusive. Reasonableness is important because the person who takes the initiative in resolving the conflict wants to maintain a harmonious working relationship with the other party. During the confrontation, one person decides to work cooperatively and confronts the second person. At this point, the person confronted may indicate a willingness to accept the confrontation or may decide to gloss over its seriousness. Often the conflict is resolved at this step, particularly if it is not serious or complicated.

After the confrontation the two parties discuss their own opinions, attitudes, and feelings in relation to the conflict, attempting to identify the real issue. For example, the real cause of conflict between a manager and a team member might be that they have a different concept of what constitutes a fair day's work. After understanding the real issue, the parties attempt to develop specific means of reducing or eliminating the cause of the conflict. If the cause cannot be changed (such as changing one's opinion of a fair day's work), a way of working around the cause is devised. If both parties agree on a solution, then the confrontation has been successful. After the solution has been implemented, both parties should check periodically to ensure that their agreements are being kept.

The collaborative style of conflict resolution meshes with confrontation and problem solving. A major factor is that trust builds between two parties as they search for the real reason for conflict.

Confront, Contain, and Connect for Anger

A variation of confrontation and problem solving has been developed specifically to resolve conflict with angry people, and it involves confronting, containing, and connecting. You *confront* by jumping right in and getting agitated workers talking to prevent future blowups. The confrontation, however, is not aimed at arguing with the angry person. If the other person yells, you talk more softly. You *contain* by moving an angry worker out of sight and out of earshot. At the same time, you remain impartial. The supervisor is advised not to choose sides or appear to be a friend. Finally, you *connect* by asking open-ended questions such as "What would you like us to do about your concern?" to get at the real reasons behind an outburst. Using this approach, one worker revealed he was upset because a female coworker got to leave early to pick up her daughter at day care. The man also needed to leave early 1 day a week for personal reasons but felt awkward making the request. So instead of asserting himself in explicit and direct fashion about his demands, he flared up.

An important feature of the confront, contain, and connect technique is that it provides angry workers a place where they can vent their frustrations and report the outbursts of others. Mediator Nina Meierding says: "Workers need a safe outlet to talk through anger and not feel they will be minimized or put their job in jeopardy."[23]

Structural Methods

A structural method of resolving conflict emphasizes juggling work assignments and reporting relationships so that disputes are minimized. One structural method for resolving conflict is for a manager to have direct control over all the resources he or she needs to get the job done. In this way, the manager is less likely to experience conflict when attempting to get the cooperation of people who do not report directly to him or her.

Conflict can often be reduced or prevented by one or more members from one organizational unit exchanging places with those of another unit; for example, shifting from purchasing to manufacturing. Working in another unit can foster empathy. Reassigning people in this way can also encourage people to develop different viewpoints in the affected groups. As the group members get to know one another better, they tend to reduce some of their distorted perceptions of one another. (As described previously, cross-functional teams accomplish the same purpose.) Exchanging members works best when the personnel exchanged have the technical competence to perform well in the new environment.

In some firms, top management maintains an **open-door policy,** in which any employee can bring a gripe to attention without checking with his or her immediate manager. The open-door policy is a popular grievance procedure because it allows problems to be settled quickly.

A long-standing structural approach to conflict resolution is an appeals procedure. When the person cannot resolve a problem with his or her manager, the person appeals to a higher authority. The higher authority is ordinarily the next level of management or a member of the human resources department. When a dispute (conflict) involves a union worker, the higher authority would be a union representative. The ability to help two group members in dispute resolve their conflicts is considered a high-level management skill. Exhibit 13-3 presents some of the

Exhibit 13-3

Managerial Ways of Intervening in Conflicts between or among Other People

295

- Clarify the issues and interests at stake.
- Examine the interrelationships between interests and their degree of convergence or divergence.
- Facilitate the choice of the relevant approach for resolving the conflict.
- Identify appropriate conflict-resolution processes.
- Clarify the dynamics of interaction and implications for resolving the conflict.
- Identify assumptions, and reframe the understanding of the conflict.
- Identify and reexamine mutual stereotypes and perceptions.
- Facilitate communications.

- Model appropriate communications through restating, reflecting, and summarizing.
- Propose appropriate communication processes and procedures.
- Identify inappropriate behaviors, and propose more effective ones.
- Increase awareness of the conflict's real cost and benefits.

Source: Republished with permission of the Academy of Management Executive from Patrick Nugent, "Third-Party Interventions for Managers," *Academy of Management Executive,* February 2002, p. 147. Permission conveyed through Copyright Clearance Center, Inc.

competencies and strategies required to help subordinates resolve their conflicts. Few managers would have the time to learn all these competencies, but listening to the disputants and helping them to understand the true problem facing them would be a useful start.

An effective method for resolving disputes between workers and managers minimizes the instances in which a company is served with a complaint or a notice of a claim before a state or federal agency. Most top-level managers would prefer to learn about an employee dispute themselves early in the dispute so the problem can be resolved, rather than from a lawyer representing the individual.[24]

DEALING WITH DIFFICULT PEOPLE

A challenge all workers face from time to time is dealing constructively with workers who appear intent on creating problems. For a variety of reasons, these difficult or counterproductive people perform poorly themselves or interfere with the job performance of others. A **difficult person** is an individual who creates problems for others, yet has the skill and mental ability to do otherwise. The bully mentioned earlier is an example of a difficult person. Another of many examples is the yes-person who will agree to any commitment and promise any deadline, but will rarely deliver. Some well-known executives are sometimes difficult people in their interactions with work associates. Although Steve Jobs of Apple Computers and Pixar may be a charismatic and visionary leader, he is prone to temper tantrums. As one of his detractors states, "His capacity for cruelty runs the gamut from verbal lashings of his own customers to rumored summary dismissals for the sin of having brought him the wrong brand of bottled water."[25]

The techniques described next have wide applicability for helping difficult people change to a more constructive behavior pattern.

1. *Use tact and diplomacy in dealing with annoying behavior.* Coworkers who irritate you rarely do annoying things on purpose. Tactful actions on your part can sometimes take care of these annoyances without having to confront the problem. For example, point to the telephone in your hand if noisy coworkers are gathered outside your cubicle. When subtlety does not work, it may be necessary to proceed to the confrontation tactics described earlier. Tact and diplomacy can also be incorporated into confrontation. In addition to confronting a person, you might also point out an individual's good qualities.

2. *Use nonhostile humor.* Nonhostile humor can often be used to help a difficult person understand how his or her behavior has blocked others. Also, the humor will help defuse conflict between you and that person. The humor should point to the person's unacceptable behavior, yet not belittle him or her. Assume that you and a coworker are working jointly on a report. Whenever you turn over a portion of your work for her to review, she finds some fault. You point out lightly that her striving for perfection is admirable but the striving is creating stress for you.

3. *Give recognition and attention.* Counterproductive or difficult people, like misbehaving children, are sometimes crying out for attention. By giving them recognition and attention, their counterproductive behavior will sometimes cease. If their negative behavior is a product of a more deeply rooted problem, recognition and attention alone will not work. Other actions will need to be taken, such as referring the person for counseling.

4. *Help the difficult person feel more confident.* Many counterproductive employees are simply low in self-confidence and self-efficacy. They use stalling and evasive tactics because they are afraid to fail. You might be able to arrange a project or task in which you know the difficult person will succeed. With a small dose of self-confidence and self-efficacy, the person may begin to complain less. With additional successes, the person may soon become less difficult.[26] Building self-confidence takes time. However, self-efficacy can build more quickly as the person learns a new skill.

5. *Reinforce civil behavior and good moods.* In the spirit of positive reinforcement, when a generally difficult person behaves acceptably, recognize the behavior in some way. Reinforcing statements would include, "It's enjoyable working with you today," and "I appreciate your professional attitude."

NEGOTIATING AND BARGAINING

Conflicts can be considered situations calling for **negotiating and bargaining,** conferring with another person in order to resolve a problem. When you are trying to negotiate a fair salary for yourself, you are simultaneously trying to resolve a conflict. At first the demands of the two parties may seem incompatible, but through mutual-gains negotiation, a salary may emerge that satisfies both parties. The term *mutual gains* refers to the idea that both parties win.

Be aware of basic negotiating and bargaining techniques to resolve conflict.

Compromise

In compromise, one party agrees to do one thing if the other party agrees to do something else. "I'll get my reports to you on time if you agree to get them back to me with your suggestions within 10 days." Compromise is a realistic approach to resolving conflict and is almost inescapable in our culture. People enter into negotiation and bargaining sessions expecting a compromise solution. Assume, for example, that a company has agreed to have a custom-designed machine built for a certain price. The buyer does not expect to get all the features desired at that price, while the seller anticipates throwing in more features than he or she first offered.

The major problem with compromise is that the two parties may wind up with a solution that pacifies both but does not solve the problem. One example would be buying two department heads half the equipment that each requests. As a result, neither department really shows the productivity gain that would have been possible if the full request had been granted to either side.

Allow Room for Negotiation, but Be Plausible

The basic tactic of compromise is to begin with a demand that allows you room for compromise and concession. Anyone who has ever negotiated for the price of an automobile or house recognizes this basic approach. If you think your 10-speed bicycle is worth $400, you might put it on sale for $500. A potential buyer makes an initial offer of $300. After negotiation you wind up with an offer of $400, precisely what you wanted. However, be prepared to go beyond common sense. Most people believe that allowing room for negotiation includes beginning with an extreme demand or offer. (An example would be the seller asking $850 for the bicycle, or the potential buyer offering $150.) The final compromise will therefore be closer to your true demand or offer than if you opened negotiations more realistically. But a plausible demand is better because it shows you are bargaining in good faith. Also, if a third party has to resolve the conflict, a plausible demand or offer will receive more sympathy than an implausible one.

Focus on Interests, Not Positions

Rather than clinging to specific negotiating points, keep your overall interests in mind and try to satisfy them. Remember that the true object of negotiation is to satisfy the underlying interests of both sides. Here is how this strategy works:

> While job hunting, you are made an offer for a position you really want. You have a certain starting salary in mind, which is $3000 more per year than the job offers. Your real interests are probably to be able to live a particular lifestyle with your salary, whereas your position is to attain a particular start-ing salary. Your interests are best served by examining the total compensa-tion package, including employee benefits, along with the cost of living in the area. Agreeing to a starting salary lower than you had planned might serve your true interests best.

A key benefit of focusing on interests rather than positions is that it helps place the emphasis away from winning and toward what you really want to achieve. If you focus on mutual interests, your intent will be to solve a problem rather than to out-maneuver the other side. For example, if a customer makes an unrealistic demand, your best interest is to somehow satisfy that demand without losing money and retain the customer.

Make Small Concessions Gradually

Making steady concessions leads to more satisfactory agreements in most situa-tions. Gradually, you concede little things to the other side, such as throwing in an air pump and a backpack if the person agrees to move up the offer for the 10-speed bike. The small-concession tactic is described as a soft approach to bar-gaining. The hard-line approach is to make your total concession early in the negotiation and grant no further concessions. In our example, "My bike is for sale at $400 including an air pump and a backpack. I will keep the bike rather than let it go for less."

Use Deadlines

Giving the other side a deadline is often helpful in winning a negotiation or resolv-ing a conflict. Deadlines often force people into action because they require some type of external control or motivation. Here is an example of how you might be able to use deadlines to gain advantage in your negotiation: "Will I be receiving a promotion to project leader by December 31? If not, I will be forced to accept employment at another company that has offered me such a promotion."

Ask the Other Side, "What Do You Want Me to Do?"

An effective tactic for both negotiation and other forms of conflict resolution is to ask the other side what he or she would like you to do in order to reach an agreement.

If you do what the other side wants, you will often have reached an agreement. The underlying psychology is that having suggested the solution, the other side will feel committed. Here is an example:

> Your teammates and you are dividing up the work for a large task. It appears that several of your teammates do not think you are making an equitable contribution. After negotiating your contribution for about 30 minutes, you find that negotiations are stalled. You then ask, "What would you people like me to do?" Because you are so cooperative, the other team members will probably not make an outrageous demand. Also, they will probably regard your contribution as equitable because they formulated it.

Make a Final Offer

In many instances, presenting a final offer will break a deadlock. You might frame your message something like this: "I am willing to set up your Web page for $450. Call me when you are willing to pay that much for this specialized piece of work." Sometimes the tactic will be countered by a final offer from the other side. "Thanks for your interest in helping me set up a Web page. But the maximum price I am willing to pay is $250. Call me or send me an e-mail if that price is acceptable to you." One of you will probably give in and accept the other person's final offer.

After having studied negotiating and bargaining tactics, along with other techniques of conflict resolution, now do the accompanying skill-development exercise. It deals with the most important goal of negotiation.

The accompanying Organizational Behavior in Action box illustrates how one company has decided to resolve its difference of opinion with a small segment of its workforce.

SKILL-DEVELOPMENT EXERCISE

Mutual Gains Bargaining

Organize the class into groups of six, and divide each group into negotiating teams of three each. The members of the negotiating teams would like to find integrative (win–win) solutions to the issue separating them. The team members are free to invent their own pressing issue or choose one from among the following:

- Management wants to control costs by not giving cost-of-living adjustments in the upcoming year. The employee group believes that a cost-of-living adjustment is absolutely necessary for its welfare.
- The marketing team claims it could sell 250,000 units of a toaster wide enough to toast bagels if the toasters could be produced at $13 per unit.

The manufacturing group says it would not be feasible to get the manufacturing cost below $18 per unit.

- Blockbuster Video would like to build in a new location, adjacent to a historic district in one of the oldest cities in North America. The members of the town planning board would like the tax revenue and jobs that the Blockbuster store would bring, but they still say they do not want a Blockbuster store adjacent to the historic district.

After the teams have arrived at their solutions through high-level negotiating techniques, the creative solutions can be shared with teammates.

Collaboration

ORGANIZATIONAL BEHAVIOR *In Action*

Scotts Miracle-Gro Looks to Stop Its Employees from Smoking

Scotts Miracle-Gro Co. took its campaign to stamp out smoking among its workers to an unusual length: It's threatened to fire smokers beginning in fall 2006. The threat represents another attempt by an employer to try to reduce health-care costs by targeting smokers.

Scotts, which has 5300 U.S. workers, is one of the largest companies so far to have put an outright ban on smoking even off the job.

Scotts offers to pay for smoking-cessation programs and products, too. But the ultimatum of October 2005 "is way over the top by today's standards," said Helen Darling, president of the National Business Group on Health, a coalition of major corporations. "Most employers are still in the mode of 'You've got to have positive incentives,'" and help employees to improve their health.

Some lawyers said Scotts could be vulnerable to disability challenges if it fires people who smoke. "Once you start regulating outside conduct, the question is where do you stop?" says Marvin Gittler, an employment law specialist.

Smokers who are "really trying" to quit, even after the deadline, won't have to worry, allows Jim Hagedorn, Scotts's chief executive. "If you work with us, and we know you're working with us, I don't think you're going to end up getting fired."

Still, the lawn and gardening products company emphasizes that it expects employees to make a good-faith effort to improve their health. Scotts estimates that about 30% of its workers smoke. Scotts says it will begin randomly testing about 20% of its workforce nationwide where it's legal to do so to identify employees who are still lighting up. The company says it hasn't worked out the details of how to test employees. Workers found to be still smoking or using other tobacco products habitually could be fired, Scotts says, as long as they work in states where that termination is legal.

Scotts's wellness program includes a $5 million fitness gym and health clinic opened in 2005 near the company's Marysville, Ohio, headquarters. Employees on the company's medical plan will have free access in the clinic to a physician, nurse practitioners, diet and fitness experts and a pharmacy with generic drugs.

In return, every year employees will face a strict requirement: Take a health assessment through a program affiliated with medical-information Web site WebMDHealth Corp.— or pay $40 extra a month in health-care costs. The health assessment starts with filling out a form online. Then a "health coach" contacts the employee and arranges a treatment regimen for any health issues. The employee must again follow through with the recommendations or pay higher premiums.

Scotts's Hagedorn said he's "gotten pretty religious" about employees' health. A few years ago, the company abolished smoking from its corporate campus, and the company cafeteria has cut down on fried food, instead offering up baked salmon and other fish. Vending machines dispense more "granola stuff," he said. By company mandate, employees who leave work during the work day for the gym will not be penalized.

Hagedorn, 50 years old, once smoked two packs of cigarettes a day but quit 20 years ago after his mother died of lung cancer. He said he understands how difficult it is to quit smoking but also how important it is. "Are we going to stand by and watch our people get sick? The answer is no," he said. "Success here is not firing anybody."

Some smokers at headquarters are concerned about the company's deadline, said Linda Sutkin, an employee who successfully stopped smoking. "The consensus is like, is this the end or is it going to lead to something else?" she says. "Are they going to watch what we eat?"

ORGANIZATIONAL BEHAVIOR *In Action*

(Continued)

Questions

1. What is the conflict between Scotts's management and its employees who smoke?
2. How successful do you think Scotts's ban on smoking will be?

3. How else might Scotts resolve its conflict with employees who smoke?

Source: Reprinted with permission from Ilan Brat, "A Company's Threat: Quit Smoking or Leave," *The Wall Street Journal*, December 20, 2005, p. D1.

WORK STRESS

Stress is closely related to conflict because conflict is a major contributor to stress. As used here, **stress** is the mental and physical condition that results from a perceived threat that cannot be dealt with readily. Stress is therefore an internal response to a state of activation. The stressed person is physically and mentally aroused. Stress will ordinarily occur in a threatening or negative situation, such as worrying about losing one's job or being reprimanded. However, stress can also be caused by a positive situation, such as receiving a large cash bonus.

Understand the nature, causes, and consequences of work stress.

The topic of work stress is of enormous interest to managers and other professionals because of its impact on productivity and its legal and human consequences. Companies lose an estimated $200 billion annually because of stress, taking into account below-standard job performance, tardiness, and workers' compensations claims.[27]

Our study of work stress centers on its consequences and sources, along with individual and organizational methods for managing stress. Because stress deals heavily with personal perceptions, you will be invited to take two questionnaires, starting with the stress questionnaire in the accompanying self-assessment quiz.

Symptoms and Consequences of Work Stress

A person experiencing stress displays certain symptoms indicating that he or she is trying to cope with a **stressor,** any force creating the stress reaction. These symptoms can include a host of physiological, emotional, and behavioral reactions. A problem with stress symptoms is that they lead to an adverse impact on employee health and well-being.

Physiological symptoms of stress include increased heart rate, blood pressure, breathing rate, pupil size, and perspiration. Men, in particular, who respond most intensely to mental stress have a higher risk of blocked blood vessels, which increases their risk of heart attack and stroke. If stress symptoms are severe or persist over a prolonged period, the result can also be other stress-related disorders, such as hypertension, migraine headache, ulcers, colitis, and allergies. Stress also leads to a chemical imbalance that adversely affects the body's immune system. Thus, the overly stressed person becomes more susceptible to disease and suffers more intensely from existing health problems.

SELF-ASSESSMENT

The Stress Questionnaire

Directions: Apply each of the following questions to the last 6 months of your life. Check the appropriate column.

	Mostly Yes	Mostly No
1. Have you been feeling uncomfortably tense lately?	☐	☐
2. Are you engaged in frequent arguments with people close to you?	☐	☐
3. Is your social life very unsatisfactory?	☐	☐
4. Do you have trouble sleeping?	☐	☐
5. Do you feel apathetic about life?	☐	☐
6. Do many people annoy or irritate you?	☐	☐
7. Do you have constant cravings for candy and other sweets?	☐	☐
8. Is your cigarette or alcohol consumption substantially up?	☐	☐
9. Do you find yourself checking your e-mail or cell phone every few minutes even when not a business or social necessity?	☐	☐
10. Do you find it difficult to concentrate on your work?	☐	☐
11. Do you frequently grind your teeth?	☐	☐
12. Are you increasingly forgetful about little things such as mailing a letter or responding to an important e-mail message?	☐	☐
13. Are you increasingly forgetful about big things such as appointments and major errands?	☐	☐
14. Are you making too many trips to the restroom?	☐	☐
15. Have people commented lately that you do not look well (or "good")?	☐	☐
16. Do you get into verbal fights with people too frequently?	☐	☐
17. Have you been involved in more than one physical fight lately?	☐	☐
18. Do you have a troublesome number of tension headaches?	☐	☐
19. Do you feel nauseated frequently?	☐	☐
20. Do you feel light-headed or dizzy almost every day?	☐	☐
21. Do you have churning sensations in your intestines too often?	☐	☐
22. Are you in a big hurry all the time?	☐	☐
23. Are far too many things bothering you?	☐	☐
24. Do you frequently feel exhausted for no particular reason?	☐	☐
25. Do you have difficulty shaking colds or other infections?	☐	☐

Scoring: The following guidelines are only of value if you answered the questions sincerely:

0–7, Mostly Yes answers: You seem to be experiencing a normal amount of stress.

8–17, Mostly Yes answers: Your stress level seems high. Become involved in some kind of stress-management activity, such as those described later in this chapter.

18–25, Mostly Yes answers: Your stress level appears much too high. Discuss your stress levels with a mental health professional or visit your family doctor (or both).

Emotional symptoms of stress include anxiety, tension, depression, discouragement, feeling unable to cope, boredom, prolonged fatigue, feelings of hopelessness, and various kinds of defensive thinking. Behavioral symptoms include nervous habits such as facial twitching, as well as sudden decreases in job performance due to forgetfulness and errors in concentration or judgment. If the stress is particularly uncomfortable or distasteful (large and enduring discrepancies), it will lower job performance. The effect is greater for more-complex jobs. An example of a stressor

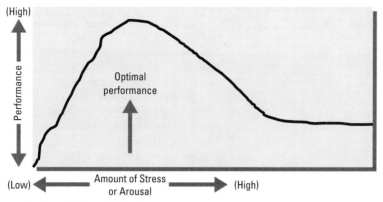

Source: Developed by Robert M. Yerkes and John D. Dodson, Department of Psychology, Harvard University, 1908.

Exhibit **13-4**

*The Yerkes–Dodson Law
for a Complex Task*

*A certain amount of stress
is needed to perform well,
but a very high stress level
interferes with perfor-
mance, particularly on a
complex task such as
preparing a budget.*

that will lower job performance for all people is a bullying, abrasive boss who wants to see the employee fail. Also, an 8-hour meeting on a Monday is a stressor for most managers and professionals who have other urgent work to perform.

Similar to conflict, not all stress is bad. People require the right amount of stress to keep themselves mentally and physically alert. The approximate relationship between stress and performance is known as the Yerkes–Dodson law. As the task becomes more complex, less arousal or stress can be tolerated to achieve optimal performance, as illustrated in Exhibit 13-4. Yet, individual differences are important. For some people, a high amount of stress increases their ability to process informa- tion and get a complex task accomplished.[28]

A person's perception of something or somebody usually determines whether that person or thing will be a positive or negative stressor. For example, one man- ager might perceive a quality audit by a corporate executive to be so frightening that he is irritable in dealing with team members. Another manager might welcome the visit as a chance to proudly display her department's high-quality performance.

After prolonged exposure to job stress, a person runs the risk of feeling burned out—a drained, used-up feeling. **Burnout** is a pattern of emotional, physical, and mental exhaustion in response to chronic job stressors. The same syndrome (collec- tion of symptoms) is sometimes regarded as work exhaustion. Cynicism, apathy, and indifference are the major behavioral symptoms of the burned-out worker. Personal accomplishment finally diminishes as a result of burnout.[29]

A study of workers and their supervisors in a hospital verified that work exhaustion can have negative consequences for the individual and the organization. Employees completed questionnaires measuring emotional exhaustion, organiza- tional commitment, and turnover intentions. Supervisors rated the same employees on job performance and organizational citizenship behavior. The major findings of the study were that emotional exhaustion led to lower commitment to the organi- zation and a higher rate of intention to leave the organization. Exhaustion also led to lower job performance and lower organizational citizenship behavior in terms of helping both the supervisor and the organization.[30] An important implication of this study is that burnout can adversely affect behavior and attitudes.

Factors Contributing to Work Stress

A host of a person's internal factors, as well as adverse organizational conditions, can cause or contribute to job stress. As with sources of conflict, the list is dynamic. New sources of stress surface as the work environment changes. For example, today

303

The numbers to the right of each life event represent the scale value in life-change units.

1. Death of a spouse (100)
2. Divorce (73)
3. Marital separation (65)
4. Jail term/imprisonment (63)
5. Death of a family member (63)
6. Major personal injury or illness (53)
7. Marriage (50)
8. Fired from job (47)
9. Marital reconciliation (45)
10. Retirement (45)
11. Major change in health of family member (44)
12. Pregnancy (40)
13. Sexual difficulties (39)
14. Change in financial state (38)
15. Change in number of arguments with spouse (35)
16. Mortgage or loan for major purpose (31)
17. Foreclosure of mortgage or loan (30)
18. Change in responsibilities at work (29)
19. Son or daughter leaving home (29)
20. Trouble with in-laws (29)
21. Outstanding personal achievement (28)
22. Spouse, or partner begins or stops work (26)
23. Begin or end school (26)
24. Change in living conditions (20)
25. Revision of personal habits (15)

Source: These stressors have changed over time. This version is from Thomas H. Holmes and Richard H. Rahe, "The Social Adjustment Rating Scale," *Journal of Psychosomatic Research,* 15, 1971, pp. 210–223, with permission of Elsevier; with an interview updating it from Sue MacDonald, "Battling Stress," *Cincinnati Enquirer,* October 23, 1995.

Exhibit 13-5

The Top 25 Stressors as Measured by Life-Change Units

thousands of industrial and retail salespeople feel less job security because so much of the sales function has moved to the Internet.

Factors within the Individual

A general stressor that encompasses both individual and organizational factors is having to cope with significant change. The more significant the change you have to cope with in a short period of time, the greater the probability that you will experience a stress disorder.[31] Exhibit 13-5 presents the impact of various life changes, measured in life-change units. Hostile, aggressive, and impatient people, labeled as having Type A personalities, find ways of turning almost any job into a stressful experience, in contrast to their more easygoing Type B personality counterparts. In addition to being angry, the outstanding trait of Type A personality people is their strong sense of time urgency, known as "hurry sickness." This sense of urgency compels them to achieve more and more in less and less time. Type A personality people are prone to cardiovascular disorders, particularly when the individual is hostile. A study of 774 males found that hostility (being cynical and negative) was a good predictor of who would have heart disease 3 years later.[32]

Recognize, however, that not every hard-driving, impatient person is correctly classified as having a Type A personality. Managers and professionals who love their work and enjoy other people are not particularly prone to heart disease. These people experience more positive emotion than hostility and anger.

Having an external locus of control predisposes people to job stress because they do not believe they can control key stressors in their environment. Managers and professionals with a limited tolerance for ambiguity are prone to frustration and stress because high-level job responsibilities are often ambiguous. **Negative lifestyle factors** also predispose one to job stress. Among them are poor exercise and eating habits and heavy consumption of caffeine, alcohol, tobacco, and other drugs. Another factor predisposing a person to stress is a pessimistic attitude. Being optimistic, in contrast, helps you ward off stress.

Adverse Organizational Conditions

Under ideal conditions, workers experience just enough stress to prompt them to respond creatively and energetically to their jobs. Unfortunately, high stress levels

	Low Job Demands	High Job Demands
Low Control	Passive Job	High-Strain Job
High Control	Low-Strain Job	Active Job

Exhibit **13-6**

The Job Demands–Job Control Model

created by adverse organizational conditions lead to many negative symptoms. According to the **job demands–job control model,** workers experience the most stress when the demands of the job are high yet they have little control over the activity[33] (see Exhibit 13-6). A customer service representative dealing with a major blooper by the firm would fit into this category. In contrast, when job demands are high and the worker has high control, the worker will be energized, motivated, and creative. An industrial sales representative who decides which customers to call on might fit here.

A major contributor to work stress is *role overload*. Demands on managers and professionals are at an all-time high, as companies attempt to increase work output and decrease staffing at the same time. Better financial results are achieved by having fewer employees accomplish more work, thereby fostering role-overload stress. Worrying about being next on the "hit list" during downsizing is another major job stressor. In contrast to being overloaded, many other workers suffer from role underload (too little to do) or the job monotony associated with repetitive work. In one situation, a manager left town for 3 weeks, without giving his newly hired executive assistant an assignment. The assistant suffered anxiety attacks after the fifth day of make-work activities.

A long-recognized contributor to work stress is **role conflict**—having to choose between competing demands or expectations. We have already touched on role conflict in the study of value conflicts in Chapter 4 and work–family conflicts in this chapter. If a person complies with one aspect of a role, compliance with the other is difficult. *Person–role* conflict occurs when the role(s) an employer expects a worker to perform conflict with the person's basic values. An office assistant in the bursar's office at a vocational technical school in Montreal experienced role conflict because the administration asked her to pressure students to pay their outstanding bills. The woman, herself in poor financial condition, sympathized with the students.

Another role-related stressor is **role ambiguity,** a condition in which the job holder receives confusing or poorly defined expectations. Role ambiguity involves several factors. First, there is insufficient information about the worker's expected performance. Second, there is unclear or confusing information about expected job behaviors. Third, there is uncertainty about the outcome (such as promotion or dismissal) of certain on-the-job behaviors.[34] The person facing extreme role ambiguity proclaims, "I don't know what I'm supposed to be doing or what will happen to me if I do it."

A powerful stressor for knowledge workers is information overload, as described in Chapter 8. Workers have to process so much information in the form of e-mail messages, text messages, websites, written reports, and job-related news that their brain circuits become overloaded, leading to stress and lowered concentration. Many workers encourage overload by multitasking while receiving information. Stress caused by information overload is sometimes referred to as "technostress," caused by having to cope with ever-changing technology and the deluge of data stemming from information technology.[35]

A final organizational stressor mentioned here is being part of a culturally diverse workforce. Although cultural diversity brings many advantages to organizations (as will be described in Chapter 17), it may lead to interpersonal stress. As analyzed by Richard S. DeFrank and John M. Ivancevich, these stressors include competition among groups for attention and resources and decreased interaction because of the perceived need for political correctness in dealing with demographic groups other than one's own. Not knowing how to respond well in a diverse setting is also a stressor; for example, a 55-year-old white man feeling awkward because his manager is a 25-year-old African-American woman. Furthermore, it is stressful for a person to feel that he or she is not a good cultural fit with most members of the organization.[36]

ORGANIZATIONAL APPROACHES TO STRESS MANAGEMENT

Explain what organizations can do to manage and reduce stress.

Negative stress is disruptive to both productivity and employee well-being. As a consequence, organizations are actively involved in stress management. Several illustrative approaches to stress management include providing emotional support to employees, sponsoring a wellness and fitness program, giving on-site massages, and providing the opportunity to take nap breaks on the job. Creating a high-job-demand, high-control job, as described previously, is also an approach to stress prevention.

Emotional support from an immediate superior can help group members cope better with job stress. One study compared the illness rate between two groups of employees who faced comparable heavy stressors. Employees who felt they had their manager's support suffered only half as much illness in 12 months as those who felt they lacked such support. The most helpful managers ask themselves the question, "How can I make my subordinates feel as effective as I do?" Supportive behaviors that help employees feel more effective include (a) keeping communication channels open, and (b) providing the right kind of help (such as verbal encouragement or time off from work to recover from a heavy stressor).[37]

To help combat negative stress, as well as to promote wellness, many employers offer programs that encourage employees to stay in good physical and mental shape. A **wellness program** is thus a formal organization-sponsored activity to help employees stay well and avoid illness. Workshops, seminars, activities, and medical procedures offered in a wellness program include the following: medical examinations, stress-management techniques, smoking-cessation programs, and preventive health care. Scotts Miracle-Gro, as described in the chapter opener, offers a wellness program.

A study conducted by the Nevada Stress Center demonstrated that employees who participated in a stress-management program had fewer sick days than those who did not participate. Furthermore, the stress-center participants visited physicians 34% less often than did their nonparticipating counterparts.[38] At the same time, one could ask the question, Are employees who are healthier to begin with more likely to participate in stress-management programs?

An emerging approach to help employees combat stress is to give them the opportunity to nap on company premises. Napping is one of the most effective methods of treating and preventing stress. Everyday job stress can often be alleviated by taking a 15- to 20-minute nap to restore alertness and memory and to decrease the effects of fatigue. Naps beyond 30 minutes place people in their normal sleep cycle, with people often waking up feeling groggy and disoriented. For career-minded people, the slogan "You snooze, you win" replaces "You snooze, you lose."

A macro approach for reducing stress is for an organization to practice justice with respect to policies and managerial actions. According to Jared Greenberg, employees will experience less stress if managers take the following actions to promote justice: (1) Explain the reasoning behind the allocation of resources, such as bonuses and budgets, in a dignified and respectful manner; (2) give employees an opportunity to express their opinions on key issues, referred to as having a *voice;* and (3) use accurate, unbiased procedures and implement them openly. Examples of unbiased procedures include the accurate calculation of overtime, and not basing performance evaluations on favoritism.[39]

INDIVIDUAL APPROACHES TO STRESS MANAGEMENT

Techniques individuals can use to manage stress can be divided into three categories: control, symptom management, and removal of the stressor.[40]

Do a more effective job of managing your own stress.

Control

Methods of controlling and reducing stress include getting the right emotional support. Receiving social support—encouragement, understanding, and friendship—from other people is a key strategy for coping with work and personal stress.

An equally important control technique is to practice good work habits and time management. By establishing priorities and minimizing procrastination, people can gain better control of their lives. Gaining control is especially important because feeling out of control is a major stressor. The lowly to-do list could thus save you an ulcer or heart attack! Demanding less than perfection from oneself can also help prevent stress. Decreasing clutter in your life can also reduce stress by improving concentration and reducing the feeling of being overwhelmed. Periodically throwing out information, including hard-drive and e-mail documents, and physical possessions you do not need is an effective method of reducing clutter. Not measuring up to one's own unrealistically high standards is a substantial stressor.

Symptom Management

Dozens of symptom-management techniques have been developed, and no stress-management program is complete without using at least one. Getting appropriate physical exercise is an excellent starting point in symptom management. Physical exercise helps dissipate some of the tension created by work stress and also helps the body ward off future stress-related disorders. One way in which exercise helps combat stress is by releasing endorphins. These are morphine-like chemicals produced in the brain that act as painkillers and antidepressants.

Another widely applicable symptom-management technique is the **relaxation response,** a general-purpose method of learning to relax by yourself that could be considered a form of meditation. The key ingredient of this technique is to make yourself quiet and comfortable. At the same time, think of the word *one* (or any simple chant or prayer) with every breath for about 10 minutes. The technique slows you down both physiologically and emotionally and at the same time reduces the adverse effects of stress. A major contribution of the relaxation response is that it is a physical state of deep rest that counteracts the harmful effects of fighting stressors.[41]

- Take a nap when facing heavy pressures. Napping is one of the most effective techniques for reducing and preventing stress.
- Give in to your emotions. If you are angry, disgusted, or confused, admit your feelings. Suppressing your emotions adds to stress. Talk to a friend or counselor about your problems.
- Take a brief break from the stressful situation and do something small and constructive such as washing your car, emptying a wastebasket, or cleaning out a drawer.
- Get a massage, because it can loosen tight muscles, improve your blood circulation, and calm you down.
- Get help with your stressful task from a coworker, manager, or friend.
- Concentrate intensely on reading, a sport, a hobby, or surfing the Internet. Contrary to common sense, concentration is at the heart of stress reduction such as in meditation or yoga.

- Have a quiet place at home and enjoy a brief idle period there every day.
- Take a leisurely day off from your routine, or at least take a brief walk during a particularly stressful day.
- Finish something you have started, however small. Accomplishing almost anything reduces some stress, particularly if you are goal oriented.
- Stop to smell the flowers, make friends with a young child or elderly person, or play with a kitten or puppy (if you like domestic animals).
- Strive to do a good job, but not a perfect job.
- Work with your hands, doing a pleasant task.
- Find somebody or something that makes you laugh, and have a good laugh.
- Minimize drinking caffeinated or alcoholic beverages, and drink fruit juice or water instead. Eat fruits or vegetables for snacks rather than junk food.

Exhibit 13-7

Stress Busters

Much of the benefit of the relaxation response can also be achieved by napping or visualizing a pleasant fantasy for about 10 minutes. Yoga offers many of the benefits of the relaxation response; however, pushing yoga too far can be dangerous for people with high blood pressure or disorders of the joint. The relaxation response is physically harmless. The stress busters listed in Exhibit 13-7 are mostly aimed at symptom management.

Removal of the Stressor

Removal-of-the-stressor methods of stress management are actions and reappraisals of situations that provide the stressed individual some escape from the stressor. Eliminating the stressor is the most effective escape technique. For example, if a manager experiences stress because of serious understaffing in his department, he should negotiate to receive authorization to hire additional staff. Mentally blocking out a stressful thought is another removal technique, but it may not work in the long run. Without constructive action about the problem, a stressor will usually return.

The accompanying skill-development exercise takes you step by step through an advanced stress-management technique.

IMPLICATIONS FOR MANAGERIAL PRACTICE

1. A manager's goal should be to maintain optimal levels of conflict and stress in his or her unit. Sometimes this will involve the reduction of conflict; at other times, a modest amount of conflict stimulation may be necessary.
2. Approximately 20 to 30% of a manager's time involves resolving conflict. It is therefore important for a manager to develop effective conflict-resolution skills. A good starting point is to use confrontation and problem solving.
3. Given that an optimal amount of stress facilitates performance, a manager should strive to design the appropriate amount and kinds of stressors for both

SKILL-DEVELOPMENT EXERCISE

The Freeze-Frame Technique for Managing Stress

A scientifically based method of stress reduction that emphasizes reappraisal, along with some symptom management, is the *freeze-frame technique,* developed by the HeartMath Institute. To use this technique to learn to better manage stress, try it out during your next stressful episode, such as receiving a negative performance evaluation, appearing in court for a speeding ticket, or terminating your relationship with someone you have been dating for a while.

The method proceeds as follows:

Step One. *Recognize the stressful feeling and freeze-frame it.* See your problem as a still photo, not a movie. Stop the inner conversation about it.

Step Two. Make a sincere effort to *shift your focus* away from the racing mind or disturbing emotions in the area around your heart. Pretend you are breathing through your heart to help focus energy in this area. Stay focused there for 10 seconds or more.

Step Three. *Recall a positive fun feeling or time* you've had in your life and visualize experiencing it again.

Step Four. Using your intuition, common sense, and sincerity, *ask your heart what would be a more efficient response* to the situation—one that will minimize future stress.

Step Five. *Listen to what your heart says* in answer to your question. Here you are using an in-house source of common-sense solutions.

You may hear nothing, but at least you will feel calmer. You may receive confirmation of something you already know. Equally important, you may gain a perspective shift and see the problem in a different way. Although we may not have control over the event, we do have control over how we perceive it.[42] Any complex skill takes practice, so if the technique appeared to have any value in reducing stress the first time you tried it, use it again in the future.

---

individuals and groups. Manipulating stressors is much like manipulating the challenge level of a job. Stress can be increased or decreased by manipulating the amount of job responsibility, goal difficulty, tightness of deadlines, amount of supervision, and critical feedback.

4. Managers should encourage team members to embark on a systematic program of stress management, considering today's turbulent work environment. Workers who are already managing stress well should be encouraged in their efforts.

SUMMARY OF KEY POINTS

 Understand the nature of conflict in organizations and its leading causes.

Workplace conflict has many sources, including the following: perceived adverse changes; line versus staff differentiation; sexual harassment; factional groups; competing work and family demands; and incivility, personality clashes, and workplace bullies. Task conflict focuses on substantive, issue-related differences. Relationship conflict focuses on personalized, individually oriented issues that are dealt with more emotionally than intellectually. Conflict in small doses leads to positive outcomes such as increased creativity. Negative consequences of conflict include wasted resources.

 Have the necessary information to resolve many workplace conflicts, including dealing with difficult people.

Five styles of handling conflict based on a combination of assertiveness (looking out for oneself) and cooperativeness have been identified: competitive, accommodative, sharing, collaborative (win–win), and avoidant. A widely applicable approach to re-solving conflict is confrontation and problem solving, in which the true source of the conflict is identified and then resolved systematically. The recommended confrontation approach is a gentle and tactful one. To resolve conflict with an angry person, you might confront him or her, contain the angry situation, and connect with the person.

A structural method of resolving conflict empha-sizes juggling work assignments and reporting rela-tionships so that disputes are minimized. An appeals procedure is a structural approach. Techniques for dealing with difficult people include using tact and diplomacy, using nonhostile humor; giving recogni-tion and attention; helping the difficult person feel more confident; and reinforcing civil behavior and good moods.

 Be aware of basic negotiating and bargaining tech-niques to resolve conflict.

Negotiating and bargaining techniques include com-promise, allow room for negotiation but be plausible, focus on interests not positions, make small conces-sions gradually, use deadlines, and ask the other side "What do you want me to do?", and make a final offer.

 Understand the nature, causes, and consequences of work stress.

Stress is an internal response to a state of activation, ordinarily occurring in a threatening or negative situ-ation. Stress symptoms include a host of physiologi-cal, emotional, and behavioral reactions. Many of these symptoms can adversely affect job perfor-mance. After prolonged job stress, a person may experience burnout. A general stressor that encom-passes both individual and organizational factors is having to cope with significant change. Factors within a person contributing to work stress include a Type A personality, an external locus of control, nega-tive lifestyle factors, and a pessimistic attitude.

Adverse organization conditions are another set of stressors. According to the job demands–job control model, workers experience the most stress when the demands of the job are high yet they have little control over the activity. Other stressors include role overload and worry about potential job loss. Role conflict, role ambiguity, and information overload are other stressors of significance. Another potential stressor is being part of a culturally diverse group.

 Explain what organizations can do to manage and reduce stress.

Organizational approaches to stress management in-clude providing emotional support to employees, establishing a wellness program, allowing for nap-ping on the job. and creating a just organization.

 Do a more effective job of managing your own stress.

Individual methods of preventing and controlling stress can be divided into three categories: attempts to control stressful situations, symptom manage-ment, and removal of the stressful situation. Specific tactics include eliminating stressors, getting suffi-cient physical exercise, using relaxation techniques, getting emotional support from others, and improv-ing work habits. Also see the stress-buster list in Exhibit 13-7.

KEY TERMS AND PHRASES

Conflict, 285
The opposition of persons or forces giving rise to some tension, or a disagreement between two or more parties who are interdependent.

Downsizing, 285
The laying off of workers to reduce costs and increase efficiency.

Sexual Harassment, 286
Unwanted sexually oriented behavior in the workplace that results in discomfort and/or interference with the job.

Work–Family Conflict, 289
Conflict that ensues when the individual has to perform multiple roles: worker; spouse; and, often, parent.

Personality Clash, 290
An antagonistic relationship between two people based on differences in personal attributes, preferences, interests, values, and styles.

Task Conflict, 291
Conflict that focuses on substantive, issue-related differ-ences related to the work itself.

Relationship Conflict, 291
Conflict that focuses on personalized, individually oriented issues.

Win–Win, 293
The belief that, after conflict has been resolved, both sides should gain something of value.

Confrontation and Problem Solving, 294

A method of identifying the true source of conflict and re-solving it systematically.

Open-Door Policy, 295

An understanding in which any employee can bring a gripe to the attention of upper-level management without checking with his or her immediate manager.

Difficult Person, 296

An individual who creates problems for others, yet has the skill and mental ability to do otherwise.

Negotiating and Bargaining, 297

Conferring with another person in order to resolve a problem.

Stress, 301

The mental and physical condition that results from a per-ceived threat that cannot be dealt with readily.

Stressor, 301

Any force creating the stress reaction.

Burnout, 303

A pattern of emotional, physical, and mental exhaustion in response to chronic job stressors.

Negative Lifestyle Factors, 304

Behavior patterns predisposing a person to job stress, including poor exercise and eating habits and heavy con-sumption of caffeine, alcohol, tobacco, and other drugs.

Job Demands–Job Control Model, 305

An explanation of job stress contending that workers experience the most stress when the demands of the job are high yet they have little control over the activity.

Role Conflict, 305

Having to choose between competing demands or expec-tations.

Role Ambiguity, 305

A condition in which the job holder receives confused or poorly defined role expectations.

Wellness Program, 306

A formal organization-sponsored activity to help employ-ees stay well and avoid illness.

Relaxation Response, 307

A general-purpose method of learning to relax by oneself, which includes making oneself quiet and comfortable.

DISCUSSION QUESTIONS AND ACTIVITIES

1. Get together in a small group to present evidence that being effective at resolving conflict is still a major problem in business and society.

2. In what way does the presence of *spam* advertising on e-mail represent conflict? Who are the parties in conflict?

3. Conflict is said to have some functional conse-quences. Describe an example of how conflict has ever improved your work or personal life.

4. Why do so many workers at all organizational lev-els still commit sexual harassment despite all the information available about its illegality and immorality?

5. Why are entrepreneurs and other business owners more likely to experience work–family conflict than corporate employees?

6. Give an example from your personal experience of how too much stress can lead to problems that dam-age a person's career.

7. Identify a job in any field of business that you think creates negative stress for most incumbents, and pinpoint the stressors.

CASE PROBLEM: Hard Charger Turned Soccer Mom

I was an extremely shy, awkward kid. I'm 5-foot-10, and I've had the feeling of being 5-foot-10 since I was 10 years old. It wasn't until I got to college that I developed a lot of self-confidence. I went to an obscure but wonderful small college, Lynchburg College in Virginia, much to my parents' chagrin. My mother had gone to Purdue, my dad to Carnegie Mellon. They wanted me to go to a school with a big name. But I had a lot of support at college.

I have worked since I was 15, so early on I had a sense of how to support myself. My parents had rough times financially. I was the oldest of three girls. We weren't poor, but we went without the nicest clothes; we didn't go on elaborate vacations or buy brand-new cars. I thought I'd really made it when I got to college and was able to buy Pepperidge Farm instead of day-old bread. My first job after college was at Chevy Chase Savings Bank in Washington, as a management trainee.

(continued)

CASE PROBLEM (Continued)

The day my son, Will, was born, I worked all day and then drove myself to the hospital in Wilmington, Delaware, at 2 a.m. This was 8 years ago—I was working for a bank in Wilmington and commuting to our home in Chevy Chase, Maryland, on the weekends. My husband drove up and joined me at the hospital. I was in labor for several hours, then they gave me an epidural. I couldn't feel anything. I was just waiting around for the baby to be born. So I kept on working. I had colleagues sending me faxes at the hospital. Doctors were walking into my room handing me documents I had to sign for work. The baby was born that afternoon. I took the minimum maternity leave of 6 weeks.

It took 6 months before I realized—time out! I can't be that hard-charging work-all-the-time person anymore. Before I had the baby, I was known as a straight-A student who knew all the answers and intimidated my peers. I set aggressive deadlines. I micromanaged people.

After having Will, I became a more balanced person. When you come home to a baby who demands your full attention, you stop thinking about all the issues at work. You give your brain a time out. Because I reduced my hours after having Will, I was forced to delegate more. I learned to listen, and I'm a better executive now. Had my son not come along, I doubt I would be in the position I'm in today.

The most difficult time was that first year after the baby was born. I was torn between my responsibilities on the job and my devotion to my child. My supervisor at the company I used to work for once called me at 10 on a Saturday night and told me I had to come to the office immediately. The company was in the midst of a merger. I had worked that day at home, even though my son and I were sick with the flu. My husband was out of the country on a business trip. I knew no one in town, except the people I worked with. So I told my supervisor, "No can do," but he insisted. When I asked if I could bring my son, he said it would not be appropriate. I felt under so much pressure. I knew the security officer in my building well enough, so I said, "Isaac, can you take care of the baby?" I left him there, went to work and after about an hour realized the absurdity of the situation. By then it was almost midnight, and I just left.

I've really learned to put up boundaries since then. My average day used to be from 7 a.m. to 10 p.m. Now I'll work from 7 or 8 a.m. to 7 or 8 p.m. Then I'll spend time reading to Will, have dinner, put him to bed. Once he's asleep, I'll go back to my e-mail a little bit. But I don't work weekends like I used to. I'm a soccer mom now.

Case Questions

1. What kind of conflicts and stress was the case heroine facing?
2. Has this woman really achieved an effective work–life balance?
3. What suggestions can you make the case heroine to create an even more effective work–life balance?
4. How should this woman have dealt with the late-night request by her boss?

Source: Reprinted with permission from As Told to Julia Lawlor, "A New Sense of Time," *The New York Times* (*nytimes.com*) March 27, 2005.

ENDNOTES

1. Yuhyung Shin, "Conflict Resolution in Virtual Teams," *Organizational Dynamics*, 4(2005), p. 332.
2. David M. Noer, *Healing the Wounds: Overcoming the Trauma of Layoffs and Revitalizing Downsized Organizations* (San Francisco: Jossey-Bass, 1993).
3. Marjorie L. Icenogle, Bruce W. Eagle, Sohel Ahman, and Lisa A. Hanks, "Assessing Perceptions of Sexual Harassment Behaviors in a Manufacturing Environment," *Journal of Business and Psychology*, Summer 2002, pp. 601–616.
4. These rulings are summarized in Jennifer Laabs, "What You're Liable for Now," *Workforce*, October 1998, pp. 34–42.
5. Kimberly T. Schneider, Suzanne Swan, and Louise F. Fitzgerald, "Job-Related and Psychological Effects of Sexual Harassment in the Workplace: Empirical Evidence from Two Organizations," *Journal of Applied Psychology*, June 1997, p. 406.
6. Carra S. Sims, Fritz Drasgow, and Louise F. Fitzgerald, "The Effects of Sexual Harassment on Turnover in the Military: Time-Dependent Modeling," *Journal of Applied Psychology*, November 2005, pp. 1141–1152.
7. Jana L. Raver and Michele J. Gelfand, "Beyond the Individual Victim: Linking Sexual Harassment, Team Processes, and Team Performance," *Academy of Management Journal*, June 2005, pp. 387–400.
8. Joann S. Lublin, "How to Get a New Job after Reporting a Case of Sexual Harassment," *The Wall Street Journal*, October 4, 2005, p. A17.
9. Jiatao Li and Donald C. Hambrick, "Factional Groups: A New Vantage on Demographic Faultlines, Conflict, and Disintegration in Work Teams," *Academy of Management Journal*, October 2005, pp. 794–813.

10. Linda Elizabeth Duxbury and Christopher Alan Higgins, "Gender Differences in Work-Family Conflict," *Journal of Applied Psychology,* February 1991, p. 64.

11. "When Work and Private Lives Collide," *Workforce,* February 1999, p. 27.

12. Virginia Smith Major, Katherine J. Klein, and Mark G. Ehrhart, "Work Time, Work Interference With Family, and Psychological Distress," *Journal of Applied Psychology,* June 2002, pp. 427–436.

13. Leslie B. Hammer, Talya N. Bauer, and Alicia A. Grandey, "Work-Family Conflict and Work-Related Withdrawal Behaviors," *Journal of Business and Psychology,* Spring 2003, pp. 419–436.

14. Timothy A. Judge and Jason A. Colquitt, "Organizational Justice and Stress: The Mediating Role of Work-Family Conflict," *Journal of Applied Psychology*, June 2004, pp. 395–404.

15. Keith H. Hammonds, "Balance Is Bunk," *Fast Company,* October 2004, p. 72.

16. Christine M. Pearson and Christine L. Porath, "On the Nature, Consequences and Remedies of Workplace Incivility: No Time for 'Nice'? Think Again," *Academy of Management Executive*, February 2005, pp. 7–18; Lynne M. Andersson and Christine M. Pearson, "Tit for Tat? The Spiraling Effect of Incivility in the Workplace," *Academy of Management Review,* July 1999, pp. 452–471.

17. Julie Ellis, "Knock Down Workplace Bullying; Improve Office Morale," *Managing Workplace Conflict,* sample issue, Arlington, VA: Dartnell Corporation, 2002.

18. Arthur H. Bell, *You Can't Talk to Me That Way* (Franklin Lakes, NJ: Career Press, 2005).

19. Allen C. Amason, Wayne A. Hockwarter, Kenneth R. Thompson, and Allison W. Harrison, "Conflict: An Important Dimension in Successful Management Teams," *Organizational Dynamics* (Autumn 1995), pp. 20–33; Carlsen K. W. De Dreu and Laurie Weingart, "Task versus Relationship Conflict, Team Performance, and Team Member Satisfaction: A Meta-Analysis," *Journal of Applied Psychology*, August 2003, pp. 741–749.

20. De Dreu and Weingart, "Task versus Relationship Conflict," p. 746.

21. Mary Ann Von Glinow, Debra L. Shapiro, and Jeanne M. Brett, "Can We *Talk*, and Should We? Managing Emotional Conflict in Multicultural Teams," *Academy of Management Review*, October 2004, pp. 578–592.

22. Kenneth Thomas, "Conflict and Conflict Management," in Marvin D. Dunnette (ed.), *Handbook of Industrial and Organizational Psychology* (Chicago: Rand McNally College Publishing, 1976), pp. 900–902.

23. The quote and technique are both from Kathleen Doheny, "It's a Mad, Mad Corporate World," *Working Woman,* April 2000, pp. 71–72.

24. F. Peter Philips, "Ten Ways to Sabotage Dispute Management," *HR Magazine*, September 2004, p. 163.

25. Rich Karlgaard, "Vladimir Ilyich Jobs?" *The Wall Street Journal,* May 3, 2005, p. A16.

26. "How to Deal with 'Problem' Workers," *Positive Leadership,* sample issue, distributed 2001 by Ragan Communications, Inc. 316 N. Michigan Ave., Suite 300, Chicago, IL 60601.

27. Michelle Conlin, "Meditation; New Research Shows That It Changes the Brain Waves in Ways that Alleviate Stress," *Business Week,* August 30, 2004, p. 137.

28. Daniel C. Ganster, "Executive Job Demands: Suggestions from a Stress and Decision-Making Perspective," *Academy of Management Review,* July 2005, p. 497.

29. Cynthia L. Cordes and Thomas W. Dougherty, "A Review and Integration of Research on Job Burnout," *Academy of Management Review,* October 1993, p. 622.

30. Russell Cropanzano, Deborah E. Rupp, and Zinta S. Byrne, "The Relationships of Emotional Exhaustion to Work Attitudes, Job Performance, and Organizational Citizenship Behavior," *Journal of Applied Psychology,* February 2003, pp. 160–169.

31. Rabi S. Bhagat, "Effects of Stressful Life Events on Individual Performance and Work Adjustment Processes within Organizational Settings: A Research Model," *Academy of Management Review,* October 1983, pp. 660–671.

32. Research reported in Etienne Benton, "Hostility Is Among Best Predictors of Heart Disease in Men," *Monitor on Psychology,* January 2003, p. 15.

33. Marilyn L. Fox, Deborah J. Dwyer, and Daniel C. Ganster, "Effects of Stressful Job Demands and Control on Physiological and Attitudinal Outcomes in a Hospital Setting," *Academy of Management Journal,* April 1993, pp. 290–292.

34. J. B. Teboul, "Facing and Coping with Uncertainty during Organizational Encounter," *Communication Quarterly, 8* (1994), pp. 190–224.

35. Keith Newman, "Information Overload—Overcoming Techno Stress," *iStart*, http://www.istart.co.nz.

36. Richard S. DeFrank and John M. Ivancevich, "Stress on the Job: An Executive Update," *Academy of Management Executive,* August 1998, p. 56.

37. Sandra L. Kirmeyer and Thomas W. Dougherty, "Work Load, Tension, and Coping: Moderating Effects of Supervisor Support," *Personnel Psychology,* Spring 1988, pp. 125–139.

38. Kathryn Tyler, "Cut the Stress," *HR Magazine,* May 2003, p. 101.

39. Jerald Greenberg, "Stress: Fairness to Fare No Stress: Managing Workplace Stress by Promoting Organizational Justice," *Organizational Dynamics, 4* (2004), pp. 352–363.

40. The framework for this section is from Janina C. Latack, "Coping with Job Stress: Measures and Future Directions for Scale Development," *Journal of Applied Psychology,* August 1986, pp. 522–526.

41. Reported in "A Conversation with Mind/Body Researcher Herbert Benson," "Are You Working Too Hard?" *Harvard Business Review*, November 2005, p. 54.

42. Bruce Cyer, Rolling McCraty, and Doc Childre, "Pulling the Plug on Stress," *Harvard Business Review*, July 2003, pp. 102–107; http://www.HeartMath.org, 2006.

313

14

Organization Structure and Design

In August 2005, five state emergency managers brought a tough message to a meeting in Washington with Homeland Security Secretary Michael Chertnoff and his top deputies. "We told them straight out that they were weakening emergency management with potentially disastrous consequences," says Davie Liebersbach, the director of Alaska's Division of Homeland Security & Emergency Services. The department's focus on terrorism was undermining its readiness for other catastrophes, said the visiting officials—who included emergency managers from Mississippi and Alabama.

With the Gulf Coast flooded and New Orleans in ruins, the question ricocheting around the world and the nation was: How could the world's largest superpower fail so badly in protecting and rescuing its residents from a natural disaster so frequently foretold?

The answer was to receive intense scrutiny in Congress and around the nation. "We are going to take a hard, hard look at our disaster response procedures," said Republican Majority Leader Bill Frist of Tennessee, as he assisted patients in the New Orleans Airport.

A preliminary analysis revealed that a major problem was the decision to transform the Federal Emergency Management Agency (FEMA) from a cabinet-level agency reporting directly to the president to just one agency within the gargantuan Department of Homeland Security, which diluted FEMA's effectiveness at preparing for natural disasters.

Source: Robert Block, Amy Schatz, Gary Fields, and Christine Cooper, "Hard, Hard Look: Behind Katrina Response, A Long Chain of Weak Links," *The Wall Street Journal*, September 6, 2005, p. A1.

OBJECTIVES

After reading and studying this chapter and doing the exercises, you should be able to:

1. Identify and define the foundation concepts of organization structure, including the informal organization.

2. Specify the basic features of the bureaucratic form of organization structure, including how it is divided into departments.

3. Describe two key modifications of a bureaucratic structure: matrix and flat.

4. Describe the nature of outsourcing and how it influences organization structure.

5. Describe the two contemporary organization designs referred to as horizontal structures and network structures.

6. Specify the criteria for an effective organization design.

Now Ask Yourself: **What is the point of this story about weak disaster preparedness?** It illustrates how organization structure influences organizational behavior. Buried deep within a gargantuan bureaucracy, FEMA had lost the flexibility and nimbleness necessary to move quickly and intelligently when disaster strikes. In this chapter, we describe organization structure because understanding structure is part of organizational behavior. Structure and behavior influence each other. For example, a loose organization structure, such as a collection of teams, requires employees to work productively without the benefit of close supervision. In contrast, some employees need careful guidelines for conducting their work, and therefore need a tighter structure, such as a bureaucracy.

Another example of how structure influences behavior is that workers are shaped by their positions.[1] Some workers are seen as being mean and uncaring when it is really their position that dictates their behavior, such as a government case worker refusing welfare payments to an applicant who has not submitted the necessary paper work. Also, an executive who lays off 1000 workers might seem heartless, yet his or her position demands taking extreme steps to earn a profit.

The purpose of this chapter is to understand the various types of organization structures and factors that influence the structure for a given purpose. Three terms need to be clarified first. An **organization** is a collection of people working together to achieve a common purpose (or simply a big group). **Organization structure** is the arrangement of people and tasks to accomplish organizational goals. The structure is usually indicated on the organization chart, along with specifying who reports to whom. **Organization design** is the process of creating a structure that best fits a purpose, strategy, and environment. For example, a giant motor company like Ford Motors emphasizes organization by product, such as having a separate division for Jaguar Motors.

FOUNDATION CONCEPTS OF ORGANIZATION STRUCTURE

Identify and define the foundation concepts of organization structure, including the informal organization.

Organizations are so complex that many different variables are required to describe them, similar to describing people or machines. To get started understanding how organizations are structured, we look at five key concepts: mechanistic versus organic, formal versus informal, degree of formalization, degree of centralization, and complexity. You will observe that several concepts about organization structure overlap, thereby simplifying the understanding of organizations.

Mechanistic versus Organic

A major variable for understanding organization structure is whether it is mechanistic or organic. A **mechanistic organization** is primarily hierarchical, with an emphasis on specialization and control and vertical communication and a heavy reliance on rules, policies, and procedures. An old-fashioned manufacturing organization such as the General Motors of yesteryear is an example of a mechanistic organization. The Coca-Cola Company of today is also a mechanistic organization. The term *mechanistic* has become synonymous with the term *bureaucracy*.

An **organic structure** is laid out like a network and emphasizes horizontal specialization, extensive use of personal coordination, and extensive communication among members, with loose rules, policies, and procedures. Knowledge resides wherever it is most useful to the organization. Organic structures are known for their responsiveness to a changing environment. A small high-tech start-up would be an example of an organic structure. Also, a shop that makes custom racing cars would have an organic form.

Formal versus Informal Structure

Understanding the difference between the formal and informal structure is akin to understanding the difference between formal and informal groups, as described in Chapter 9. The **formal organization structure** is an official statement of reporting relationships, rules, and regulations. The rules and regulations are designed to cover all the events and transactions that are likely to take place in conducting the business of the organization. For example, the formal organization structure tells managers how to respond to employee requests for a leave of absence to acquire an education or what to do with damaged parts from vendors.

The **informal organization structure** is a set of unofficial working relationships that emerges to take care of the events and transactions not covered by the formal structure. The informal structure supplements the formal structure by adding a degree of flexibility and speed. A widespread application of the informal structure is the presence of "tech fixers" in most firms, who supplement the technical support center. For example, marketing assistant Rick might be skilled at resolving Internet-related problems. As a consequence, many people call on Rick for some quick assistance even though the formal organization indicates that they should use the tech support center for help with Internet problems.

Another perspective on the informal organization structure is that all companies have hidden shadow organizations where much of the real work gets accomplished. The shadow organization is revealed by social network analysis, which traces who talks to whom, who listens, and how most of the information and influence really flows. Consultants Ernst & Ernst LLP reported finding opportunities to save a large auto industry supplier more than $14 million by using social network analysis to uncover inefficient communication that was deterring innovation.[2]

Social network analysis reveals the informal social relationships and the unofficial communication channels, so it also helps in understanding informal groups and informal communication channels. Tracking the informal relationships within an organization can help explain how and why new hires either succeed or fail to assimilate into the corporate culture. Workers who connect to the right information flow will perform better because of the connections they make.

Network mappers begin by surveying company employees to find answers to several key questions. The basic one is, "To whom do you go for information about what's going on?" Other questions are asked about the frequency of interaction or are used to differentiate between requests for information and requests for influence. Based on the answers, the mappers draw diagrams that graphically show who is connected to whom.[3]

Social network analysis can benefit managers by revealing if people are getting the information they need to perform their jobs well. The same analysis can point to which employees are in the best position to disseminate useful information to other workers.

Degree of Formalization

The dimension of **formalization** is the degree to which expectations regarding the methods of work are specified, committed to writing, and enforced. The more policies, rules, and procedures there are specifying how people should behave, the more formalized the organization. An organization with a high degree of formalization is likely to have a high degree of specialization of labor and high delegation of authority. A more formal organization is more mechanistic and bureaucratic. A motor vehicle bureau usually has a high degree of formalization, especially in dealing with the public. (People cannot order vanity license plates without paying a fee, no matter how sweetly they ask!) A specific example of formalization would be a company allocating specific meal allowances rather than permitting business travelers to be reimbursed for whatever meal expenses they incur.

Degree of Centralization

Centralization refers to the extent to which executives delegate authority to lower organizational units. The smaller the amount of delegation, the more centralized the organization. In a decentralized firm, however, some decisions are more centralized than others. Strategic decisions—those involving the overall functioning of the firm—are more likely to be centralized than operational decisions. An organization that relies heavily on functional (specialized) units will be more centralized because top management needs to coordinate the functions of the various units.

Domino's Pizza is a highly centralized firm. Company headquarters makes all the major decisions about matters such as the menu and décor of its establishments, the quality of its products, and the speed of its deliveries. An example of a highly decentralized firm is Tyco, a worldwide collection of loosely associated business firms (a conglomerate) engaged in both manufacturing and services. CEOs of the affiliated companies have considerable latitude in running their businesses, yet must meet financial targets set by headquarters.

Decentralization helps make large organizations more democratic because more managers throughout the company have more decision-making authority. Yet decentralization can lead to duplication of effort and high costs. For many years General Motors Corp. granted executives in places like Australia and Sweden considerable autonomy over the design of new vehicle models. GM recently reversed that policy by insisting that its worldwide units cooperate to design vehicles that can be sold, with minor variation, anywhere on the globe. A specific example is that GM wanted to reduce the types of radios it uses in its cars to 50 from 270, resulting in a savings of 40% in radio costs.[4]

The accompanying Organizational Behavior in Action box illustrates how tweaking a decentralized firm is sometimes necessary to encourage cooperation among the various units.

Complexity

Complexity refers to the number of different job titles and organizational units. Large organizations often have hundreds of departments and thousands of job titles. In a complex organization, many of the job titles are esoteric, such as "risk analyst," "contract administrator," and "fleet manager." The more complex the organization, the more difficult it is to manage. Complexity typically increases in direct proportion to size. Small organizations have fewer job titles and departments.

The concept of *differentiation* is closely linked to complexity. A horizontally differentiated organization has many different job titles, and many different departments doing separate work, whereas a vertically differentiated organization has many levels. A giant bureaucracy such as Citigroup has considerable horizontal and vertical differentiation.

ORGANIZATIONAL BEHAVIOR *In Action*

Major Advertising Firm Modifies Organization Structure to Enhance Cooperation among Units

In a move that challenges the traditional notions about how ad agencies are structured, WPP Group's Young & Rubicam Advertising (Y&R) is eliminating its regional fiefdoms and streamlining its operations.

The organization currently is made up of six North American offices in major cities that each operate as a separate company. Y&R is taking down such borders, challenging the agency model that exists at most large U.S. ad firms. The expectation is that a shared bottom line will spur cooperation among the agencies and prevent the bickering and internal competition that often hamper agency performance. The move runs counter to the way most ad firms are structured and comes as clients are increasingly questioning the ad-agency model, looking instead for nimble firms that can serve them in the quickly changing media landscape.

"Having worked on the business side, I know you have to push creative ideas beyond the television set," says Y&R Chairman and Chief Executive Ann Fudge, a former Kraft Foods executive. Fudge is creating a special team

of five Y&R executives who will work with all Y&R clients. The group, dubbed the Catalyst Team, will help offer clients business ideas that go well beyond the traditional 30-second ad—something clients increasingly are demanding of their agencies.

The restructuring is the boldest move yet by Fudge, who joined the agency 2 years ago. One new-business consultant was impressed by the changes. "It's about time ad agencies woke up to being clientcentric and not egocentric," says Linda Fidelman, the head of a New York firm that counsels marketers on ad-agency relationships.

Questions

1. In what way does the restructuring of Y&R represent a move in the direction of centralization?
2. How will the Catalyst Team contribute to centralization?

Source: Excerpted from Suzanne Vranica, "Y&R Streamlines Against the Flow: Agency Drops Office Borders In Challenge to Model Used at Other Big U.S. Shops," *The Wall Street Journal,* July 29, 2004, p. B3.

THE BUREAUCRATIC FORM OF ORGANIZATION

Specify the basic features of the bureaucratic form of organization structure, including how it is divided into departments.

As already implied, a **bureaucracy** is a rational, systematic, and precise form of organization in which rules, regulations, and techniques of control are precisely defined. *Bureau* is the French word for office, indicating that a bureaucracy is a form of organization with many different offices. Exhibit 14-1 depicts the basic concept of the bureaucratic form of organization. A bureaucracy was conceived of by Max Weber to be the ideal organization, having the following characteristics:

- Rules and procedures controlling organizational activities
- A high degree of differentiation among organizational functions
- A high degree of job specialization
- An organization of offices determined by hierarchy, with each unit reporting to a higher unit and no unit free-floating
- A heavy emphasis on rules and norms to regulate behavior
- Interpersonal relations characterized by impersonality in place of favoritism

Exhibit **14-1**

The Bureaucratic Form of Organization

In a bureaucracy, power is concentrated at the top. Note that team leaders are typically found at the first level or middle level of management.

- Selection and promotion based on merit
- All administrative actions recorded in writing[5]

The ideal organization just described is called a **machine bureaucracy,** because it standardizes work processes and is efficient. It is best suited to large organizations whose work is largely performed by production, technical, and support workers. In contrast, a **professional bureaucracy,** composed of a core of highly trained professionals, standardizes skills for coordination. Professional bureaucracies include organizations such as accounting firms, consulting firms, hospitals, and universities. Because it is difficult to regulate the work of professionals performing complex work, the professional bureaucracy decentralizes decision making and is less formal than a machine bureaucracy. The professional bureaucracy is relatively flat, with considerable differentiation across units.[6]

In visualizing a typical bureaucracy, it appears that one person is in charge of every function, including running the enterprise. In reality, authority is shared to some extent in top-level positions. You will recall the existence of top management teams as described in Chapter 10, in which major executives share responsibility for directing an enterprise. A dual-executive team is becoming more frequent in major corporations. A company founder will often divest day-to-day responsibilities to another executive so that the former can concentrate more on strategy and building relationships with the outside world.

Dividing up executive responsibilities in one position is now referred to as **two in a box.** Two managers are given the same responsibilities and the same title, and are expected to divide the work of the job between them. Among the companies using the two-in-a box approach are Intel, Goldman Sachs Group, Dell, and Cisco systems. When the technique is used carefully, it can ease the transition from one leader to another, allowing the new incumbent to learn from the more experienced executive. When a position calls for extensive global travel, one executive can be on hand to take care of daily issues, while the other is conducting business in another country. Two in a box also allows for skill division. For example, one executive might concentrate on technical decisions while the other concentrates on business decisions.

The two-in-a-box arrangement carries risks, including confusion, conflicting objectives, and clashing egos.[7] Paying two executives to accomplish the same job is also a major financial investment unless they both agree to half-pay. Kraft Foods Inc. gave up on the idea of sharing the CEO position and then returned to relying on one CEO, partially because outstanding results were not forthcoming.

Before reading about the good and bad side of bureaucracy, do the accompanying self-assessment quiz. It will help you assess how well you might fit into a bureaucracy.

SELF-ASSESSMENT

The Bureaucratic Orientation Scale

Directions: Answer each question "mostly agree" (MA) or "mostly disagree" (MD). Assume the mindset of attempting to learn something about yourself rather than attempting to impress a prospective employer.

	MA	MD
1. I value stability in my job.	☐	☐
2. I like a predictable organization.	☐	☐
3. I enjoy working without the benefit of a carefully specified job description.	☐	☐
4. I would enjoy working for an organization in which promotions are generally determined by seniority.	☐	☐
5. Rules, policies, and procedures tend to frustrate me.	☐	☐
6. I would enjoy working for a company that employed 95,000 people worldwide.	☐	☐
7. Being self-employed would involve more risk than I'm willing to take.	☐	☐
8. Before accepting a job, I would like to see an exact job description.	☐	☐
9. I would prefer a job as a freelance Web designer to one as a supervisor for the Department of Motor Vehicles.	☐	☐
10. Seniority should be as important as performance in determining pay increases and promotion.	☐	☐
11. It would give me a feeling of pride to work for the largest and most successful company in its field.	☐	☐
12. Given a choice, I would prefer to make $125,000 per year as a vice president in a small company than $150,000 per year as middle manager in a large company.	☐	☐
13. I would feel uncomfortable if I was to wear an employee badge with a number on it.	☐	☐
14. Parking spaces in a company lot should be assigned according to job level.	☐	☐
15. I would generally prefer working as a specialist instead of performing many different tasks.	☐	☐
16. Before accepting a job, I would want to make sure that the company has a good program of employee benefits.	☐	☐
17. A company will not be successful unless it establishes a clear set of rules and regulations.	☐	☐
18. Regular working hours and vacation are more important to me than finding thrills on the job.	☐	☐
19. You should respect people according to their rank.	☐	☐
20. Rules are meant to be broken.	☐	☐

Scoring and Interpretation: Give yourself one point for each question that you answered in the bureaucratic direction:

1. Mostly agree	8. Mostly agree	15. Mostly disagree
2. Mostly agree	9. Mostly disagree	16. Mostly agree
3. Mostly disagree	10. Mostly agree	17. Mostly agree
4. Mostly agree	11. Mostly agree	18. Mostly agree
5. Mostly disagree	12. Mostly disagree	19. Mostly agree
6. Mostly agree	13. Mostly disagree	20. Mostly disagree
7. Mostly agree	14. Mostly agree	

15–20: You would enjoy working in a bureaucracy.

8–14: You would experience a mixture of satisfaction and dissatisfaction if you were working in a bureaucracy.

0–7: You would most likely be frustrated by working in a bureaucracy, especially a large one.

Source: Updated from *Human Relations: A Job Oriented Approach,* 5th ed., by Andrew J. DuBrin ©1988. Reprinted by permission of Pearson Education, Inc., Upper Saddle River, NJ.

The Contribution of Bureaucracy

Bureaucratic forms of organization have persisted because, used properly, they make possible large-scale accomplishments that cannot be achieved by small groups of people working independently. The Social Security Administration is an example of a large bureaucracy that accomplishes an astonishing amount of work each month in paying benefits to approximately 60 million Americans. Elliot Jacques has aptly expressed the contribution of bureaucracy:

> Thirty-five years of research has convinced me that managerial hierarchy (or bureaucracy) is the most efficient, hardiest, and in fact the most natural structure ever devised for large corporations. Properly structured, hierarchy can release energy, creativity, and rational productivity and actually improve morale.[8]

An analysis by Paul S. Adler also points to the important contributions of bureaucracy. One of his major arguments is that slashing bureaucracy can backfire. Many firms have discovered that the layers of managers eliminated to reduce bureaucracy are often the repository of precious skills and expertise.[9] After many middle manager positions have been eliminated, their loss is recognized and regretted.

A similar argument is that dumping the policies and procedures characteristic of a bureaucracy can weaken an organization. In many cases, these procedures embody a vast organizational memory of best practices. Having tossed out the manuals, many organizations discover that their employees are frustrated because they have to improvise with little guidance. A lot of time is wasted in reinventing and redeveloping useful procedures that have been discarded. For example, a newly appointed credit manager might not have a policy for dealing with a long-term, reliable customer who suddenly becomes delinquent with payments.

The hierarchical form of organization called bureaucracy emerged from necessity. It is the only form of organization that enables a firm to employ large numbers of people and still hold them clearly accountable for their results. Bureaucracy is also important for the emotional reason that it fulfills our deep need for order and security.[10] As an employee, it is comforting to know that there is an efficient system in place to deposit your pay directly into your bank twice per month, and that if the fluorescent bulb in your office burns out, you know which office (bureau!) to call.

Potential Dysfunctions of a Bureaucracy

Not all bureaucracies work as Max Weber intended. The major problem is that members of the bureaucracy often carry out its characteristics to the extreme. Organizations that rely heavily on formal controls to direct people sometimes suppress initiative and decision making at lower levels of management. Too many controls and too much review of decisions can also lower productivity. A bureaucracy is subject to rigidity in handling people and problems. Although a bureaucratic design is supposed to hold people accountable for results, some people in large bureaucracies tend to *pass the buck,* or claim that a particular problem is the responsibility of another department or person. A bureaucracy's well-intended rules and regulations sometimes create inconvenience and inefficiency.

A major problem within large bureaucracies is that they are clumsy and slow, often prompting companies to go outside when they need something done in a hurry, such as developing a prototype of a new product. (As described later, almost all bureaucracies have built-in structures to overcome the slowness problem.) Business writer Keith H. Hammonds has expressed the extreme negative view of large bureaucracies as inefficient and monolithic entities: "Big companies are broken. Nearly a century old, the modern business organization is nearing the end of its useful life. The old model is dying."[11] (Has Hammonds visited a Wal-Mart lately?)

Even hugely successful business firms often fall victim to the problems associated with bureaucracy. As Microsoft Corp. hit 30 years of age, it transformed quite naturally into a large, complex organization. According to one analysis, the company's growing pains have delayed product introductions, leaving the door open for Microsoft to be beaten to market by younger, more nimble competitors like Google and Yahoo. Among the specific bureaucratic problems have been miscommunication and different units working on overlapping technology without adequate cooperation.[12] We will explain later how Microsoft has changed its structure to deal with these problems.

Another frequent problem in a bureaucracy is high frustration accompanied by low satisfaction. The sources of these negative feelings include red tape, slow decision making, and an individual's limited influence on how well the organization performs.

Two Types of Departmentalization

In bureaucratic and other forms of organization, the work is subdivided into departments or other units. The departmentalization capitalizes on the classic bureaucratic principle of specialization and also helps avoid confusion. Can you imagine the chaos if all the workers in an organization of more than 50 people worked in one large department? The process of subdividing work into departments is called **departmentalization.**

Here we will use charts to illustrate two frequently used forms of departmentalization: functional and product/service. Most organization charts show a combination of these two types, along with other forms of departmentalization, such as dividing into geographic regions.

Functional Departmentalization

Functional departmentalization involves grouping people according to their expertise. Bureaucracies are almost always organized into functional departments. Within a given department, the work may be further subdivided. For instance, finance may include subunits for accounts receivable, accounts payable, and payroll. The names of functional departments vary widely with the nature of the business or enterprise. Exhibit 14-2 illustrates a representative type of functional structure. The advantages and disadvantages of functional departmentalization follow those of a bureaucracy.

Exhibit 14-2

Functional Departmentalization within the Davenport Machine Company

Observe that each box below the level of chief executive officer (CEO) indicates an executive in charge of a specific function or activity, such as having responsibility for sales and marketing.

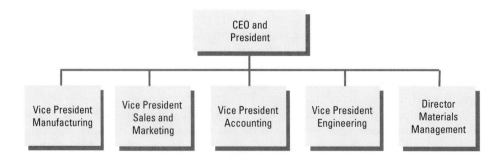

Product/Service Departmentalization

Product/service departmentalization is the arrangement of departments according to the products or services they provide. When specific products or services are so important they almost become independent companies, product departmentalization makes sense. Exhibit 14–3 presents a version of product/service departmentalization at Microsoft. In 2005, top-level management at Microsoft created a streamlined product and service organization by dividing Microsoft's business into three major units. The reorganization had two major purposes. One was to compete more effectively with companies using the Internet to deliver software and related services. For example, MSN could be used as a mechanism for distributing future Windows features. The second purpose was to hasten decision making in a company of 60,000 employees. The intent was to push decision making further down into the organization.[13] Another purpose of the new structure was to help the company reestablish its nimbleness, while at the same time encouraging cooperation among the various product divisions. You will recall that the new structure at Y&R had the same goal in mind.

Line versus Staff Units

In Chapter 13, line and staff groups were mentioned in relation to conflict. Line and staff groups are present in most forms of departmentalization, yet the organization chart rarely makes such designations. In Exhibit 14-2, the manufacturing, sales and marketing, and materials management units would all be considered line units. The accounting and engineering groups would *sometimes* be considered staff groups. If a sixth box were added, human resources, we would definitely have a staff group.

The distinction between line and staff is often blurred. (Line groups are responsible for the primary purposes of the firm, whereas staff groups are responsible for the secondary purposes.) Members of some departments are not sure if they are perceived as line or staff by top management, and this leads to role ambiguity. A marketing executive said, "The key purpose of our firm is to provide goods to customers. Yet when cutbacks take place, marketing people get chopped first. It makes no sense to me."

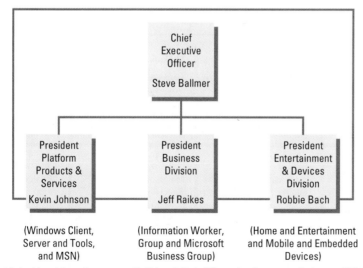

Exhibit 14-3

Product and Service Organization Structure at Microsoft

323

Sources: Chart derived from information presented in Robert A. Guth, "Microsoft to Restructure Businesses," *The Wall Street Journal,* September 21, 2005, pp. A3, A5; http://www.microsoft.com.; Allison Linn, "Microsoft Realigns Execs as Windows Update Lags," The Associated Press, March 24, 2006. As with any organization chart, the arrangement of people and the names of units are subject to frequent change.

KEY MODIFICATIONS OF THE BUREAUCRATIC STRUCTURE

Describe two key
modifications of a
bureaucratic structure:
matrix and flat.

To overcome several of the disadvantages of the bureaucratic and functional forms of organization, several other structures have developed. Typically these less bureaucratic structures are used to supplement or modify the bureaucratic structure. Teams, as described in Chapter 10 in the context of job design, have emerged as the most widely used supplement to the bureaucratic structure. In the Organizational Behavior in Action scenario of the advertising firm, the Catalyst Team was formed to provide advice to clients beyond what the various divisions of the agency might be offering. Task forces and projects follow a similar departure from bureaucracy as do teams. Here we describe the matrix organization structure and the flat structure as organizational arrangements.

Matrix Organization Structure

Traditional organizations can be slow to respond to change. A frequently used antidote to this problem is the **matrix organization structure,** which consists of a project structure superimposed on a functional structure. A **project** is a temporary group of specialists working together under one manager to accomplish a fixed objective, such as launching a major new product. The word *matrix* refers to the feature of something contained in something else, similar to a grid with numbers in the cells (Exhibit 14-4).

The distinguishing feature of the matrix organization is the responsibility of the project or program manager to achieve results through employees who also report directly to another manager or have dual reporting responsibilities. For example, a person assigned to a project in a matrix organization might report to both the project manager and the manager in his or her regular department.

Exhibit **14-4**

*Matrix Organization in
an Electronics Company*

*In a matrix organization,
a project structure is
superimposed on a
functional structure.*

324

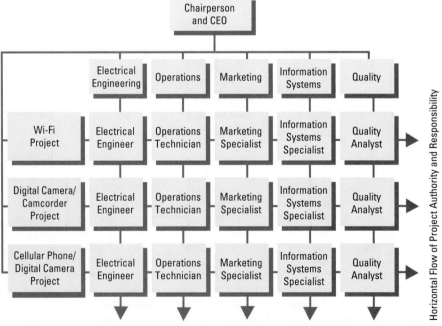

A major purpose of the matrix organization is to allow the firm to take advantage of new opportunities and solve special problems. Instead of developing a new organization containing functional departments, the firm leaves the original organization intact. The project or program managers within the matrix structure have access to the resources of the functional departments. A key advantage of the matrix organization is its ability to implement important projects that demand intense, sustained attention for a limited time. It has been used, for example, to build a prototype for an e-commerce system. On the negative side, the matrix structure often creates problems because people assigned to projects within the matrix have a dual reporting relationship.

The matrix organization highlights the importance of project structures, because projects are embedded in the matrix. In recent years, projects have been elevated in status because they are used to accomplish important goals, such as launching a new product or diversifying a workforce culturally. The position of project manager is also seen as excellent training and experience for growth into higher management.[14] To be an effective project manager, the individual must use a high level of interpersonal skill (such as the ability to resolve conflict) as well as technical skill to achieve goals. The project manager needs good technical skills because he or she interacts directly with skilled professionals, and must also provide technical input to decisions.

Flat Organization Structures and Downsizing

A **flat organization structure** is one that has relatively few layers. A flat structure is less bureaucratic for two reasons. First, few managers in this form of organization are available to review the decisions of other people. As a by-product, customer service is often improved because many customer problems can be resolved without waiting for layers of approval. Second, because the chain of command is shorter, there is less concern about authority differences among people. Most large organizations have moved toward flatter structures, continuing a trend that began over 25 years ago. Part of the success of Samsung Electronics Company has been attributed to its flat structure. Samsung uses a lean corporate structure with considerable authority delegated to front-line managers around the world.[15]

Small and medium-size businesses have held on to their traditionally flat structures, which are usually imposed by not having enough money to build management depth. To minimize the number of managers needed to run a business, small businesses often rely on information technology to supply workers with all the information they need instead of consulting with a supervisor. Yet with organizations of all types, too little hierarchy may lead to decisions not getting made or made wrongly by employees who lack the appropriate experience, motivation, and accountability to do the work of missing managers.[16]

Flatter organization structures created by downsizing lead to greater organizational efficiency about half the time. GE, one of the world's most successful companies, has downsized by over 100,000 workers in the past two decades. A controversial aspect of flat structures created by downsizing is that they result in substantial human suffering. Even when jobs are plentiful, losing a job can result in considerable emotional turmoil for the individual. Survivors of the downsizing also experience problems, such as guilt. On a larger scale, when large numbers of companies and government agencies downsize, a recession is perpetuated because fewer people have strong purchasing power. A continuing recession leads to more job insecurity and more layoffs, intensifying human suffering. More will be said about the problems associated with downsizing as a change strategy in Chapter 16.

An important implication for managers when creating flat structures is to deal with the human element. A study about downsizing concluded that maintaining an open dialogue with employees and providing them with opportunities to affirm themselves in a positive manner helps eliminate some of the negative outcomes that accompany layoffs.[17]

OUTSOURCING AS AN ORGANIZATIONAL ARRANGEMENT

Describe the nature of outsourcing and how it influences organization structure.

Log on to **www.thomsonedu .com/infotrac**. Locate recent articles on the outsourcing of white-collar work. Where are most of the jobs going and what are the reasons for sending them there?

A widespread practice among organizations of all types and sizes is to **outsource,** or have work performed for them by other organizations. When the work is performed by a company in an overseas location, the process is often referred to as **offshoring.** Outsourcing, including offshoring, is an integral part of the globalization of business. Instead of performing all the manufacturing or service work domestically, the global enterprise has some of the work performed in other countries. An overseas call center is an example of the globalization of service.

Outsourcing is linked to organization structure because it is a method of dividing work: Certain activities are assigned to groups outside the organization. Another way of framing outsourcing is that it is a vast network of interconnected enterprises that depend on one another for services. By outsourcing, a company can reduce its need for employees and physical assets and reduce payroll costs. Many firms outsource the development and start-up phases of their e-commerce units to outside information technology consultants.

Here we describe three aspects of outsourcing that impact human behavior in organizations: the scope of outsourcing, its time zone advantages, and homesourcing.

The Scope of Outsourcing

Outsourcing has advanced so far that some companies do little more than develop an idea for a product, with product development, manufacturing, and marketing being done by other firms. Performing outsourced work for other companies has become an industry of its own, including companies that fulfill orders for online stores (e-tailers). United Parcel Service (UPS) exemplifies how far outsourcing has advanced. The world's largest delivery company provides a wide variety of services for other companies through its subsidiary, UPS Supply Chain Solutions. The services other companies outsource to UPS include performing emergency electronic repairs, fixing laptops, installing giant x-ray machines, operating customer-service hotlines, packaging consumer electronics, and issuing corporate credit cards. The type of work Supply Chain provides lends itself to domestic outsourcing because much of the work is needed urgently. UPS stores every conceivable part in its giant warehouse in Louisville, Kentucky, so that it can perform repairs quickly. The highly regarded brand name UPS has facilitated the growth of the outsourcing business.[18]

Even activities as complex as research and the design of products are sometimes outsourced. A company might design its own core product and have less important products designed by another firm. The purpose of outsourcing design is to have products designed at high speed and low cost by a smaller firm—one with an organic structure! Even the manufacture of luxury goods is sometimes outsourced; for example, part of the Giorgio Armani collection is constructed in Eastern Europe rather than Italy.

Much to the chagrin of labor unions and local workers, many companies outsource work to geographic areas where workers are paid lower wages. Among the many examples of outsourcing would be for a small company to hire another company to manage its payroll and employee benefits and for a large manufacturing firm to have certain components made by another firm. Even IBM is a contractor for other employers—for example, IBM makes the hard drives for other computer manufacturers or manage other companies' computer systems. A new thrust in outsourcing is for U.S. firms to send white-collar professional jobs overseas, including software development and financial services. In the 4 years following the recession of 2001–2002, the information technology industry in the United States had seen very little job growth.[19] Overall, the outsourcing movement has been a boon for small and medium-size firms who perform stable work for larger organizations.

A key implication of outsourcing as an organization design strategy is that people over whom you have no direct control perform work for your company. Other managers are responsible for leading and managing employees who perform important functions for the organization. A frequent concern in the clothing, toy, and consumer electronics industries is that subcontractors sometimes engage in unsavory practices, such as violating wage and child-labor laws. Outsourcing has led to sweatshops, as smaller firms compete to offer the lowest possible price for manufacturing goods. Outsourcing can therefore create ethical dilemmas.

Another key human aspect of outsourcing is that it breeds conflict over which functions should be outsourced. Labor unions vehemently oppose a company sending jobs to lower-wage countries in order to save money, which results in job loss for union members. Department heads within a company fight to defend themselves against being outsourced, such as outsourcing the training function of the human resources department. Another example would be the head of a software development unit in a U.S. company struggling against a plan to outsource software development to an Indian company. Proponents of global outsourcing argue that it enables the domestic company to remain competitive, thereby saving jobs. Also, many overseas companies, such as Toyota, export thousands of jobs to other countries, including the United States.

Time Zone Advantages of Outsourcing

When knowledge work needs to be performed in a sequence, with one person or group building on the output of the previous person or group, outsourcing offers a unique advantage. While one group is off duty, another group in a different time zone in a distant country prepares the input the first group will need by the morning. A more complex possibility is that work can be performed in sequence across three time zones. A person in one time zone collects the data for a key report and transmits the data to a person in the next time zone, who translates the data into PowerPoint slides. The slides and backup data are then transmitted to a third person in another time zone, who prepares the final report. Instead of the project taking three work days, it is all accomplished within 24 hours.

As mysterious as this aspect of globalization appears, it is not much different in concept from night shift workers, handing over their input in the morning to day shift workers. On an international level, here is an example: Sandra, a virtual team member in Boston finishes her part of a project at 5 P.M. EST. She sends her output to Ben, a team member in Seoul, South Korea, and it arrives 7 A.M. his time. Ben finishes his contribution to the project at 3 P.M. his time, and sends his output to Claire, a member of the virtual team, at 7 A.M. Paris time. Claire finishes her work and sends it back to Sandra at 5 P.M. Paris time, and it arrives at Sandra's desktop 11 A.M. EST, so she can have the input before noon. (All this is very confusing, but international workers keep several clocks with different time zones going at the same time.) The general idea is that workers across the globe can collaborate 24/7, even if the time zones do not match precisely.

Homesourcing Instead of Offshoring

Offshoring has its problems, such as the language barrier of the call-center workers not speaking English in a manner comprehensible to English-speaking people in the United States. A similar problem is not understanding the culture, such as the caller making reference to a major sporting events or an athletic team. Another challenge is coordinating and managing the work of people in another county. To deal with this problem, many firms, including Office Depot and Sears Holdings Corp., are outsourcing customer service work to people at home, referred to as **homesourcing.** Outsourcing to homes has been facilitated by expanded broadband access to the Web, less-expensive computer technology, and advanced call-routing systems. Home (or virtual) agents typically work for low pay, and no benefits, and have to deal with many irate customers.

The work of home agents is carefully monitored, and background noise such as dogs barking and children playing is usually not allowed. Nevertheless, the appeal of working at home is so strong for so many people that the industry is expanding rapidly. Virtual agents have considerable flexibility in their choice of when to work. About 70 to 80% of home agents have college degrees, in comparison to 30 to 40% of call-center workers. Turnover among home agents is much less than for their call-center counterparts.[20]

LEADING-EDGE ORGANIZATION STRUCTURES

Describe the two contemporary organization designs referred to as horizontal structures and network structures.

Spin-offs from traditional organization structures continue to emerge as organizations strive to improve their efficiency and effectiveness. A major reason for these changes is that a traditional mechanistic organization can be too cumbersome to respond to changes in the environment. Two leading-edge forms are the horizontal structure and the network organization.

The Horizontal Structure

A major current development in organization design is to work horizontally rather than vertically. A **horizontal structure** is the arrangement of work by teams that are responsible for accomplishing a process. The virtual organization is thereby similar to the establishment of work teams. A major difference, however, is that team members are responsible for a process rather than for a product or service. The difference is subtle; the team aims at delivering a product or service to a customer rather than focusing on the product or service itself. Instead of focusing on a specialized task, all team members focus on achieving the purpose of all the activity, such as getting a product in the hands of a customer. In a horizontal structure or process organization, employees take collective responsibility for customers.[21]

One approach to switching from a task emphasis to the process emphasis in a horizontal structure is through **reengineering,** the radical redesign of work to achieve substantial improvements in performance. Reengineering searches for the most efficient way to perform a large task. The emphasis is on uncovering wasted steps, such as people handing off documents to one another to obtain approval.

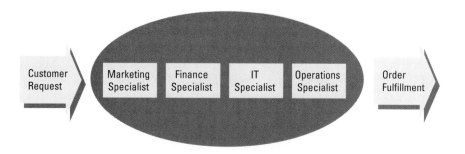

Exhibit **14-5**

A Horizontal Structure

In a horizontal structure, even though specialists are assigned to the team, they are expected to understand one another's tasks and to perform some of those tasks as needed.

Eliminating workers who perform nonessential tasks is another goal of reengineering. E-commerce can be considered a way of reengineering the work of sales representatives. If goods are exchanged over the Internet, the need for industrial sales representatives shrinks considerably. Also, fewer purchasing agents are needed because buying over the Internet is more efficient than speaking directly to sales representatives.

As a result of reengineering, work is usually organized horizontally rather than vertically. The people in charge of the process act as team leaders who guide the team toward the completion of an important core process, such as new product development or filling a complicated order. Key performance objectives for the team would include "reduce cycle time," "reduce costs," and "reduce throughput time." Exhibit 14-5 illustrates the horizontal structure, as do the projects embedded in the matrix organization shown in Exhibit 14-4.

A caution to managers and prospective managers is to recognize that the push toward the horizontal structures and reengineering should not be embraced without qualification. Having a "task mentality" is still important because expertise is crucial in many endeavors. A surgical team, for example, still relies on highly proficient specialists, such as a brain surgeon and an anesthetist. Also, wouldn't you prefer that a specialist had designed the operating system on your cell telephone when you need to call somebody to rescue you from a life-threatening situation?

The Network Structure

Another fast-growing development in organization structure is for organizations to affiliate with one another based on their need to share resources. Few companies have all the assets and resources in their firm to accomplish new endeavors. The best resources and talents are borrowed as needed. A **network structure (or virtual organization)** is a temporary association of otherwise independent firms that are linked by technology to share expenses, employee talents, and access to one another's markets.[22] Outsourcing is somewhat like forming a network structure, except that the relationship is more limited and contractual.

A pure network structure would have neither corporate headquarters nor an organization chart. Hierarchy would be sacrificed to speed of decision making, and vertical integration would be supplanted by horizontal integration across company boundaries. Each contributor to the network would stick to its core competency—what it does best, such as manufacturing a particular component, marketing the finished product, or new product development.

For most organizations, the network structure supplements the regular structure, much like a large project. Many large organizations have small units that use the network structure for forming strategic alliances with other companies. Digital cameras, for example, are typically the product of a strategic alliance among several companies. Strategic alliances are also formed to market products. For example, Xerox formed a strategic alliance with several office products stores to provide new channels through which customers can obtain many Xerox products. Also, many companies form partnerships with Internet portals to one another's advantage. A portal such as Yahoo! benefits because a link on the website of the partner drives traffic to the portal.

Proponents of the network structure see it as a fluid and flexible entity taking the form of a group of collaborators who link to capitalize on a specific opportunity. After the opportunity has been met, the venture will typically disband. However, some alliances and partnerships are relatively permanent. An essential requirement is that members of the alliance must trust one another. One incompetent or dishonest member of the network can ruin or severely damage the multiple venture. It is not uncommon for an overseas member of a strategic alliance to steal the other's technology and become a direct competitor.

The horizontal and virtual structures place additional demands on the interpersonal skills of the workers involved. Relationships tend to be more stable in a functional structure, whereas horizontal and virtual structures involve more temporary relationships. A person has to get up to speed quickly in establishing working relationships. Furthermore, the authority structure is less clear, so the individual may have to rely more on informal influence tactics. Personal power becomes more important than positional power.

THE CRITERIA FOR AN EFFECTIVE ORGANIZATION DESIGN

Specify the criteria for an effective organization design.

One way to integrate information about organization design is to specify what makes for an effective design. Based on their consulting and first-hand research, Michael Goold and Andrew Campbell conclude that most organization structures evolve in fits and starts, shaped more by organizational politics than policies.[23] An example of designing an organization on the basis of politics would be to have a minor functionary report directly to the CEO because the division head in question was a good friend of the CEO. Goold and Campbell present a number of tests that can be used to evaluate an existing design or create a new one. Here we look at the five *good design* tests, as outlined in Exhibit 14-6.

First comes the *specialist cultures test,* which asks, "Does your design protect units that need distinct cultures?" For example, the company might have a new-product development group that requires a highly organic design, as opposed to a more

Exhibit 14-6

Five Criteria for an Effective Organization Design

Good Design

1. Specialist Cultures
2. Difficult-Links
3. Redundant Hierarchy
4. Accountability
5. Flexibility

Well-Designed Organization

Source: Diagram developed from text information presented in Michael Goold and Andrew Campbell, "Do You Have a Well-Designed Organization?" *Harvard Business Review*, March 2002, pp. 117–124.

mechanistic design for the rest of the company. Next is the *difficult-links test,* which asks, "Does your design provide coordination solutions for the unit-to-unit links that are likely to be problematic?" Typically, the majority of these links are best handled through self-managed networking among the units. When the units do not link well, it might be necessary to have a clearly defined arbitration process for resolving disputes.

The *redundant hierarchy test* asks, "Does your design have too many parent levels and units?" An upper-level unit must add value to lower-level units (by at least 10%) to justify having that layer of management. The *accountability test* asks, "Does your design support effective controls?" (A control is a way of measuring performance against a standard.) Ensure that each unit is accountable for its results, and cannot blame poor performance on problems created by other units. Finally comes the *flexibility test,* which asks, "Does your design facilitate the development of new strategies and provide flexibility required to adapt to change?" See if your design would support the pursuit of future opportunities, such as having a business development unit that has the resources to research the future.

A management team would need to invest considerable time in investigating these five criteria for an effective organization design. Yet the result could be a superior design that would take into account both organization structure and human capabilities.

IMPLICATIONS FOR MANAGERIAL PRACTICE

1. An overriding decision in organization design is the choice between a mechanistic or an organic structure. Mechanistic structures are better suited to repetitive tasks in a stable environment, in which centralized control is desirable.
2. A design decision for a large organization is usually not an issue of mechanistic versus organic but instead choosing which units should be mechanistic and which should be organic.
3. Organization structure influences behavior in many ways. A key factor is that specialization can lead to job dissatisfaction and boredom for many workers. An exception is that some highly trained workers prefer to be superspecialists, such as a package designer.
4. Leading-edge organization designs are becoming increasingly popular. Managers and nonmanagers alike need high-level interpersonal skills to function effectively in such structures because they must often rely more on informal than formal authority.

Machado & Silvetti Associates, Inc.
Take a look at the Boston-based architectural firm Machado and Silvetti at **www .thomsonedu.com/ management/dubrin**. Please watch the video. Where would you place the firm on a continuum from mechanistic to organic? From formal to informal?

331

SUMMARY OF KEY POINTS

 Identify and define the foundation concepts of organization structure, including the informal organization. Organization structure is the arrangement of people and tasks to accomplish organizational goals, whereas organization design is the process of creating an appropriate structure. Mechanistic organizations are hierarchical, with an emphasis on special-

ization and control, as well as rules and regulations. In contrast, an organic structure is laid out like a network and is much looser. An informal organization emerges to take care of the events and transactions not covered by the formal structure. Social network analysis is useful in depicting the informal structure. The more formalized an organization, the more it is mechanistic and bureaucratic. The more centralized an organization, the more extensively top managers delegate responsibility. Organizations vary in their complexity, or differentiation among subunits.

 Specify the basic features of the bureaucratic form of organization structure, including how it is divided into departments.

A bureaucracy is a rational, systematic, and precise form of organization. In it, rules, regulations, and techniques of control are defined precisely. Properly used, bureaucracy allows for large-scale accomplishments. Problems associated with bureaucracy include suppression of initiative through overcontrol, high job frustration, and low job satisfaction. A bureaucracy can also be clumsy and slow.

Departmentalization is the grouping of work into manageable units. Two key forms of departmentalization are functional and product/service. Most firms use several types of departmentalization. The functional organization has both the advantages and disadvantages of a bureaucracy. Line and staff units are frequently built into a departmentalized structure.

 Describe two key modifications of a bureaucratic structure: matrix and flat.

Bureaucratic structures are commonly supplemented by organic, or highly adaptable, organizational units. A matrix structure consists of a project structure imposed on a functional structure. The matrix manager must achieve results through employees who are also responsible to another manager. A flat structure has relatively few layers, which speeds up decision making.

 Describe the nature of outsourcing and how it influences organization structure.

Outsourcing is an arrangement whereby one organization has work performed by another, including offshoring. Outsourcing is linked to structure because it is a method of dividing work. Outsourcing has advanced to the point at which performing work for other industries has become an industry of its own, and complex activities like research and design are outsourced. Outsourcing leads to conflict over lost jobs, and which jobs should be outsourced.

Outsourcing allows for completing segments of projects around the clock because of time zone differences among the countries where the work is performed. The homesourcing movement involves moving work into the homes of virtual agents. Although the work is low paid, the demand for these jobs is high.

 Describe the two contemporary organization designs referred to as horizontal structures and network structures.

Two leading-edge organization structures are the horizontal structure and the network structure. A horizontal structure arranges work by teams that are responsible for accomplishing a process. A network structure, or virtual corporation, is a temporary association of otherwise independent firms that join forces to exploit an opportunity. Each network member contributes its core competency.

 Specify the criteria for an effective organization design.

To produce a well-designed organization, managers are advised to answer five "good design" tests. The good design tests deal with specialist cultures, difficult links among the units, redundant hierarchy, accountability, and flexibility.

KEY TERMS AND PHRASES

Organization, 315
A collection of people working together to achieve a common purpose (or simply a big group).

Organization Structure, 315
The arrangement of people and tasks to accomplish organizational goals.

Organization Design, 315
The process of creating a structure that best fits a purpose, strategy, and environment.

Mechanistic Organization, 315
A primarily hierarchical organization with an emphasis on specialization and control and vertical communication and a heavy reliance on rules, policies, and procedures.

Organic Structure, 315
An organization laid out like a network, emphasizing horizontal specialization, extensive use of personal coordination, extensive communication among members, and loose rules, policies, and procedures.

Formal Organization Structure, 316
An official statement of reporting relationships, rules, and regulations.

Informal Organization Structure, 316
A set of unofficial working relationships that emerges to take care of the events and transactions not covered by the formal structure.

Formalization, 316
The degree to which expectations regarding the methods of work are specified, committed to writing, and enforced.

Centralization, 317
The extent to which executives delegate authority to lower organizational units.

Complexity, 317
The number of different job titles and units within an organization.

Bureaucracy, 318
A rational, systematic, and precise form of organization in which rules, regulations, and techniques of control are precisely defined.

Machine Bureaucracy, 319
An ideal organization that standardizes work processes and is efficient.

Professional Bureaucracy, 319
An organization composed of a core of highly trained professionals that standardizes skills for coordination.

Two in a Box, 319
Dividing up executive responsibilities in one position.

Departmentalization, 322
The process of subdividing work into departments.

Functional Departmentalization, 322
The grouping of people according to their expertise.

Product/Service Departmentalization, 323
The arrangement of departments according to the products or services they provide.

Matrix Organization Structure, 324
An organization consisting of a project structure superimposed on a functional structure.

Project, 324
A temporary group of specialists working together under one manager to accomplish a fixed objective.

Flat Organization Structure, 325
An organization structure with relatively few layers.

Outsource, 326
The practice of having work performed by groups outside the organization.

Offshoring, 326
The practice of having work performed by a company in an overseas location.

Homesourcing, 328
The practice of outsourcing work to homes.

Horizontal Structure, 328
The arrangement of work by teams that are responsible for accomplishing a process.

Reengineering, 328
The radical redesign of work to achieve substantial improvements in performance.

Network Structure (or Virtual Organization), 329
A temporary association of otherwise independent firms linked by technology to share expenses, employee talents, and access to one another's markets.

DISCUSSION QUESTIONS AND ACTIVITIES

1. Many readers of this textbook are not yet in a position to lay out an organization structure. How might they make use of information about organization structure and design?

2. Explain whether Starbucks (or choose Pizza Hut or McDonald's) is a mechanistic or an organic organization. Compare your answer with that of another student who has analyzed the same business.

3. What hints would you look for to analyze the degree of formalization in the company for which you were being interviewed?

4. Why do you think homesourcing jobs attract such a high percentage of people with college degrees?

5. Explain how a worker in an entry-level position could be a systems thinker.

6. Why is it that so many business owners who say they do not like bureaucracy nevertheless welcome large bureaucratic organizations, like DaimlerChrysler, as customers?

7. Microsoft, as well as several other information technology companies, advertise that its software systems make companies less bureaucratic. How might this claim be true?

CASE PROBLEM: The J&J Organization Design Team

You and several classmates are seated in a large conference room at the worldwide headquarters of Johnson & Johnson, the medical products giant. Chairman and CEO William C. Weldon addresses the group in a serious yet excited tone: "We are privileged to be here today at a historic moment in the history of J&J, the company we all love and admire. I say with confidence that there is not a person in this room, nor his or her loved ones, who have not used J&J products at some point in their life, perhaps even this week. Can anybody present today say he or she has never used a Band-Aid, or Johnson & Johnson Baby Powder? Is there anybody here who has never used Tylenol or Motrin?

"But I am not here to be sentimental. Rather, I am here to take action. We have a great company with one of the best brands in the world. Johnson & Johnson has been around a long time, and we have taken good care of our customers, employees, and stockholders. Our products have reduced human suffering and saved hundreds of thousands of lives. But I think we can do better.

"Please study our organization chart carefully. [Larsen begins a PowerPoint presentation of the organization structure, as shown in Exhibit 14-7.] As you students of organization structure and design can easily recognize, we emphasize a product structure because our products are so vital, and so distinguishable. We know, for example, that personal care products are a different animal from professional pharmaceuticals. Yet what I am asking this design team to do is give me a new organization structure. That's right—redesign the Johnson & Johnson worldwide organization structure. Give me a design by geographic region, give me a design by function. Or whatever else you can dream up. Do what you want.

"I and the other members of the executive team may not accept your first attempt at redesign, but at least we will be getting started in the direction of organization redesign. A great organization explores the possibility of change regularly. The breakout rooms are equipped with paper, pencils, transparency masters,

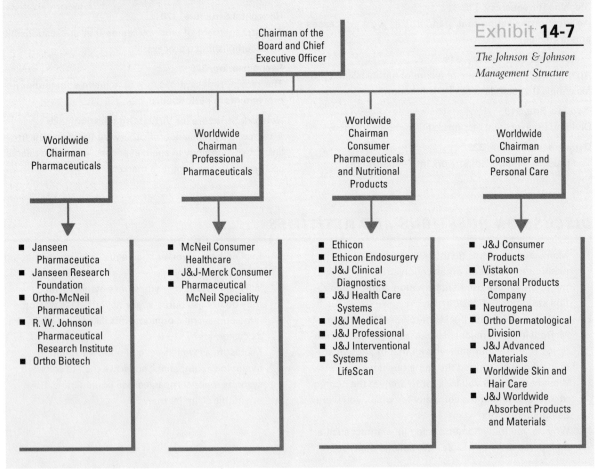

Exhibit 14-7

The Johnson & Johnson Management Structure

CASE PROBLEM (Continued)

laptop computers, and chalkboards. However, the message is more important than the medium. Bring me back your first efforts in 30 minutes."

Your Task

Draw a new organization structure for Johnson & Johnson (http://www.jnj.com) by working in a small group to discuss your redesign. Drawing your final design on a transparency for an overhead projector is often the easiest and quickest method. Sketching directly on a chalkboard or flip chart also works well. After the design teams have completed their tasks, a team leader presents the findings to the entire class. In this way, the various designs can be compared. Speculate about the potential advantage of your design over the existing design.

Collaboration

ENDNOTES

1. Interview by Shelia M. Puffer, "Changing Organizational Structures: An Interview with Rosabeth Moss Kanter," *Academy of Management Executive,* May 2004, p. 99.
2. Mark Henricks, "The Shadow Knows," *Entrepreneur,* January 2000, p. 110.
3. Ibid., p. 112.
4. Lee Hawkins, Jr., "Reversing 80 Years of History, GM Is Reining In Global Fiefs," *The Wall Street Journal,* October 6, 2004, p. A1.
5. Max Weber, *The Theory of Social and Economic Organization* (New York: Free Press, 1947).
6. Henry Mintzberg, *Structure in Fives: Designing Effective Organizations* (Upper Saddle River, NJ: Prentice-Hall, 1983), pp. 189–214.
7. Scott Thurm, "Power-Sharing Prepares Managers," *The Wall Street Journal,* December 5, 2005, p. B4.
8. Elliot Jacques, "In Praise of Hierarchy," *Harvard Business Review,* January–February 1990, p. 127.
9. Paul S. Adler, "Building Better Bureaucracies," *Academy of Management Executive,* November 1999, p. 36.
10. Harold J. Leavitt, "Why Hierarchies Thrive," *Harvard Business Review,* March 2003, p. 98.
11. Keith H. Hammonds, "Size Is Not a Strategy," *Fast Company,* September 2002, p. 80.
12. Allison Linn, "Internal Tape Bogs Down Microsoft," The Associated Press, October 10, 2005.
13. Robert A. Guth, "Microsoft to Restructure Businesses," *The Wall Street Journal*, September 21, 2005, pp. A3, A5.
14. Lee Meadows, "Project Management Is New Career Frontier," *The Detroit News* (http://www.detnews.com), August 26, 2005.
15. James Brooke and Saul Hansell, "Samsung Is Now What Sony Once Was," *The New York Times* (http://www.nytimes.com), March 10, 2005.
16. Mark Henricks, "Falling Flat?" *Entrepreneur,* January 2005, p. 69.
17. Barbara J. Petzall, Gerald E. Parker, and Philipp A. Stoeberl, "Another Side to Downsizing: Survivors' Behavior and Self-Affirmation," *Journal of Business and Psychology,* Summer 2000, p. 601.
18. Chuck Salter, "Surprise Package," *Fast Company*, February 2004, pp. 62–66.
19. "Open Debate," *Fast Company,* January/February 2006, p. 108.
20. Sue Shellenbarger, "Outsourcing Jobs to the Den: Call Centers Tap People Who Want to Work at Home," *The Wall Street Journal,* January 12, 2006, p. D1.
21. Ann Majchrzak and Qianwei Wang, "Breaking the Functional Mind-Set in Process Organizations," *Harvard Business Review,* September–October 1996, p. 93.
22. William H. Davidow and Michael S. Malone, *The Virtual Corporation: Structuring and Revitalizing the Corporation for the 21st Century* (Edward Burlingame Books/Harper Business, New York, NY, 1992).
23. Michael Goold and Andrew Campbell, "Do You Have a Well-Designed Organization?" *Harvard Business Review,* March 2002, pp. 117–124.

15

OBJECTIVES

After reading and studying this chapter and doing the exercises, you should be able to:

1. Describe three aspects of organizational culture: how it is determined, its dimensions, and how it is learned.

2. Describe how organizational culture can also be understood in terms of organizational types.

3. Explain some of the major consequences and implications of organizational culture.

4. Describe the 4I framework of a learning organization and components of the learning organization.

5. Pinpoint strategies and techniques for knowledge management.

6. Specify methods for sharing information within an organization.

Organizational Culture and Knowledge Management

As new Sony Corp Chief Executive Officer Howard Stringer prepared to implement the business turnaround he unveiled when starting his new job, his biggest challenge appeared to be winning over his own management team. His goal was simple enough: to boost results at the flagging electronics and entertainment giant, pushing sales to an annual 8 trillion yen ($71.6 billion) by within a 3-year period, up from 7.1 trillion yen the previous year, and operating profit to a margin of 5%, up from 1.6%.

But whereas plenty of Western executives would just decide how to execute the plan and order the deputies to do it, Stringer, who took over as Sony's first foreign CEO in June 2005, had to use a more subtle approach. Through a mix of discussion and compromise, he was attempting to coax his top lieutenants to take the tough steps needed to turn around the company—cutting 10,000 jobs (nearly 7% of Sony's workforce), discarding unprofitable product lines and shaking up a corporate culture long centered around proud, autonomous business units.

Source: Phred Dvorak, "Culture Clash Crimps Sony CEO," *The Wall Street Journal*, September 24–25, 2005, p. A6

Now Ask Yourself: **How important it is for a leader to understand a company's culture in order to bring about improved results?** In this chapter we discuss organizational culture and how to understand it. In the next chapter we deal more specifically with bringing about organizational change. The present chapter also emphasizes a topic closely related to culture and change—how an organization as a entity makes good use of knowledge, including getting workers to effectively share their knowledge with each other.

ORGANIZATIONAL CULTURE

As implied in previous mentions of the term, **organizational culture** is a system of shared values and beliefs that influence worker behavior. Edgar Schein was the first management theorist to define the corporate culture and to explain how the culture is such a dominant force in organizations. Much of his original thinking has influenced these more recent ideas about organizational culture.[1] Organizational culture may be considered a soft concept, yet the culture itself is quite durable. An entrenched culture might take 10 years to change, such as a smug and insular company becoming more open to ideas and new ways of doing things.[2] A specific example is the difficulty top management at the Coca-Cola company has faced in getting people to believe that for the company to continue to prosper in the long run it must not rely so heavily on carbonated beverages for its revenues.

Our study of organizational culture focuses on its determinants, its dimensions, how it is learned, and its consequences.

DETERMINANTS OF ORGANIZATIONAL CULTURE

Many forces shape a firm's culture. Often its origin lies in the values, administrative practices, and personality of the founder or founders. Also, the leader's vision can have a heavy impact on culture, such as John Chambers's dream of Cisco Systems becoming one of the world's greatest companies. A much-publicized example of the impact of a leader on culture is Herb Kelleher, the founder of Southwest Airlines, who is considered pivotal in shaping one of the most distinctive organizational cultures. Up until Kelleher's retirement several years ago, Southwest was considered very dependent on his personality and character. After his retirement for health reasons, his personality could still be felt. At the core of Southwest are the values of humor and altruism. For example, Southwest employees have established a catastrophe fund to help workers who need more assistance than usual employee benefits cover. Also, flight attendants and pilots use jokes and games to put customers at ease (a practice now copied by JetBlue Airlines).[3]

Organizational culture responds to and mirrors the conscious and unconscious choices, behavior patterns, and prejudices of top-level managers. As the founders leave or become less active, other top-level managers help define the culture. One of the ways in which Lou Gerstner, the former CEO and chair of IBM, changed the IBM culture was to relax its dress standards. His intent was to create a more relaxed (and less rigid) atmosphere at IBM. His successor, Sam Palmasano, has continued the tradition.

The culture in which a society operates also helps determine the culture of the firm. Sooner or later, society's norms, beliefs, and values find their way into the firm. Societal values are communicated through means such as the media, conversations, and education. The emphasis on sexual and racial equality in U.S. society has

Describe three aspects of organizational culture: how it is determined, its dimensions, and how it is learned.

become incorporated into the value culture of many employers. The emphasis on collegiality translates into harmony and cooperation in the workplace at many Scandinavian companies, including Nokia. Another perspective on national culture is that the introduction of values from another society into a retail business can be a competitive advantage. For example, the Japanese values of high quality and reliability, and spotless factories, have helped fuel the success of the Toyota car brand in the United States.

The industry to which a firm belongs helps shape its culture; for example, the culture of a high-tech information technology firm is quite different from that of a meat-packing facility. A public utility will have a culture different from a food manufacturer of comparable size. Heavy competition and low profit margins may force the food manufacturer to operate at a faster pace than the utility, which has more limited competition.

Dimensions of Organizational Culture

The dimensions, or elements, of culture help explain the nature of the subtle forces that influence employee actions. For example, a culture that values risk taking encourages employees to try new ways of doing things. The employees will do so without concern that they will be punished for failed ideas. The following list describes nine influential dimensions of culture:

1. *Values.* The foundation of any organizational culture is values. A firm's philosophy is expressed through values, and values guide behavior on a daily basis. Values also contribute directly to the ethical atmosphere within a firm. A study demonstrated, for example, that when top management has a lax attitude toward honesty, employee theft increases above the norm of 30%.[4] (Two previous studies have shown that about 30% of respondents admitted to having stolen from their employers.)

   A positive value that contributes to a healthy organization culture is a high regard for human welfare, exhibited in programs and policies that enhance employee health and well-being. One of many examples is Liberty Precision Industries. The company helps its employees develop versatile job skills. A consulting psychologist works with Liberty employees to identify specific areas in which they can improve job performance.[5]

2. *Organizational stories with underlying meanings.* Stories are circulated in many organizations to reinforce principles that top management thinks are important. An oft-repeated story is how company officials or other workers inconvenienced themselves to satisfy a customer or client need, such as foraging through a salvage yard to find a replacement part for a customer's old machine.

3. *Myths.* Myths are dramatic narratives or imagined events about the firm's history. (A myth is more exaggerated than an organizational story.) Myths contribute to corporate legends, help unify groups, and can build competitive advantage. At United Parcel Service (UPS), for example, stories are repeated about drivers overcoming severe obstacles or reaching inaccessible locations to deliver packages.

4. *Degree of stability.* A fast-paced, dynamic firm has a different culture from that of a slow-paced, stable one. Top-level managers send out signals by their own energetic or lethargic stance regarding how much they welcome innovation. The degree of stability also influences the strength of a culture and whether or not a culture can take root.

338

5. *Resource allocations and rewards.* The ways in which money and other resources are allocated have a critical influence on culture. The investment of resources sends a message about what the firm values.

6. *Rites and rituals.* Part of a firm's culture is made up of its traditions, or its rites and rituals. Few companies think they have rites and rituals, yet an astute observer can identify them. Examples include regular staff meetings, company picnics, retirement banquets (even for fired executives), and receptions for visiting dignitaries.

7. *A sense of ownership.* The movement toward stock ownership for an increasing number of employees has created an ownership culture in many firms, in which workers are inspired to think and act like owners. An ownership culture includes increased loyalty, improved work effort, and the alignment of worker interests with those of the company. An ownership culture can be reflected in everyday actions such as conserving electricity, making gradual improvements, and not tolerating sloppy work by coworkers. An ownership culture can backfire, however, if employee wealth stays flat or decreases as a result of stock ownership.[6]

8. *Belief in a higher purpose.* A dominant characteristic of many of the companies judged to be The 100 Best Companies to Work For is that employees have a sense of purpose. Employees derive deep satisfaction from feeling what they do is good and right. A belief in a higher purpose is easy to understand if one works for a pharmaceutical company. Yet employees of some financial services firms believe that they are occupying a useful role in society. For example, at Vanguard, the mutual fund giant, helping people pay for retirement is part of the mission.[7]

9. *Innovativeness.* A cultural dimension of significance in most fields is the innovative spirit of the workforce. As described in Chapter 5 our study of creativity, an environment that encourages innovation contributes to individual creativity. Bill Ford said in 2006 that the driving force for strengthening of Ford Motor Company will be the innovation. He noted furthermore that innovation is very much the history of the company, going all the way back to the Model T and the assembly line.[8]

In addition to the dominant culture of a firm, the subculture also influences behavior. A **subculture** is a pocket in which the organizational culture differs from the dominant culture, as well as other pockets of subculture. In a bank, the consumer loan division may have a culture different from that of the mortgage group, because the consumer group has to work with much shorter time frames in processing loans.

Exhibit 15-1 presents key aspects of the organizational culture of business firms most likely to be familiar to you. Scanning the exhibit, combined with other references to culture in this chapter and elsewhere in the book, will add to your understanding of organizational culture.

How Workers Learn the Culture

Employees learn the organizational culture primarily through **socialization,** the process of coming to understand the values, norms, and customs essential for adapting to the organization. Socialization is therefore a method of indoctrinating employees into the organization in such a way that they perpetuate the culture. The socialization process takes place mostly by learning through imitation and observation.

Another important way in which workers learn the culture is through the teachings of leaders, as implied in the cultural dimension of resource allocations and

Exhibit **15-1**

*A Sampling of
Organizational Cultures
of Well-Known
Companies*

IKEA	Very informal culture with roots in Swedish culture. Emphasis on informality, cost-consciousness, and a humble, down-to-earth approach. Workers are allowed considerable responsibility.
Nike	Go-it-alone, insular culture characterized by a desire for growth within, rather than taking on the hassles of integrating a merger with another company. Very difficult for outside executives to be accepted by the inner circle.
Home Depot	Rowdy corporate culture, with the idea of growing big and fast. Workers used to drive forklift trucks through aisles with customers around. Before former GE exec Bob Nardelli took over in 2001, the culture permitted casual attitudes toward costs.
Coca-Cola	Bureaucratic, slow-moving, with major changes taking a long time to implement. Continuing profits from beverages help keep key employees from seeing the need for change. For many years it had a bloated corporate staff. Gradually shifting to a faster-moving culture.
Southwest Airlines	Strong, trusting partnerships between managers and workers and unions that allow all concerned to execute the intricacies of an airline running smoothly. Strong emphasis on valuing human resources and intrinsic job satisfaction. Positive job attitude a key hiring factor.
United Airlines	Ailing culture, long plagued by tension between management and unions. Employees are hired for functional skills rather than relational skills. Performance is measured in a functionally specific, divisive way rather than allowing cross-functional responsibility for performance.

Sources: Katarina Kling and Ingela Goteman, "IKEA CEO Anders Dahlvig on International Growth and IKEA's Unique Corporate Culture and Brand Identity," *Academy of Management Executive,* February 2003, pp. 31–37; Douglas Robson, "Just Do . . . Something," *Business Week,* July 2, 2001, pp. 70–71; Aixa M. Pascual, "Tidying Up at Home Depot," *Business Week,* November 26, 2001, pp. 102–104; Dean Foust, "Gone Flat," *Business Week,* December 20, 2004, pp. 76–82; Tom Belden, "Will Fun Be Enough?" http://www.philly.com, January 24, 2006; Patrick J. Kiger, "Unite or Die," *Workforce,* February 2003, pp. 26–29.

rewards. Organizational members learn the culture to some extent by observing what leaders pay attention to, measure, and control.[9] Suppose a coworker of yours is praised publicly for doing community service. You are likely to conclude that an important part of the culture is to help people outside the company. Senior executives will sometimes publicly express expectations that help shape the culture of the firm. At Paychex Inc., the chairman and founder, Tom Golisano, sets the tone for a practical-minded, action-oriented culture, with dedicated managers. He reflects:

> We expect our senior management to be hands on. And I think when you talk to a lot of people who come from larger organizations, a lot of times they come from a different culture and it's hard for them to adapt. They expect in most cases a much healthier benefits and wage package, okay? They expect larger support staffs. They expect a little more freedom in their time and movement than we're willing to give them.[10]

Describe how organizational culture can also be understood in terms of organizational types.

The Organizational Culture as Organizational Types

Closely related to organizational culture is the idea that organizations have personalities, similar to the human personality. The consulting firm Booz Allen Hamilton has recently reinvented this long-standing idea as organizational types, resembling personality.[11] The seven types summarized in the following list are based on the results of over 30,000 surveys completed online. All of these organizational types might also be considered different types of cultures. The first three are healthy types, and the last four unhealthy.

1. *Resilient.* "As good as it gets." A resilient organization is highly adapted to shifts in the external market, yet stays focused on a coherent business strategy, like being a cost leader. Resilient organizations are flexible, forward thinking, and attract team players. Such an organization also bounces back from problems such as a product recall.

2. *Just-in-Time.* "Succeeding by the skin of our teeth." The just-in-time firm is not always prepared for change but can arise to an unforeseen challenge without losing sight of the overall picture. Successes are pulled off at the last minute, and there is a can-do attitude. The hectic nature of the just-in-time organization promotes employee burnout.

3. *Military Precision.* "Flying in formation." Everyone in a military-precision organization knows his or her role and implements it well, as characteristic of a successful bureaucracy. This type of firm is dominated by a small, committed team. The basis of its success is superior execution and the efficiency of its operating model. However, the military-precision organization type is not so nimble at dealing with the unanticipated.

4. *Passive-Aggressive.* "Everyone agrees, but nothing changes." Here is the seething, smiley-faced organization. Workers are congenial and seemingly conflict free, and consensus is easily achieved. A major problem is the poor implementation of agreed-upon plans. Corporate initiatives are often passively ignored, so change and progress is difficult to come by. Senior management accepts the idea that the organization is apathetic.

5. *Overmanaged.* "We're from corporate, and we're here to help." An overmanaged organization has multiple layers of management, analyzes problems to the point of diminishing returns, and emphasizes politics in decision making. Managers spend so much time checking the work of subordinates that they neglect to scan the external environment for opportunities or threats.

6. *Outgrown.* "The good old days meet a brave new world." This type of organization has become too large and complex to be effectively managed by a small team, yet has not decentralized and democratized decision making. Top management resists suggestions for change stemming from below, and reacts slowly to market developments, such as getting beyond an outdated technology.

7. *Fits and Starts.* "Let 1000 flowers bloom." Here we find an organization with loads of smart, motivated, and talented people who rarely coordinate their efforts to achieve important goals. A person can take an idea and run with it, yet direction from above is confusing, and a solid core of values is absent from below, so most initiatives falter.

According to the survey by Booz Allen Hamilton, the most common organizational type is the passive-aggressive. The passive-aggressive organization would need to undergo organizational change to become more successful. If the survey is valid, too many firms are ineffective based on a flawed personality. The survey, however, did not take into account financial results, which many analysts consider to be an important measure of organizational health.

The Consequences and Implications of Organizational Culture

Depending on its strength, a firm's organizational culture can have a pervasive impact on organizational effectiveness. Employees of a firm with a strong culture will follow its values with little questioning. A weaker culture provides only broad

341

Explain some of the major consequences and implications of organizational culture.

Exhibit **15-2**

*Consequences and
Implications of
Organizational Culture*

guidelines to members. Six major consequences and implications of organizational culture are outlined in Exhibit 15-2 and summarized next.

1. *Competitive advantage and financial success.* The right organizational culture contributes to gaining competitive advantage and therefore achieving financial success. A study of 34 firms investigated the relationship between a high-involvement/participative culture and financial performance. Firms perceived by employees to link individual efforts to company goals showed higher returns on investments and sales than firms without such linkages.[12]

2. *Productivity, quality, and morale.* A culture that emphasizes productivity, including high quality, encourages workers to be productive. Productivity and competitive advantage are closely linked because high-level productivity contributes heavily to gaining on the competition. A culture that values the dignity of human beings fosters high morale and job satisfaction. The consistently strong performance of Southwest Airlines is partially attributed to its humane and fun-loving culture that leads to high job satisfaction and motivation, often resulting in high productivity.

3. *Innovation.* A major contributor to innovation is a corporate culture that encourages creative behavior. Gary Hamel has identified specific features of a culture that inspire innovation, including the setting of very high expectations, creating a cause that workers can be passionate about, encouraging radical ideas, and allowing talented people in the company to easily transfer to different business areas within the firm. Also, innovators must be paid exceptionally well. As Hamel states, "Entrepreneurs won't work for peanuts, but they'll work for a share of the equity, a piece of the action."[13]

4. *Compatibility of mergers and acquisitions.* A reliable predictor of success in merging two or more firms is the compatibility of their respective cultures. When the cultures clash, such as a mechanistic firm merging with an organic one, the result can be negative synergy. A consultant who contributed to a major study on mergers and acquisitions said, "Many deals fail to capture the expected synergies due to incompatible cultures, the loss of key talent or clashes of management style." He recommends, therefore, that human resource professionals become an integral part of the merger and acquisition team.[14] One of the biggest disappointing mergers of all time was the union of AOL and Time Warner, and its problems were attributed to a culture clash. The AOL culture was epitomized by "all-elbows business practices," while Time Warner was characterized as a tradition-bound media giant. Five years after the merger, AOL was finally on its way back to health as it stopped charging fees for so many basic services.

5. *Person–organization fit.* An important success factor for the individual is finding an organization that fits his or her personality. Similarly, an organization will be

more successful when the personality of most members fits its culture. In one study, organizations were measured on dimensions such as stability, experimenting, risk taking, and an orientation toward rules. The preferences of professional employees regarding culture were measured and compared with the culture of their firms. Good person–organization fits result in more commitment and higher job satisfaction.[15] At times a good fit for the organization can be a heterogeneous group, as described in the accompanying Organizational Behavior in Action box.

6. *Direction of leadership activity.* Much of a top-level manager's time is spent working with the forces that shape the attitudes and values of employees at all levels. A key leadership role is to establish what type of culture is needed for the firm and then shape the existing culture to match that ideal. Charles D. Moran, the

ORGANIZATIONAL BEHAVIOR *In Action*

Virgin Mobile Manager Seeks Out the Right Mix of Employees

"The power of any group of people is the power of the mix," says Renée Wingo, chief people officer [a trendy name for a human resources director] at Virgin Mobile USA of Warren, New Jersey. "You may do all right, but you're not going to create any magic as a manager unless you bring together people with diverse perspectives who aren't miniversions of you."

When hiring her own staff of 10 human-resource professionals, she says she tried to create "a stew that wasn't mushy but distinct, where we could all taste the carrots, potatoes, and other ingredients." Her staff includes employees with experience ranging from 30 years down to 18 months; people who are technology-oriented and those we are service-oriented; full- and part-timers; and extraverts as well as introverts. "There are folks who would be inclined to party in New York on weekends and others who prefer sitting by a warm fire with a dog on their feet," she says.

This mix serves a vital business function, she argues, "because if we come together and represent all these different points of view, we can better appreciate and serve" Virgin Mobile's diverse workforce. But it makes her own job as a manager more difficult, she acknowledges. At weekly meetings at which her staff discuss

problems and projects, she says she has to encourage an airing of different opinions but also keep everyone focused enough to make decisions. "It's kind of like being with a group of people who are debating where to go to dinner, and one person is insisting, 'We have to go to the East Side,' and another says, 'No, the West Side,' and it's my role to ask, 'Why don't we talk about what we want to eat?'" she says.

One common quality all her employees share is a desire to work in a diverse group. Ms. Wingo says she screens this quality during job interviews by asking candidates to describe how they have made decisions and what they have valued most in their jobs. "It's a positive when they say they loved coming together as a team and learned things they never knew about," she says. "But if they say, 'Well, things kept changing and I didn't agree with people I worked with,' I question whether they'd fit here."

Questions

1. What type of person–organization fit is Wingo looking for?
2. How might the diversity Wingo establishes in the group enhance group effectiveness?

Source: Carol Hymowitz, "Managers Err if They Limit Their Hiring to People Like Them," *The Wall Street Journal*, October 12, 2004, p. B1.

top executive at Acxiom Corp., sums up the link between culture and company leadership in these words: "Your culture should be everything you do as a business. It should be how you solve problems, build products and work in teams. For the CEO and other leaders, it's about how you lead."[16] You will recall that the new CEO of Sony described in the chapter opener realized that he would have to shake up the corporate culture.

THE LEARNING ORGANIZATION

Closely related to organizational culture and change is the idea that an effective organization engages in continuous learning by proactively adapting to the external environment. A **learning organization** is one that is skilled at creating, acquiring, and transferring knowledge; and at modifying behavior to reflect new knowledge and insights.[17] Although we speak of organizational learning, it is still individual people who create the conditions for such learning. Our approach to understanding the learning organization will be to first describe a recent model framework of a learning organization, followed by a sampling of building blocks or components. Before proceeding, however, the accompanying self-assessment quiz will give you a sense of the day-to-day characteristics of a learning organization.

SELF-ASSESSMENT

Do You Work for a Learning Organization?

Directions: Indicate for each of the following statements whether it is mostly true or mostly false in relation to your current or most recent place of work. Indicate a question mark when the statement is either not applicable or you are not in a position to judge.

	Mostly True	?	Mostly False
1. Company employees often visit other locations or departments to share new information or skills they have learned.	☐	☐	☐
2. Our company frequently repeats mistakes.	☐	☐	☐
3. We get most of our market share by competing on price.	☐	☐	☐
4. Many people in our organization are aware of and believe in our vision.	☐	☐	☐
5. Top management assumes that the vast majority of employees are experts at what they do.	☐	☐	☐
6. Almost all of our learning takes place individually rather than in groups or teams.	☐	☐	☐
7. In our company, after you have mastered your job you do not have to bother with additional learning such as training programs or self-study.	☐	☐	☐
8. Our firm shies away from inviting outsiders into our company to discuss our business because few outsiders could understand our uniqueness.	☐	☐	☐
9. If it weren't for a few key individuals in our company, we would be in big trouble.	☐	☐	☐
10. Our new product launches go smoothly and quickly.	☐	☐	☐
11. Our company creates a lot of opportunities for employees to get together and share information, such as conferences and meetings.	☐	☐	☐
12. We are effective at pricing the service we provide to customers.	☐	☐	☐
13. Very few of our employees have any idea about company sales and profits.	☐	☐	☐

SELF-ASSESSMENT

(Continued)

	Mostly True	?	Mostly False
14. I often hear employees asking questions about why the company has taken certain major actions.	☐	☐	☐
15. The company maintains a current database about the knowledge and skills of almost all our employees.	☐	☐	☐
16. Having specialized knowledge brings you some status in our company.	☐	☐	☐
17. It would be stretching the truth to say that many of our employees are passionate about what our organization is attempting to accomplish.	☐	☐	☐
18. Our performance-appraisal system makes a big contribution to helping employees learn and improve.	☐	☐	☐
19. Following established rules and procedures is important in our company, so creativity and imagination are not encouraged.	☐	☐	☐
20. Most of our employees believe that if you do your own job well, you don't have to worry about what goes on in the rest of the organization.	☐	☐	☐
21. We get loads of useful new ideas from our customers.	☐	☐	☐
22. I have frequently heard our managers talk about how what goes on in the outside world has an impact on our company.	☐	☐	☐
23. We treat customer suggestions with a good deal of skepticism.	☐	☐	☐
24. During breaks, you sometimes hear employees discussing the meaning and implication of the work they are doing.	☐	☐	☐
25. Employees at every level tend to rely on facts when making important decisions.	☐	☐	☐
26. If a process or procedure works well in our company, we are hesitant to experiment with other approaches to a problem.	☐	☐	☐
27. Our company treats mistakes as valuable learning experiences about what not to do in the future.	☐	☐	☐
28. Our company rarely copies ideas from the successful practices of other companies.	☐	☐	☐
29. Each time we face a significant problem, our company seems to start all over to find a solution.	☐	☐	☐
30. It's a waste of time to be reading about a learning organization, when my real interest is in learning how to prevent problems.	☐	☐	☐

Total score: _____

Scoring and Interpretation:

A. Record the number of Mostly True answers you gave to the following questions: 1, 4, 5, 10, 11, 12, 14, 15, 16, 18, 21, 22, 24, 25, 27.
B. Record the number of Mostly False answers you gave to the following questions: 2, 3, 6, 7, 8, 9, 13, 17, 19, 20, 23, 26, 28, 29, 30.
C. Add the numbers for A and B.
D. Add half of your "?" responses to A, and half to B.

25 or higher: You are most likely a member of a learning organization. This tendency is so pronounced that it should contribute heavily to your company's success.

13–24: Your company has an average tendency toward being a learning organization, suggesting an average degree of success in profiting from mistakes and changing in response to a changing environment.

0–12: Your firm is definitely not a learning organization.

Source: Andrew J. DuBrin, *Looking Around Corners: The Art of Problem Prevention* (Madison, WI: CWL Publishing Enterprises, 1999), 181–183. Used with permission of the publisher.

4

THE 4I FRAMEWORK OF A LEARNING ORGANIZATION

Describe the 4I frame-
work of a learning
organization and com-
ponents of the learning
organization.

The 4I framework is instructive because it describes the processes involved in a firm making systematic use of information. A portion of the model that appears most useful to practitioners is presented here and shown in Exhibit 15-3. A premise behind this framework is that organizational learning that results in organizational renewal encompasses the entire enterprise, not simply the individual or group. Another premise is that the organization operates in an open system, rather than having solely an individual focus. As is well known, an organization must satisfy the demands of the external world or it will perish.

As explained by Mary M. Crossan, Henry W. Lane, and Roderick E. White, organizational learning is composed of four processes: intuiting, interpreting, integrating, and institutionalizing.[18] The four processes work together to link the individual, group, and organizational levels. The four processes are the glue that binds the structure together. The three learning levels define the structure through which organizational learning takes place (as does all of organizational behavior).

Individual level: Intuiting and interpreting take place at the individual level. *Intuiting* is the preconscious (not quite explicit or conscious) recognition of the pattern and/or possibilities inherent in a personal stream of experience. *Intuiting* is essentially intuition, and it relies on hunches about events taking place in the organization. *Interpreting* is explaining through words and/or actions an insight or idea to oneself and to others. A manager might develop the intuition that the company is not getting its fair share of repeat business. He might then say to coworkers, "Could we be facing some problem with our products that prompts many customers to forget about us after one try?"

Group level: Integration takes place at the group level. This is the process of developing shared understanding among individuals and of taking coordinated action. Dialogue about the problem and joint action are critical to the development of shared understanding. The group might bat around the problem by asking "What is it about us that prompts so many customers to try us once and not come back?"

Organization level: Institutionalization takes place at the organization level. This is the process of ensuring that routine actions occur. At first, the integrating taking place at the group level will be ad hoc and informal. However, if the coordinated action is recurring and substantial, it will become institutionalized. Tasks become defined, actions specified,

Exhibit **15-3**

*The 4I Framework of
Organizational Learning*

*Organizational learning
takes place at three levels
and involves four processes.*

346

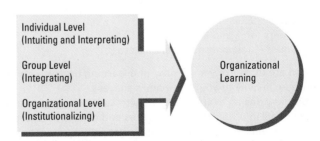

Source: Mary M. Crossan, Henry W. Lane, and Roderick E. White, "An Organizational Learning Framework: From Institution to Institution," *Academy of Management Review,* July 1999, p. 525.

and organizational mechanisms put in place to ensure that certain actions occur.

Institutionalizing can also be regarded as the process of embedded learning achieved by individuals and groups into the organization. In the example at hand, an institutionalized process might be to follow up with first-time customers regarding the reasons they intend to return or not return.

An implication of the 4I framework for managers is that for organizational learning to take place, individuals should be encouraged to share their intuition and insights with other individuals and the group. In this way, the best insights will eventually become institutionalized. A more recent line of investigation emphasizes the importance of both transformational and transactional leadership in encouraging the institutionalization of learning. Transformational leadership might point the way for the new learning, while transactional leadership would help reinforce the institutional learning at the work-group level.[19] The supervisor, for example, might reward a worker for using recently acquired knowledge about better handling inquiries.

An update of the 4I framework emphasizes that political tactics provide the social energy that translates the insights of individual and groups into the institutions of an organization. Without a key player exerting influence, a useful idea might never become institutionalized. The idea becomes neglected in the press of everyday activities. Instead, if a champion of the idea keeps pushing for its acceptance, the idea may become institutionalized.[20] An example might be a business analyst in a large firm continually pushing the company to use ethanol fuel in more of its hundreds of vehicles to help reduce pollutants sent into the air. In addition to being smart, the innovation champion would need good connections in the company.

BUILDING BLOCKS OF A LEARNING ORGANIZATION

To become and remain a learning organization, certain characteristics and behaviors are required of organizational members, as described next.[21] Although organizational theorists speak of a learning organization, the workers do the learning. The collective wisdom of the workers might then translate into a learning organization.

Double-Loop Learning

An in-depth, nondefensive type of learning takes place in a learning organization. **Double-loop learning** occurs when people use feedback to confront the validity of the goal or the values implicit in the situation. When you engage in double-loop learning, you change the governing values or assumptions themselves. As a result, you change your actions. A conventional-thinking manager (one who engages in single-loop learning) at a tire distributor observes that sales have been declining (feedback from the environment). The manager then asks, "How can we more effectively market retread tires for automobiles?" As a double-loop learner, the same manager might ask, "Why are we even selling retreads for the automotive market? The demand is declining and they are not very safe." Note that the sales manager is being open and nondefensive about his or her product line, and is changing the assumption that retreaded tires even make a contribution to society.

Systems Thinking

In the learning organization, members regard the organization as a system in which everybody's work affects the activities of everybody else. Systems thinking also means keeping the big picture foremost in everybody's mind and being keenly aware of the external environment. This is true because the organization is part of a system that includes the outside world. A systems thinker at Brooks Brothers said a few years ago, "The trend even among affluent businesspeople is away from our ultraconservative image. Our customer base is declining. If we don't want Brooks Brothers to be perceived as a museum of fashions past, we had better modify our product line." Brooks Brothers was able to modify its product image just enough to satisfy the modern conservative dresser without alienating its remaining die-hard ultraconservatives. Each store has elegant products to satisfy the conservative and ultraconservative dresser.

Team Learning

A learning organization emphasizes collective problem solving. Members freely share information and opinions with one another to facilitate problem solving. The team learning can take place in several ways. The basic approach is to use group problem solving throughout the firm. However, a large firm might bring people together at a retreat, where they work in teams to reflect on ways of improving the organization.

Personal Mastery of the Job

Continuous learning usually is required to master a job in the modern organization. Two major examples are learning new information technology as it applies to the job, and learning more about different cultures. For continuous learning to take place, each member must develop expertise. Quite often this detail is overlooked because of the emphasis on learning in groups. Collective learning is much more productive when every member of the group brings something valuable to the table.

Translation of New Knowledge into New Ways of Behaving

Given that learning involves a change in behavior, a true learning organization translates knowledge into action. Learning at a superficial level would occur if managers attended a seminar on expectancy theory and simply retained key principles. Members of a learning organization would *apply* expectancy theory.

Learning from Other Organizations

Some of the best insights an organization can acquire stem from studying competitors and other firms. Borrowing ideas from the competition, also known as *benchmarking*, took place long before the concept of a learning organization arose. A learning organization systematizes the process while at the same time attempting to be ethical. "Learning from others" is most ethical when the learning does not directly capitalize on an idea a competitor spent considerable time and money developing.

Substantial learning can take place in copying the practices of firms not directly in your line of business. Suppose you would like to establish a worldwide method of distributing hard-to-get automobile parts, like a carburetor for a 1956 Edsel. You carefully study the marketing techniques of Amazon.com and BarnesandNoble.com, distributors of books, music, and other products. You set up an elaborate system, copy the order and shipping process of these firms, and call yourself Oldautoparts.com. Since you do not distribute books, music, and videos and your benchmarking targets do not distribute hard-to-find auto parts, nobody gets hurt. You are a learning organization without directly copying another company's ideas.

Is there any research evidence that organizations can really learn? A study was conducted in an auto parts manufacturing company about the impact of gainsharing on organizational performance. The learning involved concerned the implementation of suggestions leading to reduction in the costs per unit produced. Overall, the results of the study indicated that it is possible to ramp up organizational learning through introducing a planned performance program such as gainsharing.[22]

KNOWLEDGE MANAGEMENT

A major consequence of a learning organization is that knowledge is managed more effectively. **Knowledge management (KM)** is a systematic approach to documenting, applying, and transferring the know-how and experience of employees.[23] A major objective of knowledge management is to make effective use of the vast store of useful information experience possessed by employees. Often this knowledge has to be transferred to affiliates in another country and culture. Managing knowledge well achieves goals such as innovation, nonduplication of effort, and competitive advantage. When knowledge is managed effectively, information is shared as needed whether it is printed or stored electronically or in the brains of workers.

The justification for knowledge management is that intellectual capital is a resource that allows for survival and competitive advantage. **Intellectual capital** is knowledge that transforms raw materials and makes them more valuable. It is also a capital asset consisting of intellectual material.[24] The intellectual capital of many firms, consisting of the know-how and intelligence of the workers, is far more valuable than their physical assets, consisting mostly of a handful of machines and furniture. Firms high in intellectual capital and low in physical capital include software development companies, consulting firms, and advertising agencies. Knowledge management also helps deal with the problem of knowledge loss when competent employees leave the firm. If the employee's useful knowledge, including creative ideas, is documented by the firm, a knowledgeable employee's departure is a less serious problem.

Pinpoint strategies and techniques for knowledge management.

Log on to **www.thomsonedu .com/infotrac**. Find examples of ways companies have attempted to use knowledge management to capture unstructured knowledge that resides in people's heads.

Knowledge-Management Strategies and Techniques

Given that knowledge management has become one of the fastest-growing trends in management, various strategies and techniques have been developed to foster the process. The building blocks of a learning organization are also closely tied in with the knowledge-management strategies and techniques to be described next.

Hire the Right Persons

Hiring people who are good at learning and teaching makes a substantial difference in the effectiveness of knowledge management. Thomas H. Davenport explains: "Not enough companies have built into their competency models how well people learn and pass on their knowledge informally on the job. If you've got people who are hungry to learn and people who are good at transferring knowledge, the organization will be much more alive."[25] People with the right stuff for KM are most likely to be those who have demonstrated intelligence, accumulated knowledge, and displayed intellectual curiosity in the past.

Create Knowledge

Creating knowledge is an important first step for managing knowledge. The strategy is easily stated but not so easy to implement. First, you need intelligence to create the knowledge, and you also need the conditions favoring creativity and innovation described in Chapter 5. The 4I model of organizational learning provides a partial explanation of how knowledge is created. To understand the need for creating new knowledge, it is useful to perceive every product, service, and work process as a bundle of knowledge. For example, the Chrysler PT Cruiser is the intelligence bundled in the ability to transform a 67-year-old design to fit modern tastes for the retro look, do the appropriate engineering and manufacturing, and market and distribute the product to customers.

Closing the Gap between Knowing and Doing

Why don't companies accomplish more if they have so much knowledge and expertise? Jeffrey Pfeffer and Robert I. Sutton believe that companies have fallen into the knowing–doing gap because doing something requires the hard work of making something happen. Managing knowledge is not enough; it must be converted into action. It is easier and safer to have intellectual discussions, to gather large databases, and to invest in technical infrastructure than it is to actually execute. The challenge for companies and the people in them is to build a culture of action.[26] Often this means taking decisive action that results in repeat business, such as an airline having a high percentage of on-time flights or a retailer offering commissions to sales representatives in the stores.

METHODS OF SHARING INFORMATION

Specify methods for sharing information within an organization.

A major goal of the learning organization and knowledge management is for organizational members to share relevant information. Many of the strategies and techniques already described in this chapter contribute directly or indirectly to information sharing. Although knowledge management does not appear to be highly complicated, few organizations have figured out how to share knowledge among employees, or to pass it on when one employee transfers or quits.[27] Here we describe briefly five focused methods for sharing information.

1. *In-house Yellow Pages.* The basic idea of company Yellow Pages is to compile a directory of the skills, talents, and special knowledge of employees throughout the firm. To be useful, the Yellow Pages have to go far beyond basic information and job experience. The directory should indicate the specialized knowledge of the people listed and their level of expertise. When faced with a problem requiring specialized talent, employees can consult the Yellow Pages for a person who can help.

2. *Intranet communication systems.* A growing number of firms use intranets and online forums to spread and share knowledge. Google's idea search starts with an internal web page that takes a few minutes to set up. Using a program called Sparrow, even Google employees without Internet savvy can create a page of ideas. Every Google employee spends a fraction of his or her time on research and development.[28]

3. *Personal explanations of success factors.* An advanced method of information sharing is for key organizational members to teach others what they know through explanations of success factors. Noel Tichy refers to these stories as the *teachable point of view* because they help leaders become teachers. The teachable point of view is a written explanation of what a person knows and believes about what it takes to succeed in his or her own business, as well as in business in general. About two pages in length, the document focuses on critical success factors such as "What would it take to knock out the competition?" Tichy claims that this hard-hitting method of information sharing is used in hundreds of companies.[29]

4. *Foster dialogue among organization members.* To promote the importance of information sharing, company leaders should converse about the importance of intellectual capital and the development of core competencies.[30] At the same time, workers throughout the firm should be encouraged to share useful suggestions, tidbits of knowledge, and success stories about problem solving. This type of information sharing can take place face to face, but e-mail exchanges also play a vital role. The most consistent observation about knowledge management and information sharing is that the human touch is more important than technology. David Gilmour, the president of a knowledge systems company, advises that technology should not flood people with information or take it from them. It is better to identify connections that are valuable to the people who are being connected.[31]

5. *Shared physical facilities and informal learning.* An important method of fostering dialogue is to develop shared physical facilities as described in Chapter 10 regarding teamwork development. Considerable information sharing is likely to take place in a snack lounge or company information resource center. At the same time, informal learning takes place, which is almost synonymous with information sharing. A survey of 800 managers found that 78% share information through personal and information communication, compared with 19% that rely on formal or technology-driven processes. (Three percent don't bother with knowledge sharing.)[32]

IMPLICATIONS FOR MANAGERIAL PRACTICE

1. To manage organizational culture, one must first understand the culture of the firm and then use that knowledge to guide one's own behavior and that of group members. For example, an executive might resist downsizing as a way to reduce costs because laying off productive and loyal employees conflicts with the firm's values.

2. The biggest challenge in implementing workplace innovations is to bring about cultural change. Workers' attitudes and values have to change if the spirit of innovation is to keep smoldering. An effective vehicle for bringing about such change is for top-level managers and others to exchange ideas. Formal arrangements, such as regularly scheduled staff meetings, facilitate exchanging ideas, reflecting on values, and learning what behavior is in vogue. Encouraging informal meetings can often achieve the same purpose with a higher degree of effectiveness.

3. The most important and the most practical aspect of the learning organization and knowledge management is for workers to share useful information with one another. In your role as a manager, you should therefore make a systematic

PLAY VIDEO >>

Fannie Mae Promotes a Diverse Workforce

Visit **www. thomsonedu.com/ management/dubrin** and watch the video for this chapter. What are some of the challenges that mid-level managers at Fannie Mae might face in managing a diverse group of workers?

effort to ensure that information is shared in the total organization or your organizational unit. Establish both formal steps (for example, an intranet) and informal methods (such as simply encouraging people to exchange good ideas) to accomplish information sharing.

4.   Several theorists have mentioned that a company's true competitive advantage derives from intellectual capital. If this observation is valid, then one of the highest organizational priorities is to recruit and retain knowledgeable and intelligent workers. Even during a downsizing, maximum effort should be invested in retaining the best thinkers and most knowledgeable people in the company.

SUMMARY OF KEY POINTS

① Describe three aspects of organizational culture: how it is determined, its dimensions, and how it is learned.

The origins of organizational culture often lie in the values, administrative practices, and personality of its founders. Other key influences are the societal culture, the industry, and the organization's code of conduct. Organizational culture has various dimensions, such as the values, stories, and myths maintained by the organization; the sense of ownership within the firm; belief in a higher purpose; and innovativeness. The culture is taught primarily through socialization and the teaching of leaders.

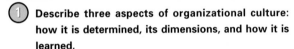

② Describe how organizational culture can also be understood in terms of organizational types.

Organizations have been divided into types, similar to personalities. The healthy types are resilient, just-in-time, and military precision. The unhealthy types are passive-aggressive, overmanaged, outgrown, and fits and starts. Passive-aggressive is the most common type of organization.

③ Explain some of the major consequences and implications of organizational culture.

The consequences and implications of organizational culture include competitive advantage, productivity and morale, innovation, compatibility of mergers and acquisitions, the person–organization fit, and the direction of leadership activity.

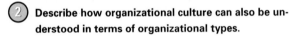

④ Describe the 4I framework of a learning organization and components of the learning organization.

According to the 4I framework, organizational learning that results in organizational renewal encompasses the entire enterprise. Organizational learning

is composed of four processes: intuiting, interpreting, integrating, and institutionalizing. The four processes work together to link the individual, group, and organizational levels. Intuiting and interpreting take place at the individual level; integrating takes place at the group level; and institutionalizing takes place at the organizational level. Both transformational and transactional leadership can facilitate the institutionalization of knowledge. Political skill is also necessary to institutionalize knowledge.

Components of the learning organization include (a) double-loop learning, (b) systems thinking, (c) team learning, (d) personal mastery of the job, (e) translation of new knowledge into new ways of behaving, and (f) learning from other organizations.

⑤ Pinpoint strategies and techniques for knowledge management.

Strategies and techniques for knowledge management include (a) hiring the right people, (b) creating knowledge, and (c) closing the gap between knowing and doing.

⑥ Specify methods for sharing information within an organization.

Information sharing is at the heart of a learning organization and knowledge management. Five specific methods are (a) in-house Yellow Pages, (b) intranet communication systems, (c) personal explanations of success factors, (d) the fostering of dialogue among organizational members, and (e) shared physical facilities and organizational learning. The human touch is more important than technology in sharing information.

KEY TERMS AND PHRASES

Organizational Culture, 337
A system of shared values and beliefs that influence worker behavior.

Subculture, 339
A pocket in which the organizational culture differs from the dominant culture, as well as other pockets of subculture.

Socialization, 339
The process of coming to understand the values, norms, and customs essential for adapting to an organization.

Learning Organization, 344
An organization that is skilled at creating, acquiring, and transferring knowledge and at modifying behavior to reflect new knowledge and insights.

Double-Loop Learning, 347
A change in behavior that occurs when people use feedback to confront the validity of the goal or the values implicit in the situation.

Knowledge Management (KM), 349
The systematic sharing of information to achieve advances in innovation, efficiency, and competitive advantage.

Intellectual Capital, 349
Knowledge that transforms raw materials and makes them more valuable; it is also a capital asset consisting of intellectual material.

DISCUSSION QUESTIONS AND ACTIVITIES

1. How would you describe the organizational culture of Wal-Mart (or any other retailer) based on whatever evidence you have? If necessary, visit your local Wal-Mart (or other retailer) to make firsthand observations.

2. Why do so many CEOs believe that their primary responsibility is managing organizational culture? What happened to making a profit?

3. Identify any organization you know about that you think would best fit your personality. Justify your reasoning.

4. How might you be able to use a few concepts from the learning organization and knowledge management to manage your career more effectively?

5. Why do mental models sometimes interfere with the goals of diversity?

6. What is your evaluation of McDonald's as a learning organization? Support your conclusion with a few observations.

7. Ask an experienced manager what type of information should be included in the in-house Yellow Pages. Be prepared to share your findings with classmates.

CASE PROBLEM: The Corporate Culture Picnic

Matt Larson is the CEO of Exterior Light Inc., a company that manufactures and installs external lighting for municipalities, malls, and athletic stadiums. Working closely with Helen Ono, the vice president of administration and human resources, he organizes a company picnic every summer. The tradition has endured for 25 years.

Four hundred of the company's 440 people attended the picnic this year, held at Larson's summer home on lakefront property. The picnic facilities featured a volleyball area, a 22-foot inflatable slide, pony rides, face painters, temporary tattoos, miniature golf, food bar for children, an open beer-and-wine bar for adults, and a fully stocked Good Humor truck. Larson, Ono, and the other corporate officials worked the grill, which included meat products as well as vegetarian choices.

According to the accounting department, the picnic cost $43,000, including reimbursed travel costs for employees working in field locations.

Perry Sanders, an accounts payable specialist attending the picnic, commented to Larson, "Geez Matt, I hope you and the over four hundred people stuffing themselves today are getting a bang for the buck. Today's fun will probably run a tab of over $40,000. Those bucks would look pretty good if they were used to fatten our bottom line."

Larson retorted, "Perry, take off your accountant's hat for a few moments. Our annual picnic sends a clear signal that it's part of our culture to treat people well, and for our employees to work together in a friendly, cooperative environment."

(continued)

CASE PROBLEM (Continued)

After the last guest had left, Larson and Sanders chatted more about the value of the picnic, and they were joined by Ono. When she heard about the challenge to the picnic, she chimed in, "I'm a human resources professional, not a drumbeater for the company picnic. Yet, I like Matt's point about the picnic communicating the culture. Setting up lighting systems requires a lot of cooperation across department and geographic lines. Seeing so many of your colleagues in person sets up a climate for a culture of cooperation and teamwork."

Barbara Lyons, the director of marketing, said, "I saw a little of this friendliness go too far. The open bar led to too much random hugging, kissing, and patting. If you get sexually harassed at a company picnic, it is as serious as harassment in the office."

Ono replied, "Good point, Barbara. I think I know who you are talking about. Some of our field technicians get a little too macho at the picnic. We'll have to send out a polite reminder before next year's picnic."

Larson rested his chin on the thumb of a clenched fist, and said, "So you folks think there might be less expensive and time-consuming ways of communicating

our culture of caring and teamwork? Let's leave the door open on this topic and return to it at a staff meeting."

Sanders said, "I don't want to be the Abominable Snowman, but we need to calculate the return on investment from these picnics. Are we getting a cultural bang for the buck?"

Case Questions

1. Do Sanders, Ono, and Lyons have the right to challenge the value of the annual company picnic in communicating the corporate culture values?

2. How would company management at Exterior Lighting know if the picnic was an effective way of communicating the cultural values of caring for people and engaging in teamwork?

3. What, if anything, should management do about possible sexual harassment at the company picnic?

4. Aside from a picnic, how might top management communicate the company's culture?

Source: A few of the facts in this case are from Maryann Hammers, "Impervious to the Call for ROI, the Company Picnic Is Alive and Well," *Workforce Management*, July 2004, pp. 70–73.

ENDNOTES

1. Edgar Schein, "Careers, Culture, and Organizational Learning," in *Business: The Ultimate Resource* (Cambridge, MA: Perseus Books Group, 2002), p. 1044.
2. Interview of Heinrich von Pierer, "Transforming an Industrial Giant," *Harvard Business Review*, February 2005, p. 122.
3. Katrina Brooker, "Can Anyone Replace Herb?" *Fortune*, April 17, 2000, pp. 186–192; Tom Belden, "Will Fun Be Enough?" http://www.philly.com, January 24, 2006.
4. John Kamp and Paul Brooks, "Perceived Organizational Climate and Employee Counterproductivity," *Journal of Business and Psychology*, Summer 1991, p. 455.
5. Mark Greer, "A Happier, Healthier Workplace," *Monitor on Psychology*, December 2004, p. 29.
6. Scott Hays, "'Ownership Cultures' Create Unity," *Workforce*, February 1999, pp. 60–64.
7. Geoff Colvin, "The 100 Best Companies to Work For," *Fortune*, January 23, 2006, p. 74.
8. "My Goal is to Fight Toyota," *Time*, January 30, 2006.
9. Literature reviewed in Gerard George, Randall G. Sleeth, and Mark A. Siders, "Organizing Culture: Leader Roles, Behaviors, and Reinforcement Mechanisms," *Journal of Business and Psychology*, Summer 1999, p. 548.
10. Quoted in Andy Meisler, "Spare Him the Gurus," *Workforce*, June 2003, p. 36.
11. "About Organizational DNA," http://www.OrgDNA.com; Gary L. Neilson, Bruce A. Pasternak, and Karen E. Van Nuys, "The

Passive-Aggressive Organization," *Harvard Business Review*, October 2005, p. 85.
12. Daniel R. Denison, *Corporate Culture and Organizational Effectiveness* (New York: Wiley, 1990).
13. Gary Hamel, "Reinvent Your Company," *Fortune*, June 12, 2000, pp. 97–118. The quote is from page 118.
14. Quoted in Jeffrey A. Schmidt, ed., *Making Mergers Work* (Alexandria, VA: Towers/Perrin/SHRM, 2002).
15. Charles A. O'Reilly III, Jennifer A. Chatman, and David F. Caldwell, "People and Organizational Culture: A Profile Comparison Approach to Assessing Person-Organization Fit," *Academy of Management Journal*, September 1991, pp. 487–516.
16. Charles D. Moran, "Culture Change/Culture Shock," *Management Review*, November 1998, p. 13.
17. David A. Garvin, "Building a Learning Organization," *Harvard Business Review*, July–August 1993, p. 80.
18. Mary M. Crossan, Henry W. Lane, and Roderick E. White, "An Organizational Learning Framework: From Intuition to Institution," *Academy of Management Review*, July 1999, pp. 522–537.
19. Vera Dusya and Mary Crossan, "Strategic Leadership and Organizational Learning," *The Academy of Management Review*, April 2004, p. 235.
20. Thomas B. Lawrence, Michael K. Mauws, Bruno Dyck, and Robert F. Kleysen, "The Politics of Organizational Learning: Integrating Power into the 4I Framework," *Academy of Management Review*, January 2005, pp. 180–191.

21. Robert M. Fulmer and Philip Gibbs, "The Second Generation Learning Organizations: New Tools for Sustaining Competitive Advantage," *Organizational Dynamics,* Autumn 1998, pp. 7–20; Chris Argyris, "Double-Loop Learning, Teaching and Research," *Academy of Management Learning & Education,* December 2002, pp. 206–218.

22. Jeffrey B. Arthur and Christopher L. Huntley, "Ramping up the Organizational Learning Curve: Assessing the Impact of Deliberate Learning on Organizational Performance under Gainsharing," *Academy of Management Journal*, December 2005, pp. 1159–1170.

23. Book review in *Academy of Management Executive,* February 2002, p. 161.

24. Thomas A. Stewart, "Intellectual Capital," in *Business: The Ultimate Resource,* p. 159.

25. Quoted in Louisa Wah, "Making Knowledge Stick," *Management Review,* May 1999, p. 27.

26. Cited in Alan Webber, "Why Can't We Get Anything Done?" *Fast Company,* June 2000, pp. 168–180.

27. Scott Thurm, "Companies Struggle to Pass on Knowledge that Workers Acquire," *The Wall Street Journal*, January 23, 2006, p. B1.

28. Fara Warner, "How Google Searches Itself," *Fast Company*, July 2002, pp. 50–52.

29. Noel Tichy, "The Teachable Point of View," *Harvard Business Review,* March–April 1999, p. 82.

30. William Miller, "Building the Ultimate Resource," *Management Review,* January 1999, p. 45.

31. David Gilmour, "How to Fix Knowledge Management," *Harvard Business Review*, October 2003, pp. 16–17.

32. Pamela Babcock, "Shedding Light on Knowledge Management," *HR Magazine*, May 2004, p. 49.

16

Organizational Change

For Ken Lewis, CEO of Bank of America, the era of big deals in U.S. retail banking is over. Federal law prohibits any acquisition that would give a bank 10% or more of total U.S. deposits. BofA is at the limit, and the new mission became to grow fast anyway.

To make this happen, Lewis wants to build the most efficient bank in the United States. To do so, he has poached 100 Six Sigma–trained GE people, even though he regards CEO Jeff Immelt as both a friend and a business hero. Refined at GE during the Jack Welch era, Six Sigma is a method of improving operating efficiencies. Six Sigma–trained "black belts" help rank-and-file employees improve every step of their work processes—in BofA's case, from collecting bad loans to writing mortgages. The payoff is more production and fewer errors—all traced by sophisticated statistical measures. This regimen is light years ahead of the traditional coffee-and-cookies approach to getting new business.

Lewis deployed Six Sigma to derive a metric that BofA had never before considered: the number of products each banker sells each day. He found that 20% of the employees in a branch were selling 80% of the mortgages, loans, and credit cards, and that many employees sold almost nothing. Now he imposes minimum daily sales quotas—typically, around a half-dozen products a day—for every banker. There's a carrot to match the stick: New incentives mean star producers can earn half their base pay in bonuses.

Source: Shawn Tully, "Banker of America," *Fortune*, September 5, 2005, p. 111.

Now Ask Yourself: **Why is this story about a giant bank relevant to the study of organizational change?**   The CEO in question faced the serious change of no longer being able to grow much by purchasing other banks. So he turned to a highly disciplined method of organization development (or change), Six Sigma, to improve the productivity of bank branch employees. In this chapter we describe five key aspects of organizational change: (1) two models of the change process, (2) an analysis of resistance to change and overcoming change, (3) forces that create change, (4) organization development, and (5) dealing with change at a personal level.

TWO MODELS OF THE CHANGE PROCESS IN ORGANIZATIONS

Present two models of the change process in organizations.

"The only constant is change" is a frequently repeated cliché in the workplace. To meet their objectives, managers and professionals must manage change effectively almost daily. Even companies that appear from the outside to work in a stable environment are faced with change. A surprising example is Hershey Foods Corporation, which has been making chocolate products since 1905—including the remarkably stable brands Hershey's milk chocolate and Reese's Peanut Butter Cups. However, the technology for distributing chocolate products, including Internet sales, has created enormous challenges for the chocolate maker. A company executive said almost a decade ago, "Keeping up with the technology is probably the greatest challenge. Imagine how different it is to make chocolate now than when Milton Hershey was making his first caramel. From the time chocolate is made to the time it reaches the consumer, it's dealing with new technology the whole way."[1]

Competitive threats are a primary mover for changes within an organization, even for market leaders. For example, Microsoft now faces stiff competition from Google because the latter is now able to preload its software into some new PCs. Linux, the free operating system—not counting service fees—is another competitive threat to the dominance of Microsoft.

The many other types of change in organizations include changes in technology, organization structure, and the people with whom one works, such as customers and company insiders.

Organizational change has been studied from different perspectives. Collectively, the two models described next help explain change from the organizational and individual perspectives.

The Growth Curve Model of Change in Organizations

The **growth curve model** traces the inevitability of change through a firm's life cycle, as shown in Exhibit 16-1. According to this model, businesses pass through three phases in sequence.[2] First is the *formative phase,* characterized by a lack of structure, trial and error, and the presence of entrepreneurial risk taking. Mistakes are seen as learning opportunities, and innovation is extremely important. The firm focuses on its market, with the goal of becoming predictable, stable, and successful.

Second is the *normative phase,* in which stability occurs. An emphasis is placed on maintaining the existing structure and developing predictability. Mistakes are frowned upon and perhaps punished, which leads to less risk taking. The firm becomes more bureaucratic, and innovation is mostly given lip service or relegated to the research and development unit. The goal is survival, and the focus is less on

Exhibit **16-1**

*The Growth Curve
Model of Organizational
Change*

*Organizations go through
predictable life stages.*

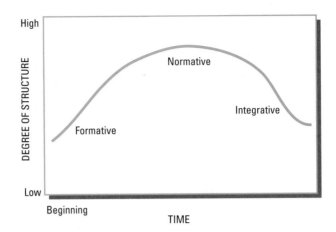

the market and more on maintaining the status quo. However, changes continue to occur in the environment, which forces this phase to end.

Third is the *integrative phase*, in which the firm redefines itself and finds a new direction. During this phase, top-level managers attempt many changes, such as introducing a new vision and policies. At the same time, the most resistance to change occurs at this stage, as many members of the firm attempt to resist the discomfort change brings. The integrative phase is associated with ambiguity and uncertainty. In addition, the firm experiences an "organ rejection" of the new systems. During this phase, leadership, inspiration, and interpersonal skills become more important than routine management and technical skills.

During the integrative phase, there is a pulling and tugging between forces for and against change. According to the **force-field theory,** an organization simultaneously faces forces for change (the driving forces) and forces for maintaining the status quo (the restraining forces). Forces for change include new technology, competition from other groups, and managerial pressures. Forces for the status quo include group performance norms, fear of change, employee complacency, and well-learned skills. Considerable managerial skill is required in order for driving forces to outweigh restraining forces. As managers push for change, there is an equal push in the opposite direction from those who want to maintain the status quo.[3]

Another observation about change is that the ability to change is somewhat related to size: Large organizations are more resistant to change than are small or medium-size organizations. In the Microsoft example just cited, the inference could be made that CEO thought the bigness of the company was making it less nimble.

The Unfreezing–Changing–Refreezing Model

Psychologist Kurt Lewin presented a three-step analysis of the change process.[4] His **unfreezing–changing–refreezing model** is widely used by managers to help bring about constructive change. Many other approaches to initiating change stem from this simple model, illustrated in Exhibit 16-2. Unfreezing involves reducing or

Exhibit **16-2**

The Change Process

*Change is a three-step
process.*

eliminating resistance to change. As long as employees oppose a change, it will not be implemented effectively.

Changing, or moving on to a new level, usually involves considerable two-way communication, including group discussion. According to Lewin, "Rather than a one-way flow of commands or recommendations, the person implementing the change should make suggestions. The changees should be encouraged to contribute and participate." *Refreezing* includes pointing out the success of the change and looking for ways to reward people involved in implementing the change. For the change process to be complete, refreezing must take place.

WHY PEOPLE RESIST CHANGE

Before a company's managers can gain support for change, they need to understand why people resist change. People resist change for reasons they think are important, the most common being the fear of an unfavorable outcome. This outcome could be less money, personal inconvenience, more work, and so forth. People also resist change for reasons such as not wanting to disrupt social relationships and not wanting to break well-established habits.

Describe why people resist change and how to manage such resistance.

A deep-level reason many employees resist change is that they face competing commitments. Even if the worker wants to go along with a workplace change, he or she might direct productive energy toward a hidden competing commitment. Organizational psychologists Robert Kegan and Lisa Laskow Lahey explain that an employee who moves slowly on a project may have an unrecognized competing commitment to avoid an even tougher assignment that might follow. If he performs well on the present project he might be given an even greater challenge that he fears might be beyond his potential.[5] The competing commitment functions as an immunity to change. Another example of a competing commitment is that a worker might resist performing well in a new supervisory position; if she performs well as a supervisor, she might be perceived as being disloyal to members of the work group of which she was a well-accepted member.

Even when people do not view a change as potentially damaging, they may sometimes resist it because they fear the unknown. People will sometimes cling to a system they dislike rather than change. According to folk wisdom, "People would rather deal with the devil they know than the devil they don't know." Workers may also resist change because they are aware of weaknesses in the proposed changes that may have been overlooked or disregarded by management.[6]

> A sales manager resisted her company's proposal to shift a key product to dealer distribution. She explained that dealers would give so little attention to the product that sales would plunge. Despite her protests, the firm shifted to dealer distribution. Sales of the product did plunge, and the company returned to direct selling.

Another subtle reason for resisting change is that the change might be perceived as damaging the person–environment (or organization) fit. This conclusion was based on a study of 34 separate work units experiencing 21 different organizational changes, including reengineering projects, reorganization, and implementation of new technology.[7] Suppose an Avon representative has built a successful business, relying heavily on her network of personal contacts. She particularly enjoys visiting the homes of customers and placing orders by hand on order forms. The representative now learns that customers should be encouraged to place their replacement orders on the Avon website. Although the representative will still receive commissions on these sales, she resists getting her customers to shift to placing their orders on the Internet. The Avon rep feels that the new work environment is not a good fit for her skills.

Gaining Support for Change

Gaining support for change, and therefore overcoming resistance, is an important managerial responsibility. Here we look at nine of these techniques for gaining support for change. Exhibit 16-3 provides an overview of several of these methods plus a few others, as described in a classic article.

1. *Allow for discussion and negotiation.* Support for change can be increased by discussing and negotiating the more sensitive aspects of the change. The two-way communication incorporated into the discussion helps reduce some employee concerns. Discussion often leads to negotiation, which further involves employees in the change process. Town-hall meetings between senior executives and workers in different locations of a company have become a popular vehicle for gaining acceptance of change. During the meetings, the executives field questions from the local workers. In the words of Anne M. Mulcahy, the Chairman and CEO of Xerox Corp. who led the company

Exhibit 16-3

Methods for Dealing with Resistance to Change

Approach	Commonly Used	Advantages	Drawbacks
Education and communication	When there is a lack of information or inaccurate information and analysis.	Once persuaded, people will often help with the implementation of the change.	Can be very time-consuming if lots of people are involved.
Participation and involvement	When the initiators do not have all the information they need to design the change, and when others have considerable power to resist.	People who participate will be committed to implementing change, and any relevant information they have will be integrated into the change plan.	Can be very time-consuming if participants design an inappropriate change.
Facilitation and support	When people are resisting because of adjustment problems.	No other approach works as well with adjustment problems.	Can be time-consuming, expensive, and still fail.
Negotiation and agreement	When someone or some group will clearly lose out in a change, and when that group has considerable power to resist.	Sometimes it is a relatively easy way to avoid major resistance.	Can be too expensive in many cases if it alerts others to negotiate for compliance.
Manipulation and co-optation	When other tactics will not work or are too expensive.	It can be a relatively quick and inexpensive solution to resistance problems.	Can lead to future problems if people feel manipulated.
Explicit and implicit coercion	When speed is essential, and the change initiators possess considerable power.	It is speedy and can overcome any kind of resistance.	Can be risky if it leaves people mad at the initiators.

Source: Adapted and reprinted by permission of *Harvard Business Review*. From "Choosing Strategies for Change" by John P. Kotter and Leonard A. Schlesinger, March–April 1979, p. 111. Copyright © 1979 by the President and Fellows of Harvard College, all rights reserved.

360

through massive changes, "Change doesn't happen if you don't work at it. You've got to get out there, give people the straight scoop, and get buy-in. It's not just good-looking presentations; it's doing town meetings and letting people ask the tough questions. It's almost got to be done one person at a time."[8]

2. *Allow for participation.* The best documented way of overcoming resistance to change is to allow people to participate in the changes that will affect them. A powerful participation technique is to encourage people who already favor the change to help in planning and implementation. These active supporters of the change will be even more strongly motivated to enlist the support of others. A related approach is to grant responsibility for change to workers who have a capacity to find unique ways to look at problems that seem impossible to solve. Labeled *positive deviants,* these individuals are able to see solutions in places where others do not. An example of this approach took place at Hewlett Packard, where management wanted to bring about changes in the way computers were manufactured so they would not overheat when left running. (Overheating increases the failure rate.) Most engineers, however, were not much interested in this mundane problem. Using the positive deviant tactic, managers turned over the problem to an "positive deviant" engineer who galvanized other HP engineers around the globe to create cooler and less failure-prone machines.[9]

3. *Point out the financial benefits.* Because so many employees are concerned about the financial effects of work changes, it is helpful to discuss these effects openly. If employees will earn more money as a result of the change, this fact can be used as a selling point. For example, the CEO of a small company told his employees, "I know you are inconvenienced and ticked off because we have cut way back on office support. But some of the savings will be invested in bigger bonuses for you." Much of the grumbling subsided.

4. *Avoid change overload.* Too much change in too short a time leads to negative stress. So it is helpful to avoid overloading employees with too many sweeping changes in a brief period. Too much simultaneous change also causes confusion, leading to foot-dragging about the workplace innovation. The more far-reaching the innovation is, such as restructuring a firm, the greater is the reason for not attempting other innovations simultaneously.

5. *Gain political support for change.* Few changes get through organizations without the change agent forming alliances with people who will support his or her proposals. Often this means selling the proposed changes to members of top-level management before proceeding down the hierarchy. It is much more difficult to create change from the bottom up.

6. *Provide education.* A standard method of reducing resistance to change is through education and communication of relevant information. The method is likely to be the most effective when people resist change because they lack sufficient information. For example, workers may resist making the necessary preparations for outsourcing part of their work until they are informed about the scale of the outsourcing program and how it will affect their jobs.

7. *Avoid citing poor performance as the reason for change.* Instead of criticizing, the change agent should accurately describe market challenges or budget restraints and show employees why change is necessary for survival. For example, do not say to employees, "If things hadn't become so sloppy around here, we wouldn't need to change." Instead, tell them, "Our competitors can deliver finished product in half the time because of this new technology. If we don't make the change, too, we'll lose all our key accounts."[10]

SKILL-DEVELOPMENT EXERCISE

Gaining Support for Change

One student plays the role of a team leader who is to meet today with team members to sell them on the idea that the company plans to shift from a standard workweek to a 4/40 workweek (work 10 hours per day, 4 days per week). About six other students play the role of the team members, several of whom have mixed reactions to the proposed change. The team leader should use the techniques for gaining support for change described in this section. Team members who do not like the contemplated change should express what they consider valid reasons for resisting the change. Other class members should observe and then provide feedback.

Collaboration

8. *Incorporate the human touch.* Some changes are resisted because they are perceived to diminish valued human contact. Many workers and customers may be impressed with an information technology device that eliminates having to deal with a human to complete a transaction. The same workers, however, may resist the change because they enjoy human contact. Perhaps employees might be able to receive counseling about their benefits through an interactive computer program, or a voice recognition system, yet they would *prefer* to interact face-to-face with a benefits counselor.

9. *Pay attention to the emotional aspects of change.* Another aspect of behavior that must be dealt with in overcoming resistance to major change is emotion. Too often the manager attempting to sell the change focuses on cognitive aspects alone, such as making a rational presentation of the merits of the change. One example of paying attention to emotion would be to enable workers to express tension and anxiety they have about the change, such as worrying about whether a merger with another company will make them second-class citizens. Another way of paying attention to emotion is to formulate a metaphor that evokes positive feelings.[11] In the merger situation, the manager might talk about the group becoming part of a bigger family with room for everyone.

To practice the concepts of managing change, do the accompanying skill-development exercise.

③ FOUR MAJOR FACTORS THAT CREATE ORGANIZATIONAL CHANGE

Describe four major factors that create organizational change.

Many forces can create change in organizations. Here we pinpoint four representative forces: downsizing, information technology, and a shift in work roles. A fourth, more subtle, force is a value shift within the organization.

Downsizing and Restructuring as a Change Strategy

Downsizing has already been mentioned as a significant stressor and as a method of achieving a flat structure. Downsizing is also the most often used deliberate organizational change in the past 25 years, even during times of relative prosperity for companies. Governmental and educational institutions also downsize in response to financial pressures. The merger of companies is also a force for downsizing because of duplications in positions, such as having two human resource and information technology departments in the merged firm. Many downsizings come about because many fields have consolidated, such as retail chains buying each other and a major retailer like Wal-Mart or Target driving other retailers out of business.

Cost reductions are often necessary because the survival of the firm is at stake. Laying off workers can sometimes make a firm more competitive by lowering costs, but at the same time this causes enormous confusion and resentment. Downsizing can also leave a firm so understaffed that it cannot capitalize on new opportunities. Another concern is that downsizing depletes human assets and interferes with organizational learning because so much information stored in people's memories leaves the firm.[12]

An important perspective on downsizing as a change strategy is to specify the conditions under which it has the best chance of contributing to organizational effectiveness.[13] To begin with, top management should ponder whether downsizing can be avoided. Instead of laying off employees, a way should be sought to better use their expertise. Some cost cutting can be achieved by involving employees in improving work methods and processes. Under ideal circumstances, key people can look to penetrate new markets. As a last-ditch maneuver to avoid downsizing, a company might reduce the salaries of all workers, or place workers on a 4-day workweek, thereby having enough money to pay a full workforce.

The first key to a successful restructuring is to integrate downsizing with the company's long-term strategies. The firm must determine in what direction the business is headed and which employees are needed to ensure that future. The company must identify and protect high-potential individuals who are needed to carry the firm forward. After delayering, firms must decentralize and empower key individuals to conduct their jobs. The downsizing survivors must be revitalized by redefining their positions. (A problem is that survivors often have to assume the workload of several people.) It is therefore essential to eliminate low- and no-value activities such as multiple reviews of other people's work and meetings without meaningful agendas.

After restructuring, teamwork must be emphasized more than previously because much cooperation is required to accomplish the same amount of work with fewer human resources. The downsized organization may require a new structure. It should be redesigned to reflect the changed jobs, processes, and responsibilities. Horizontal as well as vertical relationships must be specified. Considerable attention must be paid to the human element before and after downsizing. A carefully implemented system of performance evaluation increases the chances that good work performance and the possession of vital skills should receive more weight than favoritism in retaining employees.

A progressive approach is to offer training to employees designated for downsizing so they might qualify for any vacant positions in the company. Downsizing survivors in all companies need an outlet to talk about their grief and guilt in relation to laid-off coworkers. As is often done, laid-off workers should be given assistance in finding new employment and redirecting their careers.

Information Technology and Organizational Change

Advances in information technology have facilitated a variety of profound changes in organizations. Your knowledge of information systems and information technology will help you visualize many organizational changes created by digitalizing information. A major change is that electronic access to information has made possible much of the delayering of organizations. Many middle management and coordinator positions have been eliminated because there is less need for people to act as conduits of information. Instead, information seekers obtain information via computers. Information technology has forced hundreds of companies to change their product offerings. Two small examples are that people purchase fewer hard-copy roadmaps today, and fewer low-priced watches are sold because many people use their cell phones to tell time.

Information technology has played a key role in making organizations more democratic. Democracy is enhanced because more people have access to information. E-mail makes it easier for lower-ranking members to communicate directly with higher-ranking members. Before the surge in information technology, such direct interaction was rare in large firms.

Although information technology has made organizations more democratic, many communications are also more impersonal. E-mail messages and other communication software such as shared web pages have replaced many conversations that might have profited from face-to-face interaction. Self-service systems for key functions, such as filing travel and expense reports and obtaining information about benefits, make it difficult to chat with someone about a problem. (At the same time, these impersonal systems save the organization time and money, such as through hiring fewer people to work on expense accounts.)

The Internet has substantially changed the nature of many businesses, such as companies interacting more directly with customers and suppliers. Many retail sales positions and industrial sales positions have been eliminated by e-commerce. The Internet has transformed some industries. A good example is the newspaper industry, whose changes mirror what is happening in other industries. To survive, the industry has had to rely on its traditional strength of offering detail and depth. Services must now also be offered in both hard copy and online. Newspapers were among the first commercial entities on the Internet. Information on the Net is now offered free, by pay-per-view, and by subscription. Similar to newspapers, advertising agencies have to cope with a major shift away from print ads toward advertising on the Internet.

Enterprise software that links the various functions of the enterprise to one another and to customers affects job behavior. A smaller number of managers are needed because fewer employees are needed when enterprise software is fully implemented. The remaining key workers must be skilled in information technology, problem solving, and interpersonal skills.

Information technology has created substantial changes in how long and where people work. Accessing and responding to e-mail has added hours to the workweek of many employees. Another change is that managers and professionals feel obliged to stay in frequent contact with the office, even during nights, weekends, and vacations. A report on technology in the 21st century put it this way:

> The problem today is that we haven't yet learned to manage technology. All too often our cellular telephones and notebook computers control us. Increasingly, we work all the time, everywhere. We use every available second to handle and prioritize voice mail, e-mail, and paperwork. In the Information Age, it's becoming impossible to know when work is completed. And unless something changes, all this ultimately affects everything from customer service to burnout.[14]

The Transition from Carrying Out a Job to Performing Work

A subtle change in the workplace is that traditional job descriptions are becoming too rigid to fit the flexible work roles carried out by many workers. An emerging trend is for companies to hire people to "work" rather than to fill a specific job slot. At both Amazon.com and Koch Industries, job descriptions are rarely used. At Amazon, a person might still hold the same essential job but 3 months later perform entirely different work. The "Amazonian" might be working out a software glitch one day and helping to lay out a new wing of a distribution center the next.

This sea change in work design can be overwhelming for people whose paradigm is to think of work as occupying a particular job. A starting point in the shift is to think about how to accomplish work rather than fill a job. Both Koch and Amazon have developed a model to make this shift from filling a job to carrying out a work role. These companies look more for a good person–organization fit than for candidates to fill a particular job. At Amazon, this means hiring people with entrepreneurial drive who are customer focused. The director of strategic growth (human resources) says, "We try not to be too rigid about qualifications, but [sic] the kind of people we hire and how they can apply what they know."[15]

To make this approach to work roles function well, the organization structure has to be flexible and employees have to have access to different opportunities. Also, managers have to be willing to let employees experiment and work in different positions. A cornerstone idea is that workers' skills have to be matched to the project. For example, a creative person from anywhere in the firm might be assigned to a cross-functional product-development team.

The implication for managers is that shifting away from relatively fixed job descriptions to emphasizing work roles is part of dealing with change in organizations. For many managers, this shift is difficult because job descriptions are the essence of bureaucracy.

Changing the Values of an Organization

A less tangible way in which an organization might change is to make a value shift. Workers who had different values must now change their values to prosper. A classic example is that banks had to learn to value customers more as regulations allowed a larger range of players into the mortgage business. Instead of doing customers a favor by granting them a mortgage, banks had to curry favor with potential mortgage customers. The value shift was from indifference toward high concern for customer service.

A current example is the value shift IBM underwent a few years ago. The company's long-standing values grew out of traditions begun in 1914. The three principles known as *Basic Beliefs* at the time were (a) respect for the individual, (b) the best customer service, and (c) the pursuit of excellence. Over time these values were changed into a sense of arrogance and entitlement throughout IBM. In 2003, CEO Sam Palmisano spearheaded a change in values using a computerized tool that collected employee input. Over a 72-hour period, thousands of IBM employees participated in an intranet discussion called "ValuesJam." A small team, with input from the CEO, arrived at a new set of new corporate values:

- Dedication to every client's success
- Innovation that matters—for our company and the world
- Trust and personal responsibility in all relationships

These values are supposed to drive operational decisions made by IBM employees. Today more than two-thirds of IBM's revenues stem from software and services (such as consulting). The values have become so important because IBM customers are buying more knowledge than hardware. IBM is therefore selling knowledge contained in the brains of employees.[16] A translation of a value into decision making would be for an IBM sales representative to think, "What service would best help my customer become more profitable?" rather than thinking, "How much IBM hardware can this customer possibly afford to buy?" Another example is that the new values would encourage IBM workers to develop innovations for noble purposes such as improving medical services and combating terrorism. The third value would translate into behaviors such as pricing products and services fairly.

The accompanying Organizational Behavior in Action box illustrates how a company in the consumer products field must adjust to changes in the environment.

ORGANIZATIONAL BEHAVIOR *In Action*

Unilever Executive Deals with a Changing World

Niall FitzGerald, cochairman of global consumer-products giant Unilever, sat down with *The Wall Street Journal* to discuss the tough business of running a global consumer-goods company. (Among the Unilever brands are Skippy, Lipton, and Hellman's.)

WSJ: Can a company like Unilever ever reach a point where its product portfolio is stable?

FitzGerald: You're never done because the world is changing all the time. You can be the best surfer in the world. But if you sit with your surfboard on a flat ocean, you won't go very far. What we have to do with the portfolio is consistently seek where the waves are going, and be there.

WSJ: How do you keep people motivated during times of upheaval?

FitzGerald: I try to make very clear that change is not criticism of the past. It's not what you did in the past was rubbish. It wasn't. It was absolutely relevant to the past and worked beautifully. Unilever had been around 75 years, so clearly a lot of things were done very well in the past. But the future's going to be different and we need to equip ourselves for the future.

When I visit a country now, I spend the first day nowhere near the company. I visit retailers and talk about what we're not doing right. I'll spend several hours with young managers on my own, with their bosses or their bosses' bosses. I say, "Come on, I want to hear it from you. How do you feel about things?"

WSJ: How do you keep the people who manage the brands fresh and focused on consumer needs?

FitzGerald: A brand will remain relevant as long as you keep innovating and you're absolutely ruthless about not allowing your resources to be dissipated elsewhere. There are no tired brands, only tired brand managers. Sometimes they've lost touch with the consumer. They've probably spent a lot of time reading market research reports and going to consumer panels. But they don't really know who the consumers are. Now at Unilever you have to have your "market's license" and demonstrate that you've spent 200 hours talking with consumers before you can talk about a marketing issue.

To be a successful marketer you have to be prepared to live with failure. If you try to take [sic] a decision without having 40% of what you need, you're in trouble. And if you wait until after you've got 70%, it's too late. So be brave enough to take your decisions in the 40% to 70% zone.

WSJ: How do you encourage managers to take risks?

ORGANIZATIONAL BEHAVIOR *In Action*

(Continued)

FitzGerald: I was a living, breathing example of someone who had taken risks and who had failed spectacularly. In 1994 we had been losing the laundry battle to Procter & Gamble and we came up with a breakthrough called the [Persil] accelerator which cleaned clothes. The problem was that, if you used it under the wrong conditions, it washed away not just the dirt but the clothes themselves. So, one of our friendly competitors placed in the newspapers pictures of knickers with holes in them that had been washed in our product.

I decided I want to be on the front line with guys and girls, in hand-to-hand combat to show them I would lead by doing what I was asking them to do. But I wasn't doing what a leader should do under those circumstances, which was to stand right back, survey the field of battle and then take [sic] judgments.

Scientifically, the product was unmatchable. Now, after successful marketing initiatives the Persil business is healthier than it was before. The turnaround was a statement to the business, showing that when this guy failed, the business didn't throw him out. The business actually made him chairman. Had I tried to create an example to make the point, I couldn't have done it any better.

Questions

1. Why does this story belong in a textbook about organizational behavior? Shouldn't it be in a marketing text?
2. What has risk taking got to do with managing or coping with change?

Source: Excerpted from Deborah Ball, "Stocking a Global pantry: Unilever's Niall FitzGerald On Buy-and-Purge Strategy, Need to Keep Changing," *The Wall Street Journal*, May 24, 2004, B1, B3.

ORGANIZATION DEVELOPMENT AS A CHANGE STRATEGY

When it is necessary to bring about long-term, significant changes in a firm, a formal method of organizational change is sometimes used. **Organization development (OD)** is any strategy, method, or technique for making organizations more effective by bringing about constructive, planned change. You might think of a clinical psychologist or executive coach working with the individual to bring about change, whereas an organization development professional focuses on improving the entire organization. OD applies principles of human behavior to promote healing, growth, and constructive change in organizations.[17] In its ideal form, organization development attempts to change the culture toward a more democratic and humanistic model. At other times, organization development aims to help change the technology or structure of the firm.

An appreciation of the number of OD techniques available can be gained from studying Exhibit 16-4. Various techniques are grouped according to whether they deal primarily with individuals, small groups, or the total organization. Several of the techniques, such as team development, conflict resolution, and stress management, have been described in previous chapters. Labeling all of these interventions as organization development is somewhat arbitrary because they are practiced in organizations not even aware of the existence of such a label. Here we describe a process model of organization development, followed by more information about four other OD approaches.

Explain the nature of organization development.

Log on to **www.thomsonedu.com/infotrac**. Can you find specific examples of organization development in some of the world's biggest companies?

367

Individual Level	Small-Group Level	Organizational Level
Executive (or business) coaching	Team development	Six Sigma
Employee assistance programs (EAPs)	Diversity training	Gainsharing
Career development programs	Modified work schedules	Survey feedback (attitude surveys)
Emotional intelligence training	Creativity training	Action research (employees participate
Cultural intelligence training	Intergroup conflict resolution	in implementing changes identified
Wellness programs, including stress	Self-managing teams	as needed by a consultant)
reduction		Knowledge management
Sexual harassment avoidance training		

Exhibit **16-4**

A Sampling of Organization Development Interventions

A wide range of organizational behavior and psychological techniques can be considered techniques of organization development.

Exhibit **16-5**

A Process Model of Organization Development

A formal program of organization development follows certain steps.

A Process Model of Organization Development

A process model of organization development has been advanced that incorporates the important features of many different OD change efforts.[18] The model builds on earlier strategies for organization development and is flexible enough to diagnose problems in most organizations. A key feature is that the OD specialist and staff members are both involved in bringing about constructive change. The model, which is summarized here, is outlined in Exhibit 16-5.

Preliminary Identification
of a Problem

↓

Managerial Commitment

↓

Data Collection and Analysis

↓

Data Feedback

↓

Identification of Specific
Problem Areas

↓

Development of Change Strategies

↓

Initiation of Behavior

↓

Evaluation

Source: Joseph A. Young and Barbara Smith, "Organizational Change and the HR Professional," *Personnel*, October 1988: p. 48. Reprinted with the permission of *Personnel* published by the Society for Human Resource Management, Alexandria, VA.

Step 1: Preliminary Problem Identification

The manager recognizes that a problem exists that interferes with work effectiveness. The problem could include the manager's behavior, such as the manager not making effective use of input by group members in his or her planning.

Step 2: Managerial Commitment to Change

The manager must commit to taking the steps necessary to implement the change program. The manager is warned that the change program could involve negative feedback about his or her behavior.

Step 3: Data Collection and Analysis

Before organization development can proceed, the climate must be assessed through interviews, observations, and a written survey. Information is obtained about topics such as the manager's alertness and open-mindedness, cooperation with other departments, problem-solving ability, and trust. This information is used to develop objectives for constructive changes. Many OD practitioners believe that collecting data is an important part of an effective change effort.[19] The alternative is for the change agent to simply use his or her judgment about what needs improvement. As implied previously, the data can take the form of interview summaries, and more objective data from questionnaires.

Step 4: Data Feedback

Data collected in Step 3 are shared with the manager and staff members. In this way, staff members can compare their perceptions with those of others, and the manager shows ownership of the problem.

Step 5: Identification of Specific Problem Areas

The OD specialist helps staff members give the manager feedback regarding strengths and weaknesses. Although the manager may not agree with the feedback, he or she must accept the perceptions. Problem areas among the staff members can also be identified in this step.

Step 6: Development of Change Strategies

The emphasis is on identifying root problems and developing action steps. A spirit of teamwork often develops as problems are identified that can be attributed to both the manager and staff members.

Step 7: Initiation of Behavior

An action step(s) is selected and implemented that seems to be the best solution to the problem. The behavioral change strategy considers who, what, when, and where. For example, the manager (who) will make sure that the planning and priority setting (what) are accomplished during staff meetings (when) in the conference room (where).

Step 8: Evaluation

An attempt is made to evaluate whether the behavior changes made in Step 7 by both the manager and staff members have improved behavior and work results. Evaluation data may be collected through more interviews and observations, including speaking to the manager's superior.

Process Consultation

A widely used OD intervention at the small-group level is called **process consultation.** Using this technique, the OD specialist (process consultant) examines the pattern of a work unit's communications. A team leader typically asks for process consultation because team meetings have not been highly productive. The process consultant directly observes team meetings. At opportune times, the consultant will raise questions or make observations about what has been happening. The role of the process consultant is to challenge the status quo by asking questions such as:

- "Why doesn't anybody ever respond to Larry's questions?"
- "How come nobody challenges Jennifer's remarks when she is way off base?"
- "Why does everybody nod their heads in agreement when the CEO speaks? Are you all yes-people around here?"
- "How much multitasking do you folks want in a meeting? I see people checking their text messages, and opening websites not related to the meeting."

Why process consultation makes a contribution has been explained in these terms: "It points out the true quality of the emperor's new clothes even when everyone is pretending they are quite elegant." Also, the process consultant can be helpful in changing a closed communication style.[20]

Large-Scale Organizational Change

At best, organization development is a method of change aimed at breathing new life into a firm. **Large-scale organizational change** is the method used to accomplish a major change in the firm's strategy and culture. The process is sometimes referred to as *bending the frame,* to indicate that the firm is changed in a significant way.[21] A company needs large-scale organizational change, or a turnaround, when it faces major internal or external problems. A high turnover rate suggests that the company is not a good place to work for a variety of possible reasons. When a company develops a reputation for high turnover, it will be difficult to attract talented, motivated replacements. Loss of established business and the failure to obtain new business is virtual proof that the company is in trouble.

Shifting from an authoritarian (or command and control) style organization to a team-based organization would be a typical example of a large-scale change. Closely related is the shift from a slow-moving bureaucracy to a more nimble, entrepreneurial-style firm. One of the most stunning turnarounds of all was Continental Airlines, which went from an airline headed for its third bankruptcy—with low morale and poor customer service—to becoming an industry leader. A key part of the large-scale organizational change was to establish a results-oriented culture. Two components of the culture change were to (a) let people do their job without interference, and (b) treat one another with dignity and respect.[22] The case problem at the end of the chapter describes Ford Motor Company's plans to engage in large-scale organizational change, yet the company never slid to the depths that Continental Airlines did.

A starting point in bringing about large-scale organizational change is to place a transformational leader in charge. Another important consideration, as advanced by the research and analysis of Larry Hirschorn, is to organize the transformational effort into three campaigns: political, marketing, and military. Following these procedures will help bring order to the chaos often associated with a large-scale change initiative.[23] The *political campaign* creates a coalition strong enough to support the initiative, and also to receive guidance from the people involved in the change. The change initiator may have to inspire others at first, and then build consensus at a later point. At other times, a change in organization structure might be necessary to help build the coalition. For example, a layer of management might be eliminated so division heads can interact directly with the CEO who spearheads the large-scale organizational change.

The *marketing campaign* is designed to publicize and sell the benefits of the initiative. The campaign concentrates on listening to ideas that surface from the field as well as on working with lead customers to design the initiative. (A lead customer makes an advanced use of a product or service, or uses it in an imaginative way— such as closing wounds with duct tape!) Another approach to receiving input is to observe directly what is happening in the field. For example, top management at a large insurance company wanted to enhance productivity throughout the organization. During field visits, organizational behavior specialists discovered that in the most successful offices, managers held huddles rather than formal meetings at the beginning of each day, covering the same topics as the meetings would. The huddles were then recommended to all branch offices. The marketing campaign also includes giving a theme to the change initiative, such the classic "Work-Out" theme at GE, meaning that executives would help lower-ranking managers resolve problems and eliminate unnecessary work.

The *military campaign* is aimed at deliberately engaging with others to overcome resistance, using many of the ideas just described for winning support for change. It is essential for the change initiator to stay closely involved with the change effort because many large-scale initiatives fail simply because they are neglected shortly after the kickoff.

A final consideration here about large-scale organizational change is to involve as many people as feasible. Richard H. Axelrod explains that efficient and effective implementation of change requires a critical mass of people throughout the organization who are committed to the outcomes; not just consultants and leaders, but everyone.[24] (Knowledge of individual differences suggests that such total commitment to improving the organization is highly unlikely, even though it is an ideal worth striving for.)

As with most forms of organization development, an external or internal consultant is usually required to bring about large-scale change. Line managers may be responsible for implementing the change, but advisors trained in organizational behavior help in the process.

Six Sigma as Organization Development

The shift to a more quality-conscious firm can be classified as a total systems approach to organization development. Having high-quality goods and services is considered a necessary minimum to compete effectively. Most customers today require high-quality standards from vendors. One such standard is six sigma, or 3.4 errors in 1 million opportunities. (The figure is derived from the area under the normal curve from −6 to +6 standard deviations from the mean.) This quality standard has taken the form of company-wide programs for attaining high quality.

With capital first letters, Six Sigma® also refers to a philosophy of driving out waste, and improving quality and the cost and time performance of a company. Examples of companies with Six Sigma programs in some or all of their divisions are Motorola, GE, 3M, Home Depot, and Bank of America, as described in the chapter opener. (Six Sigma is a registered trademark of Motorola Inc., based on the statistical techniques developed by Joseph Juran.) Six Sigma is widely used in both manufacturing and service settings, such as improving employee benefits programs.

Six Sigma is regarded as a data-driven method for achieving near-perfect quality, with an emphasis on preventing problems. The approach emphasizes statistical analysis and measurement in design, manufacturing, and the entire area of customer-oriented activities. Six Sigma also has a strong behavioral aspect, with an emphasis on motivating people to work together to achieve higher levels of productivity. The system creates specialized positions in the company instead of placing additional responsibility on already overburdened managers and specialists. Employees choose to be "black belts," or Six Sigma specialists, and work full time as Six Sigma project leaders. Six Sigma teams carry out most of an organization's quality-improvement efforts. Nevertheless, everybody in the company is supposed to be involved in the change effort.[25] As with all programs of organizational improvement, commitment from top management is vital.

Six Sigma is seen as a fusion of technical and social systems because of the emphasis on both technical programs and creating a culture of quality. Without a shift to a culture that believes in and practices quality, it is difficult to sustain the shift to high quality. Six Sigma teams are formed to carry out most of the quality improvement.

An example of the application of Six Sigma to fix a quality problem took place in a manufacturing unit of Xerox. Software for translating technical manuals into foreign languages could not deal with some of the engineering jargon. Identifying and eradicating the problem phrases led to more rapid translations, fewer errors, and savings of up to $1 million.[26]

Six Sigma, as with other quality programs, can help an organization achieve reliable products and services. However, the program must fit into the company culture. When Ann Fudge, a former Kraft Foods Inc. executive, joined the advertising giant Young & Rubicam Inc., she was intent on implementing Six Sigma. Disliking the discipline of the system, many of the free spirits in the advertising firm referred to program as Sick Sigma. However, Fudge persisted and Six Sigma soon gained some acceptance among the advertising specialists.[27]

Linkage Analysis to Spread the Effects of OD

A major challenge in bringing about organizational change is that improvements in one unit do not necessarily spread to other units, or the organization as a whole. A frequent occurrence is that the advantages derived from downsizing one unit of a multinational firm do not necessarily improve overall firm performance. To deal with the challenge of getting the positive results from a change effort in one unit to spread to the firm as a whole, Paul S. Goodman and Denise M. Rousseau have developed a tool labeled **linkage analysis.** The general idea is to create linkages in the change pathway that translate gains within smaller organization units into benefits for the larger firm. Successful change efforts in one unit do not spread to the entire firm because organizations are so complex and use different metrics of good performance.[28]

Linkage analysis traces the connections between business units and the organization as a whole. A *change pathway* is a causal model that spells out the practices needed to build links between successful changes in one unit and the entire firm. Step 1 in the process is to understand the change pathway. Answers to four questions about features of the organization must be answered.

1. *How is the firm organized?* When organizational units are relatively independent, changes in one unit are more easily extended to other units. When the units are

more dependent on each other, changes in one unit tend to complicate the links between each other.

2. *Are the performance metrics similar?* When the performance metrics from one unit to another are the same, it is easier to trace the results from lower- to higher-level units in the organization. For example, if Six Sigma triples the profits of one region of Bank of America, these good results can easily be measured in terms of the overall performance of the bank because measures of profitability are standard throughout the bank.

3. *What is a unit's functional (discipline-related) contribution to overall firm performance?* In an organization with units of approximately equal size, and performing similar types of work, the proportional contribution is easier to measure. Starbucks can readily measure the contribution of each of its 6000 stores to the overall profitability of the firm. It would be much more difficult to measure the functional contribution of a research laboratory within 3M. (The functional contribution of a Starbucks unit is selling company products, whereas the functional contribution of a research laboratory is contributing marketable ideas.)

4. *What are the time lags between the change and observable results?* One consideration in a time lag is what activities must transpire between a unit-level change and the firm-level change. For example, will unit representatives have to spend a lot of time coaching and training other units about the new changes? If a Six Sigma initiative helps five Bank of America units, what has to be done to transfer the quality initiatives to other units of the bank? Another concern is how much time will elapse before changes in unit results lead to changes in the firm. If one unit of the firm receives training in ethics, how long will it take for the entire firm to behave more ethically?

Step 1 is understanding the change pathway including how one unit of the firm links to another. In Step 2 the manager and consultant must identify obstacles to the links. An example of a useful linkage would be the unit that has changed to share this knowledge with other units and the firm as a whole. An obstacle might be that the second unit was too busy to capitalize on knowledge sharing. Step 3 is to build stronger linkages by introducing mechanisms that will remove obstacles and increase the firm's ability to capitalize on local performance improvements. One approach is to build a shared multilevel motivation system, such as a bonus plan. Ideally workers and managers are rewarded for individual, group, plant or division, and corporate performance.

The mechanisms in linkage analysis create linkages in the change pathway that translate gains within work groups and units into benefits for the larger firm. The authors of the method provide case history evidence, including organizational improvements at Champion International Paper. A complicated organization development system of this type, however, requires an organizational culture quite sympathetic to experimentation.

MANAGING CHANGE YOURSELF   ⑤

A major factor in managing change is coping well with change yourself. All the approaches to organizational and small-group change described in this chapter work more effectively with individuals predisposed to managing change well. Our approach to providing insight into self-managing change is divided into relevant research and personal suggestions. To help you think through your flexibility about dealing with change, do the accompanying self-assessment quiz.

Develop useful insights into managing change in your job and career.

373

SELF-ASSESSMENT

How Flexible Are You?

To succeed as a managerial worker, a person needs a flexible attitude, an ability to be open to others, and a willingness to listen. Where do you stand on being flexible? Test yourself by answering Often, Sometimes, or Rarely to the following questions.

	FREQUENCY		
	Often	Sometimes	Rarely
1. Do you tend to seek out only those people who agree with your analysis on issues?	☐	☐	☐
2. Do you ignore most of the advice from coworkers or other students about doing your work more efficiently?	☐	☐	☐
3. Do your team members go along with what you say just to avoid an argument?	☐	☐	☐
4. Have people referred to you as "rigid" or "close-minded" on several occasions?	☐	☐	☐
5. When presented with a new method, do you immediately look for a flaw?	☐	☐	☐
6. Do you make up your mind early with respect to an issue and then hold firmly to your opinion?	☐	☐	☐
7. When people disagree with you, do you tend to belittle them or become argumentative?	☐	☐	☐
8. Do you often feel you are the only person in the group who really understands the problem?	☐	☐	☐
9. Do you prefer to keep using old software even though more than one new update has been published?	☐	☐	☐
10. Do you resist trying new foods?	☐	☐	☐

Check Your Score: If you answered "Rarely" to eight questions, you are unusually adaptable and therefore probably cope well with change. If you answered "Sometimes" to at least six questions, you are on the right track, but more flexibility would benefit your ability to deal with change. If you answered "Often" to five or more questions, you have a long way to go to improve your flexibility and adaptability to change. You are also brutally honest about your faults, which could be an asset.

Empirical Research about Coping with Organizational Change

A study involving over 500 employees in six organizations and five countries supported the well-accepted belief by practicing managers that some employees adapt better to organizational change than others. The ability to cope with change was measured both by self-reports and managerial assessments of how the workers coped with change. Seven personality factors presumed to be related to change were measured: locus of control, generalized self-efficacy, self-esteem, positive affectivity (similar to optimism), openness to experience, tolerance for ambiguity, and risk aversion. The seven traits were reduced to two factors: positive self-concept and risk tolerance.

A key result was that having a positive self-concept and a tolerance for risk were positively related to both measures of coping with change. The strongest and most consistent dispositional, or personality, variables among the seven traits in terms of their relationship to coping with change were tolerance for ambiguity and positive affectivity.[29] The implication supports what you probably suspected: People who can tolerate a lack of clarity and structure, and who are optimistic, cope well with change.

Suggestions for Coping with Change

The research just reported has a few implications for your ability to manage change well: Practice dealing with ambiguous tasks (such as unclear assignments) and work on having a positive general disposition. Consider also the following practical suggestions: *Look for the personal value that could be embedded in a forced change*.[30] If you are downsized, take the opportunity to assume responsibility for your own career rather than being dependent on the organization. Many downsizing victims find a new career for themselves that better fits their interests, or try self-employment in search of more job security.

When faced with a significant change, *ask "What if?" questions* such as "What if my company is sold tomorrow?" "What if I went back to school for more education?" and "What if I did accept that one-year assignment in China?" When confronting major change, *force yourself to enjoy at least some small aspect of the change*. Suppose the edict comes through the organization that purchases can now only be made over the Internet. This means you will no longer be able to interact with a few of the sales reps you considered to be buddies. With the time you save, however, you will have spare hours each week for leisure activities.

You are less likely to resist change if you *recognize that change is inevitable*. Dealing with change is an integral part of life, so why fight it? Keep in mind also to *change before you have to, which can lead to a better deal*. If your manager announces a new plan, get on board as a volunteer before you are forced to accept a lesser role. If your company has made the decision to start a Six Sigma program, study the subject early and ask for a role as a facilitator or team leader. Stop trying to be in control all the time because you cannot control everything. Many changes will occur that you cannot control, so relax and enjoy the ride. Finally, recognize that change has an emotional impact, which will most likely cause some inner turmoil and discomfort. Even if the change is for the better, you might remain emotionally attached to your old system—or neighborhood, car, or PC.

Continuous learning has been cited at several places in this textbook as a positive force in the individual's career. Continuing to acquire useful knowledge is also helpful in dealing with change because you have the new knowledge at hand to get past the change.[31] When digital photography became dominant, the operators of many portrait studios felt threatened and were too slow to offer digital services to their customers. Many of these photographers who waited too long to offer digital services were forced out of business. In contrast, many other portrait photographers were early learners of digital technology, and survived the transition well.

Dealing with Changes Created by the Flat World

The best seller *The World Is Flat: A Brief History of the Twenty-First Century*, by Thomas L. Friedman, has made thousands of educators and individuals aware of the potential changes imposed on us by globalization and outsourcing (as described in Chapter 14). One key point of the book is that the global economic playing field has been leveled by information technology that enables people to collaborate regardless of their location. Another key point is that the success of individual workers will depend on the development of specialized skills. Furthermore, to cope with these changes workers must constantly upgrade their skills. At the same time they should search for jobs that cannot be outsourced, or that are anchored because they must be done at a specific location, such as calling on an industrial customer.[32]

Many personal service jobs cannot be outsourced or sent offshore, among them being a hair dresser, massage therapist, custodial technician, and auto mechanic. Yet even here, some personal service workers in North America complain that residents from lower-wage countries are willing to perform these services at lower wages. Some corporate professional jobs are more difficult to outsource than others. The positions less likely to be outsourced are those requiring the combination of technical (or discipline skills) plus connections with people.[33] A real-estate agent with hundreds of personal contacts cannot be replaced by a website. An information systems specialist who performs hands-on work with internal clients cannot be replaced by an IT specialist working 7000 miles away in another country. The change-management lesson here is that building relationships with work associates helps ward off some of the threats of the "flat world."

IMPLICATIONS FOR MANAGERIAL PRACTICE

Peter Pan Offers a Safe Ride

Visit **www. thomsonedu.com/ management/dubrin** and watch the video for this chapter. What might be some sources of resistance to the changes in Peter Pan's safety and security practices?

1. The biggest challenge in implementing workplace innovations is to bring about cultural change. Workers' attitudes and values have to change if the spirit of innovation is to keep smoldering. An effective vehicle for bringing about such change is for top-level managers and others to exchange ideas. Formal arrangements, such as regularly scheduled staff meetings, facilitate exchanging ideas, reflecting on values, and learning what behavior is in vogue. Encouraging informal meetings can often achieve the same purpose with a higher degree of effectiveness.

2. Learning how to cope well with change yourself is a key part of managing change. Typical of such change would be dealing with the change of an employer cutting way back on paying for your health insurance and expecting you to pay a larger share.

SUMMARY OF KEY POINTS

 Present two models of the change process in organizations.

The growth curve model of change in organizations traces the inevitability of change through a firm's life cycle. During the integrative phase, there is a pulling and tugging between forces for change and against change. Another model of change views it as a three-step process: the unfreezing, changing, and refreezing of behavior.

 Describe why people resist change and how to manage such resistance.

People resist change for a variety of reasons they think are important, the most common being the fear of an unfavorable outcome. Also, facing competing commitments may create immunity to change, and the change might be perceived as damaging the person–environment fit. Techniques for overcoming resistance include (1) allowing for discussion and negotiation, (2) allowing for participation, (3) pointing out financial benefits of a change, (4) avoiding change overload, (5) gaining political support for change, (6) providing education, (7) avoiding citing poor performance as the reason for change, (8) incorporating the human touch, and (9) paying attention to the emotional aspects of change.

 Describe four major factors that create organizational change.

Downsizing as a change strategy is most likely to be effective when it is integrated into the company's long-term strategies. Low-value work must be eliminated, teamwork must be emphasized, and considerable attention must be paid to the human element. Information technology has facilitated change in organizations, including making them more democratic because of the increased accessibility of information. The Internet is changing the nature of many businesses, such as allowing companies to interact more directly with customers and suppliers. Information technology has created substantial changes in how long and where people work. Another force for change in organizations is the transition from a jobholder meeting the demands of a job description to a person carrying out a variety of work roles, or different kinds of work. Changes in behavior of workers can also stem from a value shift in the organization, such as becoming more dedicated to every client's success.

 Explain the nature of organization development.
Organization development brings about constructive, planned change, including modifying the culture. Using the process model of organization development, both the OD consultant and staff members are involved in bringing about constructive change. Process consultation is used to examine the pattern of a work unit's communications. Large-scale organization development is used to accomplish a major change in the firm's strategy and

culture. The large-scale change effort should be organized into three campaigns: political, marketing, and military. As many people as feasible should be involved in the change effort. Six Sigma programs stem from total quality management, and are an important organization development strategy. Six Sigma is also a philosophy of driving out waste, improving quality and the cost and time performance of a company. Linkage analysis is a tool for translating gains in one part of the organization to the firm as a whole.

 Develop useful insights into managing change in your job and career.
People who score high on the personality factors of positive self-concept and risk tolerance adapt better to change. Two specific traits related to dealing well with change are tolerance for ambiguity and positive affectivity. Among the suggestions for managing change well are searching for the personal value that could be embedded in forced change, asking "What if," forcing yourself to enjoy at least some small aspect of the change, recognizing that change is inevitable, and understanding that change has an emotional impact. To help cope with possible changes caused by outsourcing and offshoring of one's job, it is important to incorporate the building of relationships into one's job.

KEY TERMS AND PHRASES

Growth Curve Model, 357
A model that traces the inevitability of change through a firm's life cycle.

Force-Field Theory, 358
The theory contending that an organization simultaneously faces forces for change (the driving forces) and forces for maintaining the status quo (the restraining forces).

Unfreezing–Changing–Refreezing Model, 358
A three-step analysis of the change process based on the idea that change involves unfreezing, followed by changing and refreezing.

Organization Development (OD), 367
Any strategy, method, or technique for making organizations more effective by bringing about constructive, planned change.

Process Consultation, 370
An intervention in which the organization development specialist examines the pattern of a work unit's communications.

Large-Scale Organizational Change, 370
The method used to accomplish a major change in the firm's strategy and culture.

Six Sigma, 372
A data-driven method for achieving near-perfect quality, with an emphasis on preventing problems.

Linkage Analysis, 372
An organization development technique designed to create linkages in the change pathway that translate gains within smaller organization units into benefits for the larger firm.

DISCUSSION QUESTIONS AND ACTIVITIES

1. Approximately 30 years ago many managers and scholars were concerned that the computerization of the workplace would lead to enormous resistance to change. Whatever happened to resistance to computers in the workplace?

2. How can a manager tell if an employee is resisting change?

3. In recent years many people have had to cope with the change of now being managed by somebody who is much younger than themselves. Why are many of these people uncomfortable about being managed by a younger person?

4. Why might the transition from "jobs to work" lead to resistance to change for many people?

5. How does organization development at the individual level contribute to organizational change?

6. Why is *linkage analysis* important when conducting organization development?

7. Identify a major change you will have to cope with in the next several years and describe your plan of action for coping with it.

CASE PROBLEMS: Big Changes at GM and Ford

"Change or die" is the mantra of Mark Fields, the Ford Motor Co. president who crafted the automaker's latest restructuring plan. But with Asian competition seemingly a step ahead in introducing new models that consumers want and a powerful union that will fight to protect jobs and benefits, some question how much Ford and U.S. automakers can really change.

Ford announced a plan in to cut up to 30,000 jobs and close 12 plants in North America by 2012. The plan echoed General Motor Corp.'s restructuring effort announced 2 months previously, which will cut 30,000 jobs and close 12 North American plants by 2008.

GM's shares fell after analysts said its plan didn't go far enough. Ford's shares rose, but several analysts were unconvinced the plan will make the company's North American division profitable by 2008, as promised.

"Ford's restructuring plan was widely anticipated, but was more vague and protracted than we expected, which is disappointing, Goldman Sachs analyst Robert Barry said in a note to investors. "We also see sizable North American share loss continuing, weighing on earnings and offsetting many restructuring benefits."

GM and Ford announced the plans as their combined U.S. market share fell to an unprecedented low of 43% in 2005, down from 52% 5 years earlier. By contrast, Asian brands enjoyed a surge and now control nearly 37% of the U.S. market.

GM and Ford say they're going to the very core of their businesses to turn things around. They're vowing to work more closely with suppliers to cut costs, a tactic borrowed from Japanese rivals. They expect to save billions in development costs by sharing components globally and making plants more flexible, and they're promising to rely less on costly incentives.

"At both companies, they're very much attacking the culture of the organization," said David Cole, chairman of the Center for Automotive Research in Ann Arbor, Michigan. "I think they've got real possibilities."

Ford says it's taking on a top-down corporate culture that has stifled innovation. It's developing an appeals process to make sure employees' ideas are heard even if they're rejected by a manager, and it will judge employees on innovative thinking in performance review. "We're going to be a big company that thinks like a small company," Ford Chairman and CEO Bill Ford told employees a week ago.

But others aren't sure GM and Ford will be able to attract consumers despite new vehicles. GM has put low sticker prices on most of its vehicles and is retooling its marketing. Ford plans to make more distinction among its Ford, Lincoln, and Mercury brands and will emphasize its American heritage.

Case Questions

1. Offer Bill Ford a couple of suggestions for bringing about the culture changes he is aiming for.

2. What gains and losses might be forthcoming from the downsizings at Ford and GM?

3. What type of changes in attitudes and behavior will production and office workers at GM and Ford have to make for their employers to attain their new goals?

Source: Adapted from Dee-Ann Durbin, "U.S. Automakers Find Change Hard, Payoff Uncertain," The Associated Press, January 29, 2006.

ENDNOTES

1. "Hershey Thinks Its Delivery Problems Are Now Over," Associated Press, April 20, 2000.
2. Harry Woodward and Steve Bucholtz, *Aftershock: Helping People through Corporate Change* (New York: Wiley, 1987).
3. Kurt Lewin, *Field Theory in Social Science: Selected Theoretical Papers* (New York: Harper & Brothers, 1951).
4. Kurt Lewin, *Field Theory and Social Science* (New York: Harper & Row, 1951), Chapters 9 and 10.
5. Robert Kegan and Lisa Laskow Lahey, "The Real Reason People Won't Change," *Harvard Business Review,* November 2001, pp. 84–92.
6. James A. F. Stoner and R. Edward Freeman, *Management,* 4th ed. (Upper Saddle River, NJ: Prentice Hall, 1989), p. 369.
7. Steven D. Caldwell, David M. Herold, and Donald B. Fedor, "Toward an Understanding of the Relationship among Organizational Change, Individual Differences, and Changes in Person–Environment Fit: A Cross-Level Study," *Journal of Applied Psychology,* October 2004, pp. 868–882.
8. Interview with Anne M. Mulcahy by Keith H. Hammonds, "What I Know," *Fast Company*, March 2005, p. 98.
9. Richard Tanner Pascale and Jerry Sternin, "Your Company's Secret Change Agents," *Harvard Business Review*, May 2005, pp. 72–81.
10. "When Employees Resist Change," *Success Workshop,* A supplement to *Manager's Edge,* January 2000, p. 1.
11. Shaul Fox and Yair Amichai-Hamburger, "The Power of Emotional Appeals in Promoting Organizational Change Programs," *Academy of Management Executive,* November 2001, pp. 84–93.
12. Susan Reynolds Fisher and Margaret A. White, "Downsizing in a Learning Organization: Are There Hidden Costs?" *Academy of Management Review,* January 2000, pp. 244–251.
13. Sherry Kuczynski, "Help! I Shrunk the Company," *HR Magazine,* June 1999, pp. 40–45; "Layoffs Are Not Inevitable," The Associated Press, November 19, 2001.
14. Samuel Greengard, "How Technology Will Change the Workplace," *Workforce,* January 1998, p. 78. Used with permission.
15. Shari Caudron, "Jobs Disappear: When Work Becomes More Important," *Workforce,* January 2000, pp. 30–32.
16. Interview with Samuel J. Palmisano by Paul Hemp and Thomas A. Stewart, "Leading Change When Business Is Good," *Harvard Business Review,* December 2004, pp. 60–70.
17. Book review by Rick Tallarigo, Sr., in *Personnel Psychology,* Winter 2002, p. 1033.
18. Joseph A. Young and Barbara Smith, "Organizational Change and the HR Professional," *Personnel,* October 1988, p. 46; Wendell L. French, "Organization Development, Objectives, Assumptions, and Strategy," *California Management Review, 2*(1969), p. 26.
19. Janine Waclawski and Allan H. Church (Editors), *Organization Development: A Data-Driven Approach to Organization Change* (San Francisco, CA: Jossey-Bass, 2002).
20. Leonard D. Goodstein and W. Warner Burke, "Creating Successful Organizational Change," *Organizational Dynamics,* Spring 1991, p. 14.
21. Goodstein and Burke, "Creating Successful Organizational Change," p. 4.
22. Greg Brenneman, "Right Away and All at Once: How We Saved Continental," *Harvard Business Review,* September–October 1998, pp. 162–179.
23. Larry Hirschorn, "Campaigning for Change," *Harvard Business Review,* July 2002, pp. 98–104.
24. Richard H. Axelrod, *Terms of Engagement: Changing the Way We Change Organizations* (Williston, VT: BK Publishers, 2000).
25. Sara Fister Gale, "Building Frameworks for Six Sigma Success," *Workforce,* May 2003, pp. 64–69.
26. Faith Amer and Adam Aston, "How Xerox Got Up to Speed," *Business Week,* May 3, 2004, p. 104.
27. Diane Brady and Brian Grow, "Act II," *Business Week,* March 29, 2004, p. 76.
28. Paul S. Goodman and Denise M. Rousseau, "Organizational Change That Produces Results: The Linkage Approach," *Academy of Management Executive*, August 2004, pp. 7–19; and Executive Commentary to the article by Allan H. Church, pp. 20–21.
29. Timothy A. Judge, Carl J. Thoresen, Victor Pucik, and Theresa M. Welbourne, "Managerial Coping with Organizational Change: A Dispositional Perspective," *Journal of Applied Psychology,* February 1999, pp. 107–122.
30. The first two items on the list are from Fred Pryor, "What Have You Learned from Change?" *Manager's Edge,* September 1998, p. 2.
31. Al Siebert, *The Resiliency Advantage* (San Francisco, CA: Berrett-Koehler, 2005).
32. Thomas L. Friedman, *The World Is Flat: A Brief History of the Twenty-first Century* (New York: FSG, 2005).
33. Peter Svensson, "Hands-On Jobs May Be the Safest," Associated Press, July 4, 2004.

17

OBJECTIVES

After reading and studying this chapter and doing the exercises, you should be able to:

1. Understand the scope, competitive advantages, and potential problems associated with cultural diversity.

2. Identify and explain key dimensions of cultural differences.

3. Describe what is required for managers and organizations to become multicultural.

4. Be more aware of barriers to good cross-cultural relations.

5. Explain how motivation, ethics, appropriate negotiation skills, conflict resolution, and empowerment practices can vary across cultures.

6. Appreciate the nature of diversity training and cultural training, including cultural intelligence training.

Cultural Diversity and Cross-Cultural Organizational Behavior

Steven S. Reinemund has built PepsiCo Inc. into much more than a purveyor of junk food standards. Through constant innovation and savvy moves like the $14 billion acquisition of Quaker Oats Co., Reinemund, 56, has created a nimble, $27 billion food and beverage giant. Every year, PepsiCo adds more than 200 product variations to its global portfolio of brands, which includes Frito-Lay snacks, Pepsi-Cola sodas, Gatorade sports drinks, and Tropicana juice. Many are aimed at wooing ethnic tastes as well as satisfying health-conscious consumers.

But Reinemund's greatest achievement is in developing people more than products. While some rivals are mired in management challenges, PepsiCo has developed one of the deepest executive benches in Corporate America. Moreover, the diversity of that bench has proved to be an asset in tapping new markets. As Reinemund puts it: "To be a leader in consumer products, it's critical to have leaders who represent the population we serve." He personally takes a major role in mentoring and teaching staff—both formally and informally. He also demands that everyone in the senior ranks do the same.

The payoff: consistent double-digit earnings growth and solid sales at a time when many of the company's staple products are under threat from fears over childhood obesity and other heath concerns. One reason for heavy growth in earnings per share is the increasing strength of operations in foreign markets such as India and China, thanks largely to the talent of local teams.

Source: Adapted from "The Best Managers" (Steven Reinemund), *Business Week*, January 10, 2005, p. 57.

Now Ask Yourself: **What does this story about the continuing success at PepsiCo tell us about cultural diversity and international organizational behavior?** To be an internationally prominent business firm, it helps to have diverse leadership, who in turn can guide the company toward success in culturally diverse domestic and international markets. We have already mentioned demographic and cultural diversity at several places in this textbook. Chapter 2 included a description of demographic factors as a source of individual differences, Chapter 8 described cross-cultural communication barriers, Chapter 15 described how cross-cultural differences can hamper a merger, and cross-cultural issues were raised in relation to many other concepts throughout the book. One purpose of this chapter is to provide additional insights managers and professionals can use to capitalize on diversity within and across countries.

The fact that business has become increasingly global has elevated the importance of understanding cross-cultural and international organizational behavior. Furthermore, the U.S. workforce continues to be more culturally diverse. Our description of cultural diversity and cross-cultural organizational behavior will include a presentation of key concepts, as well as ideas for developing diversity and cross-cultural skills. Before reading on, do the accompanying self-assessment quiz on skills and attitudes. It will help you think through how multicultural you are now.

CULTURAL DIVERSITY: SCOPE, COMPETITIVE ADVANTAGES, AND POTENTIAL PROBLEMS

Cultural diversity can be approached from many different perspectives relating both to its interpersonal and business aspects. In this section, we describe the scope and goals of cultural diversity and how it affects business results, as well as potential problems with a culturally diverse workforce. Diversity training is given separate attention later.

Understand the scope, competitive advantages, and potential problems associated with cultural diversity.

The Scope and Goals of Cultural Diversity

Improving cross-cultural relations includes understanding the true meaning of appreciating demographic and cultural diversity. To appreciate diversity, a person must go beyond tolerating and treating people from different racial and ethnic groups fairly. Recognize, however, that some people criticize the diversity movement for being overly inclusive instead of assisting people who have been held back or discriminated against because of demographic factors such as race or age. The true meaning of valuing diversity is to respect and enjoy a wide range of cultural and individual differences, thereby including everybody. Some diversity specialists now prefer the term *inclusion* to *diversity,* and focus on the *similarities* among people rather than on the differences among them.

To be diverse is to be different in some measurable way. Although the diversity factor is measurable in a scientific sense, it may not be visible on the surface. Upon meeting a team member, it may not be apparent that the person is diverse from the standpoint of being dyslexic, color-blind, gay, lesbian, or vegetarian. However, all of these factors are measurable.

As just implied, some people are more visibly diverse than others because of physical features or disabilities. Yet the diversity umbrella is supposed to include everybody in an organization. The goal of a diverse organization is for persons of all cultural backgrounds to achieve their full potential, not restrained by group identities such as sex, nationality, or race.[1]

SELF-ASSESSMENT

Cross-Cultural Attitudes and Skills

Listed here are various skills and attitudes that employers and cross-cultural specialists think are important for relating effectively to coworkers in a culturally diverse environment. Check the appropriate column.

	Applies to Me Now	Not There Yet
1. I have spent some time in another country.	☐	☐
2. At least one of my friends is deaf, blind, or uses a wheelchair.	☐	☐
3. Currency from other countries is as real as the currency from my own country.	☐	☐
4. I can read in a language other than my own.	☐	☐
5. I can speak in a language other than my own.	☐	☐
6. I can write in a language other than my own.	☐	☐
7. I can understand people speaking in a language other than my own.	☐	☐
8. I use my second language regularly.	☐	☐
9. My friends include people of races different from my own.	☐	☐
10. My friends include people of different generations.	☐	☐
11. I feel (or would feel) comfortable having a friend with a sexual orientation different from mine.	☐	☐
12. My attitude is that although another culture may be very different from mine, that culture is equally good.	☐	☐
13. I would be willing to (or already do) hang art from different countries in my home.	☐	☐
14. I would accept (or have already accepted) a work assignment of more than several months in another country.	☐	☐
15. I have a passport.	☐	☐

Scoring and Interpretation: If you answered "Applies to Me Now" to 10 or more of these statements, you most likely function well in a multicultural work environment. If you answered "Not There Yet" to 10 or more of these statements, you need to develop more cross-cultural awareness and skills to work effectively in a multicultural work environment. You will notice that being bilingual gives you at least five points on this quiz.

Sources: Some of the statements are derived from Ruthann Dirks and Janet Buzzard, "What CEOs Expect of Employees Hired for International Work," *Business Education Forum,* April 1997, pp. 3–7; Gunnar Beeth, "Multicultural Managers Wanted," *Management Review,* May 1997, pp. 17–21.

Also, the concept of diversity continues to evolve. The director of diversity and work environment at Merck & Co. recently stated that "We've gone from the '80s understanding of diversity, where the goal was making the affected groups feel better, to where we connect it more to our business and hold managers accountable."[2] Diversity is therefore seen as a mechanism for business success, including generating more ideas and serving customers better.

An important distinction exists between diversity and diversity management. *Diversity* focuses on differences among people, whereas *diversity management* involves systematic strategies and tactics designed to improve interaction among people and groups so that they function more effectively.[3]

Exhibit 17-1 presents a broad sampling of the ways in which work associates can differ from one another. Studying this list can help you anticipate the types of differences in cultural as well as individual factors. Individual factors are also important because people can be discriminated against for personal characteristics as well as

Exhibit **17-1**

The Diversity Umbrella

Diversity has evolved into a wide range of group and individual characteristics.
- Race
- Sex or gender
- Religion
- Age (young, middle-aged, and old)
- Generation differences, including attitudes (for example, Baby Boomers versus Generation X and Generation Y)
- Ethnicity (country of origin)
- Education
- Abilities
- Mental disabilities (including attention-deficit disorder)
- Physical status (including hearing status, visual status, able-bodied, wheelchair user)
- Values and motivation
- Sexual orientation (heterosexual, homosexual, bisexual, transgender or transsexual)
- Marital status (married, single, divorced, cohabitating, widow, widower)
- Family status (children, no children, two-parent family, single parent, grandparent, opposite-sex parents, same-sex parents)
- Personality traits
- Functional background (area of specialization, such as marketing or human resources)
- Technology interest (high-tech, low-tech, technophobe)
- Weight status (average, obese, underweight, anorexic)
- Hair status (full head of hair, bald, wild hair, tame hair, long hair, short hair)
- Style of clothing and appearance (dress up; dress down; professional appearance; casual appearance; tattoos; body piercing, including multiple earrings, nose rings, lip rings)
- Tobacco status (smoker versus nonsmoker, chewer versus nonchewer)
- Your addition(s) to the list

group factors. Many people, for example, believe they are held back from promotion because of their weight-to-height ratio.

The Competitive Advantage of Diversity

Encouraging cultural and demographic diversity within an organization helps an organization achieve social responsibility goals. Also, diversity sometimes brings a competitive advantage to a firm. Before diversity can offer a competitive advantage to a firm, it must be woven into the fabric of the organization. This stands in contrast to simply having a "diversity program" offered periodically by the human resources department. Instead, the human resource efforts toward accomplishing diversity should be managed as part of organizational strategy. Thomas A. Kochan conducted a 5-year study of the impact of diversity on business results. The study examined large firms with positive reputations for their long-standing commitment to building a culturally diverse workforce and managing diversity effectively. Kochan concluded that diversity can enhance business performance only with proper training and an organizational culture to support it.[4]

The potential competitive (or bottom-line) benefits of cultural diversity, as revealed by research and observations, are described next.[5]

1. *Managing diversity well offers a marketing advantage, including increased sales and profits.* Allstate Insurance Company invests considerable effort into being a culturally diverse business firm. More than coincidentally, Allstate is now recognized as the nation's leading insurer of African Americans and Hispanics. Appeals to specific cultural groups, including websites written in the language of the target group,

have enhanced sales substantially. As IBM has increased the number of women and minorities in its management ranks, the company has dramatically increased the amount of business it does with small and midsize minority- and women-owned business firms.[6] A study of Fortune 500 companies by the research firm Catalyst indicates that the companies with the highest representation of women in senior ranks have a 35% higher return on equity and a 34% higher return to shareholders than companies with fewer women in top-level positions.[7] (It is also possible that more profitable companies are more willing to invest in diversity.)

2. *Effective management of diversity can reduce costs.* More effective management of diversity may increase job satisfaction for diverse groups, thus decreasing turnover and absenteeism and their associated costs. A diverse organization that welcomes and fosters the growth of a wide variety of employees will retain more of its minority and multicultural employees. Also, effective management of diversity helps avoid costly lawsuits over being charged with discrimination based on age, race, or sex.

3. *Companies with a favorable record in managing diversity are at a distinct advantage in recruiting talented people.* Companies with a favorable reputation for welcoming diversity attract the strongest job candidates among women and minorities. The recruitment and retention of global talent has become an essential element of corporate success in today's economy. A shortage of workers gives extra impetus to cultural diversity. In recent years the driver-starved trucking industry has been recruiting in urban Hispanic communities, advertising in Spanish, reaching out to high-school students, and setting up booths at job fairs. So far a driver shortage remains, but the results are encouraging. Part of the appeal has been to those Hispanics searching for higher-paying jobs that do not require fluent English.[8]

4. *Workforce diversity can provide a company with useful ideas for favorable publicity and advertising.* A culturally diverse workforce or its advertising agency can help a firm place itself in a favorable light to targeted cultural groups. During Kwanzaa, the late-December holiday celebrated by many African Americans, McDonald's Corp. has run ads aimed at showing its understanding of and respect for African Americans' sense of family and community. For such ads to be effective, however, the company must also have a customer-contact workforce that is culturally diverse. Otherwise, the ads would lack credibility.

5. *Workforce heterogeneity may also offer a company a creativity advantage.* As mentioned in relation to effective groups (Chapter 9), creative solutions to problems are more likely when a diverse group attacks a problem. A pioneering study of organizational innovation found that innovative companies had above-average records on reducing racism, sexism, and classism.[9] A more recent study, however, of management groups in banks found that the relationship between heterogeneity and productivity is complex. It was found that in banks with more entrepreneurial strategies, both low and high management group heterogeneity were associated with higher productivity than was moderate heterogeneity.[10] Conceivably, moderate heterogeneity just created confusion within the group with respect to producing useful ideas.

Potential Problems Associated with Diversity

In addition to understanding the competitive advantages of diversity within an organization, a brief look at some of the potential problems is also helpful. Cultural diversity initiatives are usually successful in assembling heterogeneous groups, but the group members do not necessarily work harmoniously. The potential for conflict is high. In general, if the demographically different work-group members are supportive toward each other, the benefits of group diversity such as more creative problem solving will be forthcoming. Group members must also share knowledge with each other for the heterogeneous groups to be successful. Another problem is that diverse groups may be less cohesive than those with a less diverse composition.

A study of 60 work units in New York State shed light on the potential problems with work-group diversity. Most of the groups studied were composed of Caucasian, and African American workers. It was found that the true benefits of diversity surface only when there are support-based relations among dissimilar workers. Furthermore, it was found that heterogeneous peers supported each other more when the task was interdependent and when a high-support climate prevailed. However, there was a tendency for supportive relationships to decrease when the proportion of racially different others increases. For example, a group that was composed of 25% minority group members would be likely to have more supportive relationships than in a group with 50% minority group members. Another curious finding was that when groups were composed of African Americans as well as other minority group members, relationships were more supportive.[11]

Denny's restaurant presents a case history of how a diverse workforce does not inevitably contribute to increased business. In the early 1990s, Denny's settled antidiscrimination lawsuits by African American customers. By 2000, the company was considered a positive model of diversity, being named the Fortune No. 1 company for minorities based on Denny's investing millions on a wide range of diversity initiatives. Denny's management is proud to be such a culturally diverse and socially responsible company but has yet to see any positive financial results. CEO Nelson Marchioli says, "If you think diversity is going to sell one more pancake, you're crazy."[12]

CROSS-CULTURAL VALUES

Useful background information for understanding how to work well with people from different cultures is to examine their values. We approach this task by first looking at how cultures differ with respect to certain values; and second, how cultural values shape management style. As described in Chapter 4, values are a major force underlying behavior on and off the job.

Key Dimensions of Differences in Cultural Values

One way to understand how national cultures differ is to examine their values. Here we examine 10 values and how selected nationalities relate to them, based on the work of several researchers.[13] Geert Hofstede conducted the pioneering work in value dimensions in research spanning 18 years, involving over 160,000 people from over 60 countries. Some of his original work is presented here, along with updating and refinements by other researchers. Differences in cultural values are stereotypes, reflecting how an average person from a particular culture might behave. Cultural values follow a normal curve, as do personality traits. People within a culture are likely to vary considerably; for example, many Latin Americans have casual attitudes toward time, with others placing a high value on being punctual and making effective use of time. A summary of these cultural values is presented next.

Identify and explain key dimensions of cultural differences.

Log on to **www.thomsonedu. com/infotrac**. Locate articles related to significant differences amongst national cultures. Are cultural values changing in any particular part of the world?

1. *Individualism versus collectivism.* At one end of the continuum is **individualism,** a mental set in which people see themselves first as individuals and believe that their own interests take priority. At the other end of the continuum, **collectivism** is a feeling that the group and society should receive top priority. Members of a society that values individualism are more concerned with their careers than with the good of the firm. Members of a society that values collectivism, in contrast, are typically more concerned with the organization than with themselves. Highly individualistic cultures include the United States, Canada, Great Britain, Australia, and the Netherlands. Japan, Taiwan, Mexico, Greece, and Hong Kong are among the countries that strongly value collectivism. The current emphasis on teamwork, however, is softening individualism in individualistic cultures.

2. *Power distance.* The extent to which employees accept the idea that members of an organization have different levels of power is referred to as **power distance.** In a high-power-distance culture, the boss makes many decisions simply because she or he is the boss. Group members readily comply because they have a positive orientation toward authority. In a low-power-distance culture, employees do not readily recognize a power hierarchy. They accept directions only when they think the boss is right or when they feel threatened. High-power-distance cultures include India, France, Spain, Japan, Mexico, and Brazil. Low-power-distance cultures include the United States, Israel, Germany, and Ireland. According to the GLOBE (Global Leadership and Organizational Behavior Effectiveness) studies of 62 societies, organizational practices in most countries support a generally high level of power distance (as well as materialism, as listed below).[14]

3. *Uncertainty avoidance.* People who accept the unknown and tolerate risk and unconventional behavior are said to have low **uncertainty avoidance.** In other words, these people are not afraid to face the unknown. A society ranked high in uncertainty avoidance contains a majority of people who want predictable and certain futures. Low uncertainty-avoidance cultures include the United States, Canada, Australia, and Singapore. Workers in Israel, Japan, Italy, and Argentina are more motivated to avoid uncertainty in their careers.

4. *Materialism versus concern for others.* In this context, **materialism** refers to an emphasis on assertiveness and the acquisition of money or material objects. It also means a de-emphasis on caring for others. At the other end of the continuum is **concern for others,** an emphasis on personal relations and a concern for the welfare of others. Materialistic countries include Japan, Austria, and Italy. The United States is considered to be moderately materialistic. Scandinavian nations all emphasize caring as a national value.

5. *Long-term orientation versus short-term orientation.* Workers from a culture with a **long-term orientation** maintain a long-range perspective, and thus are thrifty and do not demand quick returns on their investments. A **short-term orientation** is characterized by a demand for immediate results and a propensity not to save. Pacific Rim countries are noted for their long-term orientation. In contrast, the cultures of the United States and Canada are characterized by a more short-term orientation.

6. *Formality versus informality.* A country that values **formality** attaches considerable importance to tradition, ceremony, social rules, and rank. At the other extreme, **informality** refers to a casual attitude toward tradition, ceremony, social rules, and rank. Workers in Latin American countries highly value formality, such as lavish public receptions and processions. Americans, Canadians, and Scandinavians are much more informal. The workplace across the world is becoming

much more informal, with workers at all levels making less use of titles and last names. The informality of communication by Internet has fostered informality.

7. *Urgent time orientation versus casual time orientation.* Individuals and nations attach different importance to time. People with an **urgent time orientation** perceive time as a scarce resource and tend to be impatient. People with a **casual time orientation** view time as an unlimited and unending resource and tend to be patient. Americans are noted for their urgent time orientation. They frequently impose deadlines and are eager to get started doing business. Asians and Middle Easterners, in contrast, are patient negotiators.

8. *High-context versus low-context cultures.* Cultures differ in how much importance they attach to the surrounding circumstances, or context, of an event. **High-context cultures** make more extensive use of body language. Some cultures, such as the Asian, Hispanic, and African American cultures, are high context. In contrast, northern European cultures are **low context** and make less use of body language. The American culture is considered to be medium-low context. People in low-context cultures seldom take time in business dealings to build relationships and establish trust.

9. *Work orientation/leisure orientation.* A major cultural value difference is the number of hours per week people expect to invest in work instead of leisure or other non-work activities. American corporate professionals typically work about 55 hours per week, take 45-minute lunch breaks, and take 2 weeks of vacation annually. Japanese workers share similar values with respect to the amount of work per week. European professionals, in contrast, are more likely to work 40 hours per week, take 2-hour lunch breaks, and take 6 weeks of vacation annually. European countries have steadily reduced the work week in recent years, while lengthening vacations, accounting for much of Europe's productivity deficit compared with the United States.[15]

10. *Performance orientation.* A recently labeled cultural difference stemming from the GLOBE study of 62 cultures is the degree to which the culture encourages and rewards group members for performance improvement and excellence. The value is imposed on schoolchildren, university students, and workers. Many Asian countries, including China, Hong Kong, Japan, Korea, Singapore, and Taiwan, rank high on performance orientation.[16]

Although the dimensions of cultural values just described are broad national stereotypes, they still relate to meaningful aspects of organizational behavior. A study on the impact of cultural values investigated how similarity to peers and supervisors influences career advancement in an individualistic versus a collectivistic society. The study participants were bank tellers working for the same multinational bank in Hong Kong and the United States. Both personality and individualism versus collectivism were measured by questionnaires. The researchers did not assume that work units in Hong Kong banks were collectivistic, nor that work units in the United States were individualistic. One major finding was that having a personality similar to peers was positively associated with promotion in units with high individualism. In units with high collectivism, having a personality similar to the boss was instead positively associated with advancement.[17] (The lesson here is that if you find yourself in an individualistic work group, emphasize personality traits that match your coworkers'. In a collectivistic work group, do what you can to emphasize personality traits that are similar to your supervisor's.)

How might a person use information about cultural differences to enhance interpersonal effectiveness? A starting point would be to recognize that a person's national values might influence his or her behavior. Assume that the managerial worker wanted to establish a good working relationship with a person from a high-context culture. To begin, he or she might emphasize body language when communicating with the individual.

Another application would be to recognize that many Asian Americans may need to be encouraged to talk in meetings because they have been taught to respect authority and to defer to elders. Consultant Jane Hyun observes, "Unfortunately this reticence gets mistaken for aloofness or arrogance or inattention, when it is usually just the Asian habit of respecting authority. We wait for our turn to speak—and often our turn just never comes."[18]

Culturally Based Differences in Management Style

The impact of culture on management and leadership style is another important influence of culture on organizational behavior. Although personality factors are a major contributor to management style, culture is also important because it serves as a guide to acceptable behavior. Culture provides the values that guide behavior. For example, a person raised in a collectivist culture would find it natural to be a consensus-style manager/leader. Because management deals so heavily with people, it is part of the society in which it takes place. To be effective, a manager transplanted to a different culture may have to make some concessions to the national stereotype of an effective leader. National stereotypes of management styles, according to the research of Geert Hofstede and his collaborators, are as follows[19]:

1. *Germany:* German managers are expected to be primarily technical experts, or meisters, who assign tasks and help solve difficult problems. More recent data stemming from the GLOBE indicate that a strong performance orientation is the most pronounced German value, with German managers not being overly considerate of others.[20]
2. *Japan:* Japanese managers rely on group consensus before making a decision, and the group controls individual behavior to a large extent. Japanese managers are perceived as more formal and businesslike, and less talkative and emotional, than their American counterparts. Japanese managers in large, successful firms are more likely to fit the consensus stereotype. Many Japanese managers in family-owned businesses have imperial attitudes and behaviors and have strong sexist attitudes toward women.

    The emphasis on consensus management in Japan does not mean that the pattern cannot be changed. Carolso Ghosn, a Brazilian-born executive, converted an almost bankrupt Nissan Motors into an industry leader in less than a decade. Reflecting on his management style, Ghosn said it was imperative that he move quickly to avoid being caught up in the quicksand of consensus. "This idea that no step can be taken without unanimous agreement was, in any case, largely a myth."[21]
3. *France:* French managers, particularly in major corporations, are part of an elite class (having attended select business schools called *Les Grandes Écoles*). As a consequence, they behave in a superior, authoritarian manner. The rigid class distinctions of French society also help shape the managers' attitudes and behaviors. Higher-level managers perceive themselves to be superior to managers at lower levels.
4. *The Netherlands:* Dutch managers emphasize quality and consensus, and do not expect to impress group members with their status. Dutch managers give group members ample opportunity to participate in problem solving. Following the tradition of consensus, most problems are resolved through lengthy discussion.

5. *China:* Many managers from China work in Pacific Rim countries such as Taiwan, the city of Hong Kong, Singapore, Malaysia, and the Philippines. In companies managed by Chinese, major decisions are made by one dominant person, quite often people over 65. The Chinese manager maintains a low profile.

The GLOBE study suggests that certain leadership and management styles may be favored in a cluster of countries. For example, participative leadership was the most culturally acceptable in the Germanic Europe cluster of countries (Austria, Germany, Netherlands, and Switzerland). In contrast, participative leadership was the least acceptable from a cultural standpoint in the Middle Eastern cluster of countries (Egypt, Kuwait, Morocco, Qatar, and Turkey).[22]

MULTICULTURAL MANAGERS AND ORGANIZATIONS

A major message from the study of international and cross-cultural organizational behavior is that managers and their organizations need to respond positively to cultural diversity. Here we look separately at the multicultural manager and the multicultural organization.

Describe what is required for managers and organizations to become multicultural.

The Multicultural Manager

The **multicultural manager** has the skills and attitudes to relate effectively to and motivate people with little regard to race, gender, age, social attitudes, and lifestyles. A multicultural manager has the ability to conduct business in a diverse, international environment. Achieving such competence requires a combination of many factors, including some of the traits associated with effective leadership described in Chapter 11. A few skills and attitudes are especially relevant for achieving the status of a multicultural manager.

A good starting point is to make strides toward becoming bilingual. International businesspeople respect the fact that a managerial worker is bilingual even if the second language is not their primary language. For example, if an American speaks French, the American can relate well to Italians and Spanish people. The tortuous reasoning is that many Italians and Spanish speak French as a third language, and respect the American who speaks a little French.

A major requirement for becoming a multicultural manager is to develop **cultural sensitivity,** an awareness of and a willingness to investigate the reasons why people of another culture act as they do.[23] A person with cultural sensitivity will recognize certain nuances in customs that will help build better relationships with people from cultural backgrounds different from his or her own. A positive example is that for an executive to conduct business successfully in China, he or she must build a *guanxi* (a network of relationships or connections among parties). The *guanxi* must be established internally with subordinates, peers, and superiors as well as externally with clients, suppliers, and government officials. Relationship building of this type takes time, but it is a cultural imperative in China.[24]

In addition to being culturally sensitive, the multicultural manager avoids cultural insensitivity. An example of cultural insensitivity follows:

A manager in a telecommunications in firm in Washington, DC, wanted to recognize the outstanding accomplishments of a worker, who was born and raised in India, on a major project. The manager offered the worker guest coupons to a steakhouse, not stopping to think that an Indian raised in India probably does not eat steak. The worker appreciated the recognition but laughed with his coworkers in describing the incident.

Dorothy Manning of International Business Protocol suggests adhering to the following dos and don'ts in the countries indicated. Remember, however, that these suggestions are not absolute rules.

Great Britain

DO say please and thank you often.

DO arrive promptly for dinner.

DON'T ask personal questions, because the British protect their privacy.

DON'T gossip about British royalty. Allow the British to take the initiative with respect to gossiping about royalty, such as mentioning juicy stories in the tabloids.

France

DO shake hands when greeting. Only close friends give light, brushing kisses on cheeks.

DO dress more formally than in the United States. Elegant dress is highly valued.

DON'T expect to complete any work during the French 2-hour lunch.

DON'T chew gum in a work setting.

Italy

DO write business correspondence in Italian for priority attention.

DO make appointments between 10:00 A.M. and 11:00 A.M. or after 3:00 P.M.

DON'T eat too much pasta, as it is not the main course.

DON'T hand out business cards freely. Italians use them infrequently.

Greece

DO distribute business cards freely so people will know how to spell your name.

DO be prompt even if your hosts are not.

DON'T expect to meet deadlines. A project takes as long as the Greeks think is necessary.

DON'T address people by formal or professional titles. The Greeks want more informality.

Japan

DO present your business cards with both hands and a slight bow as a gesture of respect.

DO present gifts, American made and wrapped.

DON'T knock competitors.

DON'T present the same gift to everyone, unless all members are the same organizational rank.

Source: *TWA Ambassador* October 1990, p. 69; *Inc. Magazine's Going Global: Japan Inc.*, January 1994; plus updates from direct observation in the present.

Exhibit 17-2

Protocol Dos and Don'ts in Several Countries

Exhibit 17-2 provides specific examples of nuances to consider. In addition, the information in Chapter 8 about overcoming cross-cultural communication barriers is directly relevant. Being able to deal effectively with cultural differences can be a make-or-break factor (or mediating variable) in the success of overseas ventures. Applying the information in Exhibit 17-2 will be the most effective when you understand the cultural values driving the behavior. For example, the information about the importance of business cards in Japan is generated in part because Japanese people value power distance, and the company a person works for helps determine his or her status. The value of collectivism also fosters the exchange of cards.[25]

An effective strategy for becoming a multicultural manager is simply to respect others in the workplace. To respect another culture is to recognize that although the other culture is different, it is equally as good as your own. A person from one culture might therefore say, "Eating rattlesnakes for dinner is certainly different from my culture, yet I can see that eating rattlesnakes is as good as eating cows." (Which living organisms constitute palatable food is a major day-to-day cultural difference.) Respect comes from valuing differences. Respecting other people's customs can translate into specific attitudes such as respecting one group member for wearing a yarmulke on Friday or another for wearing an African costume to celebrate Kwanzaa.

The Multicultural Organization

As more workers in a firm develop multicultural skills, the organization itself can achieve the same skill level. A **multicultural organization** values cultural diversity and is willing to encourage and even capitalize on such diversity. Developing a

MONOCULTURAL	NONDISCRIMINATORY	MULTICULTURAL
Exclusion of minorities and women from power	Unfair advantage of majority group removed, but no culture change	Shares power and influence with all; major culture change

Exhibit 17-3

Developmental Stages for the Multicultural Organization

multicultural organization helps achieve the potential benefits that come with valuing diversity. In addition, the multicultural organization helps avoid problems that crop up when managing for diversity, such as increased turnover, interpersonal conflict, and communication breakdowns.

An organization passes through developmental stages as it moves from a monocultural organization to a multicultural one, as shown in Exhibit 17-3. At the *monocultural level,* there is implicit or explicit exclusion of racial minorities, women, and other groups underrepresented in powerful positions in society.

The *nondiscriminatory* level is characterized by a sincere desire to eliminate the majority group's unfair advantage. Yet the organization does not significantly change its culture. The organization may strive to ensure that the racial and ethnic mix matches the racial and ethnic mix of society in general or its customer base. The organization may also attempt to influence its climate so it is not a hostile environment for the new members of the workforce. Full compliance with a government-mandated affirmative action program helps an organization reach the nondiscriminatory level.

At the *multicultural level,* the organization is becoming or has become profoundly diverse. The organization reflects the contributions and interests of the diverse cultural and social groups in the organization's mission, operations, products, and services. A pluralism exists when both minority and majority group members are influential in creating behavioral norms, values, and policies. Another characteristic is full structural integration. This term means that that no one is assigned a specific job just because of his or her ethnicity or gender.[26] The multicultural organization strives to be bias free, because bias and prejudice create discrimination.

To move toward being a multicultural organization, business firms take a variety of diversity initiatives. For example, the MGM Mirage's Bellagio in Los Vegas runs a 9-month executive mentoring program to ready high-potential minority workers in management positions for advancement into the executive suite. The hotel also offers a 6-month Management Associate Program—6 months of training to prepare recent minority graduates for careers in management through mentoring, classroom instruction, job shadowing, and hands-on experience.[27] Later in this chapter we describe diversity and cultural training. Also of importance are a variety of initiatives related to various demographic groups, as listed in Exhibit 17-4. An age initiative, for example, would be to ensure that in downsizing, senior employees are not overrepresented. At the same time, junior candidates should not be overrepresented in hiring.

As judged by *Hispanic Business Magazine,* three top multicultural firms, particularly in relation to Hispanic employees and customers, are McDonald's, Bank of America, and SBC Communications. For example, Bank of America opens retail and small-business outlets in Hispanic neighborhoods and hires Spanish-speaking associates.[28] The accompanying Organizational Behavior in Action box illustrates how one of the best-known companies in the world strives to be multicultural and diverse.

Exhibit **17-4**

Diversity Initiatives at
Major Business Firms

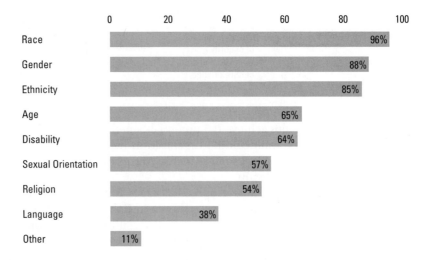

Race	96%
Gender	88%
Ethnicity	85%
Age	65%
Disability	64%
Sexual Orientation	57%
Religion	54%
Language	38%
Other	11%

Note: Figures indicate percentage of companies responding that they address certain issues through diversity initiatives.

Source: "Impact of Diversity on the Bottom Line," an SHRM/Fortune survey reflecting the responses of 121 HR professionals from 1,000 companies on *Fortune* magazine's list of the "100 Top Companies to Work For." Presented in Lin Grensing-Pophal, "Reaching for Diversity," *HR Magazine*, May 2002, p. 56. Reprinted with the permission of HR Magazine published by Society for Human Resource Management, Alexandria, VA.

ORGANIZATIONAL BEHAVIOR *In Action*

Starbucks Extends Its Reach to People with Disabilities

If Starbucks has its way, its future workforce will look more like Michelle Penman. Thirty-six-year-old Penman, who has cerebral palsy, spends 3 hours getting ready for work every morning. Because she has trouble speaking and limited mobility, customers write down their orders and place them on her wheelchair. She returns with their coffee and food on a tray or in a backpack affixed to her motorized wheelchair.

The Seattle-based coffee giant has already turned Penman into something of a company icon. The Starbucks CEO mentions her in his speeches as an example of the devotion of the company's workforce, and says he keeps her picture in his office. Now Starbucks wants to make Penman a literal model employee. As the company expands its outlets, it is trying to tap into the growing pool of job seekers with disabilities. The goal: to make its stores more inviting to customers with disabilities, as well as their caretakers, family members, and friends.

"This is a group that most businesses have not addressed," says May Snowden, Starbucks's vice president, global diversity. "As I look at changes in demographics, it is one of the groups that are very important."

Indeed, people with disabilities have discretionary spending power of $220 billion annually, according to the American Association of People with Disabilities. Of the 70 million families in the United States, more than 20 million have at least one member with a disability, according to the association.

For Starbucks, the equation is simple. "Customers tend to patronize a business that is like them," says Jim Donald, president and chief executive officer.

A Wake-Up Call

The Starbucks effort, which is still in the early stages, is proceeding on a couple of fronts. The company recently hired Marthalee Galeota, who worked with Seattle-area nonprofits on

ORGANIZATIONAL BEHAVIOR *In Action*

(Continued)

disability matters, as senior diversity specialist in charge of disability issues. The job goes beyond making sure Starbucks complies with the Americans With Disabilities Act, and the law that mandates equal access to jobs and services for the disabled. Galeota focuses on establishing a companywide etiquette for a range of issues.

For instance, she has changed the labels on tables designed for wheelchair users to read, "For a customer with a disability," instead of "Disabled customers." The company has also designed its counters at a height that is easily reached by customers in wheelchairs, and the majority of its roughly 10,000 stores around the world have at least one handicapped-accessible entrance.

In addition, Galeota is working to incorporate disability etiquette into employee training. For example, employees should ask a customer with a disability if he or she would like help, rather than automatically lending a hand; they should also refrain from petting a working service dog for the blind. Then there are day-to-day matters. Galeota fields calls from employees with disabilities as well as store managers to give advice about potentially tricky situations—for example, what a manager should do if an employee goes deaf.

Beyond the Coffee Line

Starbucks faces a higher hurdle than most companies when it comes to recruiting people with

disabilities. Its workers are constantly interacting with the public in its fast-paced, high-volume stores. Some Starbucks employees with disabilities acknowledge the challenges—but also the rewards.

Jim Donald, the president and CEO, attended Michelle Penman's 10th anniversary party at the store. Michelle has been the subject of a local newspaper story and television news spot, her mother says. "People talk about Starbucks in such a positive way, they say 'That's where Michelle works,'" her mother says. She says she knows her daughter is giving the company a wealth of positive press, but she doesn't mind. "If they want to be selfish and do it for them, that is OK. The person with the disability is winning too."

Questions

1. What effects on profitability might the initiative toward persons with disabilities have for Starbucks?
2. What impact, if any, might this story have on your propensity to be a Starbucks customer?
3. Is Starbucks exploiting Michelle Penman?
4. Why is "For a customer with a disability," preferable to "Disabled customers" as a term to place on tables at Starbucks?

Source: Excerpted from Michael Corkery, "A Special Effort: Starbucks Is Reaching Out to People with Disabilities—Both as Employees and Customers," *The Wall Street Journal*, November 14, 2005, p. R8.

BARRIERS TO GOOD CROSS-CULTURAL RELATIONS

An important part of achieving a multicultural organization and good cross-cultural relations in general is to understand barriers to such harmony. Major barriers of this type are described as follows[29]:

Be more aware of barriers to good cross-cultural relations.

1. *Perceptual expectations.* Achieving good cross-cultural relations is hampered by people's predisposition to discriminate. They do so as a perceptual shortcut, much like stereotyping. An example would be a sales representative encountering a man apparently in his 80s when visiting an important customer. The sales rep

begins to patronize the old man, talking to him in a child-like manner. The rep is then informed that the person he is patronizing is the chairman of the board, and still quite active. (Oops, a lost sale!) Because people are not naturally nondiscriminatory, a firm has to put considerable effort into becoming multicultural.

2. *Ethnocentrism.* The multicultural manager avoids **ethnocentrism,** the belief that the ways of one's culture are the best ways of doing things. Most cultures consider themselves to be the center of the world. One consequence of this attitude is that people from one culture prefer people from other cultures more similar to themselves. English people would therefore have more positive attitudes toward the Scottish than they would toward Brazilians. Despite this generalization, some countries that appear to have similar cultures are intense rivals. Many Japanese dislike Korean people, and vice versa, as do French and Belgians.

3. *Intergroup rather than interpersonal relations.* In intergroup relations, we pay attention only to the group membership of the person. In interpersonal relations, we pay attention to a person's characteristics. An interpersonal relationship requires more effort because we have to attend to details about the other person. Automobile manufacturers have in recent years developed extensive training programs to help sales representatives develop interpersonal rather than intergroup relations with women buyers. In the past, many sales reps would lose valuable sales prospects because they assumed that women were not the decision makers about an automobile purchase.

4. *Stereotypes in intergroup relations.* As a result of stereotypes, people overestimate the probability that a given member of a group will have an attribute of his or her category. People tend to select information that fits the stereotype and reject inconsistent information. As a consequence, we readily draw conclusions about people from other cultural groups without carefully listening and observing. As a Chinese American woman reports, "I'm tired of people assuming that I like math and science and that I'm good with details. I'm a people person with a creative bent. I actually hate math." (A problem here is that the woman may be excluded from job assignments that fit her true capabilities.)

5. *Language differences.* A major barrier to good cross-cultural relations is language differences. When people do not understand each other's languages, the possibility for misunderstanding multiplies. A team member who was a native of France on assignment in the United States said the boss was *retarded,* so the meeting would have to wait. The other team members thought this was an insult, but *en retard* in French refers to being late. On a more somber note, language barriers cause many industrial accidents in the United States. Hispanics in the United States are frequently employed in dangerous industries, particularly construction. Language barriers between workers and supervisors make safety training exceptionally difficult. Also, safety instructions are sometimes not written in both Spanish and English.[30]

6. *Cultural assumptions.* A **cultural assumption** is a form of stereotype in which we attribute attitudes and behaviors to members of a group without verifying our information. Making this assumption could create a communication and personal barrier between you and that other individual. A naïve assumption is that a Chinese visitor to your company would like to dine at a Chinese restaurant. A more serious assumption is that all African Americans are liberal (or all blacks think alike). In reality, many blacks are quite conservative. As noted by social scientist Mark A. Williams, "African Americans tend to be progressive on issues related to civil rights. But when other issues are introduced into the mix, like gay marriage, abortion and prayer in schools, these themes resonate with about a third of the African American community."[31]

CROSS-CULTURAL PROCESSES

Another approach to understanding international and cross-cultural organizational behavior is to examine similarities and differences in important processes. Five such areas in which cross-cultural differences may surface are motivation, ethics, negotiations, conflict resolution methods, and empowerment practices.

Explain how motivation, ethics, appropriate negotiation skills, conflict resolution, and empowerment practices can vary across cultures.

Cross-Cultural Motivation

For managers to effectively lead and influence workers from another culture, they must use a motivational approach that fits the culture in question. Motivational concepts apply across cultures providing that the manager has relevant information about two key factors. The manager must know which needs the people are attempting to satisfy and which rewards will satisfy those needs. A case in point is reinforcement theory. All human beings are motivated by rewards, yet the specific rewards with high valence varies across cultures. An American worker might respond well to individual recognition, while a South Korean worker might respond better to sharing a reward with the group.

In support of the idea that people in different cultures have similar needs, a study of global leadership by Manfred F. R. Kets De Vries and Elizabeth Florent-Treacy indicates that workers have basic motivational needs. One such need is the *attachment/affiliation need,* which is expressed as a drive for connecting with other people, such as identifying with a group or feeling a sense of community. Another universal need, according to these researchers, is exploratory/assertive and is closely associated with cognition and learning. These needs constitute the foundation for play, creativity, and innovation, thereby being a new label for intrinsic motivation and openness.[32] The similarity of needs across cultures is not surprising when you consider that the Five Factor Model can describe the personality structure of people in different continents (as discussed in Chapter 2).

A two-country study found that cultural factors influence the effectiveness of participative management as a motivational technique. The participants in the study were junior workers in the Hong Kong and U.S. branches of a large multinational bank. Four variables were studied in addition to participative decision making and performance: (1) self-efficacy about participative decision making, (2) group efficacy about participation (believing that the group is competent), (3) *ideocentrism* (viewing the self as separate from others, with an orientation toward personal accomplishment), and (4) *allocentrism* (viewing the self as inseparable from others in the in-group). A major finding of this complex study was that for employees with allocentric beliefs, a strong positive relationship was found between an opportunity to participate and group performance—assuming the participants had high participation efficacy. Also, in groups scoring low on allocentrism, there was no relationship between participative decision-making opportunity and group performance.[33] In short, when people believe in collective effort, it helps them benefit from participative decision making.

Cross-Cultural Ethics

Coping with cross-cultural ethical codes challenges many international managers. When faced with an ethical dilemma, should managers abide by ethical codes of their own country or those of the country they are visiting? A recurring ethical dilemma is that in many countries, including Pakistan and Mexico, government officials demand payments to expedite certain transactions. In the United States, direct payments to government officials to win contracts are illegal and unethical. The Foreign Corrupt Practices Act does not outlaw payment to foreign government officials, providing such payoffs are part of the country's business practices. To get around the direct payment prohibitions, some countries demand that large American companies donate technology to the foreign country, with China being a leading example. Money is not exchanged, but the foreign country receives side benefits from dealing with a U.S. company.

The challenge of cross-cultural ethics received considerable publicity in relation to censoring of the Internet. A few years ago, four U.S. high-tech companies were branded as collaborators with the Chinese government to suppress dissent in return for access to a fast-growing Internet market. House of Representative members condemned the practices of Microsoft Corp., Yahoo Inc., Cisco Systems Inc., and Google Inc. According to the State Department, China is increasingly manipulating the Internet. Yet the Chinese government says its measures are intended to protect its citizens from "immoral and harmful content." Yahoo helped the Chinese government locate Shi Tao, a journalist and Yahoo user who wrote critically about the anniversary of the Tiananmen Square massacre. As a result, he was captured and sentenced to 10 years in prison.

The American companies defended themselves. A Google vice president said the company's decision to censor its Chinese Internet search engine was "not something we did enthusiastically or something we're proud of." A Microsoft spokesperson said his company would stay in China, with its 110 million Internet users. "We think the benefits far outweigh the downside, in terms of promotion freedom of expression."[34]

One questionable way in which managers cope with cross-cultural differences in ethics is to outsource to another country work that would be unethical, or illegal, in their own countries. A lethal example is the recycling of automobile and truck batteries. During recycling, acid leaks from these batteries and the fumes are extraordinarily toxic. Several countries, including Australia, contract with small firms in India to recycle these batteries. The small Indian firms take virtually no safety precautions for the workers.

Cross-Cultural Negotiations

As world trade increases, so does the need for negotiating with people from different cultures. Negotiation is one of the single most important skills for the international manager or specialist. A major challenge in skill development is that negotiation styles vary from one culture to another. Managers should negotiate when the value of the exchange and the relationship is important.

Managerial negotiation requires significant adaptation when conducted in a foreign culture. A do-or-die attitude is often self-defeating. A list of suggestions for negotiation abroad follows. Each of the first five points includes the American attitude that could be self-defeating and explains how it can be improved.[35]

1. *Use a team approach.* Most American managers are convinced they can handle any negotiation by themselves, while other countries rely on negotiation teams. Bringing several Americans to the negotiating table may convey a seriousness of purpose and commitment.
2. *Be patient.* A striking difference between American negotiations and those in many foreign cultures concerns time. Japanese, Chinese, and Arab negotiators, for example, are willing to spend many days negotiating a deal. Much of their

negotiating activity seems to be ceremonial (including elaborate dining) and unrelated to the task. This often frustrates the "strictly business" American.

3. *Learn to tolerate less than full disclosure of information.* Many Americans believe that "laying one's cards on the table" is a valuable negotiating tactic. As a consequence, they expect honest information and are frustrated when it is not forthcoming. Because many foreign negotiators routinely practice small deceptions at the negotiating table, less than full disclosure must be tolerated.

4. *Accept silence as part of negotiating.* Unlike Asian negotiators, Americans often become uncomfortable when more than 10 seconds elapses without somebody making a task-related comment. It is sometimes fruitful to remain silent and wait for the other side to make an offer or to reveal the nature of its thinking.

5. *Take no for an answer sometimes.* American are highly competitive in a negotiating session and take each loss personally. Foreign customers and suppliers, in contrast, are often willing to lose one negotiating session to build a solid long-term relationship among people and firms.

6. *Learn about the other culture's negotiating style in advance.* Part of doing your homework for negotiating in another culture involves having an awareness of negotiating stereotypes for the other culture. A few possibilities: Japanese prefer an exchange of information to confrontation; Russians love combat; Spanish negotiators are individualistic; Koreans are team players; Asians are high in context so you have to watch the body language and what is *not* said.[36]

A useful perspective on these suggestions is that a person is rarely on a level playing field when negotiating in another country. Adapting to the other side's negotiating tactics may help to place negotiations on an equal footing. However, Americans should not necessarily be the only group adapting their negotiating tactics to fit different cultures. Businesspeople from around the world may have to develop a cross-cultural negotiating style.

Conflict Resolution Models across Cultures

Research provides some quantitative evidence that national culture influences which method of conflict resolution a manager chooses. Catherine Tinsley sorted conflict resolution models into three types: resolving conflict by (a) deferring to status power, (b) applying regulations, and (c) integrating interests. According to her observations, preference for a model, or method, is influenced by culture which filters information and guides members toward a particular model. The 396 participants in the study were managers from Japanese, German, and American cultures. All participants had been educated by business programs in their culture and were currently working for a company in their culture. Participants completed surveys about resolving conflict over different approaches to solving a business problem.

A major finding was that Japanese, German, and American managers tended to use different models when resolving workplace conflict. Half the variance (reasons for something taking place) in choosing a conflict model could be accounted for by a manager's cultural group membership. Japanese preferred a status power model (using their authority). Germans preferred a regulations model (appealing to rules and regulations), and Americans preferred an interests (win–win) model. Tinsley cautions that these cross-cultural differences may complicate the work life for expatriate managers who find themselves trying to manage conflict in a foreign cultural system. A particular concern is that American managers may be surprised to learn that colleagues from Japanese and German cultures do not favor the interests model.[37]

Empowerment and Continuous Improvement across Cultures

A team of researchers investigated how well the management practices of empowerment and continuous improvement fit different cultures. Data were collected from employees from a United States–based multinational corporation with operations in the United States, Mexico, Poland, and India. The major findings were as follows:

- Continuous improvement was related to high levels of satisfaction with coworkers and the work itself in all four countries. No negative findings were associated with continuous improvement in any country, suggesting that continuous improvement and self-development are a good fit in all the cultures studied.
- The outcomes associated with empowerment varied with the country and culture. Workers in the United States, Mexico, and Poland had favorable views of their supervisors when they used a high degree of empowerment. Indian employees, however, rated their supervisors low when empowerment was high. (Indians value high power distance, and therefore expect the supervisor to retain most of the power.)
- In the United States and Mexico, empowerment was unrelated to coworker satisfaction, yet in Poland, empowerment was positively related to coworker satisfaction. In India, empowerment was shown to have a negative impact on coworker satisfaction.[38]

In general, the results of the study suggest that multinational managers should consider the cultural context of the management practices they implement. In particular, empowerment may backfire when used in a high-power-distance culture. The study might also be interpreted as more evidence of the universal need for personal growth.

DIVERSITY TRAINING, CULTURAL TRAINING, AND CULTURAL INTELLIGENCE TRAINING

Appreciate the nature of diversity training and cultural training, including cultural intelligence training.

Many training programs have been developed to help employees value diversity and improve cross-cultural relations, especially overseas relations and foreign-language development. The emphasis in these programs is to improve relationships between people of different cultural and demographic groups, rather than an emphasis on overcoming discrimination. The type of information presented so far in this chapter is likely to be included in such programs. In this section, we describe a diversity training program along with cultural training for improving cross-cultural relations, including the development of cultural intelligence.

Diversity Training

Cultural training aims to help workers understand people from other cultures. Understanding can lead to dealing more effectively with them as work associates or customers. **Diversity training** has a slightly different purpose. It attempts to bring about workplace harmony by teaching people how to get along better with diverse work associates. Quite often the program is aimed at minimizing open expressions of racism and sexism. All forms of diversity training center on increasing people's awareness of and empathy for people who are different from themselves.

Diversity training sessions focus on the ways in which men and women or people of different races reflect different values, attitudes, and cultural backgrounds.

SKILL-DEVELOPMENT EXERCISE

Developing Empathy for Differences

Class members come up to the front of the room one by one and give a brief presentation (perhaps 2 or 3 minutes) about any way in which they have been perceived as different and how they felt about this perception. The difference can be of any kind, relating to characteristics such as ethnicity, race, choice of major, physical appearance, height, weight, hair color, or body piercing. After each member of the class has presented (perhaps also the instructor), class members discuss what they learned from the exercise. It is also important to discuss how this exercise can improve workplace relationships.

Here are several points of analysis:

* What is the most common difference to which people refer?
* What type of being different appears to make the person most uncomfortable?
* Are all the differences people refer to physical and speech factors? Or are some of the differences related to attitudes, values, and behaviors?

Collaboration

Some diversity programs deal specifically with generational differences, so people with different values based on age can work harmoniously. Diversity training sessions can vary from several hours to several days.

An essential part of relating more effectively to diverse groups is to empathize with their point of view. To help training participants develop empathy, representatives of various groups explain their feelings related to workplace issues. A concern about diversity training is that it exaggerates stereotypes in order to promote understanding, such as propagating that Latinos do not start meetings on time.[39] The accompanying skill-development exercise provides an opportunity to simulate a diversity training program.

Training in Cross-Cultural Relations

For many years, companies and government agencies have prepared their workers for overseas assignments. The method most frequently chosen is **cultural training,** a set of learning experiences designed to help employees understand the customs, traditions, and beliefs of another culture. The globalization of business has created an impetus for cultural training. A representative example is that when Intel developed a new leadership program for mid-level managers, it made firsthand exposure to different cultures a cornerstone. Mid-level leaders travel to weeklong seminars out of their home regions to participate in cultural training.[40]

A major goal of cultural training, especially for workers on overseas assignments, is to help them avoid **culture shock.** The condition refers to a group of physical and psychological symptoms that can develop when a person is abruptly placed in a foreign culture. Among the symptoms are excessive hand washing and concern for sanitation, fear of physical contact with others, fear of being mugged, and strong feelings of homesickness.[41] A partial explanation for culture shock is that when placed in an unfamiliar environment, and when people behave in ways we do not understand, we feel out of control. Culture shock is a major contributor to the high failure rate of overseas assignments. Attention has also been paid to the culture shock problems of employees from other countries transferring to the United States. Such employees are referred to as *inpatriates*. One problem is that inpatriates may find no fellow members of their country in the United States, whereas Americans can always find Americans in other countries. Another problem is that many people fear their children will be shot at on the way to or from school.[42] Again, perceptions have a major influence on attitudes and actions, whether or not they are correct.

Learning a foreign language is often part of cultural training, yet it can also be a separate activity. Knowledge of a second language is important because it builds better connections with people from other cultures than does having to rely on a translator. Many workers in addition to international business specialists choose to develop skills in a target language. Speaking another language can help build rapport with customers and employees who speak that language.

Cultural Intelligence Training

An advanced form of learning how to deal effectively with people from other cultures is cultural intelligence training. **Cultural intelligence (CQ)** is an outsider's ability to interpret someone's unfamiliar and ambiguous behavior the same way that person's compatriots would. Similar to emotional intelligence, cultural intelligence encompasses several different aspects of behavior. The three sources of cultural intelligence relate to the cognitive, emotional/motivational, and the physical, explained as follows[43]:

1. *Cognitive (the head).* The cognitive part of CQ refers to what a personal knows and how he or she can acquire new knowledge. Here you acquire facts about people from another culture, such as their passion for football (soccer in North America), their business practices, and their promptness in paying bills. Another aspect of this source of cultural intelligence is figuring out how you can learn more about the other culture.

2. *Emotional/motivational (the heart).* The emotional/motivational aspect of CQ refers to energizing one's actions and building personal confidence. You need both confidence and motivation to adapt to another culture. A man on a business trip to Africa might say to himself, "When I greet a work associate in a restaurant, can I really pull off kissing him on both cheeks? What if he thinks I'm weird?" With strong motivation, the same person might say, "I'll give it a try. I kind of greet my grandfather the same way back in the United States."

3. *The body (physical).* The body aspect of CQ is the action component. The body is the element for translating intentions into actions and desires. Kissing the same-sex African work associates on both cheeks is the *physical* aspect just mentioned. We often have an idea of what we should do, but implementation is not so easy. You might know, for example, that when entering an Asian person's home you should take off your shoes, yet you might not actually remove them—thereby offending your Asian work (or personal life) associate.

A key part of the training is to learn the three contributors to CQ—head, heart, and body. Instead of learning a few simple guidelines for working effectively with people from another culture, the trainee is taught strategies for sizing up the environment to determine which course of action is best. The culturally intelligent overseas worker would learn how to figure out how much humor to interject into meetings, what kind of handshake is most appropriate, and so forth. The following excerpt will give you a feel for what is involved in cultural intelligence training:

> A Canadian manager is attempting to interpret a "Thai smile." First, she needs to observe the various cues provided in addition to the smile gesture

itself (e.g., other facial or bodily gestures, significance of others who may be in proximity, the source of the original smile gesture) and to assemble them into a meaningful whole and make sense of what is really experienced by the Thai employee. Second, she must have the requisite motivation (directed effort and self-confidence) to persist in the face of confusion, challenge, or apparently mixed signals. Third, she must choose, generate, and execute the right actions to respond appropriately.

If any of these elements is deficient she is likely to be ineffective in dealing with the Thai employee. A high CQ manager has the capability with all three facets as they act. in unison.[44]

To practice high cultural intelligence, the mind, heart, and body would have to work together. You would have to figure out how you have to act with people from another culture; you would need motivation and confidence to change; and you would have to translate your knowledge and motivation into action. So when you are on a business trip to New Deli, India, go ahead and hold your fork in your left hand!

Workers do not benefit equally from cultural training, as shown by a study of European managers participating in a cross-cultural training program in Japan. The personality factor, openness to experience, was significantly related to cross-cultural training performance, whereas cognitive ability (or general intelligence) was significantly correlated with learning Japanese. Training performance was rated by instructors, and exams were used to measure language knowledge. A straightforward interpretation of these findings is that you have to be intellectually curious to learn about another culture, and you have to be bright to learn a complex second language.[45]

IMPLICATIONS FOR MANAGERIAL PRACTICE

1. As a manager or cultural diversity specialist, it is important to keep selling the idea that diversity initiatives do not regard white males as the enemy. In contrast, diversity is meant to be inclusive. Many white males are concerned that diversity initiatives are a form of reverse discrimination and that they will be accused of being "advantaged" because of their skin color.[46]
2. A managerial success factor is to become multicultural in terms of conducting business effectively with people from different cultures. The demand for multicultural managers continues to increase as the business world becomes increasingly global.
3. To perform well in many positions in the modern world, it may be necessary for you to develop a global mindset, a feeling of comfort and confidence in dealing with workers from diverse countries. Developing a global mindset requires perspective, a sincere interest in another country, and a sense of humor to recover from obvious slips.[47]

SUMMARY OF KEY POINTS

 Understand the scope, competitive advantages, and potential problems associated with cultural diversity.
The true meaning of valuing diversity is to respect a wide range of cultural and individual differences. To be diverse is to be different in some measurable, although not necessarily visible, way. Encouraging cultural diversity within an organization is socially responsible and also offers these potential advantages:

increased sales and profits, cost reduction associated with turnover and lawsuits, better employee recruitment, better ideas for publicity and advertising, and creativity. A potential problem with diversity is that the diverse members of a group do not necessarily get along well together unless supportive relationships are in place. Also, increased profits are not inevitable.

 Identify and explain key dimensions of cultural differences.
Ten values particularly helpful in understanding how national cultures differ are as follows: individualism versus collectivism, power distance (respect for hierarchy), uncertainty avoidance, materialism versus concern for others, long-term versus short-term orientation, formality versus informality, urgent time orientation versus casual time orientation, high-context versus low-context cultures, work orientation/leisure orientation, and performance orientation.

The impact of culture on management and leadership style is another important influence of culture on organizational behavior. Culture serves as a guide to acceptable behavior. For example, a person raised in a collectivist culture would find it natural to be a consensus-style manager/leader. Also, participative leadership is least acceptable from a cultural standpoint in the Middle Eastern cluster of countries.

 Describe what is required for managers and organizations to become multicultural.
Multicultural managers have the skills and attitudes to relate effectively to and motivate people across race, gender, social attitudes, and lifestyles. Multiculturalism is enhanced by bilingualism, cultural sensitivity, and an absence of parochialism and ethnocentrism. A multicultural organization values cultural diversity and is willing to encourage and even capitalize on such diversity. The developmental stages of such an organization are monocultural, nondiscriminatory, and multicultural. To move toward becoming multicultural, business firms can take a variety of initiatives, including not targeting senior employees for downsizing.

 Be more aware of barriers to good cross-cultural relations.
Barriers to the good cross-cultural relations required of a multicultural organization include perceptual expectations that lead to discriminatory stereotypes and ethnocentrism, intergroup (based on group differences) versus interpersonal (based on individual differences) relations, language differences, and cultural assumptions.

 Explain how motivation, ethics, appropriate negotiation skills, conflict resolution, and empowerment practices can vary across cultures.
Certain motivational approaches can apply cross-culturally. Some psychological needs, such as attachment/affiliation, apply across cultures. A cultural belief in collective effort enhances the effectiveness of participative decision making. Coping with cross-cultural ethical codes challenges many international managers. A major issue is whether to abide by the home ethical codes or those of the foreign company and country.

Managers need good negotiating skills to achieve their objectives in international business. Americans must adapt their traditional negotiating tactics to fit other cultures. For example, people from other cultures may want to work more slowly than Americans on reaching agreement. When working in other countries, managers must be sensitive to differences in the preferred model of resolving conflict. One study showed that Japanese managers preferred a status power model of conflict resolution, Germans preferred to appeal to rules and regulations, and Americans preferred an interests model. Empowerment is likely to work poorly in a high-power-distance culture such as India. However, continuous improvement works across cultures.

 Appreciate the nature of diversity training and cultural training, including cultural intelligence training.
Diversity training attempts to bring about workplace harmony by teaching people how to get along better with diverse work associates. Cultural training is helpful in overcoming culture shock and contributing to better relations with various groups at home. Learning a foreign language is often part of cultural training, yet it can also be a separate activity. An advanced form of learning how to deal effectively with people from other cultures is cultural intelligence training, in which you learn to interpret subtle behaviors.

KEY TERMS AND PHRASES

Individualism, 386
A mental set in which people see themselves first as individuals and believe that their own interests take priority.

Collectivism, 386
A value emphasizing that the group and society should receive top priority.

Power Distance, 386
The extent to which employees accept the idea that members of an organization have different levels of power.

Uncertainty Avoidance, 386
The extent to which people accept the unknown and tolerate risk and unconventional behavior.

Materialism, 386
An emphasis on assertiveness and the acquisition of money and material objects. Usually measured along a continuum, with concern for others at the opposite end.

Concern for Others, 386
An emphasis on personal relations and a concern for the welfare of others. Usually measured along a continuum, with materialism at the opposite end.

Long-Term Orientation, 386
In describing national culture, taking a long-range perspective.

Short-Term Orientation, 386
In describing a national culture, a demand for immediate results.

Formality, 386
Attaching considerable importance to tradition, ceremony, social rules, and rank.

Informality, 386
A casual attitude toward tradition, ceremony, social rules, and rank.

Urgent Time Orientation, 387
The perception of time as a scarce resource, therefore leading to impatience.

Casual Time Orientation, 387
The perception of time as an unlimited and unending resource, leading to patience.

High-Context Culture, 387
A culture that makes more extensive use of body language.

Low-Context Culture, 387
A culture that makes less use of body language.

Multicultural Manager, 389
A manager with the skills and attitudes to relate effectively to and motivate people across race, gender, age, social attitudes, and lifestyles, and to conduct business in a diverse, international environment.

Cultural Sensitivity, 389
An awareness of and a willingness to investigate the reasons why people of another culture act as they do.

Multicultural Organization, 390
An organization that values cultural diversity and is willing to encourage and even capitalize on such diversity.

Ethnocentrism, 394
The assumption that the ways of one's culture are the best ways of doing things.

Cultural Assumption, 394
A form of stereotype in which we attribute attitudes and behaviors to members of a group without verifying our information.

Diversity Training, 398
Training that attempts to bring about workplace harmony by teaching people how to get along better with diverse work associates.

Cultural Training, 399
Training that attempts to help workers understand people from other cultures.

Culture Shock, 399
A group of physical and psychological symptoms that can develop when a person is abruptly placed in a foreign culture.

Cultural Intelligence (CQ), 400
An outsider's ability to interpret someone's unfamiliar and ambiguous behavior the same way that person's compatriots would.

DISCUSSION QUESTIONS AND ACTIVITIES

1. What steps can you take to better prepare yourself to become a multicultural manager?
2. Commercial airlines go out of their way to be culturally homogeneous for certain positions. For example, the flight attendants on Singapore Airlines are from Singapore, Air India flight attendants are from India, and the Air France attendants and flight crew all speak French. Explain whether these airlines should be accused of practicing job discrimination and avoiding cultural diversity.

3. Diversity specialists argue that a firm's employee mix (or base) should match its customer mix. Assume you are the general manager of a nursing home or a retirement village. Explain whether your employee base (or mix) should match your client base.

4. If you knew that group members all had "a strong leisure orientation," how would this information help you do a better job as a manager?

5. Working in a small group, think through the many group projects you might have had in school or on the job. Brainstorm a list of the advantages and disadvantages that have stemmed from having diverse groups.

6. Software is available to translate documents from one language into another, and devices are for sale that will give you a voice translation from one language to another. With this technology available, why should the multicultural worker bother learning another language?

7. A criticism made of cultural training and diversity training is that they usually emphasize Americans adjusting to other cultures rather than the reverse. Where do you stand on this issue?

CASE PROBLEM: What to Do about Louie?

Louie is the manager of a Mighty Muffler Brake service center in the Great Lakes Region of the United States. Mighty Muffler Brake offers a wide range of services for vehicles, including muffler and exhaust system replacement, brake systems, oil change, lubrication, tune-ups, and state inspections. Louie's branch is located close to a busy highway, yet stores and residential neighborhoods are also close by. His store is among the chain's highest-volume and most profitable units. The fact that Louie's Mighty Muffler Brake is located in a region that heavily salts the streets and highways during periods of snow and ice contributes to the steady influx of business at Louie's store.

Management at Mighty Muffler Brake is pleased with the financial management of Louie's store, yet complaints have surfaced about aspects of his relationships with employees and customers. Emma, the human resources and marketing manager for the company, was recently poring over the results from customer-satisfaction cards mailed back to the company. She found that a few of the customer comments suggested that Louie might have made a few inappropriate comments, as reflected in these remarks:

"You did a wonderful job in replacing my brakes, and fixing a rattle in my exhaust system. But the manager insulted me a little by suggesting that I talk over with my husband whether or not to get a new exhaust system now."

"I have no complaints about the repairs you did or the price you charged. However, you had better replace that manager of yours, who is definitely out of touch with the times. My partner and I are proud of our gayness, so we don't attempt to hide occasional public displays of affection. When your manager saw me giving my partner a peck on the cheek, he asked if we were from San Francisco."

"When I came to pick up my car, I had to wait 2 hours even though I was told the car would be ready by 3:00 in the afternoon. I also found some smudge marks on the beige leather seats. When I complained to the manager, he said, 'Granny, watch your blood pressure. It's not good for a senior citizen to get too excited.' I was never so insulted."

Concerned about these comments, Emma scheduled a trip to Louie's store to investigate any possible problems he might be having in managing cultural diversity among employees. Emma explained to Louie that the home office likes to make periodic trip to the stores to see how well employee relations are going, and how well employees are working together. Louie responded, "Talk to anybody you want. I may joke a little with the boys and girls in the shop, but we all get along great."

In Emma's mind, her informal chats with workers at Louie's store suggested that employee relations were generally satisfactory, but she did find a few troublesome comments. A young African American noted that when he does something particularly well, or Louie agrees with him strongly, Louie gives him a "high-five." In contrast, Caucasian or Hispanic workers will receive a congratulatory handshake.

A female brake technician said that Louie is a kind-hearted boss but that he is sometimes patronizing or insulting without realizing it. She volunteered this

CASE PROBLEM (Continued)

incident: "During breaks I sometimes enter the waiting room area because we have a vending machine up front that sells small bags of nuts and raisins, which I particularly like. One day I was about to enter the waiting room, when Louie tells me to stay in the back. He said that there was a Hell's Angel–type guy waiting for his truck to be repaired, and he probably wouldn't appreciate it if he thought that a 'girl' was working on his truck. How could anybody be that sexist in today's world?"

Emma went back to the home office to discuss her findings with the CEO and the vice president of administration. Emma said that Louie is making a contribution to the firm, but that some changes needed to be made. The two other executives agreed that Louie should become a little more multicultural, but that they didn't

want him to upset him too much because he could easily join a competitor. Emma concluded, "So I guess we need to figure out what to do about Louie."

Case Questions

1. Does Louie have a problem, or are the people who made the negative comments about Louie just being too sensitive?

2. If you were the CEO of Mighty Muffler Brake, would the profitability of Louie's store influence your decision about approaching him on his ability to relate to culturally diverse people?

3. What improvements might Louie need to make to become a truly multicultural manager?

4. What activity would you recommend to help make Louie more culturally sensitive?

ENDNOTES

1. Joan Crockett, "Winning Competitive Advantage through a Diverse Workforce," *HRfocus,* May 1999, p. 9.
2. "Making Best Practices Even Better," *Hispanic Business,* January/February 2005, p. 54.
3. Book review by James L. Outtz in *Personnel Psychology,* Winter 2004, p. 1042.
4. Study reported in Fay Hansen, "Diversity's Business Case Doesn't Add Up," *Workforce,* April 2003, pp. 28–32.
5. Debbe Kennedy, "Boosting Business Success through Diversity," pp. 29–30; *Business: The Ultimate Resource* (Cambridge, MA: Perseus Books, 2002), pp. 31–32; Hansen, "Diversity's Business Case," pp. 28–32; Jeffrey Pfeffer, "Recruiting for the Global Talent War," *Business 2.0,* August 2005, p. 56.
6. Carol Hymowitz, "The New Diversity," *The Wall Street Journal,* November 14, 2005, p. R3.
7. Patricia Sellers, "By the Numbers," *Fortune,* February 9, 2004, p. 22.
8. Marc Levy, "Trucking Industry Looks to Hispanics to Drive Growth," Associated Press, July 12, 2005.
9. Rosabeth Moss Kanter, *The Change Masters* (New York: Simon & Schuster, 1983).
10. Orlando C. Richard, Tim Barnett, Sean Dwyer, and Ken Chadwick, "Cultural Diversity in Management, Firm Performance, and the Moderating Role of Entrepreneurial Dimensions," *Academy of Management Journal,* April 2004, p. 263.
11. Samuel B. Bacharach, Peter A. Bamberger, and Dana B. Vashdi, "Diversity and Homophily at Work: Supportive Relations among White and African-American Peers," *Academy of Management Journal,* August 2005, pp. 619–644.
12. Irwin Speizer, "Diversity on the Menu," *Workforce Management,* November 2004, pp. 41–45. The quote is from page 42.
13. Geert Hofstede, *Culture's Consequences: International Differences in Work-Related Values* (Beverly Hills, CA: Sage, 1980); updated and expanded in "A Conversation with Geert Hofstede," *Organizational Dynamics* (Spring 1993), pp. 53–61; Jim Kennedy and Anna Everest, "Put Diversity in Context," *Personnel Journal,* September 1991, pp. 50–54.
14. Robert J. House et al., *Culture, Leadership, and Organizations: The GLOBE Study of 62 Societies* (Thousand Oaks, CA: Sage, 2004).
15. Stephen Power and Marcus Walker, "Less Leisure in Germany," *The Wall Street Journal,* July 26, 2004, p. A13.
16. Mansour Javidan, Güter K. Stahl, Felix Brodbeck, and Celeste P. M. Wilderom, "Cross-Border Transfer of Knowledge: Cultural Lessons from Project GLOBE," *Academy of Management Executive,* May 2005, p. 75.
17. John Schaubroeck and Simon S. K. Lam, "How Similarity to Peers and Supervisor Influences Organizational Advancement in Different Cultures," *Academy of Management Journal,* December 2002, pp. 1120–1136.
18. Anne Fisher, "Piercing the 'Bamboo Ceiling,'" *Fortune,* August 22, 2005, p. 122.
19. Geert Hofstede, "Cultural Constraints in Management Theories," *Academy of Management Executive,* February 1993, pp. 81–94; Hofstede, "The Universal and the Specific in 21st-Century Global Management," *Organizational Dynamics,* Summer 1999, pp. 35–41.
20. Felix C. Brodbeck, Michael Frese, and Mansour Javidan, "Leadership Made in Germany: Low on Compassion, High on Performance," *Academy of Management Executive,* February 2002, pp. 16–30.
21. Ken Belson and Todd Zaun, "Land of the Rising Gaijin Chief Executive," *The New York Times* (http://www.nytimes.com), March 27, 2005.
22. House et al., *Culture, Leadership, and Organizations.*
23. Arvand V. Phatak, *International Dimensions of Management* (Boston: Kent, 1983), p. 167.
24. Jaun Antonio Fernandez and Laurie Underwood, "Succeeding in China: The Voices of Experience," *Organizational Dynamics,* 4(2005), pp. 404, 411–414.
25. Jack Scarborough, *The Origins of Cultural Differences and Their Impact on Management* (Westport, CT: Quorum, 2000).
26. The model in Exhibit 17-4 is an integration of Badi G. Foster, Gerald Jackson, William E. Cross, Bailey Jackson, and Rita

Hardiman, "Workforce Diversity and Business," *Training and Development Journal,* April 1988, pp. 39–40; and Taylor Cox, "The Multicultural Organization," *Academy of Management Executive,* May 1991, pp. 34–47.

27. Janet Perez, "A Fresh Deck: Publicly Traded MGM Mirage Begins Dealing Diversity," *Hispanic Business,* January/February 2006, p. 62.

28. "2005 *Hispanic Business Magazine* Top 40," *Hispanic Business,* September 2005, p. 32.

29. Harry C. Triandis, *Culture and Social Behavior* (New York: McGraw-Hill, 1994). pp. 249–259.

30. Julie Dunn, "Death Rate for Hispanics on Job Climbs in Colorado," *The Denver Post,* April 28, 2005.

31. Quoted in Sonia Alleyne, "Zoning in On Cultural Differences," *Black Enterprise,* April 2005, p. 55; Mark A. Williams, *Your Identity Zones: Who Am I? Who Are You? How Do We Get Along?* (Sterling, VA: Capital Books, 2004).

32. Manfred F. R. Kets De Vries and Elizabeth Florent-Treacy, "Global Leadership from A to Z: Creating High Commitment Organizations," *Organizational Dynamics,* Spring 2002, pp. 295–309.

33. Simon S. K. Lam, Xiao-Ping Chen, and John Schaubroeck, "Participative Decision Making and Employee Performance in Difficult Cultures: The Moderating Effects of Allocentrism/Idiocentrism and Efficacy," *Academy of Management Journal,* October 2002, pp. 905–914.

34. "U.S. Firms Accused of Aiding China's Internet Censorship," *Associated Press,* February 16, 2006; Jason Dean and Kevin J. Delaney, "Limited Search: As Google Pushes into China, It Faces Clashes with Censors," December 16, 2005, p. 1A.

35. John L. Graham and Roy A. Herberger, Jr., "Negotiators Abroad—Don't Shoot from the Hip," *Harvard Business Review,* July–August 1983, p. 167.

36. Marc Diener, "Culture Shock," *Entrepreneur,* July 2003, pp. 77.

37. Catherine Tinsley, "Models of Conflict Resolution in Japanese, German, and American Cultures," *Journal of Applied Psychology,* April 1998, pp. 316–323.

38. Christopher Robert et al., "Empowerment and Continuous Improvement in the United States, Mexico, Poland, and India: Predicting Fit on the Dimensions of Power Distance and Individualism," *Journal of Applied Psychology,* October 2000, pp. 643–658.

39. Gillian Flynn, "The Harsh Reality of Diversity Programs," *Workforce,* December 1998, p. 27.

40. Ed Frauenheim, "Crossing Cultures," *Workforce Management,* November 21, 2005, p. 1.

41. Triandis, Culture and Social Behavior, p. 263.

42. Carroll Lachnit, "Low-Cost Tips for Successful Inpatriation," *Workforce,* August 2001, pp. 42–47.

43. P. Christopher Earley and Elaine Mosakowski, "Toward Culture Intelligence Training: Turning Cultural Differences into a Workplace Advantage," *Academy of Management Executive,* August 2004, pp. 154–155.

44. P. Christopher Earley and Randall S. Peterson, "The Elusive Cultural Chameleon: Cultural Intelligence as a New Approach to Intercultural Training for the Global Manager," *Academy of Management Learning and Education,* March 2004, p. 6.

45. Filip Lievens, Michael M. Harris, Etienne Van Keer, and Claire Bisqueret, "Predicting Cross-Cultural Training Performance: The Validity of Personality, Cognitive Ability, and Dimensions Measured by an Assessment Center and a Behavior Description Interview," *Journal of Applied Psychology,* June 2003, pp. 476–489.

46. Gillian Flynn, "White Males See Diversity's Other Side," *Workforce,* February 1999, pp. 52–55.

47. Mildred L. Culp, "New Mentality Compels Business Effectiveness . . . Global Mind-Set: Don't Leave Home without It," Work-Wise®, December 6, 1998.

Glossary

A

Active Listening Listening for full meaning without making premature judgments or interpretations.

Administrative Management A school of management thought concerned primarily with how organizations should be structured and managed.

Attitude A predisposition to respond that exerts an influence on a person's response to a person, a thing, an idea, or a situation.

Attribution Theory The process by which people ascribe causes to the behavior they perceive.

Avoidance Motivation Rewarding by taking away an uncomfortable consequence.

B

Behavioral Approach to Leadership An attempt to specify how the behavior of effective leaders differs from their less-effective counterparts.

Behavioral Approach to Management The belief that specific attention to the workers' needs creates greater satisfaction and productivity.

Behavioral Decision Model An approach to decision making that views managers as having cognitive limitations and acting only in terms of what they perceive in a given situation.

Blame The tendency to place the responsibility for a negative outcome on a person, a thing, or the environment.

Bounded Rationality The idea that people's limited mental abilities, combined with external influences over which they have little or no control, prevent them from making entirely rational decisions.

Bureaucracy A rational, systematic, and precise form of organization in which rules, regulations, and techniques of control are precisely defined.

Burnout A pattern of emotional, physical, and mental exhaustion in response to chronic job stressors.

C

Casual Time Orientation The perception of time as an unlimited and unending resource, leading to patience.

Centralization The extent to which executives delegate authority to lower organizational units.

Charisma The ability to lead others based on personal charm, magnetism, inspiration, and emotion.

Classical Decision Model An approach to decision making that views the manager's environment as certain and stable and the manager as rational.

Coaching (in relation to teams) A direct interaction with the team with the intention of improving team processes to enhance performance.

Coercive Power Controlling others through fear or threat of punishment.

Cognitive Dissonance The situation in which the pieces of knowledge, information, attitudes, or beliefs held by an individual are contradictory.

Cognitive Learning Theory A theory emphasizing that learning takes place in a complicated manner involving much more than acquiring habits and small skills.

Cognitive Skills Mental ability and knowledge.

Collectivism A value emphasizing that the group and society receive top priority.

Complexity The number of different job titles and units within an organization.

Concern for Others An emphasis on personal relations and a concern for the welfare of others. Usually measured along a continuum, with materialism at the opposite end.

Conflict The opposition of persons or forces giving rise to some tension.

Confrontation and Problem Solving A method of identifying the true source of conflict and resolving it systematically.

Consideration The degree to which the leader creates an environment of emotional support, warmth, friendliness, and trust.

Contingency Approach to Management The viewpoint that there is no one best way to manage people or work but that the best way depends on certain situational factors.

Contingency Theory of Leadership The position that the best style of leadership depends on factors relating to group members and the work setting.

Creative Self-Efficacy The belief that one can be creative in a work role.

Creativity The process of developing good ideas that can be put into action.

Crew A group of specialists each of whom has specific roles, performs brief events that are close synchronized with each other, and repeats these events under different environmental conditions.

Cross-Functional Team A work group composed of workers with different specialties but from about the same organizational level, who come together to accomplish a task.

Cultural Assumption A form of stereotype in which we attribute attitudes and behaviors to members of a group without verifying our information.

Cultural Intelligence (CQ) An outsider's ability to interpret someone's unfamiliar and ambiguous behavior the same way that person's compatriots would.

Cultural Sensitivity An awareness of and a willingness to investigate the reasons why people of another culture act as they do.

Cultural Training Training that attempts to help workers understand people from other cultures.

Culture Shock A group of physical and psychological symptoms that can develop when a person is abruptly placed in a foreign culture.

D

Decision The act of choosing among two or more alternatives in order to solve a problem.

Decision Criteria The standards of judgment used to evaluate alternatives.

Delphi Technique A group decision-making technique designed to provide group members with one another's ideas and feedback while avoiding some of the problems associated with interacting groups.

Demographic Diversity Differences in background factors about the workforce that help shape worker attitudes and behavior.

Departmentalization The process of subdividing work into departments.

Difficult Person An individual who creates problems for others, yet has the skill and mental ability to do otherwise.

Diversity Training Training that attempts to bring about workplace harmony by teaching people how to get along better with diverse work associates.

Double-Loop Learning A change in behavior that occurs when people use feedback to confront the validity of the goal or the values implicit in the situation.

Downsizing The laying off of workers to reduce costs and increase efficiency.

E

E-learning A web-based form of computer-based training.

Emotion A feeling such as anger, fear, joy, or surprise that underlies behavior.

Emotional Intelligence Qualities such as understanding one's own feelings, empathy for others, and the regulation of emotion to enhance living.

Emotional Labor The process of regulating both feelings and expressions to meet organizational goals.

Empowerment The process of sharing power with group members, thereby enhancing their feelings of self-efficacy.

Equity Theory The theory that employee satisfaction and motivation depend on how fairly the employees believe that they are treated in comparison to peers.

Ethics An individual's moral beliefs about what is right and wrong or good and bad.

Ethnocentrism The assumption that the ways of one's culture are the best ways of doing things.

Expectancy A person's subjective estimate of the probability that a given level of performance will occur.

Expectancy Theory The theory that motivation results from deliberate choices to engage in activities in order to achieve worthwhile outcomes.

Experience of Flow Being "in the zone"; total absorption in one's work.

Expert Power The ability to influence others because of one's specialized knowledge, skills, or abilities.

Extinction Weakening or decreasing the frequency of undesirable behavior by removing the reward for such behavior.

F

Feedback Information about how well someone is doing in achieving goals. Also, messages sent back from the receiver to the sender of information.

Filtering The coloring and altering of information to make it more acceptable to the receiver.

Flat Organization Structure An organization structure with relatively few layers.

Force-Field Theory The theory contending that an organization simultaneously faces forces for change (the driving forces) and forces for maintaining the status quo (the restraining forces).

Formal Communication Channels The official pathways for sending information inside and outside an organization.

Formal Group A group deliberately formed by the organization to accomplish specific tasks and achieve goals.

Formal Organization Structure An official statement of reporting relationships, rules, and regulations.

Formality Attaching considerable importance to tradition, ceremony, social rules, and rank.

Formalization The degree to which expectations regarding the methods of work are specified, committed to writing, and enforced.

Frame of Reference A perspective and vantage point based on past experience.

Functional Departmentalization The grouping of people according to their expertise.

Fundamental Attribution Error The tendency to attribute behavior to internal causes when focusing on someone else's behavior.

G

***g* (general) Factor** A major component of intelligence that contributes to problem-solving ability.

Gainsharing A formal program of allowing employees to participate financially in the productivity gains they have achieved.

Goal What a person is trying to accomplish.

Grapevine The major informal communication channel in organizations.

Group A collection of people who interact with one another, work toward some common purpose, and perceive themselves as a group.

Group Cohesiveness A situation that takes place when members work closely with each other, in a unified, cooperative manner.

Group Norm The guidelines for acceptable and unacceptable behaviors that are informally agreed on by group members.

Group Polarization A situation in which postdiscussion attitudes tend to be more extreme than prediscussion attitudes.

Groupthink A deterioration of mental efficiency, reality testing, and moral judgment in the interest of group cohesiveness.

Growth Curve Model A model that traces the inevitability of change through a firm's life cycle.

H

Hawthorne Effect The tendency of people to behave differently when they receive attention because they respond to the demands of the situation.

Heuristics Simplified strategies that become rules of thumb in decision making.

High-Context Culture A culture that makes more extensive use of body language.

Homesourcing The practice of outsourcing work to homes.

Horizontal Structure The arrangement of work by teams that are responsible for accomplishing a process.

Human Relations Movement An approach to dealing with workers based on the belief that there is an important link among managerial practices, morale, and productivity.

I

Implicit Leadership Theory An explanation of leadership contending that group members develop prototypes specifying the traits and abilities that characterize an ideal business leader.

Individual Differences Variations in how people respond to the same situation based on personal characteristics.

Individualism A mental set in which people see themselves first as individuals and believe that their own interests take priority.

Informal Communication Channels The unofficial network of channels that supplements the formal channels.

Informal Group A group that emerges over time through the interaction of workers, typically to satisfy a social or recreational purpose.

Informal Learning A planned learning that occurs in a setting without a formal classroom, lesson plan, instructor, or examination.

Informal Organization Structure A set of unofficial working relationships that emerges to take care of the events and transactions not covered by the formal structure.

Informality A casual attitude toward tradition, ceremony, social rules, and rank.

Information (or Communication) Overload A situation that occurs when people are so overloaded with information that they cannot respond effectively to messages, resulting in stress.

Initiating Structure The degree to which a leader establishes structure for group members.

Instrumentality The individual's subjective estimate of the probability that performance will lead to certain outcomes.

Intellectual Capital Knowledge that transforms raw materials and makes them more valuable; it is also a capital asset consisting of intellectual material.

Intelligence The capacity to acquire and apply knowledge, including solving problems.

Intrinsic Motivation A person's beliefs about the extent to which an activity can satisfy his or her needs for competence and self-determination.

Intuition An experience-based way of knowing or reasoning in which weighing and balancing evidence are done automatically.

J

Job Characteristics Model A method of job design that focuses on the task and interpersonal demands of a job.

Job Crafting The physical and mental changes workers make in the task or relationships aspects of their job.

Job Demands–Job Control Model An explanation of job stress contending that workers experience the most stress when the demands of the job are high yet they have little control over the activity.

Job Enrichment The process of making a job more motivational and satisfying by adding variety, responsibility, and managerial decision making.

Job Satisfaction The amount of pleasure or contentment associated with a job.

K

Knowledge Management (KM) The systematic sharing of information to achieve advances in innovation, efficiency, and competitive advantage.

L

Large-Scale Organizational Change The method used to accomplish a major change in the firm's strategy and culture.

Leader–Member Exchange Model The model that recognizes that leaders develop unique working relationships with each group member.

Leadership The ability to inspire confidence and support among the people on whose competence and commitment performance depends.

Leadership Grid® A framework for classifying leadership styles that simultaneously examines a leader's concerns for task accomplishment and people.

Leadership Style The relatively consistent pattern of behavior that characterizes a leader.

Learning A relatively permanent change in behavior based on practice or experience.

Learning Organization An organization that is skilled at creating, acquiring, and transferring knowledge and at modifying behavior to reflect new knowledge and insights.

Learning Style A person's particular way of learning, reflecting the fact that people learn best in different ways.

Legitimate Power Power based on one's formal position within the hierarchy of the organization.

Linguistic Style A person's characteristic speaking pattern, involving the amount of directness used, pacing and pausing, word choice, and the use of jokes, figures of speech, questions, and apologies.

Linkage Analysis An organization development technique designed to create linkages in the change pathway that translate gains within smaller organization units into benefits for the larger firm.

Locus of Control The way in which people look at causation in their lives.

Long-Term Orientation In describing national culture, taking a long-range perspective.

Low-Context Culture A culture that makes less use of body language.

M

Machiavellianism A tendency to manipulate others for personal gain.

Machine Bureaucracy An ideal organization that standardizes work processes and is efficient.

Management by Walking Around The process of managers intermingling freely with workers on the shop floor, in the office, and with customers.

Maslow's Hierarchy of Needs A classical theory of motivation that arranges human needs into a pyramid-shaped model, with basic physiological needs at the bottom and self-actualization needs at the top.

Materialism An emphasis on assertiveness and the acquisition of money and material objects. Usually measured along a continuum, with concern for others at the opposite end.

Matrix Organization Structure An organization consisting of a project structure superimposed on a functional structure.

Mechanistic Organization A primarily hierarchical organization with an emphasis on specialization and control, vertical communication, and heavy reliance on rules, policies, and procedures.

Message A purpose or an idea to be conveyed in a communication event.

Meta-Analysis A quantitative or statistical review of the literature on a particular subject; an examination of a range of studies for the purpose of reaching a combined result or best estimate.

Meta-Communicate To communicate about your communication to help overcome barriers or resolve a problem.

Micromanagement Supervising group members too closely and second-guessing their decisions.

Mixed Signals Communication breakdown resulting from the sending of different messages about the same topic to different audiences.

Modeling Imitation; learning a skill by observing another person performing that skill.

Motivation In a work setting, the process by which behavior is mobilized and sustained in the interest of achieving organizational goals.

Multicultural Manager A manager with the skills and attitudes to relate effectively to and motivate people across race, gender, age, social attitudes, and lifestyles, and to conduct business in a diverse, international environment.

Multicultural Organization An organization that values cultural diversity and is willing to encourage and even capitalize on such diversity.

Multiple Intelligences A theory that proposes that people know and understand the world in distinctly different ways according to the varying degrees to which they possess eight faculties: linguistic, logical–mathematical, musical, spatial, bodily–kinesthetic, intrapersonal, interpersonal, and naturalist.

N

Need for Achievement The desire to accomplish something difficult for its own sake.

Need for Affiliation The desire to establish and maintain friendly and warm relationships with others.

Need for Power The desire to control other people, to influence their behavior, and to be responsible for them.

Negative Lifestyle Factors Behavior patterns predisposing a person to job stress, including poor exercise and eating habits and heavy consumption of caffeine, alcohol, tobacco, and other drugs.

Negotiating and Bargaining Conferring with another person in order to resolve a problem.

Network Organization A spherical structure that can rotate self-managing teams and other resources around a common knowledge base.

Network Structure (or Virtual Organization) A temporary association of otherwise independent firms linked by technology to share expenses, employee talents, and access to one another's markets.

Noise Anything that disrupts communication, including the attitude and emotions of the receiver.

Nominal Group Technique (NGT) An approach to developing creative alternatives that requires group members to generate alternative solutions independently.

Nonprogrammed (or Nonroutine) Decision A unique response to a complex problem.

Nonverbal Communication The transmission of messages by means other than words.

Normative Decision Model A contingency viewpoint of leadership that views leadership as a decision-making process in which the leader examines certain situational factors to determine which decision-making style will be most effective.

O

Offshoring The practice of having work performed by a company in an overseas location.

Open-Door Policy An understanding in which any employee can bring a gripe to the attention of upper-level management without checking with his or her immediate manager.

Operant Conditioning Learning that takes place as a consequence of behavior.

Organic Structure An organization laid out like a network, emphasizing horizontal specialization, extensive use of personal coordination, extensive communication among members, and loose rules, policies, and procedures.

Organization A collection of people working together to achieve a common purpose (or simply a big group).

Organization Design The process of creating a structure that best fits a purpose, strategy, and environment.

Organization Development (OD) Any strategy, method, or technique for making organizations more effective by bringing about constructive, planned change.

Organization Structure The arrangement of people and tasks to accomplish organizational goals.

Organizational Behavior The study of human behavior in the workplace, the interaction between people and the organization, and the organization itself.

Organizational Behavior Modification (OB Mod) The application of reinforcement theory for motivating people in work settings.

Organizational Citizenship Behavior Behaviors that express a willingness to work for the good of an organization even without the promise of a specific reward.

Organizational Culture A system of shared values and beliefs that influence worker behavior.

Organizational Effectiveness The extent to which an organization is productive and satisfies the demands of its interested parties.

Organizational Politics Informal approaches to gaining power through means other than merit or luck.

Outsource The practice of having work performed by groups outside the organization.

P

Paradigm A model, framework, viewpoint, perspective, or frame of reference.

Path–Goal Theory of Leadership An explanation of leadership that specifies what the leader must do to achieve high morale and productivity in a given situation.

Perception The various ways in which people interpret things in the outside world and how they act on the basis of these interpretations.

Personality The persistent and enduring behavior patterns of an individual that are expressed in a wide variety of situations.

Personality Clash An antagonistic relationship between two people based on differences in personal attributes, preferences, interests, values, and styles.

Personalized Power The use of power primarily for the sake of personal aggrandizement and gain.

Person–Role Conflict A condition that occurs when the demands made by the organization or a manager clash with the basic values of the individual.

Positive Organizational Behavior The study and application of human resource strengths and psychological capacities that can be measured, developed, and managed for performance improvement.

Positive Reinforcement The application of a pleasurable or valued consequence when a person exhibits the desired response.

Power The potential or ability to influence decisions and control resources.

Power Distance The extent to which employees accept the idea that members of an organization have different levels of power.

Problem A discrepancy between the ideal and the real.

Process Consultation An intervention in which the organization development specialist examines the pattern of a work unit's communications.

Procrastinate Delaying to take action without a valid reason.

Product/Service Departmentalization The arrangement of departments according to the products or services they provide.

Professional Bureaucracy An organization composed of a core of highly trained professionals that standardizes skills for coordination.

Programmed (or Routine) Decision A standard response to an uncomplicated problem.

Project A temporary group of specialists working together under one manager to accomplish a fixed objective.

Punishment The presentation of an undesirable consequence for a specific behavior.

R

Reengineering The radical redesign of work to achieve substantial improvements in performance.

Referent Power The ability to influence others that stems from one's desirable traits and characteristics; it is the basis for charisma.

Reinforcement Theory The contention that behavior is determined by its consequences.

Relationship Conflict Conflict that focuses on personalized, individually oriented issues.

Relaxation Response A general-purpose method of learning to relax by oneself, which includes making oneself quiet and comfortable.

Resource Dependence Perspective The need of the organization for a continuing flow of human resources, money, customers, technological inputs, and material to continue to function.

Reward Power Controlling others through rewards or the promise of rewards.

Role Ambiguity A condition in which the job holder receives confused or poorly defined role expectations.

Role Conflict Having to choose between competing demands or expectations.

S

***s* (special) Factors** Components of intelligence that contribute to problem-solving ability.

Satisficing Decision A decision that provides a minimum standard of satisfaction.

Scientific Management The application of scientific methods to increase workers' productivity.

Self-Awareness Insightfully processing feedback about oneself to improve personal effectiveness.

Self-Determination Theory The idea that people are motivated when they experience a sense of choice in initiating and regulating their actions.

Self-Efficacy The feeling of being an effective and competent person with respect to a task.

Self-Managed Work Team A formally recognized group of employees responsible for an entire work process or segment that delivers a product or service to an internal or external customer.

Self-Serving Bias An attribution error whereby people tend to attribute their achievements to good inner qualities, whereas they attribute their failures to adverse factors within the environment.

Semantics The varying meanings people attach to words.

Servant Leader A leader who serves constituents by working on their behalf to help them achieve their goals, not the leader's own goals.

Sexual Harassment Unwanted sexually oriented behavior in the workplace that results in discomfort and/or interference with the job.

Shaping Learning through the reinforcement or rewarding of small steps to build to the final or desired behavior.

Short-Term Orientation In describing a national culture, a demand for immediate results.

Situational Control The degree to which the leader can control and influence the outcomes of group effort.

Situational Leader II (SLII) A model of leadership explaining how to match the leadership style to the capabilities of group members on a given task.

Six Sigma A data-driven method for achieving near-perfect quality with an emphasis on preventing problems.

Social Learning The process of observing the behavior of others, recognizing its consequences, and altering behavior as a result.

Social Loafing Freeloading, or shirking individual responsibility when placed in a group setting and removed from individual accountability.

Social Responsibility The idea that firms have an obligation to society beyond their economic obligations to owners or stockholder and also beyond those prescribed by law or contract.

Socialization The process of coming to understand the values, norms, and customs essential for adapting to an organization.

Socialized Power The use of power to achieve constructive ends.

Stock Option A financial incentive that gives employees the right to purchase a certain number of company shares at a specified price, generally the market price of the stock on the day the option is granted.

Stress The mental and physical condition that results from a perceived threat that cannot be dealt with readily.

Stressor Any force creating the stress reaction.

Subculture A pocket in which the organizational culture differs from the dominant culture, as well as other pockets of subculture.

Substitutes for Leadership Factors in the work environment that provide guidance and incentives to perform, making the leader's role almost superfluous.

Superordinate Goals Overarching goals that capture the imagination of people.

T

Task Conflict Conflict that focuses on substantive, issue-related differences related to the work itself.

Team A special type of group in which the members have complementary skills and are committed to a common purpose, a set of performance goals, and an approach to the task.

Team Efficacy A team's belief that it can successfully perform a specific task.

Teamwork A situation in which there is understanding and commitment to group goals on the part of all team members.

Telecommuting Working at home and sending output electronically to the office.

Territorial Games Also known as turf wars, territorial games refer to behaviors involving the hoarding of information and other resources.

Transformational Leader One who helps organizations and people make positive changes in the way they conduct their activities.

Triarchic Theory of Intelligence The theory that intelligence is composed of three different types of intelligence: analytical, creative, and practical.

Two-Factor Theory of Work Motivation Herzberg's theory contending that there are two different sets of job factors. One set can satisfy and motivate people (motivators or satisfiers); the other set can only prevent dissatisfaction (dissatisfiers or hygiene factors).

Two in a Box Dividing up executive responsibilities in one position.

U

Uncertainty Avoidance The extent to which people accept the unknown and tolerate risk and unconventional behavior.

Unfreezing–Changing–Refreezing Model A three-step analysis of the change process based on the idea that change involves unfreezing, followed by changing and refreezing.

Urgent Time Orientation The perception of time as a scarce resource, therefore leading to impatience.

V

Valence The value a person places on a particular outcome.

Value The importance a person attaches to something that serves as a guide to action.

Value Judgment An overall opinion of something based on a quick perception of its merit.

Virtual Team A group that conducts almost all of its collaborative work via electronic communication rather than face-to-face meetings.

Virtuous Circle The idea that corporate social performance and corporate financial performance feed and reinforce each other.

W

Wellness Program A formal organization-sponsored activity to help employees stay well and avoid illness.

Whistle-Blower An employee who discloses organizational wrongdoing to parties who can take action.

Win–Win The belief that, after conflict has been resolved, both sides should gain something of value.

Work–Family Conflict Conflict that ensues when the individual has to perform multiple roles: worker; spouse; and, often, parent.

burnout, 303
Burns, James McGregor, 250
business acumen, 5

C

Caliper, 275
Campbell, Andrew, 330
Carty, Donald J., 264
Cascio, Wayne F., 192
case studies, 3
casual time orientation, 387
Catalyst, 384
Center for Workforce
    Development, 46
centralization, 317
certainty associated with
    decisions, 90
challenger, 196
Chambers, John, 263, 337
Champion International Paper, 373
chance encounters, 173
charisma
    charismatic leadership, 252–254
    definition, 250
    evil, 252
Chertnoff, Michael, 314
Chrysler PT Cruiser, 350
Cisco Systems, 263, 319, 337, 396
Citigroup, 276, 317
classical approach to management,
    8–9
classical decision model, 90
coaching, 217–219
Coca-Cola Company, 315, 337
codes of conduct, 80
coercive power, 264
cognitive skills and cognition,
    45–47, 233
    cognitive conflicts, 291
    cognitive dissonance, 64
    cognitive intelligence, 25, 37, 94,
        95, 233
    individual differences, 25–29
    personality, 95
    see also learning
collective problem solving, 217
collectivism, 386
commitment to firm, individual
    differences, 21
common sense, 7–8

communication
    barriers to communication,
        174–177
    body language, 168–170
    computer-mediated, impact,
        167–168
    cultural differences, 179–181
    directions, 173–174
    gender differences, 179
    information technology. See
        information technology and
        communication
    interpersonal, 161–187
    listeners. See listeners
    nonverbal, 168–170
    open, 278
    organizational channels, 170–174
    overcoming barriers to,
        176–177
    overload, 175
    process, 162–163
communion striving, 131
company blogs, 164–165
complexity, 317
components of intelligence, 26–27
compromise, 297
    see also negotiation
computers and communication. See
    information technology and
    communication
concern for others, 386
conflict
    cognitive, 291
    consequences, 291–292
    definition, 285
    difficult people and, 296–297
    management styles, 293–297
    resolution methods, 294–296
    sources and antecedents, 285–291
    structural methods for resolving,
        295–296
    task versus relationship
        conflict, 291
    and tension in creativity, 103–104
    work-family, 289
confrontation
    confront, contain, and connect
        for anger method, 294–295
    problem solving, 294
conscientiousness, 30, 33, 131
consideration, 240

consistency, 235
consultative coaching, 218
Continental Airlines, 370
contingency approach to
    management, 11
contingency theories of leadership,
    243–249
conventional level of moral
    development, 75
Corning, Inc., 194
Couch, Richard, 222
CQ (cultural intelligence), 400–401
creativity
    characteristics of creative people,
        100–102
    conflict and tension, 103–104
    creative process, 100
    definition, 98
    encouragement from others, 104
    enhancing and improving,
        105–109
    environmental needs, 103
    intelligence and intellectual
        abilities of creative people,
        27, 101
    knowledge of creative people, 101
    mood, 104
    necessary conditions, 102–103
    personality of creative people,
        101–102
    self-efficacy, 101
    steps in creative process, 100
    "thinking outside the box," 105
    thinking skills, 102
    time pressures, 104
    training, 109
    see also ideas; thinking
credibility, 175
Crest, 98
crews, 193
criterion, 3
cross-cultural relations
    barriers, 393–394
    conflict resolution models, 397
    empowerment issues, 398
    ethics, 395–396
    motivation, 395
    negotiations, 396–397
    values, 385–388
cross-functional teams,
    190–191

word fluency, 26
work-family conflict, 289
work groups. *See* groups
work stress
   contributing factors, 303–306
   control, 307
   individual approaches to
     management, 307–308
   management of, organizational
     approaches, 306–307
   organizational conditions,
     adverse, 304–306
   stressors, 301, 308

symptom management,
   307–308
symptoms and consequences,
   301–303
World Is Flat, The: A Brief History of the Twenty-First Century, 375
Wright, Laura, 266
Wrzesniewski, Amy, 143

X

Xerox, 330, 372

Y

Yahoo Inc., 322, 330, 396
Yerkes-Dodson law, 303
Young & Rubicam Advertising
   (Y&R), 318, 323, 372

Z

Zhou, Jing, 104